ESSENTIALS OF
AMATEUR SPORTS LAW

ESSENTIALS OF AMATEUR SPORTS LAW

GLENN M. WONG
University of Massachusetts

Auburn House Publishing Company
Dover, Massachusetts

To Paula and Ernest Glenn

Copyright © 1988 by Auburn House Publishing Company.

Library of Congress Cataloging in Publication Data

Wong, Glenn M.
  Essentials of law in amateur sports / Glenn M. Wong.
      p.   cm.
  Includes index.
  ISBN 0-86569-131-2
  1. School sports—Law and legislation—United States.   2. Sports-
  w and legislation—United States.   I. Title.
  4166.W66   1988
  .73'077—dc19
  7.30477]   87-24620
                                                            CIP

ited in the United States of America

PREFACE

In my several professional roles as attorney, teacher, and consultant, I meet frequently with individuals and groups active in amateur sports. Athletic administrators and others around the country have repeatedly expressed a need for a "practitioner's" book because sports law has become such an integral part of their day-to-day operation. They want to have a background on sports law before they deal with attorneys on legal issues. Even more important, they want to attempt to avoid litigation. The interest and concerns of these people motivated the writing of this book.

I started with the concept that the book should be written for those affected by sport law issues who are not necessarily lawyers, including college or high school athletic administrators or coaches, student-athletes, school board members, institutional representatives, and those involved in amateur sports organizations. There is, for example, a chapter on the court system, a glossary, and an appendix of sample forms that can be used by practitioners as starting points for developing their own forms. The major intercollegiate and interscholastic amateur sports organizations, such as the U.S. Olympic Committee and the National Collegiate Athletic Association, are described in detail. All new legal concepts and issues are discussed, as are basic tort law, contract law, trademark law, and constitutional law. Each of the chapters has been designed as a self-contained unit that can be used as a quick reference. Case citations and brief summaries of cases (rather than lengthy discussions) have been included in the notes. The notes also include law review articles, names and addresses of relevant organizations, and other information which can lead the reader to additional sources of information.

I would like to thank some of the many people who have been instrumental in assisting me with *Essentials of Amateur Sports Law*. First, Margaret M. Kearney, the editor, helped express the thoughts and principles in this book. In addition, she kept the project moving and made sure that legalese was eliminated. As for research and writing, I would like to thank and acknowledge the work of Professor Richard J. Ensor of the University of Massachusetts, Amherst. He co-authored Chapter 9 (sports broadcasting) and Chapter 10 (trademark law). His numerous reviews of the manuscript and comments were invaluable in that he provided the perspectives of a sports lawyer and of an experienced athletic administrator. I also acknowledge the contributions of several research assistants: David Knopp, William Hubbard, Scott Proefrock, and Scott Zuffelato. The many drafts of the manuscript were typed by Susan McBride, to whom I am grateful. Several others, too numerous to mention individually, also contributed in various ways to this project. And, finally, I would like to thank Professor Robert Berry of Boston College Law School for getting me started in sports law.

THE AUTHOR

CONTENTS

CHAPTER 7

Application of Tort Law   335

CHAPTER 8

Sex Discrimination Issues   405

Chapter 1

OVERVIEW OF AMATEUR ATHLETICS AND SPORTS LAW

Introduction
The National Collegiate Athletic Association
     (NCAA)
The National Federation of State High School
     Associations (NFSHSA)
The International Olympic Committee (IOC)
The United States Olympic Committee (USOC)
National Governing Bodies (NGBs)
The Pressure to Succeed
  Impact on Coaches
  Impact on Institutions
  Impact on Student-Athletes
Overview of Topics

INTRODUCTION

The scope, financial stakes, and power of amateur athletic organizations in the United States and worldwide have expanded tremendously over the last quarter century. In the United States alone, amateur athletics encompass organizations that involve themselves in the lives of people from their childhoods (e.g., Pop Warner Football and Little League) through high school years (e.g., National Federation of State High School Associations) through college days (e.g., National Collegiate Athletic Association) and beyond (e.g., United States Olympic Committee). The purpose of this overview is to give the reader a sense of the size of amateur athletics in the United States, the involvement of the national amateur athletic organizations, and the financial impact these organizations have in the world of athletics.

To assist the reader with the overview, the major amateur athletic organizations referred to in the book are briefly introduced in the following sections. Chapter 1 then examines how pressure to succeed affects various constituencies of amateur athletics—the coaches, the institutions, and the student-athletes. The last section of Chapter 1 gives an overview of the topics covered in each of the succeeding chapters.

THE NATIONAL COLLEGIATE ATHLETIC ASSOCIATION (NCAA)

The National Collegiate Athletic Association (NCAA) is an organization founded in the early 1900s whose members are four-year colleges and universities and two-year upper-level collegiate institutions in the United States. Member schools—and there are now over 1,000—agree to be bound by NCAA rules and regulations and are obligated to administer their athletic programs in accordance with NCAA rules.

As the NCAA has grown, its financial base has expanded (see Chapter 4). Operating funds for the NCAA are in part accumulated through membership dues that are figured on a sliding scale based on the type of membership held. Funds also accrue from television coverage of intercollegiate football and basketball. In fact, prior to the 1984–1985 academic year, the NCAA had been financed in part by its percentage share of the national television contracts for intercollegiate football. However, on June 27, 1984, the U.S. Supreme Court in a 7–2 decision struck down the NCAA's 1982–85 Football Television Plan because it violated the federal Sherman Antitrust Act. (This decision and other broadcasting matters are discussed in Chapter 9.)

The NCAA conducts many different championships, including men's basketball, women's basketball, swimming, track and field, and baseball. Although some of the revenues are retained for the NCAA's operating expenses (40 percent of the NCAA Basketball Tournament's net receipts go to the NCAA), most of the monies are distributed. For instance, participants in the 1985 NCAA Basketball Tournament received from $153,080 for first-round losers to $751,899 for the final four teams. These figures increased to $211,205 for first-round losers to $1,056,027 for the final four teams in the 1987 NCAA Basketball Tournament (see Exhibit 1–1). Similarly, in intercollegiate football during 1985, the Cherry Bowl participants received $750,000 each, and the teams in the Rose Bowl collected $5.1 million each. During 1987, the payouts to the participants ranged from $300,000 per team in the Hall of Fame Bowl to $6.0 million per team in the Rose Bowl (see Exhibit 1–2). These large sums of money have put enormous pressure on coaches to succeed and some believe may be the root cause for many of the rules violations that occur.

In addition to the financial issues, a major problem facing the NCAA in recent years has been in the area of recruiting violations by member schools. "I believe there is a growing acceptance of the belief that the conditions of intercollegiate athletics are such that you have to cut corners, you have to circumvent the rules," stated Walter Byers, executive director of the NCAA from 1951–1987. He added, "there seems to be a growing number of coaches and administrators who look upon NCAA penalties as the price of doing business: If you get punished, that's unfortunate, but that's part of the cost of getting along." In 1984, there were, at one point, 13 NCAA institutions on probation. As of October 1987, 21 are on NCAA probation, and a number of other schools have just ended their probation periods.

One concern of the NCAA, which involves both the financial aspects and recruiting areas, is the subject of booster organizations. Booster organizations serve as support groups for specific sports in an athletic department. Their primary purpose is to raise monies for the sport in the form of direct contributions or indirect support through the purchase of season ticket packages and dinner tickets, or by providing employment opportunities for the student-athletes on the team. While estimates are that in 1985 college sports generated $1,064,749,000 million in revenues, only 37 percent of all NCAA institutions had revenues exceed expenses. Booster organizations thus become increasingly important and can play a significant role in generating additional income for the athletic department. In 1985, contributions from alumni, as a revenue

TOURNAMENT PARTICIPANTS
TO SHARE IN $24.8 MILLION

More than 87 percent of Division I basketball-playing institutions will share in the proceeds from the 1987 Division I Men's Basketball Championship, according to Association Controller Louis J. Spry.

Based on projections Spry made last July, . . . 253 of the 290 Division I members will receive a share of the tournament's receipts.

A conference-by-conference breakdown shows that the Big East, with five teams in the 1987 play-offs, will get the largest amount—in excess of $3.6 million.

Only the Big South, Gulf Star and Metropolitan Conferences and 17 independents are not represented in the distribution.

The 64-team field included 22.1 percent of Division I members, which is a participation ratio of 1 to 4.5.

Projected Distribution of Net Receipts

Conference or Institution	Total Members	Number of Entrants and Rounds Reached	Total Units	Projected Distribution
Big East	9	5-5-4-2-2	18	$ 3,612,150
Big Ten	10	5-4-2-2-2-1	16	3,210,800
Southeastern	10	4-3-3-2-1-1	14	2,809,450
Atlantic Coast	8	4-3-1-1-1-1	11	2,207,425
Big Eight	8	3-3-2-1	9	1,806,075
Western Athletic	9	3-2-1	6	1,204,050
Pacific Coast	10	5	5	1,003,375
Southwest	9	2-1-1	4	802,700
Atlantic 10	10	2-1	3	602,025
DePaul	1	3	3	602,025
Notre Dame	1	3	3	602,025
Ohio Valley	9	2-1	3	602,025
Pacific-10	10	2-1	3	602,025
Sun Belt	8	2-1	3	602,025
Mid-Continent	8	2	2	401,350
Midwestern	7	2	2	401,350
Missouri Valley	8	1-1	2	401,350
New Orleans	1	2	2	401,350
West Coast	8	1-1	2	401,350
Big Sky	8	1	1	200,675
Colonial	8	1	1	200,675
East Coast	8	1	1	200,675

Exhibit 1-1 Distribution of Proceeds for the 1987 NCAA Division I Men's Basketball Championship *Source: The NCAA News,* April 18, 1987, p. 1.

source, represented 11 percent of the total revenues of athletic department budgets.

Some booster organizations have violated NCAA rules and regulations and subsequently caused the involved programs to be put on NCAA probation. Sanctions range from total prohibition of an entire program to an individual team being excluded from intercollegiate competition (the so-called "death penalty") or championship play, to prohibition from television appearances, to merely a warning. In 1987, Southern Methodist University (SMU) became the first football program to receive the NCAA's "death penalty" (Kentucky's basketball program was suspended for the 1952–53 season because of booster payments to athletes, and Southwestern Louisiana's basketball program was suspended for 2 seasons—1973–1975—because of more than 100 NCAA violations involving recruiting and academics). The ruling barred SMU from all football competition in 1987, allows only seven games in 1988 (SMU subsequently decided not to play football in the 1988 season), prohibits television or bowl appearances until 1989, restricts off-campus recruiting and the number of assistant coaches until 1989, and allows for only 15 football scholarships per year through the 1988–89 academic year. SMU was caught breaking NCAA rules for a record seventh time—while the football program was already on three years' probation for recruiting violations cited in 1985. Athletic departments rely on booster organizations for several reasons, among them the emergence of women's athletic programs, the increased costs of running all programs, and the need for new or improved facilities, all of which require additional monies. Boosters were recently banned from recruiting (NCAA Bylaw 1-2-b, 8/1/87).

An example of the high cost of a big-time athletic program is Rutgers University. In 1984, Rutgers, which is the State University of New Jersey, decided to upgrade its football program. For years it had languished at the bottom of NCAA Division I-A programs. After hiring a new coach, Rutgers immediately spent $3 million to build a new outdoor practice field, a bubble-enclosed indoor practice field, and a new $1.5 million scoreboard. The university also renovated the locker room, bought $50,000 worth of Nautilus equipment, and hired a full-time strength and conditioning coach. The next phase in upgrading the Rutgers program involved the construction of a $5 million football complex consisting of a locker room, weight room, trainer's room, coaches' offices, and meeting facilities. In addition, lighting was installed at Rutgers Stadium, increasing the seating capacity in the stadium from 23,000 to about 40,000 seats, and a new press box was built.

Another grave concern of the NCAA involves drug abuse by athletes. Drug abuse, whether recreational or sports-related, has become a very large problem for all athletic organizations, including the NCAA. In 1985, the NCAA released a drug survey of 2,000 athletes: 27 percent smoked marijuana, 12 percent used cocaine, 11 percent used major pain killers, and an overwhelming 82 percent used alcohol. NCAA research coordinator Eric Zemper noted: "I don't think the results are that surprising. The numbers

The Lineups and Money for This Season's Bowl Games

Bowl	Date	Time (EST)	Location	Teams	Estimated payment per team
All-American	Dec. 22	8:00 pm	Birmingham, Ala.	Brigham Young vs. Virginia	$ 800,000
Aloha	Dec. 25	3:45 pm	Honolulu	Florida vs. UCLA	500,000
Bluebonnet	Dec. 31	7:00 pm	Houston	Pittsburgh vs. Texas	500,000
Cotton	Jan. 1	1:30 pm	Dallas	Notre Dame vs. Texas A&M	2,200,000
Fiesta	Jan. 1	1:30 pm	Tempe, Ariz.	Florida State vs. Nebraska	2,100,000
Florida Citrus	Jan. 1	Noon	Orlando, Fla.	Clemson vs. Penn State	1,000,000
Freedom	Dec. 30	8:00 pm	Anaheim, Cal.	Air Force vs. Arizona State	500,000
Gator	Dec. 31	2:30 pm	Jacksonville, Fla.	Louisiana State vs. South Carolina	1,000,000
Hall of Fame	Jan. 2	1:00 pm	Tampa, Fla.	Alabama vs. Michigan	300,000
Holiday	Dec. 30	7:30 pm	San Diego	Iowa vs. Wyoming	750,000
Independence	Dec. 19	8:00 pm	Shreveport, La.	Tulane vs. Washington	500,000
Liberty	Dec. 29	8:00 pm	Memphis	Arkansas vs. Georgia	1,000,000
Orange	Jan. 1	8:30 pm	Miami	Miami (Fla.) vs. Oklahoma	2,500,000
Peach	Jan. 2	1:00 pm	Atlanta	Indiana vs. Tennessee	800,000
Rose	Jan. 1	5:00 pm	Pasadena, Cal.	Michigan State vs. Southern California	6,000,000
Sugar	Jan. 1	3:30 pm	New Orleans	Auburn vs. Syracuse	2,650,000
Sun	Dec. 25	2:35 pm	El Paso	Oklahoma State vs. West Virginia	850,000

Exhibit 1-2 College Football Bowls (1987–1988)

are certainly higher than we hoped, but it's a pervasive problem throughout society." As of April 1987, in its first season of drug testing, only 2.2 percent of the student-athletes tested by the NCAA had been ruled ineligible because of positive tests (33 of 1,528 tested). Only two of those tested positive were from street-related drug use. All the other positive tests were for steroid-related abuses. The drug abuse and the testing for drugs in athletics that have become areas of focus and controversy for the NCAA have led to a new area of litigation in the 1980s. Drug testing and defending litigation will bring about additional financial problems for athletic programs. The governance authority of the NCAA is discussed in Chapter 4, litigation involving student-athletes is discussed in Chapter 5, and drug testing is dealt with in Chapter 12.

THE NATIONAL FEDERATION OF STATE HIGH SCHOOL ASSOCIATIONS (NFSHSA)

The National Federation of State High School Associations (NFSHSA) consists of the 50 individual state high school athletic and/or activities associations and the association of the District of Columbia. Also affiliated are nine interscholastic organizations from the Canadian Provinces of Alberta, British Columbia, Manitoba, New Brunswick, Newfoundland-Labrador, Nova Scotia, Ontario, Prince Edward Island, and Saskatchewan, as well as the Canadian School Sports Federation and the associations of the Republic of the Philippines, Okinawa, Guam, and St. Thomas.

These associations have united to secure the benefits of cooperative action which eliminate unnecessary duplication of effort and which increase efficiency through the pooling and coordinating of ideas of all who are engaged in the administration of high school athletic and activities programs.

The NFSHSA had its beginning in a meeting at Chicago on May 14, 1920. L. W. Smith, secretary of the Illinois High School Athletic Association, issued invitations to neighboring states, and state association representatives came from Illinois, Indiana, Iowa, Michigan, and Wisconsin. The primary purpose of the meeting was to discuss problems which had resulted from high school contests which were organized by colleges and universities or by other clubs or promoters. In many cases, little attention was paid to the eligibility rules of the high school associations or to other school group regulations, and chaotic conditions had developed. At this first meeting, it was decided that the welfare of the high school required that a more active part in the control of such athletic activities be exercised by the high school through the state associations, and this control necessitated the formation of a national organization. A constitution and bylaws were adopted, and the group decided on the name "Midwest Federation of State High School Athletic Associations." Principal George Edward Marshall, Davenport, Iowa, was elected secretary-treasurer.

In 1921, four states, Illinois, Iowa, Michigan, and Wisconsin, continued their interest and became charter members through formal ratification of the constitution. Largely due to their efforts, the national organization grew during the early years.

In 1922, the Chicago annual meeting was attended by representatives from 11 states, and the name of the National Federation of State High School Associations was adopted. A number of college and university representatives who attended the meeting expressed sympathy for an interest in the efforts to introduce a high degree of order in the regulation of interscholastic contests.

Since that time, the National Federation has had a healthy growth to its present nationwide membership. By 1940, a national office with a full-time executive staff became necessary, and such an office was established in September of that year.

The legislative body is the National Council made up of one representative from each member state association. Each representative must be a state association chief executive officer or governing board member. The executive body is the Executive Committee of at least eight members from the eight territorial sections as outlined in the constitution. Their election is by the National Council at its summer meeting.

The purpose of the National Federation of State High School Associations is to coordinate the efforts of its member state associations toward the ultimate objectives of interscholastic activities. It shall provide a means for state high school associations to cooperate in order to enhance and protect their interscholastic programs. In order to accomplish this, the National Federation is guided by a philosophy consistent with the accepted purposes of secondary education. Member state associations' programs must be administered in accordance with the following basic beliefs:

> Interscholastic activities shall be an integral part of the total secondary school educational program which has as its purpose to provide educational experiences not otherwise provided in the curriculum, which will develop learning outcomes in the areas of knowledge, skills and emotional patterns and will contribute to the development of better citizens. Emphasis shall be upon teaching "through" activities in addition to teaching the skills of activities.
>
> Interschool activities shall be primarily for the benefit of the high

school students who participate directly and vicariously in them. The interscholastic activity program shall exist mainly for the value which it has for students and not for the benefit of the sponsoring institutions. The activities and contests involved shall be psychologically sound by being tailored to the physical, mental and emotional maturity levels of the youth participating in them. . . .

The state high school associations and the National Federation shall be concerned with the development of those standards, policies and regulations essential to assist their member schools in the implementation of their philosophy of interscholastic activities.

Nonschool activities sponsored primarily for the benefit of the participants in accordance with a philosophy compatible with the school philosophy of interscholastics may have values for youth. When they do not interfere with the academic and interscholastic programs and do not result in exploitation of youth, they shall be considered as a worthwhile supplement to interschool activities.

The welfare of the school demands a united front in sports direction policies and the high school associations provide opportunity for this unity. They must be kept strong.

THE INTERNATIONAL OLYMPIC COMMITTEE (IOC)

The International Olympic Committee (IOC) "governs the Olympic movement and exercises all rights over the Olympic Games. Every organization that plays any part in the Olympic movement must accept the authority of the IOC and be bound by the rules of the IOC."

Since the revival of the Olympic Games in 1896, the IOC has enforced a strict amateur code for athletes to be eligible to participate, which on occasion has given rise to litigation from athletes seeking to participate. However, in 1982 the IOC relaxed its rules and asked the individual amateur governing bodies, such as the International Football Federation (FIFA), which governs the sport of soccer, to propose their own eligibility codes. At the 1984 Winter Olympic Games at Sarajevo, Yugoslavia, IOC president Juan Antonio Samaranch said: "I think the IOC must do its best to give to all the athletes from all over the world and from all the political systems the same right to participate in the Games. We are going step by step, bit by bit, but I should like to say that I wish we could go faster."

Rule 26 of the IOC, which was instituted in 1982 to effect the change in emphasis, reads:

A competitor must observe and abide by the rules of the IOC and in addition, his or her international federation as approved by the

IOC, even if the federation's rules are more strict than those of the
IOC.

A competitor must not have received any financial rewards or
material benefit in connection with his or her sports participation
except as permitted in the bylaws to this rule.

In 1985, the IOC moved even further in relaxing its eligibility
rules, voting to allow professionals under the age of 23 to participate in the 1988 Winter and Summer Olympic Games, in the
sports of tennis, ice hockey, and soccer. Samaranch noted: "This
decision is only for 1988. After 1988 we will see. The Olympic
movement must go with the times." Throughout 1986 and 1987,
the IOC has been considering a revision of the Olympic charter
which would allow each international federation to determine its
own eligibility rules for the Olympic Games. This would, in effect,
turn Olympic participation from being strictly amateur to "open to
all," since many international federations already allow professionals to compete in their sports. Robert M. Helmick, president of
the United States Olympic Committee (USOC), endorsed the
change. He commented: "This step recognizes that each sport is
different and should have the freedom to run its own sport. This is
a most positive step because it will take the hypocrisy out of
sports" (*Boston Globe*, February 13, 1986, pp. 57, 67).

One major problem for the IOC, which has led to some litigation
in American courts, has been the boycotting of the Olympic Games
for political reasons by various countries, most significantly the
United States in 1980 (Moscow Summer Games) and the Soviet
Union in 1984 (Los Angeles Summer Games). The problem facing
the IOC is that participation in the Olympics is voluntary and not
compulsory. However, it has been proposed that the IOC should
penalize countries which boycott the Olympic Games by restricting
future participation.

Chapters 4 and 5 examine the Olympic movement in regards to
how the American court system has handled litigation involving
the governance authority of the IOC, the U.S. Olympic Committee
(USOC) and national governing bodies (NGBs), and the rights of
the individual Olympic athletes.

THE UNITED STATES OLYMPIC COMMITTEE (USOC)

The United States Olympic Committee (USOC) is the National
Olympic Committee for the United States representing the coun-
try's interest with the IOC. The USOC is recognized as the United
States National Olympic Committee (NOC) pursuant to IOC Rule

24. The court, in *U.S. Wrestling Federation v. Wrestling Division of the AAU, Inc.*, noted that

> each nation wishing to participate in the Olympic Games must maintain a National Olympic Committee ("NOC") recognized by the IOC. Each NOC must enforce the rules and bylaws of the IOC. The IOC recognizes the USOC as the NOC for the United States.

The USOC was formed as

> a corporation chartered by the United States Congress in 1950. P.L. 81-805 (81st Cong. 2d Sess.) September 21, 1950; 64 Stat. 889. In 1978, the USOC Congressional Charter was amended by a legislative enactment popularly called "The Amateur Sports Act of 1978." P.L. 95-606 (95th Cong. 2d Sess.) November 8, 1978; 92 Stat. 3045 ("the Act"). USOC's principal place of business is located at Colorado Springs, Colorado, and it operates in all fifty states and the District of Columbia.

The USOC operates its main Olympic Training Center in Colorado Springs, Colorado, and others in Lake Placid, New York, and Marquette, Michigan. Funds for the center come primarily from corporate sponsorship. For example, the Miller Brewing Company donated $3.3 million to sponsor the Olympic Training Centers in the quadrennial leading up to the 1984 Olympic Games in Los Angeles and will continue its support through 1988. An additional $15,081,900 was raised from corporate funds and other income sources, and the money was distributed by the USOC to the various national governing bodies to support their operations. In comparison, between 1961 and 1964, the total development money distributed by the USOC was only $50,000. From 1965 to 1968, the sum was $300,000; from 1969 to 1972 it was $800,000; from 1973 to 1976 it was $2.2 million; and from 1977 to 1980 it was $9.2 million.

The operating budget for the USOC has also experienced similar growth. In 1972, the USOC budget was $9 million, in 1976, $43 million, in 1980, $88.7 million, and for the 1985–1988 quadrennium, $125 million. Thirty-eight percent of the 1981–1984 income came from corporate programs, 36 percent from general contributions, 8 percent from TV rights to the Olympic Trials and National Sports Festivals, 4 percent from the Olympic Society, and 14 percent from other sources (licensing/marketing). The USOC is the only National Olympic Committee among the 160 in the world that does not receive continuing financial support from its national government.

In the 1985–1988 four-year period, the USOC will make more than $65 million available to assist athletes in the form of cash and

resources, such as the elite athlete program, development grants
to national governing bodies, sports medicine, national training
centers, and travel expenses.

As with other amateur athletic associations, the USOC is very
concerned about increasing drug use in sports. The USOC in 1985
decided to upgrade its drug-testing program to include every major
athletic competition it sanctions prior to the Olympic Games, with
stiff penalties for violations. The testing for drugs and controversies
over drug test results may be an area of increased litigation for the
Olympic movement (see Chapter 12).

NATIONAL GOVERNING BODIES (NGBs)

The IOC, in addition to recognizing a NOC in each participating
nation, also designates an International Federation which governs
each Olympic sport. The International Federation establishes rules
and regulations for the sport it governs, including eligibility rules
for athletes. The International Federation also elects one amateur
organization from each nation as its affiliate member for that
nation. The selected national amateur organization is the sport's
national governing body (NGB) for Olympic competition.

The court, in *U.S. Wrestling Federation v. Wrestling Division of
the AAU, Inc.*, noted:

> IOC by-law V(5) to Rule 24 provides that a NOC (such as the USOC)
> "must not accept as members more than one national federation for
> each sport, and that federation must be affiliated to the relevant
> (international federation) recognized by the IOC."
>
> Pursuant to its Congressional Charter and the published rules
> and regulations of the International Olympic Committee, the USOC
> recognizes one United States amateur sports organization as the
> national governing body ("NGB") for each Olympic sport, 36 U.S.C.
> section 391. The national governing body ("NGB") so recognized is
> the member in the United States of the international sports federa-
> tion recognized by the International Olympic Committee for the
> purpose of administering the competitions on the Olympic program.
> USOC Const. Art. IV, section 4. Each NGB so recognized is the
> USOC's "Group A" member for its sport.
>
> Under Section 203 of the Amateur Sports Act, 36 U.S.C. section
> 393, each USOC-recognized NGB is authorized to exercise certain
> powers, including without limitation representing the United States
> in the international sports federation for its particular sport.

THE PRESSURE TO SUCCEED

Impact on Coaches

The pressure to succeed in athletics forces head coaches and their staff to spend enormous amounts of time and money in developing quality programs, particularly in recruiting "blue chip" athletes. Bobby Ross, while the Maryland football coach, stated: "I'm not that good a coach that I can do it without the players." In explaining Boston College's system, football recruiting coordinator Barry Gallup stated: "We have a mailing list of 250, but some of the bigger programs have a much larger list."

In intercollegiate athletics, recruiting becomes a year-round enterprise. There is extensive travel by the staff, numerous phone calls and letters, and on-campus visits by potential players. The costs of recruiting can be enormous, and there is no guarantee that the sought-after recruits will eventually agree to attend the recruiter's institution. The athlete being recruited may visit a number of different institutions and then decide which one to attend to the exclusion of the other schools. Such uncertainty can cause a coach to look for an edge on other recruiters by providing extra inducements to the recruited athlete which are not allowed under NCAA rules.

The need for "blue chip" athletes has forced coaches to search worldwide. Basketball, soccer, and track and field coaches have all gone abroad to recruit athletes. The potential for abuse and confusion is greater in situations where language problems, customs, distance, and ignorance of the NCAA's rules exist. It can also prove diplomatically embarrassing. In the past, recruiters have been accused of paying recruits from other countries to attend their institutions, among them athletes who have deserted military service to enroll at American schools. Recruiters have also been accused of falsifying immigration records in order to get the recruited athlete into the country.

The problems associated with the recruitment of student-athletes and their continued athletic and academic eligibility while attending school have come under increasing examination by many of the individual school's chief executive officers. James H. Zumberge, president of the University of Southern California, made this observation:

> Several institutions of higher learning, USC among them, have come under recent scrutiny for rules violations in the area of intercollegiate athletics. These violations appear to have been the result of malfeasance by a small number of individuals. Nevertheless, the fact

that so many similar incidents should have occurred, at so many institutions, suggests that higher education may well have come to a turning point in its relationship to competitive sports. It would seem that the pressures demanding performance, in many instances, have overwhelmed the forces of responsibility and integrity within the system as a whole and within the institutions in question. ["Academic Conduct, Admission, Advisement and Counseling of Student-Athletes at the University of Southern California," by James H. Zumberge, President USC, October 12, 1980]

One does not have to search far for examples of the incidents mentioned by President Zumberge. At the University of Maryland, only a few days after Len Bias died of cocaine intoxication in June 1986, it was revealed that 5 out of the 12 players on the basketball team had flunked out the previous semester, that 1 out of every 5 Maryland athletes had either been given an academic warning or had been dismissed by the end of the 1984–85 academic year, and that a teaching assistant claimed she had been approached by athletic department officials who asked her to change an athlete's grade the previous year. At the University of Georgia, it was discovered that university officials changed the failing grades of 9 football players so they could remain eligible for the 1982 Sugar Bowl. Jan Kemp, an English coordinator in the Developmental Studies program, who was demoted and later dismissed as an instructor in retaliation for her protests against such preferential treatment of athletes at Georgia, was awarded $2.57 million for lost wages, mental anguish, and punitive damages in her successful suit against University of Georgia officials.

Tulane University was also rocked by a scandalous incident in March 1985. Several members of the men's varsity basketball team at Tulane were arrested for accepting bribes to shave points in two home games. This was followed by revelations that the coaching staff had been making improper payments to a few players for an extended period of time. It was also discovered that Tulane had seriously compromised its professed academic and admissions standards for student-athletes. All of these incidents indicate the disastrous consequences from the immense pressure to succeed.

At USC an advisory committee studied the problems mentioned by President Zumberge, and in their investigative report to him noted:

Higher education today may have reached a crossroads in its relationship to big-time athletics. The major spectator sports have taken on an existence and momentum entirely of their own and drifted away from the procedures and academic philosophies of the institutions which spawned them. If the present trend is allowed to continue, the potential exists for gradually undermining the integrity and credibility of the educational enterprise as a whole. Therefore, individual institutions, and the intercollegiate athletic system of which they are a part, must explore ways of restoring clear purposes and goals for competitive sports which are consistent with broader educational purposes and societal needs. ["Academic Conduct . . . ," Zumberge]

The pressures noted above, which are associated with big-time athletic recruiting and administration, take a terrific toll on the individual coaches who work under them on a daily basis. "I was on a treadmill," former University of Notre Dame football coach Ara Parseghian recalls. "You go from fall season to recruiting to fund raising to golf outings back to fall season again. The pressure I felt was just immense. There's no way to explain what your stomach feels like every day of the week."

Bill Battle, former football coach at Tennessee, described the pressure this way:

It was the staggering investment of time with uncertain results, particularly the endless recruiting dance, which I found "insane, bordering on ridiculous." You want to do what you have to do to beat the competition, so you invest months of time and effort into recruiting a prospect. Then he starts to lean the other way and you try to do what you have to do, within the bounds of your own ethics and morality, to keep him interested. I finally decided I didn't want to spend that much time trying to sign 17- and 18-year-olds that your livelihood depended upon who were not necessarily the most stable guys in the world.

Marv Harshman, who retired as basketball coach of the University of Washington after the 1984–85 season, had this to say:

In the old days, I don't think any school expected to make money. Now sports has become like the professional arm of a school. We have 22 men and women sports at Washington. The money has to come from somewhere, and that somewhere is football and basketball.

I used to enjoy recruiting and talking to the youngsters, but I stopped liking it when it turned into a salesman's job. Everybody is looking for something. . . . A lot of assistants will tell them anything because their job is to get players.

Joe Mullaney, who retired as basketball coach at Providence College after the 1984–85 season, noted:

Everybody has to win these days and nobody can afford to lose. It has changed recruiting. . . . I feel sorry for assistant coaches.

Recruiting is a tough way to pay your dues in order to become a head coach.

The continuous pressure on coaches exhibits itself in many ways. Fred Jacoby, executive officer of the Southwest Conference, notes that even game officials are not spared:

What a coach gets paid in salary and what he realizes is so much greater. There is a shoe endorsement, camps, clinics and speaking engagements. When a coach jumps all over an official, it's like he's saying "you're meddling with my income."

Such pressures may have led in the 1984–85 season to the one-game suspension of Indiana coach Bobby Knight, who received that penalty for tossing a chair across a basketball court after a displeasing call by an official.

Indicative of the problems facing intercollegiate athletics was the 1985 scandal involving the Baylor University basketball team. In that sad incident, Baylor basketball coach Jim Haller was secretly recorded by one of his players, reserve center John Wheeler, as he gave the student-athlete a university check for $172 to make car payments and talked of having the strength coach dispense anabolic steroids to Wheeler. Coach Haller, who resigned at the end of the season, later stated:

[I]n my mind I know how I've lived my life and I'm not going to apologize to anybody for it. I'm not going to apologize except for a couple of situations I got myself into here lately.

. . . It wasn't going to help me. It wasn't going to help our basketball team. I was doing it to help an individual.

The pressure on coaches is not limited to coaches of men's sports. With the development and expansion of women's athletic programs, women's sports coaches have also experienced pressure. Former Louisiana Tech women's basketball Coach Sonja Hogg has stated that "there is tremendous pressure—it's do or die." Indicative of the year-long nature of recruiting is the statement of Marianne Stanley, women's basketball coach at Old Dominion University, who noted: "The camps (summer) are so valuable. I can see 250 kids at one time." The pressure may be even greater for women's sports coaches because of smaller recruiting budgets and less available information. However, at least one coach, Linda Sharp at the University of Southern California, has stated that the pressure has not reached an uncomfortable level. Sharp, who snared Cheryl Miller, the top female recruit in 1982, had this to say:

Even though there were teams from all over the country competing for her, I don't think she received the same intense recruiting pressure as, say, a Patrick Ewing did, or a Ralph Sampson.

The other day, I understood one of our assistant men's coaches had been gone eight days trying to recruit a player, watching him play in state playoffs, letting him know they're very, very interested.

I haven't done that—haven't sent an assistant out for eight days just to get one individual.

Impact on Institutions

Bill L. Atchley, former president of Clemson University, made the following comment a few years ago:

> The NCAA regulations remind me of the proverbial horse that was put together by a committee, and ended up as a camel. This complex body of rules must be streamlined and then disseminated with a strong educational campaign directed not only at college coaching and recruiting staffs, but also at potential recruits.

Clemson has had its share of trouble with the NCAA, including sanctions against its football team for illegal recruitment of athletes. In 1985, yet another scandal hit the Clemson athletic program, this time involving the dispensing of illegal drugs to student-athletes by Clemson coaches. Atchley resigned as an indirect result of the scandal after the university's board of trustees refused to remove the Clemson Athletic Director, Bill McLellan, as Dr. Atchley recommended they do because of the continuing problems with the program under McLellan.

As previously mentioned, the University of Maryland also fell on unfortunate times in regard to its athletic program. In the aftermath of the Len Bias drug-related death, athletic director Dick Dull stepped down from his position, emotionally and physically burned out from the daily pressures of the Bias controversy. During the same month, long-time Maryland basketball coach Lefty Driesell resigned from his coaching position under pressure from Maryland Chancellor John Slaughter. Slaughter, chairman of the NCAA President's Commission, also received sharp criticism of the school's athletic policies and lack of reform.

Clemson University and the University of Maryland are not alone in having problems with their athletic departments. The Southwest Athletic Conference and many of its member institutions, especially Southern Methodist University, are currently having problems. In August 1980, the University of Southern California (USC) and four other Pacific Athletic Conference (PAC-10) member institutions had their football programs disqualified from the PAC-10 football championship. The penalty was imposed by the presidents and chancellors of the conference schools. Although the penalty was for academic violations, the study commissioned by USC following the sanctions was charged with investigating all aspects of the USC athletic department. Excerpts from that report that deal with the areas of recruitment and admissions are reprinted here ("Academic Conduct, Admission, Advisement and Counseling of Student-Athletes at the University of Southern California," by James H. Zumberge, President USC, October 12, 1980):

. . . The present crisis appears to be related to at least five major weaknesses. All of these, to one degree or another, have been manifested in the recent so-called "scandals" besetting intercollegiate athletics. Some of these weaknesses have been prevalent at USC.

First, institutional and individual integrity has not always guided action. Colleges and universities have too often taken advantage of athletes either through failing to assist those with marginal skills or failing to confront the less able early in their academic careers with an awareness that academic success may not be viable. Too often, the practice has been to admit athletes with marginal academic motivations and abilities, permit them to drift through the curriculum and, once athletic eligibility is used up, to cast them aside with neither a degree nor much hope of attaining one. The failure to offer opportunities and incentives to students to become academically successful is itself a weakness. But, the failure to confront a student-athlete early with the realities of his or her true potential for academic survival is unethical. Such practices are tantamount to exploitation and are unacceptable.

A second prominent weakness has been a failure to understand the seriousness of the present situation. A similar shakeup in college sports occurred during the early 1950s as a result of recruiting violations and classroom cheating. The proportions of the national scandal in 1980 are substantially larger and far less innocent. Today's scenario includes not only cheating and recruiting violations, but manipulation of courses by faculty and coaches, forgery of admissions credentials by outside "merchants," financial mismanagement by athletic program administrators, and more.

A third weakness has been a failure to comprehend the significance of changes that have occurred in competitive sports in America during the past three decades. Colleges and universities today must come to grips with these changes because they are the source of much of the malaise that afflicts intercollegiate athletics today. The earlier brief crisis of the 50s came at a time when national television played a small part; when pro-football and basketball were in a fledgling state, and big-time professional tennis and golf were almost unimaginable; when the largest pro-contracts might total $30,000 per year and agents to negotiate them were non-existent; when the egalitarian "Great Society" reforms of the 60s, which broadened higher education's accessibility, had not yet begun; when literacy levels in elementary and secondary schools were not declining; and, when Las Vegas-style gambling on collegiate sports outcomes was less prominent. Higher education must begin to comprehend the implications of these major developments if it is to begin to deal more adequately with the present crisis.

A fourth common weakness is that of failing to understand more clearly the purposes served by intercollegiate athletics. Much has been made of the importance of intercollegiate sports for institutional name recognition and fund raising. Such purposes, while often part of the institutional *raison d'etre* for sponsorship, have been largely overstated in comparison to the many individual and social values that are derived. Consequently, intercollegiate athletics have remained curiously tangential and their status indefinite. What often has been projected by institutions is doubt, uncertainty, and ambivalence about the relationship between higher education and athletics.

Excellence on the field and excellence in the classroom are not inherently incompatible. Indeed, they often are mutually reinforcing in individual development. The rapid acquisition of new skills; the management of time and energy; the development of collaborative abilities; the development, clarification, and testing of values; and the testing of personal limits of physical and psychological endurance encountered in athletic competition all provide rare learning opportunities for the student-athlete.

Intercollegiate athletics also serve broader institutional and social interests. The role played by sports in providing a common meeting ground, in overcoming racial barriers, and in bridging the generations often have been overlooked and/or significantly understated. The importance of play in human life and education also has too often been given short shrift in discussions of the role of sports. More precision about these and other positive aspects of intercollegiate athletics should help clarify both their relationship to higher education and the reasons for institutional commitment to athletes and athletic competition.

Fifth, strong university leadership has been lacking. Presidents, coaches, athletic directors, admissions officers, academic deans, advisers, and faculty—everyone connected with the enterprise— must share in the responsibility for individual and institutional conduct. Too often, there has been a tendency to adopt an attitude of *laissez faire* toward athletes and athletics. This attitude has permitted drift within the system when the mounting pressures and abuses have called for firm action. Each individual, and most certainly presidents of institutions, must accept more active responsibility than in the past for the tenor and conduct of intercollegiate athletics within individual institutions and the system as a whole. . . .

Principles and Responsibilities of Proper Conduct

These weaknesses notwithstanding, it is abundantly clear that there is far more that is positive about intercollegiate athletics today than negative. Proper reforms, diligently implemented, can have immediate, positive effects in reversing the general drift and restoring the public's confidence in the capacity of higher education for self-correction and ethical conduct.

University Conduct

1. Admission standards and procedures for student-athletes should be fully consistent with University-wide standards and procedures for all students.
2. All matters of eligibility and academic progress must be under the direct supervision and control of faculty and staff outside the department of athletics. . . .

Reforms and Actions: Admissions

6. Responsibility for the admission of all students (including athletes) shall rest solely with the Office of Admissions acting in accordance with established University policies and procedures governing appeals and referrals.
7. The Admission Policy of the University of Southern California is to identify students who can both contribute to, and benefit from, its special ambiance by their individual excellence and intellectual promise. Admission to USC is not determined by a rigid formula. University-wide admissions standards are presently under discussion within the University Admissions Committee. A proposed policy governing regular admission has been forwarded to the President's Advisory Council. The Admissions Committee will consider policies governing Special Action admissions later this Fall.

   In the interim, the Office of Admission has been directed by the President to adhere to the following criteria for Special Action: Applicants falling below a minimum high school grade point standard of 2.7 on a 4.0 scale and combined Scholastic Aptitude Test scores of 800 *normally* shall not be admitted to the University. (The average freshman today enters USC with a 3.4 high school GPA and combined SAT scores of 1040.)

However, applicants falling below these minimums may, in certain cases, be admitted by Special Action to regular standing providing such students are able to demonstrate, through admissions credentials, potential for academic success at USC. Applicants subject to Special Action consideration shall be closely evaluated, in addition to grades and SAT (or equivalent ACT) scores, on the basis of trends in past academic performance, writing samples, personal interviews, cultural factors, class rank, extracurricular involvement, intensiveness of secondary school training, and statements of teachers and counselors regarding academic potential.

Circumstances justifying Special Action review will vary, but may include special talent, i.e., musical, dramatic, athletic, and scientific. All students admitted by Special Action are required to enter an appropriately designated support program designed to encourage academic success.

8. All student-athletes transferring after two years at a community or four-year college or university shall satisfy standard academic admission criteria without consideration of other factors that may be taken into account for students entering as freshmen.

9. The Office of Admissions shall, in conjunction with appropriate student support personnel, determine the placement of Special Action admissions within available support programs in the USC academic support system. . . .

Problem Areas: Admission and Retention

An *Ad Hoc* Committee on Student-Athlete Advisement and Counseling was charged with examining the current status of academic advisement and counseling of student-athletes at USC and to make recommendations for improvement, if warranted.

During its deliberations, the Committee found it appropriate to expand its inquiries and recommendations to the area of University admissions criteria and practices due to the intrinsic relationship between admissions standards and the potential for academic success. Clearly, the matter of appropriate advisement and counseling for student-athletes is closely linked to standards and practices of admission.

With regard to admission and retention it has been found that:

• For several years, the University, while adhering to NCAA admission standards for athletic eligibility, admitted some athletes who fell below normal USC standards of admission. (This practice also was applied to some non-athlete student applicants.) Between 1970 and 1980, these exceptions averaged 33 student-athletes per year (in all sports).

- Academically, marginal athletes have been admitted to USC in the past based chiefly on athletic prowess as judged by the Athletic Department, and without normal Admissions Office review.
- Although the retention and graduation rate of USC student-athletes during the past decade has been approximately the same as for the undergraduate student body as a whole, only a small number of athletes admitted as exceptions have ever graduated from the University.

The USC report gives an overview of many of the "academic" problems associated with intercollegiate athletics. A more individualized problem in intercollegiate athletics that threatens to tarnish the image of many institutions involves drug abuse among athletes. Already noted were the cases involving Clemson University and University of Maryland athletes and coaches. Also in 1985, Arizona State University became embroiled in controversy when baseball coach Jim Brock disclosed that many of his players used a mood-altering drug dispensed by a psychiatrist who served as a part-time consultant to the program. Vanderbilt University was also involved in a drug controversy in 1985—the same year the Tulane University gambling scandal was revealed and the underlying cause was identified as being cocaine abuse by the basketball team members.

However, although an institution can put its reputation in intercollegiate athletics at stake through involvement in academic, recruiting, or other scandals, it can also enhance its reputation by well-known programs. As an example, Georgetown University's director of annual giving, Patrick J. McArdle, credits the success of the basketball team in recent years for "geometric" increases in contributions. It has been estimated that in 1984 the Georgetown basketball team generated $3 million for the school in direct revenue. The university's 33 percent increase in admissions applications since 1983 is also indirectly credited to the team's success.

In balancing the positive and negative aspects of an intercollegiate athletic program, an institution must realize that the chances of becoming embroiled in some controversy are quite likely. Litigation is becoming more prevalent in intercollegiate athletics, and institutions should be aware of the potential areas of litigation. Chapters 4 and 5 examine some of the problems that face institutions in regard to these controversies.

Impact on Student-Athletes

The pressure to succeed in intercollegiate athletics can also severely affect the student-athlete. In particular, the impact of recruiting violations on student-athletes can be tremendous. It can affect all aspects of their lives, education, family, and careers. Consider this statement by Alan Page, a former football player for the Minnesota Vikings:

> We had each spent four years in colleges with decent reputations. I remember that two of us could read the playbook, three others had some trouble with it but managed, and four of my teammates couldn't read it at all. It was embarrassing. . . . There were no big words and not a lot of syllables. They all understood the concept when spoken, so it's not that they were dumb. I don't think you can be dumb to play football. Maybe I'm wrong, but if you can understand the intricacies of X's and O's, then you should be smart enough to learn to read and write. The problem seems to be that these athletes—and there are many more like them, blacks and whites—were never expected to learn to read and write. They've floated through up to this point because they were talented athletes.

This special treatment because of athletic talent may lie at the root of other problems plaguing intercollegiate athletics today. As columnist George Will has stated, "Many athletes live in an atmosphere of permanent exemption—exemption from all rules and rigors of academic life. Not surprisingly, some young people come to think they are exempt also from physiological limits."

Ned Bolcar was one of the most sought-after high school football recruits of the 1985 recruiting season. The Phillipsburg, New Jersey, high school player, who finally chose Notre Dame, made this comment about his recruitment:

> Intelligent players know what recruiters are trying to do. You believe some, you let some go by. But you are always polite. If people aren't polite to me, I will hang up. I don't want any pressure. They look out for their business, and I look out for mine.

Once in college, athletes are finding that there is greater emphasis on academics than in the past. In 1985, Kentucky running back George Adams noted:

> Around here, they emphasize that you get the grades and that degree. We're assigned counselors, and they keep an eye on us and our grades. Coach Claiborne keeps emphasizing that life is a bigger game, and that you can't be a player all your life.

Unfortunately, for some the new emphasis on academics causes hardship. Former University of Tennessee basketball player Gary Carter was declared academically ineligible his senior year and left school without graduating. He commented:

I found out in December of my senior year that I was ineligible.
The new rule went into effect. . . . I was off the team. They could
have put me on probation and let me get my grades up, but they
didn't. It hurt because I wanted to be drafted by the NBA.

. . . They could have spent more time with the players and made
sure they kept their grades up, rather than wait till it's too late.
Athletes know they have to get the grades, and there is emphasis on
grades but you could see they really wanted you to be good in
basketball.

The areas of recruitment and academic eligibility will remain a
constant problem in the years ahead for athletes and litigators.
Chapter 5 examines these subjects in detail, noting the various
types of litigation that can be pursued by the student-athlete.

Donn C. Renwick, chair of sports management at the U.S.
Sports Academy, summarized the impacts of the pressure to win
and offered a solution to the problem:

We place coaches, management and players under tremendous
pressure to produce and to be winners. An unholy amount of
attention from fans, the media, men and women on the street, and
critics is directed toward these games designed for children. All
participants are judged, criticized and adored by a public whose
loyalties are as fragile as the last victory. The pressure to destroy, to
defeat and to win at all cost has forced undue strain on those
associated with sports. The breaking point has been reached. Their
values are put aside. In the name of winning, sports have become a
spectacle.

Scandal ensues. How do we correct this behavior and return
sports to what they were meant to be? It begins with redefining
"success" and "winning." Parents, athletes, coaches and athletic
administrators must realize that the road to success or winning is a
journey rather than a destination. How we get there is important,
because along the way we learn teamwork, loyalty, belief in ideas
and integrity. Through sports, we educate young men and women
to know and realize their capabilities. We teach them to work
cooperatively in striving for obtainable goals that are important only
for an instant. We should cheer success, praise effort and revel in
the enjoyment these games provide.

More importantly, if we are to return competition through sports
to its original intent, we should reemphasize that the integrity of
individuals, institutions and ideas is paramount. It is up to each of
us to protect the other's integrity. We no longer can condone those
who use sports and give nothing back. For coaches, we must curtail
the amount of public pressure, insist upon their maintaining the
rules, separate the positions of coach and athletics administrator,

and punish rule offenders. Athletes must learn that the purpose of games is to gain an understanding of themselves, their teammates and their opponents. They must know that effort, sportsmanship and loyalty are more important than a victory. They must be academically prepared to be students. ["The Emphasis on Winning Must Be Redirected," *The NCAA News*, February 26, 1986, p. 2]

OVERVIEW OF TOPICS

The structure and governance of amateur athletics in the United States affects many individuals, participants, administrators, and coaches. This book has been written for the aforementioned, as well as for faculty advisers, school boards, player representatives, lawyers, sporting goods manufacturers, and others who are involved in amateur athletics. Of particular concern is the growth in amateur athletics and the corresponding increase in litigation, which has come about, in part, because of the rising financial stakes for amateur athletic organizations and amateur athletes. Recruiting violations, sanctions against coaches and institutions, and the use of ineligible players are all sources of litigation in intercollegiate and interscholastic athletics.

To establish a foundation upon which such litigation can be understood and possibly avoided, Chapter 2 introduces the basics of the court and the legal system, and Chapter 3 introduces the fundamental aspects of contract law. How the courts view litigation in intercollegiate and interscholastic athletics and the effect litigation has on amateur athletic associations are examined in Chapter 4. Chapter 5 focuses on how these areas can affect the rights and remedies under the law of individual student-athletes and how courts have decided the complex and conflicting interests involved.

Chapter 6 introduces the theory of tort liability as it relates to sports, and Chapter 7 examines the many tort liability questions that affect coaches, athletic administrators, and others. Chapter 8 discusses the rise in intercollegiate athletic opportunities for women and the sex discrimination issues that have accompanied this growth in women's sports. Chapter 9 discusses the various legal theories involving television and the media in the sports context. Chapter 10 examines the legal principles of trademark law, and Chapter 11 focuses on the issues and considerations an amateur athlete is faced with before deciding to turn professional. The drug-testing issue, so often in the headlines of sports news today, is explored in Chapter 12. Chapter 13, the final chapter, discusses various legal considerations involving violence, gambling, taxes, and antitrust law.

Chapter 2

THE COURT AND LEGAL SYSTEM IN THE UNITED STATES

INTRODUCTION

Directors of amateur athletic organizations need a fundamental understanding of the legal system in the United States to deal effectively with the wide variety of legal matters they face today. The overview given in this chapter is brief and general in nature, but the reader can consult the notes for source materials that provide greater detail.

The American legal system is based primarily on the common law tradition established in England. *Common law* is to be distinguished from *legislative law* in that it is based on legal custom and precedent. The influence of English common law in our American legal system goes back to colonial America, with its English laws, customs, and language.

Two fundamental concepts, precedent and stare decisis, are associated with the common law tradition. *Precedent* is the example established in an earlier case law that is followed by the courts in future cases that arise under similar circumstances. *Stare decisis* is the following by the court of a principle of law established previously. Understanding these two concepts will help amateur athletic administrators and coaches to avoid mistakes made in the past by other administrators and coaches which have been litigated in the courts.

The legal system in the United States is generally viewed as having three functions: (1) administering the laws of the country or individual states, (2) serving as a conflict resolver of private civil suits among parties, and (3) interpreting the legislative intent of a law in deciding a case.

There are two basic legal systems in the United States: the federal system and the state system. Chapter 2 begins with a description of the federal court system, which includes the U.S. Supreme Court, U.S. courts of appeals, U.S. district courts, and several administrative agencies. The chapter next discusses the state legal system, which consists of the primary sources of law in each state's constitution and court decisions in each state. Naturally, there is variation among state legal systems.

Just as important as understanding the legal system in the United States is knowing how to find legal information. The next section of Chapter 2 identifies and describes all sorts of legal sources that coaches and administrators may find useful. The last section of Chapter 2 describes the ten steps in the trial system—information that will reduce the fear often associated with "going to court."

THE FEDERAL COURT SYSTEM

The federal court system in the United States consists of the Supreme Court, 12 courts of appeals, 91 district courts, and certain specialized courts, and administrative agencies (Exhibit 2–1). Federal cases usually are first heard in a district court, although certain cases are initiated in the higher courts of appeals or in the Supreme Court. Cases that are appealed after being heard in the district courts usually go to a court of appeals, or in rare cases, directly to the Supreme Court. The 12 courts of appeals (representing 11 judicial circuits and the District of Columbia) also review orders issued by administrative agencies such as the Securities and Exchange Commission, the Federal Trade Commission, the Internal Revenue Service, and the National Labor Relations Board.

The special federal courts include the U.S. Court of Claims, the U.S. Customs Court, the U.S. Court of Military Appeals, the Tax Court of the U.S., and the U.S. Court of Customs and Patent Appeals. The jurisdiction of these courts is rather narrow. For example, the U.S. Court of Claims only hears cases in which individuals have some claim against the federal government, and the U.S. Court of Customs and Patent Appeals only hears patent and trademark cases. These courts generally are not of concern to athletic administrators.

The U.S. Supreme Court

The Supreme Court is the highest court in the United States and the ultimate dispute arbitrator. Once the Supreme Court decides an issue, all other federal courts must interpret the law by its lead. The Supreme Court has two types of jurisdiction: original and

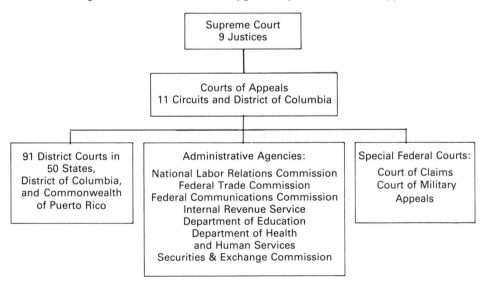

Exhibit 2-1 The Federal Court System

appellate. *Original jurisdiction* covers two types of cases: those involving ambassadors, ministers, and consuls, and those involving a state as one of the parties to a lawsuit. The Supreme Court hears very few cases under original jurisdiction. *Appellate jurisdiction* covers cases tried or reviewed by the individual state's highest court involving federal questions, including those bearing on the U.S. Constitution, congressional acts, or foreign treaties. It also covers cases tried or reviewed by the U.S. courts of appeals or the U.S. district courts. Appellate jurisdiction constitutes the vast majority of cases reviewed by the Supreme Court.

Nine justices sit on the U.S. Supreme Court, including a chief justice and eight associate justices. The Supreme Court justices are appointed by the President of the United States and confirmed by the United States Senate. They serve lifetime tenures. The chief justice receives a salary of $115,000, and the associate justices receive $110,000 each (1987).

The Supreme Court generally reviews cases brought before it by writ of appeal or writ of certiorari. There is little significant difference between the two procedures, but they may be distinguished as follows. A *writ of appeal* applies when:

1. A state supreme court has held a federal act to be unconstitutional.
2. A state supreme court has held a state action to be constitutional.
3. A lower federal court has decided against the United States in a criminal case.
4. The United States has brought suit under the Interstate Commerce Act.
5. A federal district court has heard a suit that involves a restraint on enforcement of a state or federal statute on the grounds that it is unconstitutional.

A *writ of certiorari* allows the Court to hear cases not covered by the writ of appeal. It is a written order to call up for review a case from a lower court. Four of the nine Supreme Court justices have to vote to review a case under a writ of certiorari. Certiorari gives the Supreme Court broad discretion in deciding which cases to review. It can be employed by the Court to review:

1. Any civil or criminal case in the federal court of appeals, no matter which party petitions the Court.
2. Any state court decision in which a federal statute or treaty is questioned.
3. Any state court decision that rules a state statute unconstitutional under the federal Constitution.

The Supreme Court hears oral arguments from the attorneys for the parties when it decides to hear a case. The parties also submit *briefs*, or written arguments, to the Court. Sometimes the Court allows a brief termed *amicus curiae*, or "friend of the court," to be submitted by third parties who believe that they (or the organization they represent) may be affected by the Court's decision in a case. For instance, in a 1984 Supreme Court case not directly involving athletics, *Grove City College v. Bell* (see Chapter 8), the Council of Collegiate Women's Athletic Administrators submitted an *amicus curiae* brief because it feared that opportunities for women in intercollegiate athletics would be diminished, based on an adverse Court decision.

Supreme Court decisions are made after the justices have heard the oral presentations and reviewed the briefs from both parties. Each justice renders an opinion on why a certain decision should be made, and then the justices vote in order of seniority. After a decision has been reached by majority vote, a justice is chosen to write the *opinion of the Court*. A justice who disagrees with the opinion and who did not vote with the majority may write a *dissenting opinion*. A justice who agrees with the majority opinion but not with the reasons it was reached may write a *concurring opinion*. All opinions that result from a case are reported in the following publications:

1. *United States Reports* (official edition), cited U.S.
2. *United States Supreme Court Reports* (Lawyers Co-operative Publishing Company), cited L. Ed. or L. Ed. 2d.
3. *Supreme Court Reporter* (West Publishing Company), cited Sup. Ct. or S. Ct. The *United States Reports* (official edition), cited U.S., the *United States Supreme Court Reports* (Lawyers Co-operative Publishing Company), cited L. Ed. or L. Ed. 2d, and the *Supreme Court Reporter* (West Publishing Company), cited Sup. Ct. or S. Ct., are published in order to publicize the opinions of the Supreme Court. The *United States Reports* is the official set of the three and is cited by the *United States Supreme Court Reports* and the *Supreme Court Reporter*. Most lawyers and researchers use the unofficial sets because they include editorial features, known as annotations, which make the opinions easier to read. The *Commerce Clearing House, Supreme Court Bulletin*, cited S. Ct. Bull., provides the reader with a table that outlines current cases pending in court.
4. *United States Law Week* (Bureau of National Affairs), cited U.S.L.W. or U.S.L. Week. The *United States Law Week* is published by the Bureau of National Affairs in Washington,

D.C. The publication is composed of two looseleaf volumes; one contains the current opinions of the United States Supreme Court, and the other volume deals with matters that do not relate to the United States Supreme Court.

Only a small percentage of cases that are filed on the trial level ever reach the Supreme Court for the following reasons: cases are settled, parties do not believe they will be successful on appeal, costs can be prohibitive, and appellate courts can refuse to hear an appeal. Cases that the appellate courts do review are those in which there may have been an error at the trial court level or ones that may involve important questions of law. Even so, Warren Berger, Chief Justice from 1969 to 1986, often complained that the U.S. court system does not filter out enough cases and that the Supreme Court is overburdened. Some critics of the judicial system believe an additional level of judicial review is needed between the courts of appeals and the Supreme Court.

U.S. Courts of Appeals

The United States is divided into 11 judicial districts, one of which is the District of Columbia (Exhibit 2–2). Each of these districts, called circuits, has a U.S. Court of Appeals. The appeals courts have one type of jurisdiction, *appellate*. That means they review cases tried in the federal district courts and cases heard and decided by the federal regulatory commissions mentioned earlier. Decisions of the appeals courts (also called appellate courts) are reported in the *Federal Reporter* (West Publishing Company) and

Circuits	Location
District of Columbia	Washington, D.C.
First	Boston
Second	New York
Third	Philadelphia
Fourth	Richmond, Asheville
Fifth	New Orleans, Fort Worth, Jackson
Sixth	Cincinnati
Seventh	Chicago
Eighth	St. Louis, Kansas City, Omaha, St. Paul
Ninth	San Francisco, Los Angeles, Portland, Seattle
Tenth	Denver, Wichita, Oklahoma City
Eleventh	Atlanta, Jacksonville, Montgomery

Exhibit 2-2   U.S. Courts of Appeals Locations

are cited F. or F.2d, depending on the date of the court decision. The *Federal Reporter* has now limited the number of published opinions because of the caseload. Additional cases for the athletic administrator to review would be found in the Temporary Emergency Court of Appeals, which are published in the *Federal Reporter*.

U.S. District Courts

The district courts are the trial courts of the federal court system. Each state has at least one district court, and some of the larger states have as many as four. A total of 91 district courts cover the 50 states, the District of Columbia, and the Commonwealth of Puerto Rico (see Exhibit 2–3). Each district court has at least one federal district judge, and some have as many as 27 federal judges.

The decisions of the district courts are reported in the *Federal Supplement* (West Publishing Company) and are cited F. Supp. In a district court opinion, the district involved is always included as a part of the citation. For example, D.N.J. 1985 is the citation for District of New Jersey, 1985. When there is more than one federal district court in a state, the particular district involved in the decision is cited. For example, S.D.N.Y. 1985 is the citation for Southern District of New York, 1985, which differentiates it from the Northern District of New York, 1985, or N.D.N.Y. 1985.

Administrative Agencies

Rulings made by federal agencies such as the Federal Trade Commission, the Internal Revenue Service, and the National Labor Relations Board fall into the category of administrative law. For a number of reasons, notably specialization, efficiency, and flexibility, Congress and the state legislatures decided to grant certain judicial powers to administrative agencies such as those named in Exhibit 2–1. These agencies are allowed to formulate rules for the administrative area they regulate, enforce the rules, hold hearings on any violations, and issue decisions, including penalties. This delegation of the power to adjudicate controversies has been generally held to be constitutional, although the agencies must follow specific guidelines in their administration of these delegated powers. On the federal level, Congress has enacted the Administrative Procedure Act, which sets guidelines for the agencies to follow. Many states have similar state statutes. A party to an administrative law decision can appeal such decisions and sometimes obtain judicial review, depending on the nature of the

Alabama	3 districts (Northern, Middle, and Southern)
Alaska	1 district
Arizona	1 district
Arkansas	2 districts (Eastern and Western)
California	4 districts (Northern, Eastern, Central, and Southern)
Colorado	1 district
Connecticut	1 district
Delaware	1 district
District of Columbia	1 district
Florida	3 districts (Northern, Middle, and Southern)
Georgia	3 districts (Northern, Middle, and Southern)
Hawaii	1 district
Idaho	1 district
Illinois	3 districts (Northern, Central, and Southern)
Indiana	2 districts (Northern and Southern)
Iowa	2 districts (Northern and Southern)
Kansas	1 district
Kentucky	2 districts (Eastern and Western)
Louisiana	3 districts (Eastern, Middle, and Western)
Maine	1 district
Maryland	1 district
Massachusetts	1 district
Michigan	2 districts (Eastern and Western)
Minnesota	1 district
Mississippi	2 districts (Northern and Southern)
Missouri	2 districts (Eastern and Western)
Montana	1 district
Nebraska	1 district
Nevada	1 district
New Hampshire	1 district
New Jersey	1 district
New Mexico	1 district
New York	4 districts (Northern, Southern, Eastern, and Western)
North Carolina	3 districts (Eastern, Middle, and Western)
North Dakota	1 district
Ohio	2 districts (Northern and Southern)
Oklahoma	3 districts (Northern, Eastern, and Western)
Oregon	1 district
Pennsylvania	3 districts (Eastern, Middle, and Western)
Puerto Rico	1 district
Rhode Island	1 district
South Carolina	1 district
South Dakota	1 district
Tennessee	3 districts (Eastern, Middle, and Western)
Texas	4 districts (Northern, Southern, Eastern, and Western)

Exhibit 2-3 U.S. District Court Locations

Utah	1 district
Vermont	1 district
Virginia	2 districts (Eastern and Western)
Washington	2 districts (Eastern and Western)
West Virginia	2 districts (Northern and Southern)
Wisconsin	2 districts (Eastern and Western)
Wyoming	1 district

Exhibit 2-3 Continued

dispute and whether all administrative remedies have been exhausted.

THE STATE COURT SYSTEM

Generally, each of the 50 states has a three-tiered court system, with a trial court level, appellate level, and supreme court level of review. Each state judicial system hears cases and reviews the law, based on its state constitution, state statutes, and court decisions. In addition, a state court must often interpret the federal constitution and/or federal statutes, based on how they impact on state criminal or civil laws that are reviewed under its jurisdiction. The structure of the state court system, in which the more important the court the fewer they are in number, is very similar to the federal court structure (see Exhibit 2–4).

State court decisions can be reported (although only a small percentage are) in a state or regional collection of reports called a *reporter*. A regional reporter groups decisions from a number of states in one publication. The regional reporters as a group are termed the *National Reporter System,* which is published by the West Publishing Company and includes West's federal law reports and some additional special court reporters. The *National Reporter System* provides a quick method of making the opinions of the state courts known to the public. The seven regional reporters are listed in Exhibit 2–5.

SOURCES OF LEGAL INFORMATION

The athletic administrator should know how to find legal information. Sources include legal dictionaries, directories, encyclopedias, indexes, treatises, guides, and law reviews; state and federal constitutions and legislation; federal administrative rules and regulations; and case law.

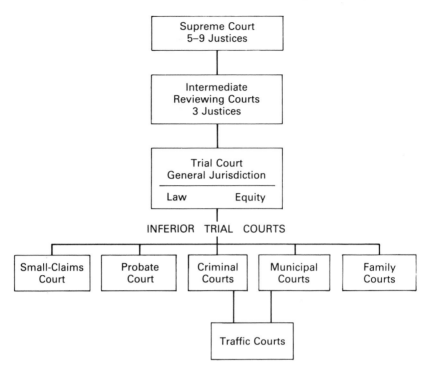

Exhibit 2-4 A Typical State Court System

Pacific Reporter (P. or P.2d)	Alaska, Arizona, California to 1960, Colorado, Hawaii, Idaho, Kansas, Montana, Nevada, New Mexico, Oklahoma, Oregon, Utah, Washington, and Wyoming
North Western Reporter (N.W. or N.W.2d)	Michigan, Minnesota, Nebraska, North Dakota, South Dakota, and Wisconsin
South Western Reporter (S.W. or S.W.2d)	Arkansas, Kentucky, Missouri, Tennessee, and Texas
North Eastern Reporter (N.E. or N.E.2d)	Illinois, Indiana, Massachusetts, New York, and Ohio
Atlantic Reporter (A. or A.2d)	Connecticut, Delaware, Maine, Maryland, New Hampshire, New Jersey, Pennsylvania, Rhode Island, Vermont, and District of Columbia Municipal Court of Appeals
South Eastern Reporter (S.E. or S.E.2d)	Georgia, North Carolina, South Carolina, Virginia, and West Virginia
Southern Reporter (So. or So. 2d)	Alabama, Florida, Louisiana, and Mississippi

Exhibit 2-5 Regional Reporters

Legal Reference Materials

Legal Dictionaries

Legal dictionaries contain definitions of words and functions that are commonly used in the legal system in the United States and other common law jurisdictions, such as Great Britain, Canada, and Australia. The following are three of the best and most popular legal dictionaries:

1. *Black's Law Dictionary*, 5th ed. (St. Paul, Minn.: West Pub. Co., 1979).
2. *Ballentine's Law Dictionary*, 3d ed. (Rochester, N.Y.: Lawyers Cooperative Pub. Co., 1969).
3. *Modern Legal Glossary* (Charlottesville, Va.: Michie Co., 1980).

Lawyer Directories

Lawyer directories are published lists of lawyers by states or regions. The *Martindale-Hubbell Law Directory*, published by Martindale-Hubbell, Summit, New Jersey, is an annual publication that lists all the lawyers in the United States. Another useful directory is published by Legal Directories Publishing Company, Los Angeles, California. It publishes many state directories (e.g., the *Texas Legal Directory*) and regional directories (e.g., the *New England Legal Directory*).

Legal Research Guides

Legal research guides are texts that explain how to do legal research. They include instruction on different sources of law and how best to utilize the sources. The athletic administrator will find the following guides most helpful:

1. Price and Bitner, *Effective Legal Research*, 4th ed. (Boston, Mass.: Little, Brown, 1979). A guide that gives the athletic administrator an in-depth description of the types of sources available for law research by providing separate chapters geared to the individual source.
2. Jacobstein and Mersky, *Fundamentals of Legal Research*, 2d ed. (Mineola, N.Y.: Foundation Press, 1981). An excellent guide to legal research. This book is very well organized for the person who is learning how to do legal research.
3. Cohen, *How to Find the Law*, 8th ed. (St. Paul, Minn.: West Publishing, 1983). A guide that trains the student and non-lawyer how to research law.

4. Cohen, *Legal Research in a Nutshell,* 4th ed. (St. Paul, Minn.: West Publishing Co., 1985). A condensed guide that briefs the reader on how to perform legal research. This book may be most appropriate for the athletic administrator's introduction to legal research material.

Annotated Law Reports

The *American Law Reports (ALR)* gives comprehensive annotations on legal subject matters. It consists of five series. An *annotation* is a commentary on how a particular legal subject developed and the current status of the law on that subject. The annotations in the *ALR* often include a list of cases that have discussed the point of law that the annotation explains. For a good example of an *ALR* annotation, see "Tort Liability of Public Schools and Institutions for Accidents Occurring During School Athletic Events," 35 *ALR* 3d 725.

Legal Encyclopedias

Legal encyclopedias are texts designed to give the reader a broad view of the law on any given legal subject. The following are two of the best:

1. *Corpus Juris Secundum (C.J.S.)* (St. Paul, Minn.: West Publishing Company, 1936–current date). This encyclopedia is a compilation of the entire body of American law from the first case to present cases. There are approximately 150 volumes of this text.
2. *American Jurisprudence (Am. Jur.,* 2d) (Summit, N.J.: Lawyers Cooperative Publishing Company and the Bancroft-Whitney Company, 1962–current date). *American Jurisprudence* differs from *Corpus Juris Secundum* in that it only publishes selected court decisions; it provides quick answers to problems that can then be explored more fully.

Treatises

Treatises are texts designed to give the user legal information in one particular legal subject. Treatises can be in the form of casebooks, textbooks, or hornbooks. *Casebooks* are compilations of cases and narrative on a particular subject (see, for example, Berry and Wong, *Law and Business of the Sports Industries,* Vols. 1 and 2 [Dover, Mass.: Auburn House, 1985]). *Textbooks* are narratives on a particular area of law (see, for example, Weistart and Lowell, *The Law of Sports* [Indianapolis, Ind.: Bobbs-Merril, 1979]). *Horn-*

books are texts designed to give rudimentary knowledge on a particular subject of law (see, for example, Biederman et al., *Law and Business of the Entertainment Industries* [Dover, Mass.: Auburn House, 1987]).

Legal Indexes

Legal indexes are lists of articles that contain information on legal subjects, case decisions, and general legal information that has been published in law reviews and other legal periodicals. The following are two good legal indexes:

1. *Index to Legal Periodicals* (Bronx, N.Y.: H. W. Wilson Company, 1908–current date). Includes periodicals published in the United States, Canada, Great Britain, Ireland, Australia, and New Zealand, and is therefore comprehensive in nature.
2. *Index to Periodical Articles Related to Law* (Dobbs Ferry, N.Y.: Glanville Publishers, 1958–1968, Vols. 1–10). Contains articles that appear to be of value and are not covered by the *Index to Legal Periodicals*. This index is useful in locating newly developing areas of law.

Citation Form

One of the most intimidating tasks for any student of the legal system is learning how to cite a case properly. Probably the best reference for checking the correct citation form for legal decisions or writings is the "Blue Book," *A Uniform System of Citation*, 14th ed. (Cambridge, Mass.: Harvard Law Review Association, 1986).

Law Review Articles

Law reviews, published by law schools and administered by a student editorial board, contain current or historical articles that relate to the study of law and law making (for example, legal, legislative, entertainment, and sport law). A school may publish more than one type of law review.

Law reviews are designed to add to the process of developing a better understanding of law and the legal process. This is accomplished by reviewing cases and the impact of decisions, analyzing the legal reasoning behind court decisions, reviewing legislative enactments, proposing reforms, and reviewing legal writings through book reviews.

Shepard's Citations

Shepard's Citations is a system that is used to research reported case decisions to see if the case being researched has been cited as authority by another court, or whether a reported case has been overruled, modified, or questioned in a later decision. *Shepard's*, or "shepardizing," provides a complete history of any case since it was first reported. *Shepard's* is available in hard copies in all law libraries and is also incorporated into the two major legal computer services described below.

Legal Computer Services

Legal computer services offer subscribers access through remote terminals to federal and state court decisions, annotated reports, statutes, law reviews, and so forth, stored within their systems. They generally are the most up-to-date source for legal information, but unfortunately they are not readily available to the lay person. Further, they are expensive and require some training to use easily.

The two major legal computer services are *Lexis*, Mead Data Central, New York, New York, and *Westlaw*, West Publishing Company, St. Paul, Minnesota.

Constitutions

A constitution is the written instrument that serves as the ultimate source of legal authority by which a government and the courts derive their power to govern and adjudicate. The courts in the United States use the federal Constitution or a state constitution as the source for interpreting whether enacted laws are constitutional and whether individual rights granted to a state's citizens are legal. The laws and actions of a government must be consistent with the constitution of that government to be considered legal. A constitution may not always contain language that covers specifically every governmental action, and in such instances the courts must interpret the constitution broadly to include certain governmental actions that are not specifically covered in the constitution. Constitutions can be amended.

Legislation

Legislation is the process by which laws are enacted. Laws are also referred to as *statutes*. Federal legislation is enacted by the U.S. Congress. Very little federal legislation is geared specifically to amateur athletics. One notable exception is the Amateur Sports Act of 1978 (36 U.S.C. §§ 371–396), which governs some of the operation of amateur athletics, especially the U.S. Olympic efforts, in the United States. It should be noted that nonsport-specific legislation may be applied to athletics. An example is Title IX, which governs education and applies to athletics as athletics applies to the educational mission of an institution. Bills can be introduced by individual representatives or senators or groups of commissioned representatives or senators. Copies of pending legislation can be obtained by writing to the following addresses (enclose a self-addressed gummed return label):

Senate Document Room	House Document Room
B-04, Hart Senate Office Bldg.	H-226, U.S. Capitol
Washington, D.C. 20510	Washington, D.C. 20515
(202) 224-7860	(202) 225-3456

The public may receive up to six different items per request, but only one request per day will be filled. Also, only one copy of an individual item will be distributed at a time.

When legislation is enacted and first issued, it is called a *slip law*. Once a session of Congress ends, all the slips laws are published as a group and called *U.S. Statutes at Large*. This is a chronological list of legislation that has been enacted. Every six years, the *U.S. Statutes at Large* is codified—that is, arranged by subject—and published as the *United States Code* (U.S.C.). The *United States Code* includes the public and permanent laws in effect, arranged alphabetically under 50 different titles. The annotated codes are also published by private firms; for example, the *United States Code Annotated* (U.S.C.A.) is published by West Publishing Company, and the *United States Code Service* (U.S.C.S.), *Lawyers Edition*, is published by the Lawyers Cooperative Publishing Company and the Bancroft-Whitney Company.

State legislation is enacted by the legislature in each state. As with federal legislation, very little state legislation is geared specifically to athletics. However, one example is Louisiana's Bribery of Sports Participants Law (L.S.A.—R.S. 14: 118.1), which concerns gambling on sports events. On the state level, bills are also introduced by individual legislators or groups of legislators. Copies of legislation can usually be obtained from the legislators or from the state office that handles legislative services. Each state publishes all the laws that it passed in a given year. These are called *session laws*. Session laws are compiled into statutes, which may be single or multivolume editions. Annotated editions are usually available from private publishing companies.

Federal Administrative Rules and Regulations

Federal administrative rules and regulations attempt to translate enacted laws into practices that must be followed in order to comply with the law. For instance, when Congress enacted Title

IX of the Education Amendments of 1972—a federal statute which prohibited sex discrimination in education (see Chapter 8)—the Department of Health, Education and Welfare had to develop rules and regulations to be followed in order to comply with the new law. An administrative agency which promulgates rules and regulations publishes them in the *Federal Register* (Fed. Reg.). This information is periodically organized by subject (codified) and published in the *Code of Federal Regulations* (C.F.R.).

Case Law

Although this book is not written as a case law text, case law is often cited to give the athletic administrator a better understanding of a legal point in amateur sports law by providing an actual set of circumstances tried before a court. In the notes sections, case law is provided to give the athletic administrator a source for further information on a sports law subject. A case law citation consists of a case title and case citation, which includes the court reporter in which the decision can be found, the court which made the decision, the year of the decision, the volume, and the page number. For example, *Shelton v. National Collegiate Athletic Ass'n* 539 F.2d 1179 (9th Cir. 1976) was a case decided in the federal court of appeals (denoted by F.2d, which is the *Federal Reporter, Second Series*), volume 539, page 1179; the case was heard in the Ninth Circuit Court of Appeals and was decided in 1976.

Often a case is reported in more than one court reporter. A case may be repeated in a state reporter and/or a regional reporter. In the case of the U.S. Supreme Court, a case *can be* reported in as many as five reporters. When a case is reported in more than one court reporter, the multiple cites are termed *parallel citations*. For example, *University of Nevada-Las Vegas v. Tarkanian*, 95 Nev. 389, 594 P.2d 1159 (1979) was a case heard in the state court system in Nevada. The case is reported in two different places. The first is the *Nevada State Reporter* (denoted by Nev.), volume 594, page 1159; the case was decided in 1979. The *Pacific Reporter* (denoted by P.2d) contains appellate-level decisions of several states, including Nevada; it is the second place this case was reported.

Sometimes a case citation will involve multiple courts, which explains how the case fared through judicial review. For example, this district court decision was affirmed by the court of appeals: *Parish v. National Collegiate Athletic Ass'n*, 361 F. Supp. 1214 (N.D. La. 1973), *aff'd*, 506 F.2d 1028 (5th Cir. 1973).

Depending on the nature of the trial—that is, whether it is a civil or a criminal trial—a citation's case name will reflect the type of case involved. For example, the case names in a civil case would look like this:

1. *Jones v. Smith* (individual suing another individual)
2. *Jones v. NCAA* (individual suing an organization)

In a criminal case, the case names will look like this:

1. *State v. Smith* (state criminal law case)
2. *U.S. v. Jones* (federal criminal law case)

Most case decisions can be broken down into the following parts:

1. Case title and citation.
2. Case summary. Gives brief synopsis of case and decisions.
3. The facts. Gives the facts of the case, identifies the parties involved, and reviews any case history, including the lower court decisions.
4. The issues. Presents the issue or issues before the court to be decided.
5. The reasoning. Gives the explanation of the court for its decisions on the issues presented by the parties.
6. Conclusion. A case may contain a final conclusion by the court, which may include the disposition of the case.
7. Majority, dissenting, or concurring opinions. A case on the appellate or supreme court level may contain the majority (the deciding opinion), concurring (in agreement with decision but on different or additional reasoning), or dissenting (does not agree with majority decision) opinions.

THE TRIAL SYSTEM

For many nonlawyers, a group which includes most amateur athletic administrators, the threat of litigation, including the possibility of having to go to trial, is a very upsetting proposition, with the potential of great expense. However, with some basic information about how the trial system works, the athletic administrator will realize that dealing with the trial system is not so difficult after all.

An athletic administrator should follow these basic rules when there is a possibility of a lawsuit developing:

1. Know your organization's attorney and insurance carrier. If some event occurs that may lead to litigation, inform them immediately so that they can take steps to protect your organization's interests.
2. In preparing for litigation, do not hide from your attorney.

Be honest and open about the facts of the case and be prepared to supply any information or records that are needed for trial.
3. Do not talk to outsiders about the pending litigation, especially the media.
4. If possible, review any alternatives for possible settlement of the litigation before it goes to trial.

The steps in the trial system can be broken down into ten parts:

1. the complaint
2. the summons
3. the answer
4. court jurisdiction
5. discovery
6. the parties
7. the type of court
8. the trial
9. the judgment
10. the appeals process

The Complaint

The *complaint*, the initial pleading in a trial, is filed by the plaintiff in a civil case and the prosecutor (e.g., attorney general, district attorney) in a criminal case. *DeFrantz v. United States Olympic Committee*, 492 F. Supp. 1181 (D.D.C. 1980), is an example of a *civil case*. The plaintiffs, 25 athletes who wished to participate in the 1980 Summer Olympic Games in Moscow, filed a civil complaint against the U.S. Olympic Committee for its participation in a boycott of the Olympics. To illustrate an example of a *criminal case*, in 1985, the Orleans Parish district attorney's office issued criminal complaints against Tulane University basketball players for allegedly fixing games ("point shaving") for gambling purposes.

The Summons

When filing a complaint, the plaintiff must make sure that notice of the legal action being instituted against the defendant is served. The *summons* is the actual serving of notice. The plaintiff (or prosecutor) serves a summons on the defendant ordering the defendant to "answer" the charge by a certain date. Often the summons is served by a process server or officer of the court, such as a sheriff. Until a complaint is lawfully served to the defendant, a court has no jurisdiction to review the dispute.

The Answer

The *answer* is the defendant's initial pleading on the alleged violation of criminal or civil law. The defendant may deny or admit to the allegations made by the plaintiff and state his or her own facts about the matter in dispute. In some instances, a defendant may also file a *counterclaim* against the plaintiff, which essentially means the defendant admits no guilt and, in fact, has been injured by the plaintiff.

Court Jurisdiction

Two types of jurisdiction must be satisfied before a court can hear a case: personal and subject matter. *Personal jurisdiction* means that a court must have sufficient contact with the defendant to bring the defendant into its jurisdiction. Simply stated, the defendant must have some contact within the boundaries of that court's jurisdiction to be eligible to be brought into it for a trial. Some criteria that would be considered by a court to establish personal jurisdiction would be residency, voter registration, driver's license, or business activity. *Subject matter jurisdiction* means that the court must have authority to hear the subject matter that is being tried. For instance, a state court would not be the correct jurisdiction in which to bring a suit involving a federal law, which is within the subject matter jurisdiction of the federal courts.

Discovery

Discovery is a pretrial procedure by which each party to a lawsuit obtains facts and information about the case from the other parties in the case in order to assist the party's preparation for trial. Discovery is designed to:

1. Discover facts and evidence concerning the case. It apprises the parties to the lawsuit of the nature of the claim to be litigated.
2. Bind the other party to a legal position. It is advantageous for the litigant to have the other party's legal position clearly stated in advance, so as to anticipate what legal arguments are likely to be argued and what witnesses and evidence will be introduced at the trial.
3. Seek out weaknesses in the other party's legal position.
4. Perpetuate testimony that may become unavailable at trial.
5. Narrow the issues in contention.

A party can ascertain information about the case being litigated from the other party to the lawsuit using a number of methods.

The two most common discovery techniques are depositions and interrogatories. A *deposition* is an out-of-court examination of a witness to a lawsuit, under oath, during which questions and answers are recorded by a notary public or a court official. An *interrogatory* is a set of written questions sent by one party involved in a lawsuit to another party involved in the litigation. The questions must be answered under oath and must be returned within a specified time period.

The Parties

The *plaintiff* is a person or party that initiates a legal action by bringing a lawsuit against another person or party. The *defendant* is the person or party against whom relief or recovery is sought in a legal action or lawsuit. The defendant does the defending or denying of the charges brought by the plaintiff.

On the trial level of review, a case citation usually notes the plaintiff first and the defendant second. For example, in *Kupec v. Atlantic Coast Conference*, 399 F. Supp. 1377 (M.D.N.C. 1975), Kupec is the plaintiff and the Atlantic Coast Conference is the defendant. Sometimes another party will be joined to litigation as a *third-party defendant* when its involvement is such as to make its presence at trial imperative. Athletic associations such as the National Collegiate Athletic Association (NCAA) are often named as a third-party defendant. For instance, a student-athlete who is suing the school over an eligibility matter as a third-party defendant often names the NCAA (or athletic governing organization), because the NCAA implements or oversees the regulations being enforced by the school against the student-athlete.

The Type of Court

The *trial court* is the court of original jurisdiction where all issues are brought forth, argued, and decided on by either a judge or jury. The *appeals court* is the court of review where issues decided at trial are reviewed for error. No new evidence or issues may be entered. Generally, in order to be reviewed, an issue must have been objected to and put on the record at trial.

In the federal court system, original jurisdiction is limited to all criminal cases involving a federal law and civil cases that fall into the following categories:

1. A suit brought by the United States against a citizen or group of citizens.
2. Litigation between citizens of the same state in which the

amount in controversy is over $10,000 (designed to prevent the use of federal courts for frivolous lawsuits).
3. A lawsuit between citizens who reside in two different states.
4. A case brought by a citizen of one state against a foreign nation or citizen of a foreign nation.

In the state court system, original jurisdiction exists for all state law matters, including disputes among the state's citizens and disputes between one of its citizens and a citizen of another state when the out-of-state party has made itself amenable to the jurisdiction of the suing party's state courts. For example, the NCAA, which is located in Kansas, is often a party in state court actions because it is a national organization with members in all the states and therefore has the requisite contact with each state to make it amenable to each state's jurisdiction.

The Trial

Trials can involve a jury or they can take place without a jury present. Whether a trial will be a jury or a nonjury trial depends on the nature of the trial. Federal criminal cases require a trial by a jury of 12 persons. State criminal cases generally require a jury of no less than 6 persons. If a defendant pleads guilty, a jury is not required. In civil cases a trial by jury is not always required and may be waived. Jury size in civil cases may also vary.

Pretrial motions are proposed by either side concerning any number of legalities—for example, a motion to dismiss. In a motion, one of the parties to the suit is attempting to gain a better strategic position for the upcoming trial, or trying to have certain procedural matters settled prior to trial. For instance, a defendant may try to make a motion to dismiss because of a lack of sufficient grounds for the suit. Often, a judge will hold a pretrial conference in the judge's chambers in an effort to attempt to resolve the dispute or elements of the dispute before trial.

The state prosecutor in a criminal case or the plaintiff in a civil suit gives the *opening statement* to the court; then the defendant may do the same. The opening statement is designed to alert the triers of fact (either the judge or the jury, depending on the type of trial) to the nature of the case and to the types of evidence that will be presented during trial. Such statements set expectations and when delivered correctly can serve as the basis for a persuasive argument that will be presented during the trial.

After the opening statements have been made, the plaintiff (or the prosecutor) presents the case first. The plaintiff calls witnesses and examines them; the witnesses are cross-examined by the defendant (or the defense attorney), re-directed by the plaintiff, and re-crossed by the defendant. The defendant then repeats the whole process—that is, the defendant calls and examines witnesses, and these witnesses are cross-examined by the plaintiff. After the witnesses are re-directed by the defendant and re-crossed by the plaintiff, both parties are allowed to call rebuttal witnesses.

At the conclusion of the trial, the defendant (or defense attorney) gives a closing statement first. Then the plaintiff (or prosecutor) gives a closing argument.

The Judgment

After the closing statements when a trial is being argued before a jury, the judge instructs the members of the jury on their options in reaching a decision based on the applicable state and/or federal law or laws. These instructions can be quite involved and are often a subject of appeal by the losing party. Case law and precedent are noted in the instructions. If any statutes are involved, they are read to the jury. After deliberation, the jury renders a decision.

In a trial without a jury, the judge can either recess the court while reaching a decision, or the judge may render a decision immediately on completion of closing statements. Some decisions are given orally; others are written. In rendering a decision, the judge will often cite case law or statutes.

The Appeals Process

Many judgments by trial courts are *appealed*—that is, the party who lost the case requests that the trial proceedings be reviewed by a higher court in the hopes that the decision will be reversed. Among the reasons allowed for an appeal are the following:

1. The plaintiff did not have an opportunity to state his or her case at trial.
2. Evidence was incorrectly allowed into or disallowed at the trial.
3. The judge interpreted the law incorrectly.

The party who takes an appeal from one court to another—the losing party at trial—is called the *appellant*. The party in a case against whom an appeal is taken—the winning party at trial—is called the *appellee*.

In an appeals procedure, no new jury, no new witnesses, and no new facts are allowed to be introduced. The basis for appeal is the record, which may include copies of the testimony, exhibits, and any other evidence introduced at trial. Attorneys for the appellant and the appellee may appear before the court, argue their cases, and submit briefs.

An appeals court may *reverse* (disagree with) a lower court's ruling totally or in part. It may *remand* (return) the case back to the lower court for further proceeding, or it may *affirm* (agree with) the lower court's decision. After a decision has been rendered, the case may be appealed again, either to a state supreme court or the U.S. Supreme Court, depending on what court system is involved. (State supreme court cases involving a federal question—for example, a constitutional law claim—may also in some circumstances be appealed to the U.S. Supreme Court.)

NOTES

1. Exhibit 2–6 contains a list of some of the legal and sports-related abbreviations used frequently in this text and in reported case decisions.

2. A good research source for sports law issues that an athletic coach or administrator might wish to review is Uberstine, *Covering All the Bases: A Comprehensive Research Guide to Sports Law* (Buffalo: William S. Hein Co., 1985).

3. A good research source about governmental policy toward sports issues and potential legislative issues involving amateur athletics is Johnson and Frey, *Government and Sports* (Tutowa, N.J.: Rowman and Allanheld Publishers, 1985).

4. In any research involving a legal issue, or in preparation for litigation, an athletic administrator should attempt to answer some basic questions, including the following:

- Who are the plaintiffs in the case?
- Who are the defendants in the case?
- What are the legal theories of the plaintiffs?
- What are the defenses raised by the defendants?
- Is it state or federal court?
- Is it an administrative agency?
- Is it a trial or appellate level decision?
- What issue or issues did the judge have to decide in the case?
- For whom did the judge rule?
- What was the rationale for the judge's ruling the way he or she did?
- What is the impact of the case?

AAU	Amateur Athletic Union	**LPGA**	Ladies Professional Golf Association
ABA	American Bar Association	**maj**	majority view
ABA	American Basketball Association	**min.**	minority view
AE	assignee	**MISL**	Major Indoor Soccer League
aff'd	affirm(ed)	**MLB**	Major League Baseball
AFL	American Football League	**MLBPA**	MLB Players Association
agt	agent	**n/a**	not applicable
AIAW	Association of Intercollegiate Athletics for Women	**NAIA**	National Association of Intercollegiate Athletics
ans	answer	**NASL**	North American Soccer League
AR	assignor		
a/r	assumption of risk	**NBA**	National Basketball Association
b/c	because		
b/p	burden of proof	**NBPA**	National Basketball Players Association
br/K	breach of contract		
c/a	cause of action	**NCAA**	National Collegiate Athletic Association
CBA	Continental Basketball Association	**NFHSAA**	National Federation of High School Athletic Associations
c/c	counterclaim		
c/d	corpus delicti	**NFL**	National Football League
c/l	common law	**NFLPA**	NFL Players Association
c/n	contributory negligence	**NGB**	National Governing Bodies (Olympics)
c/p	condition precedent		
c/s	condition subsequent	**NHL**	National Hockey League
c/x	cross examination	**NHLPA**	NHL Players Association
Con	constitutional(ity)	**NJCAA**	National Junior College Athletic Association
corp	corporation		
ct	court	**neg**	negligence
d>	distinguish (compare)	**OE**	offeree
d/x	direct examination	**OR**	offeror
D	defendant	**P**	plaintiff
dem	demurrer	**PE**	promisee
eq	equity	**PGA**	Professional Golf Association
ev	evidence	**PR**	promisor
g/r	general rule	**p/f**	prima facie or partner(ship)
int	interest	**Q**	question (or issue)
IOC	International Olympic Committee	**R**	rule (or holding)
		rd/x	redirect examination
J	judgment	**rem**	remanded
J/D	judgment for defendant	**rev'd**	reversed
J/P	judgment for plaintiff	**RIL**	res ipsa loquitur
J/aff'd	judgment affirmed	**RS**	restatement
J/rev'd	judgment reversed	**S**	statute
K	contract	**S/F**	statute of frauds
lcc	last clear chance	**TC**	trial court

Exhibit 2-6 Glossary of Legal and Sports-Related Abbreviations

TP   third party

TPB   third party beneficiary

UCC   Uniform Commercial Code

USBL   United States Basketball League

USFL   United States Football League

USOC   United States Olympic Committee

v   versus

w   with

w/a   weight of authority

WBL   Women's Basketball League

WFL   World Football League

WHL   World Hockey League

w/i   within

w/o   without

xn   action

Exhibit 2-6   Continued

Chapter 3

CONTRACT LAW APPLICATIONS TO AMATEUR ATHLETICS

INTRODUCTION

Amateur athletic administrators are likely to have regular dealings with contract law when they handle game contracts, officiating contracts, personnel contracts, television and radio contracts (see Chapter 9), facility lease agreements, and scholarships. (Although scholarships are viewed as financial aid, they have many features similar to those of contracts, as shown in Chapter 5.) For this reason athletic administrators should have a working knowledge of contract law terminology and its many applications in sports law. Athletic administrators who do not pay careful attention to the contracts they enter into on behalf of the amateur organization they represent can anticipate potentially disastrous results. Teams don't show up for scheduled games, referees don't show up to officiate athletic events, insurance premiums aren't paid, and injury claims can't be paid. The problems can be endless.

Contract law forms the basis for many of the daily activities of an athletic organization. This chapter therefore begins with an introduction to contract law. Then it provides a checklist of information the person preparing the contract should consider and a checklist of typical clauses that are included in most contracts. The last section examines the different types of contracts an athletic administrator may need to review. Examples are included of each type of contract discussed.

CONTRACT LAW

The simplest way for an amateur athletic administrator to consider a contract is as an agreement between parties which is enforceable under the law. A contract can be either written or oral, and it must contain a promise to do something in the future. There are three major sources of contract law:

1. *Common law*. Common law is based on previous court decisions regarding fact situations not specifically dealt with by statute. These previous court decisions provide guidelines in determining the legality of a contract.
2. *Restatement of Contracts*. The American Law Institute (ALI) first published *Restatement of Contracts* in 1932. It has organized and summarized this country's common law concerning contracts. Attorneys and the judiciary rely on it for precedent.
3. *Uniform Commercial Code* (U.C.C.). The U.C.C., a uniform statute that every state except Louisiana has enacted, in-

volves the sale of goods (not land or services). Athletic administrators most often would deal with the U.C.C. art. 2, which specifically covers sales—for example, of sporting goods and game tickets.

Legal Concepts of a Contract

The major legal concepts involved in the formation of a contract are offer, acceptance, consideration, legality, and capacity.

Offer

For a contract to come into existence, the parties must agree on terms. To reach the stage at which there is mutual assent, the parties must go through a process of offering terms and accepting terms. To form a contract the parties must not necessarily agree on all the terms of a contract but rather only on the major or essential terms. The terms of a contract are interpreted objectively, and questions concerning the terms of a contract are often answered in keeping with the intent of the parties forming the contract.

An *offer* is a conditional promise made by the offeror to the offeree. It is conditional because the offeror will not be bound by the promise unless the offeree responds to the offer in the proper fashion. *The Second Restatement of Contracts* defines an offer as "the manifestation of willingness to enter into a bargain, so made as to justify another person in understanding that his assent to that bargain is invited." An offer usually includes the following essential terms: (1) the parties involved, (2) the subject matter, (3) the time (and place) for the subject matter to be performed, and (4) the price to be paid. For example, School A offers to play at School B in football on January 1, 1990 at 2 P.M. for the sum of $100 plus complimentary tickets. School B accepts the offer and signs a written contract with School A. Here, an exchange of promises has been made, and the essential terms of parties, time, place, performance, and price have been incorporated. Note, however, that the number of complimentary tickets has not been specified. By itself this would not void a contract; rather, it would be expected that this number would be the number of tickets usually given to the opposing team as a standard practice in football games.

Most offers contain a pair of promises—a conditional promise made by one party that is premised on the second party's promising to do some act in return. This exchange of promises is categorized as a *bilateral contract*. When an offer is made by one party to a proposed contract to the second party to the contract, it creates a *power of acceptance*, because if the second party accepts the offer, a contract is formed. For example, A promises to pay B $100 if B promises to officiate a basketball game for A. This would be a bilateral contract.

A *unilateral contract* is a contract that does not involve an exchange of promises. It instead involves an exchange of a promise in return for an act by a second party. The second party is not bound to do anything, but if the second party chooses to do the requested act, the first party is bound to the terms of his or her promise. For example, a promoter promises Fighter A that if he will box Fighter B, the promoter will pay A $100. A has not agreed to fight B, but if A does fight B, then the promoter is bound to pay A $100.

An *option contract* involves an offer by one party to keep an offer open exclusively to a second party, for a stated period of time, if the second party pays a fee (or some consideration) to the first party for keeping the offer open. For example, A offers B the opportunity to buy 100 baseball bats at $10 each and also offers that if B will pay A $1, the price quote will remain fixed at $10 per bat (up to 100 bats) for six months.

An offer made in jest is not a valid offer and creates no power of acceptance in the second party. Similarly, an offer is not made if it is just an expression of opinion. It is also important to distinguish preliminary negotiations from an offer that creates a power of acceptance. Consider the following situation: The athletic director of School A calls the athletic director of School B and says School A would be interested in playing School B in men's basketball during the 1990 season. School B's athletic director then sends out a game contract to School A's athletic director which states: "I accept your offer and will play you on December 1, 1990 at 8 P.M. at Madison Square Garden for $1,000." School A has not entered into the contract since its athletic director's call was but a solicitation of a contest and not an offer creating the power of acceptance in School B's athletic director. School A may still agree to the date, but it is under no obligation to do so.

Advertisements are not considered offers to sell but rather are viewed as an invitation to the public to buy. For example, a school advertises an upcoming football game in the town newspaper. The game is a sellout. A fan wants to buy a ticket to the game. The school is under no obligation to sell the fan a ticket since its advertisement was just an invitation for the public to buy tickets— not an offer specifically to sell the fan a ticket.

Acceptance

An *acceptance* can only be made by the party to whom the offer was made. For example, a school's equipment manager offers to buy 10 football helmets from Manufacturer A for $100 each. Unknown to the equipment manager, Manufacturer B has bought Manufacturer A's business. The equipment manager has dealt with Manufacturer B's company before and does not like its warranty policy. Manufacturer B accepts the order from the equipment manager. However, the equipment manager refuses to accept delivery from Manufacturer B and does not have to do so since the offer to purchase was made to Manufacturer A and does not create a power of acceptance in Manufacturer B.

The party accepting the offer, the *offeree*, may be required to accept the offer from the party making it, the *offeror*, in a certain specified manner (e.g., by letter). In some instances, which may depend in part on the past practice between the parties, an offer may be accepted in silence (offeree makes no response to offeror). This is why all athletic administrators should always respond to any offer made, whether to reject or accept, in writing or by telephone, and keep a record of the response made.

One major problem that often arises in athletic administration is when an acceptance varies in its terms from the initial offer. Historically, the acceptance had to be a mirror image of the offer (common law). However, it is possible under the U.C.C. for an acceptance that differs from the offer to be acceptable (for sale of goods) as long as the acceptance is not expressly conditioned on the offeror's accepting the new terms. This is particularly so when one party to the contract is not a merchant. This example illustrates the problems: an equipment manager orders two dozen football helmets with face guards and chin straps attached for $100 each. The manufacturer accepts the order but notes on its order acknowledgment form that chin straps are not usually included but that they will be included in this sale for an additional $1 per helmet. Under U.C.C. art. 2-207, this is considered "a proposal for addition to the contract" because the equipment manager is not a merchant. It may not become part of the contract unless the equipment manager agrees to it. If the question of chin straps is essential to the formation of the entire contract, then a contract may be deemed not to have come into existence at all.

The offeree's power of acceptance can be terminated in four ways:

1. By rejection or counteroffer by the offeree.
2. By the lapse of time.
3. By revocation by the offeror.
4. By death or incapacity of either party to the contract.

The following examples illustrate these reasons for termination.

- School A offers to play School B in field hockey on October 15, 1990. School B rejects the October 15 date and instead offers to play on October 16. The offer by A is terminated by B's rejection and counteroffer.
- School A sends a letter of intent to a proposed scholarship student-athlete, which notes that if the letter of intent is not signed by a certain date, it is no longer valid. Student-athlete is considering a number of other scholarships and allows School A's letter of intent to lapse. Student-athlete later reconsiders and requests a new letter to be sent. School A has subsequently offered the scholarship to another individual and notifies the initial offeree that its offer of a scholarship has lapsed because of time.
- The Meadowlands Arena contacts School A and offers to schedule the school to play there on June 1, 1990 at 8 P.M. for $1,000 against a specified school. School A says it's interested but wants to think it over. While considering the offer, School A's 7-foot All-American center declares his intent to play in the NBA for the upcoming season. The Meadowlands immediately calls up School A upon hearing the news of the student-athlete's decision and revokes its offer.
- Smith, a sole proprietor, offers to print all the tickets for Home State University's athletic contests for the upcoming school year in exchange for $500. Smith dies before Home State can accept the offer. Home State's power of acceptance is terminated because Smith's death makes the performance of a contract impossible.

Consideration

In addition to mutual assent, the offer, and acceptance, it is essential for the formation of most contracts that there be some form of consideration. *Consideration* is defined abstractly, and there are various definitions of the term. It is often described as a "legal detriment." It involves an exchange of value wherein one party agrees through a bargaining process to give up or do something in return for another party's doing the same. For example, Bob offers Scott a book in exchange for $25. Scott accepts. This is a binding contract. Bob is giving up his book in exchange for Scott's giving up $25. Each party has pledged to give up something to benefit the other. An example in athletic administration would involve a coach who agrees to work at School A, to the exclusion of all other schools, for a period of two years; in return, School A agrees to pay the coach the sum of $100,000 per year. Consideration is often viewed as the essential term needed in a contract to make it legally enforceable. Without consideration, there may be a promise to do an act, but it may not be legally enforceable as a contract.

Consideration can be contrasted to the giving of a gift, which may involve a promise to give something of value but involves no promise to do anything in return for receiving it. Generally, past consideration cannot be a basis for enacting a legally binding current contract. Past consideration is an act that could have served as consideration if it had been bargained for at the time but that was not the subject of a bargain. The following situation illustrates this point: School A played School B at School A's home court in basketball the previous season under a single game contract. The following year School A agrees to a return game at School B under a separate game contract. There is no further remuneration or benefit accrued to School A for returning the date. Subsequently, School A decides to cancel the game with School B. School B will not be able to have the game contract legally enforced if it was not receiving any consideration for playing at School B. The previous year's game will not be deemed to be consideration, since it occurred in the past and was not part of the current contract with School B.

Legality

Another requirement for a valid contract is the *legality* of the underlying bargain. The general rule is that the courts will not enforce an illegal contract. The courts hope that by not enforcing illegal contracts they will discourage unlawful behavior. In addition, the honoring of such contracts would be demeaning to the judiciary. The courts are concerned with two types of illegalities: statutory violations and violations of public policy not expressly declared unlawful by statute. The former include gambling contracts, contracts with unlicensed professionals (doctors, lawyers, accountants, etc), Sunday contracts, and a variety of contracts that violate laws regulating consumer credit transactions ("loan sharks," etc.). Contracts that violate public policy include many types of "covenants not to compete," provisions that waive tort liability (discussed in Chapters 6 and 7), and contracts that interfere in family relationships.

With these contracts, no general rule for determining their legality can be given, except to say that the harsher the restrictions or interference the less likely they will withstand judicial scrutiny. Although both types of illegal contracts are generally unenforceable, the severity of this approach has led courts to seek ways to moderate the impact. The principle of restitution has been used to accomplish this moderation. *Restitution* requires that no one who has conferred a benefit or suffered a loss should unfairly be denied compensation. In a case where even though the underlying bargain of the contract is illegal, the court may find it appropriate to reimburse or "make whole" a party who unfairly suffered a loss.

Capacity

In addition to the offer and the acceptance, the capacity of a party to make or accept an offer is an important factor in the formation of a valid contract. *Capacity* is defined as the ability to understand the nature and effects of one's acts. In regard to contracts, the general rule is that anyone who has reached the age of majority (18 in most states) has the capacity to enter into a contract. An exception to this rule is an intoxicated individual. If a person is so drunk that he has no awareness of his acts and the other person knows this, there is no contract. A minor, or an individual who has not yet reached the age of majority, may disaffirm a contract anytime before reaching majority and for a reasonable period of time after reaching majority.

In addition to individual capacity, members of organizations can have the capacity to bind a corporation to a contract. A corporate agent can be a natural person or another corporation that is authorized to act for the corporation, as for example, in accepting a summons. An athletic director is authorized to bind the school in certain areas; thus the athletic director has corporate capacity to act on behalf of the athletic department and/or the school.

Mistakes in Contracts

Mistakes occur in the contracting process on a frequent basis. In fact, much litigation surrounds contractual mistakes. In the past, the courts put a lot of emphasis on whether a contractual mistake was unilateral or mutual. *Unilateral mistakes*, or those made by one party, were often granted no relief from the courts. For example, Powerhouse University is eager to schedule its junior varsity basketball team and sends a game contract to Pushover University seeking to schedule Pushover's varsity team. Pushover, anxious to play Powerhouse to gain prestige for its program, readily accepts by signing the game contract without reading it. Pushover believes it will be playing Powerhouse's varsity team. When Pushover's mistake is discovered, Pushover will not be able to avoid the contract. Pushover is bound to play Powerhouse's junior varsity, because it did not read the contract before signing it.

Mutual mistakes occur when both parties make a mistake about a basic assumption of the contract. The contract is voidable by the party that is adversely affected. For example, Wahoo University entered into an agreement to purchase 125 football helmets from Tribex Corporation made of a compound called "plastex." Unbeknownst to the buyer and the seller, two different compounds called "plastex" could be used to make football helmets. Wahoo University thought it was ordering one form of the compound, while Tribex made the helmet out of the only form of the compound it knew of, the other form. There would be no contract upon discovery of the mutual mistake; since neither party was aware of the ambiguity, there was no common assent to the terms of the agreement. Today, the courts tend to examine the underlying merits of any litigation involving contractual mistakes.

The Parol Evidence Rule

When a written contract is finalized and the parties agree that it represents the final expression of their agreement, the contract may be considered to be an *integration of the agreement*. Often a contract will contain an integration clause that stipulates that the written document represents the total agreement between the parties. When this occurs, the contract is considered the *total expression of the agreement*.

The parol evidence rule prohibits the admission of oral statements, preliminary agreements, or writings made prior to or at the time of signing that would in any way alter, contradict, or change the written contract. However, any evidence may be introduced to show the intention of the parties whenever the object of the contract cannot be ascertained from the language employed. In its strictest form, the parol evidence rule bars any evidence of preliminary agreements, writings, or oral understandings between the parties to an agreement from being introduced in court when the contract was considered integrated at its signing. For example, School A negotiates with School B to have School B play a soccer match at School A. In preliminary negotiations, there was some discussion about School A returning the match at School B for the season following the year School B plays at School A. The final contract makes no mention of a return match. The final contract contains an integration clause. School B is barred under the parol evidence rule from introducing any evidence in court about any oral negotiations concerning a return of the match by School A.

Conditions of a Contract

Usually in a contract one or more conditions must be met by each of the parties in order for each party to be in compliance with the

contract. The nonoccurrence of a condition by either party operates to discharge a contractual duty by the other party. Consider
the following situation. School A has a medical insurance policy
that covers injury to its student-athletes. Payment of medical
expenses by the insurance company is conditioned on an accident
being reported within 30 days of its occurrence. If a claim is not
filed within that period, the insurance company is discharged from
its duty to pay the medical expenses incurred by the student-
athlete.

Conditions may be expressed, stated directly in the agreement,
implied (tacitly understood between the parties as part of the
agreement), or constructive (not agreed upon at all by the parties
but imposed by a court in order to ensure fairness).

Breach of Contract

A *breach of contract* is a failure to perform a duty imposed under
the contract. A contract may be totally or partially breached by a
party to it. A total breach discharges the aggrieved party of any
duty to perform, and the aggrieved party may immediately file
suit. A partial breach may not discharge the aggrieved party from
a duty to perform, but the aggrieved party may file suit immediately to collect any damages that are due. The following two
situations illustrate breach of contract:

- State U agrees in 1988 to play Private U in a home-and-away
  series of football games, with State U playing at Private U in
  September 1990 and Private U returning the game the following year at State U. In June 1990, State U informs Private U
  that it cannot afford to travel to Private U and cancels the
  game set for September. The total breach by State U discharges Private U from any duty to play at State U in 1991,
  and Private U may immediately sue for any damages it may
  have suffered because of State U's actions (lost ticket revenue,
  concession revenue, television revenue, parking revenue,
  etc.).
- Pushover University agrees in 1988 to play Powerhouse University in a home-and-away series of football games, with
  Pushover hosting Powerhouse in 1990 and paying Powerhouse
  a $500,000 guarantee within a year of the contest, and with
  Powerhouse hosting Pushover in 1991 but paying no guarantee. (Powerhouse is a national football power, while Pushover
  is trying to develop such a program.) Powerhouse travels in
  1990 to Pushover and trounces them in a game that sports
  writers considered amateurish. Two weeks after the first game,

Powerhouse cancels its home game with Pushover in 1991 but will play in 1995 or sooner if Pushover becomes ranked in the top 20. Pushover, which has not yet paid Powerhouse its guarantee for the game played in 1990, may still have to do so despite the partial breach of contract. However, Pushover can immediately file suit for any damages it suffered because of the partial breach by Powerhouse.

The Statute of Frauds

Certain types of contracts are unenforceable under the statute of frauds unless they are in writing. The statute of frauds has its roots in English common law. Certain types of contracts were required to be in writing to prevent injustices resulting from fraudulent claims or promises that were never kept. The U.C.C. in art. 2-201 states that a contract for the sale of goods over $500 is not enforceable by way of either action or defense unless there is some writing sufficient to indicate that there was a contract for sale between the parties now contesting the arrangement. Contracts involving an "interest" in land are also subject to the statute of frauds and must be in writing. An "interest" in land includes the sale, mortgaging, and leasing of real property and the creation of easements. Additionally, any contract that cannot be fully per-formed within one year shall not be enforceable unless it is in writing.

Two types of contracts athletic administrators might enter into that would fall under this statute would be a contract that is not to be performed within one year from the making (e.g., future game contracts or coaches' contracts) and land contracts that involve the sale of an interest in land (e.g., facility site land purchases).

Remedies for a Breach of Contract

Remedies for a breach of contract usually entail monetary damages awarded by the court to the aggrieved party. The philosophy of monetary damages is to compensate the injured party for economic losses. The problem with monetary damages is that the aggrieved party must be able to translate the injury into a financial sum and be able to justify that amount to the court.

With the exception of some land sale contracts, the courts are extremely reluctant to require specific performance of a contract. *Specific performance* requires the performance of a contract in the specific form in which it was made. It is generally invoked by the courts when damages would be an inadequate compensation for the breach of an agreement—for example, a specific piece of land is ordered to be conveyed under the terms of the original agreement. The court rarely requires a contract for personal services, like a coach's contract, to be specifically performed. The courts usually reason that this would be a form of involuntary servitude.

Courts will usually award contract damages based in whole or in part on three legal economic interests: expectations, reliance, and restitution. An *expectation interest* is the benefit that was bargained, and the remedy is to put the party breached in a position equal to the position had the contract been performed. A *reliance interest* is the loss suffered by relying on the contract and taking actions consistent with the expectation that the other party will abide by it; the remedy is reimbursement that restores the promisee to his or her position before the contract was made. A *restitution interest* is that which restores to the promisee any benefit the promisee conferred on the promisor.

PREPARING AND REVIEWING A CONTRACT

In many athletic organizations an administrator may routinely draft and/or review documents such as game contracts or facility leases. It is suggested that an attorney always review such documents to see if they would withstand legal review. At a minimum all standard form contracts should be reviewed at least once annually. In preparing a contract it is critical for the athletic administrator to provide the attorney drafting the contract with as many pertinent facts as possible so that the attorney can fully protect the amateur athletic organization's rights under the agreement. Since many of the contracts used in amateur athletics are unique to the industry, the attorney will require significant input from the athletic administrator in order to draw up a proper contract. Athletic administrators should be prepared to provide such data and to review drafts of contracts to check for errors. The following is a checklist of information that an amateur athletic organization should consider when developing contracts for use by the organization.

1. If there have been prior dealings between the parties, the lawyer drafting the new contract should be informed of the nature of these dealings in order to decide if they have any bearing on the new contract.
2. If the contract can only be performed by the original parties to the contract, the lawyer should be informed so as to state in the contract that it will not be assignable.
3. If any party is to be required to furnish a bond or to make a deposit, this information needs to be incorporated into the agreement.

4. If the parties have agreed to any special conditions, the lawyer drafting the contract must know of the conditions in order to include them in the agreement.
5. The consideration for the contract needs to be identified.
6. A description of the subject matter of the contracts should be provided. If property is the subject matter, then a description of the property should be furnished.
7. If there are any circumstances that would excuse either party from performing the contract, these circumstances should be explained in detail and included in the agreement.
8. The lawyer must be informed if the parties to the agreement need to view each others' books and records.
9. The attorney should know the means of payment agreed to between the parties for the subject matter of the contract, any agreement as to the payment of attorney's fees should a breach occur, and any agreement as to the payment of any resulting taxes.
10. The attorney should have the name, capacity, and residence of each party to the agreement and information regarding their ability to sign the contract and bind themselves or the organization they represent.
11. The effective date of the contract, the duration of the contract, and how the contract can be terminated before it runs its stated length all need to be incorporated into the agreements.
12. The attorney must be informed of the liabilities of both parties to the agreement and whether the liability of either party is to be limited under the agreement.

With all of the above information in hand, the attorney can proceed with drafting the contract document. The following is a general checklist of typical clauses that are included in most sports contracts (see Exhibit 3–1):

1. *Opening*. Identifies the parties to the agreement and also the date of the contract and its effective date.
2. *Representations and warranties*. Contains information regarding the rights and qualifications of the parties to enter into an agreement and also any express or implied warranties regarding the subject matter of the contract.
3. *Operational language*. Contains the subject matter of the contract. The precise rights and duties of the parties under the contract are explained.
4. *Other clauses*. Certain other clauses may be included, depending on the nature of the contract. Compensation, rights

CONTRACT

<table>
<tr><td>*Opening*</td><td>This Agreement made and entered into this __1st__ day __September__ , 19 __XX__ , by and between the athletic authorities of the Powerhouse University and the athletic authorities of __Anyschool University__ , stipulates:</td></tr>
<tr><td>*Representations & Warranties*</td><td>First: Whereas, Powerhouse University and Anyschool University are the owners to the rights for their individual basketball teams to compete in NCAA intercollegiate competition.
Second: That the __basketball (men's)__ teams representing the above named institutions shall __meet and play__ at _____ (site) _____ on _____ (date) , 19____ , and at _____ _____ on _____ , 19____ .</td></tr>
<tr><td>*Operational Language*</td><td>Third: That in consideration of playing this game,
(1) That the Host Team shall provide the Visiting Team one rights-free radio outlet for the broadcast of the game by its designated radio station and/or network.
(2) That television rights to the game remain the property of the Big Time Conference and the Powerhouse University.
(3) That the Host Team shall provide the Visiting Team with forty (40) complimentary tickets.
(4) That a minimum of 200 tickets shall be made available for sale to the Visiting Team, but that unsold tickets be returned to the Home Team no later than 72 hours prior to the game.</td></tr>
<tr><td>*Other Clauses*</td><td>Fourth: That officials for the game shall be provided by the conference.
Fifth: That the game shall be played under the eligibility rules of the respective institutions.</td></tr>
<tr><td>*Termination*</td><td>Sixth: Either party failing to comply with condition of Article One, either by cancellation or failure to appear, shall forfeit money in the amount of __Big $$__ unless such cancellation shall be by mutual consent, in which case this agreement shall be null and void.</td></tr>
<tr><td>*Entire Agreement and Amendments*</td><td>Seventh: This agreement constitutes the entire agreement and understanding between Powerhouse University and Anyschool University and cancels, terminates and supersedes any prior agreement or understanding relating to the game contest. There are no representations, agreements, warranties, covenants or undertakings other than those contained herein. None of the provisions of this Agreement may be waived or modified except expressly in writing signed by both parties. However, failure of either party to require the performance of any term in this Agreement or the waiver by either party of any breach</td></tr>
</table>

Exhibit 3-1 Typical Clauses in a Sports Contract

thereof shall not prevent subsequent enforcement of such term nor be deemed a waiver of any subsequent breach.

Closing

Witnessed by: Powerhouse University

_____   _____
Business Manager   Director of Athletics
of Athletics

_____
                                     Anyschool University
Witnessed by: (Visiting Institution)

_____   _____
Business Manager   Director of Athletics
of Athletics

Exhibit 3-1 Continued

to arbitration for any disagreements, and the right to assign the contract are typical examples of other clauses.

5. *Termination.* Discusses the length of the contract and the means of ending the agreement.
6. *Entire agreement and amendments.* Details the comprehensiveness of the contract and its relation to other agreements and also the methods by which the contract can be amended.
7. *Closing.* Contains the signatures of the parties to the contract, any acknowledgments, and the signatures of any witnesses.

TYPES OF ATHLETIC CONTRACTS

An athletic administrator needs to be a contract expert. Typically, an administrator will routinely deal with contracts governing game contests, personnel contracts involving coaches or physicians, facility leases agreements, etc. Administrators need to utilize contracts in such situations to protect both the organization and the administrator himself. The following sections present an administrator with some examples of the types of contracts and language that should be used in situations such as those just described. Additional examples of athletic contracts appear in Appendix B. (See Chapter 5, for a review of scholarship agreements, Chapter 9 for television and radio licensing agreements, and Chapter 10 for a licensing agreement involving trademarks and logos.) The examples described in the following sections are for informational purposes only and an administrator should consult with the organization's attorney before utilizing any of the language of the examples to ensure the language covers the organization's legal needs.

Coaches' Contracts

Major college and university athletic coaches in the revenue-producing sports (basketball and football) are changing the face of contracts between institutions and the coaches who work for them. Recent lawsuits and the resulting out-of-court settlements should have placed athletic directors across the country on notice. The negotiation of a coaching contract is a serious business. Coaching is a profession, and the men and women who pursue it as such may be formidable opponents at the negotiating table. Several coaches at the intercollegiate level hire attorneys to represent them in contract negotiations. Great care should be taken in drafting the agreement to protect the school's best interests.

Basically, a coach's contract is similar to any other employment contract. It sets forth the nature and duration of the employment, the compensation to be paid to the employee, and any other terms and conditions of the employment that might be relevant (see Exhibit 3–2).

The employer-employee relationship between the institution and the coach is similar to the typical employer-employee relationship found in the business world; nevertheless, some unique aspects of the coach's employment should be considered before an institution signs a coach to an employment contract. Coaches at all levels of competition are under tremendous pressure to win. The pressure to win at the high school level may not be as great as the pressure at a major university, but it exists nonetheless. The ability to produce a winning program is usually the measure of a good coach. A coach who is not successful in producing a winning program is likely to be fired, often before the contract has expired. In this instance, the institution has breached the contract and is liable for damages. In the past, these damages have consisted of either a lump-sum payment by the institution to the coach of the dollar value of the remaining years of the contract or simply a continuance of payments under the contract as if the coach were still working.

However, recent litigation, which has been settled out of court, has shown that the institution may be liable for more than the face value of the coaching contract. Coaching at a major university provides an individual with many other outside opportunities to enhance his or her income. Television shows, radio shows, and

EMPLOYMENT CONTRACT

Agreement made this_____day of_____, 19   , by and be-tween _____ *University* and _____, supersedes a con-tract agreement dated November 22, 1982, a copy of which is attached hereto.

The University hereby continues the employment of _____ as Head Coach of Football for the period beginning this date and ending on the 30th day of June, 19   . The Coach hereby agrees to and does accept paid employment for the designated period, subject to the provisos below. The termination date of this agreement may be exended on a year-to-year basis at the agreement of the Uni-versity and Head Coach, in accordance with Paragraph 6.

The University may suspend the Head Coach for a reasonable period of time without compensation, or terminate his employment, if he is found to be in delib-erate or serious violation of NCAA regulations.

The Head Coach agrees that he will devote full time to his football responsibilities during the practice and game seasons. The Head Coach agrees that he will under-take no paid public speaking engagements during the fall practice and game seasons, unless specifically authorized to do so by the Director of Athletics, whose permission shall not be unreasonably withheld.

If the University ceases to engage in Intercollegiate Football through its own election, or chooses to terminate the Coach's coaching responsibilities prior to the expiration of the Contract, the University will provide a responsible administrative position to the Coach for the duration of the Contract. If the Coach desires to leave under these circumstances for another assignment which does not offer the salary compensation at the same level as the University does, then the University will provide the financial difference during the length of the Contract.

The University shall have the ability to extend this Contract for a period of one year, and for additional one year periods thereafter, provided the University gives the Coach written notice of its desire to extend the Contract at least 19 months in advance of the termination date of this Contract. The Coach shall then either accept or reject in writing the extension of this Contract within four weeks after receipt of the University's intent to extend this Contract, or two weeks after the completion of the football game season, whichever is later.

The Coach agrees that he will not seek, negotiate for or discuss other full time employment of any nature during the football game season, without the express written permission of the Executive Vice President or his designee prior to the expiration of this Contract, whose permission shall not be unreasonably withheld.

The parties agree that in the event of the death or disability of the Head Coach rendering it impossible for him to perform his duties as set forth herein, but not including any disability arising out of or in the course of his employment, _____ *University* shall be entitled to cancel this Agreement or suspend the operations of this Agreement for the duration of said disability. However, the employee will be eligible to apply for and receive disability payments through the University's nor-mal disability insurance plan.

In witness whereof, the parties have caused this Contract to be signed and sealed by their respective officers hereunto duly authorized the _____ day of _____, 19   .

For the University   *Coach*

_____   _____
Executive Vice President   Head Coach-Football

Exhibit 3-2   A Coach's Contract

shoe contracts are a few examples. In addition, wealthy boosters may see fit to provide the coach with a free car, free housing, stock options, or cash gifts. All these perquisites are available as a result of the position the coach holds. When the institution terminates the agreement prematurely, the coach suddenly loses all these additional benefits. As a result, coaches have sued their universities for these benefits in addition to the face dollar value of their contracts. Pepper Rodgers, who was coaching Georgia Tech at the time he was fired, sued the school for $496,000 in damages relating to the perquisites he lost as a result of his firing (see *Rodgers v. Georgia Tech Athletic Ass'n,* 303 S.E.2d 467 [Ga. App. 1983]). He gained a substantial out-of-court settlement after the Georgia court of appeals ruled that the inclusion of the word "perquisite" in Rodgers's contract might permit a jury to award Rodgers some of the damages he was requesting (see Exhibit 3–3).

In an attempt to monitor and control these outside sources of income, the NCAA has recently passed legislation requiring more institutional involvement in this area. Coaches must now receive prior approval from the school before using the school's name or logo in endorsing commercial products or services. Coaches are also required to get the institution's approval before accepting any compensation from an athletic shoe, apparel, or equipment manufacturer in exchange for the institution's use of such equipment. The new legislation also prohibits coaches from accepting any sort of compensation for the scheduling of contests or for arranging for particular student-athletes to participate in an event. Finally, the NCAA passed a proposal which requires the institution's chief executive officer to be informed annually of coaches' athletically related income and benefits. While these new rules may make it easier for the institutions to track the coaches' outside income, the institutions may be subjecting themselves to even more liability for these perquisites because of the increase in control they exercise over these additional sources of income for the coaches.

In addition to damages over and above the face value of the contract, institutions should be aware of the potential for a coach to sue the school for defamation. The high visibility of a coach and the large amount of publicity surrounding the team at a major university magnifies this problem. The institution must be careful in announcing the firing and in disclosing the reasons for the firing. Being fired means the coach was not doing the job adequately. Joe Yukica, the Dartmouth football coach, claimed that in being dismissed from his job before the end of his contract "the damage to the plaintiff's professional career and opportunities will be irreparable" (petition for declaratory judgment). Yukica brought action against the athletic director and college (*Yukica v. Leland,* No. 85-

Pepper Rodgers was fired in December, 1979 with two years of his contract remaining. Rodgers received his salary through December 1981 but sued for his perquisites. They included the following:

A. benefits and perquisites received by Rodgers directly from the Georgia Tech Athletic Association:
   (1) gas, oil, maintenance, repairs, other automobile expenses;
   (2) automobile liability and collision insurance;
   (3) general expense money;
   (4) meals available at the Georgia Tech training table;
   (5) eight season tickets to Georgia Tech home football games during fall of 1980 and 1981;
   (6) two reserved booths, consisting of approximately forty seats at Georgia Tech home football games during the fall of 1980 and 1981;
   (7) five season tickets to Georgia Tech home basketball games for 1980 and 1981;
   (8) four season tickets to Atlanta Falcon home football games for 1980 and 1981;
   (9) four game tickets to each out-of-town Georgia Tech football game during fall of 1980 and 1981;
   (10) pocket money at each home football game during fall of 1980 and 1981;
   (11) pocket money at each out-of-town Georgia Tech football game during fall of 1980–1981;
   (12) parking privileges at all Georgia Tech home sporting events;
   (13) the services of a secretary;
   (14) the services of an administrative assistant;
   (15) the cost of admission to Georgia Tech home baseball games during the spring of 1980–1981;
   (16) the cost of trips to football coaches' conventions, clinics, and meetings and to observe football practice sessions of professional and college football teams;
   (17) initiation fee, dues, monthly bills, and cost of memberhip at the Capital City Club;
   (18) initiation fee, dues, monthly bills, and cost of membership at the Cherokee Country Club;
   (19) initiation fee and dues at the East Lake Country Club.

B. benefits and perquisites received by Rodgers from sources other than the Georgia Tech Athletic Association by virtue of being head coach of football:
   (1) profits from Rodgers' television football show, "The Pepper Rodgers Show," on Station WSB-TV in Atlanta for the fall of 1980–1981;
   (2) profits from Rodgers' radio football show on Station WGST in Atlanta for the fall of 1980 and 1981;
   (3) use of a new Cadillac automobile during 1980–1981;
   (4) profits from Rodgers' summer football camp, known as the "Pepper Rodgers Football School," for June 1980 and June 1981;
   (5) financial gifts from alumni and supporters of Georgia Tech for 1980–1981;
   (6) lodging at any of the Holiday Inns owned by Topeka Inn Management, Inc. of Topeka, Kansas, for the time period from December 18, 1979 through December 31, 1981;
   (7) the cost of membership in Terminus International Tennis Club in Atlanta for 1980 and 1981;
   (8) individual game tickets to Hawks basketball and Braves baseball games during 1980–1981 seasons;
   (9) housing for Rodgers and his family in Atlanta for the period from December 18, 1979 through December 31, 1981;
   (10) the cost of premiums of a $400,000.00 policy on the life of Rodgers for the time period from December 18, 1979 through December 31, 1981.

Rodgers v. Georgia Tech Athletic Ass'n, 303 S.E. 2d 467 (6A. App 1983).

Exhibit 3-3 Perquisites in Pepper Rodgers' Georgia Tech Coaching Contract

E-191 [Super. Ct. N.H. 1985]), to retain his position as head
football coach until his contract ran out. A New Hampshire superior court granted an order restraining the athletic director from
firing Yukica, because Yukica showed that the athletic director did
not have the right to fire Yukica under the contract Yukica had
signed with Dartmouth in 1978 and renewed for two additional
years in 1985. The *Rodgers* and *Yukica* cases are prime examples
of what can happen when the terms of an agreement are not
specific enough or misunderstood.

If a coach breaches his or her contract with an institution, the
institution also has legal remedies against the coach. However,
unlike coaches, universities have been reluctant to pursue legal
remedies. If the coach is leaving for a better position, it would be
bad publicity for the school to hold the individual back. Also,
finding a replacement for the departed coach might be more
difficult if it appears that the university is not willing to allow its
personnel to advance to better positions. In addition, it is difficult
for the university to prove monetary damages. The most the
university could hope for would be the cost of searching for a new
coach. The loss of revenue for the school due to the loss of a
successful coach is very difficult to quantify and prove. And finally,
if a coach does not want to work for a particular institution, the
institution is not likely to force the issue; an unhappy employee is
generally less productive.

Although the previous discussion has focused on college coaches
and their contracts, high school administrators must also be aware
of certain legal issues, especially those related to the hiring and
firing of coaches in the high schools. High school coaches, unlike
their collegiate brethren, are generally teachers first and coaches
second. Most have separate *divisible* contracts involving the two
jobs. As a teacher, the high school coach is usually eligible to gain
tenure after a specified number of years of teaching. With a coach,
however, this is not usually the case. Most states do not grant
tenure for coaches. A practical problem arises when a coach is
dismissed from his or her job as coach but has tenure as a teacher
and decides to remain at the school in that capacity. Unless there
is another teacher already in the school system who can take over
the coaching duties, it may not be feasible to go out and hire
another coach other than on a part-time basis, because there will
not be a teaching position to go along with the coaching job. In
addition, depending on the circumstances surrounding the dismissal, it may be awkward to have the ex-coach continue to teach
at the school.

In order to address the problem of divisible teaching-coaching
contracts, many school districts require the individual to sign an

indivisible contract. Under this type of an agreement, the loss of either position results in the loss of both positions. The indivisible contract solves the problem of having a teaching position available for the new coach and also reduces the potential for ill will as discussed earlier. The issue of tenure and its relationship to coaching in secondary schools has resulted in some litigation, and athletic administrators should be aware of their school district's policies before entering into any coaching agreement.

Physicians' Contracts

The need to have a physician on duty at athletic events is obvious. Injuries are a possibility in all athletic contests, and the immediate treatment and diagnosis of an injury by a qualified doctor is desirable and often critical. The presence of a physician at certain athletic contests may be a requirement of most schools' insurance policies. However, it is important from the standpoint of the school to acquire the doctor's services as an independent contractor and not as an employee. If the doctor is an employee of the institution or school district, the school could be held vicariously liable for a tort (discussed in Chapters 6 and 7) committed by the doctor in the performance of medical duties for the school. If the doctor is an independent contractor, however, the school will not be at risk.

The key difference between an employee and an independent contractor is the degree of control and direction exercised over the individual worker by the institution. An employee is subject to a much higher degree of control than an independent contractor. Because of the high degree of control, the employer can be held responsible for the acts of the employee in the performance of the employee's assigned duties. The independent contractor's actions generally cannot be attributed to the institution that contracted for his or her services (see Exhibit 3–4).

Officials' Contracts

As with physicians, the need to have officials at athletic events is obvious. There has to be someone present to enforce the rules of the game—someone who is independent from the participants. The referee or official can be involved in two distinct areas where tort liability can arise. The first is personal injury of participants and/or spectators, and the second is judicial review of a decision of an official. (Both are discussed in Chapters 6 and 7.) In order to protect the school or college from being held vicariously liable for the actions of officials, it is important that the officials be deemed independent contractors. Exhibit 3–5 is an example of a model

AGREEMENT

STATE_____

COUNTY_____

THIS AGREEMENT made and entered into the _____day of _____, 19xx, by and between _____, a college having its principal place of business in ____ _____ (hereinafter referred to as "College"), and DR. _____, a citizen and resident of _____, (hereinafter referred to as "Physician").

WITNESSETH:

WHEREAS, College is desirous of obtaining the services of Physician in connection with its intercollegiate sports program, and

WHEREAS, Physician is skilled in the practice of medicine and is willing to assist College with its medical programs in its intercollegiate sports program,

NOW THEREFORE, in consideration of the convenants and promises contained herein, the parties agree as follows:

1. College hereby retains and Physician agrees to be retained by College as College's consultant in College's intercollegiate sports program for the school year 1985–86.

2. Physician will act as a consultant with the College's coaches, trainers, athletes and other personnel with regard to medical problems incurred by athletes in the College's intercollegiate sports program. Physician's consulting services shall include attendance at home football games whenever possible. In Physician's absence, he will attempt to find qualified medical help to attend. Physician will be available for consultation one day per week.

3. Physician agrees to review participation medical records on a yearly basis.

4. Physician shall make recommendations to the coaching staff, trainers, and other personnel as to the handling of all medical matters with regards to the athletes in the College's intercollegiate sports program. Such recommendations shall include prescribing treatment for injuries and other medical problems, and recommendations for surgical and other hospital procedures when necessary. All physician charges for such surgery and other hospital procedures are not covered under the terms of this agreement.

5. Physician shall make decisions on athletes practicing, returning to practice or playing in athletic contests. In absence of Physician, he will delegate authority to another physician, head trainer or sports medicine coordinator.

6. Physician will supervise student trainers and graduate assistants through the head athletic trainer and sports medicine coordinator.

7. Physician will make the decision to send an athlete to another physician or delegate that decision to another individual.

8. If an athlete seeks a second opinion without consent of team physician, payment is not guaranteed.

9. As compensation for all consulting services rendered hereunder, College agrees to pay to Physician the sum of $_____ to be paid upon execution of this agreement.

10. It is understood and agreed that Physician is an independent contractor with regard to all consulting services to be rendered hereunder, and is not acting as College's agent, employee or servant. It is also understood that Physician is not an insurer of results in any medical treatment rendered under the terms of this agreement.

11. This agreement is to be construed under and governed by the laws of the State of _____.

IN WITNESS WHEREOF, the parties hereto have executed this agreement in duplicate originals on the day and year first above written.

_____COLLEGE   DR: _____

By: _____   By: _____

Exhibit 3-4 A Physician's Contract

contract between schools and sports officials. Particular attention should be given to clause 3, "official status," which clearly states that the official has agreed to work as an independent contractor. The independent contractor status is beneficial for the school because it shields the school from attempts to hold the school liable for improper actions of the official and avoids any liability for workers' compensation should the official be injured.

Facility Contracts

When an institution competing in athletics does not own its own arena or stadium, it is necessary to enter into agreements for the use of these types of facilities. In reaching an agreement for the use of a facility, the athletic administrator should take great care in detailing the responsibilities and duties of both parties to the contract. In addition to the use of the facility, consideration should be given to the amount of rent charged, the method of payment, and the specific services provided for the rent. The responsibility for the promotion of the event, the setting up of the arena for the event, and the provision of personnel to run the arena (such as a security force, ticket takers, a public address announcer, and various work crews) need to be addressed in the contract. The time of the event itself and the availability of the arena for warm-ups before the event should also be explicity stated in the contract. In addition, any potential conflicts between multiple lessees should be addressed in the drawing of an agreement.

Third-party agreements, such as radio or television contracts between the institution and the media, also need to be considered in the drafting of a contract for the use of a facility in case certain accommodations are necessary. Insurance requirements must also be considered. Generally, facilities require specific types of insurance coverage to be carried by the institution before they will allow the institution to use their facilities for a particular event. A review of the insurance carried by the institution should be carried out before an agreement is reached. Exhibit 3–6 is an example of a facility contract.

NOTE _____

1. For further information, see the following law review article: Graves, "Coaches in the Courtroom: Recovery in Actions for Breach of Employment Contracts," 12 *Journal of College and University Law* 545 (1986).

MODEL CONTRACT BETWEEN
SCHOOLS AND SPORTS OFFICIALS

Please note that this is a "Model" and may have to be modified to fit the particular circumstances of your local association and/or schools at which you officiate. Also, it is based upon general principles of law; therefore, you should review it with a local attorney prior to using it due to differences of state law.

The _____ (home school) [hereinafter "School"] of _____
(city and state) and _____ (official's name) of _____ (official's address) [hereinafter "Official"] enter into the following Agreement:

1. CONTEST. The Official agrees to officiate a _____ (level) _____
(sport) contest between _____ (home school) and _____
(visitor school) at _____ (place) _____ (city and state)
on _____ (date) at _____ (time). The other official(s) is/are _____
_____.

2. PAYMENT. In consideration of such services, the _____ (home
school) will pay the Official within _____ days of the game date a fee of _____
(amount), plus mileage at the rate of 20 cents/mile for _____ miles, in the amount
of $_____.

3. OFFICIAL'S STATUS. The Official agrees to work this game as an independent contractor.

4. OFFICIAL'S REPRESENTATION. The Official represents that he/she is, or will be by the date of the contest, a duly licensed official in this state authorized to officiate this contest. If it is found to be otherwise, this Agreement shall become null and void.

5. INTERPRETATION. The Constitution, By-Laws and rules and regulations of the ____
(state association) and of the _____ (local association) are considered a part of this Agreement and shall govern, except as modified by this Agreement, any disputes arising out of this Agreement. Both parties to this Agreement agree to be so bound.

6. VOIDING OF CONTRACT. This contract shall become null and void upon probation or suspension of either the School or the Official by the _____ (state association).

7. CANCELLATION/POSTPONEMENT. This contract may be canceled at any time by the mutual written consent of both parties. This contract is voidable if either party cannot comply with its terms for any sufficient reason.

   A. Sufficient Reason. If the contest is canceled by mutual written consent or for sufficient reason (including, but not limited to, unfavorable weather, illness, accident, or injury) and the Official is not notified in time to prevent travel to the game site, the Official shall be paid the round-trip mileage at the rate of 20 cents/mile. If the contest begins, but is then canceled due to unfavorable weather, the Official shall be paid the fee and mileage expenses set forth in Paragraph 2.

   B. Insufficient Reason. If the game is canceled for any insufficient reason, or if either school participating in the contest no longer desires the Official to officiate, the Official shall be paid the fee.

   C. Rescheduling. If the contest is postponed and rescheduled, the Official shall be paid the fee set forth in Paragraph 2. If the agreed time of the contest is changed, the Official will be given the first opportunity to officiate at the new time, but if the Official is unable to do so, the Official shall be paid the fee set forth in Paragraph 2.

   D. Official's Failure To Officiate. If the Official fails to officiate the game for a reason other than a sufficient reason, then the Official shall pay the school an amount equal to the fee within _____ days of the game date.

   E. Payment. Payment of the fee and/or mileage as a result of cancellation, rescheduling, or postponement shall be made by the School and received by the Official within _____ days after the original date set for the game.

Exhibit 3-5 An Official's Contract

F. Notification. All notification concerning the provisions of this paragraph shall be in writing to the below address. If initial notification is by phone then a written confirmation shall thereafter be sent within seven days.

8. ACCEPTANCE. This contract is void if not signed by the Official and the School on or before _____ (date).

Date: _____   Date: _____

School: _____   Official: _____

By: _____   Address: _____

     (Name),   (Title)   _____

Address: _____   Business Phone: _____

_____   Home Phone: _____

School Phone: _____

Home Phone: _____

Copyright © 1985 by Melvin S. Narol, Esquire. Jamieson, Moore, Peskin, and Spicer, Princeton, New Jersey. Permission to use and reproduce this Model Contract is hereby granted provided the above copyright notice is set forth on the document.

National Association of Sports Officials, 2017 Lathrop Avenue, Racine, WI 53405.
Phone (414) 632-5448.

Exhibit 3-5 Continued

LEASE AGREEMENT
NASSAU VETERANS MEMORIAL COLISEUM
HYATT MANAGEMENT CORPORATION OF NEW YORK, INC.
UNIONDALE, NEW YORK 11553

Lease _____

THIS AGREEMENT made this _____ day of _____, 19_____ between Hyatt Management Corporation of New York, Inc., d/b/a Nassau Veterans Memorial Coliseum (hereinafter referred to as COLISEUM) and _____(hereinafter referred to as LESSEE) whose address is _____

WITNESSETH:

AREA RENTED—DATES RESERVED
1. In consideration of the sums hereinafter specified, COLISEUM grants to the LESSEE the use of the following facilities in the Nassau Veterans Memorial Coliseum:

ARENA ☐   EXHIBITION HALL ☐   OTHER ☐

SQUARE FOOTAGE RENTED:

_____

for the following program and/or event: _____

on the following dates: _____

RENT
2. (a) The LESSEE agrees to pay by check, payable to Hyatt Management Corporation of New York, Inc., as rent for said space the following: _____

A non-refundable deposit of $_____ shall be paid when this agreement is executed and the balance as follows: _____

(b) For purposes of this agreement, "gross receipts" shall mean the entire proceeds from the sale of tickets of admission, less any admissions taxes.

(c) Final settlement between LESSEE and COLISEUM of all monies owing under this agreement shall be effected on or before: _____

(d) (I) If the LESSEE cancels this agreement or otherwise fails to comply with its terms, the aforesaid non-refundable deposit, at the option of COLISEUM, shall be retained by COLISEUM without any claim therefor by the LESSEE. COLISEUM, however, has the option to elect to commence a suit or other action against the LESSEE by reason of such cancellation or failure to perform, for the balance of any unpaid rent plus any resulting damages.

(II) In case suit or other action is instituted by COLISEUM against LESSEE as a result of LESSEE'S failure to comply with the terms of this agreement, COLISEUM shall recover all damages provided by law, all costs and disbursements provided by statute and all costs usually incurred, including reasonable attorney's fees.

(e) LESSEE assumes full responsibility for all customer's checks returned by the bank because of insufficient funds and the total sum thereof shall be charged against LESSEE'S share of the gross receipts.

Exhibit 3-6 A Facility Contract

BOX OFFICE/TICKETS

3. The LESSEE must use the COLISEUM Box Office and only ticket agencies approved by COLISEUM. LESSEE will reimburse COLISEUM for such Box Office use. (See "Rules, Regulations and Conditions for Lessees of the Coliseum."

INSURANCE AND INDEMNITY OF LESSEE

The LESSEE shall be liable for all damages to building and equipment, normal wear and tear excepted, and agrees to indemnify and hold COLISEUM harmless from any claims or suits arising out of injury or death to any person or damage to property resulting from use of said building. LESSEE will be required to furnish an appropriate certificate of insurance showing that there is in effect, and will remain in effect throughout the term of the Lease, comprehensive general liability insurance, including public liability and property damage, written by an insurer, authorized to do business in the State of New York, in the following amounts:

Comprehensive General Liability—(Including Personal Injury, Contractural, and Products

Liability) _____

Bodily Injury (each occurrence) _____ Property Damage (each occurrence) _____

Aggregate _____ Workmen's Compensation (Statutory) _____

The LESSEE shall name as additional insured, Hyatt Management Corporation of New York, Inc., its officers, agents, employees and the County of Nassau. At least fourteen (14) days prior to the commencement of this Lease, the LESSEE shall deliver to COLISEUM certificates of insurance, with the limits specified above, evidencing that the policies hereby required by LESSEE will be in full force and effect through the lease term. COLISEUM may obtain said policies at LESSEE'S expense or cancel subject event(s).

ASSIGNMENT

The LESSEE shall not assign or sublet to others the space covered by this Lease Agreement without written consent of COLISEUM.

COMPLIANCE WITH LAWS AND REGULATIONS

(a) Compliance with Laws: LESSEE shall comply with all laws of the United States, of the State of New York, and all local statutes and ordinances, and all rules and regulations established by any authorized officer or department of said entities; LESSEE will not suffer or permit to be done anything on said premises in violation of any laws, statutes, ordinances, rules, or regulations.

(b) Licenses: LESSEE shall obtain all necessary permits or licenses required by such laws, statutes, ordinances, rules and regulations. If proper required licenses and permits are not obtained by LESSEE, then COLISEUM may obtain same and LESSEE will be responsible for reimbursement of all associated costs.

(c) Compliance with Rules and Regulations: LESSEE shall, and shall cause its servants, agents, employees, licensees, patrons and guests, to abide by such reasonable rules and regulations as may from time to time be adopted by COLISEUM for the use, occupancy and operation of the COLISEUM.

CONCESSIONS SALES

Except as specifically provided for herein, COLISEUM reserves unto itself, or its assigned agents, the sole rights: (a) to sell or dispense programs, librettos, periodicals, books, magazines, newspapers, soft drinks, flowers, tobacco, candies, food, novelties, or any related merchandise commonly sold or dispensed in the auditorium: (b) to rent and/or sell opera glasses, cushions and other articles; (c) to take and/or sell photographs; (d) to operate the parking lots and checkrooms.

HANDLING FUNDS

In the handling, control, custody and keeping of funds, whether the same are received through the box office or otherwise, COLISEUM is acting for the accommodation of LESSEE, and as to such funds, COLISEUM shall not be liable to LESSEE nor to any other person for any loss, theft, or defalcation thereof, whether such loss, theft or defalcation is caused or done by employees of COLISEUM or otherwise; nor shall any officer, agent, employee or servant of COLISEUM be liable for any loss, theft, or defalcation of such funds unless he willfully caused or permitted to be caused the same or unless it was proximately caused by his own gross negligence.

Exhibit 3-6 Continued

CONTROL OF BUILDING

The COLISEUM and premises, including keys thereto, shall be at all times under the control of the General Manager, and he or other duly authorized representatives of COLISEUM shall have the right to enter the premises at all times during the period covered by this contract. The entrances and exits of said premises shall be locked and unlocked at such times as may be reasonably required by LESSEE for its use of the COLISEUM; but LESSEE, at its own expense, must at all times place proper watchmen at all entrances and exits when the same are unlocked.

LICENSOR/LICENSEE

(a) It is expressly understood that COLISEUM shall not be construed or held to be a partner, agent or associate by joint venture or otherwise of LESSEE in the conduct of its business, it being expressly understood that the relationship between the parties hereto is and shall remain at all times that of licensor and licensee.

(b) It is understood and agreed that no agent, servant, or employee of LESSEE or any of its subcontractors shall under any circumstances be deemed an agent, servant or employee of COLISEUM.

COMPLIMENTARY TICKETS

LESSEE agrees that COLISEUM is entitled to receive and retain, for its own use or for the use of others, complimentary tickets to the Event in locations to be designated by COLISEUM; provided however, that the number of such complimentary tickets should not exceed one-half of one percent (0.5%) of the total number of tickets printed.

EXISTING UTILITIES

The rental includes the permanently attached electric lights, heat and/or air conditioning needed for the presentation of the attraction; however, failure to furnish any of the foregoing from circumstances beyond the control of the COLISEUM shall not be construed a breach of agreement.

OCCUPANCY DISRUPTION

In the event the COLISEUM or any part thereof shall be destroyed or damaged by fire, act of God, or any other cause, or if any other casualty or unforeseen occurrence of any kind shall render the fulfillment of this contract by COLISEUM reasonably or practically impossible, including without limitation thereto, the requisitioning of the premises by the United States Government, or any arm thereof, or by reason of labor disputes, then and thereupon, this contract shall terminate and LESSEE shall pay rental for said premises only up to the time of such termination, at the rate herein specified, and LESSEE hereby waives any claim for damages or compensation should this contract be so terminated.

COLISEUM'S RIGHT TO TERMINATE

It is agreed that without prejudice to any other rights and remedies that may be available to COLISEUM, in the event of the breach by LESSEE of one or more of the provisions of this Lease Agreement of any misrepresentations in obtaining said Lease Agreement, COLISEUM may refuse to allow the LESSEE to take possession of the premises, or if LESSEE is already in such possession, may stop all activities of LESSEE on premises and oust LESSEE therefrom. COLISEUM and its agents and employees shall in no way be responsible to the LESSEE for doing any or all of the things authorized by this paragraph. THIS AGREEMENT IS SUBJECT TO EACH AND EVERY TERM AND CONDITION OF THE FOLLOWING:

(a) Agreement of Lease between the County of Nassau and Hyatt Management Corporation of New York, Inc. dated October 15, 1979, on file with the Nassau County Board of Supervisors;

(b) Any Rider annexed to this agreement and made a part thereof;

(c) All rules, regulations, terms and conditions set forth in a booklet entitled: "NASSAU VETERANS MEMORIAL COLISEUM RULES, REGULATIONS AND CONDITIONS FOR LESSEES OF THE COLISEUM" delivered to the LESSEE at the time of the execution of this agreement. Receipt of booklet is acknowledged by the LESSEE by the execution of this agreement.

(a) Unless this contract is returned duly by LESSEE to COLISEUM on or before _____, it shall be deemed to be outstanding, and the contract becomes null and void and of no force and effect.

(b) This contract shall not be effective or binding upon COLISEUM until such time as it has been duly executed by an authorized officer of COLISEUM and an executed copy thereof delivered to the LESSEE.

Exhibit 3-6 Continued

This agreement shall be construed under the laws of the State of New York.

IN WITNESS WHEREOF, the parties have affixed their signatures as follows:

LESSEE:　　　　　　　　　　　　　HYATT MANAGEMENT CORPORATION OF NEW
　　　　　　　　　　　　　　　　　　　　　　YORK, INC.

_____　　　　_____
(SIGNATURE OF AUTHORIZED OFFICER)　　　　(SIGNATURE)

ADDENDUM TO LEASE AGREEMENT
NASSAU VETERANS MEMORIAL COLISEUM
HYATT MANAGEMENT CORPORATION OF NEW YORK, INC.
UNIONDALE, NEW YORK 11553

This addendum hereby becomes a part of Lease Agreement Number: _____

between Hyatt Management Corporation of New York, Inc. and _____

_____

whose address is _____

_____

dated _____ of _____ 19_____.

LESSEE: _____　　HYATT MANAGEMENT CORPORATION OF
　　　　　SIGNATURE OF AUTHORIZED　　　　　　　NEW YORK INC.
　　　　　　　　OFFICER

_____　　BY: _____
(COMPANY)

Exhibit 3-6　Continued

Chapter 4

AMATEUR ATHLETIC ASSOCIATIONS

INTRODUCTION

Amateur athletics are an integral part of American life both inside and outside educational institutions. They have, over time, become complex. Increasingly, certain amateur athletics bear a resemblance to big business, and the ineligibility or unavailability of an individual athlete or program can result in a large financial loss for the institution or the forfeiture of a chance to pursue a sports career for the athlete.

The organizations that govern amateur athletics are collectively referred to in this chapter as "amateur athletic associations." For our purposes, amateur athletic associations include high school and college athletic associations like the National Federation of State High School Associations (NFSHSA), the National Collegiate Athletic Association (NCAA), the National Association of Intercollegiate Athletics (NAIA), and the National Junior College Athletic Association (NJCAA); high school and college athletic conferences like the Big Ten and the Pac-10; and national and international governing bodies like the United States Olympic Committee (USOC), the Amateur Athletic Union (AAU), the International Amateur Athletic Federation (IAAF), and The Athletics Congress (TAC).

Besides these organizations, interscholastic and intercollegiate athletics are governed in this country by three other groups: the educational institutions, athletic directors, and coaches. These groups, together with amateur athletic associations, operate in a pyramidlike fashion: athletic associations set certain minimum standards and requirements for participation, conferences and educational institutions may impose stricter obligations on their student-athletes, and athletic directors and coaches may further demand stringent requirements that they judge to be necessary for successful performance in their individual sport or for proper functioning of the educational department as a whole. Since educational institutions and coaches must act within the scope of association and conference regulations, our focus will be primarily on the activities, rules, and governance of amateur athletic associations and conferences.

Chapter 4 analyzes the impact of the law on amateur athletics and notes the growing power of organizations that govern amateur athletics. Traditionally, these organizations have not been challenged in terms of legal accountability, but their pervasive influence has recently led to increasing legal scrutiny. Some argue that this has resulted in better protection of individual rights from arbitrary or unfair actions on the part of governing organizations, institutions, schools, or coaches and teachers. Others argue that this increased judicial presence is an unwarranted intrusion into amateur athletics.

The chapter begins with a discussion of the various definitions of an amateur athlete. While the amateur athlete is the topic of Chapter 5, the definitions of "amateur" are discussed here because the various definitions and interpretations of an amateur athlete have sparked controversy among the many amateur athletic associations that promulgate, interpret, and enforce the eligibility rules and regulations affecting amateur athletes.

The chapter then discusses three basic legal principles that often are the focus of court rulings and decisions concerning amateur athletic associations: judicial review, standing, and injunctive relief. This section is followed by information about major categories of voluntary amateur athletic organizations: the U.S. Olympic Committee, collegiate athletic associations such as the NCAA, and high school athletic associations. The public responsibilities of these categories of amateur athletic organizations are also discussed.

The chapter continues with the constitutional law aspects of athletics. The focus is on the amateur organization as a defendant or potential defendant in a court case. The last section of Chapter 4 discusses association authority with respect to promulgating and enforcing rules and regulations. The NCAA is used as the primary example of an amateur association's authority in this area.

The material covered in Chapter 4 is very important to athletic administrators. High school and college athletic administrators must deal with amateur athletic associations on a frequent basis, covering topics such as eligibility requirements, rule interpretations, student-athlete rights, and compliance and enforcement processes and procedures. Increasingly, athletic administrators have also become involved with athletic associations in a record number of lawsuits. Consequently, it has become essential for these administrators to understand as much about sports law and athletic associations as possible. The information in this chapter and in Chapter 5 can assist high school and college administrators to eliminate or minimize potential litigation by sensitizing them to the manner in which the courts view certain athletic organizations, their rules, and their authority to establish regulations on various topics. In addition, for the athletic administrator who becomes involved in a lawsuit as a representative of the student-athlete or the institution, familiarity with the legal terms and concepts introduced in the chapter is essential.

DEFINITIONS OF "AMATEUR"

In times past, most amateur athletic organizations refused to allow
amateur athletes to receive any money at all in compensation for
their time or expenses. In fact, this restriction was the basis for
distinguishing the amateur from the professional athlete. Increasingly, however, amateur athletes are receiving compensation for
certain living, training, and competition expenses. The amount
and type of reimbursement allowed is determined by the governing athletic organization. For example, The Athletics Congress
(TAC) has established a Trust Fund Program to enable TAC-
registered athletes to receive fees for product endorsements or
expenses from event promoters and still maintain their amateur
track eligibility (see Notes 2 and 4 and Appendix A).

The compensation issue has made the line between professional
and amateur more difficult to draw. While the definitions of
"amateur athlete" offered by various amateur athletic associations
have not changed much over the years, the interpretations of these
definitions have become more liberal to allow reimbursement of
expenses. The following are several examples of the definitions of
"amateur":

- National Collegiate Athletic Association. "An amateur student-
  athlete is one who engages in a particular sport for the
  educational, physical, mental and social benefits derived
  therefrom and to whom participation in that sport is an
  avocation." [*1987–88 NCAA Manual*, Constitution 3-1]
- International Olympic Committee. "[An amateur is] one who
  has participated in sports as an avocation without having
  received any remuneration for this participation." [Rule
  26(III)(3)] (See Note 3.)
- United States Olympic Committee. "Amateur athlete means
  any athlete who meets the eligibility standards established by
  the national governing body for the sport in which the athlete
  competes." [Chapter 17, U.S.C.A. sec. 373(1)] (See Note 1.)
- Amateur Athletic Union. "[An amateur is a] person who engages in sports solely for the pleasure and physical, mental, or
  social benefits he desires therefrom and to whom sport is
  nothing more than an avocation." [Code/Art. 1, sec.
  101.3(I)(1675)]
- Massachusetts Interscholastic Athletic Association. "An amateur athlete is one who engages in athletic competition solely
  for the physical, mental, social, and pleasure benefits derived
  therefrom." [*MIAA Rules and Regulations Governing Athletics
  1987–88*, Part II(16)]

- United States Swimming, Inc. "An amateur swimmer is one who engages in athletic competition solely for pleasure and the physical, mental and social benefit derived therefrom, and to whom swimming is nothing more than recreation for which no remuneration is received." [*United States Swimming Rules and Regulations 1985*, art. 43—Eligibility, sec. 343.1]
- American Hockey Association of the United States. "An amateur hockey player is one who is registered with the national association governing amateur hockey and is not engaged in playing organized professional hockey under contract to a professional club. Any player having completed his/her contractual obligations to a professional club may apply to the AHAUS for reinstatement of his/her amateur status. Fee— $100.00." [*1982–83 Official Guide*, Rules and Regulations No. XI]
- United States Tennis Association. "Any tennis player is an amateur who does not receive and has not received, directly or indirectly, pecuniary advantage by the playing, teaching, demonstration or pursuit of the game (meaning that the amateur has not in any way used his tennis skills for pecuniary advantage), except as expressly permitted by the USTA." [*1982 Yearbook: Standing Orders of the USTA*, art. II(B)]

These definitions have sparked a lively controversy because of the serious consequences of defining an amateur athlete. At the international level, the International Olympic Committee in 1986 endorsed a proposed rule change to eliminate the distinction between amateur and professional athletes. Although the individual international sports federations retain the power to say who can compete in the Olympic Games, it is likely that the Games will be open to professional athletes, at least in some sports. In 1987, for example, the International Tennis Federation (ITF) and the IOC approved a code of tennis eligibility that would permit the sport's millionaire stars to play in the 1988 Games. The IOC also allowed former World Hockey Association (WHA) players to compete at Sarajevo in 1984, and the International Hockey Federation (IHF) already allows NHL players to compete in its annual world championships. In soccer, a professional can compete unless he has played in the World Cup for a European or South American nation according to the Federation Internationale de Football Association (FIFA).

High school and collegiate athletic administrators must be familiar with these definitions because student-athletes who receive money or products related to a TAC-approved competition, or compete with professionals on a team in an IHF annual world championship, may lose their eligibility under NCAA or high school regulations. Athletic administrators should also be aware that professionalism in one sport may impact amateur status in another sport. A case in point is that of Renaldo Nehemiah, a former world class hurdler who joined the San Francisco Forty-Niners of the National Football League. Nehemiah lost his amateur track status for several years as a result of his pro football affiliation; he was later reinstated after he retired from football. More recently, Willie Gault, a professional on the Chicago Bears National Football League team, also competed as an amateur, in this case in the sport of bobsledding.

Athletic administrators would be wise to explore the details and the interpretations of the definitions of "amateur" for those associations with which their student-athletes become involved. The definitions can be found in association bylaws or constitutions, and interpretations can be obtained by contacting the organization's rule interpretation department or attorney. Again, let us emphasize that the definitions of "amateur" have not changed as much as the interpretations of those definitions.

NOTES ───

1. The United States Olympic Committee, in conjunction with Canteen Corporation, operates a Job Opportunities Program for amateur athletes with high Olympic potential. The program has serviced over 200 athletes since 1977. The job matching service attempts to find employment for amateur athletes while they train. During the period between 1977 and 1980, athletes employed by various corporations received an average annual salary of approximately $14,500.

2. The Athletics Congress, America's national governing body for track, operates a trust fund from which athletes can receive certain financial payments as a result of athletic activity and competition in accordance with regulations of the TAC/TRUST agreement, which has been approved by the International Amateur Athletic Federation (see Appendix A).

3. In 1985, as an experiment, the International Olympic Committee voted to allow professionals under the age of 23 to participate in the 1988 Winter and Summer Games in the sports of ice hockey, tennis, and soccer.

4. The Athletics Congress approved an agreement proposed by Eastman Kodak, by which three leading 1984 Summer Olympic participants—Mary Decker, Edwin Moses, and Alberto Salazar—served as "Olympic representatives" in exchange for a consulting fee. The three appeared in television commercials as part of the deal.

5. For further information concerning the governance of amateur athletic associations, see "Government of Amateur Athletics: The NCAA-AAU Dispute," 41 *Southern California Law Review* 464 (1968).

LEGAL PRINCIPLES PERTAINING TO AMATEUR
ATHLETIC ASSOCIATIONS

Amateur athletic associations are a pervasive part of American society. Individuals in the United States begin participating in such organizations at an early age (Pop Warner Football, Biddy Basketball, etc.) and can continue to do so through adulthood (NFSHSA, NCAA, AAU Master's Program, etc.). This section explores the mechanisms and principles of law as they pertain to amateur athletic associations, examines the structure of some of the organizations, and reviews litigation involving these organizations. A listing of various athletic organizations appears in Exhibit 4–1.

As college and high school athletics administration becomes increasingly complex and accountable with regard to legal issues, a basic knowledge of law becomes a necessary tool for all athletic administrators. For example, when revoking a student-athlete's scholarship, an administrator must be attentive to due process considerations. Or, when an interscholastic eligibility rule must be established with regard to married student-athletes or transfer student-athletes, the high school administrator should be aware of the potential for claims of equal protection violations.

Three legal concepts that are particularly important in the application of the law to the areas of amateur athletics are limited judicial review, standing, and injunctive relief. The concept of *limited judicial review* derives from a theory that courts should not review every legislative judgment of an organization but rather defer to the organization's decisions. The legal system intervenes as a general rule through judicial review only when legislative actions violate rights guaranteed by the Constitution, rights granted by the institution concerned, or basic notions of fairness. It should be noted that federal courts possess a more limited power of review than do state courts. This means that only cases involving certain constitutional issues will be heard at the federal level, while most others are deferred to the state level. The federal courts may thus be prevented from reviewing cases that might be subject to review at the state court level. A case in which an action by the state violates a federal constitutional right is, however, usually subject to judicial review at the federal level.

Standing is a procedural device that must be demonstrated prior to the initiation of any lawsuit. The requirement of standing is based on the theory that all cases brought before the legal system must be part of a current or an ongoing controversy. Academic curiosity or contrived situations are not sufficient requisites for a plaintiff to demonstrate standing.

Council of Ivy Group Presidents
70 Washington Road, Princeton, NJ 08544. (609) 452-6426
Strives to provide sound and balanced athletic programs within an academic framework.

National Association of Intercollegiate Athletics (NAIA)
1221 Baltimore St., Kansas City, MO 64105. (816) 842-5050
Formed in 1940, the NAIA administers programs of intercollegiate athletes for over 500 member institutions.

National Christian College Athletic Association (NCCAA)
1815 Union Ave., Chattanooga, TN 37404. (615) 698-6021
Formed in 1966, the NCCAA provides Christian athletes in Christian colleges an opportunity to be a national champion.

National Collegiate Athletic Association (NCAA)
Box 1906, Mission, KS 66222. (913) 384-3220
Formed in 1905, the NCAA is the premier governing body of intercollegiate athletics.

National Collegiate Football Association (NCFA)
15 Tulipwood Drive, Commack, NY 11725. (516) 543-0730
Founded in 1976, the NCFA sponsors and encourages intercollegiate competition in nonvarsity football programs.

National Junior Colleges Athletic Association (NJCAA)
12 East 2nd, Hutchinson, KS 67501. (316) 663-5445
Formed in 1937, the NJCAA promotes and supervises a national program of junior college sports and activities.

Texas Intercollegiate Athletic Association (TIAA)
Box C-17, Alpine, TX 79830. (915) 837-8226
Sponsors intercollegiate competition among selected state schools.

National Little College Athletic Association (NLCAA)
R.R. #1, Princeton, IN 47670. (812) 385-5757
Formed in 1966, the NLCAA sponsors intercollegiate competition for smaller schools (fewer than 500 males and/or females).

United States Olympic Commitee (USOC)
1750 East Boulder St., Colorado Springs, CO 80909. (303) 632-5551
Coordinates U.S. participation in Olympics.

International Olympic Committee (IOC)
Chateau de Bidy CH-1007, Lausanne, Switzerland. Phone: 41-21-54-25-55
Governs the Olympic movement and exercises all rights over the Olympic Games.

Amateur Basketball Association of the U.S.A.
1750 East Boulder St., Colorado Springs, CO 80909. (303) 632-7687
Founded 1975; serves as a class A member of the United States Olympic Committee.

American Baseball Coaches Association (ABCA)
605 Hamilton Drive, Champion, IL 61820. (217) 371-6000
Founded 1945, the ABCA furthers the game of baseball in schools and colleges.

American Football Coaches Association (AFCA)
7758 Wallace Road, Suite I, Orlando, FL 32819. (305) 351-6113
Founded in 1922, the AFCA promotes the sport of football through the exchange of information among coaches.

College Sports Information Directors of America
Campus Box 114, Kingsville, TX 78363.
Founded 1955; provides the exchange of ideas among members of the sports information profession.

Exhibit 4-1 Amateur Athletic Associations and Organizations

Intercollegiate Association of Amateur Athletes of America (ICAAA)
P.O. Box 3, Centerville, MA 02632. (617) 771-5060
Founded 1875; sponsors intercollegiate competition in cross-country, indoor and outdoor track.

National Association of Collegiate Directors of Athletics
P.O. Box 16428, Cleveland, OH 44116. (216) 892-4000
Founded in 1965. Seeks to establish educational standards and objectives among individuals responsible for administering collegiate athletic programs.

National Association of Basketball Coaches of U.S.
12 Pine Orchard Ave., P.O. Box 307, Branford, CT 06405. (203) 488-1232
Founded 1927; provides opportunities for professional growth on all levels of coaching.

National Club Sports Association
15 Tulipwood Drive, Commack, NY 11725. (516) 543-0730
Formed 1976; promotes and sponsors intercollegiate competition in nonvarsity sports.

U.S. Baseball Federation
4 Gregory Drive, Hamilton Square, N.J. 08690. (609) 586-2381
Founded 1965; coordinates and advances amateur baseball in the United States.

National Federation of State High School Associations
P.O. Box 20626, 11724, Plaza Circle, Kansas City, MO 64195. (816) 464-5400
Founded 1920; provides sanctioning services for interstate and international events and writes the playing rules for high school athletics.

Exhibit 4-1 Continued

The type of relief to be granted is the third important legal concept. Two types of relief are commonly requested: *monetary damages* and *injunctive relief*. Since monetary damages do not always provide the plaintiff with appropriate or adequate relief, the equitable remedy of injunctive relief is often requested. Equitable remedy of injunctive relief is a fair, nonmonetary form of compensation to redress a wrong or an injury. This type of relief is particularly important in amateur sports during the period in which legal action involving that participation is being tried in the courts. Time often is of the essence, and injunctive relief may be crucial to the student-athlete, since it allows him to continue competing.

These three concepts—limited judicial review, standing, and injunctive relief—are examined in greater detail in the following subsections.

Judicial Review

College and high school athletic administrators make decisions and take actions regarding rules and regulations every day. Yet athletic administrators must realize that as decision makers they do not possess uncontroverted control over student-athletes. Some decisions may be reviewed by the courts. Historically, courts have refused to intervene in the internal affairs of organizations that govern any aspect of a school's athletic program. However, beginning in the 1960s, student-athletes began to challenge the authority that was delegated to directors of athletic programs, because these administrators had begun to regulate personal behavior, including marriage and physical appearances. Courts accepted jurisdiction over these cases and invalidated rules that interfered with the constitutional rights of individual participants.

Voluntary associations such as the National Collegiate Athletic Association (NCAA), the National Junior College Athletic Association (NJCAA), The Athletics Congress (TAC), and state high school athletic associations and conferences are ordinarily allowed to make and enforce their own rules without interference from the courts. By becoming a member of such an organization, an individual and/ or an institution agrees to be bound by the athletic association's existing rules as well as any others subsequently passed.

As a general rule, the courts will review a voluntary association's rules *only* if one of the following conditions is present:

1. The rules violate public policy because they are fraudulent or unreasonable.
2. The rules exceed the scope of the association's authority.
3. The organization violates one of its own rules.
4. The rules are applied unreasonably or arbitrarily.
5. The rules violate an individual's constitutional rights.

For example, in one high school case, the courts determined that if a rule regulating either hair length or facial hair was reasonable and advanced an educational purpose, it should be obeyed. Thus, the federal court decided to defer to the judgment of school officials. Yet, in another case, a court struck down a good conduct rule on due process and equal protection grounds because it was too broad and attempted to regulate a student-athlete's conduct during the off-season (*Bunger v. Iowa High School Athletic Ass'n*, 197 N.W.2d 555 [Iowa 1972]) (see Note 1d). The harshness of a rule is not by itself grounds for judicial relief. Relief is granted only for those rules found to be in violation of one of the above conditions.

Even if the rule is subject to review, the role of a court is very limited. A court will not review the merits of the rule involved. It will only determine if the rule is invalid by virtue of one of the five standards listed above. If a violation is found, the case is remanded or deferred back to the athletic association for further consideration based on directions from the court.

Constitutional violations that require judicial intervention are often based either on due process or equal protection considerations. Due process involves infringements on life, liberty, or property, and equal protection involves the fair application of laws to individuals. Both of these constitutional standards require that state action be present prior to judicial review. (State action is discussed later in the chapter.)

Amateur athletic associations can guard against judicial scrutiny by reviewing and updating rules and regulations so that they (1) protect the health and welfare of athletes and serve to protect a justifiable public interest and (2) are consistent with court decisions in the state, region, or nation regarding similar rules. If a case is brought, the court is then more apt to show great deference to the judgment of the athletic administrators who created these rules and are best equipped to decide controversies concerning them. Only evidence of fraud, collusion, or unreasonable, arbitrary, or capricious action will cause a court to intervene on behalf of an athlete concerning the interpretation of a rule.

NOTES

1. The courts *granted* review in the following cases.
   (a) In *California State University, Haywood v. National Collegiate Athletic Ass'n*, 47 Cal. App. 3d 533, 121 Cal. Rptr. 85 (1975), a university filed a request for an injunction to prevent the NCAA from designating the entire intercollegiate athletic program as indefinitely ineligible for postseason play. The court ruled that when a voluntary association such as the NCAA clearly violates one of its own rules, its decision is subject to judicial review.
   (b) In *Estay v. LaFourche Parish School Board*, 230 So. 2d 443 (La. Ct. App. 1969), a rule prohibiting athletic participation for married students was held to be invalid because it exceeded the scope of the school board's authority and was therefore unreasonable.
   (c) In *Dunham v. Pulsifer*, 312 F. Supp. 411 (D. Vt. 1970), a rule requiring short hair for male student-athletes was held to be invalid because it was beyond the school board's authority to make such a rule. Athletic safety was not the issue, and even if it were, the problem could be solved by a much less intrusive measure such as requiring the wearing of headbands. (See page 255.)
   (d) In *Bunger v. Iowa School Athletic Ass'n*, 197 N.W.2d 555 (Iowa 1972), a rule that denied eligibility to any student-athlete found in a car that also carried alcohol was held to be invalid. The rule was judged to be too far removed from the problem of high school drinking to be a reasonable exercise of authority. (See page 260.)
2. The courts *denied* review in the following cases.
   (a) In *Kentucky High School Athletic Ass'n v. Hopkins County Board of Education*, 552 S.W.2d 685 (Ky. Ct. App. 1977), a high school transfer student-athlete sought to prohibit the school from enforcing the state high school athletic association bylaw under which he was declared ineligible. The court held that the bylaw was

valid and that it had not been arbitrarily applied. The court reasoned as follows: "It is not the responsibility of the courts to inquire into the expediency, practicality, or wisdom of the bylaws and regulations of voluntary associations. Furthermore, the courts will not substitute their interpretation of the bylaws . . . so long as [the association's] interpretation is fair and reasonable."

(b) In *State ex rel. National Junior College Athletic Ass'n v. Luten*, 492 S.W. 2d 404 (Mo. Ct. App. 1973), a junior college filed a request for equitable relief, alleging that the NJCAA had misinterpreted one of its rules. The court ruled that "the interpretation [of the NJCAA] being a reasonable and permissible one, and no other basis for the court's interference being present, the trial court lacked the jurisdiction to prohibit the implementation of the NJCAA ruling."

(c) In *Tennessee Secondary School Ass'n v. Cox*, 221 Tenn. 164, 425 S.W. 2d 597 (1968), a lower court's review of a transfer rule based on a violation of public policy and due process was ruled invalid due to lack of jurisdiction. The court held that participation in high school athletics is a privilege, not a legally cognizable right.

(d) In *Marino v. Waters*, 220 So. 2d 802 (La. Ct. App. 1969), a high school student-athlete had transferred to another school because his marriage was a policy violation of the private school he had originally attended. The court held that the rule was not arbitrary because it was promulgated for a legitimate purpose and was not applied in a discriminatory manner. Again, the mere harshness of a rule in its application to an individual does not make it subject to proper judicial review.

(e) In *Sanders v. Louisiana High School Athletic Ass'n*, 242 So. 2d 19 (La. Ct. App. 1970), a high school student-athlete was ruled ineligible by the high school athletic association under the transfer rule, because he had been "enrolled" for a period of one year. The court held that it will not ordinarily interfere with a voluntary association unless the association deprives a property right or its actions are capricious, arbitrary, or unjustly discriminatory.

(f) In *Albach v. Odle*, 531 F.2d 983 (10th Cir. 1976), a high school student-athlete challenged the athletic association's transfer rule. The court held that unless the regulation denied the student-athlete a constitutionally protected right, the rules regarding transfer would remain within the discretion of the appropriate state board and would not be within federal jurisdiction.

(g) In *Colorado Seminary v. National Collegiate Athletic Ass'n*, 417 F. Supp. 885 (D. Colo. 1976), the court held that it should not act as arbiter of disputes between an athletic association and its member institutions.

3. For the proposition that harshness by itself is not grounds for judicial review, see the following cases.

(a) In *State v. Judges of Court of Common Pleas*, 173 Ohio 239, 181 N.E.2d 261 (1962), the state high school athletic association suspended a member high school from participating in athletics for one year and declared two boys from the high school ineligible for interscholastic athletics for failure to abide by association rules. The court held that this action should not be prohibited when, although harsh, determination was not the result of mistake, fraud, collusion, or arbitrariness.

(b) In *Shelton v. National Collegiate Athletic Ass'n*, 539 F.2d 1179 (9th Cir. 1976), the court found no violation of equal protection of an NCAA eligibility rule as applied to a college basketball player. The court did admit that "the application of such [eligibility] rules may produce unreasonable results in certain situations." Though the court recognized that the eligibility rule and its means of enforcement may not be the best way to achieve the objective of ensuring amateurism, it stated: "It is not judicial business to tell a voluntary athletic association how best to formulate or enforce its rules." (See pages 236 and 244.)

4. For further information, see the following law review articles:

(a) "Judicial Control of Actions of Private Associations," 76 *Harvard Law Review* 983 (1963).

(b) "Administration of Amateur Athletes." 48 *Fordham Law Review* 53 (1979).

(c) Lowell, "Federal Administrative Intervention in Amateur Athletics," 43 *George Washington Law Review* 729 (March 1975).

(d) Lowell, "Judicial Review of Rule Making in Amateur Athletics," *Journal of College and University Law Review* 76 (1977).

5. Certain federal statutes are commonly cited in an effort to obtain federal court jurisdiction in athletic cases. Among them are the following:

(a) 28 U.S.C. section 1343—Civil Rights and Elective Franchise

The district courts shall have original jurisdiction of any civil action authorized by law to be commenced by any person:

(1) to recover damages for injury to his person or property, or because of the deprivation of any right or privilege of a citizen of the United States, by any act done in furtherance of any conspiracy mentioned in section 1985 of Title 42 (42 U.S.C. section 1985);

(2) to recover damages from any person who fails to prevent or to aid in preventing any wrongs mentioned in section 1985 of Title 42 which he had knowledge were about to occur and power to prevent;

(3) to redress the deprivation, under color of a State law, statute, ordinance, regulation, custom or usage, of any right, privilege or immunity secured by the Constitution of the United States or by an Act of Congress providing for equal rights of citizens or of all persons within the jurisdiction of the United States; and,

(4) to recover damages or to secure equitable or other relief under any Act of Congress providing for the protection of civil rights including the right to vote.

(b) 42 U.S.C. section 1983—Civil Action for Deprivation of Rights

Every person who, under color of any statute, ordinance, regulation, custom or usage of any State or Territory, subjects or causes to be subjected any citizen of the United States or other person within the jurisdiction thereof to the deprivation of any rights, privileges, or immunities secured by the Constitution and laws shall be liable to the party injured in an action at law, suit in equity, or other proper proceeding for redress.

Standing

In spite of safeguards designed to prevent judicial review, college and high school administrators may become involved in court cases. The athletic administrator may represent the school or the conference against a student-athlete's challenge, the student-athlete's interest against a larger association like the NCAA, or the school in relation to a student-athlete's challenge of an NCAA rule. To proceed in these situations, the student-athlete and/or the school must first justify, to the satisfaction of the court, bringing the complaint to a court of law. If successful, the party bringing the suit is said to have established *standing*.

For example, in a case in which a student-athlete brought a complaint against the NCAA, the court concluded that the standing requirement was met by the student-athlete's institution. The court reasoned that since the interests of the student-athlete are "inherently intertwined with those of his team and school," procedures which allow the university to proceed on behalf of the student-athlete are justified (*Hunt v. NCAA*, No. 676-370 C.A. [W.D. Mich. 1976]).

In order to establish standing in court, the plaintiff must meet three criteria. First, a demonstration that the action in question did in fact cause an injury, whether economic or otherwise, is required. Second, the plaintiff must establish that the interest to be protected is at least arguably within the zone of interests protected by the Constitution, legislative enactments, or judicial principles. This criterion is often labeled by the phrase "substantiality of federal question." Finally, the interest to be protected must be substantial to the plaintiff bringing the suit. That is, the plaintiff must be an interested party or be otherwise directly involved. If the plaintiff has only a peripheral interest, there may be no standing. This often applies to an amateur association and one of its member institutions. An individual student-athlete therefore is not directly involved in the controversy because the individual is not a member of the amateur association. Consequently, the student-athlete who brings suit may be deemed to lack the necessary standing. An example is the NCAA, whose membership consists of colleges and universities and not of individual student-athletes.

NOTE ───

1. The following cases discuss the substantiality of federal question required for federal court jurisdiction in athletic association cases.

　　(a) In *Fluitt v. University of Nebraska*, 489 F. Supp. 1194 (D. Neb.

1980), the court found that there is a substantial federal question for two reasons: (1) the Supreme Court had not, in prior decisions, spoken so clearly on the issues raised by the college student-athlete in this case to render the claims frivolous or the subject foreclosed, and (2) the student-athlete's claim alleged that two people in the identical situation are treated differently solely on the basis of their sex, and sex discrimination is one of the categories even the tenth circuit court has held as presenting a substantial federal question. (See page 156.)

(b) In *Parish v. National Collegiate Athletic Ass'n*, 361 F. Supp. 1214 (W.D. La. 1973), *aff'd*, 506 F.2d 1028 (5th Cir. 1975), the court held that the NCAA's imposition of a rule requiring a grade point average of 1.600 for athletic eligibility does not raise a substantial federal question under the Civil Rights Act such that federal court jurisdiction would be appropriate. (See page 187.)

(c) In *National Collegiate Athletic Ass'n v. Califano*, 444 F. Supp. 425 (D. Kan. 1978), *rev'd*, 622 F.2d 1382 (10th Cir. 1980), the NCAA challenged the Department of Health, Education and Welfare's jurisdiction with regard to Title IX. On appeal, the Tenth Circuit ruled that the NCAA had standing to challenge the application of Title IX legislation to intercollegiate athletic programs. The court based its decision on the fact that individual NCAA member institutions have the necessary standing to test the validity of Title IX regulations. The court stated that the NCAA can bring suit on behalf of its member institutions if it can show that it has their support. (See page 428.)

(d) In *Georgia High School Athletic Ass'n v. Waddell*, 285 S.E.2d 7 (Ga. 1981), the court held that appeals of decisions made by football officials in game conditions are not subject to judicial review. The court ruled that were the decision to be otherwise, every error in the trial courts would constitute a denial of equal protection. The court further held that courts of equity in Georgia do not have authority to review decisions of football referees because they do not present judicial controversies.

(e) In *Watkins v. Louisiana High School Athletic Ass'n*, 301 So. 2d 695 (La. Ct. App. 1974), a spectator sought an injunction preventing an association from enforcing a ruling that prohibited her high school team from playing any athletic contests for one year if she was in attendance as a fan because of a dispute she had had with a referee. The Louisiana Court of Appeals held that the spectator had a sufficient legal interest to institute the suit, assuming a valid cause of action was alleged.

(f) In *Florida High School Activities Ass'n v. Bradshaw*, 369 So. 2d 398 (Fla. Dist. Ct. App. 1979), the court held that neither the coach nor team players had standing to assert a denial of equal protection to an individual player.

(g) In *Assmus v. Little League Baseball, Inc.*, 70 Misc. 2d 1038, 334 N.Y.S.2d 982 (1972), the court held that players who were not members of a baseball corporation did not have standing to attack the alleged illegality of the corporation's rule.

Injunctive Relief

Providing the plaintiff has been successful on the issues of limited judicial review and standing, the next step for the plaintiff is to request relief. Because enforcement of the rules and regulations of amateur athletic associations frequently prohibits athletes from competing, student-athletes and their schools often bring lawsuits to obtain relief in the form of injunctions that force the associations to allow the student-athlete to participate. These attempts to keep the student-athlete eligible are critical to the high school athlete hoping to obtain a college scholarship and to the collegiate athletic program striving for a profitable and prestigious winning team.

An *injunction* is a court order for one of the parties to a lawsuit to behave in a certain manner. Injunctive relief is designed to prevent future wrongs—not to punish past acts. It is only used to prevent an irreparable injury, which is suffered when monetary damages cannot be calculated or when money will not adequately compensate the injured party. An injury is considered irreparable when it involves the risk of physical harm and death, the loss of some special opportunity, or the deprivation of unique, irreplaceable property. For example, a high school football star may be granted an injunction to compete in an all-star game since an inability to do so may jeopardize his chances of obtaining a college scholarship.

The injunction is a form of equitable relief that can be used to force an athletic association to engage in or refrain from an action that affects an institution, an individual student-athlete, or a staff member. There are three types of injunctions: a temporary restraining order (TRO), a preliminary injunction, and a permanent injunction.

A *temporary restraining order* is issued to the defendant without notice and is usually effective for a maximum of 10 days. The defendant is not bound by the TRO until actual notice is received. After receiving notice, the defendant can immediately ask the court for a review. A *preliminary injunction* is granted prior to a full hearing and disposition of a case. The plaintiff is obligated to give the defendant notice and also to post a bond. The defendant is usually present at the preliminary injunction hearing. The hearing on the issuance of a preliminary injunction is granted only in an apparent emergency and only if the plaintiff shows a likelihood of success for winning the case on the merits. Temporary restraining orders and preliminary injunctions are also granted during the course of a trial to preserve the status quo until the rights of the litigants can be determined. A *permanent injunction* may be issued following a full hearing, and if it is issued, remains in force until the final determination of the particular suit.

The issuance of any of the three types of injunctions calls for the exercise of sound judicial discretion. A judge generally considers three factors before granting or denying any form of equitable relief: the nature of the controversy, the objective of the injunction, and the comparative hardship or inconvenience to both parties.

An excellent example of the use of a preliminary injunction may be found in the case of Greg Kite, a high school basketball player (later with the Boston Celtics). Kite was declared ineligible for his senior year after attending a basketball camp, which was against state interscholastic association rules. Kite sued and was granted a preliminary injunction to prevent the high school athletic association from enforcing its training camp rule against him. The court maintained that Kite had a strong likelihood of winning the case, that he would suffer irreparable harm if he lost his senior year of competition, that it served the public interest to have Kite eligible, and that when the hardships were balanced, he would suffer more material harm if the injunction were denied than the association would suffer in having Kite compete until the matter came to trial (*Kite v. Marshall*, 454 F. Supp. 1347 [S. D. Tex. 1978]). Two years after Kite graduated, the trial concluded and the interscholastic association won because its training camp rule was found to be constitutional (*Kite v. Marshall*, 494 F. Supp. 227 [S.D. Tex. 1980]). On appeal, the association was successful in reversing the lower court decision (*Kite v. Marshall*, 661 F.2d 1027 [5th Cir. 1981]). (Other examples dealing with injunctions were discussed in Chapter 3.)

NOTES ──

1. Injunctions were *denied* in the following cases.
   (a) In *Samara v. National Collegiate Athletic Ass'n*, 1973 Trade Cases 74, 536 (E.D. Va.), two track athletes, students at NCAA schools, wished to participate in a Russian-American meet sponsored by the Amateur Athletic Union. Under NCAA bylaws, this meet was an "extra event" that must be certified by the NCAA or the participating student-athletes would lose their NCAA eligibility. The plaintiffs sought injunctive and declaratory relief on the basis of the Sherman Act to prevent the NCAA from imposing sanctions due to their participation. Equitable relief was denied because the plaintiffs only faced a threat; they had not suffered any injury.
   (b) In *Thompson v. Barnes*, 294 Minn. 528, 200 N.W.2d 921 (1972), a student-athlete had been suspended for one year from participat-

ing in interscholastic athletics due to a second violation of the alcohol rule of the league to which his high school belonged. The student-athlete requested a temporary injunction staying his suspension until his motion for a permanent injunction could be heard. The request was denied because the student-athlete failed to show that he would have competed during the period of the suspension, that suspension would cause irreparable injury pending trial, or that the permanent injunction sought in the main action would be insufficient relief.

(c) In *Kupec v. Atlantic Coast Conference*, 399 F. Supp. 1377 (M.D.N.C. 1975), a student-athlete's request for a preliminary injunction was ruled improper when the student-athlete did not show actual harm, when harm would be done to the college athletic conference by granting an injunction, and when the student-athlete did not seem likely to succeed on the merits of his claim. (See page 202.)

(d) In *Florida High School Activities Ass'n v. Bradshaw*, 369 So. 2d 398 (Fla. Ct. App. 1979), an injunction was denied as improper when the student-athlete failed to show personal injury.

2. Injunctions were *granted* in the following cases.

(a) In *University of Nevada-Las Vegas v. Tarkanian*, 95 Nev. 389, 594 P.2d 1159 (Nev. 1979), University of Nevada at Las Vegas (UNLV) basketball coach Jerry Tarkanian was granted a temporary restraining order and then a permanent injunction barring UNLV from suspending him from his coaching duties for two years. UNLV was directed to impose the suspension by the NCAA Committee on Infractions under the show-cause provisions of the NCAA's enforcement procedures. On appeal to the Nevada Supreme Court, the permanent injunction was reversed and sent back to the Clark County District Court for further proceedings. (See page 139, Note 2.)

(b) In *Hall v. University of Minnesota*, 530 F. Supp. 104 (D. Minn. 1982), the court looked to four factors to determine whether a preliminary injunction should be issued: (1) the threat of irreparable harm to the moving party; (2) the state of balance between that harm and the injury that granting the injunction would inflict on other parties; (3) the public interest; and (4) the probability that the moving party would succeed on the merits of the claim. (See pages 191 and 272.)

VOLUNTARY ATHLETIC ASSOCIATIONS

All amateur athletic organizations are subject to fundamental legal principles. Athletic associations and conferences, such as the National Federation of State High School Associations (NFSHSA), the NCAA, and the Big Ten, although private and voluntary organizations, are nevertheless scrutinized. The courts have begun to question these supposedly "private" athletic associations and conferences for two reasons: (1) large numbers of public institutions form the membership of these organizations, and (2) these organizations are performing a traditional government or public function.

In this public function vein, a number of organizations have been created to serve different groups of individuals in a variety of athletic activities. The Amateur Athletic Union (AAU) has, for almost 100 years, dedicated itself to the development of amateur sports and physical fitness for amateur athletes of all ages (e.g., the AAU Junior Olympics and the AAU Masters Program for adults age 25 and over). The NCAA has taken upon itself the role of a coordinator and overseer of college athletics, in the interest of individuals and their educational institutions. As these organizations become more and more a part of the public domain in the eyes of the judicial system, it becomes crucial for college and high school athletic administrators to understand their nature, their composition, and their operation.

Amateur athletic organizations are often distinguished on the basis of the sport (e.g., The Athletic Congress [TAC], the national governing body for track and field), educational level (e.g., National Junior College Athletic Association [NJCAA]), or geographical location (e.g., a state high school athletic association). Some amateur sports organizations govern institutions (e.g., the NCAA governs colleges and universities), and some govern individual athletes (e.g., TAC). Belonging to such an organization does not preclude membership in another. In fact, most educational institutions belong to an allied conference (e.g., Pacific-10 Conference or Big East Conference) in addition to being a member of a national association with a broader constituency (e.g., NCAA). Allied conferences, a subset of the larger amateur sports associations, usually consist of a number of schools in a geographic area that have similar institutional goals and interests. These schools compete against each other in a number of sports and often compete for conference championships in each of the sports.

In many ways, the NCAA's functions and its relationship with its members are analogous to the federal government's relationship with the state governments. For example, the NCAA promulgates rules regarding minimum standards that must be followed by all of its members. These rules do not, however, preclude its membership from creating a stricter rule on any subject already covered by an NCAA regulation. In addition, the membership can also make and enforce any rule that does not conflict with a stated rule or policy of the NCAA.

There are many amateur organizations besides the NCAA, such as Little League baseball, Pop Warner football, and the Amateur

Softball Association (ASA). However, because of its importance and influence, the NCAA will be used as a representative example of a voluntary athletic association in this chapter's presentation of arguments that can be raised against or on behalf of a voluntary athletic association. First, however, we will take a brief look at the United States Olympic Committee and the Amateur Sports Act, which provides the basic underpinnings for amateur athletics in this country.

The United States Olympic Committee (USOC)

The Amateur Sports Act of 1978 (36 U.S.C. sections 371–396) was passed by the United States Congress to reorganize and coordinate amateur athletics in the United States and to encourage and strengthen participation of U.S. amateurs in international competition. The act concerns itself with two major areas: (1) the relationship between athletes eligible for international amateur competition and the ruling bodies that govern those competitions, and (2) the relationship between the ruling bodies themselves. The act establishes the United States Olympic Committee (USOC) as the principal mechanism for attaining these goals and assigns the USOC the following 14 objects and purposes as guidelines for its operation:

1. Establish national goals for amateur athletic activities and encourage the attainment of those goals.
2. Coordinate and develop amateur athletic activity in the United States directly relating to international amateur athletic competition, so as to foster productive working relationships among sports-related organizations.
3. Exercise exclusive jurisdiction, either directly or through its constituent members of committees, over all matters pertaining to the participation of the United States in the Olympic Games and in the Pan-American Games when held in the United States.
4. Obtain for the United States, either directly or by delegation to the appropriate national governing body, the most competent amateur representation possible in each competition and event of the Olympic Games and of the Pan-American Games.
5. Promote and support amateur athletic activities involving the United States and foreign nations.
6. Promote and encourage physical fitness and public participation in amateur athletic activities.
7. Assist organizations and persons concerned with sports in the development of amateur athletes.

8. Provide for the swift resolution of conflicts and disputes involving amateur athletes, national governing bodies, and amateur sports organizations, and protect the opportunity of any amateur athlete, coach, trainer, manager, administrator, or official to participate in amateur athletic competition.
9. Foster the development of amateur athletic facilities for use by amateur athletes and assist in making existing amateur athletic facilities available for use by amateur athletes.
10. Provide and coordinate technical information on physical training, equipment design, coaching, and performance analysis.
11. Encourage and support research, development, and dissemination of information in the areas of sports medicine and sports safety.
12. Encourage and provide assistance to amateur athletic activities for women.
13. Encourage and provide assistance to amateur athletic programs and competition for handicapped individuals, including, when feasible, the expansion of opportunities for meaningful participation by handicapped individuals in programs of athletic competition for able-bodied individuals.
14. Encourage and provide assistance to amateur athletes of racial and ethnic minorities for the purpose of eliciting the participation of such minorities in amateur athletic activities in which they are underrepresented.

The Amateur Sports Act creates a governing structure for the USOC by empowering it to select one national governing body (NGB) for each Olympic or Pan-American sport. The act enumerates specific responsibilities for an NGB, including the definition of an "amateur athlete" and the determination of eligibility of each athlete for competition in that particular sport. The NGBs do the actual organizational work of developing athletes, organizing teams, instructing coaches and officials, and scheduling events. The act details explicit requirements for amateur sports organizations to become an NGB and provides a mechanism for resolution of disputes between individual organizations wishing to be recognized as the sole NGB. One important requirement of NGBs is that they have the backing of the sport's participants in the United States; they must also be recognized by international governing bodies.

Interestingly, provisions in the Amateur Sports Act call for the encouragement and assistance to "amateur athletic programs and competition for handicapped individuals" and the promotion of "physical fitness and public participation in amateur athletic activities." This language would seem to warrant the inclusion of non-Olympic or Pan-American sports in its realm of responsibility. In the past, however, the USOC has chosen to reject this broader interpretation and has instead directed its efforts through the NGBs toward Olympic/Pan-American sports. Nevertheless, USOC membership remains open to any sport not falling into the Olympic/Pan-American classification.

Although the USOC has chosen to concentrate on Olympic/Pan-American sports, its jurisdiction in this area is not exclusive. Not only must the NGBs be approved by an international governing body, but the USOC itself must contend with and conform to the policies and regulations of the International Olympic Committee (IOC). Furthermore, the Amateur Sports Act specifies that "any amateur sports organization which conducts amateur athletic competition, participation in which is restricted to a specific class of amateur athletes (such as high school students, college students, members of the Armed Forces or similar groups or categories), shall have exclusive jurisdiction over such competition." It is only when that group wishes to become involved in international competition that the USOC may play a role through the granting of a sanction or "certificate of approval issued by an NGB," which is required for such international competition. Even here, the USOC does not have exclusive control. For instance, when the United States hosts the Olympic or Pan-American Games, the USOC must work in concert with local and state governments and also with the organizing committee of the host city.

The Amateur Sports Act defines an "amateur sports organization" as a "not-for-profit corporation, club, federation, union, association or other group organized in the United States which sponsors or arranges any amateur athletic competition." This broad definition, when taken together with the specification regarding exclusive jurisdiction over amateur athletic competition referred to above, limits the jurisdiction of the USOC by delegating the jurisdiction over competitions to any sports body that meets the definition. Yet, this broad definition also allows for a comprehensive structure of many organizations which assume a role in the regulation of amateur athletics in the United States. Exhibit 4–2 lists the various groups that comprise the USOC membership. Particular note should be given to Group B members—the NCAA, NFSHSA, NAIA, and NJCAA. Exhibit 4–3 lists the international sports federations that are recognized by the International Olympic Committee.

For high school and college administrators, the Amateur Sports Act represents the foundation upon which their athletic associations are based. Through this foundation, the various athletic associations (NCAA, NJCAA, NFSHSA, etc.) are interrelated with the USOC and the Amateur Sports Act. As athletes bring lawsuit against their governing associations, this relationship can be analyzed by the courts. Consequently, being familiar with this relationship prepares the administrator for these situations.

NOTES ───

1. For further information on the USOC and its powers, see *DeFrantz v. United States Olympic Committee*, 492 F. Supp. 1181 (D.D.C. 1980), *aff'd without opinion*, 701 F.2d 221 (D.C. Cir. 1980). The federal district court held that the Amateur Sports Act of 1978 did not establish a cause of action for 25 designated Olympic athletes who sought to prohibit the USOC from barring these American athletes from participating in the 1980 Olympic Games in Moscow. The court noted:

> We . . . conclude that the USOC not only had the authority to decide not to send an American team to the summer Olympics, but also that it could do so for reasons not directly related to sports considerations.
> We . . . find that the decision of the USOC not to send an American team to the summer Olympics was not state action, and therefore, does not give rise to an actionable claim for the infringements of the constitutional rights alleged. [See page 249.]

2. For further information on national governing bodies, review *United States Wrestling Federation v. Wrestling Division of the AAU, Inc.*, 545 F. Supp. 1053 (N.D. Ohio, 1982). The federal court prohibited one national athletic organization from being the designated NGB over another organization pursuant to the Amateur Sports Act of 1978. (See page 249.)

3. For information on how the federal courts interpret IOC decisions, see *Martin v. International Olympic Committee*, 740 F.2d 670 (9th Cir. 1984). The U.S. Court of Appeals for the Ninth Circuit turned down a request by 82 women athletes from 27 countries for an injunction that would order the IOC to let women compete in the 5,000-meter and 10,000-meter races at the 1984 Los Angeles Olympics. The court held that California civil rights law does not authorize the establishment of "separate but equal" events for men and women and that the IOC rule which governed the addition of new events to the games was applied equally to men and women and thus was not discriminatory.

4. For further information on the Amateur Sports Act, see Nafzinger, "The Amateur Sports Act of 1978," *Brigham Young University Law Review* 47 (1983).

The National Collegiate Athletic Association (NCAA)

Although not every athletic administrator may be directly involved with the National Collegiate Athletic Association, administrators of all types of amateur athletic associations should be familiar with its characteristics. Because of the NCAA's breadth and influence, it

Group A, National Governing Bodies

Archery	National Archery Association (NAA)
Athletics	The Athletics Congress of the USA (TAC)
Baseball	U.S. Baseball Federation (USBF)
Basketball	Amateur Basketball Association of the USA (ABAUSA)
Biathlon	U.S. Biathlon Association (USBA)
Bobsledding	U.S. Bobsled and Skeleton Association
Boxing	USA Amateur Boxing Federation (USA/ABF)
Canoeing	American Canoe Association (ACA)
Cycling	U.S. Cycling Federation (USCF)
Diving	U.S. Diving (USD)
Equestrian	American Horse Shows Association (AHSA)
Fencing	U.S. Fencing Association (USFA)
Field Hockey	(Men) Field Hockey Association of America (FHAA)
	(Women) U.S. Field Hockey Association (USFHA)
Figure Skating	U.S. Figure Skating Association (USFSA)
Gymnastics	U.S. Gymnastics Federation (USGF)
Ice Hockey	Amateur Hockey Association of the U.S. (AHAUS)
Judo	U.S. Judo (USJ)
Luge	U.S. Luge Association (USLA)
Modern Pentathlon	U.S. Modern Pentathlon Association (USMPA)
Roller Skating	U.S. Amateur Confederation of Roller Skating (USAC/RS)
Rowing	U.S. Rowing Association (USRA)
Shooting	National Rifle Association of America (NRA)
Skiing	U.S. Ski Association (USSA)
Soccer	U.S. Soccer Federation (USSF)
Softball	Amateur Softball Association of America (ASA)
Speedskating	U.S. International Speedskating Association (USISA)
Swimming	U.S. Swimming (USS)
Synchronized Swimming	U.S. Synchronized Swimming (USSS)
Table Tennis	U.S. Table Tennis Association (USTTA)
Taekwondo	U.S. Tae Kwon Do Union (USTU)
Team Handball	U.S. Team Handball Federation (USTHF)
Tennis	U.S. Tennis Association (USTA)
Volleyball	U.S. Volleyball Association (USVBA)
Water Polo	U.S. Water Polo (USWP)
Weightlifting	U.S. Weightlifting Federation (USWF)
Wrestling	USA Wrestling (USAW)
Yachting	U.S. Yacht Racing Union (USYRU)

Group B, National Multi-Sport Organizations

Amateur Atlantic Union of the U.S. (AAU)
American Alliance for Health, Physical Education,
  Recreation, and Dance (AAHPERD)
Catholic Youth Organization (CYO)
Jewish Welfare Board (JWB)
National Association of Intercollegiate Athletics (NAIA)
National Collegiate Athletic Association (NCAA)
National Exploring Division, Boy Scouts of America
National Federation of State High School Associations (NFSHSA)
National Junior College Athletic Association (NJCAA)
U.S. Armed Forces
Young Men's Christian Association of the USA (YMCA)

Exhibit 4-2 Membership of the United States Olympic Committee

Group C, Affiliated Sports Organizations
American Amateur Racquetball Association (AARA)
(Men) American Bowling Congress (ABC),
(Women) Women's International Bowling
    Congress (WIBC)

Group D, U.S. Olympic Committee State Fundraising Organizations
There are 54 state/area organizations in the U.S.

Group E, Handicapped in Sports
American Athletic Association of the Deaf
National Association of Sports For Cerebral Palsy
National Wheelchair Athletic Association
Special Olympics
United States Amputee Athletic Association
U.S. Association for Blind Athletes

Exhibit 4-2 Continued

affects athletes from grade school to the professional level. In addition, the way the courts approach a voluntary athletic association like the NCAA can serve as a good indicator of how the courts may deal with other organizations that embrace principles and goals similar to those of the NCAA.

The NCAA was formed in the early 1900s in response to the rugged nature of football. The flying wedge, football's major offense in 1905, and other mass formations and gang tackling led to many injuries and even deaths. As a result, many institutions discontinued football and others urged that it be reformed or abolished from intercollegiate athletics. President Theodore Roosevelt reacted by holding two White House conferences with college athletic leaders to encourage such reform. In early December 1905, Chancellor Henry M. MacCracken of New York University brought 13 institutions together to propose changes in football playing rules. At a subsequent meeting held on December 28, the Intercollegiate Athletic Association of the United States (IAAUS) was founded. When the IAAUS was officially constituted on March 31, 1906, it had 62 members. It took its present name—the National Collegiate Athletic Association—in 1910.

Initially, the NCAA was a discussion group and rules-making body. In 1921, the first NCAA national championship was held: The National Track and Field Championships. Over the years, more rules committees were formed and more championships in other athletic events were held. After World War II, the NCAA adopted the "Sanity Code," which established guidelines for recruiting and granting financial aid. Unfortunately, the code failed to curb abuses involving student-athletes. The number of postseason football games began to increase, and member institutions became more concerned about the effects of unrestricted television

INTERNATIONAL FEDERATION
For Olympic Sports

IAAF International Amateur Athletic Federation (track and field)

FITA International Archery Federation

FIBA International Amateur Basketball Federation

FIBT International Bobsleigh and Tobogganing Federation

AIBA International Amateur Boxing Association

FIAC International Amateur Cyclists Federation

FIE International Fencing Federation

FIFA International Association Football Federation (soccer)

FEI International Equestrian Federation

FIG International Gymnastics Federation

IHF International Handball Federation

FIH International Hockey Federation (field hockey)

IFWHA International Federation of Women's Hockey Associations

IIHF International Ice Hockey Federation

IJF International Judo Federation

FIL International Luge Federation

IUPMB International Union of Modern Pentathlon and Biathlon

FISA International Federation of Rowing Societies

UIT International Shooting Union

ISU International Skating Union (figure skating and speed skating)

FIS International Ski Federation

FINA International Amateur Swimming Federation (also diving and water polo)

FIVB International Volleyball Federation

IWF International Weightlifting Federation

FILA International Amateur Wrestling Federation

IYRU International Yacht Racing Union

FIC International Canoe Federation

For Pan American Games Sports

AINBA The International Baseball Association

FIRS International Roller Skating Federation

FIS International Softball Association

ITF International Tennis Federation

UNITED STATES MEMBER

NAA National Archery Association

ABAUSA Amateur Basketball Association of the USA

USCF U.S. Cycling Federation

USSF U.S. Soccer Federation

AHSA American Horse Shows Association

USGF U.S. Gymnastics Federation

USTHBF U.S. Team Handball Federation

FHAA Field Hockey Association of America (men's)

USFHA U.S. Field Hockey Association, Inc. (women's)

AHAUS Amateur Hockey Association of the U.S.

AAU Judo Div.

AAU Luge Div.

USMPBA U.S. Modern Pentathlon and Biathlon Association

NAAO National Association of Amateur Oarsmen

NRA National Rifle Association of America

USFSA U.S. Figure Skating Association

USISA U.S. International Skating Association

USSA U.S. Ski Association

AAU Aquatics Div.

USVBA U.S. Volleyball Association

AAU Weightlifting Div.

AAU Wrestling Div.

USYRU U.S. Yacht Racing Union

ACA American Canoe Association

USBF U.S. Baseball Federation

USACRS U.S. Amateur Confederation of Roller Skating

A.S.A. Amateur Softball Association of America

USTA U.S. Tennis Association

Exhibit 4-3 International Sports Federations Recognized by the International Olympic Committee and U.S. Members of the International Federations

coverage on football attendance. As the complexity and scope of these problems and the growth in membership and championships multiplied, the need for full-time professional leadership became apparent.

In 1951, Walter Byers, a former part-time executive assistant, was named executive director of the NCAA. In 1952, a national headquarters was established in Kansas City. In addition, a program to control live television coverage of football games was approved, the annual convention delegated enforcement powers to the association's council, and legislation was adopted governing postseason bowl games. By 1988, a national staff of approximately 147 employees occupied two NCAA buildings in Mission, Kansas. Dick Schultz, former athletic director at the University of Virginia, was selected to replace Walter Byers as executive director beginning in October 1987.

At the first special convention in 1973, the NCAA's membership was divided into three legislative and competitive divisions (referred to as Division I, Division II, and Division III). Subdivisions I-A and I-AA were created in the sport of football by Division I members five years later. Women joined the NCAA's activities in 1980 when Divisions II and III established 10 championships for 1981–82. At the historic 75th convention a year later, an extensive governance plan was adopted to include women's athletic programs, services, and representation. The women's championships program was expanded with the addition of 19 more events.

In 1984, the President's Commission was created in a special convention. This decisive step was taken to strengthen the association's compliance and enforcement efforts. With this presidential involvement, the NCAA has come full circle since its beginnings in 1905.

The NCAA's current voluntary membership consists of over 1,000 four-year colleges and universities and two-year upper-level collegiate institutions located throughout the United States. Member schools agree to be bound by NCAA rules and regulations and are obligated to administer their athletic programs in accordance with NCAA rules. Over half of the NCAA's members are state-subsidized universities, and most receive some form of federal financial assistance. Operating funds for the NCAA are in part accumulated through membership dues that are figured on a sliding scale based on the type of membership held. The annual dues range from $225 to $1,800 (effective 9/1/85) (*1987–88 NCAA Manual*, Bylaw 9-3[b & c]). If a school's dues are not paid, the school is denied a chance to vote at the annual convention and cannot enter teams in NCAA-sponsored competitions. In addition, if the dues are not paid within one year, the membership automatically terminates.

The NCAA does not offer membership to individual student-athletes. Instead, it uses the principle of institutional control. In essence, this means that the NCAA deals only with school administrations and not with individual student-athletes. When a violation is discovered that concerns a student-athlete, the NCAA informs the school of its findings and requests that the school declare the student-athlete ineligible. If the school does not adhere to the request, the NCAA may invoke sanctions against all or any part of the institution's athletic program.

The purposes of the NCAA are stated in its constitution:

(a) To initiate, stimulate and improve intercollegiate athletic programs for student-athletes and to promote and develop educational leadership, physical fitness, sports participation as a recreational pursuit and athletic excellence;

(b) To uphold the principle of institutional control of, and responsibility for, all intercollegiate sports in conformity with the constitution and bylaws of this Association;

(c) To encourage its members to adopt eligibility rules to comply with satisfactory standards of scholarship, sportsmanship and amateurism;

(d) To formulate, copyright and publish rules of play governing intercollegiate sports;

(e) To preserve intercollegiate athletic records;

(f) To supervise the conduct of, and to establish eligibility standards for, regional and national athletic events under the auspices of this Association;

(g) To cooperate with other amateur athletic organizations in promoting and conducting national and international athletic events;

(h) To legislate, through bylaws or by resolution of a Convention, upon any subject of general concern to the members in the administration of intercollegiate athletics; and,

(i) To study in general all phases of competitive intercollegiate athletics and establish standards whereby the colleges and universities of the United States can maintain their athletic activities on a high level. [*1987–88 NCAA Manual*, Constitution 2-1(a-i)]

In addition, the fundamental policy upon which the NCAA is based is as follows:

(a) The competitive athletic programs of the colleges are designed to be a vital part of the educational system. A basic purpose of this Association is to maintain intercollegiate athletics as an integral part of the educational program and the athlete as an integral part of the student body and, by so doing, retain a clear line of demarcation between college athletics and professional sports. [*1987–88 NCAA Manual*, Constitution 2-2(a)]

Although all members can propose new rules and revisions of old rules, the NCAA administration has overall organizational responsibility and often initiates legislation on matters of general interest to all its members. The administrative body of the NCAA consists of a 46-member Council. The Council is elected at the annual convention of the association. At least four Council seats are reserved for women. Between annual meetings, the Council is empowered to interpret the NCAA constitution and bylaws. Between Council meetings, this is done by the Legislation and Interpretation Committee. These interpretations are binding after they are published and circulated to the membership via the NCAA's weekly publication (bi-weekly in the summer), the *NCAA News*. A check on the Council's power lies in the fact that any member can request affirmation of a Council decision at the next annual convention. Approval of a bylaw can be obtained by a simple majority vote of the delegates. The Council is also responsible for facilitating cooperation with other amateur organizations, such as the National Association of Intercollegiate Athletics (NAIA) and The Athletics Congress (TAC) in promoting and conducting national or international events.

Historically, the NCAA has tried to balance the distribution of athletic talent among member institutions. It has also acted as a bargaining agent for its members concerning commercial opportunity such as television telecasts (see Chapter 9), and arranged postseason play in intercollegiate athletics. The revenue from postseason games is distributed among eligible member institutions.

Although the NCAA's major purposes include creating, administering, and enforcing rules regarding intercollegiate athletics, these purposes are not beyond judicial review. An example of how the courts may view the NCAA's rules-making authority can be seen in the case of *Justice v. National Collegiate Athletic Ass'n*, 577 F. Supp. 356 (D. Ariz. 1983). In the *Justice* case, four members of the University of Arizona's football team sought a preliminary injunction to prevent enforcement of the NCAA's sanctions against the team that would prohibit postseason play in 1983 and 1984 and television appearances for 1984 and 1985. The U.S. District Court held that:

1. The student-athletes in this case have been deprived neither of their scholarships nor their right to participate in intercollegiate athletics.

2. Whatever oral representations that were made by university coaches to the student-athletes regarding participation in post-season and televised athletic contests created a mere expectation or desire rather than a legitimate claim of entitlement based on contract.
3. A distinction must be drawn between actions that constitute punishment without personal guilt for substantive due process purposes and actions which merely affect innocent persons adversely.
4. The student-athletes' loss of the opportunity to participate in post-season and televised competition, however unfortunate and personally undeserved, does not constitute a deprivation of their due process rights.

Prior to the 1984–85 academic year, the NCAA was funded in part by its percentage share of the national television contracts for intercollegiate football. However, on June 27, 1984, the Supreme Court in a 7-2 decision in *National Collegiate Athletic Ass'n v. Board of Regents of University of Oklahoma and University of Georgia Athletic Ass'n*, 468 U.S. 85, 104 S. Ct. 2948, 82 L. Ed. 2d 70 (1984), struck down the NCAA's 1982–85 Football Television Plan because it violated the Sherman Antitrust Act (see Chapters 9 and 13). The effect of this ruling on the NCAA's budget was immediate. Estimates were that the NCAA would lose about $5 million in football television revenues, or 14 percent of its budget. In January 1985, the NCAA Executive Committee in its report to the membership reported an actual loss of $4.7 million. Fortunately for the organization, a $14 million increase in the CBS-TV fee to telecast the 1985 NCAA Basketball Championship covered the loss. A portion of this increase also went to teams in the NCAA Basketball Tournament.

The monies that the NCAA receives from its television packages are distributed mostly to the participating institutions in the NCAA championships involved. The NCAA conducts many different championships, including men's basketball, women's basketball, swimming, track and field, and baseball. While some of the revenues are retained for the NCAA's operating expenses (40 percent of the NCAA Basketball Tournament's net receipts go to the NCAA), most of the monies are distributed. For instance, participants in the 1985 NCAA Basketball Tournament received from $153,080 ($211,205 in 1987) for first-round losers to $751,899 ($1,056,027 in 1987) for the final four teams. Similarly, in intercollegiate football in 1985, the Cherry Bowl participants received $750,000 each, while the teams in the Rose Bowl collected $5.1 million each. These large stakes have put enormous pressure on coaches to succeed and, as some believe, may be the root cause for many of the rules violations that occur.

In addition to the financial issues, a major problem facing the NCAA in recent years has been in the area of recruiting violations by member schools. "I believe there is a growing acceptance of the belief that the conditions of intercollegiate athletics are such that you have to cut corners, you have to circumvent the rules," stated Walter Byers in 1984. Byers added: "There seems to be a growing number of coaches and administrators who look upon NCAA penalties as the price of doing business: If you get punished, that's unfortunate, but that's part of the cost of getting along." As of October 1987, 21 institutions were under NCAA sanctions.

One of the NCAA's concerns, which involves both the financial aspects and recruiting areas, is the subject of booster organizations. Booster organizations serve as support groups for specific sports in an athletic department. Their primary purpose is to raise monies for the sport in the form of direct contributions or indirect support through the purchase of season tickets packages and dinner tickets, or by providing employment opportunities for the student-athletes on the team. Athletic departments rely on booster organizations for several reasons, among them the emergence of women's athletic programs, the increased costs of running programs, and the need for new or improved facilities, all of which require additional monies. Estimates are that in 1982 college sports generated approximately $1,064 million in revenues, but only 37 percent of all NCAA institutions balanced their athletic budgets. Booster organizations thus become increasingly important and can play a significant role in generating additional income for athletic departments. In 1985, contributions from alumni, as a revenue source, represented 11 percent of the total revenues of athletic department budgets.

Unfortunately, some booster organizations have violated NCAA rules and regulations and subsequently caused the involved programs to be put on NCAA probation. The sanctions range from total prohibition of an entire program or an individual team from championship play to prohibition from television appearances to just a warning.

Booster organizations are not the only ones to have violated NCAA rules and regulations. With the large amounts of revenue available to winning programs from television packages, the temptation to circumvent the rules for institutional monetary gain is heightened. Coaches and boosters alike may be tempted to induce exceptional student-athletes to attend their school by offering them money, cars, girls, or jobs for their relatives.

In July 1984, the enforcement staff of the NCAA asked Walter

Byers to double its size. Byers began to make inquiries around the country about the need for a larger investigative force and the additional funding that would be necessary to support an increase in staff. In an article published in the November 7, 1984 issue of the *Chronicle of Higher Education*, Byers stated:

> It became, I think, abundantly clear that we were not keeping up with the levels of transgression. The techniques of circumventing the rules are more sophisticated and they seem to be more deliberate.
>
> I was surprised at first, and finally I became astonished at what I considered to be the deliberateness of strategies of getting around the rules. And I was also astonished at the level of it, the level of the dollar transactions. [p. 31]

Byers went on in this article to give his opinion on what had brought about such flagrant disregard for the NCAA rules and regulations and what should be done about it:

> One cause, Mr. Byers said, is the jet airplane, which "did more to complicate recruiting than any single development." Before coast-to-coast travel was so easy, most colleges recruited only in their own regions, he noted, and a coach was more likely to know a player and his family personally. Now, contacts with unknown players have become common, and the lack of personal bonds have made corruption easier, he said.
>
> The other dramatic influence on college athletics was network television, Mr. Byers said. It has brought publicity and financial rewards, making many institutions yearn for TV exposure and willing to do whatever is necessary to get it.
>
> Television has also served to dramatize the benefits that can come to a student-athlete, he said.
>
> In addition, Mr. Byers said, "athletics has moved more into the hands of managers" and is no longer controlled by coaches. "I don't believe that in the regular decision-making process, the people closest to athletics really have the influence and direction they used to have," he said.
>
> A relaxation of the definition of amateurism by other associations governing athletics has also led to the deterioration of integrity in college sports, Mr. Byers said. He noted that many U.S. athletes in the summer Olympic Games could openly receive thousands of dollars and remain amateurs.
>
> "I think that ultimately higher education has been hurt because of the rules colleges have put in effect," Mr. Byers said. Although the NCAA's members adopted those regulations to control athletics, he said, many of them not only fail to do the job, but often encourage hypocrisy.

Every year, he said, coaches, student-athletes, and college presidents sign pledges that they have abided by the rules even when there have been violations. "We're supposed to teach young people the proper, civilized way of conducting their affairs, and it is simply not right to engage them in an apparatus that is essentially deceitful."

Nor is the NCAA itself blameless, Mr. Byers said. National championships, particularly in basketball, offer a big financial incentive for winning, he said, and the rules for eligibility in different divisions create additional pressures on an institution. . . .

College presidents, Mr. Byers said, could help lead the way back to respectability for athletics. "It's my view that for a number of years there have been a number of responsible chief executive officers who have been uncomfortable with the condition of college athletics. . . . There are a substantial number of responsible, thoughtful CEOs who want to change conditions."

Three areas to which presidents and chancellors should give their attention are academics, integrity, and economics, Mr. Byers said. . . .

Mr. Byers said harsher penalties are needed for the 10 to 15 percent of NCAA institutions he calls "chronic violaters."

He wants coaches at those institutions fired when violations are found, and institutions that don't take measures to prevent violations should have their athletic schedules canceled.

Mr. Byers said he was also concerned about institutions that don't want to cheat, but that skirt the rules because of competitive pressure to do so. Those institutions have to decide on a set of rules, he said, and live by them and understand that they will be penalized for deliberate violations.

The schedule of penalties should be published, he said, so that institutions will know the price they will have to pay if they cheat.

Student-athletes who cheat should also be subject to sanctions, Mr. Byers said, though he added that colleges that pursue student-athletes are more guilty than the student-athletes they pursue.

Not all cheating will ever be eliminated from collegiate athletics, Mr. Byers said. "There are always certain people who try to beat the rules. It seems to me our job is to deal with them in the most aggressive manner we can, and, if we can't convince them to go by the rules, ostracize them and hopefully persuade the others not to follow their example.

"Higher education is a highly constructive force in this country," Mr. Byers added. "But in addition to research for knowledge and truth, it seems to me it has to stand for the proper conduct of human affairs. Whether you can have big-time athletics and still conduct your affairs in the proper manner, I suppose is the fundamental question.

"I think it can be done, but it will take a lot of vigilance." [p. 31]

Other Collegiate Athletic Associations

Several athletic organizations govern amateur sports participation in addition to the NCAA. One of these is the National Association of Intercollegiate Athletics (NAIA), an intercollegiate athletic governing organization composed of four-year institutions. The NAIA was formed in 1940 as the National Association of Intercollegiate Basketball. The association changed its name to the NAIA in 1952 as it expanded into sports other than basketball. The NAIA quickly grew from a small organization and had 487 member institutions as of December 1987.

A good description of the NAIA is contained in *Williams v. Hamilton*, 497 F. Supp. 641 (D.N.H. 1980):

> [The] NAIA is a voluntary association of 512 four-year colleges ranging in size from small (500) to moderate (1100), whose primary purpose as set forth in its constitution is "to promote the development of athletics as a sound part of the educational offerings of member institutions." The member institutions of NAIA pay dues to the Association, which are scaled by enrollment. Among other things, NAIA sets standards for recruiting and eligibility, and it sponsors post-season national championships in various collegiate sports, including soccer.
>
> NAIA is divided into several districts, each of which is governed by a "District Executive Committee." Each district has voting representation at NAIA's Annual National Convention, at which time policy decisions are made. Also at the National Convention delegates vote for new members of the National Executive Committee, the overall governing body of NAIA. . . .

The NAIA is open to any four-year, degree-granting college or university in the United States or Canada that is fully accredited by accrediting agencies or commissions of the Council on Postsecondary Accreditation. Those institutions belonging to the NAIA must operate their intercollegiate athletic programs according to the association's regulations and rules. Of course, member institutions can establish even stricter standards than those of the association. The NAIA's eligibility regulations are very similar to those of the NCAA, except that the NAIA's eligibility rules govern all play in sports recognized by the association, whereas the NCAA has special rules for postseason tournaments.

Like the NCAA, the NAIA has specific rules relating to transfer student-athlete eligibility and hardship regulations. The NAIA's eligibility regulations typically contain the following provisions:

1. Normal progress toward a recognized degree must be made, and a minimum grade point average must be maintained.
2. Twelve credits must be taken at the time of participation or during the term immediately preceding the date of athletic participation.
3. A minimum of 24 credits must have accrued between the term of competition and the earlier of the two immediate previous terms of attendance.
4. No more than 12 credit hours of summer school or nonterm courses can be counted toward the 24-credit rule.
5. Nine credit hours must have accrued between the beginning of the first term of attendance and the start of the second term of attendance for all second-term freshmen.
6. Repeated courses previously passed cannot count toward the 24-credit rule.
7. Eligibility must be established according to conference regulations.
8. Participation cannot exceed four seasons in any one sport.
9. Competition is prohibited once graduation requirements from a four-year institution are completed.
10. Amateur status in the student-athlete's sport must be maintained for the athlete to compete in that sport [*1985–86 NAIA Handbook*]

Another athletic organization that governs amateur sports participation is the National Little College Athletic Association (NLCAA). Four-year colleges with enrollments of less than 500 male and/or female undergraduate students qualify for membership. The National Christian College Athletic Association (NCCAA) offers championships to both sexes and governs athletics in four-year institutions. The NCCAA, which is 100 members strong, is only open to four-year Christian institutions that are willing to subscribe to a "Statement of Faith."

The National Junior College Athletic Association (NJCAA) is another intercollegiate organization that performs similar functions as the NLCAA and NCCAA, except it encompasses men's and women's junior college athletic programs. It was described in *State ex rel. National Junior College Athletic Ass'n v. Luten*, 492 S.W.2d 404 (Mo. Ct. App. 1973) as a

> not-for-profit corporation which coordinates the scheduling and playing of intercollegiate athletics among its member schools. In 1971–72 it had 513 member schools who agree to "supervise and to

control athletics sponsored by this corporation so that they will be administered in accordance with the eligibility rules . . . set forth in the . . . By Laws." Among its functions it issues and enforces rules relating to the eligibility of students at its member schools participating in intercollegiate athletics. . . .

The NCAA, NAIA, and the other intercollegiate athletic organizations already mentioned perform a regulatory function at the national level. However, there are other organizations that govern amateur athletics at a regional level. These regional governing bodies are typically leagues and conferences to which members belong. Regional leagues and conferences can make and enforce their own rules and regulations for the governance of athletics among themselves, but they must also comply and not conflict with the standards created by the national organization to which they belong. In addition to the right to establish and create separate rules and regulations, these leagues and conferences have enforcement authority to sanction and reprimand member institutions. The most notable difference between national association and league or conference rules is that league or conference rules impose more restrictive standards.

Intercollegiate athletics also has what are known as allied conferences. Allied conferences are associations of NCAA member schools that agree to participate against each other to determine a champion in any number of sports. These allied conferences can have significant financial resources of their own and have detailed revenue distribution requirements as noted in the following excerpt from the 1987 *Pacific 10 Conference Handbook:*

Administrative Rules, Chapter 1, Financial Distribution

1. Football Ticket Settlement. Financial settlement of traditional rival football games shall consist of a 50-50 split of the net receipts with no minimum guarantee or maximum payout. Financial settlement of all other Conference football games shall consist of a 50-50 split of the net receipts, with a minimum guarantee of $125,000 and a maximum payout of $200,000. . . .

2. Basketball Ticket Settlement. Financial settlement of traditional rival basketball games shall consist of a 50-50 split of the net receipts with no minimum guarantee or maximum payout. Financial settlement of all other Conference basketball games shall consist of a 50-50 split of the net receipts with a minimum guarantee of $12,500 and a maximum payout of $20,000. . . .

3. Football Television Income.

   a. Live Telecast. Television income resulting from an appearance by a member institution in a live telecast (other than home area telecasts), after deduction of any applicable NCAA assessment, will be divided according to the following formula:

55% to Pacific-10 participant(s)

45% to Pacific-10 members (divided 10 ways).

b. Home Area Telecast:

(1) Conference Game. Television income resulting from an appearance on a live home area telecast of a Conference game that is shown only in the home areas of the competing teams shall be divided according to the following formula:

50% to each Pacific-10 Conference participant.

(2) Non-Conference Game. Television income resulting from an appearance on a live home area telecast of a non-conference game that is shown only in the home areas of the competing teams shall be divided between the competing institutions per the provisions of their game contract. . . .

4. Basketball Television Income. Television income resulting from an appearance by a member institution in the Conference's basketball television packages shall be shared, with 50% of the appearance fee going to the participant and the remaining 50% being divided equally among the ten members. . . .

5. Football Postseason Income. A member institution which participates in a postseason football game shall choose between the following alternatives:

a. Non-January 1 Game.

(1) The participating institution will be provided a travel allowance equal to the cost of round trip air coach fares for 150 persons. The remaining revenue will be divided into 11 equal shares, with the participating institution receiving two shares and the other nine members receiving one share each; or

(2) The participating institution may elect to receive actual gross receipts from the bowl to a maximum of $500,000, and may appeal through a detailed budget process for additional expenses, not to exceed the Conference's share of the bowl game receipts. The remaining revenue shall be divided equally among the Conference's ten members.

b. January 1 Game. A member institution which participates in a postseason football bowl game on January 1 shall submit a detailed budget for approval by the Men's Administrative Committee and Council in accordance with budget procedures developed by the Conference. The Conference will consider payments for expenses for a party of 500 to be acceptable. The party would consist of the official party (President/Chancellor, trustees/regents, governor, faculty representative, etc.), the team party (players, coaches, managers, trainers, secretaries, etc.), athletic department staff, dependents and band members.

6. NACDA Kickoff Classic Income. A member institution which participates in the NACDA Kickoff Classic shall receive actual gross receipts from the game to a maximum of $450,000, with the remaining revenue being divided equally among the Conference's ten members.

7. Basketball Postseason Income:
    a. NCAA Tournament. A member institution which participates in the NCAA basketball tournament shall submit detailed expenses on the Conference's approved budget form to receive reimbursement for those expenses not covered by its NCAA reimbursement. The remaining revenue will be divided equally among the Conference's ten members. The participating institution may retain all expense monies provided by the NCAA.
    b. NIT Tournament. All revenue derived from the NIT preseason or postseason basketball tournaments shall be retained by the participating institution. . . .

NOTES ──

1. The organizational structure of the NCAA is briefly described in the following excerpts from an NCAA memorandum to its member institutions, which was published by *NCAA Publications*, June 27, 1984.

(A) President's Commission: Was created at the 1984 NCAA Convention to give the chief executive officers of NCAA member institutions a greater input into Association operations. It is composed of a board of 44 college presidents who will be chosen by the NCAA. The board can propose legislation but it cannot enact it without approval of the annual Convention delegates.

(B) NCAA Council: Includes 46 members, 22 from Division I, 11 from Division II and 11 from Division III, with the NCAA president and secretary-treasurer as ex officio members. Members are elected by their respective division round tables at the annual Convention. The president and secretary-treasurer are elected by the full Convention. Geographical and conference representation requirements are the same as for the President's Commission.

The Council establishes and directs the general policy of the Association in the interim between NCAA Conventions. In effect, the Convention establishes Association law and policy, and the Council implements and applies the Convention's decisions, and with day-to-day administration provided by the staff.

(C) Division Steering Committees: The 44 elected members of the Council represent their respective divisions as members of Council subcommittees identified as Division I, Division II and Division III Steering Committees. Each meeting of the Council includes separate meetings of the three steering committees, as well as sessions involving the entire Council.

The steering committees consider and act upon matters relating to their respective divisions, while the Council acts as one body to deal with matters of overall Association policy and interdivision interests. The steering committees report their actions to the full Council, and any division decision stands unless overruled by a two-thirds vote of the Council members present and voting.

The steering committees also plan and conduct the division meetings, review legislative proposals of interest to their divisions, and encourage communication between division members and the steering committee and Council.

(D) NCAA Executive Committee: Includes 14 members, with the NCAA president and secretary-treasurer as ex officio members. Of the remaining 12 members, eight represent Division I members, two represent Division II members and two represent Division III members. The division vice-president automatically is one of each division's members. The five officers are elected by the Convention; the other nine members are appointed by the NCAA Council.

The Executive Committee transacts the business and administers the financial and championship affairs of the Association, including employment of an executive director (with approval of the Council) and such other staff as necessary for conduct of the Association's business.

Constitution 5-2-(c) assigns certain responsibilities directly to the Executive Committee. The committee regularly reports to the Council as to all of its activities and also submits an annual report to the NCAA Convention.

(E) Other Committees: The other standing committees of the Association are in three general categories: Convention committees, Council-appointed (sometimes called general) committees and sports committees (some with rules-making responsibilities and some without). The size of the respective committees is specified in NCAA Bylaw 12. In most cases, each division is represented on a committee, unless it deals specifically with a matter involving only one division. In addition, ad hoc committees frequently are appointed to deal with specific assignments.

In general, such committees report to the NCAA Council and/or the Executive Committee. Actions of any committee are subject to review by the annual Convention.

(F) Staff: The NCAA currently employs a staff of approximately 95 [147 as of 1987], including clerical personnel. The staff administers the policies and decisions approved by the Association through the annual Convention or by the Council and Executive Committee. It also serves all NCAA committees by providing administrative services, including necessary record-keeping and continuing communications.

Operating under the executive director, the national office staff is organized in seven departments: administration, business, championships, communications, compliance and enforcement, publishing, and legislative services.

2. For further information on how the NAIA's governing authority is viewed by the courts, see *Williams v. Hamilton*, 497 F. Supp. 641 (D.N.H. 1980), in which a college student-athlete challenged the NAIA transfer rule requiring him to be in residence at his new college for 16 weeks before becoming eligible for intercollegiate athletics. The rule was

imposed, in part, to prevent "tramp athletes" from transferring from school to school for the sole purpose of participating in sports. The court held that the transfer rule was valid and did not deny due process or equal protection guarantees.

3. The National Junior College Athletic Association (NJCAA) is a nonprofit corporation with 536 (12/87) junior colleges (two-year programs of study) as member institutions. For further information on the NJCAA's governing authority as viewed by the courts, see *State ex rel. National Junior College Athletic Ass'n v. Luten,* 492 S.W. 2d 404 (Mo. Ct. App. 1973).

4. In addition to the NCAA, intercollegiate athletics has what are known as allied conferences. These are associations of NCAA member schools that agree to participate against each other to determine a champion in any number of sports. These allied conferences can have significant financial resources of their own and have detailed revenue distribution requirements. Examples would be the Pacific-10 Conference, the Big East Conference, the Atlantic Ten Conference, and the Southwest Athletic Conference.

5. The 1986–87 NCAA budget was $57,379,000. Exhibit 4–4 shows how the budget breaks down.

6. Exhibit 4–5 is a flowchart of the NCAA organization structure.

7. For further information on the governing structure of the NCAA, see the following law review articles:

(a) Philpot, "Judicial Review of Disputes Between Athletes and the NCAA," 24 *Stanford Law Review,* 903 (May 1972).

(b) Weistart, "Legal Accountability and the NCAA," 10 *Journal of College and University Law* 167 (1983–84).

(c) Greene, "The New NCAA Rules of the Game: Academic Integrity or Racism?" 28 *St. Louis University Law Journal* 101 (Fall 1984).

High School Athletic Associations

Having some knowledge about the structure and nature of high school athletic associations can help college athletic administrators as well as high school athletic administrators to better analyze the courts' conclusions regarding various interscholastic rules for comparison to intercollegiate situations and circumstances. Furthermore, an understanding of high school athletic associations can assist college athletic administrators in facilitating the transition of the student-athlete from the high school to the college ranks by creating a heightened level of awareness and possibly opening lines of communication.

High school athletic associations are voluntary associations consisting of all the high schools within a state that wish to participate in association events, agree to abide by the rules of the association, and are accepted as members. High school associations are often given authority to organize through enabling legislation, which in

Revenue

A.	Division I Men's Basketball Championship	$64,497,500	81.2%
B.	Other Division I championships	5,564,100	7.0
C.	Communications department	2,431,000	3.1
D.	Football television assessments	1,500,000	1.9
E.	Investments	1,300,000	1.6
F.	Publishing department	1,001,500	1.3
G.	Corporate sponsorships	950,000	1.2
H.	Membership dues	870,000	1.1
I.	Division II championships	637,200	.8
J.	General	362,500	.4
K.	Division III championships	311,200	.4
	Total revenue	$79,425,000	

Expenses

A.	Division I Men's Basketball Championship—distribution of receipts*	$32,150,770	40.5%
B.	Grant to National Collegiate Foundation**	6,800,000	8.6
C.	Championships—transportation guarantees*	4,666,200	5.9
D.	Championships—game and administrative expense	3,990,000	5.0
E.	Block grants to Divisions II and III reserves*	3,100,000	3.9
F.	Championships—per diem allowances*	2,955,400	3.7
G.	Communications department	2,825,650	3.6
H.	Other championships distributions*	2,170,700	2.7
I.	Drug testing and education	1,965,000	2.5
J.	Compliance and enforcement department	1,964,500	2.5
K.	Publishing department	1,867,300	2.3
L.	Legal services	1,500,000	1.9
M.	Administration department	1,503,900	1.9
N.	General	1,394,100	1.7
O.	Committees	1,272,000	1.6
P.	Championships department	1,043,700	1.3
Q.	Funded operating reserve	1,000,000	1.3
R.	Insurance—catastrophic*	947,000	1.2
S.	National Forum	950,000	1.2
T.	Insurance—general and liability	692,500	.9
U.	Legislative services department	737,700	.9
V.	Rent	732,000	.9
W.	Contingency	686,250	.9
X.	Business department	639,200	.8
Y.	Postgraduate scholarships**	600,000	.8
Z.	Royalties to members*	674,000	.8
AA.	Development—clinics and competition**	517,400	.6
BB.	Development—grants*	79,800	.1
*	Direct payments to membership	46,743,800	58.9
**	Educational benefits for students	7,917,400	10.0

Exhibit 4-4 Breakdown of 1986–1987 NCAA Revenue and Expenses Source: *The NCAA News*, September 14, 1987, p. 1.

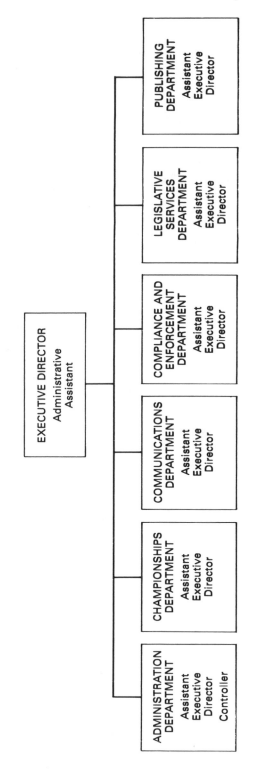

Exhibit 4-5   Organizational Structure of the NCAA

effect creates a private corporation to perform a quasi-public function.

The National Federation of State High School Associations (NFSHA) is the governing body for high school athletics. Founded in 1920, the federation was based on the belief that strong state and national high school organizations are necessary to protect the integrity of interscholastic programs and to promote healthy growth of those programs. The NFSHA as a federation has much less power than the NCAA (which has national authority). Instead, the high school athletic associations are established on an insular, state-by-state basis. Like the NCAA, they are usually funded by membership dues. Many associations charge a flat fee for each school, which includes such items as entry fees and transportation costs to association tournaments, although some states have sliding fee scales.

NFSHA services include a press service subscribed to by editors of local, state, and national publications; a national film library; national federation publications for 13 sports; national records for more than 40,000 performances as listed in the *National Interscholastic Record Book;* sanctioning of applications for interstate and international events between schools; athletic directors conferences, printed proceedings, and a quarterly magazine. The NFSHA membership serves over 20,000 high schools, 500,000 coaches and sponsors, and 500,000 officials and judges. Its structure is shown in Exhibit 4–6.

The Massachusetts Interscholastic Athletic Association (MIAA) is an example of a high school association. Its members include public and private secondary schools, as well as technical and vocational schools. Prior to membership, an applicant school must be approved by the Board of Control, which administers the rules and enforces the discipline with the association. Upon acceptance of membership, the approved school agrees to be bound by the requirements set forth in the MIAA eligibility rules. Each school is free, however, to make any other rules, including ones that are stricter than MIAA rules, as long as the school's rules do not conflict with those of the association.

The purpose of the MIAA is clearly set forth in the MIAA constitution:

> The purpose of the Association shall be to organize, regulate and promote interscholastic athletics for secondary schools of Massachusetts. In pursuing this commitment the Association shall:
> A. Provide leadership and service designed to improve inter-school relations in athletics.
> B. Foster cooperation among voluntary institutional members and the Massachusetts Secondary School Administrators As-

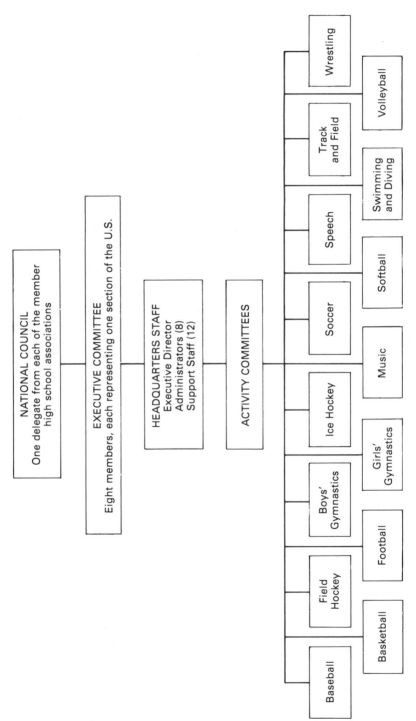

Exhibit 4-6 Organizational Structure of the NFSHSA

sociation, the Massachusetts Department of Education, Massachusetts Association of School Committees, Massachusetts Association of School Superintendents, Massachusetts Secondary School Athletic Directors Association, Massachusetts State Coaches Association, Massachusetts Division of Girls' and Women's Sports, Massachusetts State Coaches Association and with professional organizations interested in attaining common goals.

C. Secure uniform regulations and control of interscholastic participation in athletics throughout the state to provide equitable competition for students as an integral part of the education of secondary school students.

D. Promote safety and health of participants in interscholastic athletics.

E. Develop and channel the force of opinion to keep interscholastic athletics within reasonable bounds so that it will expressly encourage all that is honorable and sportsmanlike in all branches of sports for secondary youth.

F. Provide a forum for concerns related to interscholastic athletics for institutions which become voluntary members of the Association.

G. Develop uniform standards and procedures for determining championships at the end of the season. [Article II—Purpose]

Note that sections D and E expressly designate areas of concern not explicit in NCAA policies. Here, the MIAA expresses its concern for the health and safety of participating student-athletes. It also recognizes the particular problem of the effect of public opinion on presumably unsophisticated high school student-athletes.

The rules-making body of the MIAA is an assembly composed of the principals of the member schools. The assembly meets annually and is empowered with the authority to organize administrative committees as they are deemed necessary.

There are two administrative bodies of the MIAA—the Board of Control and the Eligibility Review Board (ERB). The Board of Control is composed of 17 members elected from various professional, educational, and athletic associations within the state. It is authorized to hear appeals of decisions, decide the time and place of meetings, create and appoint special committees, interpret rules and fix penalties, and issue and revise rules as necessary. The Board of Control also has the power to warn, censure, or place on probation any school, player, team, coach, or game or school official who violates any rule.

The second administrative body is the Eligibility Review Board.

The board is composed of five high school principals—one from each district in the state—who are appointed by, but are not members of, the Board of Control. It has the authority, when validated by a majority vote of its members, to set aside any rules. This action is permitted when the rule clearly fails to accomplish the purpose for which it is intended or when the application of the rule causes an undue hardship to an individual student-athlete. The granting of a waiver must not, however, result in an unfair advantage to the school or to the particular competitor seeking the waiver.

Using Massachusetts as an example, it is possible to generalize that high school associations often have a great deal of power to make decisions in the following areas: creation of rules, interpretation of rules, handling of alleged violations, eligibility of individual student-athletes, and administering tournaments.

A leading case in the area of governing authority of high school athletic associations is *Denis J. O'Connell High School v. The Virginia High School League*, 581 F.2d 81 (4th Cir. 1978), *cert. denied*, 440 U.S. 936 (1979). The case involved the league's denial of membership to a private high school. The federal appeals court ruled that a state is justified in taking any reasonable step to prevent actual or potential abuse of student-athletes. The league had defended its policy of exclusion of private schools as members because it was rationally related to the league's interest in enforcing its eligibility rules concerning transfer student-athletes. The league presented evidence that because public schools draw students from strictly defined areas while private schools are not so limited, it would be difficult to enforce transfer rules with respect to private schools.

The question of whether to allow private schools to compete against public schools is one that is drawing increasing attention. The proponents of allowing private and public school competition claim that it saves travel costs through scheduling in a smaller geographic area, and it furthermore provides a clear-cut state champion as opposed to having two teams who do not compete laying claim to a state title. Opponents argue that since private schools recruit their students (and athletes), they will have an unfair advantage against the public schools on the playing field.

As of 1987, 29 states have a single governing body for high school athletics which oversees both public and private schools. (Iowa, which does not make a distinction between public and private, has separate associations for boys and girls.) The other 20 states and the District of Columbia have separate associations governing public and private schools. Some states have three or four different governing associations defined by geographic boundaries. For example, the cities of New York and Philadelphia have separate associations that govern the city schools, and they do not compete for state titles.

Some states with more than one governing body are looking to unify them. For example, the Wisconsin legislature has introduced a bill which would allow the Wisconsin Independent School Athletic Association (private) to join the Wisconsin Interscholastic Athletic Association (public). Both associations have opposed the bill, preferring to maintain their independence.

In the future, considering steadily declining school enrollments, states could experience further pressure to have one governing body in all high school athletics. Increased competition for student-athletes and the complications caused by transfer rules make this issue one of great importance to athletic administrators.

Another area of high school athletic association authority that may come under increasing judicial scrutiny is academic requirements (see also Chapter 5). For instance, the New Jersey State Interscholastic Athletic Association (NJSIAA) in 1983 upgraded minimum academic standards for student-athletes. Under the NJSIAA rule, a student-athlete must have passed courses totaling 23 credits the last school year to be eligible to play sports. Since most New Jersey high school courses are worth five credits, at least five courses would have to be passed under the standard. The previous NJSIAA standard called for a student-athlete to pass three courses the prior school year.

Some New Jersey schools maintain higher standards than the NJSIAA requires. In Newark, for instance, a 1983 regulation requires that in addition to meeting NJSIAA standards, student-athletes must maintain a cumulative 2.0 or "C" average to be eligible for athletic competition.

In 1984, the Texas Legislature promulgated a "no pass, no play" rule, which was adopted by the State Board of Education in March 1985. Under the tough new academic standard a student must have a passing grade of at least 70 in all courses to participate in sports and other extracurricular activities. Students who fail even one course in the six-week grading period must sit out the next six-week grading period. Texas Governor Mark White noted in 1985: "We in Texas don't tell our students it's OK to flunk one course. . . . We're going to put winners in the classroom. . . . And it's going to make Texas the big winner." (See page 179.)

NOTES

1. For more information regarding the National Federation of State High School Associations, see *School Activities: The Other Half of Education* (Elgin, Ill.: NFSHA Publications, 1978).

2. At a June 26, 1984, U.S. Senate hearing, "Oversight on College Athletic Programs" (S. Hrg. 98-955, Subcommittee on Education, Arts and Humanities), Harry Edwards, Ph.D., University of California, Berkeley, Department of Sociology, made the following comments concerning high school academic requirements for student-athletes:

> But the problem does not start on the college campus. An exaggerated emphasis upon sports during the early school years, and often in the family, leads to a situation wherein by the time many student-athletes finish their junior high school sports eligibility and move on to high school, so little has been demanded of them academically that no one any longer even expects anything of them intellectually.
>
> At the high school level, the already unconscionable emphasis upon athletic development is institutionally abetted by policies which make athletic competition conditional upon minimum standards or, more typically, no standards of academic performance. As late as the Winter of 1984, it was still the case that only a handful—about forty of the nation's 16,000 plus high school districts—had set minimum academic standards for sports participation. And of those which had such standards, most required only that the student-athlete maintain a 2.0, or "C" average, or that a student-athlete's grade card show no more than one failing grade in an academic year. The problem with these minimum standards, of course, is that they have a way of becoming maximum goals. Student-athletes typically strive to achieve precisely the standards set—nothing more, nothing less.
>
> Only 5 percent of America's high school athletes ever participate in their sports at the collegiate level. Thus the lack of serious academic standards, seriously enforced as a condition of high school sports participation, impacts immediately upon the 95 percent of former high school athletes who must rely substantially upon their academic skills and records to gain college admissions. . . .

3. High school athletic association governance authority was *upheld* in the following cases.

(a) In *State v. Judges of Court of Common Pleas*, 181 N.E.2d 261 (Ohio 1962), the state high school athletic association suspended a member high school from participating in athletics for one year and declared two boys from the high school ineligible for interscholastic athletics for failure to abide by association rules. The court held that this action should not be prohibited when the determination, although harsh, was not the result of mistake, fraud, collusion, or arbitrariness.

(b) In *Mitchell v. Louisiana High School Athletic Ass'n*, 430 F.2d 1155 (5th Cir. 1970), a redshirt rule restricting all incoming high school students who voluntarily repeat eighth grade to six semesters of competition rather than to the normal eight semesters was held to be rationally related to a legitimate state interest and was declared valid.

(c) In *Walsh v. Louisiana High School Athletic Ass'n*, 428 F. Supp. 1261 (E.D. La. 1977), the court upheld the constitutional validity of a transfer rule governing high school athletics. The transfer rule was found to be rationally related to the state's valid and legitimate interest in deterring or eliminating the recruitment of promising young student-athletes by overzealous coaches, fans, and faculty members.

(d) In *Guelker v. Evans*, 602 S.W.2d 756 (Mo. Ct. App. 1980), a high school soccer player violated Missouri State High School Activities Association rules concerning school competition, the 11-day rule, and international competition when he missed 29 school days and a major part of the soccer season while participating in a tournament sponsored by the United States Soccer Federation in Puerto Rico. The court concluded that the student-athlete failed to meet requirements for a class action and thus ruled in favor of the high school activities association.

(e) In *Christian Brothers Institute v. North New Jersey Interscholastic League*, 86 N.J. 409 (1981), a suit was brought by a private high school against a high school athletic league for alleged unlawful discrimination in evaluating a membership application. The court held that a rational basis can exist for an interscholastic league limited to public schools and that such a limitation does not result per se in a denial of equal protection under the federal constitution.

(f) In *Snow v. New Hampshire Interscholastic Athletic Ass'n*, 449 A.2d 1223 (N.H. 1982), a high school track athlete claimed he would have qualified for a "Meet of Champions" if he had not been fouled in a qualified meet and finished seventh. The court supported the state association's ruling denying the student's appeal to compete in the championship meet, stating that the court was extremely limited in deciding such things as fouls in track meets.

4. The courts ruled *against* high school athletic association governance authority in the following cases.

(a) In *Alabama High School Athletic Ass'n v. Rose*, 446 So. 2d 1 (Ala. 1984), a high school football player was granted a preliminary injunction to compete despite an Alabama High School Athletic Association (AHSAA) declaration of ineligibility. The court found clear and convincing evidence of collusion perpetrated upon the student-athlete by AHSAA and its executive director.

(b) In *Florida High School Activities Ass'n v. Bryant*, 313 So. 2d 57 (Fla. Dist. Ct. App. 1975), a high school basketball player was declared eligible to play more than four years of interscholastic basketball after presenting an adequate case of undue hardship, meriting a waiver of the four-year rule. The court reasoned that basketball was vital to this student-athlete because it provided the impetus for his general scholastic, social development, and rehabilitation from prior problems of juvenile delinquency.

(c) In *Bunger v. Iowa High School Athletic Ass'n*, 197 N.W.2d 555 (Iowa 1972), a high school football player brought a suit against a high school athletic association to determine the validity of a good conduct rule. The student-athlete was declared ineligible for athletics when it was discovered that he had ridden in a car that contained a case of beer. The court stated that "school authorities may make reasonable beer rules, but we think this rule is too extreme. Some

closer relationship between the student-athlete and the beer is
required than mere knowledge that the beer is there."
(d) In *Dunham v. Pulsifer*, 312 F. Supp. 411 (D. Vt. 1970), a high
school tennis player requested an injunction to stop his high school
from enforcing an athletic grooming code. The court found that
there was no reasonable relationship between the rule and the
asserted justifications for imposing the restriction on hair length.
The court stated that when there was not even a reasonable relationship, "the code falls far short of substantial justification. It is not
essential to any compelling interest . . . and its enforcement cannot
be upheld."
(e) In *Hartzell v. Connell*, 137 Cal. App. 3d 196, 186 Cal. Rptr. 852
(1982), high school parents successfully challenged a school board's
attempt to levy a fee upon students participating in extracurricular
activities (including interscholastic athletics). The court determined
that since the fees were not authorized by the California Constitution, they were unlawful, and thus the school district could not levy
a fee on extracurricular activities at will.
   5. For further information, see the following law review article: Weistart, "Rule-making in Interscholastic Sports: The Bases of Judicial Review," 11 *Journal of Law and Education* 291 (1982).

PUBLIC RESPONSIBILITIES OF AMATEUR ATHLETIC ASSOCIATIONS

As legal bodies, amateur athletic associations may have certain
duties to fulfill for the public at large as a condition of their
corporate existence. Even a voluntary association that considers
itself a private organization may have a responsibility to the general
public. For instance, the NCAA is responsible to the public for
maintaining amateurism in college athletics, providing competition
in intercollegiate sports for both men and women student-athletes,
and most recently, allowing greater access to televised football.
   Generally, any amateur athletic organization that is public or
quasi-public in nature is a potential defendant in a public responsibility case. A case that dealt with the public responsibilities of
amateur athletic associations was *Greene v. Athletic Council of
Iowa State University*, 251 N.W.2d 559 (1977). In *Greene*, the Iowa
Superior Court ruled that an amateur college association, although
private in name, is "quasi-public" in character. The Iowa court
discussed the specific statute and decided that the controlling issue
was "whether the athletic council was a 'council' as authorized by
the laws of the state." The record showed that the ISU athletic
council was an entity established by officials of ISU to manage and
control its intercollegiate athletic program. After a discussion of
specific powers, the court found that the athletic council exercised

powers that clearly made it a governmental entity. The court went on to decide that the athletic council was granted authorization under the laws of the state which allowed the board of regents of the university to delegate responsibility to it. In conclusion, the court held that since this body was a council as authorized by the laws of the state, it was subject to the Iowa open-meeting law.

NOTE _____

1. For further information on the public responsibilities of amateur athletic associations, see Wong and Ensor, "Recent Developments in Amateur Athletics: The Organization's Responsibility to the Public," 2 *Entertainment & Sports Law Journal* 123 (Fall 1985). The article discusses in detail amateur athletic organizations as legal entities and the duties they must fulfill as a condition for retaining their nonprofit corporate status. It includes discussion on access to public records, public access to televised sporting events, public funding of athletic facilities, and delegation of public-entrusted responsibilities.

Disclosure Cases

Being designated a governmental or other public body may require an organization to be subject to any open-meeting or "sunshine" laws, which generally allow the public to attend meetings (with exceptions as included on a state-by-state basis). Thus, a quasi-public association may be subject to restrictions differing from those placed on a private organization. For instance, the quasi-public association may have to open its records for public inspection, while a private association would not have this obligation.

The degree of disclosure that a quasi-public association, conference, or institution may be required to give varies from state to state. Some state laws are more restrictive than others regarding state universities and colleges under their jurisdiction. Under the state of Florida's public records law, for example, interviews related to searches for new coaches or athletic directors are open to the media when state institutions are involved with such searches. In fact, reporters are permitted to sit in on each and every interview session, as was the case, for example, when Louisiana State University coach Bill Arnsparger was interviewed for the University of Florida's athletic director position in 1985.

For the media and the public, such laws provide factual accounts of who is actually in the running for the job, where the interviews are conducted, what is being asked, and how those being interviewed are responding. For athletic administrators and institutions, these laws put pressure on them to be unbiased, fair, evaluative, and accurate in selecting candidates for vacant positions. Athletic administrators may have to be more specific in identifying job qualifications and characteristics and the means of measuring those characteristics, in defining job responsibilities, and in establishing or refining methods of evaluating and distinguishing candidates' backgrounds and credentials.

Disclosure cases illustrate conflicts that arise concerning the right of the public to be accurately informed by athletic organizations against the need of the organization to protect the confidentiality of its files. The NCAA has argued that only through confidentiality can it investigate itself properly and thereby maintain its amateur integrity and fulfill this additional public responsibility.

The NCAA argues that opening confidential investigation files compromises the NCAA's cooperative principles, to which all member institutions agree to adhere when they join the association. The NCAA, as previously discussed, is a voluntary association whose members, by joining the organization, agree to follow certain conditions and obligations of membership, including the obligation to conduct their individual institutional athletic programs in a manner consistent with NCAA legislation. In addition, member institutions agree to be policed in regard to the organization's rule by the NCAA's enforcement staff. The key to the NCAA investigative process is the cooperative principle—that is, the accused member institution and the NCAA's enforcement staff work together to ascertain the truth of alleged infractions.

NOTES

1. The Massachusetts Interscholastic Athletic Association is subject to that state's open-meeting law. See "State Ruling Makes MIAA Records Public," *Boston Globe*, January 3, 1980, p. 37.

2. In 1981 the *MESA* (Arizona) *Tribune* was successful in a court challenge against the NCAA that involved the release of information about the association's investigation of the Arizona State football program. In "The Vow of Silence" (*The Sporting News*, April 25, 1981), the difficulties faced by the *MESA Tribune* were documented, and it was noted that:

> The newspaper encountered harassment and "stonewalling" from the very beginning of its coverage of the Frank Kush case, according to Executive Editor Max Jennings. Kush, former Arizona State football coach, faces a $2.2 million lawsuit charging that he harassed ex-ASU punter Kevin Rutledge into quitting the team and yielding his athletic scholarship. Kush has been exonerated of Rutledge's civil charge that he punched the player during a 1978 game.
>
> "Block and delay—that's the way these public institutions deny the public the right to know," Jennings recently told the Phoenix Press Club. "It's your money and my money they're spending. . . . And the NCAA doesn't want to operate in public any more than Arizona State does."

School bigwigs apparently spared no effort or expense in trying to block access to records of the investigation. The school's legal battery carried the case to the Arizona Supreme Court, claiming, among other pleas, that "the NCAA doesn't want us to reveal these documents." ASU leaders didn't bank exclusively on legal maneuvers, either. A memorandum from ASU President John Schada advised school employees to "stonewall" inquisitive reporters, Jennings said.

3. In 1984, the Miami Herald Publishing Company, the *St. Petersburg Times*, and Campus Communications, publisher of the University of Florida student newspaper *The Gator*, had a declaratory suit filed against them in Florida State District Court by the University of Florida. The university asked the court to decide what information the university could reveal to the newspapers in response to their request that files pertaining to an NCAA preliminary investigation into the school's football program be opened to the media. The University of Florida said that strict federal and state laws involving the confidentiality of student and employee records led to the decision to file the suit.

The University of Florida subsequently decided to release the requested information. The information released included the 75-page official letter of inquiry from the NCAA that listed 107 violations by Florida's football program, as well as 1,700 pages of documents about the violations. These included transcripts of interviews with a number of witnesses.

4. In the following cases, the courts required amateur athletic associations to open their records to the public under "sunshine laws."

(a) In *Seal v. Birmingham Post*, 8 Med. L. Rptr. 1633 (Dist. Ct. Kan. 1982), the newspaper sought issuance of subpoenas for NCAA files for use in its defense of a libel suit concerning a published news story. The court ruled that the interests of the newspaper in defending itself far outweighed the NCAA's need to keep such information confidential.

(b) In *Berst v. Chipman*, 8 Med. L. Rptr. 1635, 231 Kan. 369, 653 P.2d 107 (1982), the state supreme court ruled to overturn the decision in *Seal v. Birmingham Post*. After reviewing the files, the court declared that only certain specific materials were discoverable by the *Birmingham Post* and not the entire file.

(c) In *Berst v. Chipman*, 8 Med. L. Rptr. 2593 (1982), the state supreme court reiterated its opinion in *Berst v. Chipman* and affirmed the decision in *Seal v. Birmingham Post* reasoning that the needs of the newspaper outweighed those of the NCAA.

(d) In *Arkansas Gazette Company v. Southern State College*, 620 S.W.2d 258 (Ark. 1981), the newspaper brought suit against the Arkansas Intercollegiate Athletic Conference, seeking to compel it to disclose the amount of money member institutions dispensed to student-athletes during the school year. The court held that the records were not protected by the federal Family Education Rights Privacy Act of 1974, were allowed under the Arkansas Freedom of Information Act, and such disclosure did not violate student-athletes' reasonable expectation of privacy.

(e) In *Carole Kneeland et al. v. National Collegiate Athletic Ass'n and Southwest Athletic Conference*, Civil Action No. A-85-CA-616 (W.D. Texas 1986), various news organizations filed suit against the NCAA and the Southwest Athletic Conference (SWC) after their requests to inspect and copy certain information relating to possible infractions of NCAA regulations by various SWC members. The court ruled that the NCAA and SWC are governmental bodies subject to the Texas Open Records Act. The information sought by the news organizations is public information, and thus the NCAA and SWC must produce the information for an *in camera* inspection.

(f) In *Palladrium Publishing Co. v. River Valley School District*, 321 N.W.2d 705 (Mich. Ct. App. 1982), a newspaper sought declaration that the school district and board of education were required to disclose names of students suspended for alleged drug-related activities on school property. The court held that minutes of a school board must identify any student suspended by board action by name rather than student number and that the Freedom of Information Act did not prevent disclosure.

(g) In *Citizens for Better Education v. Board of Education*, 124 N.J. Super. 523, 308 A.2d 35 (1973), the court held that citywide standardized achievement tests by grade and school are subject to public inspection. Such reports were ruled to be "public records" within provision of the state right-to-know law, which states that every citizen of the state shall have the right to inspect and copy or purchase copies of public records.

(h) In *Pooler v. Nyquist*, 89 Misc. 2d 705, 392 N.Y.S.2d 948 (N.Y. Sup. Ct. 1976), the court ruled that according to the Freedom of Information Act, drop-out rates are subject to disclosure following an investigation of a complaint.

5. In the following cases, the courts ruled that amateur athletic associations do *not* have to open their records to the public.

(a) *McMahon v. Board of Trustees of University of Arkansas*, 499 S.W.2d 56 (Ark. 1973), was a suit brought to obtain the names of those persons who were given complimentary tickets and the number of tickets each person received for all University of Arkansas football games held in the state of Arkansas. The court held that such information lists are not public records under the Freedom of Information Act and dismissed the petition.

(b) In *Athens Newspaper, Inc. v. Board of Regents*, No. 42,571 (Sup. Ct. Ga. Jan. 25, 1985); *Cox Enterprises, Inc. v. Board of Regents*, No. 42,577 (Sup. Ct. Ga. Jan. 25, 1985), the University of Georgia in December 1984 agreed to release documents pertaining to an NCAA investigation of its football program, but it refused to do so in regards to an investigation of its men's basketball program. Georgia was under pressure to do so because of suits filed by Morris Communications Corp., which publishes newspapers in Georgia and Florida, including the *Athens Georgia Daily News*, and Cox Enterprises, which publishes the *Atlanta Journal* and the *Atlanta Constitution*.

In January 1985, a Georgia Superior Court refused to release the information requested by the newspaper concerning the men's basketball program because:

the ongoing investigation . . . would be impeded if statements of witnesses become available to the public before the investigation was completed or that (a) some witnesses . . . would be reluctant to furnish information if they were aware that their identity and the substance of the information they furnished would immediately become hot news; or (b) if they were aware they might be immediately subject to contact by the news media.

After the completion of the investigation, the records were released by the University of Georgia.

6. For further information on public disclosure cases and intercollegiate athletics, see Wong and Ensor, "The NCAA's Enforcement Procedure—Erosion of Confidentiality," 4 *The Entertainment and Sports Lawyer* 1 (1985).

7. Mr. Michael J. Davis, general counsel for the University of Kansas, requested an opinion of the attorney general of the state of Kansas, regarding whether certain records (vouchers, invoices, expense claims, purchase orders, and other supporting documents for checks) of the University of Kansas Athletic Corporation (KUAC) should be made available for public inspection upon request.

In the Slip Opinion dated June 5, 1980, No. 80-118, the attorney general found that the University of Kansas substantially controlled the KUAC; therefore, the KUAC fell within the public records law. The attorney general then had to determine what qualified as "public records." Using corporation (nonsports) cases as precedent, the attorney general broadly interpreted "public records" and held that they must be available to the public.

Funding of Public Facilities

A recent development with respect to public responsibilities of an amateur organization is the challenge to the use of public funds. Challenges have been made to the building of sports facilities by faculty governing bodies who have been concerned that funds would be diverted from other educational areas. In *Lester v. Public Building Authority of County of Knox*, No. 78491, Chancery Court for Knox County, Tenn. (1983), a case settled out of court, the issues raised shed light on potential problem areas in financing athletic facilities. This suit was brought by faculty members of the University of Tennessee against the university in order to block its planned funding and construction of a $30-million assembly center and sports arena. University faculty members in forcing a settlement were successful in placing pressure on school officials by commencing litigation to allow some controls and approve projects that faculty were involved with in return for the promise not to delay the financing for the assembly center and arena. "The

significant thing about the settlement," said David Burkhalter, the
faculty members' lawyer, "is that it's legally binding and sets a
clear priority. It means that the university has recognized that the
faculty has a right to say how university money should be spent,
and that's unprecedented at the University of Tennessee."

The *Lester* case was settled out of court, and the following terms
were included in the compromise agreement:

1. The University of Tennessee will make full disclosure of information concerning the funding and operation of the assembly center
   and arena to the Faculty Senate of the University of Tennessee,
   Knoxville.

2. The University of Tennessee will not make any requests of the
   Tennessee General Assembly for additional appropriations toward construction costs of the assembly center and arena over
   and above the $7 million already appropriated and allocated by
   the General Assembly and the State Building Commission for
   construction of the arena. The university will continue with its
   efforts to secure full funding for the new proposed library.

3. Construction cost overruns, if any, beyond the $30 million which
   the assembly center and arena are expected to cost, and operation and maintenance expenses of the arena following its construction, will be funded through the Athletic Department of the
   University of Tennessee, Knoxville.

4. It is presently contemplated by the University of Tennessee that
   it will request the Tennessee State School Bond Authority to
   issue revenue bonds in the amount of approximately $8 million
   to finance a portion of the University's share of the construction
   costs of the arena. The university will not request of the Tennessee State School Bond Authority the issuance in excess of $8
   million unless any amount in excess of $8 million is secured by
   sufficient revenues, gifts, or pledges of funds necessary to retire
   such bonded indebtedness. The university further agrees that all
   contributions presently pledged and gifts which have been received toward construction of the arena will be solely for the
   arena. The university further agrees that contributions currently
   pledged for the arena project, future contributions specifically
   pledged for the arena project, unrestricted gifts to the Athletic
   Department, revenues derived from the operation of the arena
   and from other operations of the Athletics Department will be
   used first to retire bonds of the School Bond Authority issued for
   the purpose of constructing the arena.

5. The University of Tennessee Guaranty will be amended prior to
   execution by inserting the following provision: "It is expressly
   understood and agreed however that for purposes of the Guar-

anty, funds legally available to the Guarantor shall not include funds appropriated by the Tennessee General Assembly for the University of Tennessee academic budgets and salaries; increases in student activity fees without consultation with the appropriate student representatives; or restricted gifts to Guarantor other than gifts to the Athletic Department of Guarantor."

For more information on the *Lester* case, see "U. of Tennessee and Professors in Accord on Arena," *Chronicle of Higher Education,* April 20, 1983, p. 13.

NOTES ─────────────────────────────────────

1. The courts will often be very protective of a perceived public interest. A key question is how much of the amateur athletic organization's power can be delegated. For an examination of this subject in regard to the Boston Marathon, see the following cases.

(a) In *Boston Athletic Ass'n v. International Marathons, Inc.*, 392 Mass. 356, 467 N.E.2d 58 (1984), the board of directors of the Boston Athletic Association (BAA) brought a lawsuit against International Marathons, Inc. (IMI) to prevent it from representing itself to the public as the association's agent. The hearing examiner found that the contract which set up the agency relationship and was signed by the president of the BAA violated state law and that the president had exceeded his authority in entering into the agreement.

(b) In *International Marathons, Inc. v. Attorney General*, 392 Mass. 376, 467 N.E.2d 55 (1984), IMI appealed the hearing examiner's decision in *BAA v. IMI*, but the court refused to review the decision because it was a moot question. The hearing examiner had disapproved the contract between IMI and BAA because it was violative of state law.

(c) In *Attorney General v. International Marathons, Inc.*, 392 Mass. 370, 467 N.E.2d 51 (1984), the attorney general brought this action seeking to enforce the provisions of state law for IMI's failure to register with the Division of Public Charities and post a necessary bond.

2. Individuals involved with a public athletic organization (administrators, coaches, etc.) should be aware that such involvement may come under a high degree of scrutiny by a court because of the "public trust" issue. For an examination of the strict standards of ethics the courts expect from an organization such as the NCAA, see *Tarkanian v. University of Nevada, Las Vegas*, Case No. A173498, 8th Judicial District Court of the State of Nevada (June 25, 1984). The University of Nevada, Las Vegas (UNLV) basketball coach successfully brought this suit to prohibit the enforcement of an NCAA-mandated sanction, which required UNLV to sever all ties with coach Tarkanian. The court held that the NCAA and UNLV acted arbitrarily and with prejudice in accepting investigative

information and reaching its decisions. The injunction was affirmed by the Supreme Court of Nevada (*Tarkanian v. National Collegiate Athletic Ass'n*, 741 P.2d 1345 [Nev. 1987]).

CONSTITUTIONAL LAW ASPECTS OF AMATEUR ATHLETICS

Athletic administrators at the high school and college level are beginning to question the frequency of claims directed against them alleging that certain penalties are violations of student-athletes' constitutional rights. Judicial decisions indicate that those administrators who seek to impose severe penalties that impair or jeopardize an individual's career should be aware of the correct procedures and limitations as imposed by law. Consequently, athletic administrators initiating disciplinary action against a coach or student-athlete must proceed in a fair and legal manner. This does not mean that an athletic administrator, athletic association, or conference cannot impose penalties. The implication is clear, however, that failure to proceed in a fair, reasonable, and constitutional manner may result in litigation brought by the student-athlete or coach.

A student-athlete involved in a dispute with an amateur organization may decide to initiate a lawsuit based on the theory that a constitutional right has been violated. In light of the problems of limited judicial review and standing, the constitutionally based claims of due process and equal protection may be the only avenues available. In addition, the constitutional law approach has other advantages. Most important, it enables the student-athlete to bring the case to a federal court, thereby utilizing the federal jurisdiction statutes of due process and equal protection. To succeed on a federal constitutional claim, however, one must show (1) that state action exists, (2) that the claim is not frivolous, and (3) that the claim concerns a right of sufficient importance to be litigated in federal court. If these three points can be established, the student-athlete can then proceed generally on an equal protection and/or a due process theory. The student-athlete may also pursue state constitutional arguments.

State Action Requirement

The constitutional safeguards of the Fifth and Fourteenth Amendments of the United States Constitution apply only when state action is present. Any action taken directly or indirectly by a state, local, or federal government is *state action* for constitutional purposes. In addition, action by any public school, state college, or state university or any of their officials is construed as state action. The issue of state action arises only when alleged wrongdoers are not acting directly on behalf of the government. In order to subject voluntary, private associations to constitutional limitations, some degree of state action must be present. Of course, actions by private organizations that are deemed to be performing a public function or are authorized under the laws of the state (quasi-public institutions) are also construed as state action. (See page 132.)

Beyond the fact that the actions taken by high school and college athletic associations are generally considered state action, it may be argued that private institutions acting in compliance with these organizations are also engaging in state action. Action by strictly private individuals does not constitute state action. Three common methods of analysis used to determine whether or not state action exists in particular circumstances are the public function theory, the entanglement theory, and the balancing approach theory.

The *public function theory* is somewhat limited and is traditionally confined to essential governmental services that have no counterparts in the public sector. A good example is American Telephone and Telegraph Company, which is a private company performing an essentially public function. The NCAA has, in at least one case, been deemed a public functionary based on its comprehensive regulation of an area that would otherwise have to be regulated by the states. The alternatives—having each state regulate college athletic programs without the existence of the NCAA—would be extremely inefficient and not a viable alternative. High school athletic association activities have also been found to be state action under the public function theory. In one case, the functions served by the high school athletic association were deemed to be so similar to the functions of the state in providing education that the association's rules were judged to be state action (see Note 3a).

In the second method of analysis, commonly known as the *entanglement theory*, the usual focal point is the amount of state and/or federal aid directly or indirectly given to the private organization. Under this view, state action issues involve a conflict between rights, and the court must balance these rights in determining whether the Constitution mandates a preference for one right over another. The receipt of such aid may subject a recipient's action to constitutional review. For this theory to be involved by the court, total state and/or federal control over the organization need not exist. Instead, the state or federal government must only have substantial influence over the association's activities. State and association actions must be intertwined to the extent that the organization's actions are supported or sanctioned by the government. State action is found based on the relationship of the association to the government.

Case law has held the NCAA's actions to be the equivalent of state action under this theory. In these cases, the rationale typically has been that over half of the NCAA's members are state-supported schools. In addition, most NCAA member schools receive federal aid, and their students receive federal financial aid (work-study, National Defense loans). Therefore, albeit indirectly, the NCAA is supported by state and federal governments. The NCAA also provides a service that is beyond the competence or authority of any one state.

High school athletic associations similarly have had their actions scrutinized under the entanglement theory. Many times high schools and their associations receive financial assistance from the state, public school or state officials may have a say in the association's policies and actions, and/or a portion of the association's membership may consist of public schools. These circumstances are sufficient to constitute state action.

The *balancing approach theory* is more general and not widely accepted. Here, if the merits of allowing the organizational practice are outweighed by the limitations on asserted/protected rights, courts have found state action which allows judicial intervention for the protection of individual constitutional rights.

In addition to these three theories, there is one more situation in which courts may intervene without a finding of state action. When an organization becomes so influential and so pervasive in an area that belonging to it is an economic necessity rather than a voluntary choice, the courts will act as necessary to equitably preserve justice. In most cases, NCAA activities have been found to be the equivalent of state action on the entanglement theory, although some early cases use the public function theory. The trend, however, seems to be toward holding the NCAA responsible for constitutional violations based on its omnipresence in collegiate athletics. (There are also cases that have held that NCAA activities are not state action.)

Most high school athletic associations are closely involved with public education and are therefore directly involved with the state. This direct connection usually provides a sufficient amount of state action to subject the high school association to constitutional limitations.

By assuming the role of a coordinator and overseer of high school athletics in the interest of its member institutions (many of which are public), high school athletic associations have generally been found to be performing traditional government functions. Yet, the Supreme Court has examined state or federal action requirements in a few nonathletic cases that may affect decisions in the amateur athletic realm. In *Blum v. Yaretsky,* 457 U.S. 991 (1982), the actions of a nursing home were not state action even though the state regulated the home. The Court stated that the plaintiff must show a greater nexus than mere acquiescence by the state. In *Rendell-Baker v. Kohn,* 457 U.S. 830 (1982), the Court ruled that a private school whose income was derived primarily from public services and whose operations were heavily regulated by state authorities did not act under state action in discharging certain employees. Conversely, in *Lugar v. Edmondson Oil Co.,* 457 U.S. 922 (1982), the conduct of a private party acting jointly with the state was found to constitute government action.

These three cases indicate how closely the Supreme Court is intending to examine claims of governmental involvement in a challenged activity. Consequently, the lower courts may reexamine the activities of athletic associations in cases based on the Supreme Court's principles. Accompany this with the fact that the courts have been inclined to defer to the decisions of amateur athletic organizations and one can conceive that the courts may not find state action on public function or any other grounds.

NOTES ————————————————————————————————

1. In the following cases, the NCAA's decisions were found to have constituted state action.

(a) In *Howard University v. National Collegiate Athletic Ass'n,* 510 F.2d 213 (D.C. Cir. 1975), the court noted that state-supported educational institutions and their members and officers play a substantial role in the NCAA's program, and that such state participation is a basis for finding state action (entanglement theory).

(b) In *Parish v. National Collegiate Athletic Ass'n,* 361 F. Supp. 1220 (W.D. La. 1973), *aff'd.,* 506 F.2d 1251 (9th Cir. 1974), the court found state action, since over half of the NCAA's members are state-supported schools and the NCAA performs a public function regulating intercollegiate athletics (entanglement theory).

(c) *Buckton v. National Collegiate Athletic Ass'n,* 366 F. Supp. 1152 (D. Mass. 1973), was the first case to declare the NCAA to be engaged in state action (public function theory). The public function theory has since been supplanted by other theories. (See page 282.)

(d) In *Regents of the University of Minnesota v. National Collegiate Athletic Ass'n,* 422 F. Supp. 1158 (D. Minn. 1976), the court acknowledged that the action taken by the NCAA has generally been accepted as the equivalent of state action. (See page 268.)

(e) In *Associated Students, Inc. v. National Collegiate Athletic Ass'n,* 493 F.2d 1251 (9th Cir. 1974), the court determined that the actions of the NCAA did constitute state action since the NCAA regulates schools and universities, at least half of which are public.

2. In the following cases, the NCAA's decisions were found to have *not* constituted state action.

(a) In *McDonald v. National Collegiate Athletic Ass'n*, 370 F.Supp. 625 (C.D. Calif. 1974), the court concluded that the NCAA is not sufficiently state supported to be considered state action, and it has an existence separate and apart from the educational system of any state. In the court's words, "if an institution is unable to concur with a voluntary organization without contravening the constitutional rights of its students, it must withdraw from the organization."

(b) In *Arlosoroff v. National Collegiate Athletic Ass'n*, 746 F.2d 1019 (4th Cir. 1984), the court stated that the "fact that NCAA's regulatory function may be of some public service lends no support to the finding of state action, for the function is not one traditionally reserved to the state."

3. The court ruled in the following cases that high school athletic associations *were acting* under color of state action.

(a) In *Barnhorst v. Missouri State High School Athletic Ass'n*, 504 F.Supp. 449 (W.D. Mo. 1980), the court found that the close identification of the functions served by the state high school athletic association with the state's provision of education (including extracurricular activities) to all children of school age is a sufficient link to transmute into state action the challenged association rule forbidding any student-athlete transferring from one member school to another member school from participating in interscholastic athletic competition for 365 days.

(b) In *Yellow Springs Exempted School District v. Ohio High School Athletic Ass'n*, 443 F. Supp. 753 (S.D. Ohio 1978), *reversed on other grounds*, 647 F.2d 651 (6th Cir. 1981), the court found that the OHSAA's conduct constituted state action because (1) the association depended on the state for operating revenue, (2) school officials were involved in the decision-making process, (3) public schools were predominant within the association membership, and (4) the association had the ability to impose sanctions upon state schools.

(c) In *Wright v. Arkansas Activities Ass'n*, 501 F.2d 25 (8th Cir. 1974), even though a voluntary, athletic association of public and parochial schools was not a state agency, its actions in regulating public school athletic activities and imposing a sanction for rule violations were found to constitute state action. The athletic association, having found a violation of "offseason" football practice rules, gave the school or school district a choice of suspending the high school from participation in association football games or not employing a particular coach as head football coach. The coach was accordingly requested to resign his coaching and teaching position and later sued the association.

4. For a case in which the court ruled that an Olympic organization was acting under color of state action, see *DeFrantz v. United States Olympic Committee*, 492 F. Supp. 1181 (D.D.C. 1980), *aff'd. without decision*, 701 F.2d 221 (D.C. Cir. 1980). Twenty-five athletes sought an

injunction to bar the USOC from boycotting the 1980 Moscow Olympics. Emphasizing that the USOC receives no federal funding and that it operates and exists independently of the federal government, the court found that the state was not in a position of interdependence with the USOC. The court also stated that the plaintiffs failed to prove that some form of control, or governmental persuasion or pressure, was behind the challenged action. (See page 249.)

5. For further information, see the following law review articles:

(a) "State High School Athletic Associations: When Will a Court Interfere?" 36 *Missouri Law Review* 400 (1971).

(b) Martin, "The NCAA and Its Student-Athletes: Is There Still State Action?" 21 *New England Law Review* 49 (1985–86).

Due Process

Constitutional guarantees afforded citizens in general apply equally as well to educational institutions, administrators, coaches, and student-athletes. The courts are reviewing with less hesitancy claims presented by aggrieved parties charging a violation of protected rights. In light of this legal development, a primary concern of athletic administrators regarding the imposition of penalties which jeopardize an individual's career should be minimum standards of "due process of law."

Due process is an elusive concept. One definition for the term *due process* is "a course of legal proceedings which have been established in our system of jurisprudence for the protection and enforcement of private rights" (*Pennoyer v. Neff*, 95 U.S. 714 [1877]). The concept may vary depending on three basic considerations: (1) the seriousness of the infraction, (2) the possible consequences to the institution or individual in question, and (3) the degree of sanction or penalty imposed.

The constitutional guarantee of due process is found in both the Fifth and Fourteenth Amendments to the U.S. Constitution. The Fifth Amendment, enacted in 1791, is applicable to the federal government. It states that "no person . . . shall be deprived of life, liberty, or property without due process of law." In 1886, the Fourteenth Amendment was ratified, reading, ". . . nor shall any state deprive any person of life, liberty, or property without due process of law . . ." This amendment extended the applicability of the due process doctrine to the states. Both amendments apply only to federal or state governmental action and not to the conduct of purely private entities. While the Constitution extends these liberties to all persons, it is also limiting in that a person must demonstrate deprivation of life, liberty, or property to claim a violation of due process guarantees.

Since athletic associations and conferences rarely deprive a person of life, the major interests that trigger application of the due process clause in the athletic context are deprivations of liberty and property. Unless an athlete or other party can establish that he has been deprived of liberty or property, he will not be able to establish a deprivation of due process.

The due process doctrine presses two inquiries. The first is *procedural due process*, which refers to the procedures required to ensure fairness. The second is *substantive due process*, which guarantees basic rights that cannot be denied by governmental action. Procedural due process has as its focal point the questioning of the decision-making process which is followed in determining whether the rule or regulation has been violated and the penalty, if any, that is imposed. Was the decision made in an arbitrary, capricious, or collusive manner? Was the accused given the opportunity to know what to defend against and to know reasonably well in advance what is thought to have been violated? Substantive due process involves the rule, regulation, or legislation being violated—namely, is it fair and reasonable? In other words, when measuring substantive due process, does the rule or legislation have a purpose and is it clearly related to the accomplishment of that purpose?

Claims to due process protection may be brought based not only on protections guaranteed by state constitutions and by federal and state statutes, but also on the regulations and constitutions of athletic institutions, conferences, and other athletic governing organizations.

Procedural Due Process

The two minimum requirements of due process are the right to a hearing and notice of the hearing's time, date, and content. The requirements are flexible, and the degree of formality depends on the nature of the right involved as well as on the circumstances surrounding the situation. If the deprivation concerned is not that of a fundamental right or is a right marginally affected by the challenged rule, only the minimal due process requirements may be necessary (see Exhibit 4–7).

On the other hand, when a fundamental right is involved or when an infringement on personal freedom is present, the hearing must be more formal, with additional safeguards. The full protections of due process include notice and the right to a hearing in front of a neutral decision maker, with an opportunity to make an oral presentation, to present favorable evidence, and to confront and cross-examine adverse witnesses. In addition, there may also be a right to have an attorney present during the proceedings, a

General Considerations
- The special requirements or procedures imposed by state law, association policy, conference policy, institution policy, or board policy regarding the declaration of student-athlete ineligibility should be determined and followed.
- The person or persons who have authority to declare a student-athlete ineligible should be identified.
- Whether the matter requires rudimentary due process or formal due process should be decided.

Due Process Procedures
- A determination should be made as to whether the alleged violation, unfulfilled requirement, or ruling is a proper basis for the proposed regulatory action.
- The person dealing with the student-athlete should promptly give the student-athlete oral or written notice of the specific violation or ruling and the proposed regulatory measure.
- If the student-athlete denies the violation or disagrees with the ruling, the individual should be provided with an explanation of the evidence which the athletic department has in its possession.
- The student-athlete should be allowed to present his or her side of the story.
- The proposed regulatory action should be imposed unless the student-athlete adequately refutes the violation or the ruling.
- The student-athlete's parents or guardian should be notified, if appropriate, of the regulatory measure being imposed.
- If requested by the student-athlete or parent, the ruling and action taken under applicable procedures should be reviewed. This may entail a verification of the ruling and action with the institution's athletic conference and/or association.

Exhibit 4-7 Minimal Due Process Checklist *Source*: Adapted from Rapp, *Education Law,* Vol. I, 3–170–175.

copy of the transcript of the hearing, and a right to a written decision based on the record (see Exhibit 4–8).

Although an individual may enjoy the guarantee of due process, the actual process is rarely spelled out. The type of due process protections guaranteed in a given situation are determined by a consideration of the importance of the right involved, the degree of the infringement, and the potential harm of the violation. As a general rule, the more an individual has at stake, the more extensive and formal are the due process requirements. Since a number of factors are involved, administrative agencies must examine the merits of each case to determine the required procedures on a case-by-case basis.

General Considerations

- The special requirements or procedures imposed by state law, association policy, conference policy, institution policy, or board policy regarding the declaration of student-athlete ineligibility should be determined and followed.
- The person or persons who have authority to declare a student-athlete ineligible should be identified.
- Whether the matter requires rudimentary due process or formal due process should be decided.

Preliminary Due Process Procedures

- A determination should be made as to whether proper grounds exist for the proposed regulatory action and, if appropriate, charges consistent with applicable procedures should be initiated.
- The student-athlete, and if a minor, the individual's parents or guardian, should be notified in writing, of the violation or ruling, the factual basis for the charges, the specific provisions of any student-athlete code, the right of the student-athlete to a hearing and the procedures to be followed at that hearing, the right of the student-athlete to be represented by an attorney or other counsel, and whether a hearing must be requested or whether one will be scheduled automatically. Also, the student-athlete, and if a minor, the individual's parents or guardian, should be given a copy of any applicable rules governing the violation or ruling and the regulatory proceedings.
- If appropriate, the written notice should be preceded or followed by a telephone or personal conference with the student-athlete or, if a minor, the parents or guardian.
- If requested or required automatically under applicable regulatory procedures, a hearing should be scheduled.
- If requested, the student-athlete or the individual's counsel should be given the names of witnesses against him and an oral or written report of the facts to which each witness will testify, unless such disclosures may result in reprisals against the witnesses.
- A transcript or record of the hearing should be arranged for if required or desired by the student-athlete.
- All steps necessary to assure fairness and impartiality of the parties involved in the hearing should be taken.

Conduct of the Hearing

- To open the hearing, the presiding officer should declare the hearing convened, state the matter under consideration, take a roll call of the members of the board or panel, and confirm the existence of a quorum.
- All persons present should be identified and their interest in the matter verified. The meeting may be closed to the public and those without a proper interest in the matter.
- The presiding officer should summarize the procedures to be followed.

Exhibit 4-8 Full Due Process Checklist *Source*: Adapted from Rapp, *Education Law,* Vol. I, 3–170–175.

- The student-athlete or the individual's counsel should be asked whether any objections exist with regard to the time, place, or procedures of the hearing.
- The student-athlete or his counsel should be allowed the opportunity to raise any questions regarding the impartiality of any member of the tribunal or the hearer.
- The charges or ruling against the student-athlete should then be read and the student-athlete requested to confirm that he or she has received a copy of the charges.
- If the parties to the matter have stipulated or agreed on any facts or exhibits in the case, they should be requested to present them.
- Each party should be provided an opportunity to make opening statements.
- Subject to the applicable rules of evidence, the person bringing the charges or ruling and, thereafter, the student-athlete, should be allowed to present any relevant material and reliable evidence, generally subject to a right of cross-examination by the other.
- Following the initial presentation of evidence, the parties should be allowed to present rebuttal and surrebuttal evidence.
- At the close of all the evidence, the parties should be invited to make closing statements or arguments.
- The hearing should then be closed with an explanation of the timetable and procedures to be used for rendering a decision.

Posthearing Procedures
- Deliberations of the case should commence.
- Only the members of the tribunal or hearer and their attorneys or advisers should be allowed to participate in or attend the deliberations.
- Once decision is reached, it should be reduced to writing, setting forth findings of fact, the basis of the decision, and the regulatory measure imposed.
- The student-athlete and, if a minor, the individual's parents or guardian, should be notified of the decision.
- Consistent with applicable procedures, the student-athlete should be advised of any available administrative review and provided that review.
- All parties should realize that the student-athlete may always seek appropriate judicial relief.

Exhibit 4-8 Continued

The Supreme Court has further applied a three-pronged inquiry to determine what is due process: the private interest that will be affected by the official action; the risk of an erroneous deprivation of such interest through the procedures used and the probable value, if any, of additional or substitute procedural safeguards; and the government's interest, including the function involved and the fiscal and administrative burdens that the additional or substitute procedural requirement would entail (*Mathews v. Eldridge*, 424 U.S. 319, 96 S. Ct. 893, 47 L.Ed.2d 18[1976]). Some have suggested that athletic organizations fashion a set of notice and hearing procedures that will withstand constitutional scrutiny. The benefits to establishing a set of procedures include the following:

1. Establishing procedures may be fairer to student-athletes, thereby building goodwill.
2. Courts, which are already inclined to defer to athletic decision makers, will in most cases find the procedures adequate, particularly if the procedures are originally fashioned in light of the *Mathews* case.
3. Provided that the procedures are basically fair and balance the factors outlined in *Mathews*, they are less likely to be challenged by the student-athletes themselves because some due process will already have been afforded the aggrieved party.
4. Establishing procedures would contribute some certainty to an area otherwise fraught with ambiguity.

Having a set of notice and hearing procedures would benefit the organization as well as the athlete, thereby reducing the role of the courts in fashioning and implementing required procedures.

NOTES _____

1. In *Behagen v. Intercollegiate Conference of Faculty Representatives*, 346 F. Supp. 602 (D. Minn. 1972), two college basketball players who had been suspended for the season sought to prohibit the ICFR (also known as the Big Ten Conference) from enforcing their suspension until they were granted due process. The court found it consistent with the powers of the commissioner to suspend the players temporarily pending a hearing, if such action was not arbitrary or capricious and was done to protect the interest of the conference. However, due process could not be denied since the suspensions bordered on punitive action, with a notable concern being that the players were prevented from displaying skills that could lead to future economic rewards as professionals.

2. In *Southern Methodist University v. Smith*, 515 S.W.2d 63 (Tex. Civ. App. 1974), the court held that no due process is required if the facts are not disputed, or if the issues have already been resolved (see *Graesen v. Pasquale*, 200 N.W.2d 842 [1978]).

3. In *Regents of University of Minnesota v. National Collegiate Athletic Ass'n*, 560 F.2d 352 (8th Cir. 1977), the court held that due process requires notice and a hearing.

4. In *Kelley v. Metropolitan County Board of Education of Nashville*, 293 F. Supp. 485 (M.D. Tenn. 1968), plaintiff high school student-athlete was suspended from athletic competition by the Board of Education

without being formally charged with a rule violation. The court held that due process involves the right to be heard before being condemned. Due process requires published standards, formal charges, notice, and a hearing. The court granted an injunction that prevented the enforcement of the suspension.

5. In *Pegram v. Nelson*, 469 F. Supp. 1134 (M.D.N.C. 1979), the court held that a short suspension (less than 10 days) from participation in after-school extracurricular activities requires only an informal hearing.

6. In *Mitchell v. Louisiana High School Athletic Ass'n*, 430 F.2d 1155 (5th Cir. 1970), the court of appeals ruled that the association's eligibility rules did not violate students' rights under due process and equal protection clauses of the Fourteenth Amendment since a substantial federal question was not raised.

7. In *O'Connor v. Board of Education*, 65 Misc. 2d 140, 316 N.Y.S.2d 799 (1970), a high school student-athlete was deprived of his athletic award (letter) after his coach turned him in for allegedly violating a "no drinking" rule. The court held that the process required a hearing prior to revocation of a high school athlete's letter.

8. In *Taylor v. Alabama High School Athletic Ass'n*, 336 F. Supp. 54 (M.D. Ala. 1972), plaintiff high school was prohibited from hosting or participating in invitational basketball tournaments for one year due to the "misconduct and unruliness" of spectators at one of its games. The Alabama High School Athletic Association violated the plaintiff's due process rights for the following reasons:

    (a) There were no preexisting standards;
    (b) No punishments were provided for violation of the rules;
    (c) No specific charge was made;
    (d) No notice was given;
    (e) There was no opportunity for an adequate hearing;
    (f) The hearing was not convened as required by the association's rules.

The court also found that the penalty imposed exceeded any other previously imposed penalty.

9. In *Hamilton v. Tennessee Secondary Athletic Ass'n*, 552 F.2d 681 (6th Cir. 1976), the court of appeals ruled that the privilege of participating in interscholastic athletics is outside the protection of due process.

10. In *Duffey v. New Hampshire Interscholastic Athletic Ass'n*, 446 A.2d 462 (N.H. 1982), the New Hampshire Supreme Court ruled that student-athlete plaintiff had been denied procedural due process because the New Hampshire Interscholastic Athletic Association failed to state the reasons for denial of eligibility.

11. In *Wright v. Arkansas Activities Ass'n*, 501 F.2d 25 (8th Cir. 1974), the court of appeals ruled that a rule prohibiting football practice prior to a certain date may provide fair notice that a school may be sanctioned. However, imposition of a sanction resulting in the loss of a coaching/teaching position denied the coach due process. The rule gave no notice of the fact that the coach could be subject to a sanction, resulting in unemployment.

12. In *Marcum v. Dahl*, 658 F.2d 731 (10th Cir. 1981), college basket-

ball student-athletes claimed their right to due process had been violated when they were dropped from the team for disciplinary reasons without a hearing. The court held that the college had offered the opportunity for a hearing, but the student-athletes had failed to take advantage of it, thus freeing the college of any further due process responsibilities.

13. An example of a hearing and appeal process which can be made available to an athlete by an amateur sports organization is the one below implemented by the United States Swimming Association.

Article 50: Hearings and Appeals

450.1 General—As hereinafter set forth, the Corporation may censure, suspend for a definite or indefinite period of time with or without terms of probation, or expel any member of the Corporation, including any athlete, coach, manager, official member of any committee, or any person participating in any capacity whatsoever in the affairs of the Corporation, who has violated any of its rules or regulations, or who has acted in a manner which brings disrepute upon the Corporation or upon the sport of swimming. The Corporation may also conduct hearings on any matter affecting the Corporation as the national governing body for swimming.

450.2 Jurisdiction of the Local Swimming Committees (LSC)—For those matters requiring a hearing and arising solely within the geographical boundaries of an LSC, the procedure to be taken and the rules to be followed for hearing shall be as set forth in Part Five, Article 71.

450.3 Jurisdiction of the Corporation—In those matters in which athlete(s) or other member(s) of the Corporation from more than one LSC is involved, or in matters involving such persons during a national or international athletic event, an investigation and report of the facts shall be made to the President as hereinafter set forth. If in the opinion of a majority of the elected officers of the Corporation a hearing or further investigation is then warranted, the matter shall be submitted to the National Board of Review for hearing and decision.

(1) Where persons or entities from more than one LSC are involved, the investigation and report shall be made by the Executive Director.

(2) In those matters occurring during the course of a national, regional, or zone event, the Senior Division or Age Group Division, as the case may be, shall make the investigation and report.

(3) In those matters occurring during the course of an international event, the Olympic International Division shall make the investigation and report.

450.4 National Board of Review—The Board of Review shall be comprised of the General Counsel of the Corporation, all associate counsels, one (1) athlete representative from each of the four zones (elected by the Athletes Committee), and such other members as may be recommended by the President and approved by the Board of Directors. The President shall appoint the chairman and shall have the authority to designate a panel of no less than three members, one of whom shall be an athlete representative, to hear and decide any case before the Board of Review.

450.5 Authority of National Board of Review—The National Board of Review has the authority to:

(1) Impose and enforce penalties for any violation of the rules and regulations, administrative or technical, of the Corporation;

(2) Determine the eligibility and right to compete of any athlete;

(3) Vacate, modify, sustain, stay or reverse any decision or order properly

submitted for review, or remand the matter for further action;

(4) Investigate any election impropriety or cause for removal of a national committeeman or national officer and take corrective action;

(5) Interpret any provision of the rules and regulations of the Corporation with the exception of the technical rules (Part One);

(6) Review any revocation, suspension or reinstatement of membership to assure due process; and

(7) Reinstate any athlete to amateur status subject to ratification by no less than 2/3 vote of the House of Delegates of the Corporation.

450.6 Procedure for Review

(1) Every appeal to the Board of Review shall be instituted by a petition served upon the Executive Director and accompanied by a $50 filing fee payable to the Corporation. The fee shall be returned if the petition is upheld, but forfeited if it is rejected or abandoned. The Board of Review may assess costs against the losing party.

(2) The Executive Director shall send a copy of the petition for review to the respondent and chairman of the Board of Review immediately upon receipt. The respondent shall within 30 days following receipt of the petition file a written response with the Executive Director, the petitioner and the chairman. The petitioner may within 10 days following receipt of a copy of the response file a written rebuttal with the Executive Director, the respondent and the chairman. The chairman may decrease or increase the time limits for any of the foregoing upon request of either party and if circumstances should warrant it.

(3) A final and binding decision shall be rendered within 75 days from date of filing of the petition by a majority of the acting panel based on the record submitted for review and on evidence submitted at such hearing as may be required by the panel. A written decision shall be sent to all parties. Petitions once reviewed and decided shall not be reopened for consideration by the Board of Review, except by direction of the Board of Directors of the Corporation, or upon showing of sufficient cause to the chairman of the Board of Review.

450.7 Appeal to the Board of Directors—Any real party in interest may appeal to the Board of Directors for review of any decision of the National Board of Review within thirty (30) days of the date of decision.

450.8 Original Jurisdiction—Upon a majority vote of the officers, the Board of Directors or the National Board of Review may be assigned original jurisdiction at any stage of any matter within the purview of this Article 50 when the best interests of the Corporation will be served thereby. If original jurisdiction is so assigned, compliance shall be made in every instance with all requirements of procedural due process as set forth in this Article 50. [1982 Code]

14. The NCAA in its recommended policies suggests in regard to the question of due process and student-athletes that:

In the administration of their athletics programs in accordance with NCAA regulations and their conditions and obligations of membership in the Association, members institutions may find it necessary, from time to time, to terminate or suspend the eligibility of student-athletes for participation in intercollegiate competition and organized athletic practice sessions. In any such case, the member institution should notify the student-athlete concerned and afford the student-athlete an opportunity for an informal hearing before the faculty athletic representative, director of athletics or other appropriate institutional authority before action is taken, it being understood that the hearing opportunity shall not delay or set aside the member's obligations required by NCAA Constitution 4-2-(a)-0-1.11 and Section 9 of the Association's enforcement procedures. This hearing opportunity will avoid possible mistaken actions affecting the student-athlete's eligibility and should satisfy due process procedures if any are required.

See *1987–88 NCAA Manual*, NCAA Recommended Policies and Practices for Intercollegiate Athletics, Policy 11, Due Process.

15. For further information, see Lowell, "Federal Administrative Intervention in Amateur Athletes," 43 *George Washington Law Review* 729 (1975).

Substantive Due Process

If the court finds that the right deprived involves life, liberty, or property, then full due process rights may be granted to the individual (see Exhibit 4–8). In sports cases, the interest most commonly cited is the property interest, although in some instances the personal liberty interest is involved (see hairlength cases in Chapter 5). For the purposes of the due process clause, types of property are not distinguished. Therefore, the first problem encountered in many of these cases is a determination of whether the interest involved constitutes property.

Traditionally, *property* has been defined as all valuable interests that can be possessed outside of oneself, which have an exchangeable value or which add to an individual's wealth or estate. Since 1972 in the Supreme Court's decision in *Board of Regents v. Roth*, 408 U.S. 564, 33 L.Ed.2d 548, 92 S. Ct. 2701 (1972), property has been defined as all interests to which an individual could be deemed "entitled." Entitlements occur only if there is some form of current interest in or current use of the property. For example, a holder of a scholarship has a property right because he is currently entitled to benefits derived from it. Once this entitlement is established, there is a property right. Due process protections are triggered only when there is an actual deprivation of the entitled rights. This "entitlement" standard does not encompass wishes that do not come true or expectations that fail to materialize; an entitlement to property must be more than an abstract need or desire for it.

The property right involved in amateur sports is the right to participate in athletic activities. The major controversy revolves around the question of whether participation is an individual protectable right or a privilege that is unprotected. This question is analyzed differently depending on whether the athletic activity is on the high school or college level. On both levels defendants have argued that participation in athletics is a privilege and therefore falls outside the parameters of the due process clause.

In the collegiate area, however, plaintiffs have been successful in claiming a property interest based on the proximity of monetary benefits currently or potentially available to the student-athlete. A property interest has been found in athletic participation because there exists a potential economic benefit to the student-athlete in the form of either a scholarship or a future professional contract. A current holder of a scholarship who would be deprived of that scholarship has a well-defined property interest based on the present economic value of the award.

A college student-athlete may also have a protectable interest in a future professional contract, as in *Behagen v. Intercollegiate Conference of Faculty Representatives* (see page 150). Some courts, however, by looking at a statistical analysis of the percentage of people who successfully enter professional sports, have discounted a legitimate property interest in a future professional contract as being too speculative. Also, at least one court has indicated that it would find a protectable property interest only if there were a professional league in that particular sport. (See *Fluitt v. University of Nebraska*, Note 1.)

In the interscholastic area, the right or privilege dichotomy is analyzed differently. A high school student-athlete with only the possibility of obtaining a scholarship generally has no present economic interest, and the possibility of obtaining a scholarship is too speculative an interest to receive protection. Similarly, a high school student-athlete is usually considered to have an entirely speculative interest in a future professional contract.

In high school cases, the right versus the privilege controversy involves the student-athlete's argument that he or she has a right to an education and that participation in interscholastic athletics is included in that right. The threshold issue is whether there is a right to an education. The Supreme Court has specifically denied a general constitutional right to education (see *San Antonio Independent School Dist. v. Rodriguez*, 411 U.S. 1, 36 L.Ed.2d 16, 93 S. Ct. 1278 [1973]). Even though the right to an education is not grounded in federal law, a state may grant a right to an education either explicitly or implicitly by requiring school attendance. Through this measure, the state effectively gives each child within its boundaries an interest in the education provided. This interest has been held to be a type of property interest protected by the due process clause. (See *Pegram v. Nelson*, 469 F. Supp. 1134 [M.D.N.C. 1979] and *Goss v. Lopez*, 419 U.S. 565, 39 L.Ed.2d 465, S. Ct. 1405 [1974].) Whether a right is stated explicitly or implicitly, once it has been established, it cannot be limited or removed without due process protections.

After finding a right to education based on statutory attendance requirements, a determination must then be made of whether or not that right includes participation in extracurricular activities. If the right to education means a right to the "total" educational process provided by a school, the courts may find participation in athletic competition to be a right. The right to participate would then be protected by due process considerations. Many courts, however, interpret educational rights as encompassing only class-room learning and view all other activities as unprotected privi-leges.

NOTES

1. In *Fluitt v. University of Nebraska*, 489 F. Supp. 1194 (D. Neb. 1980), a fifth-year college student-athlete requested one additional year of eligibility due to an injury that terminated his freshman season, but was denied. The court reasoned that the Faculty Committee was solely responsible for all determinations of hardship, a procedure that had been followed for at least 25 years. Any denial of due process at a first hearing was remedied at the second hearing, and thus, no violation of due process occurred.

2. The following cases are examples of a property interest argument in intercollegiate athletics.

(a) In *National Collegiate Athletic Ass'n v. Gillard*, 352 So. 2d 1072 (Miss. 1977), the court ruled that a player's right to play intercolle-giate football was not a property right to be protected by due process guarantees. The court ruled that the denial of player's eligibility to compete for having accepted clothing at a discount did not infringe on the plaintiff's constitutional rights to due process.

(b) See *Gulf South Conference v. Boyd*, 369 So. 2d 553 (Ala. 1979), on page 194.

(c) See *Hall v. University of Minnesota*, 530 F. Supp. 104 (D. Minn. 1982), on pages 191 and 272.

(d) See *Behagan v. Intercollege Conference of Faculty Representa-tives*, 346 F. Supp. 602 (D. Minn. 1972).

3. The following cases are examples of the property interest argument in interscholastic athletics.

(a) In *Stock v. Texas Catholic Interscholastic League*, 364 F. Supp. 362 (N.D. Tex. 1973), the court held that the plaintiff high school student-athlete's interest in playing interscholastic football was too insignificant to justify federal court jurisdiction. The plaintiff failed to show that he had been deprived of a right under color of state law such that jurisdiction under 42 U.S.C. section 1983 should be granted. The court held that: "Nowhere in the Constitution is there any guarantee of a right to play football. . . . [E]ven if the participation was thwarted under color of state law, the interest at stake was still too insignificant to justify jurisdiction."

(b) See *Gulf South Conference v. Boyd*, 369 So.2d 553 (Ala. 1979), on page 194.

(c) In *Scott v. Kilpatrick*, 286 Ala. 129, 237 So. 2d 652 (1970), a high school football player contended that the transfer rule of the high school athletic association was unconstitutional since the student-athlete's desire to compete in high school football involved a property right, which was alleged to be the opportunity to compete for a college football scholarship. The court found that participation in high school athletics was a privilege and not a property right.

(d) In *Robinson v. Illinois High School Ass'n*, 45 Ill. App. 2d 277, 195 N.E.2d 38 (1963), plaintiff high school student was denied eligibility because he was over the age limit set by the defendant association. The court held that no property interest was sufficient to justify judicial intervention when the association's determination of eligibility did not show fraud, collusion, or unreasonable or arbitrary acts.

(e) In *Taylor v. Alabama High School Athletic Ass'n*, 336 F. Supp. 54 (M.D. Ala. 1972), the district court held that participation in interscholastic athletics is a privilege. The mere chance of receiving a college scholarship based upon display of athletic ability at tournaments is not a protectable property right.

(f) In *Moran v. School District #7, Yellowstone County*, 350 F. Supp. 1180 (D. Mont. 1972), the court held that the right to attend school includes the right to participate in extracurricular activities. The court reasoned that sports are an integral part of the total educational process. This educational process is extremely important, and sport participation may not be denied when there is no reasonable basis upon which to distinguish among the various parts of the educational process.

4. For further information, see the following articles:

(a) "Judicial Review of Disputes Between Athletes and the National Collegiate Athletic Association," 24 *Stanford Law Review* 903 (1972).

(b) Comment, "A Student-Athlete's Interest in Eligibility: Its Context and Constitutional Dimensions," 10 *Connecticut Law Review* 318 (1975).

(c) Martin, "Due Process and Its Future within the NCAA," 10 *Connecticut Law Review* 290 (1978).

(d) "High School Athletes and Due Process," 15 *New England Law Review* 597 (1978).

(e) "NCAA, Amateurism, and the Student-Athletes' Constitutional Rights Upon Eligibility," 15 *New England Law Review* 597 (1978–80).

(f) "Entitlement, Enjoyment and Due Process of Law," 89 *Duke Law Journal* 101 (1974).

(g) Monaghan, "Of Liberty and Property," 62 *Cornell Law Review* 405 (1977).

(h) "Jocks Are People Too," 13 *Creighton Law Review* 843 (1979).

(i) "High School Athletics and Due Process Notice of Eligibility Rules," 57 *Nebraska Law Review* 877 (1978).

(j) "Judicial Review of NCAA Decisions: Does the College Athlete

Have a Property Interest in Interscholastic Athletics?" 10 *Stetson Law Review* 483 (1981).

Equal Protection

Through the equal protection clause of the Fourteenth Amendment of the U.S. Constitution, student-athletes and coaches are provided with the means to challenge certain rules and regulations that are of a discriminatory nature. This source of law forbids discrimination of one form or another in various contexts and thus serves to limit the regulatory power of amateur athletic organizations controlling sports activities.

Equal protection is the constitutional method of checking on the fairness of the application of any law. This independent constitutional guarantee governs all federal, state, and local laws which classify individuals or which impact on individual rights. The equal protection guarantee is found in the Fourteenth Amendment of the U.S. Constitution. It reads: "No state shall . . . deny to any person within its jurisdiction the equal protection of the laws." It is specifically applicable only to the states, but the federal government is held to similar standards under the due process clause of the Fifth Amendment. Equal protection requires that no person be singled out from similarly situated people, or to have different benefits bestowed or burdens imposed, unless a constitutionally permissible reason exists for doing so.

Different standards of review are used under equal protection analysis. The highest standard of review is that of *strict scrutiny*. Application of the strict scrutiny standard by the court means that the rule challenged will be invalidated unless the defendant can demonstrate that the rule is supported by a compelling state interest. When a rule abridges a fundamental right or makes a distinction based on suspect criteria, the defendant has the burden of proof. This standard tests only whether a classification is properly drawn, not whether an individual is properly placed within that classification. This type of review is triggered by the use of either a suspect class or fundamental interest.

The Supreme Court has found three suspect classes: alienage, race, and national origin. Any time a rule impacts directly or indirectly on any of these suspect classifications criteria, the strict scrutiny standard will be applied.

There are a number of fundamental interests, and the vast majority of these rights arise expressly from the U.S. Constitution. They include the First Amendment guarantees, such as the right to freedom of religion, speech, and press, as well as the right to assemble peaceably and to petition the government for redress of grievances. In addition to these specific rights, the Supreme Court has found three other fundamental rights: the right to travel, the right to vote, and the right to privacy (which involves decisions about marriage, abortion, and other family choices).

Some interests have been specifically found to be nonfundamental; these include subsistence and welfare payments, housing, government employment, and education. The fact that education has been deemed a nonfundamental interest is particularly important in cases involving high school or college athletic associations. This designation makes it difficult for the student-athlete plaintiff to establish participation as a fundamental interest.

The second standard of review under the equal protection guarantee is that of *rational basis*. This standard requires only that the rule have some rational relationship to a legitimate organizational purpose. It is used in the absence of a classification defined as a suspect criteria or as a fundamental right. Rules reviewed under this standard are difficult for a plaintiff to challenge successfully since the defendant is generally able to present some rational relationship between the restriction and a legitimate governmental objective. The rational basis test is the most commonly applied constitutional standard.

The third standard of review or category of classes imposes an *intermediate test*, which falls between the strict scrutiny and rational basis tests. It requires that rules classifying certain groups satisfy an "important" but not necessarily a "compelling" interest. Two "quasi-suspect" classifications have been established: gender and legitimacy. Use of either gender- or legitimacy-based classifications will trigger this intermediate standard of review. To date, the difference between "compelling" and "important" has not been made explicit and remains the subject of much examination and speculation.

Equal protection does not bar states from creating classifications. Instead, it requires that classifications not be predicated on race, alienage, or national origin. It also requires that the criteria bear a reasonable relationship to the purpose of the law. Otherwise, the distinction is automatically suspect. Once a law is suspect, it will be held valid only if a compelling interest is established and there is no less intrusive means by which the same end may be achieved. The burden of proof is on the states to establish the compelling nature of the interest. The same analysis is used when a fundamental interest is infringed upon by a state law. In summary, the theory of equal protection is used to protect individuals by ensuring that they are fairly treated in the exercise of their fundamental rights and by assuring the elimination of distinctions based on constitutionally impermissible criteria.

The equal protection guarantee relates to classes and distinctions inevitably drawn whenever a legislative body makes rules relating to specific groups. One method typically employed to challenge a rule under the equal protection clause is that which claims either under- or overinclusiveness. Under- or overinclusiveness can result in a rule being impermissibly discriminatory. *Overinclusiveness* means that the legislative class includes many people to whom the rule in question lacks a rational relationship. In other words, at least some of the class of affected individuals are not part of the problem addressed by the rule, and the rule as applied to these people has no relationship to its purpose. A rule's validity depends not on whether classes differ but on whether differences between the classes are pertinent to the subject with respect to which the classification is made. Whereas overinclusiveness exists when a rule creates a class more extensive than necessary to effectuate the purpose of the rule, *underinclusiveness* exists when a class does not contain all the members necessary to effectuate the rule's purpose.

It is possible for a rule to be both over- and underinclusive. For example, consider the following rule: "All transfer students from public high schools will not be eligible for interscholastic play for one year from date of entry." This rule is overinclusive regarding public school transfers that were made for reasons unrelated to athletics. It would be underinclusive, however, if it permitted immediate eligibility for transfer students from private schools who might be transferring solely for athletic reasons.

To draw perfect classifications that are neither over- nor underinclusive is extremely difficult. In light of this, when no important constitutional rights are involved, the courts can and do uphold both over- and underinclusive categories as long as they can find a rational relationship between the rule and its purpose. For example, only when an athletic association cannot demonstrate the connection between the rule and its purpose will the court find that an equal protection violation has occurred.

Another reason why the court will uphold rules that do not make perfect classifications is to allow athletic associations to deal with problems on an individual basis. Associations or legislatures do not have to create perfect solutions prior to attacking specific problems. In many cases, the court will not decide if the rule itself is invalid but may conclude that its application to a specific individual violates the person's civil rights. The court can therefore pay deference to the legislative judgment initiating the rule while simultaneously upholding the rights of the individual.

Technically, there is a two-tiered system for equal protection analysis; however, the trend may be toward a sliding scale that would dissolve the absolute categories of fundamental rights and interests. The advantage of a sliding-scale approach is that it is much more flexible and would in effect create a flexible scale of rights and/or classes that would be directly compared with the governmental interest involved.

NOTES ———

1. In the following cases, violations of equal protection were found in the application of an athletic association's rules or decisions.

(a) In *Buckton v. National Collegiate Athletic Ass'n*, 366 F. Supp. 1152 (D. Mass. 1973), Canadian ice hockey players were denied eligibility because they had received funding from junior league hockey teams in Canada rather than from high schools, as is the custom in the United States. The court prohibited the NCAA from enforcing ineligibility, because the rule in effect discriminated against plaintiffs on the basis of the suspect criteria of national origin.

(b) In *Indiana High School v. Raike*, 164 Ind. App. 169, 329 N.E.2d 66 (1975), a public high school rule which prohibited married students from participating in any extracurricular activities was held invalid, even though the court decided the right to marry was not a fundamental right. The court, in using a sliding scale approach, held that the rule denied equal protection because there was no fair and substantial relationship between the classification (married students) and the objective sought (preventing dropouts).

(c) In *Baltic Independent School District No. 115 v. South Dakota High School Activities Ass'n*, 362 F. Supp. 780 (D.S.D. 1973), the court held that an association's rule of classifying high schools for speech activity bore no rational relationship to the objective of promoting fair competition. The court found the right to participate was constitutionally protected, even though debating was a voluntary extracurricular activity.

(d) In *Rivas Tenorio v. Liga Atletica Interuniversitaria*, 554 F.2d 492 (1st Cir. 1977), the trial court, in dismissing the complaint which questioned the constitutionality of an athletic association's regulation banning non-Puerto Ricans from competing in intercollegiate athletics if they enrolled in member institutions after their 21st birthday, erred in failing to subject the regulation to strict constitutional scrutiny in view of the fact that it discriminated, on its face, against aliens. The case was reversed and sent back to the district court.

(e) In *Howard University v. National Collegiate Athletic Ass'n*, 510 F.2d 213 (D.C. Cir. 1975), the court applied strict scrutiny in striking down the NCAA's "Foreign Student Rule" because the classification was based on alienage. Even though the court accepted the purpose of the rule, it held that the rule was not closely tailored to achieve its goal, since it penalized foreign student-athletes for activities that citizens participated in without penalty.

2. In the following cases, violations of equal protection were *not* found in the application of an athletic association's rules or decisions.

(a) *Mitchell v. Louisiana High School Athletic Ass'n*, 430 F.2d 1155 (5th Cir. 1970), was a case litigated on the theory that there was discrimination against students who chose to repeat a junior high school grade because of academic or personal reasons. The court held that allowing those who failed a year to still have four years of high school eligibility, while reducing eligibility to three years for those who chose to repeat a year, had a rational relationship with regard to the problem of redshirting (see page 204). Therefore, it was not appropriate for the judiciary to intervene, even when the rule was unduly harsh on the individual.

(b) In *Moreland v. Western Pennsylvania Interscholastic Athletic League*, 572 F.2d 121 (3rd Cir. 1978), a high school basketball player claimed denial of equal protection when he was prohibited from competing in postseason play because he was absent from school for more than 20 days, a violation of a league rule. The court held that the rule was rationally related to the purpose of safeguarding educational values, cultivating high ideals of good sportsmanship, and promoting uniformity of standards in athletic competition.

ASSOCIATION ENFORCEMENT AUTHORITY

The authority for amateur athletic associations to regulate their membership originates from two sources. First, as corporate bodies, amateur athletic organizations must be recognized as entities by the state. Second, in order for the association to govern, the membership must have agreed to be so regulated. Most high school athletic associations and conferences do not have the resources to enforce and review compliance of rules and regulations of their organization on a first-hand basis. They rely primarily on the concept of institutional control. However, on the collegiate level, the large stakes of the revenue-producing sports like football and basketball have made it necessary to police more stringently a university's athletic program for rules violations. In this section, the legal relationships among the state government, the intercollegiate association, and the membership are examined using the NCAA as an example.

The NCAA, as described earlier in this chapter, is a voluntary association whose members agree to follow certain conditions and obligations of membership, including the obligation to conduct their individual institutional athletic programs in a manner consistent with NCAA legislation. This legislation is enacted by a majority vote of delegates at either the annual convention, held each January, or at special conventions called by the NCAA Council.

The rules of organization are published annually in the *NCAA Manual*, which is available to every member of the organization.

Member institutions agree when they join the NCAA to be policed in regard to the organization's rules by the NCAA's enforcement staff, which is given policy guidance by the NCAA's Committee on Infractions. The committee is composed of six members, one of whom serves as chair. Committee members may serve up to but not exceeding nine years. The enforcement staff conducts all NCAA investigations based on allegations of infractions by a member institution. Some investigations may involve only one or two allegations, while others may include as many as 100 or more.

The first NCAA enforcement program was enacted by the association in 1948. Called the "Sanity Code," it was designed to correct recruiting abuses. In addition, the NCAA created a Constitutional Compliance Committee, which was designed to interpret the new code and investigate violations.

The Constitutional Compliance Committee was replaced in 1951 by the Committee on Infractions. This committee was given broader investigative powers. In 1973, the NCAA membership voted to divide investigative and hearing duties so that the NCAA assumed investigation responsibilities and the Committee on Infractions handled hearings. This remains the basic structure of today's enforcement programs.

In response to increasing criticism of its enforcement procedures, the NCAA in the last few years has taken steps to improve its procedures. These steps have included expanding its staff of professional investigators (who are often former FBI agents) and interviewing highly recruited student-athletes in an attempt to uncover possible recruiting violations. Investigators attempt to develop close relationships with highly recruited "blue chip" student-athletes in hopes that the student-athlete will inform them of any illegal offers they receive from recruiters.

As a result of the "integrity crisis," the NCAA called a special summer convention in 1985 (only the fifth in its history) and enacted stronger enforcement and penalty procedures for member schools that violate NCAA regulations. The so-called "death penalty" includes suspension for an athletic team for as long as two seasons if it is found guilty of major NCAA rule infractions twice in a five-year period (retroactive to September 1980) and sanctions against student-athletes who knowingly violate NCAA rules.

Southern Methodist University (SMU), whose football program has been on probation six times—the most of any school in the United States—became the first victim of the death penalty in 1987. Since allegations of NCAA violations surfaced in November

1986, SMU's president, athletic director, and football coach have all resigned.

The NCAA also instituted mandatory reporting requirements for member institutions in regard to student-athlete academic progress and independent financial audits of athletic department budgets. As Dr. John W. Ryan, president of Indiana University and chairman of the NCAA's President's Commission, noted at the special convention that enacted the new enforcement rules, "the nation's presidents and chancellors are going to determine the direction and major policies of college athletics and . . . we are not going to condone any failure to comply with these policies."

In conjunction with the programs approved by the June 1985 NCAA special summer convention, the Executive Committee expanded the previous NCAA enforcement department and renamed it the Compliance and Enforcement Department. A compliance services staff has also been created to assist chief executive officers in compliance matters such as (1) questions and problems encountered in completing the self-study, financial audit, and academic-reporting requirements; (2) provision of compliance models in such key areas as financial aid, eligibility, and recruiting to assist member institutions in confronting problems that may arise; (3) organization of campus visitations to aid in analyzing the structure and administration of the athletics program; (4) assistance to member institutions that have been penalized under the association's enforcement procedures in correcting the problems that resulted in rules violations; and (5) cooperation with member conferences with full-time administrators in the development of conference compliance programs.

The new NCAA legislation also calls for an "institutional self-study to enhance integrity in intercollegiate athletics." Each member institution is required to undertake the self-study at least once every five years. By undertaking the candid self-examination, the chief executive officer and athletic administrators will be alerted to a broad spectrum of measurable indicators designed to minimize and perhaps eliminate the potential for rules violations.

The constitution also requires an annual independent financial audit to provide detailed information concerning revenues and expenditures for or on behalf of an intercollegiate athletic program, including funds received and expended by outside organizations in support of intercollegiate athletics. This requirement is designed to assist chief executive officers in determining the extent to which their athletic programs rely on outside financial support and in assuring that such support does not compromise the premise or the fact of institutional control.

An NCAA bylaw also requires of Division I members the compilation and reporting of data concerning admissions standards, the academic qualifications of entering recruited student-athletes, academic progress, and the graduation rate of student-athletes. All data are compiled across member institutions and then distributed to all Division I members to permit comparisons with similar institutions.

The key to the NCAA investigative process is the cooperative principle, whereby the accused member institution and the NCAA's enforcement staff work together to ascertain the truth of alleged infractions. An NCAA enforcement program consists of the following six steps:

1. *A preliminary inquiry.* A preliminary inquiry is initiated by the NCAA enforcement staff if alleged violations seem serious and plausible. A preliminary inquiry letter notifies the school that enforcement staff members will be on campus in the near future investigating alleged infractions of the NCAA's rules. This preliminary inquiry letter does not specify the nature of the allegations. In response to a school's request for further information, allegations will be made specific as to time, place, and personnel; however, at no time will the source of these allegations be revealed. In some cases the source becomes obvious and may involve one of the school's own student-athletes. Additional sources of information are other institutions and coaches.

If the preliminary inquiry indicates that allegations of wrongdoing may be valid, the enforcement staff will elect either to deal with the issue using a summary procedure before the Committee on Infractions or undertake an official inquiry.

2. *Official inquiry (OI).* An official inquiry is authorized by the NCAA's Committee on Infractions based on the results of the enforcement staff's preliminary inquiry. The OI is primarily a second letter to the institution listing specific allegations of infractions and directing the school, under obligation of NCAA membership, to conduct its own investigation immediately. Initially, the school has 60 days to respond, although extensions are frequently granted.

The OI breaks down into three parts: the overture, the allegations, and the coda. The *overture* consists of four questions requesting information about how the athletic programs are organized and administered at the accused institution. The *allegations*, the heart of the OI, list the specific charges. They also cite the rules that have been violated and identify those believed to be involved. An allegation might take the following form:

It is alleged that in January 1979, through the arrangements of head football coach Neils Thompson, student-athlete Charles Wright re-

ceived the benefit of one-way commercial airline transportation at
no cost to him between Ardmore, Pennsylvania, and Austin, Texas,
in order to travel to the University following a visit to his home.
Please indicate whether this information is substantially correct and
submit evidence to support your response.

Also provide the following:

a. The actual date of this transportation.
b. The reasons Wright was provided commercial airline transportation at no personal expense to him on this occasion.
c. A statement indicating the actual cost of this transportation and
   the source of funds utilized to pay the resultant cost.
d. The identity of all athletic department staff members involved
   in or knowledgeable of these arrangements for Wright, and a
   description of such involvement or knowledge prior to, at the
   time of, and subsequent to this trip.

There may be one or many of these allegations. They can name
student-athletes, potential recruits, coaches, alumni, and boosters.

The *coda*, the third part of an OI, is directed at the president of
the institution. Since 1974, the NCAA has required the chief
executive officer of each member institution to certify through a
signed statement that the institution is complying with NCAA
rules. In addition, since 1975, all members of an institution's
athletic department staff have been required to sign a statement
that they have reported their knowledge of and involvement in any
violation of NCAA legislation. Both of these statements—the institutional and the athletic department certifications of compliance—
comprise the coda.

The NCAA has a gag rule in effect on its involvement in an
investigation. It remains in effect throughout the entire procedure
(see *1987–88 NCAA Manual*, Enforcement, section 11). The NCAA
will not even comment on the existence of an investigation unless
it is in response to information released by the institution (see
1987–88 NCAA Manual, Enforcement, section 12-[a]-[15]).

The enforcement procedures also provide that the NCAA's
primary investigator will be available to meet with the institution
to discuss the development of its response and to assist in the case
(see *1987–88 NCAA Manual*, Enforcement 12-[a]-[14]). The two
parties attempt to reach agreement on certain facts of the case in
order to streamline the hearing process. Statements of persons
interviewed on behalf of the institution by the NCAA investigator
will be presented as part of the institution's response to the OI.

The institution must then carry out its own investigation and
draft its response to the NCAA allegations. This response, which
may be hundreds of pages long, is sent to the NCAA and to the
members of the Committee on Infractions.

3. *Committee on Infractions hearings.* Committee on Infractions hearings are usually held at the NCAA offices in Mission, Kansas. These meetings are closed and confidential. Present at the hearings are members of the Committee on Infractions, the delegation from the institution, and the NCAA enforcement staff members. The procedure begins with opening statements by a spokesperson from the institution, often an attorney, who is then followed by a spokesperson for the enforcement staff. These opening statements express the overall position of the university and of the enforcement staff. The heart of the official inquiry is a detailed review of the allegations, which includes determining which allegations are and are not in dispute. The enforcement staff presents all evidence it has, regardless of whether it supports or refutes the allegations. The institution's spokesperson then responds and may wish to refer to or add to the school's written response. This is an informal procedure, with frequent verbal exchanges between committee members and the university. Rigid rules of evidence are not enforced at these hearings, which may proceed for several days until all allegations have been covered. After the closing statements, the chairman of the committee advises the university of the next steps in the case, including the university's opportunity to appeal to the NCAA Council if it is dissatisfied with the committee's findings, its penalty, or both. Following this, the hearing is adjourned.

4. *Findings.* Findings are made after the members of the Committee on Infractions have deliberated over the case on an individual basis, reviewing each allegation. Sometimes additional information is needed, often from previous cases. The NCAA has charged the committee to base its findings on information it determines to be "credible, persuasive and of a kind on which reasonably prudent persons rely on in the conduct of serious affairs" (*1987–88 NCAA Manual,* Enforcement, section 4-[b]-[2]). Once the members of the committee reach a consensus, all findings are compiled into a confidential report. The report is then sent to the institution's president.

5. *Penalties.* If warranted, penalties are included in the Committee on Infraction's final report. These may include prohibiting an institution's team or teams from television appearances, taking away athletic scholarships, and barring teams from postseason play. Such actions are often referred to as being put on probation. There is a trend toward making individual coaches accountable when rule violations are discovered. Possible penalties may include freezing salary levels, limiting expense accounts, and restricting recruitment travel. At its 1983 convention, the NCAA passed a requirement that all coaches' contracts include a stipulation that the coach

can be suspended without pay or fired if he or she is involved in "deliberate and serious violations of NCAA regulations." The proposal was submitted by the College Football Association and was sponsored by Georgia, Nebraska, North Carolina, Penn State, Rutgers, and Tulane.

In some cases when violations are deemed to be less severe, the penalty imposed by the NCAA may take the form of a private reproach.

6. *Appeal (optional)*. An institution has an automatic right of appeal to the NCAA Council. It is heard "de novo"—that is, the matter is heard as if for the first time. The Council can reverse, expand, contract, or completely change the finding of the Infractions Committee. The option of appealing to the courts also remains.

After the appeals process has been exhausted, the NCAA will issue a press release announcing any allegations found to be true and what penalties have been imposed (see *1987–88 NCAA Manual*, Enforcement 12-[f]).

NOTES

1. For a case that examines the NCAA enforcement procedures, see *Trustees of the State Colleges and Universities v. National Collegiate Athletic Ass'n*, 82 Cal. App. 3d 451, 147 Cal. Rptr. 187 (Ct. App. 1978). Although a university's NCAA appeal involved only the penalty imposed and not the findings for an alleged failure to comply with a decision regarding the eligibility of two student-athletes, this did not bar relief on the grounds of failure to exhaust administrative remedies. The court's reasoning was that the internal appeal presented all circumstances of the university's reliance on a letter of the executive director of the NCAA and afforded the NCAA full opportunity to review the merits of its proposed disciplinary action in light thereof.

2. For a critical analysis of the NCAA's enforcement procedures, see *Enforcement Program of the National Collegiate Athletic Association: A Report Together with Minority Views* by the Subcommittee on Oversight and Investigations of the Committee on Interstate and Foreign Commerce, House of Representatives, Ninety-Fifth Congress, Second Session, December 1978 (Washington, D.C.: U.S. Government Printing Office, 1978). (See Committee Print 95–69.)

3. For further information of association enforcement authority, see the following law review articles:

(a) Wright, "Responding to an NCAA Investigation, or What to Do When an Official Inquiry Comes," *Entertainment and Sports Law Journal*, vol. 1, no. 1 (Spring 1984), pp. 19–33.

(b) "The NCAA: Fundamental Fairness and the Enforcement Program," 23 *Arizona Law Review* 1065 (1981).

(c) "The Enforcement Procedures of the NCAA: An Abuse of the

Student-Athlete's Right to Reasonable Discovery," *Arizona State Law Review* 133 (1982).

(d) Remington, "NCAA Enforcement Procedures Including the Role of the Committee on Infractions," 10 *Journal of College and University Law* (1983–84).

4. In the National Association of Intercollegiate Athletics (NAIA), procedures for rules infractions are much simpler than in the NCAA. Each of the NAIA's 32 districts has an eligibility committee, usually composed of faculty members of member association schools. Most infractions involve satisfaction of academic requirements or improper institution eligibility certificates. District officials settle most cases on that level, usually by asking for an explanation from the student-athlete or athletic director from the involved college. The district eligibility committee (three members) then makes a recommendation to a national panel, which makes its decision to the NAIA's executive committee. Standard penalties include forfeiture of games, loss of student-athlete's eligibility, and probation and suspension of athletic programs from participation in NAIA competition.

Chapter 5

THE AMATEUR ATHLETE

INTRODUCTION

The athletic associations define "amateur athlete" and then interpret and enforce the definitions (see Chapter 4), but the rules and regulations are what most directly impact the student-athlete and are the subject of this chapter. Chapter 5 first discusses individual eligibility requirements for the student-athlete. Many of the requirements, such as academic progress, redshirting, and pay, are problems and thus the NCAA is often used as an example. However, other eligibility requirements—grade point average, transfer rules, scholarship and financial aid, and professional contracts—concern college, high school, and other amateur athletes.

Although this chapter primarily examines individual eligibility requirements for participation at the high school and college level, a brief section is devoted to the eligibility requirements for Olympic competition. The significance of this topic is not confined to the Olympic arena, because participation in Olympic competition may affect a student-athlete's participation in interscholastic or intercollegiate competition.

The next major section of Chapter 5 covers freedom of expression, hair length, rules relating to high school marriages, and alcohol and drug rules. It focuses on the coach-athlete relationship in high schools and colleges. The courts have attempted to balance the rights of the individual student-athlete with the right of the coach to instruct and supervise the student-athlete.

In some cases, student-athletes do not always meet the individual eligibility requirements that are established for them by high school and college amateur athletic conferences and associations. Student-athletes may knowingly or unknowingly violate eligibility rules and regulations, and it is the responsibility of the institution and/or governing athletic association to take appropriate disciplinary action. The next section of Chapter 5 examines the penalties or sanctions levied against the student-athlete, and in some cases the institution. These penalties and sanctions may be reviewed by the courts if the student-athlete challenges the decision.

Of course, before a student-athlete can be disciplined, a violation must be found. At the collegiate level, the NCAA has established an enforcement program designed to produce compliance with its complex set of rules and regulations—the next topic of Chapter 5. The chapter then discusses the Buckley Amendment. Athletic administrators should be aware of the Buckley Amendment and its restrictions because the investigation of alleged violations may require review of student-athletes' records.

The final sections of this chapter involve two areas in which student-athletes have brought lawsuits against their high schools and colleges. Both of these areas—failure to provide an education and participation in summer camps and on independent teams—portray activities that exist on the perimeter of the amateur athletic sphere but still remain within the realm of high school and college athletic governance.

INDIVIDUAL ELIGIBILITY REQUIREMENTS: COLLEGE AND HIGH SCHOOL

For athletic administrators individual eligibility requirements are a major area of concern because they impact both the student-athlete and the institution. For instance, intercollegiate athletics, primarily football and basketball, may be financially lucrative and lead to career advancement for the individual. The monetary rewards to the institution are also great for the successful programs. To capture these financial benefits, there are several different ways an athletic department can be set up. Some departments operate under the university budget, with revenues going directly to the general fund and expenses covered as line items; others are operated like businesses; still others are separately incorporated and are responsible for covering the expenses of the department solely with revenues taken in by the department. As football and basketball have become more lucrative, the stakes in intercollegiate athletics have become higher, and the pressure to be successful and to attract the top-notch student-athlete has increased. Consequently, athletic excellence has been pursued in several instances at the expense of academic performance. College and high school athletic associations have tried to address this problem by establishing academic eligibility requirements. The grade point average requirement is one method used by the NCAA to ensure that entering student-athletes are academically qualified to participate. The grade point average is also used by some conferences to prevent participation while the student-athlete is enrolled at the university or the high school.

Rules regarding grade point average requirements have been subject to judicial review. One issue the courts have faced is the type of courses to be included in the computation of the grade point average. For example, should physical education courses involving athletic skills be included? One question is whether each university or high school should be allowed to compute grade point averages according to its own guidelines or whether the computation should be standardized according to rules promulgated by athletic associations.

The NCAA passed a controversial rule in 1983 requiring that an incoming freshman student-athlete achieve both a certain grade point average and certain scores on standardized examinations (SATs and ACTs). Although the rule went into effect in August 1986, several universities whose enrollments have historically been composed of black students have discussed challenging the rule.

A second individual eligibility requirement used by the NCAA is the rule requiring sufficient academic progress by the student-athlete. The rule was promulgated when it was discovered that a number of student-athletes maintained their eligibility with respect to grade point average by taking introductory level courses in a number of areas in the university. While this strategy enabled the student-athletes to maintain academic eligibility in accordance with grade point average requirements, it oftentimes left the student three or four semesters short of graduation after the individual's playing eligibility expired, because many upper-level course requirements in the student-athlete's major had not been fulfilled before athletic eligibility and scholarship funds ceased. Interestingly, the NCAA is not the only organization to have promulgated academic progress rules; many individual intercollegiate and interscholastic conferences have also instituted such rules—several of them more rigorous than the NCAA rules.

The third eligibility requirement deals with transfer rules that place restrictions on certain student-athletes who transfer from one school to another. The reasons behind the transfer rules are twofold: first, to discourage coaches from recruiting student-athletes who are enrolled in another school; and second, to prevent student-athletes from jumping from school to school primarily for athletic reasons. Many transfer student-athletes have sued their high school or college athletic associations in an attempt to obtain immediate playing eligibility at their new school. The result of such litigation is that many amateur athletic associations have redefined transfer rules more narrowly. While the revised rules may still be overinclusive in that the rule makes ineligible certain student-athletes who were not recruited and who did not transfer for athletic reasons, they usually allow immediate athletic eligibility for student-athletes who meet certain objective criteria.

The fourth individual eligibility requirement is the practice of redshirting. "Redshirting" is a term used to describe the practice of extending the playing career of a student-athlete by postponing or passing over a year of interscholastic or intercollegiate participation while not affecting the student-athlete's maximum allowable time for participating in high school or college athletics. The reasons for redshirting are varied and include medical, academic, and coaching factors. Many of the legal challenges on the intercollegiate level deal with situations in which the student-athlete is requesting either an additional year or a hardship year in a season in which he or she has already participated to some degree (less than 20 percent of the season).

The fifth area of individual eligibility requirements concerns financial considerations for the NCAA student-athlete. The NCAA has promulgated guidelines concerning scholarships and financial aid and pay. If the university is found to be in violation of any of these rules, it may forfeit games and/or face NCAA sanctions and penalties. On the other hand, the student-athlete who has violated the rules may be ruled ineligible for NCAA competition by the university or the NCAA. Furthermore, violations of certain NCAA rules while the student-athlete was in high school can make the student-athlete ineligible when he or she is in college. For example, the student-athlete who is deemed to have received pay from a professional team is considered a professional and will no longer be eligible for intercollegiate athletics in that particular sport. If a student-athlete participates in NCAA games after receipt of money from a professional team, the NCAA may ask the university to forfeit those games. Thus, it becomes very important for the athletic administrator to police the program in order to escape potential association sanctions and to maintain the eligibility of the student-athlete.

A key legal issue with respect to athletic scholarships is whether they are to be construed as contracts. The ramifications of a determination that the athletic scholarship is an employment contract are potentially great: the value of the scholarship becomes taxable income for the student-athlete, and as a result of receiving income, the student-athlete may no longer be deemed an amateur athlete in accordance with NCAA regulations. In addition, the student-athlete may be eligible for workers' compensation benefits, and the university athletic departments may be responsible for obtaining workers' compensation insurance.

The sixth individual eligibility requirement deals with student-athletes who have signed professional contracts. In addition to the aforementioned increased stake in a successful intercollegiate athletic program, there has been a concomitant rise in professional sports salaries. Larger television contracts, cable television, increased attendance, increased ticket prices, and competing leagues have all contributed to the pressure of placing a successful professional team on the field while leading to increased salaries. Therefore, the teams, leagues, and player agents who compete for these athletes may sign or attempt to sign the student-athletes before their college eligibility has expired. This practice may be in violation of the NCAA rules governing amateurism, since the student-athlete, at the time of commitment, in effect becomes a paid professional. (See Chapter 11 for a discussion of professional careers, drafts, contracts, and player representatives.)

The seventh individual eligibility requirement deals with player agents (see Chapter 11). The representation of these athletes has become a very lucrative area, and the competition among player agents for student-athletes has become extremely intense. As a result, some player agents are signing student-athletes before their intercollegiate eligibility has expired, thus rendering them ineligible for future NCAA competition and possibly causing forfeiture of past school victories and/or loss of financial receipts from NCAA-sponsored championships.

Many standards must be maintained by individual student-athletes in order for them to be eligible for intercollegiate and interscholastic practice and/or competition. Each school, conference, or association such as the NCAA has rules and regulations that extend its authority to various areas surrounding sports activities. For collegiate and high school student-athletes there are usually academic standards, rules governing personal conduct, and rules for each individual sport. Individual institutions on the collegiate and scholastic level may also establish eligibility requirements that are stricter than the minimum standards imposed by that institution's conference or association. In addition, a conference may impose a stricter rule than its association.

Under a principle called "institutional control," it is the institution's responsibility to determine which of its student-athletes meet, and do not meet, the eligibility standards. The process of determining eligibility for each student-athlete may be very time-consuming for an institution's athletic department, depending on the number of student-athletes participating, the number of sports offered by the institution, and the complexity of institutional, conference, and association rules, regulations, and interpretations.

In some cases, an institution's conference may assist member institutions in keeping track of the eligibility status of every student-athlete. The most a conference might do in this area is to recheck, confirm, and correct, when necessary, all institutional information. Conferences may aid in the complex process of eligibility determination because correct eligibility status may be the best, if not the first, preventative to rules violations.

An institution's athletic association is usually the primary governing body, and it is responsible for enforcing the rules and regulations relative to the eligibility of student-athletes. Penalties or sanctions may be levied against a student-athlete and the team and/or institution for knowingly or unknowingly competing in spite of the student-athlete's ineligible status. In addition to enforcement, college and high school athletic associations recommend changes in rules, make policy decisions, and render interpretations of the eligibility rules and regulations.

Eligibility rules that are enacted by a college or high school athletic association are instituted to protect student-athletes and institutions and to promote amateur athletics. Consistent with these objectives, individual eligibility requirements are established with regard to grade point average, academic progress, transferring, age restrictions, years of athletic participation, professional pay, drug use, and full-time student status among others.

Florida State University, in response to allegations of NCAA violations, examined many of these areas in a 1984 report entitled, "Student Athletes at the Florida State University: Planning Responsibility." In part, the report noted the following:

> This report is concerned with institutional responsibility. The word responsibility is a moral term. Basic to any moral understanding of responsibility, institutional or otherwise, is the question, "To whom or to what are we responsible?" We assume that the officers, faculty and staff of the Florida State University are primarily responsible to their respective academic disciplines and professional communities, to their students, to the people of Florida through their elected and appointed representatives, and to others whose welfare is affected by their policies and performance.
>
> The primary responsibilities of the University community are academic research, teaching, and service. All other responsibilities are secondary. The educational mission at Florida State is the unifying cause to which we are loyal, and all other activities must be ordered under this primary loyalty. It is from this primary commitment that we should view our participation in intercollegiate sports.
>
> Contemporary intercollegiate sport, played at Division I-A level, is characterized by specialization, commercialization, and bureaucratic organization. Sport participation makes increasingly totalistic claims on the student-athlete's life. Florida State currently has 388 young women and men who are participating in varsity athletics. Our student-athletes are receiving $1,113,600.00 in scholarship aid. The athletic budget for the academic year 1983–84 is $7,121,988.00.
>
> Concern has been expressed from a variety of sources that programs of such size can virtually become autonomous units, thus subverting the University's primary mission. There is an increasing demand for assurance that the faculty and administration are in control of the non-athletic dimension of the student-athlete's university experience and that neither institutional nor academic integrity are compromised.
>
> Our work has required that we address the following questions: (1) What is Florida State's responsibility to student-athletes? (2)

How are we presently meeting this responsibility? (3) What changes need to be made with regard to policies toward student-athletes?

This report concludes that educational institutions have a responsibility to their students, student-athletes, and members of the surrounding community to fulfill their educational mission. Because athletics can, for some individuals, tend to distract them from educational goals, rules and regulations regarding grade point averages, academic progress, and transferring have become necessary tools for the institutions and athletic organizations involved to adhere to the educational mission.

NOTES ————————————————————————————————————

1. For further information, see the following law review article: "Administration of Amateur Athletics: The Time for an Amateur Athlete's Bill of Rights Has Arrived," 48 *Fordham Law Review* 53 (1979). The article argues that the Amateur Sports Act of 1978 fails to provide adequate protection for the interests of student-athletes. The background describes the relevant athletic organizations and federal legislative involvement, including the 1978 Act and the Amateur Athletic Act of 1974. A discussion of judicial intervention in sports cases suggests that participation is a constitutional right that, because it is not recognized by the courts, should be codified by Congress. The appendix to this article offers suggested legislation.

2. For further information, see the following law review articles:

   (a) "Collegiate Athletic Participation: A Property or Liberty Interest?" 15 *Pacific Law Review* 1203 (July 1984).

   (b) Waicukauski, "The Regulation of Academic Standards in Intercollegiate Athletics," 1982 *Arizona State Law Journal* 79 (1982).

   (c) "Judicial Review of NCAA Decisions: Does the College Athlete Have a Property Interest in Interscholastic Athletics?" 10 *Stetson Law Review* 483 (1981).

   (d) Springer, "A Student-Athlete's Interest in Eligibility: Its Context and Constitutional Dimensions," 10 *Connecticut Law Review* 318 (1977).

   (e) "Judicial Review of Disputes Between Athletes and the National Collegiate Athletic Association," 24 *Stanford Law Review* 903 (1972).

3. See Exhibit 5–1 for the NCAA form for the student-athlete statement of eligibility.

4. See Exhibit 5–2 for an example of a form used by a conference for determining eligibility.

Grade Point Average

The grade point average, or GPA, has long been used and recognized as a measure of a student's academic achievement. To compute a student's GPA, each letter grade in a course is converted to the 4.000 scale (A = 4, B = 3, C = 2, D = 1, F = 0). If a different number of credits are issued for some of the courses, the letter grades and resulting grade points must be weighted according to the proportion of credits issued in the course to the number of credits granted for a normal course. The points are then totaled for the courses to be included in the computation, and that total is divided by the number of courses. A student's GPA is usually calculated for each academic term, each year, and cumulatively for the student's entire high school or college career. The method and the subjects to be considered in the computation of a student's GPA vary from school to school.

In an attempt to guarantee academic achievement for their student-athletes, a number of high schools have adopted grade point average standards. These rules serve the dual purpose of assuring that their student-athletes make sufficient academic progress during high school and that they are eligible for participation in intercollegiate athletics as incoming freshmen. It is important to realize that this dual purpose contains two separate requirements, since freshman intercollegiate eligibility in the NCAA is dependent on both standardized test scores and grade point average.

Certain states have proposed or established academic standards governing eligibility for high school sports and other extracurricular activities. Texas legislators in 1985, for example, passed such a "no pass, no play" rule requiring all students involved in extracurricular activities to maintain a minimum grade of 70 in each class to retain eligibility. A score below 70 during a six-week grading period will result in ineligibility during the next six-week grading period. The state association in Tennessee has proposed increasing the number of subjects passed from four to five, and Mississippi has considered changing to a Texas-like law requiring a C-average. Exhibit 5–3 is a state-by-state summary of academic requirements for high school athletes.

The courts have generally upheld "no pass, no play" rules as students have been found to have no right or property interest in participating in extracurricular activities. For instance, in 1986 the U.S. Supreme Court refused to hear a challenge to the Texas law citing the lack of a federal question. It thus allowed to stand the Texas court decision upholding the law. Extracurricular activities are defined to include all those activities for students that are sponsored or sanctioned by an educational institution that supplement or complement, but are not a part of, the institution's required academic program or regular curriculum. Consequently, the courts have usually reasoned that participation is a privilege which may be granted or withdrawn at the discretion of the school

Form 87-3   Academic Year 1987-88
Student-Athlete Statement

For: All student-athletes
Action: Sign and return to your director of athletics
Due date: Before you first compete each year
Required by: NCAA Constitution 3-9-(i) and 4-2-(f)
Purpose: To assist in certifying eligibility

To Student-Athlete

Name of your institution: _____

This form has three parts: a statement concerning eligibility, a Buckley
Amendment consent and a drug-testing consent. You must sign all three
parts to participate in intercollegiate competition.

Before you sign this form, you should read the Summary of NCAA Regulations provided by your director of athletics or read the sections of the
NCAA Manual that deal with your eligibility. If you have any questions,
you should discuss them with your director of athletics.

The conditions that you must meet to be eligible and the requirement that
you sign this form are spelled out in the following sections of the NCAA
Manual:

- Sections 3-1, 3-3, 3-4, 3-6 and 3-9 of the NCAA Constitution
- Sections 1-1, 1-2, 1-4, 1-5, 1-6, 1-7, 1-9, 1-10, 4-1, 5-1, 5-2 and 5-6 of the
  NCAA Bylaws
- Section 7 of NCAA Executive Regulation 1

Part I: Statement Concerning Eligibility

By signing this part of the form, you affirm that, to the best of your knowledge, you are eligible to compete in intercollegiate competition.

You affirm that you have read the Summary of NCAA Regulations or the
relevant sections of the NCAA Manual, and that your director of athletics
gave you the opportunity to ask questions about them.

You affirm that you meet the NCAA regulations for student-athletes regarding eligibility, recruitment, financial aid, amateur status and involvement in organized gambling.

You affirm that you have reported to the director of athletics of your
institution any violations of NCAA regulations involving you and your
institution.

You affirm that you understand that if you sign this statement falsely or
erroneously, you violate NCAA legislation on ethical conduct and you
will further jeopardize your eligibility.

_____   _____
Date   Signature of student-athlete

                                 _____
                                 Home address

                                 _____

Exhibit 5-1 NCAA Form for Student-Athlete Eligibility *Source*: National
Collegiate Athletic Association.

Part II: Buckley Amendment Consent

By signing this part of the form, you certify that you agree to disclose your education records.

You understand that this entire form and the results of any NCAA drug test you may take are part of your education records. These records are protected by the Family Educational Rights and Privacy Act of 1974, and they may not be disclosed without your consent.

You give your consent to disclose only to authorized representatives of this institution, its athletics conference (if any) and the NCAA, the following documents:

- this form
- results of NCAA drug tests
- any transcript from your high school, this institution, or any junior college or any other four-year institutions you have attended
- records concerning your financial aid
- any other papers or information obtained by this institution pertaining to your NCAA eligibility

You agree to disclose these records only to determine your eligibility for intercollegiate athletics, your recruitment by this institution and your eligibility for athletically-related financial aid.

_____   _____
Date   Signature of student-athlete

Part III: Drug-Testing Consent

By signing this part of the form, you certify that you agree to be tested for drugs.

You agree to allow the NCAA, during this academic year, before, during or after you participate in any NCAA championship or in any postseason football game certified by the NCAA, to test you for the banned drugs listed in Executive Regulation 1-7-(b) in the NCAA Manual.

You reviewed the procedures for NCAA drug testing that are described in the NCAA Drug-Testing Program Brochure.

You understand that if you test positive (the NCAA finds traces of any of the banned drugs in your body), you will be ineligible to participate in postseason competition for at least 90 days.

If you test positive and lose eligibility for 90 days, and then test positive again after your eligibility is restored, you will lose postseason eligibility in all sports for the current and the next academic year.

You understand that this consent and the results of your drug tests, if any, will only be disclosed in accordance with the Buckley Amendment consent.

_____   _____
Date   Signature of student-athlete

_____   _____
Date   Signature of parent if the student-athlete is a
                                minor

What to do with this form: Sign and return it to your director of athletics before you first compete.

NCAA, P.O. Box 1906, Mission, KS 66201   913/384-3220

Exhibit 5-1   Continued

Name _____ University _____

Home Town and State _____ Date _____

Date of Birth _____ Social Security Number _____
                                 School Year
Sport _____ of Residence _____

Course of Study _____

Date of Entrance   Date of First Entrance
At This University _____ at Any College or University _____

Number of Previous Seasons of
Competition Here _____ Elsewhere _____

---

1. Have you ever registered in, enrolled in or attended any classes in any other college, university, junior college, or any other institution above high school grade, or practiced or competed in any varsity or varsity reserve intercollegiate athletic contest?

(IF SO, STATE NAME OF SCHOOL, DATES, YEARS OF VARSITY INTERCOL-
LEGIATE COMPETITION, ETC.)

2. Have you ever participated as an individual or as a representative of any team in organized competition in a sport after your 20th birthday and prior to entrance at an NCAA institution?

(IF SO, STATE SPORT, NAME OF TEAM OR TOURNAMENT, DATES, ETC.)

3. Have you ever used, directly or indirectly, your skill in your sport for financial gain?

(IF SO, STATE NAME OF ORGANIZATION AWARDING FINANCIAL GAIN,
ADDRESS, DATE, AMOUNT, SPORT, ETC.)

4. Have you ever taken part in an athletic contest in your sport in which a money prize was offered (regardless of the disposition of this prize), or received expense money based upon meet results?

(IF SO, STATE SPORT, NAME OF TEAM, ADDRESS, DATES, OFFERING
ORGANIZATION, AMOUNT OF PRIZE)

5. Have ever received any remuneration for participating in an athletic contest in your sport (excluding expenses actually incurred as a partic-ipant or reasonable salary for services actually rendered on a job)?

(IF SO, STATE SOURCE, ADDRESS, DATE, AMOUNT, TYPE OF CONTEST
SPORT, ETC.)

6. Have you ever lent your name to any form of commercial advertising?

(IF SO, STATE NAME OF COMPANY OR ORGANIZATION, TYPE OF ADVER-
TISING, AMOUNT RECEIVED, DATE, ETC.)

Exhibit 5-2 Collegiate Conference Form for Student-Athlete Eligibility
Source: Big Ten Conference.

7. Have you ever signed a professional athletic contract in your sport, or been represented by an agent?

(IF SO, STATE NAME OF TEAM OR AGENT, ADDRESS, DATE, SPORT, ETC.)

8. Have you ever played in any game under an assumed name? _____

9. Have you since entering this university participated in any athletic contest, other than during summer vacations, as a representative of any team or organization other than this university?

(IF SO, STATE SPORT, NAME OF TEAM, ADDRESS, DATES, ETC.)

10. Did you play organized basketball last summer?

(IF SO, STATE NAME OF TEAM, ADDRESS, NAME OF LEAGUE, PRIZES OR AWARDS RECEIVED, SITES OF TOURNAMENTS, ETC.)

11. Did you, after completion of your high school eligibility in your sport and before graduation from high school, participate in any All Star football or men's basketball games?

(IF SO, STATE SPORT, CITY AND STATE, SPONSOR, DATES, ETC.)

12. Did you, after graduation from high school, and before entering college, participate in any All Star football or men's basketball games?

(IF SO, STATE SPORT, CITY AND STATE, SPONSOR, DATES, ETC.)

I certify, upon penalty of ineligibility for intercollegiate athletics, that the above statements are complete and accurate.

(Signed) _____

(Signed) _____ (Approved) _____
COACH   FOR FACULTY
                               COMMITTEE

Exhibit 5-2 Continued

board. The board, furthermore, has the discretion to set the qualifications necessary for students to participate when participation in extracurricular activities is considered a privilege. In reviewing such eligibility requirements, the courts will not consider whether the qualifications are wise or expedient, but only whether they are a reasonable exercise of the power and discretion of the board. As a general rule, eligibility requirements will be upheld if they are rationally related to the purpose of the extracurricular activity involved and are not arbitrary, capricious, or unjustly discriminatory. Also, as previously mentioned, a student-athlete's high school grade point average is also important for participation in intercollegiate athletics.

To represent an institution in NCAA intercollegiate athletics, a

A state-by-state summary of academic requirements for high school athletes. School districts and individual schools may have tougher standards. How credits are computed varies from state to state.

ALA.: Must pass four units in previous year.

ALASKA: Must pass four subjects in previous semester and be enrolled in four in current semester.

ARIZ.: Must pass four classes in previous semester.

ARK.: Must pass three full-credit courses in previous semester (four next year).

CALIF.: Must pass 20 credits in previous semester and be enrolled in 20 credits in current semester.

COLO.: Must not fail more than one class in previous semester.

CONN.: Must pass four subjects in previous semester.

DEL.: Must pass at least four courses in previous marking period, including two in science, math, English or social studies.

D.C.: Must pass four credits in previous semester.

FLA.: Requires 1.5 GPA on 4.0 scale in previous semester.

GA.: Must pass four credit courses in previous semester and current semester. Next year: five.

HAWAII: One-year pilot program effective in September 1986 requires 2.0 grade-point average on 4.0 scale in previous semester.

IDAHO: Must pass five classes in previous semester.

ILL.: Must pass 20 credit hours in previous semester. Weekly certification of passing work in 20 credit hours in current semester.

IND.: Must pass four full-credit subjects in previous semester.

IOWA: Must pass three courses in previous semester. Next year: four.

KAN.: Must pass five subjects in previous semester.

KY.: Must pass four classes in previous semester, and weekly certification in current semester.

LA.: Must pass five subjects, have 1.5 grade-point average on 4.0 scale in previous semester.

MAINE: No statewide requirement.

MD.: No statewide requirement.

MASS.: Must pass 20 credits each term.

MICH.: Must pass 20 credits in previous and current semesters.

MINN.: No statewide requirement.

MISS.: Must pass three major subjects (English, math, science, social studies) to be eligible following year.

MO.: Must pass four full-credit courses in previous semester.

MONT.: Must pass four credit courses in previous semester.

NEB.: Must pass 15 credit hours in previous semester.

NEV.: Must be enrolled in four courses and may not be failing any course while playing sports.

N.H.: Must pass three credits in previous period.

N.J.: Must pass 23 credit hours in previous year. Need 11.5 credits from the previous semester for second semester.

N.M.: Must pass four courses and have a 1.60 on a 4.0 scale in previous grading period.

N.Y.: No statewide requirement.

N.C.: Must pass four courses and have 75 percent attendance in previous semester.

N.D.: Must pass 15 credit hours in previous semester.

Exhibit 5-3 State Academic Standards Governing Eligibility for High School Athletics *Source: U.S.A. Today,* March 13, 1986, p. C8.

OHIO: Must pass four full-credit courses in previous grading period.

OKLA.: Must pass three full-credit course in previous semester.

ORE.: Must pass at least four subjects in previous semester.

PA.: Must pass three full-credit courses in previous marking period (four next year).

R.I.: Must pass three academic subjects, excluding physical education, in previous marking period.

S.C.: Must pass all required courses in previous semester.

S.D.: Must pass 20 hours in previous semester.

TENN.: Must pass four subjects in previous semester.

TEXAS: Must maintain grade of 70 in each class during six-week grading period to stay eligible for next six-week period.

UTAH: Must not fail more than one class in a grading period and must make up failing grade following semester.

VT.: No statewide requirement.

VA.: Must pass four subjects in previous semester.

WASH.: Must pass four full-credit subjects in previous semester.

W.VA.: Must have C average in previous semester.

WIS.: Must pass four full-credit courses in previous grading period.

WYO.: Must pass four full-credit subjects in previous semester and be passing in current semester.

Exhibit 5-3 Continued

student-athlete must be admitted in accordance with the university's regular admissions standards. Additionally, to be eligible for intercollegiate participation and athletic financial aid for the first academic year, the student-athlete must graduate from high school with a 2.0 average in a core curriculum of at least 11 academic courses. Those courses must include at least three years in English, two years in mathematics, two years in social science, and two years in natural or physical science (including at least one laboratory class, if offered by the high school). In addition, the student-athlete must score a minimum SAT score of 700 or ACT score of 15. Sliding scales are in effect until August 1, 1988, which allow a deficient score on either the GPA or the SAT/ACT to be offset by a score above the minimum on the other. The GPA and test score must be certified by the student-athlete's high school and verified by the NCAA member institution. (*1987–88 NCAA Manual*, Bylaw 5-1-[j]).

An incoming freshman who was actively recruited but did not satisfy the minimum 2.0 core grade point average and standardized test score would be ineligible for athletic financial aid, regular season competition, and practice for one academic year (*1987–88 NCAA Manual*, Bylaw 5-1-[j-[2]). Even if not recruited, the student-athlete would be ineligible for one academic year if he or she was not a 2.0 qualifier. A freshman student-athlete who fails to meet the core requirements will only have three years of athletic eligibility remaining. The student-athlete cannot practice or compete during the freshman year. During that year, the student must satisfactorily complete a minimum of 24 academic credits to be considered eligible for participation the following year (*1987–88 NCAA Manual*, Bylaw 5-1-[j]-[6]-[ii]).

A nonrecruited student-athlete who is a 2.0 nonqualifier can receive a nonathletic financial aid award (*1987–88 NCAA Manual*, Bylaw 5-1-[j]-[3]). The minimum of a 2.0 qualifier merely attempts to ensure the principle of amateurism by restricting college sports to student-athletes prepared to attend college. This principle is continued in requiring student-athletes to complete satisfactorily, stipulated credit hours in a semester and academic year.

There are two special situations in which a student-athlete's high school grades are considered differently for admission to college. The first situation involves the student-athlete who does not graduate from high school before entering a junior college. Under this circumstance, the student's junior college course grades cannot be calculated in the student's high school GPA for purposes of meeting the NCAA core requirement for freshmen, even though the junior college courses transfer to the student-athlete's high school record and satisfy requirements toward high school graduation. Upon matriculation at a four-year NCAA member institution, the student-athlete is considered a junior college transfer as opposed to a freshman. The prospective student-athlete must then meet the transfer requirement that applies to junior college transfer student-athletes who do not graduate from high school (any nonqualifiers) in order to be eligible to participate at a Division 1 institution during the first academic year in residence.

The second situation involves the student-athlete who does not graduate from high school but later obtains a state high school equivalency diploma by passing the General Educational Development (GED) test. The student-athlete's GED scores are treated as a substitute for the high school graduation and GPA. In this situation, the NCAA applies an NCAA-approved table that converts the average of the five GED scores to the high school GPA with two stipulations: (1) the scores have to have been obtained more than one calendar year from the date the student-athlete would have graduated had the student-athlete remained in high school, and (2) the student-athlete must not have graduated from high school (*1987–88 NCAA Manual*, Bylaw 5-6[b]).

An NCAA member institution can permit a student-athlete whose high school GPA and test scores have not been certified by the high school to practice, but not compete, for a maximum of two weeks. If the student-athlete's 2.00 GPA has not been certified after two weeks, the student-athlete is barred from both practice and competition. In those instances when a high school or preparatory school notifies the institution in writing that it will not provide the student-athlete's GPA or convert the GPA to a 4.00 scale, the NCAA member institution may submit the student-athlete's transcript to the NCAA Academic Testing and Requirements Committee for certification or conversion (*1987–88 NCAA Manual*, Bylaws 5-6-[b]-[1] and [2]).

A leading case in the area of academic requirements for intercollegiate participation is *Parish v. National Collegiate Athletic Ass'n*, 361 F. Supp. 1220 (W.D. La. 1973), *aff'd*, 506 F.2d 1028 (5th Cir. 1975). Parish and some fellow basketball players sought injunctive relief in this litigation to prevent member institutions from enforcing an NCAA rule that declared players ineligible if they did not predict a grade point average of 1.6 when entering college. (The 1.6 rule was the predecessor of the current 2.0 rule, and it was stricter.) The court held that the 1.6 rule limiting eligibility did not raise a federal question since there was no restriction of constitutional rights. The court ruled that judicial intervention was not required for a rule that was enacted and implemented by a private, voluntary organization. This case and several others indicate that courts will allow amateur athletic organizations to make reasonable rules relative to academic requirements.

NOTES

1. For cases in which academic requirements for *interscholastic* athletic participation were upheld, see *Bailey v. Truby* and *Myles v. Board of Education of the County of Kanawha*, 321 S.E.2d 302 (W. Va. 1984). The court stated that the State Board of Education's rule requiring a 2.000 grade point average for participation in nonacademic extracurricular activities was valid since the rule was a legitimate exercise of its power of "general supervision" over the state's educational system (*Bailey*). The Kanawha County Board of Education's rule requiring students to receive passing grades in all of their classes in order to participate in nonacademic extracurricular activities was also found to be valid (*Myles*). The county board was judged to have a legitimate concern in the encouragement of academic excellence, and regulation of such extracurricular activity was a common and accepted method of achieving that fundamental goal.

2. Academic requirements for *intercollegiate* athletic competition were upheld in the following cases.

(a) In *Ozell Jones v. Wichita State University*, 698 F.2d 1082 (10th Cir. 1983), Jones, a basketball player, sued Wichita State University (WSU) and the National Collegiate Athletic Association (NCAA), seeking to enjoin them from declaring him ineligible to practice and compete for the WSU varsity basketball team because of his failure to predict as a 2.0 qualifier. The court ruled that the NCAA "does not, and should not, tell the high schools what courses or curriculum they should utilize in figuring the GPA's of their own students" on the premise that the schools are in a better position to make this type of substantive determination.

(b) In *Associated Students Inc. v. National Collegiate Athletic Ass'n*, 493 F.2d 1251 (9th Cir. 1974), the court held that the purpose of the 1.6 GPA rule was to guarantee that only bona fide students would be eligible to participate in intercollegiate athletics in their first year, to help discourage recruiting violations, and to encourage weak students to concentrate on developing proper study skills prior to being involved in time-consuming intercollegiate athletics. The court found that the rule was reasonably related to its purposes, even as applied to students who had earned a 1.6 GPA after the first year but had failed to predict a 1.6 GPA prior to being admitted to college.

3. For further information, see the following law review articles:
   (a) Green, "The New NCAA Rules of the Game: Academic Integrity or Racism?" 28 *St. Louis University Law Journal* 101 (February 1984).
   (b) Yasser, "The Black Athletes' Equal Protection Case Against the NCAA's New Academic Standards," 19 (1) *Gonzaga Law Review* 83 (1983/1984).

Academic Progress

Academic progress rules are designed to ensure that student-athletes enroll in the type of courses required to obtain a high school diploma or college degree. At the interscholastic level, most state athletic associations do not have any academic progress rules, per se. The Massachusetts Interscholastic Athletic Association (MIAA), for example, only requires that the 20 credits in which a passing grade must be achieved be credits allowed toward a high school diploma. Furthermore, a student-athlete who repeats work for which he or she once received credit cannot count that subject a second time for eligibility *(MIAA Rules and Regulations Governing Athletics 1987–88*, Part II, Section 2[4a]). Therefore, a student-athlete who repeats a grade remains ineligible for athletic participation during that period of time.

At the intercollegiate level, the general rule for continued academic eligibility under NCAA rules (Divisions I and II) is that a student-athlete, after the first academic year, must maintain satisfactory progress toward a degree based on the member institution's academic rules of eligibility for *all* students, those specific academic eligibility rules adopted by the NCAA, and the athletic conference to which the institution belongs *(1987–88 NCAA Manual* Bylaw 5-1-[j]-[6]). The NCAA requires that a student-athlete be enrolled every semester in at least 12 credit hours, and must satisfactorily complete an average of at least 12 semester or quarter hours of course work for all regular terms, or must satisfactorily complete 24 semester or 36 quarter hours each academic year to be eligible for competition the next semester of competition (*1987–88 NCAA Manual,* Bylaw 5-1-[j]-[6]-[ii]). All minimum credit hours earned to satisfy these requirements must be in a specific baccalaureate degree program. (See Bylaw 5-1-[j]-[6]-[iii].) Correspondence, extension, and credit by examination courses are not included in the determination of academic eligibility unless the courses were completed at the school where the student-athlete was last enrolled as a full-time student.

The academic progress requirement was adopted by the NCAA in August 1981 in an effort to fight the major problem of student-athletes taking the required number of credit hours necessary to maintain eligibility but not enrolling in the type of courses necessary to satisfy degree requirements. The NCAA rule is general in nature, and many individual conferences have established stricter academic guidelines to deal with this problem at their member institutions.

Allied conferences may decide their own eligibility standards as long as they satisfy the NCAA's minimum requirements. For example, even before it became an NCAA requirement, the Big Ten Conference Committee on Academic Progress and Eligibility declared that a student-athlete "must have earned at least 24 semester hours or 36 quarter hours which are acceptable toward meeting requirements for the student-athlete's baccalaureate degree objective" to be eligible for competition during the student-athlete's second school year of residence. (See *Handbook of Intercollegiate [Big Ten] Conference,* August 1, 1986, Rule 3-2-B.) In addition, an "official interpretation" of the above rule states that "the Academic Progress and Eligibility Committee shall not grant eligibility for a second season of competition to a student-athlete who has earned less than 18 semester hours or 27 quarter hours." On entering the third year, the Big Ten requires 51 semester hours or 77 quarter hours. In the fourth year, at least 78 semester hours or 117 quarter hours are required to maintain athletic eligibility. (See *Handbook of Intercollegiate [Big Ten] Conference,* August 1, 1986, Rule 3-2-C + D.)

Another illustration of a conference which has a stricter academic progress standard is the Pacific-10 Conference (Pac-10), which requires the same number of credits entering year two (24 semester or 36 quarter hours) but expressly stipulates that the courses must have been passed. This is only implied in the Big Ten requirements. Additionally, the Pac-10 requires that a student-athlete participating in a sport after the fall term must have completed and passed a minimum of 12 units (hours) prior to the granting of eligibility. The student-athlete is ineligible if any of these units are "conditional" or "incomplete," since the individual must receive a letter grade showing that he or she passed. (See *Handbook of the Pacific-10 Conference 1986–87*, Art. 8, Sec. 4.)

A leading case in the area of academic progress is *Wilson v. Intercollegiate (Big Ten) Conference*, 668 F.2d 962 (7th Cir. 1982). Dave Wilson was injured for the entire season in his first football game at Fullerton Junior College in 1977 prior to the beginning of classes. Wilson was advised to drop out of Fullerton for the year to retain four years of playing eligibility. Wilson then enrolled at Fullerton the following year, playing football and attending classes in 1978–79 and 1979–80.

Following the 1979–80 season, Wilson transferred to the University of Illinois, where he was told that he would have only one year of eligibility because he had played in a game during the 1977 season. He was also informed that he would have to acquire senior academic year status before playing. Under Big Ten Conference rules, because he had not received a hardship waiver after being injured in the first game of the 1977–78 season, he had used three years of playing eligibility while playing at Fullerton. Since he had completed only two years of school, Wilson was subject to the Big Ten's "insufficient academic progress rule," which requires that a specific number of credits be accumulated in order for a student-athlete to be eligible for each successive playing season. Because of those alleged rule violations, the conference's faculty representatives who govern Big Ten athletics ruled that Wilson would be eligible for one season only.

In response, Wilson brought suit against the NCAA, the Big Ten, and the University of Illinois. He charged that the faculty representatives had illegally overruled their own eligibility committee, which had originally determined that he would be eligible for two seasons at Illinois. Wilson also contended that he should have been granted a hearing regarding the determination of his eligibility.

In addressing the alleged academic progress violations, Wilson argued that NCAA eligibility requirements regarding academic progress are intended to ensure a level of academic achievement for all student-athletes. In this case, considering the circumstances and the fact that he had submitted transcripts and records of his academic performance which demonstrated that he was a "serious student," the application of the rule was unnecessary.

Under several temporary court injunctions, Wilson was allowed to play football for the 1980 season, but not for the 1981 season, even though he ultimately won the case on an appeal. The Big Ten held fast to its decision to grant Wilson only one full year of eligibility, so Wilson left Illinois to pursue a career in professional football.

In addition to the *Wilson* type of case, there are the "educational exploitation" cases like *Hall* (see Note 1). The threat of litigation in this area may cause educators and athletic administrators to right many of the existing wrongs that border on unfair educational abuses. Such litigation may force the minority of educationally unsound programs to join the majority of positive programs whose academic standards are above reproach.

NOTES _____

1. For a case in which the academic progress rule was challenged, see *Hall v. University of Minnesota*, 530 F. Supp. 104 (D. Minn. 1982). Hall, a former basketball player, brought suit against the University of Minnesota for its failure to admit him to a degree-granting program, which resulted in his being declared ineligible to play basketball for his senior year. Big Ten Conference rules require a student-athlete to be enrolled in such a degree-granting program to maintain eligibility. The court found in favor of Hall, stating that a constitutionally protected property interest in a potential professional basketball contract was involved; therefore, Hall's due process rights had been violated.

2. For an example of an academic progress form used at the collegiate level, see Exhibit 5–4.

Transfer Rules

On both the intercollegiate and interscholastic level of athletic competition, the issue of student-athletes transferring from one institution to another is often troublesome and controversial. For the student-athlete, the issue centers on the individual's right to attend school and compete in athletics wherever the individual wishes. For the institution, allied conference, and national association, the issues revolve around illegal recruitment, stability of programs, and a desire to avoid an image of student-athletes being recruited from one program to another.

Transfer rules were created to deter (1) the recruiting of student-athletes by colleges or high schools that the student-athlete does not attend, and (2) the shopping around by student-athletes for institutions that seem to offer them the best opportunities for advancing their career. The courts have generally upheld transfer rules, basing their decisions on the fact that neither a suspect class has been established nor a fundamental right violated. The transfer rule needs only to be rationally related to the legitimate state interest or purpose of preventing recruitment and school hopping. The exception to this general rule is when substantial hardship or

MEMORANDUM

Date:

To: Academic Advisors

From: Academic Coordinator for Athletics

Subject: **DECLARATION OF MAJOR AND ACADEMIC PROGRESS FORM FOR STUDENT ATHLETES**

Recent legislation by the National Collegiate Athletic Association governing the eligibility of student athletes requires that in order to remain eligible in the fifth and subsequent semesters of enrollment, a student must designate in writing (Part I) the specific baccalaureate degree program he/she will pursue. Further, once the student athlete has designated a program of study, the student's satisfactory progress shall be based upon the satisfactory completion of courses in the designated program, as well as the student's overall academic record at the institution. Verification of the academic progress is required in the designated program and shall be affirmed annually by an academic official (Part II) in the major program of study.

By completing this required form no later than April 30, 1986, you will be assisting the Department of Athletics to comply with these NCAA regulations concerning academic eligibility.

Thank you for your assistance. If you have any questions, please call my office.

DECLARATION OF MAJOR AND ACADEMIC PROGRESS FORM FOR STUDENT ATHLETES

I. _____ is a member of an Intercollegiate Athletic

Team at the University of _____. His/her declared

major is _____.

_____   _____
Student Athlete Signature   Sport

II. By signing this form you will be affirming that:

1. The above named student is a declared
   major as listed.   _____   _____
                                                 YES   NO

2. He/She is making satisfactory academic
   progress toward the designated program
   of studies and is satisfying program or
   institutional requirements leading to the
   baccalaureate degree.   _____   _____
                                                 YES   NO

_____   _____   _____
Academic Official Signature   Department   Date

Exhibit 5-4   College Academic Progress Form

other mitigating circumstances can be shown to require judicial intervention. The following sections discuss in detail the problems and litigation associated with the transfer of student-athletes.

College Transfer Rules

Under NCAA regulations, a "transfer student" is one who (1) officially registers and enrolls at one institution on the opening day of classes in any quarter or semester with a minimum full-time academic load, (2) attends one or more classes, or (3) reports for regular squad practice (*1987–88 NCAA Manual*, Bylaw 5-1-[L]-[1]). A student-athlete who meets any or all of these criteria and then desires to change schools is considered by the NCAA to be a "transfer student."

Generally, as a transfer, the student-athlete must forego intercollegiate athletic competition for one full academic year, regardless of the reason for changing schools. Additionally, the student-athlete must be enrolled full-time at the new institution for the duration of that year. There are many exceptions to this rule, too numerous to detail. However, as an example, one exception to this rule occurs when a student-athlete who meets the 2.0 qualifier transfers from a two-year to a four-year college, having either graduated from the two-year institution or having a 2.0 average for a minimum of 24 credits after completion of the first year. Another exception to the rule occurs when a student-athlete transfers from a four-year to another four-year institution in order to continue participation in a sport that has been dropped by the original institution or was never sponsored on the intercollegiate level while the student-athlete was in attendance at the institution, provided the student-athlete had never attended any other institution that offered intercollegiate competition in that sport. Of course, athletic conferences may establish stricter transfer rules than those of the NCAA. However, these stricter conference eligibility rules may be subject to challenge (see Note 1a and b).

A leading case in the area of student-athlete transfer rules is *English v. National Collegiate Athletic Ass'n*, 439 So. 2d 1218 (La. App. 4th Cir. 1983). The *English* case is very important because it upholds the authority of the NCAA to regulate the very type of activity transfer rules are designed to prevent. English was an outstanding high school quarterback who entered Michigan State University in the fall of 1979 on a football scholarship. Realizing that his prospects for playing at Michigan State were poor, due in part to an injury, he enrolled at Allegheny Junior College in Pittsburgh, Pennsylvania. English attended Allegheny during the 1980–81 school year and graduated in the spring. English did not play football for Allegheny during the year he attended. In the fall of 1981, English enrolled at Iowa State University and was on the football team there during the 1981 and 1982 seasons. Once again deciding that his prospects were poor, he enrolled at Delgado Junior College in New Orleans, where his family resided and where his father had recently taken the position as head football coach at Tulane. English graduated from Delgado in the spring, and in August 1983 he enrolled in Tulane, where he sought to play football immediately but was told he was ineligible because he was a transfer.

English brought suit, contending that he was denied due process and that the NCAA's actions were arbitrary, capricious, unfair, and discriminatory. The court found from the testimony of his father that there was a question in English's mind from the very beginning about his eligibility, notwithstanding the way he wanted to read the rule. The NCAA rule in question stated that a transfer student-athlete from a junior college who had transferred from a four-year college must complete a one-year residency requirement to be eligible for NCAA postseason competition unless the student-athlete completed 24 semester hours (credits) and graduated from the junior college, and one calendar year had elapsed since the transfer from the first four-year college. English was aware of the NCAA policy of preventing a student-athlete from playing for different colleges in successive years. Since there was a question in his mind, English was also obliged to contact the NCAA national office for answers but failed to avail himself of this opportunity and instead embarked on a course he knew was perilous; therefore, he was not deprived of due process.

The court found that the NCAA rule contemplated two colleges, the first and second. A student-athlete who plays for a college one year cannot play for another college the following year. The rule does not and need not concern itself with what the court described as "the bizarre situation where one had played for yet a third college in the distant past." The court ruled that the NCAA, in adopting and implementing the transfer rule, acted reasonably in its efforts to prevent players from jumping from one school to another.

NOTES

1. In the following cases, the courts *struck down* intercollegiate transfer rules.

   (a) In *Gulf South Conference v. Boyd*, 369 So. 2d 553 (Ala. 1979), a full scholarship college football player transferred from one Gulf South Conference (GSC) institution to a junior college and then to another GSC institution. He was granted eligibility to participate after one year in varsity football at the second GSC institution since the student-athlete was in good standing, had refused the scholarship for a second year at the first GSC institution, and had not played football for two years. These conditions allowed for an exception to a conference rule that stated a student-athlete who transfers from one GSC school to another would be ineligible to participate in any sport at the second school.

(b) In *Cabrillo Community College District of Santa Cruz County v. California Junior College Ass'n*, 44 Cal. App. 3d 367, 118 Cal. Rptr. 708 (1975), the court held that a community college may not prevent a student from trying out for an interscholastic athletic program merely because that student had not lived in a college district for a particular period of time. The court stated that such athletic residency requirements were violative of state law since they imposed additional residency requirements upon students who wish to participate in community college athletic programs after they had already been duly admitted to an institution.

2. In the following cases the courts *upheld* an intercollegiate transfer rule.

(a) In *Weiss v. National Collegiate Athletic Ass'n and Eastern Collegiate Athletic Conference*, 563 F. Supp. 192 (E.D. Pa. 1983), a college tennis player, who had transferred from Arizona State to the University of Pennsylvania, brought suit claiming the one-year-loss-of-eligibility transfer rule violated antitrust law because the practice constituted a group boycott and that the rule did not fulfill its intended purpose of preventing the exploitation of college athletes by coaches attempting to raid other institutions of athletes. Weiss was neither recruited by the University of Pennsylvania nor given an athletic scholarship. The court denied the request for an injunction, finding that Weiss had not offered sufficient evidence that he would be irreparably harmed if the injunction was denied.

(b) In *Williams v. Hamilton*, 497 F. Supp. 641 (D.N.H. 1980), a college student-athlete challenged the National Association of Intercollegiate Athletics (NAIA) transfer rule requiring him to be in residence at his new college for 16 weeks before becoming eligible for intercollegiate athletics. The court held that the transfer rule was valid and did not deny due process or equal protection guarantees.

3. For further information, see the following law review article: "Williams v. Hamilton: Constitutional Protection of the Student-Athlete," 8 *Journal of College and University Law* 399 (1982).

High School Transfer Rules

High school athletic associations may restrict eligibility for student-athlete transfers in one of two ways. Some schools, in an effort to limit abuse, apply blanket restrictions on all students who change schools, regardless of their reason. This approach is often overre-strictive and unduly harsh. Even so, such rules are often upheld by the courts, and those bringing suit have failed to gain monetary or equitable relief. The rules are said to be reasonably related to alleviating recruiting problems, and courts have been reluctant to get involved with private voluntary association matters.

In some high school athletic associations, exceptions are pro-vided to allow students who transfer to schools for reasons unre-lated to athletics to have immediate athletic eligibility upon enroll-ment at the new school. Inherent in any rule which restricts eligibility with specific exceptions is the potential for inconsistency and abuse in the decision-making process. That is why many high school athletic associations simply find it easier to require all new students to meet a residency time period (usually one year) before participating in athletics.

Since there are problems with both blanket restrictions and exceptions on a case-by-case basis, some high school athletic associations have taken a third approach. This third approach allows for transfer student-athletes to be eligible immediately if certain objective criteria are met. The Massachusetts Interscholas-tic Athletic Association, for instance, has taken this third approach. To qualify for immediate athletic eligibility, the student-athlete must not have participated on the varsity level of that sport at the previous school, and the transfer must occur prior to the start of practice in the sport. If a student-athlete fails to meet these criteria, he or she must forfeit athletic eligibility for one year.

A leading case in the area of interscholastic transfer rules is *Kentucky High School Athletic Ass'n v. Hopkins County Board of Education,* 552 S.W.2d 685 (Ct. App. Ky. 1977). This case is reflective of the general rule, which allows high school athletic associations to maintain strict transfer rules. Todd Shadowen, a high school student, had parents who divorced. Legal custody was granted to Todd's mother, who moved with Todd to a new resi-dence where Todd was enrolled in high school and played varsity sports. In May 1976, for personal reasons, Shadowen moved from his mother's to his father's residence and enrolled in another school. He sought to compete in interscholastic sports during the 1976–77 school year and was denied eligibility on the basis of a Kentucky High School Athletic Association (KHSAA) transfer rule.

The Kentucky Court of Appeals found the rule was not invalid since the merits and wisdom of an association's adherence to a rule without exceptions or qualifications is not for the courts to deter-mine. The court also found that Shadowen was not compelled to change his residence because of a reason beyond his control. The change of custody was the result of Shadowen's own wishes.

Therefore, the court found that the association did not act arbitrarily in applying the transfer rule to Shadowen.

Many court cases have challenged high school transfer rules on equal protection, freedom of religion, right to travel, and due process grounds. Yet, in most instances, the courts have upheld such rules unless the student-athlete established a violation of a constitutionally protected right, or if fraud, collusion, or arbitrariness was found. Exceptions to the general rule may be found when regulations presume that all transfers are made for improper reasons (see Note 3a), and when a student-athlete moves from one state to another by virtue of change in his father's employment (see Note 3b).

States may also adopt a statute or rule preventing implementation of a transfer rule, as Oregon did in response to a suit in which it was determined that transfer rules did not violate any statutory or constitutional restrictions (see Note 2d). According to such a statute, the student who moved with his or her parents may not be declared ineligible to participate in athletics as a result of the transfer. On the other hand, the student who moved just to live with friends of the family could be declared ineligible as a result of the transfer. In addition, such a statute prohibits the declaration of ineligibility when the declaration is based solely on the fact that the student-athlete formerly participated in a given sport at another school.

NOTES

1. After deciding the essential issue, the court in *Kentucky High School Athletic Ass'n v. Hopkins County Board of Education* discussed at length a particular problem illustrated by this appeal:

> In the court's mind, this case demonstrates why courts are a very poor place in which to settle interscholastic athletic disputes, especially since this type of litigation is most likely to arise at playoff or tournament time. If an injunction or restraining order is granted erroneously, it will be practically impossible to unscramble the tournament results to reflect the ultimate outcome of the case. In almost every instance, the possible benefits flowing from a temporary restraining order or injunction are far outweighed by the potential detriment to the Association, as well as to its member schools who are not before the court. Only in a rare instance should a temporary restraining order or preliminary injunction be granted.

2. The courts *upheld* interscholastic transfer rules in the following cases.

(a) In *Scott v. Kilpatrick*, 286 Ala. 129, 237 So. 2d 652 (1970), a student-athlete contended that the transfer rule of the high school athletic association was unconstitutional, since the student-athlete's desire to compete in high school football involved a property right. The denied property right was alleged to be the opportunity for the student-athlete to compete for a college football scholarship. The court found that participation in high school athletics was a privilege and not a property right.

(b) In *Bruce v. South Carolina High School League*, 258 S.C. 546, 189 S.E.2d 817 (S.C. 1972), student-athletes who transferred voluntarily contended that, since they were not recruited and the transfer rule was designed to prevent recruiting, it should not apply to them. The court held that given the prohibitive administrative difficulties of administering such rules, the court should not question the merits or wisdom of their adoption. The court also ruled that the student-athletes had no constitutionally protected right to participate in athletics, and therefore, the court had no right to prohibit enforcement of the transfer rule.

(c) In *Walsh v. Louisiana High School Athletic Ass'n*, 616 F.2d 152 (5th Cir. 1980), parents of student-athletes brought an action on behalf of their children against the Louisiana High School Athletic Association (LHSAA). The suit alleged that the LHSAA's transfer rule unduly burdened their First Amendment right to the free exercise of their religion and deprived them of their Fourteenth Amendment right of equal protection. Several student-athletes wanted to attend a Lutheran school outside their home district, but enrollment in any high school other than a school in their home district would have resulted in their ineligibility. The appeals court held that the transfer rule was rationally related to the state's valid interest in elementary recruitment of interscholastic athletes.

(d) In *Cooper v. Oregon School Activities Ass'n*, and *Faherty v. Oregon School Activities Ass'n*, 52 Or. App. 425, 629 P.2d 386 (1981), student-athletes who transferred from a parochial to a public high school were barred from competition for a year. The court held that since the rule did not treat parochial schools differently from other schools and did not prevent parents from sending their children to parochial schools, the rule did not violate their free exercise of religion. The burden imposed on the parents and student-athletes was constitutionally permissible and justified by the state's interest in deterring the recruitment of high school athletes and the lack of an effective, workable alternative.

(e) In *Albach v. Odle*, 531 F.2d 983 (10th Cir. 1976), a federal appeals court held that a high school transfer rule was not within federal court jurisdiction. Athletic governance, supervision, and regulation was within the discretion of state boards, unless a substantial federal question was involved.

(f) In *Marino v. Waters*, 220 So. 2d 802 (La. App. 1969), a public school transfer rule, which excluded from athletic competition student-athletes who transferred between schools because of marriage, was upheld because it was applied in a nondiscriminatory manner and did not deny due process.

(g) In *Dallam v. Cumberland Valley School District*, 391 F. Supp. 358 (M.D. Pa. 1975), the court held that a transfer rule is not in violation of a recognized right or privilege protected by the constitution.

(h) In *Chabert v. Louisiana High School Athletic Ass'n*, 323 So. 2d 774 (La. 1975), the court upheld the association transfer rule. The court reasoned that in view of the avowed purpose of the rule—to prevent the evils of recruiting—the rule should be upheld. Plaintiff student-athlete lost one year's eligibility by enrolling in a parochial school located within a public school district other than the one in which he resided. If he enrolled in a parochial school within the same public school district in which he resided, he would have been eligible immediately. The court held that the rule was not arbitrary and did not abridge religious freedom, even though there was only one parochial high school in the public high school district.

(i) In *Kulovitz v. Illinois High School Ass'n*, 462 F. Supp. 875 (N.D. Ill. 1978), a rule mandating a one-year loss of eligibility due to a transfer was held constitutional when the court rejected the student-athlete's claim that such a rule deprived him of a college scholarship. The court held that expectation of an athletic scholarship is not a constitutionally protected right. In addition, the court held that the right to interstate travel is not implicitly or expressly guaranteed by the Constitution, and therefore, equal protection claims were not applicable to this case.

(j) In *Niles v. University Interscholastic League*, 715 F.2d 1027 (5th Cir. 1983), the University Interscholastic League declared a student-athlete football player ineligible to compete after he moved out of state to live with his mother during the spring term and then returned to his original school in the subsequent fall semester to participate in football. The student-athlete contended that the decision was a denial of freedom of travel and freedom of familial choice. The U.S. Circuit Court of Appeals ruled that there was no constitutional violation on which the student-athlete could base a suit.

(k) In *Kriss v. Brown*, 390 N.E.2d 193 (Ind. 1979), the Indiana Court of Appeals held that a high school basketball player was ineligible for competition after transferring to another school district because there was substantial evidence that a guardianship was created to primarily make him eligible and because the move was a result of undue influence. The court added that a determination of the Indiana High School Athletic Association that a student-athlete's desire for a scholarship was not a sufficient reason to excuse him from operation of the rules was neither arbitrary, capricious, nor unreasonable.

(l) In *re U.S. ex rel. Missouri State High Sch., etc.*, 682 F.2d 147 (8th Cir. 1982), the United States Court of Appeals held that a Missouri State High School Activities Association transfer rule did not violate the federal Constitution. It noted that the minimal impact on interstate travel of the transfer rule did not require strict judicial scrutiny normally applied to classifications that penalize exercise of the right to travel.

(m) In *Crandall v. North Dakota High School Activities Ass'n*, 261 N.W.2d 921 (N.D. 1978), a transfer rule which declared a transferring student-athlete ineligible unless the student-athlete's parents had been residents of the new high school district for 18 weeks was held not arbitrary or unreasonable. The rule was found to be reasonably related to a legitimate purpose, even though no exception was made for student-athletes who transferred solely for academic reasons.

3. The courts *struck down* transfer rules in the following cases.

(a) In *Sturrup v. Mahon*, 305 N.E.2d 877 (Ind. 1974), the court held that a transfer rule violated equal protection because it was overinclusive. The rule denied participation to a student-athlete who moved for reasons unrelated to athletics. The student-athlete moved to escape detrimental conditions at home and heavy drug use at his former school. The rule as applied was not rationally related to its stated goal.

(b) In *Sullivan v. University Interscholastic League*, 616 S.W. 2d 170 (Tex. 1981), the court held that a rule providing that a student-athlete who had represented a high school other than his present school in football or basketball was ineligible to participate for one calendar year was found to be overbroad, overinclusive, harsh, and not rationally related to the purpose of deterring high school athletic recruitment. The student-athlete had changed high schools because his father had received a job transfer.

Redshirting and Longevity

Redshirting and longevity both relate to the length of time a student-athlete has to complete his or her eligibility in interscholastic or intercollegiate competition. Redshirting and longevity rules are designed to balance the need to extend or delay a student-athlete's eligibility to compete, based on legitimate factors such as injury or academic difficulty, against potential abuse of the system by either coaches or student-athletes seeking to gain competitive advantage through an extension of a student-athlete's career.

Redshirting

Redshirting is a term used to describe the practice of extending the playing career of a student-athlete by postponing or passing over a year of interscholastic or intercollegiate participation while not affecting the student-athlete's maximum allowable time for participating in high school or college athletics. High school athletic associations and conferences, which do not allow redshirting, often employ a four-year eligibility rule. Under most high school association rules, a student-athlete has eight consecutive semesters in which to participate in interscholastic competition, beginning with the student-athlete's entry into the ninth grade.

Colleges competing under NCAA governance, on the other hand, are allowed to have their student-athletes compete in four complete seasons of play within five calendar years (in Division I) from the beginning of the semester in which the student-athlete first registers at an institution. Participation during a season in an intercollegiate sport counts as a season of competition toward the four-year total, as does any season of competition at the junior college level. The NCAA rules at Division I also state that any student-athlete who participates in any organized athletic competition after his 20th birthday shall have that participation counted as one year, but no more than one year, of varsity competition in that sport (*1987–88 NCAA Manual*, Bylaw 5-1-[d]-[3]). The only exceptions to the five-year limit are for time spent in the armed services, on official and required church missions, or with recognized foreign aid services of the United States government—for example, the Peace Corps (*1987–88 NCAA Manual*, Bylaw 4-1-[a]).

Designed to give student-athletes flexibility in completing their four seasons of eligible collegiate playing time, the five-year rule gives the student-athlete the option to postpone his or her playing career any one of the five years during which he or she has eligibility. The year postponed is commonly referred to as "redshirting." The practice of redshirting may be initiated for a number of reasons, including the following:

1. Medical reasons. Includes a serious injury or illness occurring in the off-season or before the start of the season. The student-athlete might decide it advantageous to recover fully from such a problem by postponing for a year the resumption of athletic competition.
2. Academic reasons. Includes a student-athlete becoming ineligible for play because of low grades or a student-athlete wishing to study abroad for a year of college education.
3. Transfers. The five-year rule also protects the playing career of first-time transfer students, allowing them the opportunity to switch schools once without eliminating one of their four seasons of playing time. The student-athlete may have to redshirt a year of competition while attending classes at the new institution (Division I) (*1987–88 NCAA Manual*, Bylaw 5-1-[j]-[7]).
4. Coaching strategy. The coach might ask a student-athlete to redshirt a season because the coach wants to use and schedule the player's eligibility to fit the long-term needs and requirements of the team.

In part to curb the allure of redshirting players for coaching reasons (and to reduce expenses), the NCAA membership imposed limitations on financial aid awards, including maximum (allowable) awards (*1987–88 NCAA Manual*, Bylaw 6-5). Reducing the number of scholarships a program can award has the effect of making it less advantageous for coaches to redshirt student-athletes for reasons other than those made necessary because of academics or injury. The NCAA membership has also voted to allow certain graduate student-athletes to be eligible for competition if they have playing eligibility remaining (*1987–88 NCAA Manual*, Constitution 3-3-[a-3] and Bylaw 5-1-[c]).

As a general rule, courts have upheld intercollegiate redshirt rules. A leading case is *Kupec v. Atlantic Coast Conference*, 399 F. Supp. 1377 (M.D.N.C. 1975). The *Kupec* case involved the football hardship rule of the Atlantic Coast Conference (ACC). Kupec was a college football player who sought an injunction from enforcement of the ACC eligibility rules that would not allow him to participate for a fifth year. Kupec argued that if he were not able to participate in another year of collegiate football, his professional career aspirations would be injured, he would lose his right to a tuition-free education, and the public interest would be damaged since the public wanted to see him play college football. The court stated that it would not hesitate to prohibit the ACC from an illegal practice that fell within its jurisdiction. However, the court did not see any such practices involved in this case. The court found Kupec's argument about his professional career to be too speculative. It noted that Kupec needed only to finish an incomplete course to graduate and that the loss of tuition benefits did not cause any injury.

At the interscholastic level, the practice of redshirting is not as commonplace as on the intercollegiate level, primarily because the rules do not allow the flexibility provided at the intercollegiate level. Therefore, the only alternative at the high school level in many states may be keeping back a student-athlete for an extra year before the student-athlete enters high school. This allows student-athletes another year to develop their bodies and playing skills before entering high school competition. However, the student-athlete who does this must be careful about maximum age restrictions. For instance, the Massachusetts Interscholastic Athletic Association (MIAA) does not allow students aged 19 and above to compete in high school athletics unless the student turns 19 after September 1 of the school year (*MIAA Rules and Regulations Governing Athletics 1987–88*), Section II-[6]). The MIAA also restricts competition to 12 consecutive athletic seasons (fall, winter, and spring grading semesters for four years) past the eighth grade. However, an MIAA Eligibility Review Board can authorize exceptions to the 12-consecutive-season rule because of injury or illness.

High school regulations governing the number of semesters before expiration of athletic eligibility have, like age restrictions (discussed in the next section), been justified on the basis of preventing competition between individuals with vast differences in strength, speed, and experience. Such rules are designed to promote equitable competition and player safety as well as to prevent schools from abusing athletes by holding them back a grade or "redshirting" them to allow them to mature and develop athletically. However, high school rules may make exceptions for students who academically fail a grade, enabling the student to maintain athletic eligibility since the retention was not related to athletics. Therefore, the student-athlete is allowed to compete in the fifth year but cannot compete for more than four seasons.

These rules have often been upheld by the courts when the student-athlete's delay in school was unrelated to athletics or even academic failure (see Note 2c). A few courts, however, have placed restrictions on the use of such rules when the reasons for the student's ineligibility were clearly unrelated to athletics (see Note 3b). Furthermore, at least one court has intervened to overturn an association's refusal to grant a hardship exception, since allowing a particular student to participate in basketball was crucial to his rehabilitation from juvenile delinquency (see Note 3a).

NOTES ───

1. The NCAA has what it terms a hardship exception. It is often confused with the term "redshirting." A hardship exception will be granted when:

(i) It occurs in one of the four seasons of intercollegiate competition at any four-year collegiate institution for members of Division I, or at any two-year or four-year collegiate institution for members of Divisions II or III.

(ii) Division I—It occurs when the student-athlete has not participated in more than 20 percent of the institution's completed events in his or her sport or has not participated in more than two of the institution's completed events in that sport, whichever number is greater, provided the injury or illness occurred in the first half of the season and resulted in incapacity to compete for the remainder of the season. Any contest (including a scrimmage) with outside competition is countable under this limitation. [Note: In applying the 20 percent limitation, any computation that results in a fractional portion of an event shall be rounded to the next whole number; e.g., 20 percent of a 27-game basketball schedule (5.4 games) shall be considered six games.]

(iii) Divisions II and III—It occurs when the student-athlete has not participated in more than 20 percent of the institution's completed events in his or her sport or has not participated in more than two of the institution's completed events in that sport, whichever number is greatest, provided the injury or illness occurred in the first half of the traditional playing season in that sport and resulted in incapacity to compete for the remainder of the traditional playing season. Only contests (including scrimmages) with outside competition during the traditional playing season, or, if so designated, during the official NCAA championship playing season in that sport (e.g., spring baseball, fall soccer), shall be countable under this limitation. [Note: In applying the 20 percent limitation, any computation that results in a fractional portion of an event shall be rounded to the next whole number; e.g., 20 percent of a 27-game basketball schedule (5.4 games) shall be considered as six games.]

(iv) This provision shall be administered by the conference members of the Association or, in the case of an independent member institution, by the NCAA Eligibility Committee. [*1987–88 NCAA Manual*, Bylaw 5-1-(d)-(2)]

2. In the following cases the courts *upheld* redshirt rules.

(a) In *Mitchell v. Louisiana High School Athletic Ass'n*, 430 F.2d 1155 (5th Cir. 1970), a redshirt rule which restricted all incoming high school students who voluntarily repeated eighth grade to six semesters of competition rather than the normal eight semesters was held valid since it was rationally related to a legitimate state interest.

(b) In *David v. Louisiana High School Athletic Ass'n*, 244 So. 2d 292 (Ct. App. La. 1971), a student who repeats a grade for reasons unrelated to athletics may still be validly restricted to six semesters (three years) of athletic eligibility rather than the normal eight semesters (four years).

(c) In *Smith v. Crim*, 240 Ga. 390, 240 S.E.2d 884 (Ga. 1977), a student challenged the application of a rule that counted his absence against his four-year limit of eligibility after he dropped out of school for a year to care for his invalid mother. The court, however, upheld the rule since it was rationally related to the goals of assuring fair competition and preventing redshirting.

(d) In *Alabama High School Athletic Ass'n v. Medders*, 456 So. 2d 84, 20 Educ. L. Rep. 797 (Ala. 1984), a student who had successfully completed eighth grade but voluntarily repeated eighth grade was declared ineligible to play football on the high school team during his senior year under the eight-semester rule. The court held that although the rule was susceptible to two interpretations, it had been interpreted in the same way as in the student's case for 35 years, and that interpretation fell short of fraud, collusion, or arbitrariness.

(e) In *Maroney v. University Interscholastic League*, 764 F.2d 403, 25 Educ. L. Rep. 765 (5th Cir. 1985), an 18-year-old high school football player was declared ineligible under a five-year rule which provided that students may participate in interscholastic athletics for only five years after their first enrollment in eighth grade. The court dismissed the claim for lack of a substantial federal question since the claim had no plausible foundation in law and participation in interscholastic athletics was not an interest protected by the due process clause.

3. In the following cases the courts *struck down* redshirt rules.

(a) In *Florida High School Activities Ass'n v. Bryant*, 313 So. 2d 57 (Fla. Dist. Ct. App. 1975), an association sought reversal of a final judgment which found a student eligible to play more than four years of interscholastic basketball. Affirming the judgment, the court of appeals held that for this student, basketball was vital because it provided the impetus for his general scholastic, social development, and rehabilitation from prior problems of juvenile delinquency. The student had presented an adequate case of undue hardship, meriting a waiver of the four-year rule.

(b) In *Lee v. Florida High School Activities Ass'n*, 291 So. 2d 636 (Fla. Dist. Ct. App. 1974), the student stayed out of school for 10 months to help alleviate his family's troubled financial situation. Upon returning to school, he sought a waiver of the four-year (successive) rule to participate in athletics. It was denied by the association. The court found his participation in athletics would have enhanced his chances of being admitted to college and of winning a scholarship. Except for the four-year rule, the student would have been eligible. Therefore, the court found that the denial of a waiver was a violation of due process because no justification had been given for denying eligibility in such extreme circumstances. The rule was held unconstitutional as it applied to the student.

(c) In *Duffley v. New Hampshire Interscholastic Athletic Ass'n*, 446 A.2d 462 (N.H. 1982), the court held that a student-athlete must be given procedural due process when he or she is denied a waiver of the four-year eligibility rule.

(d) In *ABC League v. Missouri State High School Activities Ass'n*, 530 F. Supp. 1033 (E.D. Mo. 1981), the student and the league were granted an injunction by the district court stopping the Missouri State High School Activities Association (MSHSAA) from enforcing a rule that would have prevented students who transferred to private schools, which form the ABC league, from participating in athletic competition when their schools played against members of the MSHSAA. The district court found that the MSHSAA rule was arbitrary, capricious, and a violation of equal protection.

4. At a June 26, 1984, U.S. Senate hearing on "Oversight on College Athletic Programs" (S. Hrg. 98–955, Subcommittee on Education, Arts and Humanities), Edward T. Foote II, President of the University of Miami noted:

> The football players in a big-time program will spend as many as 30 to 40 hours a week during the fall semester on football. Graduation in five years, not four, for those who graduate is the norm for many football programs. The practice of "redshirting" (emphasis added) freshmen encourages five years of study.

Longevity

In 1980, the NCAA enacted a new Division I bylaw (5-1-[d]-[3]) designed to address problems concerning the increasing number of older athletes being recruited, especially in the sports of track and soccer. Some member institutions believed that athletes were entering intercollegiate athletics after excessive experience in amateur leagues in the United States and more frequently in foreign countries. The "longevity" rule was initiated because it was believed that these older, more experienced athletes would place younger and more inexperienced athletes at a disadvantage in competition and when trying to gain scholarship monies.

A leading case in this area that shows how the courts view the purpose of the NCAA rule is *Butts v. National Collegiate Athletic Ass'n*, 751 F.2d 609 (3d Cir. 1984). Butts had played for the Frederick Military Academy basketball team after reaching the age of 20. When Butts entered LaSalle, a private university, it was feared that under NCAA Bylaw 5-1-(d)-(3) his post-high school experience would be counted against his four years of college eligibility. Bylaw 5-1-(d)-(3) states that "any participation by a student as an individual or as a representative of any team in organized competition in a sport during each 12-month period after his 20th birthday and prior to his matriculation at a member institution shall count as one year of varsity competition in that sport." When the NCAA indicated that Butts would be ineligible to play basketball during his senior year, he filed suit against the NCAA and LaSalle, seeking declaratory and injunctive relief. Butts alleged constitutional and statutory defects in Bylaw 5-1-(d)-(3). He claimed that the bylaw violated 42 U.S.C. § 6102 (1982), which states: "[N]o person in the United States shall, on the basis of age, be excluded from participation in, be denied the benefits of, or be subjected to discrimination under, any program or activity receiving Federal financial assistance." He also claimed that the bylaw violated 42 U.S.C. § 2000d (1982), which states: "No person in the United States shall, on the grounds of race, color, or national origin, be excluded from participation in, be denied the benefits of, or be subjected to discrimination under any program or activity receiving Federal financial assistance."

The district court concluded that Butts had shown a strong likelihood that the bylaw had a racially disparate impact (affected some races more than others even though unintentional); however, it also concluded that the NCAA had advanced a legitimate, nondiscriminatory reason for the bylaw:

> [T]he bylaw is designed and intended to promote equality of competition among its members at each level so as to prevent college athletics and access to athletic scholarships from being dominated by more mature, older, more experienced players, and to discourage high school students from delaying their entrance into college in order to develop and mature their athletic skills.

The district court held that Butts had the burden of showing that the bylaw was pretextual or that "some other, less intrusive, rule would accomplish the stated objects of the present rule." The district court found that Butts had not shown a reasonable likelihood of being able to meet this burden, and it upheld the rule and the NCAA's position and denied a preliminary injunction.

Restrictions regarding age requirements are usually related to regulations limiting the number of years a student-athlete is eligible for intercollegiate competition. For example, rules may limit eligibility to four years after reaching a designated age. These four-year eligibility rules have been held discriminatory against aliens by the courts when the age is fixed at 19 (see Note 1c). However, since many aliens attend five instead of four years of high school, the courts have upheld such rules when the age is fixed at 20. The courts have considered such rules reasonable, since fair competition in amateur athletics suggests the need to restrict those who may be excessively qualified.

A leading case involving the issue of longevity was *Spath v. National Collegiate Athletic Ass'n*, 728 F.2d 25 (1st Cir. 1984). Robert Spath was a fourth-year student at the University of Lowell in Massachusetts on an ice hockey scholarship. He was ready to begin his senior year of play (fourth year of competition) when Lowell disqualified him pursuant to NCAA Bylaw 5-1-(d)-(3). Spath, a Canadian, had played three years of intercollegiate hockey at Lowell. In addition, prior to coming to Lowell, but after his 20th birthday, Spath had played for a team in Canada for one year. Spath brought a civil rights suit in federal court against the NCAA and the University of Lowell on the grounds that the bylaws adopted by the NCAA and enforced through its member institutions deprived him of equal protection and due process of law and against Lowell on the grounds of breach of contract.

The court found nothing to justify subjecting the NCAA bylaw to a heightened level of judicial scrutiny. The court held that no fundamental right was involved in playing intercollegiate hockey. The court also found that since the bylaw was neutral on its face with respect to foreigners, to sustain an equal protection argument Spath would have to show that the NCAA purposefully discriminated against foreigners as a class. To this end, Spath presented statistics showing that Canadians were more likely to be adversely affected by the bylaw than Americans. The court held, however, that the mere fact that the bylaw disproportionately affected Canadians was not sufficient to establish discriminatory purpose. "College athletics," the court stated, "are not professional sports . . . but are, within reason, democratic opportunities for students.

Fairness suggests restrictions against those who may be excessively qualified."

Most state high school athletic associations have rules governing the age of participants, as was mentioned in the previous section on redshirting. Often students who are 19 years old or older are prohibited from participating in interscholastic athletics. These rules have been established and promulgated for a number of reasons. First, older and mature student-athletes could constitute a danger to the health and safety of younger competitors. Second, these older student-athletes are also not the typical high school student-athlete, since many college players are 19 years of age. Third, longevity rules eliminate the possibility of "redshirting" student-athletes through voluntary repetition of grades to gain advantage in competition. Last, the older student-athletes are prevented from precluding from competition the younger athletes who might otherwise be bumped from a squad with a limited size.

The courts have generally ruled that these reasons are legitimate goals for state high school athletic associations. Thus, rules excluding student-athletes from participation in interscholastic competition because of age are commonly upheld since they only need to meet a rational basis test. Challenges based on constitutional claims have been countered by the courts' rulings that athletic participation is not a property right, only a privilege; that regulations do not create a suspect class; and that age restrictions are rationally related to assuring the legitimate state interests of fair competition and student-athlete safety (see Notes 1a and b).

NOTE

1. Additional cases on longevity rules include the following.
   (a) In *Blue v. University Interscholastic League*, 503 F. Supp. 1030 (N.D. Tex. 1980), a 19-year-old high school football player sought to enjoin the University Interscholastic League from enforcing the 19-year-old eligibility rule. The U.S. District Court held that the rule did not violate due process or equal protection guarantees of the Constitution.
   (b) In *State ex rel. Missouri State High School Activities Ass'n v. Schoenlaub*, 507 S.W.2d 354 (Mo. 1974), an age rule was found reasonable, even though no hardship exception existed. The court held that an association's refusal to grant an exception was not an arbitrary or unreasonable act since the fact that this may be a hardship case did not diminish the danger to younger participants if an older athlete was allowed to compete.
   (c) In *Howard University v. National Collegiate Athletic Ass'n*, 510 F.2d 213 (D.C. Cir. 1975), the court ruled as invalid the NCAA's "Foreign Student Rule," NCAA Bylaw 4-(1)-(f)-(2), which provides

that if an alien participated in organized athletics in a foreign country, after his 19th birthday the time spent doing so counts against the athlete's period of collegiate eligibility. Even though the court accepted the rule's purpose, it held that the rule was not closely tailored to achieving its goal because foreigners were penalized for activities that citizens participated in without penalty.

(d) In *Murtaugh v. Nyquist*, 78 Misc. 2d 876, 358 N.Y.S.2d 595 (1974), a longevity rule was held not arbitrary or unreasonable when a rational basis for the rule existed. Reasons such as the prevention of delay in the educational process and the prevention of injuries to younger, less developed student-athletes were adequate to support a longevity rule. The court found this to be true even in the case of a rule which denied eligibility to students held back for academic reasons.

Scholarships and Financial Aid

In intercollegiate competition, financial matters such as scholarships and financial aid are often sources of dispute and litigation regarding an individual's athletic eligibility. In this section, these considerations are examined, as well as workers' compensation issues, the concept of scholarships as contracts, letters of intent, excess financial aid, and congressional concerns over athletic scholarships and eligibility.

The cardinal rule concerning financial aid to a student-athlete for programs within the NCAA is that the aid *must* be administered by the school. If it is administered by an outside source, such as an alumnus of the university, it jeopardizes intercollegiate eligibility. The school is required to distribute athletic scholarships through its regular financial aid channels. Donors are prohibited from making contributions to benefit specific athletes. No financial aid from an outside source can be based solely on athletic ability. Student-athletes, however, are permitted to receive aid from persons on whom they are normally dependent (i.e., family) (*1987–88 NCAA Manual*, Constitution 3-4-[a-b]).

Institutions may not pay certain preenrollment fees, application processing fees, room deposits, or dormitory damage deposits unless institutional policy specifies that the financial aid package or athletic scholarship covers these expenses. If such expenses are covered, the student-athlete can be reimbursed after payment, or the fees may be paid by the school as long as these are the policies that apply to the entire student population.

The school financial aid mechanism is required to provide the athletic scholarship recipient with an officially signed document that stipulates the amount, duration, terms, and conditions to which the parties must adhere (see Exhibit 5–5).

1987–88 ATHLETIC SCHOLARSHIP RENEWAL

NAME _____

SPORT _____

DATE _____

The Department of Athletics/Intramurals is pleased to renew your athletic scholarship for the 1987–88 school year in the amount of a FULL SCHOLARSHIP (according to NCAA rule and to include tuition, fees, room and board plus required course related books).

Recommended by: _____
HEAD COACH

Approved by: _____
ASSOCIATE ATHLETIC DIRECTOR

Approved by: _____
FINANCIAL AID OFFICE

Signed: _____
STUDENT-ATHLETE   DATE

To be signed by the student-athlete and returned to the Head Coach or Associate Athletic Director within 14 days of the above date listed.

Additional terms and conditions:

1. Renewal of an athletic scholarship:
   (a) The renewal/non-renewal of this scholarship shall be made before July 1, prior to the academic year it is to be effective.
   (b) In the event this scholarship is not renewed, you shall have the opportunity for an appeals hearing before the institutional agency that approves athletic scholarships.
   (c) The request for an appeals hearing should be filed within ten (10) days of the date you receive notification of non-renewal of your athletic scholarship.
   (d) In order to be eligible for a renewal of an athletic scholarship, you must file an application for University Financial Aid.

2. Financial aid received from any source other than the university or persons upon whom you are naturally or legally dependent must be reported to the Office of Financial Aid Services and Athletic Department. All work income (during regular term sessions/not to include breaks, holidays, or summer time) must be reported and may not exceed the limits of a full scholarship.

3. If you voluntarily withdraw from participation in the sport for which this scholarship is offered, it will be terminated.

4. This scholarship is made in accordance with the rules and regulations of the NCAA and all other athletic governing organizations to which the university subscribes. Your acceptance of this scholarship means that you accept these conditions and agree to abide by them.

Exhibit 5-5 Athletic Scholarship Renewal Form

Certain features, among them the following, make athletic scholarships different from other types of financial aid:

1. The amount of aid granted in an athletic scholarship is not dependent on need.
2. The scholarship may be withdrawn for nonacademic reasons.
3. The recipients need no special academic qualifications.
4. The athlete is expected to compete in the sports program that is granting the scholarship.

Thus, some view an athletic scholarship as payment for athletic performance.

The topic of athletic scholarships marks an area of disagreement between the NCAA and the International Olympic Committee (IOC). In its regulations the IOC states that scholarships are permitted but must be "dependent upon the fulfillment of scholastic obligations and not athletic prowess." The NCAA, on the other hand, does permit athletic ability as a determining factor in the awarding of scholarship aid. The IOC also states that "Individuals subsidized by governments, educational institutions, or business concerns because of their athletic ability, are not amateurs." Consequently, if the athletic scholarship continues to be part of higher educational aid, litigation may result regarding the definition of "amateur" between these athletic organizations.

Athletic scholarships are technically renewable each year, but after being granted, they cannot be canceled or reduced on the basis of the student-athlete's ability or contribution to the team. In addition, athletic scholarships cannot be withdrawn because of an injury to a student-athlete or for any other athletically related reasons (*1987–88 NCAA Manual*, Constitution 3-4-[c]-[1]). NCAA rules do not, however, prohibit all types of scholarship revision or rescission. Scholarship aid may be canceled or reduced immediately for any of the following reasons:

(1) Institutional aid may not be gradated or canceled during the period of its award (i) on the basis of a student-athlete's ability or contribution to a team's success, (ii) because of an injury that prevents the recipient from participating in athletics or (iii) for any other athletics reason.

(2) Aid may be gradated or canceled if the recipient (i) renders himself or herself ineligible for intercollegiate competition; or (ii) fraudulently misrepresents any information on an application, letter of intent or tender; or (iii) engages in serious misconduct warranting substantial disciplinary penalty, or (iv) voluntarily withdraws from a sport for personal reasons. Any such gradation or cancellation of aid is permissible only if such action is taken for proper cause by the

regular disciplinary or scholarship awards authorities of the institution and the student-athlete has had an opportunity for a hearing. Under (iv) above, such gradation or cancellation of aid may not occur prior to the conclusion of that term (semester or quarter). [*1987–88 NCAA Manual*, Constitution 3-4-(c)-(1-2)]

However, to protect the student-athlete, certain procedural requirements must be followed when a scholarship change or reduction is made:

> The renewal of a scholarship or grant-in-aid award shall be made on or before July 1 prior to the academic year it is to be effective. The institution shall promptly notify each student-athlete who received an award the previous academic year and who is eligible to receive an award and has eligibility remaining under Bylaw 4-1 or Constitution 3-3-(a)-(3) for the ensuing academic year whether the grant has been renewed or not renewed. In the latter event, the institution also shall inform the student-athlete that if he or she believes the grant has not been renewed for questionable reasons, the student-athlete may request, and shall have the opportunity for, a hearing before the institutional agency making the financial award. The institution shall have established reasonable procedures for the prompt hearing of such a request. [*1987–88 NCAA Manual*, Constitution 3-4-(f)]

As indicated by the NCAA rule above, the renewal or nonrenewal of a scholarship award is the responsibility of the institution (usually the head coach of the specific sport). When a scholarship is not renewed, care should be taken to provide due process in case the student-athlete chooses to request a hearing or file suit. The nonrenewal letter sent to the student-athlete should include the reasons for the action and a statement informing the athlete that he is entitled to a hearing on the nonrenewal of the scholarship. This letter should be kept on file in the athletic director's office and be available upon request to the student-athlete.

In the case of a scholarship revocation, the student-athlete should be given the opportunity for a hearing. Again, according to due process considerations, a written notice of the action, containing specific time and place, should be given to the student-athlete. The hearing, depending on the formality required, may include a presentation of statements from both parties, cross-examination of witnesses, and the right to legal counsel (see page 145 in Chapter 4).

Other suggestions that might serve to diffuse the potentially explosive situation surrounding a scholarship revocation or nonrenewal include the following:

1. The student-athlete's parents should be contacted by phone before notifying them or the student-athlete by letter.
2. The student-athlete should be told in person what the impending action is and the reasons for the action before being notified in writing.
3. The student-athlete's high school coach should be contacted in some cases to be told of the reasoning behind the action before the student-athlete has an opportunity to do so.
4. A meeting should be arranged in some cases with the assistant coach or the person who recruited the student-athlete to ensure that care is used in future recruiting in order to prevent such a situation from recurring.

These steps can serve several useful purposes. First, they allow a coach and athletic administrators the opportunity to assess, and prepare for, the possibility that the student-athlete will use the appeal process. Second, these steps may prevent an appeal by informing all interested parties of the justification for the action. Last, these steps may reduce friction with the high school coach (for recruiting purposes) and with the student-athlete's parents. These parties may be less likely to bring the matter to public attention, and the student-athlete may be less likely to pursue litigation.

Workers' Compensation

Workers' compensation is a statutorily created method for providing cash benefits and medical care to employees and their dependents when the employee has suffered personal injuries or death in the course of employment. The purpose of the benefits is to provide employees and their dependents with greater protection than they are afforded by the common law remedy of a suit for damages. Each state has its own workers' compensation act that provides a system of monetary payments for the loss of earning capacity to an employee, according to a scale established by the state. The act may also have provisions for furnishing burial, medical, or other expenses incurred by the employee.

Workers' compensation acts differ as to where the funds are derived and the method of payment used in compensating claims. Some acts require the employer to make payment directly to the employee. Other acts provide payment out of a fund from which many different employers contribute. In still other acts, the employer's private insurer makes payments.

The primary reason for passage of workers' compensation statutes was to eliminate the inadequacies of the common law remedies that resulted from the injured party having to show that the employer was negligent. Proving negligence was often difficult for the employee because of defenses available to the employer, such as contributory negligence, assumption of the risk, and co-worker negligence. Under a workers' compensation act the injured employee need only show that the employer was subject to the act, that he or she was an employee under the act's definition, and that the injury occurred during the course of employment. Fault or employer negligence is not a prerequisite to receiving workers' compensation benefits. Payments are made in intervals, when the injured party and his or her dependents need money most, instead of waiting until the completion of costly litigation. To claim a right to compensation, an employee need only fall within the terms of the statute.

This theory of compensation shifts the burden of economic loss from the employee and the employee's dependents under the common law to the employer under the act. While the employer considers workers' compensation benefits part of the production cost, it is the consumer who will most likely bear the economic burden of the cost of the benefits, since the employer adds the costs to his products or services.

Every state's workers' compensation act has the same fundamental principle—the worker's right to benefit payments for injuries arising out of the worker's employment. Although each jurisdiction varies in the details of its act, the various acts have some general similarities. For example, in all jurisdictions there is a short waiting period during which the employee must either be totally or partially incapacitated. This is to avoid small and insignificant claims. When the period ends, the worker is eligible for compensation beginning from the date of the injury. Every jurisdiction sets its own rate schedule prescribing minimum and maximum compensation amounts for either total disability, partial disability, or permanent and total disability. These amounts are determined by each state's legislature and may be revised yearly. An additional benefit, separate from weekly compensation, is added for every person wholly dependent on the injured provider. An additional sum may be awarded for certain specific injuries, such as the loss of eyesight. Each state may have its own procedure for arriving at dollar amounts depending on that state's average wage or its economy.

The issue of workers' compensation is of particular significance to amateur athletic administrators for two reasons: (1) a determination that scholarship athletes are employees of their institutions will allow injured student-athletes to collect workers' compensation benefits in appropriate situations, resulting in an expensive insurance cost for institutions and their athletics departments; and (2) injured student-athletes, if found to be employees, may bring more workers' compensation claims or costly tort actions against institutions and their personnel in order to collect workers' compensation benefits. Workers' compensation cases filed by injured student-athletes against their institutions increased during the early 1980s.

With an eye toward this trend, the NCAA in 1985 instituted a catastrophic injury protection insurance plan that could be purchased by member institutions. The NCAA's insurance policy provides benefits to catastrophically injured student-athletes regardless of fault. The NCAA program may be more attractive than a successful workers' compensation claim in many cases, since the injured student-athlete may obtain benefits immediately without the time delays, costs, and uncertainties of litigation involved in filing for workers' compensation benefits. Yet, because the scholarship athlete/employee issue has not been firmly resolved, workers' compensation cases may still be raised by student-athletes. The NCAA would rather see the costs of the benefits of the injured athlete covered by an insurance policy (like the catastrophic injury protection plan which is paid for by the NCAA member institution) than paid for through the more costly and more tenuous method of workers' compensation. The insurance plan would benefit the institution by protecting it against the sudden substantial cost of injury benefits, and the student-athlete by providing immediate benefits without having to depend on a workers' compensation board or a judge to decide the issue.

Students-athletes who receive some form of compensation (including athletic scholarships) for athletic activities have at times been considered employees by the courts, and thus entitled to workers' compensation benefits for their sports injuries. However, this is the minority position of the court.

The courts in two early cases (see Notes 2a and 2b) ruled that since the continued receipt of a job, free meals, or money was conditioned upon the student-athlete's participation in football, a contract had been created. With the employment contract established, workers' compensation benefits were payable to those employees/athletes injured or killed during the course of their employment.

In other cases, courts have found no contractual relationship based on athletic scholarships and have denied benefits to injured student-athletes. In two cases, benefits were denied because the courts believed football was not an integral, money-making part of the university's basic educational function (see Notes 1c and 1d).

Therefore, the student-athlete was employed but not in the institution's usual trade or business.

To date, the leading case in this area is *Rensing v. Indiana State University Board of Trustees*, 437 N.E.2d 78 (Ind. App. 1982), *rev'd*, 444 N.E.2d 1170 (Ind. 1983). Rensing had filed a claim for workers' compensation benefits seeking recovery for injuries and medical expenses incurred while playing varsity football for Indiana State University. In a 1976 spring practice session, Rensing was rendered a quadriplegic following a neck injury sustained while making a tackle. The Indiana Court of Appeals carefully examined the issue of the athletic scholarship as employment contract and ultimately reversed the state's industrial board decision which had denied compensation to Rensing. (The court sent the case back to the board for further proceedings.) The court stated that workers' compensation cases should be liberally interpreted in order to satisfy public policy concerns and found that the scholarship had "constituted a case for hire . . . and created an employer-employee relationship" between the parties.

On appeal, the Indiana Supreme Court reversed the appeals court decision, finding that an athletic scholarship does not constitute an employment contract. The court reasoned that the following factors suggested that the scholarship did not constitute an employment contract: (1) Rensing had not reported his benefits on his income tax returns; (2) NCAA regulations are incorporated by reference into the scholarship agreement, and since these regulations prohibit payment for athletic participation, the scholarship could not be construed as a job contract; (3) the employer's right to dismiss Rensing on the basis of poor performance was conspicuously absent; and (4) since neither party had the intent to enter into an employment contract, a contract did not exist.

NOTES

1. The courts *denied* workers' compensation to intercollegiate student-athletes in the following cases.

(a) In *Cheatham v. Workers' Compensation Appeals Board*, 3 Civ. 21975 (Ct. App. Cal. 1984), Cheatham, a wrestler who was recruited and awarded an athletic scholarship by California Polytechnic, suffered a career-ending injury during a team scrimmage. He applied for workers' compensation. In denying his request, the court noted that the state legislature had amended the California Labor Code to specifically exclude student-athletes from the definition of employee.

(b) In *Tookes v. Florida State University*, Claim No. 266-39-0855, State of Florida, Department of Labor and Employment Security, Office of the Judge of Industrial Claims, Tookes, a Florida State

University basketball player, suffered a knee injury which sidelined him for most of the 1981–82 season. As a result, he claimed he should be entitled to workers' compensation benefits and filed suit seeking payment of medical bills and "lost salary." Tookes contended that as a scholarship athlete, he was an employee of the university. The industrial claims judge found that no employer-employee relationship existed but asserted that were one present, Tookes must be considered a professional athlete and as such would be a member of a class of employee excluded under Florida law.

(c) In *State Compensation Ins. Fund v. Industrial Commission*, 135 Colo. 570, 314 P.2d 288 (1957), Ray Dennison left his job at a gas station to play football for Fort Lewis A & M College after the Fort Lewis coach offered him a job and scholarship. Dennison received a fatal head injury in a game, and the Industrial Commission of Colorado awarded death benefits to his widow. The Colorado Supreme Court reversed this decision, however, because it found that no evidence existed that Dennison's employment was dependent upon his playing football. The court also found it significant that the school did not produce a profit from its football program.

(d) In *Coleman v. Western Michigan University*, 336 N.W.2d 224 (Mich. App. 1983), workers' compensation was denied for an injury received during the course of a college football practice. The Michigan Workmen's Compensation Board denied benefits, and the Court of Appeals of Michigan upheld the decision. The court, relying on *Askew v. Macumber*, 398 Mich. 212, 247 N.W.2d 288 (1976), considered the following four factors in determining whether there existed an "expressed or implied contract for hire":

1. The proposed employer's right to control or dictate the activities of the proposed employee.
2. The proposed employer's right to discipline or fire the proposed employee.
3. The payment of "wages" and, particularly, the extent to which the proposed employee is dependent upon the payment of wages or benefits for his daily living expenses.
4. Whether the task performed by the proposed employee was "an integral part" of the proposed employer's business.

The court held that although a scholarship was "wages," the athlete receiving the scholarship was not an "employee" within the meaning of the statute. The court noted:

As to the limits on defendant's "right to control" the plaintiff's activities, plaintiff suggests that defendant had a great deal of control over plaintiff's activities as a football player. It is observed, however, that such control applied to the sports activity whether or not an athlete had the benefit of a scholarship. Plaintiff's scholarship did not subject him to an extraordinary degree of control over his academic activities. The degree of defendant's control over this aspect of plaintiff's activities was no greater than that over any other student. Moreover, the record suggests that the parties contemplated a primary role for plaintiff's academic activities and only a secondary role for plaintiff's activities as a football player. Plaintiff recognized that "you are a student first, athlete second." In this case, however, plaintiff's football playing was not essential to the business of the defendant university, which plaintiff himself recognizes "as education and research." The record supports the conclusion that defendant's academic program could operate effectively, even in the absence of the intercollegiate football program. Defendant aptly notes that "the football season lasts for only a small portion of the academic year," and contrasts this with the fact that "the greater part of the school years is devoted exclusively to obtaining a regular college education."

    2. The courts *granted* workers' compensation to intercollegiate student-athletes in the following cases.

        (a) In *University of Denver v. Nemeth*, 127 Colo. 385, 257 P.2d 423 (1953), Nemeth, a student-athlete injured during football practice, was found eligible to collect workers' compensation. Evidence showing that Nemeth was given meal money and a job on campus only if he performed well on the football field brought him within the workers' compensation act requirement of "injury arising out of and in the course of employment."

        (b) In *Van Horn v. Industrial Accident Commission*, 219 Cal. App. 2d 451, 33 Cal. Rptr. 169 (1963), Van Horn received a football scholarship from California State Polytechnic College and was killed in a plane crash while returning from a game. The Industrial Accident Commission ruled there was no contract of employment between the school and Van Horn and that his scholarship did not depend on his playing football. The District Court of Appeals overruled the commission's findings and found a contract of employment did exist dependent on Van Horn's athletic prowess, which entitled his dependents to compensation. The court stressed that his scholarship alone could be construed as an employment contract.

    3. For further information, see the following law review articles:

        (a) Steinbach, "Workmen's Compensation and the Scholarship Athlete," 19 *Cleveland State Law Review* 521 (1970).

        (b) "Workers' Compensation and College Athletes: Should Universities Be Responsible for Athletes Who Incur Serious Injuries?" 10 *Journal of College and University Law* 197 (1983).

Scholarships as Contracts

The athletic scholarship has been interpreted by some to be a contractual relationship between the student-athlete and the institution. The reasoning is that the college student-athlete who signs a scholarship agreement is contracting to perform services as an employee for the university in exchange for free room, board, tuition, and books. The scholarship student-athlete is expected to partake in a daily routine of practices or forfeit the financial aid, clearly creating an employee status. The other side of the argument is that employee status can exist only when the scholarship is based on specific performance and when there is an intent to enter into a contract.

Usually both explicit and implicit conditions must be fulfilled when an educational institution offers and a student-athlete accepts an athletic scholarship. The university relinquishes the right to demand payment for its educational services, while the student-athlete agrees to do all that is possible to maintain his or her athletic eligibility and to participate with the team in practice and in games. In essence, there is a quid pro quo, and the student-athlete is getting a benefit conditioned on participating in athletics.

According to contract theory, a contract is enforceable based on the triad of offer-acceptance-consideration. In this situation, an institution extends a scholarship (offer) to the student-athlete who chooses to attend the institution (acceptance) in exchange for participation (athlete's consideration). For consideration to exist, each party must give something to the other. On the surface, this analysis is simple and logical. However, more particular inquiries suggest problems inherent in this contractual analysis of athletic scholarships.

Several legal and practical problems are raised when the athletic scholarship is viewed as a legally enforceable contract between the student-athlete and the educational institution. First, any compensation given to induce participation or to reward the performance of an athletic skill is, theoretically, in direct violation of rules regulating amateur status, including the NCAA's own policies. A finding that athletic scholarships are contracted is arguably a violation of these rules. Also, this analysis of athletic scholarships potentially allows the institution to compel a student-athlete to perform only for it and to prevent a student-athlete from transferring to another school for the duration of his or her scholarship-contract. A finding of a contract would also seem to indicate the use of contract remedies, including litigation, if either party defaults on the agreement.

Two early cases, *University of Denver v. Nemeth* and *Van Horn v. Industrial Accident Commission*, which were reviewed in Note 2 of the previous section, demonstrate a second potential problem when scholarships are analyzed as contracts. In both these cases, the courts held that if a contractual relationship exists between a student-athlete and an institution, and if the receipt of the scholarship or other benefits is conditioned on athletic performance, the athlete is to be considered an employee of the institution for the purposes of workers' compensation. Note, however, that for an employer-employee relationship to exist, the scholarship must be granted in return for participation—not merely to defray educational expenses. Making the student-athlete an employee will effectively destroy his or her amateur status for most amateur athletic associations.

The last problem produced with a contractual analysis concerns the taxability of scholarship funds. An educational grant-in-aid is mostly nontaxable since the award is "made in the nature of a relatively disinterested, no strings, educational grant, with no requirement of any substantial quid pro quo from the recipients." If a student-athlete receives a scholarship in consideration for athletic participation, then the entire award could be considered income and, therefore, taxable in accordance with Internal Revenue Service (IRS) regulations (exclusionary rule, IRS 117[a]). IRS regulations specifically address athletic scholarships in Revenue Ruling 77-263. In that analysis, the IRS emphasizes that only when a recipient does not have to participate in athletics as a condition of the award is the award considered nontaxable.

In *The Law of Sports*, Weistart and Lowell suggest that the best method for avoiding the problems created by a contract analysis is to analyze scholarships as either conditional gifts or educational grants. These approaches also have problems which are likely to arise from determining the enforceability of the gift. It is also questionable whether this approach is in accordance with practice, since universities rarely "give" anything without expecting something in return, whether it be athletic participation or the work responsibilities required with the receipt of many educational grants-in-aid.

Much of the relationship between the student-athlete and the institution has been analyzed by the courts on a contract theory (see Chapter 3). The institution can require the student-athlete to meet certain requirements. For example, most schools require that in return for athletic scholarship benefits, the student-athlete must maintain academic eligibility, attend practices, compete in games, and follow the rules and regulations of the institution, the allied conference (if applicable), and the NCAA. Therefore, both parties to the "contract" are required to perform certain duties creating "consideration." When any integral part of the agreement is not fulfilled, or if one or both parties are unable to comply with the agreed-upon terms, the courts have allowed the institution to rescind or revoke the scholarship.

The case that is considered to have opened the door to the precedent that scholarships could be viewed as contracts is the *Taylor v. Wake Forest University* case (see Note 1). The court ruled that written and oral promises by the university to the student-athlete constituted a contract. Yet, because the athlete failed to fulfill his obligations under the contract, the university was justified in terminating the scholarship.

Another leading case which involves an analysis of an athletic scholarship as a contract is *Begley v. Corporation of Mercer University*, 367 F. Supp. 908 (E.D. Tenn. 1973). In that case, Begley, a high school student, agreed to attend Mercer University on the condition that he receive an athletic grant-in-aid worth $11,208 to pursue an undergraduate degree. Begley also agreed to participate in basketball for Mercer and agreed that he would (1) abide by all university regulations, (2) keep all training rules, (3) maintain satisfactory progress toward graduation with a minimum cumulative average of 1.6, and (4) abide by all the rules and regulations of the NCAA. Later, it was discovered that Mercer University had made a mistake in calculating Begley's high school grade point average. The corrected GPA of 1.45 rendered Begley ineligible for basketball. As a result, Mercer withdrew its offer of a scholarship.

Begley brought suit seeking money damages for a breach of contract by Mercer. The district court granted Mercer's motion to dismiss the case since the facts proved beyond a doubt that Begley could not support his claim for relief. Mercer's inability to perform its part of the contract resulted from its need to abide by the rules and regulations of the NCAA. It was obvious that Mercer contracted with Begley under the stipulation that he be bound by NCAA regulations. Mercer cannot be held to have assumed the risk that the NCAA would not permit it to perform its contract with Begley. Thus, the court held that Mercer was not liable for its inability to perform.

NOTES

1. Another case in which a court *upheld* a university's right to terminate an athletic scholarship is *Taylor v. Wake Forest University*, 16 N.C. App. 117 (1972). Taylor brought this action against Wake Forest University to recover educational expenses incurred by him and his father after the university terminated his athletic scholarship. The court of appeals ruled in dismissing the claims that the written scholarship agreement could not be construed to give the Taylors the right to determine "reasonable academic progress." Since his grade average was above the eligibility requirements of Wake Forest, he was required to attend regular practice sessions and games in order to comply with his part of the contract.

2. For further information on scholarships as contracts, see the following law review articles:

   (a) "Breach of Contract Suits by Students Against Post-Secondary Institutions: Can They Succeed?" 7 *Journal of College & University Law* 191 (1980–81).

(b) "Contract Law, Due Process and the NCAA," 5 *Journal of College & University Law* 76 (1977).
(c) Steinbach, "Workmen's Compensation and the Scholarship Athlete," 19 *Cleveland State Law Review* 521 (1970).

Letter of Intent

The national letter of intent was developed to regulate the intense competition surrounding the recruitment of talented student-athletes, commonly referred to as "blue-chippers," to play college athletics. Letters of intent first were developed on the conference level in the late 1940s during a period when intercollegiate athletics first gained national prominence.

The guiding principle behind the letter of intent or preenrollment application is that there is agreement among member institutions that subscribe to the letter of intent to place a time limit on recruiting. Yet, once the recruited student-athlete signs a national letter of intent, there are no further limits on contacting the student-athlete by the signing institution. On a given date, high school student-athletes can sign a letter of intent, and after the signing no member institution subscribing to the letter will make any effort to recruit the student-athlete. NCAA regulations, however, prohibit the use of press conferences, receptions, and dinners to announce the fact that an athlete has signed a letter of intent. A student who signs the letter, whether or not the athlete actually enrolls at the institution, is not eligible to compete at any other institution subscribing to the letter-of-intent plan for two calendar years of intercollegiate competition with certain exceptions. However, the student-athlete is free to enroll at any member institution to pursue his or her academic interests.

A letter of intent becomes invalid if any of the following circumstances exist:

1. The player does not meet minimum academic standards to play as a freshman.
2. The player attends and graduates from a junior college.
3. The player does not enroll and the institution withdraws its scholarship offer the next year.
4. The player serves in the armed forces or a church mission for at least 18 months.
5. The institution discontinues the sport.

The letter of intent is administered by the Collegiate Commissioners Association (CCA) through the commissioners of allied athletic conferences. Exhibit 5–6 is a CCA form listing policies and interpretations concerning letters of intent. An institution must be an NCAA member to belong to the program, and the national letter of intent applies only to four-year member institutions. Independent institutions that belong to the letter-of-intent program file all necessary paperwork through an allied athletic conference of their choice. The program in its present form was started in 1964 with 7 conferences and 8 independent institutions joining for a total of 68 schools. In 1982, a women's letter of intent was added. Today, 27 conferences and nearly 300 institutions belong to the program.

The letter of intent is considered a preenrollment application by the CCA, although much of the language creates the possibility that it may be construed as a contract.

The men's and women's letters of intent contain identical regulations and procedures; only the membership differs. Both have four signing dates based on sport categories of (1) mid-year junior college transfer, (2) football, (3) basketball (basketball has two signing dates—an early signing period in November and the traditional period beginning in April), and (4) all other sports. The women's national letter of intent for 1987 is reprinted in Exhibit 5–7.

In addition to the national letter of intent, many conferences have their own internal program. Conferences may have other requirements when the student-athlete wants to enroll at another institution in the same conference. For example, the Pac-10 has the following rules:

> 2. Letters of Intent. The Council may adopt legislation by a vote of a majority of its members through which a prospective student-athlete may commit to a member institution by means of a Letter of Intent in order to reduce conflicting recruiting pressures. Such legislation may provide that a student who has signed a Letter of Intent accepted by one Pacific-10 institution and who then enrolls in another Pacific-10 institution without securing favorable action on a petition for relief of penalties shall lose such eligibility for participation in Pacific-10 sports and for financial assistance as provided in such legislation. [1986–87 *Pacific 10 Conference Handbook*, Constitution article 6, section 2]

Excess Financial Aid

The subject of excess financial aid is a very important one for student-athletes, their teammates, and the institution. Not only will student-athletes lose their eligibility if their financial aid exceeds a certain limit, but the entire team may forfeit games or an entire season if the number of full scholarship equivalents

1. Each conference and participating institution agrees to abide by the regulations and procedures outlined in the National Letter of Intent Program.
2. An institution must be an NCAA member to participate in the Program, and the Letter applies only to those institutions.
3. The Steering Committee has been authorized to issue interpretations, settle disputes, and consider petitions for release from the provisions of the Letter where there are extenuating circumstances. Its decision may be appealed to the CCA, which is the final adjudication body.
4. No additions or deletions may be made to the Letter or the release form.
5. A coach is not authorized to void, cancel or give a release to the Letter.
6. A release from the Letter shall apply to all participating institutions and cannot be conditional or selective by institution.
7. When two members of the same conference are in disagreement involving the validity of a Letter, the conference commissioner shall be empowered to resolve the issue.
8. The prospect should be notified anytime his/her signed National Letter of Intent has been declared invalid or null and void.
9. In matters involving the validity of the Letter of administrative procedures between two or more institutions not members of the same conference, the appropriate conference commissioners shall take steps to ascertain the facts and apply National Letter of Intent rules. If the case cannot be settled in this manner, it shall be submitted to the Steering Committee. The prospective student-athlete may submit any information he/she desires.
10. The institution shall immediately notify a prospect if he/she fails to meet, for the fall of 1987 (or winter or spring term of 1987 for mid-year junior college transfers), its admission requirements, or its academic requirements for financial aid to athletes, or the NCAA requirement for freshman financial aid (or NCAA junior college transfer rule) if applicable. The institution shall immediately notify the appropriate conference commissioner of the prospective student-athlete's failure to meet any of these requirements, and the date on which the notification of such failure was sent to the prospect. The conference commissioner shall promptly notify all other participating conference commissioners.
11. The parent or legal guardian is required to sign the Letter regardless of the age or marital status of the prospective student-athlete.
12. If the prospect does not have a living parent or a legal guardian, the Letter should be signed by the person who is acting in the capacity of a guardian. An explanation of the circumstances should accompany the Letter.
13. If an institution (or representative of its athletic interests) violates NCAA or conference rules during the recruitment of a prospect who signed a National Letter of Intent with it, as found through the NCAA or Conference enforcement process or acknowledged by the institution, the Letter shall be declared null and void. Such declaration shall not take place until all appeals to the NCAA or conference for restoration of eligibility have been concluded.
14. It is presumed that a student is eligible for admission and financial aid at the institution for which he/she signed a National Letter of Intent until information is submitted to the contrary. This means that it is mandatory for the student to provide a transcript of his/her previous academic record and an application for admission to the institution where he/she signed a National Letter of Intent when requested.
15. The National Letter of Intent rules and regulations shall apply to all sports recognized by the member institution as varsity intercollegiate sports in which the NCAA sponsors championships or publishes the official playing rules.
16. The National Letter is considered to be officially signed on the final date of signature by the prospective student and his/hers parent or legal guardian. A National Letter is validated when name is listed on signing list that is circulated to all

Exhibit 5-6 Policies and Interpretations of the Collegiate Commissioners Association Regarding Men's and Women's National Letter of Intent

conferences. If an incomplete Letter is submitted to a conference office by an institution, the Letter may be returned and reissued. If no time of day is listed for signing of Letter it is assumed a 11:59 P.M. signing time.

17. It is a breach of ethics for an institution to sign a prospective student-athlete to an invalid second Letter for the purpose of making the prospect feel obligated to that institution.

18. If a prospect signing a Letter is eligible for admission but the institution defers his/her admission to a subsequent term, the Letter shall be rendered null and void. However, if the prospect defers his/her admission, the Letter remains valid.

19. Any prospect who signs a Letter prior to April 8, 1987 and who becomes a countable player under NCAA Bylaw 6, shall be counted in the maximum awards in the designated sport in his/her first year at the institution with which he/she signed.

20. The conditions of the National Letter of Intent Program shall not apply retroactively to an institution joining the Program.

21. A prospect who signs a professional sports contract remains bound by Letter rules when financial aid cannot be made available to him/her by the institution with which he/she signed.

22. Upon receipt of the completed Letter, the commissioner of each conference shall promptly notify the Big Ten Conference (two copies of signing lists for computer check for double signings) and one copy to the NCAA office.

23. The National Letter of Intent will carry a four year statute of limitations.

24. For a prospective student-athlete signing a National Letter of Intent as a Mid-Year Junior College Transfer, the National Letter applies for the following fall term if the student was eligible for admission, financial aid, and met the NCAA junior college transfer requirements for the winter or spring term.

Exhibit 5-6 Continued

exceeds the limits established by the NCAA for that particular sport. In most sports, there is also a limit on the value of the financial aid awards that can be in effect at one time in a given sport (*1987–88 NCAA Manual*, Bylaw 6-5-[a]). Thus, collegiate athletic administrators and coaches must be aware of the number and levels of financial aid for their student-athletes.

The amount of financial aid a student-athlete may receive from the institution or from outside sources is strictly regulated under NCAA guidelines. Scholarships may not exceed commonly accepted educational expenses (*1987–88 NCAA Manual*, Constitution 3-1-[g]); these expenses are limited to tuition and fees, room and board, and books. A school or other donor is not allowed to pay expenses exceeding these, and the student-athlete is not allowed to have any other benefits generally unavailable to all members of the student body (*1987–88 NCAA Manual*, Constitution 3-1-[g]-[1-5]).

A student-athlete may participate in *any* sport in which he or she has never participated at the professional level. However, the student-athlete who is either currently under contract to or receiving compensation from a professional organization may not receive financial aid. Nor may a student-athlete receive payment, or even

☐ **Mid-Year Junior College Transfer: Do not sign prior to 8:00 a.m. December 10, 1986 and no later than January 15, 1987**

☐ **Volleyball and Field Hockey: Do not sign prior to 8:00 a.m. February 11, 1987 and no later than August 1, 1987**

☐ **Basketball: Do not sign prior to 8:00 a.m. November 12, 1986 and no later than November 19, 1986 OR do not sign prior to 8:00 a.m. April 8, 1987 and no later than May 15, 1987**

☐ **All other sports: Do not sign prior to 8:00 a.m. April 8, 1987 and no later than August 1, 1987**

Name of student _____
(Type proper name, including middle name or initial)

Address _____ _____
Street Number   City, State, Zip Code

This is to certify my decision to enroll at _____
Name of Institution

IMPORTANT - READ CAREFULLY

It is important to read carefully this entire document, including the reverse side, before signing this Letter in triplicate. One copy is to be retained by you and two copies are to be returned to the institution, one of which will be sent to the appropriate conference commissioner.

---

1. By signing this Letter, I understand that if I enroll in another institution participating in the National Letter of Intent Program, I may not represent that institution in intercollegiate athletic competition until I have been in residence at that institution for two calendar years and in no case will I be eligible for more than two seasons of intercollegiate competition in any sport.

   However, these restrictions will not apply to me:

   (a) If I have not, by the opening day of its classes in the fall of 1987 (or the opening day of its classes of the winter or spring term of 1987 for a mid-year junior college entrant), met the requirements for admission to the institution named above, its academic requirements for financial aid to athletes, the NCAA requirement for freshman financial aid [Bylaw 5-1-(j)] or the NCAA junior college transfer rule; or

   (b) If I attend the institution named above for at least one academic year; or

   (c) If I graduate from junior college after having signed a National Letter of Intent while in high school or during my first year in junior college; or

   (d) If I have not attended any institution (or attended an institution, including a junior college, which does not participate in the National Letter of Intent Program) for the next academic year after signing this Letter, provided my request for athletic financial aid for the following fall term is not approved by the institution with which I signed. In order to receive this waiver, I must file with the appropriate conference commissioner a statement from the Director of Athletics at the institution with which I signed certifying that such financial aid will not be available to me for the requested fall term; or

   (e) If I serve on active duty with the armed forces of the United States or on an official church mission for at least eighteen (18) months; or

   (f) If my sport is discontinued by the institution with which I signed this Letter.

2. I MUST RECEIVE IN WRITING AN AWARD OR RECOMMENDATION FOR ATHLETIC FINANCIAL AID FROM THE INSTITUTION AT THE TIME OF MY SIGNING FOR THIS LETTER TO BE VALID. The offer or recommendation shall list the terms and conditions of the award, including the amount and duration of the financial aid. If such recommended financial aid is not approved within the institution's normal time period for awarding financial aid, this letter shall be invalid.

Exhibit 5-7   1987 Women's National Letter of Intent

I certify that I have read all terms and conditions on pages 1 and 2, fully understand, accept and agree to be bound by them. All three copies must be signed individually for this Letter to be valid. Do not use carbons.

SIGNED _____   _____   _____
                          Student   Date & Time   Social Security Number

SIGNED _____   _____
                    Parent or Legal Guardian   Date & Time

Submission of this Letter has been authorized by:

SIGNED _____   _____   _____
                    Director of Athletics   Date Issued to Student   Sport

NATIONAL LETTER OF INTENT REGULATIONS AND PROCEDURES

3. **I MAY SIGN ONLY ONE VALID NATIONAL LETTER OF INTENT.** However, if this Letter is rendered null and void under item 1 - (a) on page 1, I remain free to enroll in any institution of my choice where I am admissible and shall be permitted to sign another Letter in a subsequent signing year.
   JUNIOR COLLEGE EXCEPTION: If I signed a National Letter of Intent while in high school or during my first year in junior college, I may sign another Letter in the signing year in which I am scheduled to graduate from junior college. If I graduate, the second Letter shall be binding on me; otherwise, the original Letter which I signed shall remain valid.

4. I understand that I have signed this Letter with the **institution** and not for a particular sport.

5. I understand that all participating conferences and institutions (listed below) are obligated to respect my signing **and shall cease to recruit me.** I shall notify any recruiter who contacts me of my signing.

6. If my parent or legal guardian and I fail to sign this Letter within 14 days after it has been issued to me it will be invalid. In that event, this Letter may be reissued. (Note: Exception is November 12-19, 1986, signing period for basketball.)

7. My signature on this Letter nullifies any agreements, oral or otherwise, which would release me from the conditions stated on this Letter.

8. This Letter must be signed and dated by the Director of Athletics or his/her authorized representative before submission to me and my parent or legal guardian for our signatures. This Letter may be mailed prior to the initial signing date.

9. This Letter must be filed with the appropriate conference by the institution with which I sign within **21 days** after the date of final signature or it will be invalid. In that event, this Letter may be reissued.

10. If I have knowledge that I or my parent/legal guardian have falsified any part of this Letter, I understand that I shall forfeit the first two years of my eligibility at the participating institution in which I enroll as outlined in item 1.

11. A release procedure shall be provided in the event the student-athlete and the institution mutually agree to release each other from any obligations to the Letter. A student-athlete receiving a formal release shall not be eligible for competition at the second institution during the first academic year of residence and shall be charged with one season of competition. The form must be signed by the student-athlete, her parent or legal guardian, and the Director of Athletics at the institution with which she signed. A copy of the release must be filed with the conference which processes the Letters of the signing institution.

12. This letter applies only to students who will be entering a four-year institution for the first time as a full time student.

Exhibit 5-7 Continued

The following Conferences and Institutions have subscribed to and are cooperating in the National Letter of Intent Plan administered by the Collegiate Commissioners Association:

CONFERENCES:

Atlantic Coast	Continental Divide	Mid-Eastern	Southeastern
Atlantic 10	Gateway	Midwestern Collegiate	Southern
Big East	Great Lakes Valley	Missouri Intercollegiate	Southern Intercollegiate
Big Eight	Gulf South	Mountain West	Southland
Big Sky	Gulf Star	New South	Southwest
Big South	High Country	North Central	Southwestern
Big Ten	Lone Star	North Star	Sun Belt
California Collegiate	Metropolitan	Ohio Valley	Trans America
Central Intercollegiate	Mid-American	Pacific Coast	West Coast
Colonial	Mid-Continent	Pacific-10	

INDEPENDENT INSTITUTIONS:

Boston University	Gannon	Mount St. Joseph	Siena
Brooklyn	Grand Valley	New Orleans	Southern Illinois-
California Lutheran	Hartford	New York Tech	Edwardsville
Canisius	Iona	Niagara	Tampa
Central Connecticut	Kentucky State	Northeastern	Texas-El Paso
Central Florida	Lake Superior	Northern Arizona	Texas Women's
Central State (Ohio)	Liberty	Northern Illinois	Towson State
Chicago State	Loyola (MD)	Northern Michigan	Tulane
Creighton	Maine (Orono)	Oakland	Tulsa
East Carolina	Manhattan	Pace	US International
Eckerd	Marist	Pan American	Utica
Fairfield	Maryland (BC)	Quincy	Vermont
Fairleigh Dickinson	Miami (Florida)	Robert Morris	Wayne State
Florida A&M	Michigan Tech	Saginaw Valley	William and Mary
Florida Atlantic	Midwestern (TX)	St. Francis (PA)	Wisconsin-Milwaukee
Florida International	Minnesota-Duluth	Saint Leo	Wright State
Florida Southern	Missouri-Kansas City	St. Peter's (NJ)	
Fordham	Monmouth	St. Thomas (Florida)	

NOTE: Air Force, Army, and Navy are **not** members of the program.

Exhibit 5-7 Continued

a promise of payment, for playing in the sport, directly or indirectly, either before enrollment in college or during the period of eligibility (*1987–88 NCAA Manual*, Constitution 3-1-[a]-[1]). Acceptance of either payment or the promise of money for participation in a sport at the collegiate level automatically categorizes the student-athlete as a professional, and thus erases his or her amateur status. The student-athlete is also not entitled to be paid or sponsored in sporting events even though the student-athlete may not be representing the collegiate institution (unless by his natural or legal guardian). Also, the student-athlete may not receive special treatment because of his or her athletic prowess (e.g., loans on a deferred pay-back basis, automobiles, or special living quarters) (*1987–88 NCAA Manual*, Constitution 3-1-[i]-[1]-[i-v]).

Student-athletes may not participate in any competition for cash or prizes, either for themselves or for a donation on their behalf, unless they are eligible to receive such monies under the NCAA guidelines (*1987–88 NCAA Manual*, Constitution, 3-1-[i]-[g]-[5]-[i-viii]). For example, the NCAA has approved the granting of scholarship funds in a student-athlete's name if the person was selected as a most valuable player by a national advertiser or sponsor of an event. However, the NCAA has not approved a student-athlete's participation in the "Superstars" competition (ABC-TV) or similar staged sporting events. A student-athlete would also jeopardize his eligibility if he received, for example, a country-club membership as a prize or compensation.

The rule of thumb regarding payment/receipt of expenses provides that a student-athlete may not receive money for expenses that are in excess of the actual and necessary expenses involved in an activity authorized by the NCAA. Examples of prohibited expense payments include travel expenses to a special location for an article on and/or photographs of a student-athlete (unless in conjunction with the receipt of an established/authorized award at that location) and expenses from an agent seeking to represent the student-athlete in the marketing of his or her athletic skills (*1987– 88 NCAA Manual*, Constitution 3-1-[c]). The courts have historically upheld the NCAA rules restricting excess pay or financial aid unless the regulations violate constitutionally protected rights (see Notes 1 and 2).

A leading case in the area of excess financial aid is *Wiley v. National Collegiate Athletic Ass'n*, 612 F.2d 473 (10th Cir. 1979), *cert. denied*, 446 U.S. 943 (1980). An action was brought by Wiley, a student-athlete who was declared ineligible to compete because his financial aid exceeded the amount allowed by the NCAA. Wiley had been awarded a full Basic Educational Opportunity Grant (BEOG) in addition to an athletic scholarship. Taken together, these exceeded the financial limitations imposed by the institutions under NCAA regulations and made the student ineligible to compete. Wiley filed suit, and the court applied a rational basis analysis rejecting a strict scrutiny approach because poverty or wealth is not a suspect classification (see page 158). The court refused to prohibit the NCAA from enforcing its regulations on the grounds that "unless clearly defined constitutional principles are at issue, suits by student-athletes against high school athletic associations or NCAA rules do not present a substantial federal-question."

Under NCAA rules, a member school may allow a student-athlete a maximum of four complimentary admissions for each contest in his or her particular sport. However, the student-athlete's guests must sign for the admission and receive no tickets (*1987–88 NCAA Manual*, Constitution 3-1-[g]-[3]). Tickets are prohibited (Division I) since there were previous abuses by student-athletes who received compensation by scalping the tickets. A student-athlete may, however, receive free admission to a professional contest without endangering his or her amateur status and college eligibility.

NOTES

1. A case in which a court *denied* a student-athlete's eligibility based on his receipt of excess financial aid is *Jones v. National Collegiate Athletic Ass'n*, 392 F. Supp. 295 (D. Mass. 1975). An American ice hockey player brought an action against the NCAA for a preliminary injunction to prohibit the NCAA from declaring him ineligible to compete and from imposing sanctions against his college if they allowed him to play because of excess financial aid he received. Prior to entering college, the student-athlete had been compensated for five years while playing junior hockey in Canada. During one of those three years, he was paid a weekly salary and received a signing bonus. The court denied Jones injunctive relief, finding that the NCAA's rules on financial aid were reasonable.

2. A court *granted* eligibility to a student-athlete in *Buckton v. National Collegiate Athletic Ass'n*, 366 F. Supp. 1158 (D. Mass 1973), despite the NCAA's contention that the student-athlete received excess financial aid. Buckton and other Canadian ice hockey players were denied eligibility because they had received funding from Junior League Hockey teams in Canada rather than from high schools, as is the custom in the United States. The court prohibited the NCAA from enforcing ineligibility because the rule, in effect, discriminated against individuals based on national origin.

Congressional Concerns over Athletic Scholarships and Eligibility

In June 1984, the Subcommittee on Education, Arts and Humanities of the Committee on Labor and Human Resources of the United States Senate held hearings on the Oversight on College Athletic Programs. The hearings focused on a number of issues, including (1) the exploitation of athletes who clearly have the academic ability to succeed in colleges but do not because of the time demands placed upon them by athletic pursuits, (2) the dilution of academic standards to accommodate the student-athlete, and (3) the inadequacy of athletic scholarship programs to respond to the educational needs of student-athletes who no longer are able to participate—because of injury, for example—in their college athletic program.

One committee member, Senator Howard Metzenbaum of Ohio, noted during his questioning of witnesses that he was contemplating introducing a bill that would establish federal authority for the regulation of college athletic scholarships. First, the proposed legislation would require university athletic departments to maintain an accurate accounting of all student-athletes under scholarship, broken down by sport in order that their academic progress could be tracked. Second, the legislation would require institutions to make an educational commitment to the athlete at the time of the recruitment so that the athlete would be secure in the knowledge that there would always be scholarship funding for his or her education and eventual graduation. Time would not be a factor in the scholarship or loss of athletic services due to injury. And penalties would involve some impact on an institution's Title IV funds under the Federal Aid to Education Act.

The general reaction to the proposed legislation was negative, with witnesses stating that this area was not one of federal government concern. Edward T. Foote II, president of the University of Miami, noted in his statement before the committee:

> The pressures to win are great. They increase more with winning, and even faster with losing. Winning creates excitement, not only in an athletic program but throughout a university. Students like it. Alumni like it. The conventional wisdom is that a winning athletic program generates spinoff benefits, from donations to more freshman applicants.
>
> This is hardly startling news. Winning is no more fun than it was a generation ago. But in recent years, there has been a growing perception throughout higher education that something significant was changing in the equation of major, intercollegiate athletics. It was a dangerous change. If winning wasn't more fun, it was getting much more important to a lot of people. It is not a change of kind, but of intensity and magnitude.
>
> My own view is that the principal reason for the change is television, and especially the money it generates.
>
> During the past generation, as television has woven itself so tightly into the fabric of American life, perhaps no undertakings have been more dramatically affected than athletics, professional and amateur. The money television generates for the successful is immense. The going rate now for a football team's appearance on national television is $675,000, and for a regionally televised game, $350,000. The Orange Bowl paid the University of Miami and the University of Nebraska each $1,800,000 just for showing up. In addition, the University of Miami Football Hurricanes generated $1,094,910 in television income during the fiscal year that ended June 1st. The instant celebrity of athletic stars, made possible by television, translates into cash almost as fast.
>
> Money is not the only temptation presented by television. Amateur athletics are ideal fare for television's capacity to magnify and dramatize. The most mundane sporting event takes on excitement when properly narrated, packaged and hyped. Naturally exciting sports such as football and basketball assume an unnatural magic far larger than mere life itself.
>
> In summary, my message is threefold: first, the American system of big-time intercollegiate athletic competition can and sometimes

does distort important educational principles to the detriment of the nation's colleges, universities and students; second, the threat can be resisted successfully by fidelity to those principles, and the world of higher education is stiffening that resistance; third, with all due respect, the forum for addressing and resolving the problem is not the Congress of the United States.

Senator Metzenbaum himself voiced reservations but concluded that "it would be far better if the government would not be involved, and yet usually you find legislation that comes about because there is a problem and no solution is provided by those who are in a position to provide a solution. And so, out of a sense of frustration, you find a legislative approach."

Other forms of legislation have been proposed, but to date, no laws have been passed that deal with the problem of scholarships and student-athlete education. Two pieces of federal legislation were proposed in 1983 and 1985 that would have encouraged universities and professional sports teams to ensure the graduation of student-athletes (see Notes 3 and 4). Other state legislation has been proposed to discourage booster clubs and others from influencing a student-athlete's decision to attend a certain college, and to ensure academic progress at the high school level for students participating in extracurricular activities (see Note 5).

NOTES

1. At the Senate hearings just mentioned, Kevin J. Ross, a former Creighton University scholarship basketball player, gave the following testimony:

> One cannot possibly earn good grades if they have not been taught to read, and, the only other recourse is to become good in athletics and earn a scholarship to college by proving that you can conquer the world in a pair of gym shoes. Of course, being six foot nine inches helps to bring the college recruiters to your door. If these recruiters feel that you can earn extra monies for the college by lighting up the scoreboards and keeping the crowds yelling it therefore does not become necessary to function in classes.
>
> Creighton knew that I could not read or write well enough for college. In fact they saw the incompletes and poor grades that I had earned in high school. Yet they ignored these grades with the view that I could serve them well on the basketball court.
>
> Had I received a degree from Creighton University I would have been a part of our present national abuse in education. . . . I would have earned a degree, but it would have not been beneficial to those students that I worked with, nor to society. We must cease the degree factories that give out degrees to people regardless of their achievements.
>
> In fact, not much time is given one to attend classes, since most of an athlete's time is taken up in traveling across the country and in practicing to win on the basketball court.
>
> The athletic director at Creighton University never bothered with the

reality that I was an illiterate, he was only concerned with my playing ball for Creighton. The courses were selected for me by the athletic director and coaches at Creighton, and, of course, these courses were easy courses such as the theory of first aid, the theory of tennis and basketball; courses that required not one lofty thought.

If I had a paper to turn in for my classes these were done for me by the secretaries at the college. If I failed a class this was taken care of for me by the coach or athletic director.

Everything is taken care of for you academically unless you have the misfortune of becoming incapacitated to play. I was injured in my junior year, and after having knee surgery I no longer seemed to be able to do anything right. I refused to leave the college without a degree, or an explanation as to why I was considered good enough to remain at the college until my injury. To appease me the athletic director gave me an option that he knew would ridicule even the strongest of men—the option to return to a grammar school with young children whose skills made me even more inferior. In fact, I thought of suicide many times.

The athletic director called Mrs. Marva Collins of Westside Preparatory School and asked if she would accept me in the school as a student. Mrs. Collins later said that she thought surely it was a joke, but she did indicate that she would let me enroll in the school. Creighton University paid my tuition there for a year with a monthly stipend of $350.00. I, however, dared not take a job, and I had no place to live. I could not afford to work part-time since I had a full-time responsibility of recapturing sixteen years of malpractice and bad education. This was my last chance to breathe literacy.

2. At the hearings, Harry Edwards, Ph.D., Department of Sociology, University of California, Berkeley, testified:

Collegiate football and basketball players also must adjust not only to playing with pain but to living day in and day out with pain as well as in a constant state of fatigue. Neither condition is very conducive to development of study habits nor requisite levels of mental concentration demanded of students competing in the classrooms of this nation's major universities.

Under existing conditions of medical service and surveillance in intercollegiate sports, this situation seems unlikely to change in the near future. That is, in today's highly competitive collegiate sports enterprise, the line can often be intentionally or unwittingly blurred between playing with pain and playing with an injury or even a significant and life threatening illness. Within the last year alone, I have been contacted by athletes who felt pressured to play with varying medical debilities or lose their athletic grants-in-aid. In one instance, an athlete and his parents contacted me concerning a basketball coach who insisted that the young man play, though he had not fully recovered from two dislocated shoulders. In another instance, I was contacted by attorneys representing a young man who complained to his team physician about a lump on his neck in October only to be told that it was nothing of consequence. Near the end of the season, that same lump was diagnosed as cancerous. This case is now in court.

A major problem here is that team physicians are paid by athletic departments. Also, many institutions either prohibit or make it extraordinarily difficult for a student-athlete to obtain a second medical opinion on an injury or illness and even when second medical opinions are permitted, the team physician opinion prevails—not by credibility or medical convention but by the athletic department rule.

And the two most common problems that I hear from athletes—and I do get a chance to talk to athletes on most of these campuses—is, one, they are being pressured into giving up their scholarships as a result of injury or as a result of not being the blue chip that the coach thought he would be.

And the second thing that I hear most commonly is a concern about, what happens to me if I am injured. And in numerous cases I find that athletes find out too late that there is a limit on how much the school, the athletic department, will spend for them on an injury.

Virtually, no institution carries catastrophic injury insurance; the NCAA does not require it. I understand that they plan to offer it under circumstances where, I believe, the catastrophic injury—knees, shoulders, and so forth—is up about 18 percent.

In some schools they have actually written into the rules that the school will pay for no second opinions; that the school will not be liable for illness. If this athlete is ill, not as a result of a football or basketball injury, the school will not pay for it.

So, this is a major problem that has simply been swept under the rug, and because you are dealing so often with 17- to 19-year-olds or 19- to 20-year-olds, nobody takes them seriously when they raise these complaints, and they do not know what their rights are under these circumstances.

3. In February 1983, Senator Arlen Specter (Pa.) introduced legislation designed to encourage professional sports leagues to make student-athletes complete their undergraduate education before turning professional. The legislation, S. 610, was entitled the Collegiate Student-Athlete Protection Act of 1983. The legislation amended the federal antitrust laws so that they would not apply "to a joint agreement by or among persons engaging in or conducting the professional sports of football, baseball, basketball, soccer, or hockey designed to encourage college student-athletes to complete their undergraduate education before becoming professional athletes."

4. In May 1985, Congressman James Howard (N.J.) introduced legislation designed to encourage the nation's universities to make certain that the majority of student-athletes graduate from college with a degree. The legislation, H.R. 2620, was entitled the College Athlete Education and Protection Act of 1985. It was designed to amend the Internal Revenue Code of 1954 to "encourage the graduation of student-athletes by denying the deduction for contributions to athletic departments of schools not meeting certain requirements."

5. In 1986, the California Legislature considered the passage of two separate sports bills, both proposed by Assembly Speaker Willie Brown. Assembly Bill 2753, an antisports corruption bill, would prohibit the offering of money and gifts to high school athletes as incentives for their choosing a college. Violation of the prohibition would be punishable by a civil fine of up to $10,000 or three times the amount given, whichever was greater, but not less than $1,000. The bill would also prohibit a student-athlete from soliciting or accepting money for playing sports or participating in intercollegiate athletics. Violation would also be punishable by a civil fine.

The theory behind the bill was that recruiting abuses should be attacked where the corruption originates—with the boosters and alumni who supply gifts and bribes to prospective student-athletes. School policies and NCAA rules impose penalties on institutions and student-athletes, but the individuals who offer the gifts are rarely punished. The bill would have made it a misdemeanor for any person to give, offer, or promise money or anything of value to a student-athlete as inducement, encouragement, or reward for participation in intercollegiate sports.

Assembly Bill 2613 would have required that the governing board of each school district establish a policy that would ensure that high school and junior high school students make satisfactory educational progress in the previous grading period as a condition for further participation in extracurricular and co-curricular activities. "Satisfactory educational progress" included, but was not limited to, (1) maintenance of minimum passing grades (2.0 GPA) in all enrolled courses, and (2) maintenance of minimum progress toward meeting the high school graduation requirements prescribed by the governing board. The failure of the school district's governing board to establish such a policy would result in the loss of the inflation adjustment the school district receives in its state apportionment of funds.

Pay/Employment/Marketing/Expenses

Pay

Under NCAA regulations student-athletes may not receive pay that meets the following definition:

> The term "pay" specifically includes, but is not limited to, receipt directly or indirectly of any salary, gratuity or comparable compensation; division or split of surplus; education expenses not permitted by governing legislation of this Association, and excessive or improper expenses, awards and benefits. Expenses received from an outside amateur sports team or organization in excess of actual and necessary travel and meal expenses for practice and game competition shall be considered pay. [*1987–88 NCAA Manual*, Constitution 3-1-(a)-O.I.2]

This definition applies to all student-athletes competing under NCAA regulations, whether or not they are attending college on an athletic scholarship. The concept of pay deals directly with the concept of amateurism and should not be confused with employment, which is permitted under NCAA regulations.

The NCAA also considers a student-athlete who has received pay in any of the following ways ineligible:

1. Has taken pay or accepted the promise of pay in any form, for participation in a sport.
2. Has participated in a sport with the promise that compensation will be forthcoming upon the completion of intercollegiate competition.

3. Has directly or indirectly used athletic skill for pay, including payment for displaying athletic skills in the promotion of commercial products.

4. Has directly or indirectly received a salary, reimbursement of expenses, or any form of financial assistance from a professional organization based on athletic skill or participation.

The NCAA rules concerning pay were challenged in *Shelton v. National Collegiate Athletic Ass'n*, 539 F.2d 1197 (9th Cir. 1976). Lonnie Shelton, a student-athlete at the time, was allegedly persuaded to sign a professional contract by the use of fraud and undue influence on the part of an agent. After being declared ineligible by the NCAA, Shelton sued the NCAA, claiming that the rule should not be enforced against him since the misconduct of the agent rendered the contract voidable.

The court, however, after examining the rule, upheld it because the NCAA goals to protect and to promote amateurism, which were incorporated into the rule, were legitimate. Therefore, although the rule might, when applied in certain situations, produce unreasonable results, it did not violate the U.S. Constitution because the rule was rationally related to its goals (see page 244).

NOTES

1. The New Jersey Interscholastic Athletic Association has the following policy on pay and employment of high school student-athletes:

Section 2. Amateur-Athlete—An amateur-athlete is one who participates in athletics solely for the physical, mental, social and educational benefits derived from such participation. The amateur-athlete treats all athletic activities in which he/she participates as an avocational endeavor. One who takes or has taken pay, or has accepted the promise of pay, in any form, for participation in athletics or has directly or indirectly used his/her athletic skill for pay in any form shall not be considered an amateur and will not be eligible for high school interscholastic athletics in the State of New Jersey.

The following are the basic interpretations of the principles involved in the amateur code which may lead to the loss of an athlete's eligibility: . . .

B. Accepting pay or material remuneration for a display of athletic ability.

C. Any student who signs or has ever signed a contract to play professional athletics (whether for a money consideration or not); plays or has ever played on any professional team in any sport; receives or has ever received, directly or indirectly, a salary or any other form of financial assistance from a professional sports organization or any of his/her expenses for reporting to or visiting a professional team is no longer an amateur as defined by this code.

D. A Student-Athlete may participate as an individual, or as a member of a team against professional athletes, or as a member of a team on which there are some professionals who are not currently under contract with a professional team and are not receiving payment for their participation; but he/she may not participate on a professional team. [1984–85 NJSIAA Handbook, Article V. 2 B-D]

2. The U.S. Amateur Boxing Federation has the following policy concerning pay and continued eligibility:

219.7 Receiving compensation for athletic services.

(a) Any school or college teacher, including physical education teacher, whose work is educational or who is not paid more than 20 percent of their total salary or compensation directly or indirectly for coaching of athletes for competition is eligible to compete as an amateur boxer.

(b) Any person receiving compensation for officiating in boxing renders himself ineligible for further amateur competition in boxing contests sanctioned by the corporation. The Registration Committee of the local boxing committee in which such person is or was registered is empowered to approve registration or reinstatement of such person whose compensation was or is not in excess of allowable expenses under corporation regulations and who has not otherwise rendered himself ineligible.

(c) An athlete who for gain solicits publicly the employment of his athletic services shall automatically disqualify himself from further competition. . . . [*1986–87 USA/ABF Official Rules*]

Outside Employment

A student-athlete who is receiving a full athletic scholarship from an institution is not eligible for employment during the academic year except during vacation periods and then only until the first day of class begins (or practice in the case of football). The student-athlete is not eligible for employment, because under NCAA regulations, any monies or financial assistance which exceeds commonly accepted educational expenses (i.e., tuition and fees, room and board, and required course-related books) is classified as pay and renders the student ineligible to compete in NCAA athletics (*1987–88 NCAA Manual*, Bylaw 6-1-[b]-[1]).

A student-athlete who is receiving only partial financial assistance from an institution, including a partial athletic scholarship, is allowed to receive employment compensation from work-study on campus or employment off campus, up to the limit established by the institution as accepted educational expenses. This employment compensation also counts toward the value of the total financial aid awards in effect at one time for each sport (see *1987–88 NCAA Manual*, Bylaw 6-5).

Student-athletes can hold campus jobs or employment through alumni of the institution, but they must be paid only for the work actually done. Student-athletes who receive remuneration for work not performed are no longer eligible for participation in intercollegiate athletics. Furthermore, student-athletes must be paid at a rate commensurate with the going rate in the particular locality for services of a similar character (*1987–88 NCAA Manual*, Constitution 3-1-[f]).

With some exceptions (see Note 1), any compensation received over commonly accepted educational expenses as set by the individual institution must be deducted from the financial assistance package received by the student-athlete (including athletic scholarships), or else the student-athlete will be ineligible to compete for the institution.

There are limits to the types of employment a student-athlete can consider to maintain amateur status and collegiate eligibility. For example, student-athletes are not permitted to be employed by their institutions as teachers or coaches in any sport and may only be employed by other organizations as teachers or coaches in their particular sport under certain circumstances (see Note 2).

Monitoring a student-athlete's employment activities during the academic year can be a difficult endeavor for an athletic administrator. Weekend jobs, jobs with friends, or odd jobs on and off campus, while seemingly insignificant to the casual bystander or to the student-athlete, may in fact be a threat to retaining eligibility to compete in intercollegiate athletics.

NOTES _____

1. The student-athlete who is preparing to compete or has competed in the Olympic Games is entitled to recover any financial loss occurring as a result of absence from employment that is authorized by the United States Olympic Committee. The period involved in recovering the losses must "immediately" precede actual Olympic competition (*1987–88 NCAA Manual*, Constitution 3-[1]-(a)-[3]-[ii]).

2. A student-athlete cannot be employed to teach or coach in his or her particular sport unless it is part of a general physical education class in which various techniques and skills in various sports are taught. Member institutions are specifically prohibited from hiring student-athletes to coach or teach *any sport*. Student-athletes who are enrolled in a student-teacher program are permitted to be paid traveling expenses if *all* student-teachers are eligible and are part of the teacher training program (*1987–88 NCAA Manual*, Constitution 3-1-[f]).

Marketing the Athlete with Remaining Eligibility

A particularly challenging task for athletic directors, coaches, and other athletic administrators is to police the contracts between marketing organizations and student-athletes. As an aid to assist athletic administrators, the NCAA regulations in this area are very strict. Basically, the rules state that a student-athlete who contracts (orally or in writing) to be represented by an agent in the marketing of his or her athletic skills or reputation in a particular sport is ineligible in that sport. Contracts with scouting services that distribute personnel information for high school prospects to NCAA member institutions are deemed not to be marketing of the student-athlete's ability unless the company receives remuneration for placing the student-athlete in an institution as a recipient of athletically related financial aid (*1987–88 NCAA Manual*, Constitution, Article 3-1-[c]). A marketing contract that is not limited to a particular sport is considered applicable to all sports.

More specifically, once enrolled in an NCAA member institution, student-athletes cannot consent to the use of their name or picture in promoting commercial products. Doing so results in the loss of eligibility. Such activities prior to enrollment in a member institution, however, generally do not violate NCAA rules (*1987–88 NCAA Manual*, Constitution 3-1-[e]).

Certain activities in the realm of advertising will not jeopardize the student-athlete's eligibility. For example, athletic equipment manufacturers can donate equipment to member institutions and publicize the school's use of it without endangering any student-athlete's eligibility, provided that no names or pictures of team members are used.

When student-athletes' names or pictures are used for commercial purposes without their knowledge or in spite of their refusal, they are not required to take any action to preserve their eligibility. An individual or team picture can be used in an advertisement only if the primary purpose is to congratulate an achievement. There must be no indication that it is an endorsement of the advertiser's product.

Student-athletes may appear on radio or television because of their athletic abilities or performance but may not receive compensation or endorse a product or service. Student-athletes are allowed, however, to receive legitimate and necessary expenses related to the appearance (*1987–88 NCAA Manual*, Constitution 3-1-[e]-[1]).

In recent years, the NCAA has begun to enforce its marketing restrictions much more vigorously, without the leniency that characterized its earlier efforts. In 1983–84 the NCAA had 19 eligibility cases involving 74 student-athletes who were participating in the promotion of commercial products, including magazine covers, men-on-campus calendars, modeling, television commercials, newspaper advertisements, and personal appearances at commercial businesses and shopping malls (see Note 2).

NOTES _____

1. The NCAA is not alone among athletic organizations that limit their athletes' involvement in marketing in order to remain eligible for com-

petition. The United States Tennis Association (USTA) has a detailed rule for marketing amateur players who wish to retain their eligibility. According to the USTA rule, an amateur is prohibited from:

(iv) Accepting money or gaining pecuniary advantage:

   a. By permitting the taking of tennis action films or television pictures of himself;

   b. By permitting the use of his name as the author of any book or article on tennis of which he is not the actual author;

   c. For services which he does not actually render.

(v) Permitting his name or likeness to be placed on tennis equipment or tennis apparel of which he is not the actual manufacturer, wholesaler, retailer or other seller, or to be used in advertising or other sales promotion of such goods;

(vi) Permitting the advertising of his name or likeness as the user of any goods of any manufacturer, wholesaler, retailer or other seller. [*1987 USTA Official Yearbook and Tennis Guide*, Article II, Section E (iv–vi)]

2. In 1984, Olan B. Kollevoll, chair of the NCAA's Eligibility Committee, made the following comments in the *NCAA News* concerning the increase of marketing-related eligibility cases:

In most instances, the committee has felt that the member institutions attempted to inform student-athletes of the prohibition against commercial promotions; however, there is a disturbing number of cases where the student has failed to contact appropriate institutional personnel prior to participation, or misinformed staff members have authorized the promotion.

In past cases, the committee generally has restored a student's eligibility when no compensation has been provided to the student and the involved advertisement or commercial item has been removed immediately from further use or sale.

However, committee members expressed concern that publicity of several cases in which a student's eligibility has been restored without the loss of any opportunities for competition has fostered the erroneous impression that student-athletes can participate in the promotion of commercial products with impunity so long as they are not paid or identified by name.

In response, the Eligibility Committee has determined that, effective with the administration of the 1984–85 student-athlete statement, at which time student-athletes should be informed of the prohibition against involvement in the promotion of a commercial product, any violation of Constitution 3-1-(c) in which the committee concludes the student-athlete knew or should have known of the application of NCAA legislation will result in the student being charged with the loss of competitive opportunities.

Each case will be reviewed individually, based upon the facts of that case, in order to determine whether eligibility should be restored and, if so, after what period of ineligibility. ["Athletes Warned about Commercial Endorsements," *NCAA News*, August 15, 1984, p. 1]

3. The New Jersey Interscholastic Athletic Association has the following policy concerning the marketing of a high school athlete, which, if violated, results in the student-athlete's being declared ineligible:

F. If a Student-Athlete's appearance on radio or television is related in any way to his/her athletic ability or prestige, the athlete may not under any circumstances receive remuneration for his/her appearance. Under such circumstances, however, an athlete may appear on a sponsored radio or television program provided he/she does not endorse or impliedly endorse any commercial product. [*1984–85 NJSAA Handbook*, Article V, Sec. 2. F]

4. The U.S. Amateur Boxing Federation has the following policy concerning marketing of amateurs and continued eligibility:

219.8 Capitalizing on athletic fame is:

(a) Granting or sanctioning the use of one's name to advertise, recommend or promote the sale of the goods or apparatus of any person, firm, manufacturer or agent, or by accepting compensation, directly or indirectly, for using the goods or apparatus of any person, firm, manufacturer or agent unless it is in accordance with the AIBA eligibility code and approved and handled through an escrow account supervised by the corporation.

(b) Participating in radio broadcast or telecast either directly or indirectly connected with an advertisement unless special permission in writing is granted by the national Registration Committee. The advertising of any current athletic event or any civic, charitable or educational enterprise by an athlete shall not be considered a violation of the foregoing. However, the approval of the local Registration Committee must be obtained.

(c) Allowing his photograph to be taken and used for advertising or motion picture purposes (other than a news picture which may or may not be used on sponsored programs) whether or not he has received or is to receive compensation of any kind, directly from the use of such photograph, unless special written permission be granted by the national Registration Committee; provided, however, if such photograph or motion picture is in connection with regular gainful employment and not directly related to or identified with any athletic fame, then it is not a violation of this section, but local boxing committee Registration Committees should be informed of such occupational intent for record purposes prior to the first acceptance of such employment. The use of an athlete's photograph in so-called loop films or similar films for training or coaching purposes only is not prohibited by this section, provided the athlete receives no compensation of any kind, directly or indirectly for or in connection with its use. However, before such films may be sold or offered for sale, written permission must first be obtained from the national Registration Committee.

(d) Writing, lecturing or broadcasting for payment upon any athletic event, competition or sport without the prior permission of the national Registration Committee. Such permission may be given only to a person who is genuinely making his main career in one or another of such activities; shall not extend to any amateur boxing contest in which the athlete himself participates as a competitor or otherwise; and it shall be effective provided the athlete does not violate any of the other provisions of this Article, and is in accordance with the rules and regulations of the corporation. [*1986–87 USA/ABF Official Rules*]

Expenses

The issue of expenses can provide a unique source of trouble for the amateur student-athlete. In general, any amateur in a position to receive expenses, regardless of the source and prior to receiving the expenses, should distinguish between those that are permissible to receive under the athletic governing body, and more importantly, those that are not. This approach is the safest way for the amateur athlete to safeguard eligibility as an amateur and as a member of a particular athletic association (see Notes 1–3).

In the NCAA, expenses are limited to those that are actual and necessary. Actual and necessary expenses are defined by the NCAA as amounts received for reasonable travel and meals associated with practice and game competition. The NCAA considers any expenses in excess of "reasonable" to be compensation for athletic ability and warns that receipt of same can lead to a loss of eligibility. Expenses are to be paid on a regular basis and must not be determined by performance or any other incentive plan (see Note 2).

The Athletics Congress of the United States of America (TAC/USA), the national governing body for track and field, road running, and race walking events, has established a trust fund which governs finances for athletic activities while the athlete retains amateur eligibility. TAC/USA refers to this fund as TACTRUST (see Appendix A). It was passed in 1981 and later approved by the International Amateur Athletic Federation (IAAF). TACTRUST allows an athlete to set up a private trust in which deposits and withdrawals are made in accordance with TAC/USA bylaws. The deposits must consist of monies received by the athlete in the TAC/USA-sanctioned athletic event and donations. The withdrawals must be for training or expenses in connection with the TAC/USA event. TACTRUST-authorized withdrawals are permitted for (1) training, coaching, travel, lodging, equipment, and educational expenses, (2) taxes on athletic earnings, (3) professional fees, and (4) medical and dental bills. The TACTRUST agreement allows the athlete to withdraw the balance of the trust upon completion of the athlete's amateur career. TAC/USA recommends, however, that student-athletes involved in NCAA and interscholastic competition contact those organizations before setting up a TACTRUST because the NCAA and many scholastic sanctioning bodies prohibit their student-athletes from establishing such trusts.

Since the implementation of the TACTRUST program in 1982, over 700 trust fund accounts had been opened by 1983, with more than $2 million passing through the program that year. Since 1983, TAC/USA has allowed athletes to receive money from sources other than track competitions, two notable sources being product endorsements and television competitions such as the ABC network's "Superstars."

NOTES

1. The approaches to expense reimbursement vary among other governing bodies, as can be seen in the following examples:

(a) The United States Soccer Federation (USSF) requires that amateur players may not receive and retain any remuneration for playing, except expenses that have actually been incurred by the player and that are directly related to a game or games (*August 1981 Official Administrative Rulebook*, Section C-[11]-[1102]).

(b) United States Swimming, Inc. eligibility rules require that "An amateur cannot compete, train, coach or give exhibitions for payment received, directly or indirectly, in money or in kind or for material advantage or benefit." However, the organization has instituted regulations that allow for some expense monies to be received by the amateur athlete and which state in part that:

> The amateur status of a swimmer shall not be endangered: . . .
>
> (2) By accepting monetary assistance during approved periods of training, including participation in competitions approved or sanctioned by the Corporation; limited, however, to Olympic Games, World Championships, regional games, continental championships and major international competitions. Such assistance may include payment for food, lodgings, transportation, his sports equipment, coaching, medical care and insurance, and a sum per day for the number of days related to an event as an indemnity against petty expenses.
>
> (3) By accepting compensation, authorized by the Corporation to cover financial loss resulting from his or her absence from work or basic occupation, related to preparation for and participation in Olympic Games, World Championships, regional games, continental championships and major international competitions approved by the Corporation. Payment, however, shall not be in excess of the sum which the competitor would have earned in the same period of time. [*United States Swimming Rules and Regulations 1985*, Part Three, Article 43, Eligibility, Section 304.10(2-3)]

(c) The United States Tennis Association (USTA) allows an amateur reasonable expenses actually incurred in connection with participation in a tournament, match, or exhibition (*1987 USTA Official Yearbook and Tennis Guide*, Article II, Section B-1).

2. The NCAA defines permissible expenses that an institution may provide a student-athlete as follows:

> (1) Actual and necessary expenses on intercollegiate athletic trips, reasonable trips (within the state in which the member institution is located or a distance not to exceed 100 miles if outside that state) to practice sites other than those of the institution, or to transport a team a reasonable distance (not to exceed 100 miles) to an off-campus site for a post-season team award or recognition meeting; however, it shall be permissible to provide expenses when a team is invited by the President of the United States to be accorded special recognition in the national capital. . . .
>
> 0.I.6. Nationally recognized service organizations and church groups (including the Fellowship of Christian Athletes) may underwrite the actual and necessary expenses of student-athletes to attend Fellowship of Christian Athletes encampments. This interpretation specifically excludes member institutions or athletically related organizations from underwriting such expenses.
>
> (2) Actual and necessary expenses incurred by the spouse of a student-athlete in accompanying the student-athlete to a certified post-season foot-

ball game or an NCAA championship in the sport of football in which the
student-athlete is certified eligible to participate, if prescribed by the bylaws
of the Association;

(3) Actual and necessary expenses for participation in national championship events; Olympic, Pan American, and World University Games qualifying
competition, or bona fide amateur competition during the Christmas and
spring vacations as listed on the institution's official calendar. . . . [*1987–88
NCAA Manual,* Constitution 3-1-(h)-(1–3)]

3. Under NCAA regulations, a student-athlete, prior to enrollment at
a member institution, may receive one expense-paid, try-out visit from a
professional sports organization (*1987–88 NCAA Manual,* Constitution 3-
1-[b]-[1]; see also Note 2 on page 245).

Professional Contracts

A student-athlete who agrees to negotiate or signs a contract to
play for a professional sports team loses his or her eligibility to
participate in that intercollegiate sport (*1987–88 NCAA Manual,*
Constitution 3-[1]-[b]). The professed goal of the NCAA is the
promotion and preservation of amateurism in college athletics.
The reasoning behind these eligibility rules is that if the NCAA is
realistically to supervise and regulate amateur status, absolute
rules are more administratively efficient than ones that require a
consideration of mitigating factors. The contract itself does not
compromise amateur status; it is the act of signing that is the
prohibited first step toward professionalism.

For the purposes of this rule, it does not matter if the contract is
legally enforceable. A student-athlete should be wary of a professional team or agent who attempts to circumvent this rule by first
indicating that a contract signed by the student-athlete is only
legally binding when also signed by a team representative or agent,
and then, second, that the team representative or agent promises
not to sign the contract until after the student-athlete's college
eligibility has expired. Under NCAA rules, legal enforceability is
irrelevant; *merely signing the contract terminates the student-
athlete's eligibility.*

The courts have upheld rules similar to the NCAA rules on
professionalism that have been promulgated by private voluntary
associations as long as they do not violate the constitutional guarantees of due process or equal protection. The courts have said
they cannot determine the validity of a rule simply because of its
unfortunate effects on particular individuals.

The leading case in the area of intercollegiate athletic eligibility
and professional contracts is *Shelton v. National Collegiate Athletic
Ass'n,* 539 F.2d 1197 (9th Cir. 1976). This case involved an appeal
by the NCAA from a grant of preliminary injunction which sus-

pended enforcement of its amateur eligibility rule. The rule stated that a college student-athlete who signed a professional contract was ineligible to participate in intercollegiate athletics for the sport involved.

Shelton had signed a professional contract with an American Basketball Association (ABA) team and was declared ineligible by Oregon State University. He claimed that the contract was unenforceable because he had been induced to sign it by fraud and undue influence. He argued that the NCAA rule which made him ineligible, despite the alleged defects of the contract, created an impermissible, overinclusive classification and was thus violative of equal protection.

The appeals court reversed the decision of the lower court, dissolving the preliminary injunction, and thus rendered Shelton ineligible. The court decided that in the *Shelton* case, the NCAA rule on eligibility was not in violation of equal protection because the rule rationally furthered a legitimate purpose. The NCAA's goal of preserving amateurism in intercollegiate athletics legitimized the rule.

NOTES

1. In the 1971 NCAA Basketball Tournament, Villanova University finished second and received a tournament share of $68,318.84. After the tournament, it was discovered that one of Villanova's players, Howard Porter, had signed a contract with an agent and also a contract with a professional team. The NCAA ruled that Villanova had to forfeit its second-place finish and return its tournament share of the winnings.

2. Student-athletes can compete against professional athletes but not as a member of a professional team. If a student-athlete played on a professional team, eligibility is lost only if the student-athlete knew or should have reasonably known he was playing on such a team (*1987–88 NCAA Manual*, Constitution 3-[1]-[d]).

A team is professional if it is recognized as a member of an organized professional league or is supported or sponsored by a professional organization or team (e.g., minor league baseball). The team that the student-athlete plays on, however, can have a coach who also coaches a professional team (e.g., U.S. Olympic Hockey Team).

The NCAA specifically permits the student-athlete to compete in tennis or golf with persons competing for money, but the student-athlete cannot receive compensation of any kind (e.g., PGA tournaments or Pro-Am tournaments).

Teams supported by a national amateur sports administrative organization using developmental funds received from professional teams or organizations are not considered to be professional (*1987–88 NCAA Manual*, Constitution 3-[1]-[d]-0.I.4).

3. The student-athlete does not lose his eligibility if, prior to enroll-

ment in college, he had a tryout with a professional team, provided it was either at his own expense or consisted of one visit, expenses paid, lasting no longer than 48 hours. The expenses paid must be for actual and necessary expenditures. The student-athlete enrolled in a full-time course of studies cannot try out for a professional team during the academic year, unless his eligibility has been exhausted. Part-time student-athletes are permitted to try out during the academic year, provided expenses paid are only those actual and necessary. It is permissible for the student-athlete to be observed by a professional team representative during a normally scheduled workout, provided the activities observed to evaluate the student-athlete are a normal part of the workout and not conducted specifically for the observer's benefit. Special workouts after the student-athlete's eligibility has expired are permissible and are common practice with potential professional football players (*1987–88 NCAA Manual*, Constitution 3-1-[b]-[2]).

4. The U.S. Amateur Boxing Federation has the following policies relative to becoming a professional and continued eligibility:

219.10 Becoming a professional.

(a) When an athlete receives compensation to compete or participate in any professional competition or exhibition in any sport, he shall thereafter be ineligible to compete as an amateur boxer.

(b) An athlete who has entered into a tryout agreement or contract or participates in a professional training camp and who does not receive any compensation, either directly or indirectly, beyond actual expenses not in excess of the sum permitted by corporation rules may be reinstated by his local boxing committee Registration Committee upon proper application therefore at any time after thirty (30) days from the date of his first appearance with the professional group.

(c) A competitor must not:

(1) Be, or have ever been, a professional athlete in any sport, or have entered into a contract to that end prior to the official closure of the Olympic Games.

(2) Have allowed his person, name, picture or sports performance to be used for advertising, except when his IF, NOC or national federation enters into a contract for sponsorship or equipment. All payments must be made to the IF, NOC or national federation concerned, and not to the athlete.

(3) Carry advertising material on his person or clothing in the Olympic Games, world or continental championships and Games under patronage of the IOC, other than trade marks on technical equipment or clothing as agreed by the IOC with the IFs. [*1986/87 USA/ABF Official Rules*]

5. See Chapter 11 for more information regarding professional contracts for collegiate athletes.

6. The NCAA ruled that the University of Alabama must forfeit 90 percent ($253,447) of its net receipts from the 1987 NCAA Division I Basketball Championship as a result of using two student-athletes who agreed to be represented by an agent.

INDIVIDUAL ELIGIBILITY REQUIREMENTS:
OLYMPIC ATHLETES

Olympic athletes are quite scarce. Not many high schools or colleges are fortunate to have a student-athlete of Olympic quality as a member of their athletic program. Yet, the infrequency of this occurrence does not diminish the significance of being informed as to the relationship between Olympic governing bodies and amateur athletes. High school and college athletic administrators need to know how these governing bodies view the student-athletes and their eligibility, as well as how the courts view the governing bodies and their rules and regulations. The consequences of not understanding these relationships may affect a student-athlete's eligibility for interscholastic, intercollegiate, or Olympic athletics.

The Olympic Games have been run by the International Olympic Committee (IOC) since 1896. Located in Lausanne, Switzerland, the IOC controls all aspects of the Olympic operation, including eligibility to participate. The determination and enforcement of eligibility of individual athletes are delegated by the IOC to each participating country's National Olympic Committee (NOC), pursuant to IOC Rule 24, which stipulates that each NOC must enforce the rules and bylaws of the IOC.

The IOC recognizes the United States Olympic Committee (USOC) as the NOC for the United States. (The objects and purposes of the USOC are listed on page 102.) The USOC is a corporation chartered by Congress in 1950 (Pub. L. No. 81-805 [81st Cong., 2d Sess.], September 21, 1950; 64 Stat. 889). This charter was amended in 1978 by enactment of the Amateur Sports Act of 1978 (Pub. L. 95-606 [95th Cong., 2d Sess.], November 8, 1978; 92 Stat. 3045). One of the principal purposes of the Amateur Sports Act was to establish a means of resolving disputes between American sports organizations seeking to become the national governing body (NGB) for a sport as recognized by the USOC. The congressional intent was to shield amateur athletes from being harmed by these disputes.

The IOC also designates one international federation for each Olympic sport. The international federations are responsible for setting worldwide eligibility rules for each of their sports. The reason for this rule is that each sport has different circumstances, and the federations are in the best position to interpret amateur status. However, this has also had a confusing effect since there exists no uniformity among the different international federations as to what constitutes an amateur and an eligible athlete. Furthermore, as was discussed at the beginning of Chapter 4, the lack of consistency between Olympic governing bodies and domestic governing associations (like the NCAA) as to the definition and interpretation of an amateur athlete further complicates the issue.

The USOC has specific regulations that govern the eligibility of athletes who try out for a spot on the U.S. Olympic team. Any athlete who is a U.S. citizen at the time the team is selected and is eligible under the international rules of the IOC for selection for membership on the U.S. Olympic or Pan American team is allowed to try out directly or indirectly under the authority of any national governing body. All members qualifying for the Olympic or Pan American teams must pass the USOC medical examination before being accepted on the team, as well as sign an oath attesting to their eligibility (*USOC Constitution*, Chapter XXXII, Sec. 1–5).

The USOC places certain responsibilities regarding eligibility with the Committee on Eligibility, which is appointed by the president of the USOC and approved by the executive board. According to the USOC constitution, Chapter XIX, Sections 2 and 3:

> The Committee on Eligibility shall be charged with the responsibility of overseeing compliance by the several National Sports Governing Bodies, and by the individual athletes selected to represent the United States at the Olympic or Pan American Games, with the international rules of eligibility as defined by the International Olympic Committee and the Pan American Sports Organization. It shall recommend to the Executive Board such action as it deems desirable to reconcile or adjudicate any differences or conflicts that may exist between these rules and those applied by the international federations and the United States National Sports Governing Bodies, including proposals that should be made to the International Olympic Committee or Pan American Sports Organization for reform of the basic international amateur code whenever appropriate.
>
> The Committee on Eligibility shall also be charged with responsibility of reviewing the provisions of the Constitution which guarantee the right of amateur athletes to participate in protected competitions and which prevent the imposition of sanctions as a result of such participation. It shall recommend to the Executive Board such action as it deems desirable to reconcile any differences or conflicts that may exist pursuant to inconsistent rules and interpretations of Amateur Sports Organizations.

Although the specific eligibility rules and regulations are determined by the IOC and the International Federations for each sport, the USOC does play an important role in serving to reconcile differences in eligibility requirements that exist between the various amateur and Olympic governing bodies.

A leading case on amateur athletic eligibility involved Renaldo Nehemiah, who attempted to participate in amateur track and field events after he had signed a contract to play professional football with the San Francisco 49ers of the National Football League. Despite Nehemiah's arguments that his profession of football did not give him a competitive advantage in track and field, and also numerous appeals to the USOC, TAC and IAAF, and the judicial system, Nehemiah was unsuccessful in obtaining his eligibility. Nehemiah finally had his amateur eligibility reinstated after he retired from football.

This situation is indicative of the way the courts have viewed the authority of Olympic governing bodies. Generally, the courts have deferred to the powers of these governing bodies and to their authority when dealing with controversies involving amateur Olympic athletes.

NOTES

1. The following cases deal with the relationship between the athlete and Olympic governing bodies.

(a) In *Martin v. International Olympic Committee*, 740 F.2d 670 (9th Cir. 1984), women runners and runners' organizations filed suit against the IOC and sought to require the IOC to institute 5,000-meter and 10,000-meter track events for women at the 1984 Summer Olympic Games in Los Angeles. The U.S. District Court (C.D. Cal.) denied a request for a preliminary injunction, and the U.S. Court of Appeals affirmed this decision. The two courts reasoned that the IOC's Rule 32, which was the process for adding new events, was not arbitrary. In addition, it was reasoned that state law should not be applied to alter the structure of Olympic events.

(b) In *Michels v. United States Olympic Committee*, 741 F.2d 155 (7th Cir. 1984), a federal appeals court found that an individual athlete had no private cause of action (a reason or means by which to challenge the USOC's authority) against the USOC, under the Amateur Sports Act of 1978. In reversing a district court decision, the appeals court noted that the Supreme Court has emphasized congressional intent in ruling on cause of action suits and that "the legislative history of the Act clearly reveals that Congress intended not to create a private cause of action under the Act."

(c) In *DeFrantz v. United States Olympic Committee*, 492 F. Supp. 1181 (D.D.C. 1980), *aff'd without opinion*, 701 F.2d 221 (D.C. Cir. 1980), the district court held that the Amateur Sports Act of 1978 did not establish a cause of action for 25 designated Olympic athletes who sought to prohibit the USOC from barring these American athletes from participating in the 1980 Olympic Games in Moscow because of an American boycott of the event. The court concluded "that the USOC not only had the authority to decide not to send an

American team to the summer Olympics, but also that it could do so for reasons not directly related to sports considerations."

2. For a fuller discussion on the roles of the different governing bodies in the Olympic Games organization, see *United States v. Wrestling Division of the AAU*, 545 F. Supp. 1053 (N.D. Ohio 1982), in which the federal court prohibited one national sports organization (the Amateur Athletic Union) from exercising any of the national governing body (NGB) powers and ordered it to sever all ties with the international governing body for that sport pursuant to the Amateur Sports Act of 1978, since the United States Olympic Committee had selected a competing national sports organization to be the NGB. The USOC was also ordered to terminate its recognition of the AAU group as the NGB and the United States representative to the international federation. See also the companion case of *United States Wrestling Federation v. United States Olympic Committee*, Civil Action No. 13460-78, Superior Court, District of Columbia (1978), in which the USWF successfully filed suit against the USOC to compel it to recognize it as its NGB and Group A member for amateur Olympic wrestling.

3. Another major purpose of the Amateur Sports Act of 1978 was to protect the USOC's ability to raise financial revenues to field American Olympic teams which receive no direct government funding. In *United States Olympic Committee v. Intelicense Corporation*, 737 F.2d 263 (2nd Cir. 1984), the United States Court of Appeals affirmed the judgment of the district court, which ruled that pursuant to the Amateur Sports Act the USOC's consent is a prerequisite to marketing the Olympic Symbol (five interlocking rings) in the United States.

4. While Olympic symbols and trademarks may be protected by the Olympic Symbol protection provision of the Amateur Sports Act of 1978, they may also be protected under the Federal Trademark Act (Lanham Act) (15 U.S.C. § 114) or individual state trademark statutes. The following cases deal with trademark law:

(a) In *Stop the Olympic Prison v. United States Olympic Committee*, 489 F. Supp. 1112 (S.D.N.Y. 1980), an organization opposed to the postgames' use of the Lake Placid Olympic Village for a prison, filed suit to protect its First Amendment right to print and distribute a "Stop the Olympic Prison" poster. The court held that the poster did not violate the Amateur Sports Act of 1978, since the poster was not used "for the purpose of trade," or "to induce the sale of any goods or services, or to promote any theatrical exhibition, athletic performance, or competition"; nor was the poster sold or distributed commercially.

(b) See also *International Olympic Committee v. San Francisco Arts & Athletes*, Civ. Act. No. C-82-4183 (N.D. Ca. 1982) 217 U.S.P.Q. 982.

5. For further information on trademark law, see Chapter 10.

INDIVIDUAL RIGHTS OF THE STUDENT-ATHLETE

The authority of an athletic association or a coach to make rules regarding a student-athlete's private life is limited. As was the case with the rules of athletic associations and conferences, the rules of coaches and their institutions are held to the same standards of reasonableness and rational relationship to a legitimate purpose. Generally, the purpose of the rules created and enforced must be reasonably related to the pursuit of the sport itself. Without this relationship, the rule may be deemed impermissible on constitutional grounds by the courts. Even when a rational relationship to the association's or coach's purpose does exist, a rule may be impermissible if it infringes on the constitutional rights of life, liberty, and property, which are protected by due process guarantees (see Chapter 4). In other words, rules have been struck down when they deal with areas that might be loosely termed "personal choice" or "preference." In these cases, the courts have to weigh the personal freedoms of the student-athlete against the institution's or coach's regulation of athletics in the name of character building, fair play, and esprit de corps.

The personal freedoms of student-athletes that may be infringed upon by an institution's or coach's athletic rules concern the areas of freedom of expression, hair length, high school marriages, alcohol and drugs, and handicapped athletes. In these individual rights areas, the student-athlete often challenges the alleged deprivatory athletic rule by challenging the authority of the coach to carry out such a regulation. To understand these challenges, the basis for a coach's authority should be examined.

Basically, the authority of a coach is limited to the coach's position within the institution's administration. The first possible legal basis for a coach's authority within the institution is *loco parentis*. This means that the relationship between the coach or institution and the student-athlete is analogous to that of a parent and child. Although this principle would seem to give a coach virtual free reign in disciplining players, its validity, particularly as it applies to college student-athletes, many of whom are adults in the eyes of the law, has been held suspect.

The second basis for a coach's authority is the proposition that a contract exists between the student-athlete and the institution. This notion rests on the belief that education, at least at the college level, is a privilege, not a right, and that the student has access to that privilege through compliance with an institution's regulations. This doctrine has also lost favor as a college education has come to be viewed as a benefit and vital interest. However, the doctrine applies to the scholarship student-athlete if the scholarship is deemed to be a contract. Yet, if the student-athlete is perceived to be primarily a student rather than an athlete, this contract analysis will most likely be invalid.

The final possibility that might be used to justify a coach's legal authority is the argument that the coach is part of an administrative agency of the state. Educational institutions and athletic associations have in many cases been found to be engaged in state action. By extension, the authority of a department in a school or college is granted and limited by the rationale for and functions of that department. Consequently, a coach's source of authority is derived from having a role as part of the "faculty" of an athletic department, and that authority is limited to those activities of the student-athletes which are related to the purposes and goals of the department.

For example, a coach who suspends a player for wearing long hair during the off-season must show that wearing long hair runs contrary to the goals or purposes of the department. Using this perspective, one can see that different standards can exist for different teams or team members. Long hair might be allowed for baseball players or divers but not for swimmers if the coach believes that long hair slows an athlete in the water. At the same time, this does not prohibit a coach from showing that a team's conformity to grooming codes is necessary to attaining the objectives of the department or sport. Again, a coach is on solid legal ground if the goals are within the authority of the department or sport and the rules and regulations can be demonstrated as being necessary for accomplishing those goals. An internal policy statement of goals and purposes, thus, aids in determining the scope of a coach's authority.

Freedom of Expression

Freedom-of-expression issues can often be raised in the amateur athletics context whenever the athlete's or coach's right to speak is impeded. Student-athletes, coaches, and others have brought claims alleging that they lost their scholarships or jobs for engaging in expressive activity or speech that was unacceptable to their superiors. If the superior who is limiting the right to free expression is found to be engaged in state action, the student-athlete or coach may have grounds to sue the superior, using a constitutional law argument.

Freedom of expression is the cornerstone of the Bill of Rights and individual liberty under the U.S. Constitution. Freedom of expression is a broad term describing the right to free "speech." The term "freedom of expression" is used rather than "free speech" because certain nonverbal types of communication are protected under the First Amendment—for example, carrying a sign with a written message. Therefore, while the First Amendment uses the words "Congress shall make no law . . . abridging the freedom of *speech*" (emphasis added), a broader range of expression is protected.

For purposes of analysis, expression must be broken down into two component parts. First is the element of conduct or physical action, which is a necessary part of communicating a message. For example, a demonstration requires conduct by the demonstrators which can be either peaceful or violent. Violence is a noncommunicative aspect of speech that may be regulated since there are compelling government interests in peace and order involved. Second is the component that is the actual message or content of speech. This communicative aspect of speech, consisting of the thoughts or informational content of the communication, may be regulated if there is a clear and present danger of imminent lawless action—for example, shouting "fire" in a crowded theater.

Some student-athletes, coaches, and athletic personnel have been successful in challenging their termination of scholarships or suspension from their jobs on freedom-of-expression grounds (see Notes 1c and d). In analyzing these situations, the courts have examined whether or not the individual's communication involved a public or private concern. Only if the matter is of public concern have the courts been inclined to protect the individual's right to express his or her views, but this protection is not absolute. The courts must balance the speaker's interest against the other party's interest. As a general rule, the courts have favored the speaker's interest over that of the other party's. However, the courts also seem to readily allow restrictions on student-athletes' speech by deciding that players' comments (as opposed to those of students and coaches) are not matters of public concern. However, student-athletes have, on occasion, received some protection of First Amendment rights.

A leading case in the area of freedom of expression concerning athletics is *Williams v. Eaton*, 468 F.2d 1079 (10th Cir. 1972). The plaintiffs were a group of 14 black football players for the University of Wyoming. In October 1969, prior to a game against Brigham Young University, the players had approached head football coach Lloyd Eaton wearing black armbands to protest the beliefs of the Mormon Church. Coach Eaton dismissed them from the team for violating team discipline rules, which did not allow protests or demonstrations by players.

The players brought suit in district court, but their action was dismissed. The players appealed, and the court of appeals affirmed the decision in part, while sending the case back for further proceedings. Upon the second hearing, the lower court held that the players had been given a full and impartial hearing before their suspensions and that their procedural due process rights had not been violated. The court reasoned that coach Eaton's rule had not been arbitrary or capricious, and up until their action, there had been no complaint concerning the rule by any of the players. In addition, Coach Eaton, acting as an agent of the University of Wyoming and the state of Wyoming, was compelled not to allow the players, under the guise of the First Amendment rights of freedom of speech, to undertake a planned protest demonstration against the religious beliefs of the Mormon Church and Brigham Young University. The demonstration would have taken place in a tax-supported facility, and had the officials of the university acceded to the demands of the players, such action would have been violative of Brigham Young University's First Amendment rights. The court held that the rights of the players to freedom of speech as guaranteed by the First Amendment could not be held paramount to the rights of others under the same amendment to practice their religion free from state-supported protest or demonstration.

NOTE _____

1. The following cases also involve freedom of expression.
   (a) In *Menora v. Illinois High School Ass'n*, 527 F. Supp. 637 (N.D. Ill. 1981), *vacated*, 683 F.2d 1030 (7th Cir. 1982), *cert. denied*, 103 S. Ct. 801 (1983), a federal district court ruled that an Illinois High School Association (IHSA) rule that prohibited student-athletes from wearing soft barrettes or yarmulkes during basketball games violated their right to freedom of religion guaranteed by the First Amendment. Orthodox Jewish students are required by their religion to keep their head covered at all times except when unconscious, immersed in water, or in imminent danger of loss of life.
   On appeal to the court of appeals, the decision was overturned. The court ruled that the students have no constitutional right to wear yarmulkes during the basketball games. It noted that Jewish religious law requires that the head only be covered, not specifically by yarmulkes.
   (b) In *Marcum v. Dahl*, 658 F.2d 731 (10th Cir. 1981), two members of the University of Oklahoma women's basketball team had their scholarships terminated after publicly voicing opposition to the renewal of the head coach's contract. The student-athletes contended that such an action, in response to their comments, was a violation of their right to free speech under the First Amendment. The court disagreed and held that the termination of the scholarships was a result of months of dissension, and not solely a product of the players' comments.
   (c) In *Pickering v. Board of Education of Township High School District 205, Will County, Illinois*, 36 Ill. 2d 568, 225 N.E.2d 1, *rev'd*, 391 U.S. 563 (1968), the Supreme Court held that the

dismissal of a high school teacher for openly criticizing the school board's allocation of funds between athletics and education was unconstitutional on First Amendment grounds. The court reasoned that because Pickering's criticism was a matter of public concern necessary for the free and open debate which was vital to the decision-making process, it was constitutionally protected.

(d) In *Tinker v. Des Moines Independent School District*, 383 F.2d 988, *rev'd*, 393 U.S. 503 (1969), student-athletes wearing politically motivated black armbands in a public high school were found to have a constitutionally protected right of expression. The court recognized that the student-athletes' First Amendment rights do not stop at the schoolhouse or gym door, and that constitutional protection extends to forms of expression other than speech or written communication.

Hair Length

Rules regulating the length of hair for males have often led to lawsuits, especially on the high school level. Most litigation of athletic rules on constitutional grounds is based on allegations of infringement of a property interest; however, hair-length regulations have also been attacked for being infringements of personal liberty interests. Since these cases present constitutional issues, they are usually litigated in federal court. Some of the circuit courts have recognized a student-athlete's right to govern his or her personal appearance while attending public school, while other circuit courts see this liberty interest as too insubstantial to create the threshold controversy (a substantial enough federal question) necessary to attain federal jurisdiction. The courts that have upheld such rules have determined that if a rule regulating either hair length or facial hair is reasonable and advances an educational purpose, the court should defer to the judgment of school officials.

One case in which the courts viewed hair length as a constitutional issue was *Dunham v. Pulsifer*, 312 F. Supp. 411 (D. Vt. 1970). In *Dunham*, a high school student-athlete requested an injunction to stop Brattleboro (Vermont) High School from enforcing an athletic grooming code. Alleged violations of this code had resulted in dismissal of the student-athlete from the school tennis team. The court noted that although one of the asserted justifications for these rules was the promotion of closer team work and discipline, the tennis team had no such problems prior to the enactment of the dress code. "Outside of uniformity in appearance, no evidence was introduced as to advantages to be derived from the athletic code except the question of discipline for the sake of discipline."

The court reasoned that

there are few individual characteristics more basic to one's personality and image than the manner in which one wears his hair. . . .
The cut of one's hair style is more fundamental to personal appearance than the type of clothing he wears. Garments can be changed
at will whereas hair, once it is cut, has to remain constant for
substantial periods of time. Hair style has been shadowed with
political, philosophical and ideological overtones.

The court held that the enforcement of the hair code could not be
upheld.

An opposite result was reached in *Zeller v. Donegal School
Dist.*, 517 F.2d 600 (3rd Cir. 1975). In *Zeller*, a high school soccer
player sought an injunction and monetary damages under the Civil
Rights Act for his dismissal from the soccer team for noncompliance
with the athletic grooming code regulating length of hair. The
district court dismissed the complaint, and the student-athlete
appealed. The court of appeals held that the nature of constitutional interpretation calls for the making of a value judgment in
areas that are regulated by the state and in which federal courts
should not intrude, and it stated: "We hold that plaintiff's contention does not rise to the dignity of a protectible constitutional
interest." The court based its decision on the concept that a
student-athlete's liberties and freedoms are not absolute and
stated: "We determine today that the Federal System is ill-
equipped to make value judgments on hair-lengths in terms of the
Constitution." The court concluded that student-athlete hair-
length cases should be left to school regulation "where the wisdom
and experience of school authorities must be deemed superior and
preferable to the federal judiciary's."

NOTES ――――――――――――――――――――――――――――――――

1. The following cases also hold that hair-length rules *warrant* constitutional review.
    (a) In *Dostert v. Berthold Public School Dist. No. 54*, 391 F. Supp.
876 (D.N.Dak. 1975), a student-athlete sought relief from a rule
regulating hair length. The court held that the school's interest in
requiring uniformity was such a compelling part of its public educational mission as to outweigh the constitutionally protected interest of student-athletes in regards to personal appearance.
    (b) In *Long v. Zopp*, 476 F.2d 180 (4th Cir. 1973), a high school
football player challenged the denial of his football letter because of
his hair length. The court held unlawful the coach's regulation of
the hair length of his players after the end of the football season.
The holding was based on the analysis that it was reasonable for a
coach to require short hair during a playing season for health and
safety reasons. However, it was not reasonable to deny an athletic

award or an invitation to a sports banquet when a student-athlete allowed his hair to grow long after the season.

2. For another case in which a court found hair length as *insubstantial* for constitutional review, see *Davenport v. Randolph County Bd. of Education*, 730 F.2d 1395 (11th Cir. 1984). High school football student-athletes sought an injunction from the school board's decision that refused them participation in athletics unless they complied with the coach's "clean shaven" policy for football and basketball team members. The district court denied the injunction. The court of appeals affirmed the decision.

High School Marriages

Rules that relate to high school marriages have also resulted in much litigation. In the early cases, rules excluding married student-athletes from interscholastic competition were upheld under the rational relationship standard (i.e., they bore a reasonable relationship to a legitimate objective). These rules were considered reasonable because it was believed that exclusion of married students from athletics was necessary to (1) protect unmarried students from bad influences, (2) encourage students to finish high school before marriage, and (3) give married students the opportunity for more time together to develop their family life. Such exclusion from athletic participation was not considered an infringement of a constitutionally protected right since participation in extracurricular activities was not viewed as a property right but as a privilege.

More recently, however, such rules have been struck down as invalid and improper invasions of the right to marital property (i.e., the right to be married). Marriage rules have also been overturned on the basis of a property interest. In other words, the courts have reasoned that such rules deprive student-athletes of a chance for a college scholarship and therefore infringe upon their property interest of obtaining a free education (see Note 2 for the *Moran* case). Most courts have refused to accept the property interest found by *Moran*, noting that such an interest is too speculative at the high school level to merit legal protection as a property interest. However, the courts now typically hold that marital classifications are unconstitutional on equal protection grounds.

A leading case in the area of interscholastic athletic eligibility and marriage is *Estay v. La Fourche Parish School Board*, 230 So. 2d 443 (La. App. 1969). In *Estay*, a married high school student challenged his exclusion from all extracurricular participation based on a school board regulation. The court of appeals held that the school board had the authority to adopt the regulation. It found the regulation to be reasonable—not arbitrary or capricious—and enforcement of the rule did not deprive the student of any constitutional rights. The court reasoned that there was a rational relationship between the rule and its stated objective of promoting completion of high school education prior to marriage. The court held that the classification rested on a sound and reasonable basis and that the criteria were applied uniformly and impartially.

A different result was reached in *Davis v. Meek*, 344 F. Supp. 298 (N.D. Ohio 1972). In *Davis*, a married high school baseball player challenged his exclusion from the baseball team and all other extracurricular activities. The student-athlete was aware of the rule prior to his marriage and had been informed that it would be enforced against him.

The court held that extracurricular activities are an integral part of the total educational program. Therefore, the rule denied the student-athlete an opportunity which, under Ohio statutes, he had a right to receive. The issue therefore was whether the school board could enforce against the student-athlete "a rule which will in effect punish him by depriving him of a part of his education." The court held that the school board should be precluded from imposing this restriction because the deterrent effect the rule had was minimal.

NOTES

1. Rules barring married student-athletes from participation in extracurricular activities were held constitutionally *permissible* in the following cases.

(a) In *Kissick v. Garland Independent School District*, 330 S.W.2d 708 (Tex. Civ. App. 1959), the court of appeals held that the "resolution of school district providing that married students or previously married students should be restricted wholly to classroom work and barring them from participation in athletics or other exhibitions and prohibiting them from holding class offices or other positions of honor other than academic honor—was not arbitrary, capricious, discriminatory, or unreasonable."

(b) In *Starkey v. Board of Education*, 14 Utah 2d 227, 381 P.2d 718 (1963), the Utah Supreme Court held that the "rule against participation in extracurricular activities by married students bore a reasonable relationship to the problem of 'dropouts' and did not constitute an abuse of school board's discretion."

(c) In *Cochrane v. Board of Education of Mesick Consol. School Dist.*, 360 Mich. 390, 103 N.W.2d 569 (1960), proceedings were held to compel the board of education to allow married high school student-athletes to play football during the 1958 school year. On appeal, the Michigan Supreme Court affirmed the circuit court's decision and held that the "school district did not violate the statute guaranteeing to all students an equal right to public educational facilities by excluding married high school students from participation in co-curricular activities."

(d) In *State ex. rel. Baker v. Stevenson*, 270 Ohio Ap. 223, 189 N.E.2d 181 (1962), the Court of Common Pleas held that the rule precluding married high school students from participating in extracurricular activities was valid.

(e) In *Board of Directors of the Independent School District of Waterloo v. Green*, 259 Iowa 260, 147 N.W.2d 854 (1967), an action was brought to prohibit enforcement of a school board rule barring participation in extracurricular activities by married pupils. Upon appeal, the Iowa Supreme Court held that engaging in extracurricular activities, such as basketball, is a privilege which may be enjoyed only in accordance with standards set by the school district. The student did not have a "right" to participate; therefore, no violation of the equal protection clause occurred.

2. Rules barring married students from participation in extracurricular activities were held *impermissible* in the absence of a finding of a rational basis for the rules in *Moran v. School District #7, Yellowstone County*, 350 F. Supp. 1180 (D. Mont. 1972). A marriage rule was held invalid because it deprived a student-athlete of the chance for a college scholarship without showing any evidence that the presence of married students would result in a reasonable likelihood of imposing moral pollution on unmarried students. No rational basis existed upon which to restrict participation.

3. Rules barring married students from participation in extracurricular activities were held *impermissible* as violative of equal protection standards in the following cases.

(a) In *Hollon v. Mathis Independent School District*, 358 F. Supp. 1269 (S.D. Tex. 1973), the plaintiff sought a temporary injunction against the enforcement of a school district policy which prohibited married students from engaging in interscholastic league activities. The district court held that the policy was unconstitutional. The court decided "there was no justifiable relationship between the marriage of high school athletes and the overall drop-out problem; nor does it appear that preventing a good athlete, although married, from continuing to play . . . would in any way deter marriages or otherwise enhance the dropout problem."

(b) In *Romans v. Crenshaw*, 354 F. Supp. 868 (S.D. Tex. 1971), a student challenged a public high school regulation which prohibited any married or previously married student from participating in any extracurricular activity. The district court held that "absent factual support for considerations urged by the school district to sustain its regulation, the same denied equal protection"; the court granted judgment for the student.

(c) In *Indiana High School v. Raike*, 164 Ind. App. 169, 329 N.E.2d 66 (1975), a public high school rule which prohibited married students from participating in any extracurricular activities was held invalid. The court found the rule both overinclusive because it barred married students of good moral character and underinclusive because it did not bar unmarried students of questionable character. The court concluded, therefore, that the rule did not have a substantial relationship to its goal, and thus it violated the equal protection clause.

Alcohol and Drugs

Another set of rules frequently contested in the courts are those regulating the use and abuse of alcohol and other drugs. While acknowledging that a school and its coaches have a strong interest in the prevention of drug abuse (see Chapter 12), the courts have consistently required that any rule established in this area be closely related to the problem of drug abuse.

Many high schools and high school athletic associations also have "good conduct" rules. These rules can be general in nature, as opposed to specific alcohol and drug rules. These good conduct rules usually require the student-athlete to adhere to some standard of conduct. If these rules, like the alcohol and drug rules, extend to a legitimate sports-related purpose, they will most likely be upheld. If, on the other hand, the rule is too broad and attempts to regulate an athlete's conduct during the off-season or conduct not related to athletics, it will probably be struck down by the courts on due process or equal protection grounds.

A leading case in the area of alcohol and drug rules is *Bunger v. Iowa High School Athletic Ass'n*, 197 N.W.2d 555 (Iowa 1972). In *Bunger*, a high school football player brought an action to determine the validity of a good conduct rule promulgated by the state high school athletic association which prohibited the use of alcoholic beverages. In 1971, Bunger and three other minors were riding in a car which contained a case of beer. Bunger knew that the beer was in the car. The car was stopped by a state police officer, who discovered the beer and issued summonses to all four occupants for possession of beer as minors. Bunger reported the incident to his school, whereupon he was declared ineligible for athletics.

The Supreme Court of Iowa decided that based on state law, the ability to enact eligibility rules rested with the State Board of Education, not with the Iowa High School Athletic Association. Therefore, the rule was invalid because the association had no authority to make an eligibility determination. The court noted in this case that

> we are inclined to think the nexus between the school and a situation like the present one is simply too tenuous: outside of football season,

beyond the school year, no illegal or even improper use of beer. We cannot find a "direct" effect upon the school here. School authorities in reaching out to control beer in cases like this are entering the sphere of the civil authorities. We hold that the rule in question is invalid as beyond the permissible scope of school rules.

NOTE _____

1. Alcohol rules have been *upheld* by the courts in the following cases.
   (a) In *Braesch v. DePasquale*, 200 Neb. 726, 265 N.W.2d 842 (1982), the court ruled that a drinking rule served a legitimate rational interest and directly affected the discipline of a student-athlete. Such a rule was held not an arbitrary and unreasonable means to attain the legitimate end of deterrence of alcohol use.
   (b) In *French v. Cornwell*, 202 Neb. 569, 276 N.W.2d 216 (1979), a rule that allowed a school official to suspend a student for six weeks after the student admitted being arrested for intoxication was constitutionally acceptable. The court found that suspension of the student was not in violation of due process, as the student had been aware of the rule providing for the suspension and admitted his own violation of the rule.

Handicapped Student-Athletes

A policy at some high schools and colleges is to prohibit students with physical disabilities from participating in athletic activities. The rationale for this policy, which is often based on American Medical Association (AMA) guidelines that recommend barring students with particular disabilities from participating in certain interscholastic and intercollegiate sports, is that the physical requirements of certain athletic activities pose a significant degree of physical risk to the student-athlete's safety. School boards have established such rules in the face of higher injury risks to decrease the likelihood of the injured athlete suing the school for failure to take reasonable care.

The extent of a school's or association's ability to restrict the availability of athletic participation/opportunities for handicapped students is a problem which can lead to litigation by the handicapped individual seeking athletic participation. It is crucial, then, for athletic administrators to analyze the legal aspects of the legislation that applies to handicapped students in high schools and colleges in order to facilitate the making of legally sound decisions and policies.

The courts often refer to three pieces of legislation concerning physically disabled student-athletes: the Education for All Handicapped Children Act; Section 504 of the Rehabilitation Act; and the Amateur Sports Act. These pieces of legislation serve three basic functions in the sports context:

1. To ensure equal opportunities in athletic programs for participants of all ages.
2. To search out methods of organizing sports activities in order to integrate the handicapped into regular programs.
3. To provide special athletic opportunities for those unable to participate in regular athletic programs.

The Education for All Handicapped Children Act guarantees a free public education for every disabled child up to 21 years of age (25 in some states), including physical education, extracurricular activities, and interscholastic sports. The Rehabilitation Act goes even further in prohibiting discrimination against any disabled individual in any program or activity sponsored by a recipient of federal funds. The Amateur Sports Act names the USOC as the coordinator of amateur athletics in the United States (see page 102). This responsibility for coordinating athletic activities includes sports participation for individuals with disabilities. The USOC fulfills this responsibility through the Committee on Sports for the Disabled. The committee helps disabled athletes by breaking down unnecessary barriers to competition and supporting organizations that provide sports experiences for the blind, deaf, amputee, paralyzed, cerebral palsied, or mentally retarded.

Although these legislative mandates have led to significant gains for disabled student-athletes, certain problems continue to frustrate individuals with disabilities. Two types of problems commonly arise with handicapped student-athletes. First, many organizations have rules that prohibit the participation of athletes who have either lost the use of a sense (e.g., hearing or sight), or of a limb or organs. Such rules are justified on the theory that a loss of this sort creates a hazard for the affected student as well as for the other participants in that sport.

Second, a problem stems from a rule common to most high school athletic associations—limiting participation to students *19 years old or under*. Handicapped students often do not finish high school until after age 19, due to the extended length of time it might take them to complete a basic education. Age limit rules are designed to prevent the deliberate retention of students to increase a varsity team's advantage and to equalize physical size and maturity of participants in contact sports such as football. These rules, however, may seem unreasonable when applied to older handicapped students, especially in some sports like wrestling, where competitors are matched by weight.

When a student-athlete brings suit involving one of these problem areas, the courts have generally deferred to the judgment of the educational institution in upholding the disqualification from athletic participation unless the school's actions were arbitrary or capricious (see Note 1). The courts, however, have begun to recognize the rights of disabled student-athletes on the grounds of Section 504 of the Rehabilitation Act (see Note 2). Basically, the law makers and the courts want to assure that extracurricular activities are made available to handicapped students on an equal basis with nonhandicapped students. Yet, as the *Rettig v. Kent City School District*, 539 F. Supp. 768 (N.D. Ohio 1981), case showed, even though equal opportunities must be provided, extracurricular activities generally may be separate or different from those offered to nonhandicapped students, provided disabled students are allowed to participate with nondisabled students to the maximum extent appropriate to the needs of the handicapped person.

A leading case concerning the rights of handicapped athletes is *New York Roadrunners Club v. State Division of Human Rights*, 432 N.E.2d 780 (Ct. App. N.Y. 1982). This case involved an appeal by the State Division of Human Rights to allow handicapped persons in wheelchairs to participate in the New York City Marathon. The court of appeals reasoned that, "The record reveals no proof to support the Human Rights Division's finding that the respondents, New York Roadrunners Club . . . discriminated against the disabled . . ., in organizing and promoting the 1978 New York City Marathon, when it required participants to use only their feet, and not wheelchairs, skateboards, bicycles or other extraneous aids."

The court noted that the Roadrunners Club had decided to run a "traditional" marathon footrace. The club could have laid down guidelines for other competitors, but as a private, though not-for-profit, organization, it was under no legal compulsion to do so. The court further stated:

> In making these observations, we, of course, are not insensitive to the role athletic activity may play in the rehabilitation and in the lives of the handicapped. Nor do we depart from our appreciation of the special concerns committed to the expertise of the Human Rights Division to combat discrimination in the first instance. . . . Rather, we simply hold that, under the circumstances, the acts on which the complaint here was posited did not constitute an unlawful discriminatory practice.

NOTES

1. In the following cases the courts *upheld* athletic eligibility rules that barred participation by handicapped students.

(a) In *Colombo v. Sewanhaka Central High School Dist.*, 87 Misc. 2d 48, 383 N.Y.S. 2d 518 (1976), a high school student-athlete sought to overturn a school district directive which prevented him from participating in football, lacrosse, and soccer. In granting judgment for the school district, the court held that the decision of the school district to follow the advice of its medical director and American Medical Association guidelines and prohibit the 15-year-old student with a hearing deficiency from athletic participation was justified. The court believed there existed a risk of further injury to the ear in which there was only partial hearing and to which additional injury could result in irreversible and permanent damage. The court held that the prohibition was neither arbitrary nor capricious.

(b) In *Cavallaro by Cavallaro v. Ambach*, 575 F. Supp. 171 (W.D.N.Y. 1983), a handicapped 19-year-old wrestler, with neurological problems that kept him behind in school, sought a waiver of the interscholastic conference's age rule so that he could participate on the wrestling team in his senior year. After denial of the waiver by the conference's eligibility committee, the plaintiff sought judicial relief, arguing that the age rule violated his rights under the Fourteenth Amendment's equal protection clause. In denying his claim, the court noted that the student was not physically impaired and had physical skills superior to most other 19-year-old students. It noted that the age rule was designed to prevent more mature students with experience from injuring younger student-athletes in contact sports such as wrestling.

(c) In *Spitaleri v. Nyquist*, 74 Misc. 2d 811, 345 N.Y.S.2d 878 (1973), the court upheld the disqualification of a disabled student-athlete based on the American Medical Association recommendation that students with the loss of one paired organ be barred from contact sports.

(d) In *Kampmeier v. Nyquist*, 553 F.2d 296 (2d Cir. 1977), two visually impaired junior high school students brought a claim against school officials for refusing to allow them to participate in contact sports. The court permitted enforcement of the rule because testimony indicated a high risk to their good eyes. The students ultimately won their suit under state law in the state courts, even though their federal suit was unsuccessful.

2. In the following cases the courts *struck down* eligibility rules that barred participation by handicapped students.

(a) In *Wright v. Columbia University*, 520 F. Supp. 789 (E.D. Pa. 1981), a college student with vision in only one eye sued his university to play football. The district court granted a temporary restraining order forbidding the university from barring the student's participation in intercollegiate football. The court concluded that federal funds do not need to go specifically to the football program to bring it under Section 504 of the Rehabilitation Act. The court also noted that the college student was an adult who decided for himself whether to assume the risks of participation.

(b) In *Poole v. South Plainfield Board of Education*, 490 F. Supp. 948 (D.N.J. 1980), the court ruled that a student who had been born with one kidney should be permitted to participate in inter-scholastic wrestling. The court stated that the school board's only duty was to advise the family of the risks (the student and his parents signed a waiver releasing the school from liability) and not to impose its own view of proper action on the family.

(c) In *Grube v. Bethlehem Area School District*, 550 F. Supp. 418 (E.D. Pa. 1982), the court ruled that under Section 504 of the Rehabilitation Act, a high school student with one kidney should be allowed to play football if his parents signed a waiver.

(d) In *Southeastern Community College v. Davis*, 442 U.S. 397 (1979), the Supreme Court stated that Section 504 requires only that a person who is able to meet all of a program's requirements in spite of his handicap not be excluded from participation in a federally funded program "solely by reason of his handicap." This indicates that the "mere possession of a handicap is not a permissible ground for assuming an inability to function in a particular context."

3. See Education of the Handicapped Act, Pub. L. 91-230, Title VI Sec. 601, Apr. 13, 1970, 84 Stat. 175, amended Pub. L. 94-142 Sec. 3-(a), Nov. 29, 1975, 89 Stat. 774, which guarantees that all handicapped children be provided a free public education and emphasizes special education and special services designed to meet their unique needs. It also guarantees the rights of these children and parents or guardians and, while assisting states with the provision of such an educational experience, is designed to aid in the assessment of these programs.

4. Section 504 of the Rehabilitation Act of 1973 (Pub. L. 93-112), 29 U.S.C. 706, provides that "no otherwise qualified handicapped individual . . . shall, solely by reason of his handicap, be excluded from the participation in, be denied the benefits of, or be subjected to discrimination under any program or activity receiving federal financial assistance." The regulation defines and forbids acts of discrimination against qualified handicapped persons in employment and in the operation of programs and activities receiving assistance from the Department of Health, Education and Welfare (HEW). The regulation, which applies to all recipients of federal assistance from HEW, is intended to ensure that their federally assisted programs and activities are operated without discrimination on the basis of handicap. Since HEW was split, the Department of Education now has jurisdiction.

5. The New Jersey State Interscholastic Athletic Association (NJSIAA) has a policy for the use of a prosthesis (artificial limb) in high school athletic competition. The policy states, in part:

Recent federal legislation which prohibits discrimination on the basis of a physical handicap, makes it difficult for state associations to defend the former blanket prohibition of the use of a prosthesis when challenged in the courts. Football, soccer, and wrestling rules previously ruled a prosthesis to be illegal; however, these sports now have revised rules to provide "artificial limbs which, in the judgement of the rules administering officials, are no more dangerous to players than the corresponding human limb and do not place an opponent at a disadvantage may be permitted."

The NJSIAA procedure for approving the wearing of an artificial prosthesis by a student-athlete will be as follows:

(1) The member school must notify the NJSIAA and arrange for a meeting to determine the legality of the prosthesis; present at this meeting must be the school physician, athletic director, principal, coach, the chapter rules interpreter serving the area, a representative from NJSIAA, and the player who must be fully equipped as he will be when competing; an athletic trainer or other school representative may also be present.

(2) The criteria recommended as a guideline to follow in determining the legality and suitability of wearing a prosthesis in a contact sport are:

   (a) The prosthesis should be approved at any Juvenile Amputee Clinic listed in the National Directory. Kessler Institute for Rehabilitation, 1199 Pleasant Valley Way, West Orange, New Jersey 07052 is the only New Jersey clinic listed.

   (b) Restricted to below the knee prosthesis. No artificial hand, arm or above the knee prosthesis should be permitted.

   (c) Metal hinges restricted to the lateral and medial surfaces and covered with leather (similar to that required on approved knee braces).

   (d) No metal in front of the knee permitted.

   (e) Prosthesis should be wrapped with a minimum of one-half inch high-density polyurethane or foam rubber.

   (f) Signed approval by an orthopedic surgeon or physician associated with a juvenile amputee clinic and the school physician. Such approval must be presented to the officials before each game for the officials' final inspection and approval.

   NOTE: Member schools are given this advance notice to allay the possibility of having a prosthesis declared illegal, thereby preventing the player from participating until approval is granted.

DISCIPLINE OF INDIVIDUAL STUDENT-ATHLETES

The topic of discipline of individual student-athletes is a particularly important and sensitive one since the act of disciplining a student-athlete is usually the precipitating event in the decision-making process of an athlete contemplating litigation as a recourse to redress a wrong. The high school or college that fails to carry out a disciplinary action against a student-athlete, as prescribed by an association or conference, risks losing its membership in the governing athletic organization. This unpleasant alternative often places the high school or college athletic administrator in a precarious position between the student-athlete and the athletic association or conference.

The NCAA has very specific sanctions for rule violations by individual student-athletes. The association has set strict and often complicated guidelines that student-athletes *must* follow if they are to maintain eligibility for NCAA competition. Deviation from these guidelines may result in sanctions against the student-athlete, and/or the team, and/or the institution's athletic program (see the discussion on the NCAA enforcement program in Chapter 4).

The major and most common disciplinary action that the NCAA takes against individual student-athletes is to declare them ineligible for intercollegiate competition for a stated period of time. This action is enforced by the individual institution as part of its responsibilities of membership in the NCAA (*1987–88 NCAA Manual*, Constitution, 4-2).

At the high school level, student-athletes must also conform to rules and regulations as established by the institution, its athletic conference, and its athletic association. These rules run the gamut from grade point average rules to regulations governing personal appearance and good conduct. The student-athlete who fails to abide by these rules and regulations is often declared ineligible for the season in which the violation occurred or for one year from the date of the violation. In addition, the student's school is forced to forfeit all the games, matches, or events in which the ineligible student competed. High school athletic associations often possess fairly broad disciplinary powers. For example, in the Massachusetts Interscholastic Athletic Association the Board of Control is authorized to "warn, censure, place on probation or suspend up to one calendar year any player, team, coach, game or school official or school which violates any MIAA rule regarding interscholastic athletics" (*Rules and Regulations Governing Athletics MIAA 1987–88*, Part II 22[d]). High school athletic associations may also prohibit a school from participating in league championships or association-sponsored tournaments.

Other amateur athletic organizations, like national governing bodies, discipline athletes in a very similar manner. For example, the U.S. Amateur Boxing Federation states:

> The Review Section may censure, suspend for a definite or indefinite period of time with or without terms of probation, or expel any member of the Corporation (USA/ABF) and the LBC (Local Boxing Council), including any athlete, coach, manager, official, member of any committee, or any person participating in any capacity whatsoever in the affairs of the LBC, who has violated any of the rules of the Corporation or the LBC, or who has acted in a manner which brings disrepute upon the Corporation, the LBC, or upon the sport of amateur boxing. [*1986–87 USA/ABF, Official Rules*, Section 230.10(d)]

Probably the best way to illustrate the issues involved in disciplining athletes is to examine a few situations that have been litigated in the courts. In the case of the *Regents of University of Minnesota v. National Collegiate Athletic Ass'n*, 422 F. Supp. 1158 (D. Minn. 1976), the University of Minnesota challenged an NCAA sanction that placed all the university's athletic teams on indefinite probation when the university refused to declare three student-athletes ineligible for intercollegiate competition.

The student-athletes had admitted to the NCAA violations, which consisted of (1) selling complimentary season tickets; (2) accepting an invitation to stay at a cabin with all meals, lodging, and entertainment provided by a member of the booster club; and (3) using a private WATS line to place long-distance calls. After admitting to the violations, the student-athletes donated the proceeds from the sale of the tickets to charity and satisfied a university committee's punishment. However, the NCAA was not satisfied. The NCAA's proposed penalty for Minnesota's not declaring the student-athletes ineligible to compete was a three-year probation and a two-year ban on postseason play and televised games. Additionally, the NCAA imposed a two-year restriction on the granting of athletic scholarships for basketball.

Minnesota, as was its policy for all students, had afforded the three basketball players a hearing before the Campus Committee on Student Behaviors and the Assembly Committee on Intercollegiate Athletics. These committees voted not to declare the student-athletes ineligible, despite the findings of the NCAA's Committee on Infractions.

The court found that participation in intercollegiate athletics was a substantial property right entitled to due process guarantees. Thus, a student-athlete had to be afforded due process rights before the right to an education or any substantial element of it could be adversely affected. The court reasoned that the NCAA's action transgressed on the university's legal duty to afford due process hearings to student-athletes and to abide by the results of the hearing.

The court concluded that the plaintiffs had demonstrated a strong possibility of success on the merits and that Minnesota would be irreparably harmed if a preliminary injunction was not issued while the NCAA would not be harmed. The court directed the NCAA to lift the probation and temporarily prohibited the NCAA from imposing further sanctions pending a hearing on the merits of the case.

The NCAA appealed the district court's decision in *Regents of University of Minnesota v. National Collegiate Athletic Ass'n*, 560 F.2d 352 (8th Cir. 1977). The appeals court dissolved the preliminary injunction. The court noted that, as a voluntary member of the NCAA, the university agreed to adhere to association rules, including Constitution 4-2-(a), which required Minnesota "[t]o administer their athletic programs in accordance with the Constitution, the Bylaws and other legislation of the Association."

In another discipline case, *Southern Methodist University v. Smith*, 515 S.W.2d 63 (Tex. Civ. App. 1974), Southern Methodist University (SMU) appealed an order which temporarily prohibited the university from declaring student-athlete Smith ineligible to play intercollegiate football. Smith admitted to receiving financial aid in excess of the amounts allowed under NCAA rules. The NCAA ordered SMU to declare Smith ineligible. Faced with the possibility of losing its membership in the NCAA, SMU notified Smith of his ineligibility after it protested the sanction and exhausted its appeals to the NCAA Council.

Smith filed suit and claimed that he was deprived of due process when he was denied notice and a hearing concerning his violations and penalty. The court held that Smith had no legal right to a hearing by SMU. In addition, he failed to establish a constitutional or contractual right to claim a benefit or privilege from playing football. The court reasoned that the NCAA had sole authority over the eligibility decision, and its rules did not provide for the type of hearing that Smith had requested. An SMU hearing on the issues could not have declared him eligible to compete in the NCAA. Moreover, a hearing could not have afforded any relief in light of Smith's admission that he had violated the rule.

In the case of *Carlton Walker v. National Collegiate Athletic Ass'n and Officials at the University of Wisconsin*, Madison Case No. E1-C-916 (W.D. Wis. 1981), Walker, a starting guard for the University of Wisconsin football team, was declared ineligible to participate in a postseason football game (the Garden State Bowl) due to an investigation of recruiting violations. Previously, in July 1981, the NCAA had officially charged the university and its alumni with 20 violations of NCAA regulations and bylaws in connection with Walker's recruitment. Neither the NCAA nor the university charged Walker with any violation.

Walker immediately filed a motion for a preliminary injunction to gain eligibility for the postseason bowl game. Walker contended that he was not afforded due process in connection with the declaration of ineligibility since athletic participation was a property right protected by the Constitution. The district court denied Walker's motion on the grounds that he failed to establish a reasonable likelihood of success on the merits and a degree of irreparable harm necessary to afford the requested relief.

Walker, who attended the University of Wisconsin from the fall of 1980 to the spring of 1982, then transferred to the University of Utah and enrolled as a full-time student. In August 1982, pursuant to NCAA Bylaw 5-3-(3), the University of Utah requested a waiver of Walker's one-year loss of eligibility due to his transfer (NCAA Bylaw 5-1-[j]-[7]).

The NCAA Committee on Infractions reviewed the waiver request by Utah. The committee determined from the available evidence that Walker's involvement in the Wisconsin recruiting violations was not inadvertent or innocent. The waiver was denied.

Walker amended his initial complaint in November 1982, and claimed that the NCAA had tortiously and arbitrarily interfered with the contractual relations between Walker and the universities of Wisconsin and Utah, thereby depriving him of the opportunity to compete in collegiate athletics and damaging his ability to secure a professional contract.

The NCAA filed a brief in support of a motion to dismiss, or in the alternative for summary judgment. Regarding Walker's due process claims, the NCAA stated that it was well settled that a student possesses no liberty or property interest in intercollegiate athletics. Therefore, the NCAA argued, the privilege of participating in intercollegiate athletics falls outside the parameters of the due process clause.

Of course, the situations exhibited in these cases will not arise if the student-athlete can avoid being declared ineligible. This, obviously, can be accomplished if the athlete obeys the rules and regulations of the associations and conferences to which the institution belongs. This, however, is not as easy as it sounds. An athlete may unknowingly violate eligibility rules or be deceived or coerced into rules violations by a third party. Other athletes may be declared ineligible as part of a larger sanction against their high school or college, as when a football team is placed on probation and suspension of postseason competition for recruiting violations.

A student-athlete who is declared ineligible can follow a number of steps in response to such a disciplinary action. First, the athlete should exhaust all remedies available under the school's or association's policies. These remedies may include the opportunity to appeal the decision, ask for a reconsideration, or initiate other procedures for reevaluating the initial ruling of ineligibility. For example, the United States Amateur Boxing Federation, Inc. has the following appeals procedure:

> 220.6 Procedure. The procedure for reinstatement is as follows:
> (a) Application in writing shall be made to the chairman of the Registration Committee where the athlete is registered or, in the case of other members, the chairman of the local boxing committee's Registration Committee, stating the act or acts which caused the disqualification, when and where the last act was committed.

(b) When given authority, the local boxing committee Registration Committee shall render its opinion and inform the applicant in writing of its decision, forwarding a copy of the application and the committee's actions to the national Registration Committee chairman.

(c) In cases requiring action by the national Registration Committee or by the Board of Governors, the local Registration Committee will forward its recommendations to the chairman of the national Registration Committee with a copy to the applicant.

(d) The national Registration Committee shall give its findings and/or recommendations to the Board of Governors at the corporation's annual meeting whose actions shall be final and binding on all parties. [*1986–87 USA/ABA Official Rules*]

If these procedures prove fruitless, the athlete may then resort to bringing a lawsuit against the governing body. Even though most claims against the NCAA or other amateur athletic association rules have ended in unsuccessful challenges by the student-athletes involved, it is still possible for student-athletes to obtain their objective—another season of competition, in some cases. The student-athlete achieves this objective by asking the court for a preliminary injunction in response to a ruling that the particular rule violated by the student-athlete is unenforceable. To declare an eligibility rule unenforceable, the student-athlete must argue that the rule violates due process or equal protection clauses of the state and federal constitutions, or that it violates federal antitrust and other federal laws, or that it represents breach of contract. Together with this attack on the rule, the student-athlete asks for a court order to prohibit the enforcement of the rule as it is applied to his or her individual case until the case goes to trial. Since this may be months and years later, the student-athlete can compete in the interim. (These and other legal principles are discussed in Chapters 3, 4, and 13.)

NOTES

1. The discipline decisions of intercollegiate athlete associations were *upheld* in the following cases.

(a) In *Samara v. National Collegiate Athletic Ass'n*, 1973 Trade Cases 74,536 (E.D. Va.), the court upheld an NCAA decision that participation by a student-athlete in a noncertified track and field event resulted in ineligibility for further NCAA competition. The court stated that the NCAA rule and its subsequent sanctions were not illegal. This was true even though the event would have been certified if the Amateur Athletic Union (AAU) had requested the NCAA to provide such authorization.

(b) In *National Collegiate Athletic Ass'n v. Gillard*, 352 So. 2d 1072 (Miss. 1977), sanctions were imposed against a non-NCAA member player who accepted a 20 percent clothing discount. There was some evidence that this discount policy was not limited to student-athletes. The NCAA decided there was a rule transgression. The Mississippi Supreme Court held that the player's rights were adequately protected by the NCAA's procedures and that the player's right to play intercollegiate football was not a property right protected by due process guarantees.

(c) In *McDonald v. National Collegiate Athletic Ass'n*, 370 F. Supp. 625 (C.D. Cal. 1974), the court ruled that student-athletes had no due process rights infringed when the NCAA imposed sanctions against their school for bylaw violations that affected their opportunity to compete.

2. For a case in which discipline decisions of intercollegiate athletic associations have been *struck down*, see *Hall v. University of Minnesota*, 530 F. Supp. 104 (D. Minn. 1982). This case, also discussed in Note 1 on page 191, concerned a conference academic progress rule. The court was quick to point out that the student-athlete had been recruited as "a basketball player and not a scholar" and that "his academic record reflects that he has lived up to those expectations as do the academic records of many of the athletes presented to this court." The court ruled that a constitutionally protected interest was involved and Hall's due process rights had been violated. The court ordered the restoration of Hall's scholarship money and mandated his acceptance into a degree-granting program.

3. A case that involves discipline issues relating to student-athletes in interscholastic athletics is *Florida High School Activities Ass'n v. Bradshaw*, 369 So. 2d 398 (Fla. Dist. Ct. App. 1979). A high school football player sought to prohibit the state high school activities association from imposing a forfeiture of two of his team's games in which an ineligible player competed. The court upheld the penalty, reasoning that there was an absence of actual harm to the player and that the coach and other team members lacked standing to assert a claim of denial of equal protection. The court also held that the opportunity to participate is a privilege, not a constitutionally protected right; therefore, the court would not intervene in an association's discipline of its members.

4. A case that involves discipline issues relating to the Amateur Athletic Union is *Santee v. Amateur Athletic Union of the U.S.*, 2 Misc. 2d 990, 153 N.Y.S. 2d 465 (1956). The court ruled that the Amateur Athletic Union (AAU) had the authority and the jurisdiction to determine the eligibility of athletes who wished to participate in its sanctioned events. This included selection of squads for the Olympic Games, which were held under the auspices of the International Amateur Athletic Federation, from which the AAU received its sanctioning authority.

5. The New Jersey State Interscholastic Athletic Association (NJSIAA) has the following policy on reinstatement of eligibility:

Section 3. Reinstatement of Amateur Eligibility—The Executive Committee of the NJSIAA is the only body that may reinstate a Student-Athlete of a member school to eligibility status under the provisions of the organization's Constitution, Bylaws, and Rules and Regulations. In cases where the Executive Committee has determined that a Student-Athlete inadvertently participated in an activity that has caused his/her loss of eligibility, the Executive Committee may reinstate said athlete after a period of not less than one year. An application for reinstatement must be made in writing by the high school Principal to the Executive Committee and shall include all data pertinent to the case.[*1984–85 NJSIAA Handbook*, Article V. Sec. 3]

THE BUCKLEY AMENDMENT

An integral aspect of the NCAA's enforcement program is the compilation of information regarding the alleged infraction and also the operation of the institution's athletic department. Access to student-athletes' records concerning academic and financial aid information may be critical in the investigation. In order to protect against an invasion of a student's privacy and to prevent the likelihood that such information may be used in a way that hurts the student, Congress enacted the Family Educational Rights and Privacy Act (FERPA), which regulates the release and review of such records. Consequently, the NCAA and other third parties can be restricted and sometimes prevented from access to or publication of certain types of student-athlete information. The Family Educational Rights and Privacy Act of 1974 is often referred to as the Buckley Amendment.

The Buckley Amendment was designed to enhance comprehensive civil rights protections, with two objectives in mind: (1) to assure parents of students, and students themselves if they are attending an institution of postsecondary education or are 18 years old, access to their education records; and (2) to protect the students' right to privacy by restricting the transferability and disclosure of information in their records without prior consent. The procedures established by the Buckley Amendment for accomplishing these two objectives apply only to public or private educational agencies or institutions that receive funds, directly or indirectly, from a program which is administered by the secretary of education (e.g., Basic Educational Opportunity Grant [BEOG], Guaranteed Student Loan [GSL], or National Direct Student Loans [NDSL]). The agency or institution is also obligated to establish a written policy and procedures for the access, disclosure, and challenge of education records. The secretary of education has the power to withdraw federal funding from any educational agency or institution that does not comply with the Buckley Amendment.

This amendment to the General Education Provisions Act primarily involves release of information concerning a student-athlete's education records, including academic rank, biographical material, and injury and health records. This type of information is often used in athletic department publications and media releases. Sports information directors, especially, should be aware of the provisions and limitations enacted by the Buckley Amendment.

Two basic rights created under the Buckley Amendment are particularly important to athletic administrators. First, students have the right to challenge any information in their education record which they or their parents believe to be inaccurate, misleading, or in violation of the student's rights. The student can bring the challenge in a hearing, or, if the institution still refuses the challenge, the student can note his or her concerns on the education record. Second, the Buckley Amendment also protects the right to prevent personally identifiable information from being disclosed, with some exceptions, in the absence of a prior written consent of the parent or student. A school official with a "legitimate educational interest" may have access without consent.

As a general rule, information concerning student-athletes should not be disclosed unless the student has filled out and signed a consent-disclosure statement form (see Exhibit 5–8; see also Exhibit 5–1, part II). These consent-disclosure statements are intended to protect both the student-athlete and the institution. Written consent-disclosure statements must include the following information:

1. A specification of the records to be disclosed.
2. The purpose or purposes of the disclosure.
3. The party or class of parties to whom the disclosure may be made.

In addition, the form should contain language that allows for the disclosure of unforeseen events such as academic ineligibility, injury reports, and sudden illness affecting athletic involvement.

Another section of the Buckley Amendment deals with specific parties who do not have to receive a prior written authorization from the student to see the student's education files. Athletic department personnel fall into the school official exemption category and can review student-athlete files as needed to evaluate grade point average qualifiers, academic eligibility, and other matters which affect eligibility.

Athletic administrators should also be aware that some states impose additional and sometimes more restrictive requirements

ATHLETICS INFORMATION FORM

Note: This form comes under the purview of the Family Educational Rights and Privacy Act of 1974.

Principal Specification of Records: This consent statement authorizes administrative personnel of the department of intercollegiate athletics to review and to disseminate to third parties information in my personal "education records," including information contained on this form and any other education information collected and/or maintained by this institution, for public relations purposes.

Purpose(s) of Disclosure:
Information obtained from these records will assist in compilation of personal information for use in official department publications for dissemination to the news media, for purposes of nominating me for honors programs and scholarships and for general public relations purposes.

Party or Class of Parties to whom Disclosure May Be Released: By signing this consent statement, I authorize administrative personnel of the department of intercollegiate athletics to review and disseminate any information in my "education records" to third parties for general public relations purposes.

_____   _____
(Signature)   (Date)

_____   _____
(Sport)   (Effective Academic Year)

Personal Biographical Information

Full Name (Last, First, Middle)   **Nickname**   **Height**   **Weight**

Home Address   **Telephone**

Birthdate (Month, Day, Year)   **Place of Birth**

Name and Location of High School Last Attended   **Date of Graduation**

Colleges Attended   **Dates Attended**   **Degrees, If Any**

Academic Honors (Include Membership in Honor Society)

Parent or Guardian Information

Mother	Father
Name	Name
Address	Address

Telephone	Occupation	Telephone	Occupation

Exhibit 5-8   NCAA Consent-Disclosure Statement Form _Source: NCAA Public Relations and Promotion Manual_ (July 1985).

regarding the privacy of education records. However, these state statutes may not preempt the Buckley Amendment.

High school student-athletes' education records are also covered under the Buckley Amendment. A potential problem often may arise when members of a community desire access to student records to determine the effectiveness of their educational system (see Note 2).

NOTES

1. The Buckley Amendment, introduced by Senator James Buckley, appeared as an amendment to the Family Educational Rights and Privacy Act of 1974. The bill extended the Elementary and Secondary Education Act of 1965, Pub. L. No. 93-380, 20 U.S.C. §1232g(a)(4)(A).

2. For an analysis of the effect on athletics of the Family Educational Rights and Privacy Act of 1974, see the following articles:

(a) "The Buckley Amendment," *NCAA News*, October 15, 1976, p. 3.

(b) "Court Tells NCAA to Release Papers Sought in Libel Suit," *Chronicle of Higher Education*, June 9, 1982, p. 14.

3. A case that involves access to student records is *Arkansas Gazette Co. v. Southern State College*, 620 S.W.2d 258 (Ark. 1981). A newspaper publisher brought suit against an intercollegiate athletic conference seeking to compel it to disclose the amount of money its member institutions dispersed to student-athletes during the school year. The court held that records of disbursements to student-athletes by member institutions were subject to public inspection. The court reasoned that no one has a reasonable expectation of privacy concerning the amount of public funds distributed to him unless that person clearly comes within a specific exception of law, which in this case does not under the Arkansas Freedom of Information Act. The court also ruled that such records maintained by an intercollegiate athletic conference were "educational records" required to be closed under Family Education Rights Privacy Act of 1974. (See also page 133.)

ATHLETES' LAWSUITS FOR FAILURE TO PROVIDE AN EDUCATION

A more recent area of litigation is one in which former student-athletes have sued institutions for failing to provide an education. The student-athletes in such cases are claiming that they failed to receive a proper education from the college or university in exchange for their athletic participation and competition. The alleged educational exploitation of student-athletes has resulted in increasing litigation and an equal number of tragedies. In one highly publicized situation, Kevin Ross, a former Creighton University basketball star who played for three years, returned to the seventh grade in a Chicago preparatory school to improve his reading skills, which were reported to be at a second-grade level. Creighton University agreed to provide Ross with the financial help necessary for this education. Although no case was brought by Ross, this type of situation is indicative of educational exploitation. (See also page 232.)

The courts appear to be concerned with this problem. In *Sturrup v. Mahan*, 290 N.E.2d 64 (Ind. App. 1972), the court expressed its opinion on the importance of education:

> Schools are for education. There is no doubt that extracurricular athletic competition may add to the educational process, but the extracurricular activities should not take precedence over the curricular activities of the school. The sideshow may not consume the circus.

Echols v. Board of Trustees of the California State University and Colleges, (Cal. Super. Ct.) County of Los Angeles, No. C266 777 (Settled), is an example of such an educational exploitation case. Randall Echols and six other former student-athletes of California State University at Los Angeles (CSULA) brought suit against the board of trustees of CSULA, the president, the athletic director, and the basketball coach of the school. The students claimed they attended CSULA with the understanding, based upon claims by university officials, that they would receive a tuition and cost-free college education in exchange for their participation in the basketball program. All the athletes were admitted into a special program for minority students, which they claim wasted four to six years of their lives. The students were enrolled in courses such as backpacking that were designed to keep them eligible for varsity basketball.

The suit also included a claim that the university did specifically breach its portion of the athletic scholarship contracts by not providing education-related services such as adequate counseling. The students were denied access to university counselors and directed by coaches in the athletic department to enroll in nondegree requirement courses. They were never informed of various academic and course requirements as were other CSULA students and as a result were unaware of degree requirements. The students claimed they were instructed to accept grades for courses they had never attended and were therefore deprived of educational opportunities. Last, the students claimed the defendants were at all times "agents and employees" of CSULA and at all times were acting "within the course and scope of such agency and with the permission and consent" of the university. A settlement was reached with six of the seven athletes. The settlement provided them with $10,000 each and payment of loans that ranged from $2,100 to $6,000. The university also agreed "to issue a public statement expressing regret for what happened and guaranteeing that such a situation will not reoccur." In addition, the university established a scholarship fund for any of the plaintiffs who desired to continue their studies.

Although as of 1988 no court had rendered a decision on the merits of a case in this area, litigation will undoubtedly occur in the future. Legal experts predict that plaintiffs in educational exploitation cases will win if "proximate cause" can be established. If this occurs, educational institutions may be besieged by countless claims which could amount to great losses of time and money.

With the increasing threat of litigation in the area of educational exploitation, it is important to look at the related area of educational malpractice. Although the courts have not decided any sports-related educational malpractice suits, some cases outside of the sports areas do reveal the attitudes of the courts.

In the earliest case in this area, *Peter W. v. San Francisco Unified School District*, 131 Cal. Rptr. 854 (Cal. App. 1976), a student charged that the school district failed to detect his reading disability and place him in an appropriate class. The court found no standard of care against which the school district's conduct might be measured according to the principle of negligence. The court also commented that if this type of litigation were encouraged, a flood of lawsuits would result:

> Rightly or wrongly, but widely [public schools] are charged with outright failure in the achievement of their educational objectives; according to some critics, they bear responsibility for many of the social and moral problems of our society at large. . . . To hold them to an actionable "duty of care," in the discharge of their academic functions, would expose them to the tort claims—real or imagined— of disaffected students and parents in countless numbers. They are already beset by social and financial problems which have gone to major litigation, but for which no permanent solution has yet appeared. The ultimate consequences, in terms of public time and money, would burden them—and society—beyond calculation.

In a more recent case, *D.S.W. v. Fairbanks North Star Borough School District*, 628 P.2d 554 (Alaska 1981), two students' dyslexia went undetected for several years. After diagnosing the problem and giving two special courses, the school district discontinued help. The students charged that the alleged negligence caused them to suffer "loss of education, loss of opportunity for employment, loss of opportunity to attend college or post high school studies, past and future mental anguish and loss of income and income-earning ability." The court did not award the students since it believed that

> the remedy of money damages is inappropriate as a remedy for one who has been a victim of errors made during his or her education. The level of success which might have been achieved had the mistake not been made will . . . be necessarily incapable of assessment, rendering legal cause an imponderable which is beyond the ability of courts to deal with in a reasoned way. Money damages . . . are a poor, and only tenuously related, substitute for a proper education.

Educational exploitation and malpractice lawsuits have been increasing and present a threat to both the education profession and athletics. Although no appellate court has awarded damages to the plaintiffs, the increase in litigation has not been stemmed. In the present environment of academic abuses involving many student-athletes at the NCAA Division I-A level, a decision by the courts to award damages to a plaintiff in a malpractice case may lead to additional claims brought by scholarship athletes who feel they may have been held back academically because of their athletic talent.

NOTES

1. *Apuna v. Arizona State University* (pending 1984), involves claims of failure to provide an athlete with an education. A football player charges an academic adviser, the president of Arizona State University, and a former football coach with fraud, negligence, and interference with a professional contract as a result of their inducement of the student to enroll in and accept credit for a "bogus correspondence course." Apuna claims that the resulting scandal, adverse publicity, and his subsequent loss of eligibility caused him to lose his bid to play in three college all-star games and undermined his negotiating position with the National Football League. The suit also charges the university with invasion of privacy in the institution's public disclosure of plaintiff's academic records.

2. In a case related to the educational exploitation of student-athletes, Jan Kemp, a former University of Georgia remedial studies instructor, successfully sued the university's vice president for academic affairs, and the assistant vice president in charge of Georgia's developmental studies program, after Kemp was first demoted and then dismissed for speaking out against preferential academic treatment for student-athletes. One of Kemp's protests involved the changing of failing grades of nine football players so that they could remain eligible for the 1982 Sugar Bowl. The court, in agreeing with Kemp, who charged that her constitutional rights to free speech had been violated, awarded her $2.5 million for lost wages,

mental anguish, and punitive damages. One of the issues discussed in the case was whether a university should have a responsibility to graduate its student-athletes or just teach them to read, write, and communicate better. ("Protester of Georgia Grades Policy Wins Suit," *The New York Times*, February 13, 1986, p. B23)

3. At a June 26, 1984, U.S. Senate hearing on "Oversight on College Athletic Programs" (S. Hrg. 98–955, Subcommittee on Education, Arts and Humanities), Harry Edwards, Ph.D., University of California, Berkeley, Department of Sociology, gave the following testimony:

> But the problem does not start on the college campus. An exaggerated emphasis upon sports during the early school years and often in the family, leads to a situation wherein by the time many student-athletes finish their junior high school sports eligibility and move on to high school, so little has been demanded of them academically that no one any longer even expects anything of them intellectually.
>
> At the high school level, the already unconscionable emphasis upon athletic development is institutionally abetted by policies which make athletic competition conditional upon minimum standards or, more typically, no standards of academic performance. As late as the Winter of 1984, it was still the case that only a handful—about forty of the nation's 16,000 plus high school districts—had set minimum academic standards for sports participation. And of those which had such standards, most required only that the student-athlete maintain a 2.0, or "C" average, or that a student-athlete's grade card show no more than one failing grade in an academic year. The problem with these minimum standards, of course, is that they have a way of becoming maximum goals. Student-athletes typically strive to achieve precisely the standards set—nothing more, nothing less.
>
> Only 5 percent of America's high school athletes ever participate in their sports at the collegiate level. Thus the lack of serious academic standards, seriously enforced as a condition of high school sports participation, impacts immediately upon the 95% of former high school athletes who must rely substantially upon their academic skills and records to gain college admissions.

4. For a case involving alleged educational exploitation, see *Jones v. Snowdon*, (Wayne Co. Cir. Ct., N. Mich. 81-131648). An ex-high school basketball star sued his high school coaches and the University of Michigan for $15 million for exploitation of his athletic ability. Alleged learning disabilities prevented him from keeping pace academically with his classmates, but word of his outstanding athletic talent moved him from school to school to capitalize on his basketball skills. "Thoughtless and unrelenting criticism, taunts and insults" from fellow students at his junior college lead to humiliation, emotional pressure, and severe psychological illness. A Michigan district court held that the University of Michigan was a governmental agency and therefore immune from lawsuit. The Michigan Court of Appeals overturned the decision and ordered a trial on the merits.

5. The following cases are suits that involve alleged educational malpractice.

(a) In *Donohue v. Copiague Union Free School District*, 418 N.Y.S.2d 375 (N.Y. 1979), the court reasoned that judicial interference would disrupt the administration of the schools involved. In the court's words: "Recognition in the courts of this cause of action would constitute blatant interference with the responsibility for the administration of the public school system lodged by Constitution and statute in school administrative agencies."

(b) In *Hoffman v. Board of Education of the City of New York*, 424 N.Y.S.2d 376 (N.Y. App. 1979), a student of normal intelligence was placed in classes for the mentally retarded for the majority of his schooling due to a faulty diagnosis. The court awarded him $750,000 in damages, but later the court of appeals reversed this decision, denying any reward.

6. For further information, see the following law review article: Norton, "No Time for Classes: Many Athletes Go to College Hoping to Play Professionally . . . But Now They Are Suing Because They Failed to Get an Education." 4(7) *California Lawyer* 44 (1984).

SUMMER CAMPS, PARTICIPATION ON INDEPENDENT TEAMS, AND OUTSIDE ACTIVITIES

One of the more recent trends in amateur sports litigation involves high school athletes and their parents challenging rules that prohibit student-athlete participation and attendance at camps that specialize in teaching the skills of a particular sport. The rules prohibiting such attendance are relatively new. They were instituted to control overzealous coaches and parents and to equalize interscholastic competition.

One of the first rules to be challenged was one promulgated by the University Interscholastic League in Texas in the case of *Kite v. Marshall*, 494 F. Supp. 227 (S.D. Tex. 1980). The plaintiffs attacked the rule on constitutional grounds, claiming that the rule violated the constitutional rights of parents to make decisions for their children. The district court treated the rule as an infringement of a protected right and overturned it. However, the court of appeals reversed and held that the right, although important, was not a fundamental one and that the rule need only meet a rational basis test (see page 283).

The NCAA has many regulations involving summer camps. These rules involve participation by prospective student-athletes, current student-athletes, and coaching staffs. In drawing up their regulations, the NCAA divides summer camps into two categories: specialized sport camps and diversified sport camps. The specialized camps, which place special emphasis on a particular sport or sports, provide specialized instruction, practice, and usually competition. Diversified camps offer a balanced camping experience, including participation in seasonal summer sports and recreational activities, without emphasis on instruction, practice, or competition in any one sport.

Prospective student-athletes are not allowed to enroll in camps, schools, and clinics that are run by a member institution, either on or off campus, since this would be considered by the association as a tryout (*1987–88 NCAA Manual*, Bylaw 1-7-[b]). It is permissible to employ such a prospective student-athlete at a reasonable rate provided the prospect is not a high school or junior college athletics award winner (*1987–88 NCAA Manual*, Bylaw 1-7-[d]). The NCAA defines a prospective student-athlete, in terms of summer camp participation, as one who is eligible for admission to a member institution or who has started classes for the senior year in high school. Junior college student-athletes also are eligible for employment. Yet groups of prospective student-athletes who are athletics awards winners are not allowed to receive free or reduced admission to a camp, school or clinic (*1987–88 NCAA Manual*, Bylaw 1-7-[d]).

In the case of specialized camps in the sports of basketball and football, an institution cannot hire one of its own student-athletes with eligibility remaining in those sports to work at the camp (*1987–88 NCAA Manual*, Bylaw 1-7-[e]). Under special regulations, a specialized camp can hire one student-athlete from another institution from the previous year's football or basketball squad (*1987–88 NCAA Manual*, Bylaw 1-7-[g]). Diversified camps, run at a member institution, can employ one student-athlete, with eligibility remaining, from the basketball and football squads. Private camps may also do this under more stringent regulations (*1987–88 NCAA Manual*, Constitution 3-1-[f]-[3] and Bylaw 1-7-[f]).

Many high school and college athletic associations establish rules that prohibit student-athletes from participating on independent teams (YMCA, church leagues) while the student-athlete is participating in the same sport as a member of a high school or college team. The rules are intended to prevent players from obtaining unfair additional training and competition, and to keep overzealous coaches from involving student-athletes in excessive athletic participation. Not all sports are subject to these rules; golf, tennis, and swimming are often exempt.

The courts have generally upheld independent team participation rules on the grounds that the restrictions do not violate any constitutionally protected rights. In one case the court dismissed a student-athlete's complaint since the limitation on the student-athlete's participation created no circumstances violative of either state or federal constitutions (see Note 3a).

There has been one successful challenge to an independent team rule in the case of *Buckton v. NCAA*, 366 F. Supp. 1152,

1155 (D. Mass. 1973). Two resident alien college hockey players brought suit against the Eastern College Athletic Conference (ECAC) and the NCAA to challenge an ECAC and NCAA regulation which declared them ineligible because they had competed as members of the Canadian Amateur Hockey Association's major junior A classification. The challenged independent team rule stated: "Any student-athlete who participated as a member of the Canadian Amateur Hockey Association's major junior A hockey classification shall not be eligible for intercollegiate athletics" (NCAA Constitution, Article 3, Section 1, 0.I.5. [1973–74]; ECAC Bylaws, Article 3, Section 1, 0.I.5. [1972]). The court struck down the rule after finding that it violated the equal protection clause of the Fourteenth Amendment since resident aliens were granted the same constitutional right of equal protection as American citizens. The court ruled that the university must declare the student-athletes eligible, and the NCAA was prohibited from bringing sanctions against the university.

In the case of *Kite v. Marshall*, parents of high school student-athletes brought an action which challenged the constitutionality of the "summer camp rule," which was adopted by the defendant University Interscholastic League (UIL), the high school athletic association in Texas. The rationale underlying the rule's adoption was that it ensured that high school athletes would compete on a relatively equal basis. The court decided that

> the decision to send a child to summer basketball camp is important enough to warrant constitutional protection under the family's fundamental right of personal privacy. . . .
>
> Having found a fundamental constitutional right, the remaining inquiries are whether or not the UIL rule in question infringes the right and if so, whether the rule is motivated by compelling state interest and has been narrowly drawn to express only those interests.

In deciding the degree of infringement, the court stated:

> The summer camp rule is, however, directly and purposefully aimed at discouraging a specific parental decision made during the summer months when the school is not acting *in loco parentis*. The interference posed by the UIL rule . . . is neither indirect nor incidental.

The court reasoned, "As it presently reads, the summer camp rule constitutes an overbroad and unreasonable infringement on the right of a family to make decisions concerning the education of its children."

In *Kite v. Marshall*, 661 F.2d 1027 (5th Cir. 1981), UIL appealed the lower court ruling striking down its "summer camp rule." The

court of appeals held that the "summer camp rule" did not violate
either the due process or the equal protection clauses of the
Constitution. It reversed the opinion of the district court. The
court of appeals found that, "this case implicates no fundamental
constitutional right." The court subjected the rule to the rational
basis analysis.

The court also upheld a similar high school rule in *Texas High
School Gymnastics Coaches Ass'n v. Andrews*, 532 S.W.2d 142
(Tex. Civ. App. 1975). This suit was brought by parents and
coaches of gymnasts who sought to overturn a Texas High School
Gymnastics Coaches Association rule that governed dual member-
ship. The association rule read as follows:

> A Texas high school gymnast must not work out with, practice with,
> take lessons with, or compete with a private club, and be eligible
> for dual regional or state competition during the school calendar
> year of their school district.

The complaint alleged that the rule was an "unfair, unlawful and
unconstitutional restriction upon the individual rights of high
school students who . . . desire to compete in high school gymnastic competition." The trial court granted an injunction which
temporarily prohibited the association from enforcing the rule.
The association appealed.

The appeals court noted that there was not sufficient evidence
to support the conclusion that the rule is unreasonable, capricious,
or arbitrary. The court held that the rule must be upheld unless it
could be shown that the rule bears no rational relationship to the
achievement of a legitimate purpose. The court found that the
purpose of the rule was valid since it prevented inequality and
unfair advantage between students of different economic means
and schools located in different areas of economic wealth.

These cases show the reluctance of the court to overturn association rules which are reasonably related to a legitimate purpose.

NOTES

1. At the 1983 NCAA convention, the membership enacted legislation
that prohibits a member of a basketball coaching staff from being employed by a basketball camp that has been established, sponsored, or
conducted by an individual or organization that provides recruiting or
scouting services (*1987–88 NCAA Manual*, Bylaw 1-7-[h]).

2. The following cases also involve camp participation.

(a) In *Art Gaines Baseball Camp, Inc. v. Houston*, 500 S.W.2d 735
(Mo. Ct. App. 1973), a camp sought to restrain the Missouri High
School Activities Association from enforcing a rule which stated that
a student-athlete who attended a camp specializing in one sport for

more than two weeks during a summer would lose eligibility to represent his or her school in that particular sport the following school year. In affirming judgment for the high school athletic association, the court of appeals held that the rule did not infringe on public policy or law and was not unreasonable or arbitrary.

(b) In *Brown v. Wells*, 284 Minn. 468, 181 N.W.2d 708 (1970), a hockey player challenged rules excluding his participation on the high school hockey team if he participated in nonschool hockey, including hockey schools or camps. The court held that when rules are adopted for the purpose of deemphasizing extracurricular athletics that may detract from student interest in education, the court cannot deem such rules arbitrary or unreasonable. The court found that the school board had the discretion to deal with the issue as it thought best. The courts should not attempt to control the discretion of the school board.

3. The following cases deal with participation on independent teams.

(a) In *Kubiszyn v. Alabama High School Athletic Ass'n*, 374 So. 2d 256 (Ala. 1979), members of a high school basketball team were declared ineligible after playing on YMCA and church basketball teams at the same time they were playing for their high school team. The high school athletic association rule provided that any member of a high school athletic team who participated in an athletic contest as a member of a similar team, the same season, was ineligible to play for the high school team for the remainder of the season. The court found that the rule did not violate the state or federal constitution, in absence of some evidence that the student-athlete suffered some impairment of a property right, or that the acts of the athletic association were the result of fraud or collusion.

(b) In *Dumez v. Louisiana High School Athletic Ass'n*, 334 So. 2d 494 (La. Ct. App. 1976), parents of high school student-athletes who were declared ineligible to participate in interscholastic baseball athletics by an athletic association sought a permanent injunction to prohibit enforcement of the ruling. In reversing judgment for the parents, the court of appeals held that determination by the association to declare the students ineligible because they violated the "independent team rule" by participating in practice sessions held by the Babe Ruth Baseball League was not subject to judicial rescission or modification on the grounds that it constituted a serious "inequity" to the students when similar action was not taken against coaches or schools.

4. The New Jersey State Interscholastic Athletic Association (NJSIAA) has the following regulation regarding high school student-athletes who work at summer camps or recreational programs:

E. A Student-Athlete may work as a counselor in a summer camp, life guard, swimming pool attendant and swimming instructor for children without affecting his/her eligibility under the terms of this principle; he/she may work in a tennis or golf shop provided he/she does not give instruction for compensation, and he/she may obtain employment with a recreation department, his/her duties to include some officiating and coaching responsibilities; however, he/she may not be employed as an athletic coach. [*1984–85 NJSIAA Handbook*, Article V.2.E.]

5. The NCAA provides that coaches may not supervise or conduct recognized regional, national, or international training programs or competition, including prospects, unless the coaches' participation meets with the approval of the NCAA Council. If approval is not obtained, it may be considered a tryout by the prospective student-athlete (see *1987–88 NCAA Manual*, Bylaw 1-6-[c]-[6]).

Chapter 6

LEGAL PRINCIPLES
IN TORT LAW

INTRODUCTION

Tort law is an important area of sports law. There has been an upward trend in the number of cases filed based on intentional or unintentional tort theories. There are many reasons for this increase, including the astronomical rise in medical costs that injured athletes or other plaintiffs are unable to meet, along with a prevailing notion that one who injures deliberately or negligently should pay for such actions when they create serious consequences.

Civil law provides injured individuals with a cause of action by which they may be compensated or "made whole" through the recovery of damages. This cause of action comes under the general heading of torts. A *tort* is a private (or civil) wrong or injury, other than a breach of contract, suffered by an individual as the result of another person's conduct. The law of torts deals with the allocation of losses arising from human activities and provides for the adjustment of these losses via the monetary compensation of the individual for injuries sustained as a result of another's conduct.

Civil law and criminal law share the common purpose of inducing people to act for the benefit of society by preventing behavior that negatively affects society or by encouraging behavior that has a positive effect. Civil law and criminal law differ, however, in their means of achieving this similar purpose. Criminal law is designed to protect the public from harm through the punishment of conduct likely to cause harm. Civil law, on the other hand, aims to compensate (to make whole) an injured party for the harm suffered as a result of another person's conduct.

Varying interpretations of criminal and civil offenses lead to divergent methods of action in these two areas of law. Criminal actions emphasize the immorality or bad intentions of the defendants. Tort actions, on the other hand, seek to achieve desirable social results by resolving the conflicting interests of individuals. Society tends to distinguish criminal wrongs by condemning or judging the morality of the criminal more severely than that of the tortious wrongdoer. Once a crime has been discovered, the state or a subdivision of the state (e.g., county), in its capacity as protector of the public interest, brings an action against the accused. In a tort action, however, the injured party institutes the action as an individual in an effort to recover damages as compensation for the injury received.

The distinction between intentional and unintentional torts is important in the area of tort law. The responsibility of distinguishing between intentional and unintentional torts lies with the court because the court determines the manner in which it will assess the case. The degree of the defendant's intent toward the plaintiff (intent to harm) can be differentiated on the following three levels:

1. Intentional tort (e.g., assault and battery): Intent to commit the act and intent to harm the plaintiff.
2. Reckless misconduct or gross negligence: Intent to commit the act, but no intent to harm the plaintiff.
3. Unintentional tort or negligence: No intent to commit the act and no intent to harm the plaintiff, but a failure to exercise reasonable care.

Reckless misconduct (also called gross negligence) falls somewhere between intentional torts and mere ordinary negligence. It differs from negligence in degree rather than in substance. The court may view one single act either as negligent or grossly negligent, depending on the state of mind of the actor.

Intentional and unintentional torts are the most common tort actions in the sports setting. *Assault and battery,* an intentional tort, *reckless misconduct,* somewhere between intentional and unintentional torts, and *negligence,* an unintentional tort, are therefore emphasized in the first part of Chapter 6. The doctrine of *vicarious liability,* often times used in tort cases to sue an employer for the negligence of the employer's employees, is presented next. Then the less common torts of *invasion of privacy* and *intentional infliction of emotional distress* are described. The chapter concludes with a discussion of *products liability law,* an area of law that allows a party who has been injured by a product (e.g., sports equipment) that is defectively designed, manufactured, or distributed to recover damages.

Several common problems are involved in the majority of sports-related tort cases. The first is the difficulty of determining exactly what a tort is in an athletic context. There is also a public policy consideration involved in that it has been suggested in several court decisions that court interference with sports will destroy amateur athletics and unreasonably restrict the free play of sports. The third common problem is that litigation may discourage participation in the more dangerous sports. For these reasons, athletic administrators must be aware of the legal principles involved in tort liability relating to sports so that they can be better prepared to take preventive measures that will minimize the adverse effects of such litigation.

NOTES _____

1. Much of the existing case law concerning tort law and sports involves professional athletes. However, the legal ramifications are similar for

amateur athletes. For further information, see the following law review articles:

(a) "Compensating Injured Professional Athletes: The Mystique of Sport Versus Traditional Tort Principles," 55 *New York University Law Review* 971 (1980).

(b) "Comment: A Proposed Legislative Solution to the Problem of Violent Acts by Participants During Professional Sporting Events," 7 *University of Dayton Law Review* 91 (1981).

(c) Hayes, "Professional Sports and Tort Liability: A Victory for the Intentionally Injured Player," *Detroit College of Law Review* 687 (Summer 1980).

(d) Gulotta, "Torts in Sports: Deterring Violence in Professional Athletics," *Fordham Law Review* 764 (April 1980).

2. For further information, see the following texts:

(a) Weistart and Lowell, *The Law of Sports* (Indianapolis, Ind.: Bobbs-Merrill, 1979). Supplement (Charlottesville, Va.: The Michie Co., 1985).

(b) Sobel, *Professional Sports and the Law* (New York: Law Arts Publishers, 1977). Supplement, 1981.

(c) Appenzeller, *Sports and the Courts* (Charlottesville, Va.: The Michie Company, 1980).

(d) Yasser, *Torts and Sports: Legal Liability in Professional and Amateur Athletics* (Westport, Conn.: Quorum Books, 1985).

(e) Schubert, Smith, and Trentadue, *Sports Law* (St. Paul, Minn.: West Publishing Co., 1986).

(f) Boone and Nygaard, *Coaches' Guide to Sport Law* (Champaign, Ill.: Human Kinetics Publishers, 1985).

(g) Berry and Wong, *Law and Business of the Sports Industries*, Vols. I and II (Dover, Mass.: Auburn House, 1986).

THE TORTS OF ASSAULT AND BATTERY

Assault and battery can be both a criminal and a civil case; however, most people associate assault and battery with criminal law. Most state statutes broadly define criminal assault to include both attempted and actual battery. Such is not the case in civil law, where assault and battery are more specifically and narrowly defined, and where the two actions constitute separate and distinct torts. Further elaboration will clarify the distinction between the criminal and civil law definitions of assault and battery. A *civil law battery* is an unpermitted actual touching of another person, and a *civil law assault* is the apprehension of imminent harmful contact. For civil assault and battery, as for all intentional torts, there does not have to be harm to the plaintiff to establish a charge of assault and/or battery. The mere fact that a person has done and intended to do a proscribed action will suffice to provide at least nominal damages. Any harm will, however, be important in assessing monetary damages.

In torts involving intentional harm to the person, the plaintiff may recover for lost earning capacity, medical expenses, pain and suffering, and for the loss of consortium, affection, assistance, and marital fellowship. These are termed *actual damages*. Unlike negligence, however, it is not necessary in an intentional tort case to prove actual damages to recover; the plaintiff may recover substantial damages without proving specific bodily injuries. Torts involving intentional harm allow for recovery of damages for emotional suffering (i.e., humiliation, indignity, injury to feelings), as long as this suffering was proximately caused by the defendant's conduct. Certain conduct on the part of the plaintiff that is not sufficient to constitute a defense to the action may be considered in mitigation or moderation of damages. For example, although provocative words by the plaintiff do not justify the defendant's use of force, these words may be considered in mitigation of the damages awarded to the plaintiff.

In addition to actual damages, a plaintiff may recover *punitive damages* when the defendant has acted willfully or has exhibited outrageous conduct. These damages are awarded on the theory that they may help to deter future wrongful conduct. They have also been justified on the theory that they help remedy the lack of money available to pay litigation expenses, which are normally unavailable under American civil procedure. Punitive damages are awarded not according to the tort committed, although they are often given for assault and battery, but for the defendant's intentional conduct. This is usually a matter of degree, and punitive damages are awarded when the defendant's conduct is particularly reprehensible. Punitive damages are available only for intentional tort cases and are not awarded in negligence cases.

Assault

For an action to constitute assault, the following three elements must be present:

1. Intent to cause harm by the defendant.
2. Apprehension of immediate harm by the plaintiff.
3. Lack of consent by the plaintiff.

With the first element, the plaintiff does not have to prove that the defendant intended to inflict bodily harm. With the second element, the apprehension of immediate harm by the plaintiff must be reasonable, and claims that a plaintiff is extraordinarily timid will not lower the court's standard of reasonable apprehension. However, the defendant will be held responsible if the defendant knows of the plaintiff's timidness. The *apparent* ability to carry out a threat as opposed to *actual* ability is what the court relies on in determining assault. The defendant who claims that he or she had no intention of carrying out a threat will not be successful. For example, for a defendant to claim that the gun was not loaded is not a successful defense against the reasonable person's being placed in apprehension of immediate harm by the defendant because the plaintiff had no way of knowing whether or not the gun was loaded.

The third element, lack of consent by the plaintiff to the alleged assault, is extremely important in sports cases in which the court has difficulty in distinguishing among consented to contact, apprehension, and intimidation, as opposed to unconsented to activities. Actual contact between the defendant and the plaintiff need not have occurred for assault to have been committed; however, the plaintiff must be aware of the possibility of contact. The distinction between actual physical contact and the mere apprehension of it marks the dividing line between assault and battery. For example, in a high school baseball game, Freddy Fastball threw a pitch that unintentionally got away from him and passed dangerously close to Harry Hothead's head. Harry took offense at the closeness of the pitch and charged the mound and threw his bat in the direction of Freddy. The bat missed Freddy. Nevertheless, Freddy could bring suit against Harry for assault.

Battery

For an action to constitute battery, three elements must be present:

1. The intent to touch by the defendant.
2. Actual touching.
3. The lack of consent to the contact by the plaintiff.

With the first element, the plaintiff does not have to prove that the defendant intended the specific harm that the victim incurred. The rationale is that the defendant is presumed to have intended the natural and probable consequences of the act. However, a touching that results from a reflex action is not considered intentional.

With the second element, the mere apprehension of contact is not sufficient; rather, actual contact must occur for a plaintiff to prove that a defendant's action constituted battery. The plaintiff's awareness of the contact or force at the time of the battery is not essential. Plaintiffs have made successful battery claims in cases in which the contact occurred when they were asleep or under anesthesia. Contact does not necessarily have to be harmful but may instead be offensive, such as spitting at another person. The act must cause and be intended to cause an unconsented contact by the defendant.

The third element required in a battery action is lack of consent to the contact by the plaintiff. The determination of whether or not consent existed is often difficult; factors such as the time of the act and the place in which it occurred must be considered. The element of consent is crucial to both assault and battery, especially in the sports setting. In contact sports, force is expected to be used by the participants because it is one of the necessary terms and conditions of the game. The contact is justified if it is reasonable under the circumstances. Many of the contacts that occur in the sports setting would be considered batteries in a nonsports setting. However, the key distinction in sports battery cases is the determination of whether a particular contact has been consented to by the participant. If the court concludes that consent was given and the contact was reasonable, a plaintiff will not be successful in a battery case. For example, during a basketball game, Bully Smith was guarding Tommy Timid as Tommy was about to receive a pass. Without provocation, Bully intentionally pushed Tommy from behind and punched him in the back of the head. As Tommy fell, Bully hit him again, knocking Tommy unconscious. Tommy can bring suit against Bully for battery, because there was intention to harm, but not assault, because there was no apprehension of harm since Tommy did not see the punch coming.

If consent was not given or if the contact was unreasonable, then the type of contact initiated by the defendant will determine the type of damages available to the plaintiff. Any proven intentional tort provides at least nominal damages. Outrageous or extremely offensive contact will, in addition to the nominal damages, provide a basis on which to support punitive damages that may greatly increase the plaintiff's award.

NOTES

1. In *Bourque v. Duplechin*, 331 So. 2d 40 (La. Ct. App. 1976), the plaintiff sued defendant for an intentional battery that occurred during a softball game. Defendant ran into plaintiff after plaintiff second baseman had completed his throw to first base. On appeal, the court held that it was not an intentional tort because the defendant had no intent to harm the plaintiff.

2. In *Griggas v. Clauson*, 128 N.E.2d 363 (Ill. App. Ct. 1955), Griggas sued Clauson for assault and battery for injuries received when the defendant struck the plaintiff in the face several times in a basketball

game. The court found that Griggas was subjected to wanton, unprovoked, and unanticipated assault and battery and held for Griggas.

3. In *Averill v. Luttrell*, 311 S.W.2d 812 (Tenn. Ct. App. 1957), plaintiff batter, angered by the pitcher's intentionally thrown beanball, which struck him, threw his bat in the direction of the mound. The defendant catcher then stepped behind the batter and hit him with his fist. The batter sued both the catcher and the catcher's club. The court held for the plaintiff batter and found that the defendant catcher had committed assault and battery.

4. In *Manning v. Grimsley*, 643 F.2d 20 (1st Cir. 1981), defendant pitcher was sued for assault and battery for throwing a baseball from the bullpen into the stands and hitting a spectator.

5. In *Hackbart v. Cincinnati Bengals*, 435 F. Supp. 352 (D. Colo. 1977), *rev'd*, 601 F.2d 516 (10th Cir. 1979), plaintiff football player was precluded from suing for assault and battery by the statute of limitations.

6. For further information, see the following articles:
(a) "Professional Sports and Tort Liability: A Victory for the Intentionally Injured Player," *Detroit College of Law Review* 687 (Summer 1980).
(b) "Torts in Sports—Deterring Violence in Professional Athletics," 48 *Fordham Law Review* 764 (April 1980).

Defenses for Assault and Battery

The three defenses available to the defendant in an intentional harm-to-the-person action, such as assault or battery, are consent, privilege, and immunity. Consent, when given by a plaintiff, does not excuse a tort. However, because its absence is an essential element of an intentional tort, its presence will totally negate the claim of liability since the plaintiff will not be able to establish the three required elements. On the other hand, both privilege and immunity, in effect, excuse the commission of a tort after its occurrence.

Consent

Consent is a voluntary yielding of one's will to the dictates of another. It is an act of reason, accompanied by deliberation, which is made by an individual possessed of sufficient mental capacity to make an intelligent choice. To be effective, consent must be an act unclouded by fraud or duress. Consent may be expressed, or it may be reasonably implied by the circumstances surrounding the situation.

The element of consent presents a special problem in the realm of sports in general and for athletic participants in particular. The traditional interpretation in many assault and battery cases in the sports setting has been that the athlete, by participating in a given event, consents to the degree of contact commonly found within the rules of the sport. A special problem arises in the area of sports because it is often difficult to determine the extent or scope of the implied consent given. Consent implied from participation in athletic events is not a blanket consent that protects athletes from the consequences of their actions under all circumstances. Instead, many plaintiffs argue that the scope of consent is limited to acts that occur in the ordinary and normal conduct of the game.

The difficulty arises from the determination of what is "ordinary and normal conduct" in a particular game. For example, the consent defense might be employed in a sports-related assault and battery action. The defendant could claim that no tort was committed based on the nature of the relationship between himself and the plaintiff, who by his very participation in the contest consents to a certain degree of contact. Indeed, a problem in maintaining a tort action in a sports case is the difficulty of ascertaining, in the context of a game in which physical contact is allowed, exactly when or how a tort occurs.

NOTE

1. In *Tavernier v. Maes*, 242 Cal. App. 2d 532, 51 Cal. Rptr. 575 (1966), plaintiff sought recovery for injuries sustained during a family softball game. Plaintiff alleged defendant deliberately slid into him in an attempt to break up a double play. The court held that the scope of the implied consent created by plaintiff's participation, as well as the question of whether the defendant's conduct exceeded the scope of the consent given, was a matter for the jury to decide.

Privilege

A *privilege* is a particular, limited benefit enjoyed by an individual or class that extends beyond the common advantages of other citizens. In certain situations a privilege is more appropriately classified as an exemption from a burden rather than as a benefit to be enjoyed. A privilege is commonly enjoyed in situations in which the defendant has acted in defense of his or her person or property. The defendant who is successful in using the defense of privilege must bear the burden of proof to establish that a privilege existed and that the force used pursuant to the privilege was reasonable under the circumstances. The defense is denied, and the defendant will be held liable if the force used is found to be excessive or unreasonable. The defense of privilege commonly encompasses these six types of behavior:

1. self-defense
2. defense of third persons

3. corporal punishment
4. defense of property
5. effecting an arrest
6. arrest without a warrant

The privilege most commonly utilized in sports cases is that of self-defense. In order to successfully argue self-defense, the defendant must prove that no more force than was reasonably necessary was used to repel an attack.

The self-defense privilege rests on the policy that allows a person being attacked to come to his or her own defense. The privilege extends to the use of all reasonable force needed to prevent harmful bodily contact. The privilege arises when danger exists or there is a reasonable belief that danger is imminent. It is limited to the use of force that is necessary or that appears to be necessary for adequate protection. There is never any privilege to use force when the immediate danger is past.

The defense of third persons is also a potentially viable legal argument for defending against an action for assault or battery. In order for the defense to be effective, certain requirements must be met. First, the privilege extends only to the reasonable force necessary to defend another from imminent harm. The defense must occur in reaction to events as they exist at the time of the threat. There is no privilege for physical reactions to future threats or past attacks.

The privilege of third-person defense is available to anyone who reasonably defends another. There does not have to be any special relationship between the two. Some courts require that the third party take the risk that the person being defended would not be privileged to defend himself. The preferred view, however, is that an honest mistake as to the necessity for the defensive action will relieve the defendant of liability.

Immunity

Immunity is a condition that protects against a tort action. It exists because of the particular position of the defendant, and not because of any action taken by the defendant. This defense may exist either because of a relationship between the plaintiff and the defendant, or because of the capacity of the defendant. Examples of relationships that in some states permit a defense of immunity in intentional torts include those between husband and wife or between parent and child. Charitable corporations; federal, state, and municipal governments; and public officials may use this defense because of their role as protectors and defenders of the public welfare under the doctrine of charitable or sovereign immunity. (See page 356.)

THE TORT OF RECKLESS MISCONDUCT

Reckless misconduct or gross negligence falls between the unintentional tort of negligence and the intentional torts of assault and battery. Behavior in the category of reckless misconduct is characterized by intent on the part of the defendant to commit the act but no intent to harm the plaintiff by this act. Reckless misconduct means the actor has intentionally performed an act in disregard of a risk known to him where the risk is so great as to make the harm highly probable. It must usually be accompanied by a conscious disregard of the circumstances. For example, Frankie Fieldevent, after a high school track practice, was throwing the javelin at some of his teammates who were running around the track. He had no intention of hitting any of his friends, but Mikey Marathon fell while running, and the javelin pierced him in the shoulder. Mikey successfully brought suit against Frankie for reckless misconduct.

Reckless misconduct is particularly important in the area of participant-against-participant tort cases. Only recently have courts found a duty between sports participants to refrain from reckless misconduct toward another player.

To find reckless misconduct, an action must be more than ordinary inadvertence or inattention but less than conscious indifference to the consequences. It may be defined as an action that is willful, wanton, or reckless. It is not an intentional action, however, if the degree of the care exercised is so far below the usual standard that in effect it is treated as intended action. Reckless misconduct encompasses action which evidences an extreme departure from the ordinary degree of care required from the actor in the particular circumstances. However, the damages awarded, especially in the area of punitive damages, may be greater if the defendant's action is deemed grossly negligent.

NOTES _____

1. For further information, see the following law review article: "Comment, Compensating Injured Professional Athletes: The Mystique of Sport Versus Traditional Tort Principles," 55 *New York University Law Review* 971 (1980).

2. For a case in which the reckless misconduct theory was successfully applied, see *Nabozny v. Barnhill*, 334 N.E.2d 258 (Ill. App. 1975) in Chapter 7, page 340.

THE TORT OF NEGLIGENCE

Negligence is an unintentional tort which focuses on an individual's conduct or actions. Negligence must be distinguished from intentional torts, such as assault and battery, which revolve around the individual's state of mind or intent. *Negligent conduct* is defined as that which falls below the standard established by law for the protection of others against an unreasonably great risk of harm. The ability of the injured party to sue and to recover damages for negligence is based on the idea that one who acts should anticipate the consequences which might involve unreasonable danger to others.

A person must take precautions only against unreasonable risks of harm. Unreasonable risks are those whose danger is apparent or should be apparent to one in the position of the actor. The law, however, does not seek to burden the freedom of human action with excessive or unreasonable demands and restraints. Therefore, one is not expected to guard against situations or occurrences that are unlikely to happen. The standard of care required is measured by reference to the *reasonable person standard*. This hypothetical reasonable person is one who selects a course of action which would be selected by a reasonable individual residing in the affected community. The law excuses all persons from liability for accidents that are either unavoidable or unforeseeable.

Determining Negligence

The court commonly examines three factors to aid in its determination of whether or not a defendant's action constitutes negligence:

1. The extent and nature of the risk involved.
2. The social value and utility of interest advanced.
3. The availability of an alternative course of action.

With the first factor, the greater the risk of a particular action (e.g., the risk of death), the greater the extent of precautions required by the actor. Acknowledgment that as the gravity of the potential harm of a given action increases, the apparent likelihood of the occurrence lessens, does not preclude precaution regarding an action that involves great risk. In other words, if the potential risk is significant—if death is likely to occur—the court will weigh less heavily the rarity of the event and will demand a higher degree of precaution despite the low probability of the particular harm in question. For example, a school bus carrying student-athletes to a game may be required to stop at all railroad crossings. The chance of the bus being hit is extremely small, yet if a collision were to occur, the consequences could be devastating. Thus, the court would demand a high degree of precaution, even if this standard were not set by state statute. In sports, the degree of care required for archery might exceed the degree required for softball. Even though there might be the same likelihood of injury, the potential gravity of the harm in archery (death) is so much greater than for softball (broken bones) that the degree of care required may be greater.

In examining the second factor, the court will balance a consideration of the potential harm of an action and the probability of its occurrence against social value or utility in the interest which the actor seeks to advance. Swimming pools, for example, pose significant potential harm to the people who use them. Their introduction or continued use, however, may be justified in the public interest because of the tremendous amount of use and enjoyment they provide. Instead of banning swimming pools, federal and state governments may enact and impose safety regulations for their use. If the safety regulations are met and an injury occurs, the defendant will not be found negligent. In the same vein, sports will be found to have some social value or utility which will permit their continuance despite the potential for serious injury, although in theory the degree of social utility may vary from sport to sport. Thus, one issue is that of defining the extent or existence of a social value for a sport such as football which causes catastrophic injuries.

The third factor the court uses to determine whether or not an act is negligent is the availability to the actor of alternative courses of action. Different persons in the same situation may have a variety of courses of action available based on their age, knowledge, and/or experience. Acts will be negligent if the action taken is not one which is acceptable under a "reasonable person standard" and if there is an alternative available. For example, when confronted with a serious injury to an athlete, an athletic trainer may call for an ambulance or attempt to administer medical treatment without help. It may not always be reasonable to attempt to treat the injury without help. The athletic trainer may be negligent in failing to call for help if treating the serious injury (e.g., a spinal injury) is beyond his or her capability. This point leads to a discussion of the various elements and standards involved in the theory of negligence.

The following four elements must be proved by the plaintiff in order for an action to be considered negligence:

1. duty of care owed
2. breach of duty

3. actual and proximate causation
4. damages

Duty of Care Owed

The plaintiff's initial step in a negligence case is to establish the duty of care owed by the defendant. Duty is divided into two categories: a duty to act and a duty not to act in an unreasonable manner. A *duty of care* is an obligation, recognized by law, which requires an individual or a group to conform to a particular standard of conduct toward another. The duty of care required of an individual is established by reference to any special qualifications. In the case of a professional (e.g., doctor, trainer), a duty of care is determined by reference to uniform requirements that establish minimum standards of behavior. All professionals are judged not as individuals in society at large, but as members of a specified class. When acting in a professional capacity, the professional person will be judged by the standards of the profession in existence at the time.

The concept of *legal duty* is based on the relationship that exists between the parties involved. Certain relationships, such as employer-employee, principal-agent, teacher-student, and coach-athlete, establish a legal duty to act. An employer, for example, has the duty to render aid and assistance to an employee who is injured during the course of employment. However, absent a duty-imposing relationship, an individual is not liable for an omission to act. A moral obligation to act does not create a legal duty to act, and hence the individual who failed to act cannot be held liable in negligence. If one without a duty to act does undertake to act, however, that person may be held liable if he or she acts negligently. By acting, one can create a duty between oneself and another that may not have previously existed. For example, a person who undertakes to rescue another may not abandon that rescue attempt if it becomes inconvenient. By acting, the would-be rescuer has created a duty to continue to aid the person in trouble. In sports cases, the duty is often described as the "reasonable care" necessary to avoid creating risks that may result in injuries to players or spectators. For example, Peter Para suffered a serious neck injury in a high school football practice. Coach Foot attempted to provide medical assistance. In doing so, he became responsible for causing further damage which left Peter paralyzed. Peter has grounds for a suit because the coach was negligent in acting as he did if the court finds that Coach Foot did not act as a "reasonable football coach" would act in this situation.

Often liability will rest on whether the court designates the act or nonact as misfeasance, nonfeasance, or malfeasance. *Misfeasance* is the term applied to lawful conduct that is improperly done. *Nonfeasance* is an omission of an action that ought to be taken. *Malfeasance* is the doing of an act that is wholly wrongful and unlawful.

NOTES ——

  1. For a sports case in which a court decided that a legal duty was present, see *Berman v. Philadelphia Board of Education*, 456 A.2d 545 (Pa. Super. Ct. 1983). The plaintiff-student was injured during a school-sponsored floor hockey game which was supervised by a physical education instructor. A mouth guard would have prevented the injury, but Amateur Hockey Association rules did not require them at the time. The court, however, held that the board of education could not escape its duty of care for the welfare of students because of a lack of rules and standards.

  2. For a sports case in which a court decided that no legal duty was required, see *Hunt v. Scotia-Glenville School District*, 460 N.Y.S.2d 205 (N.Y. App. 1983). The court held that a basketball coach and school district were under no legal obligation to submit timely recommendations for a student-athlete applying for a college athletic scholarship. The court reasoned that there was no statute or regulation mandating such a recommendation, and the student-athlete's civil rights were not violated.

  3. For further information, see the following law review article: Harty, "School Liability for Athletic Injuries: Duty, Causation and Defense," 21 *Washburn Law Journal* 315 (Winter 1982).

Breach of Duty

Once a plaintiff has demonstrated that a duty of care was owed by the defendant, the plaintiff must prove that the defendant violated this duty. In other words, the burden of proof requires that the party on whom it rests establish the validity of the claim being made. There are three methods by which the plaintiff may sustain this burden of proof:

1. direct evidence of negligence
2. violation of a statute
3. res ipsa loquitur

Direct evidence of negligence is evidence that tends to establish actual factual occurrences through proof they happened. An example of direct evidence is eyewitness testimony. For instance, Larry Lacroix suffered an injury to his back in a high school lacrosse game. The athletic trainer told Coach Winatallcosts not to allow Larry to play and later served as an eyewitness against the coach at the trial. Coach Winatallcosts, ignoring the trainer's warning, coerced Larry to play the last 10 minutes because the state championship was on the line. As a result of further play, Larry was more severely injured. Coach Winatallcosts breached the duty of care he owed Larry. The trainer's testimony and the injury constituted the direct evidence.

When direct evidence is not available, certain procedural devices are used to enable a plaintiff to prove his or her case. One of these is presumptions. *Presumptions* are a legal fiction which requires the judge or jury to assume the existence of one fact based on the existence of another fact or group of facts. They are used in the absence of sufficient evidence to prove the fact itself. The classic example is the presumption that a person who has been gone seven years without explanation is dead. Another type of presumption involves an individual who violates a valid statute.

Violation of a statute is sometimes referred to as *negligence per se*. Negligence per se means that upon finding a violation of an applicable statute, there is a conclusive presumption of negligence. This conclusive presumption requires that a jury find for the plaintiff. It does not allow the jury to weigh all the evidence and independently determine the relative liabilities of the parties. Although in some states the violation of a valid statute may be considered negligence per se, in other states, the violation of a statute, ordinance, or even an administrative regulation is deemed only evidence of negligence. The current trend is away from viewing violations of statutes as negligence per se. When a violation is treated as evidence of negligence, it is accorded a different weight. A jury will not be required to draw any specific conclusion from the violation. Instead, a violation merely establishes an inference of negligence that may or may not be accepted by the jury.

In order for a statutory violation to provide evidence of negligence, the complaining party must establish two points. First, the statutory violation must be causally related to the plaintiff's harm. If an individual's taillights are out in violation of a statute, that violation may only be used to establish negligence when the failure of the taillights causes an accident. The second factor to be considered is that the harm must be the sort sought to be prevented by the statute. If the driver of one car pushes another car into a wall, the fact that the pusher's car headlights do not work in violation of a motor vehicle safety statute is of little or no significance.

The last method of establishing the negligence of the defendant is through the use of the legal doctrine of *res ipsa loquitur*. Res ipsa loquitur permits the fact finder to infer both negligence and causation from circumstantial evidence. It is, in effect, another type of presumption. The plaintiff must establish that more likely than not, the harm to the plaintiff was a result of the defendant's negligence. In order to defeat the application of this doctrine, the defendant must establish that there is another, equally believable explanation of the injury to the plaintiff.

Res ipsa loquitur is strictly a procedural device designed to allow a plaintiff to establish an otherwise unprovable case. In negligence cases, direct evidence of the defendant's negligence may not be available. This doctrine allows a plaintiff to recover on the basis of what probably happened.

Presumptions may be rebuttable, depending on the situation. If rebuttable, the defendant or plaintiff may counter the presumption raised by the opposition through the introduction of alternative evidence tending to dispute the validity of the presumption.

NOTES _____

1. The doctrine of res ipsa loquitur was successfully raised in the following cases:

(a) *Parker v. Warren*, 503 S.W. 2d 938 (Tenn. App. 1973). (See page 377.)

(b) *Graver v. State of New York*, 181 N.Y.S. 2d 994 (1959). (See page 371.)

2. For a case in which a court decided *not* to apply the doctrine of res ipsa loquitur, see *Jordan v. Loveland Skiing Corp.*, 503 P.2d 1034 (Colo. App. 1972). Plaintiff skier sought recovery for injuries sustained in a fall from defendant's ski lift. In ruling in favor of the defendant, the court of appeals held that the issues of the lift operator's negligence and proximate cause were properly submitted to the jury and the doctrine of res ipsa loquitur did not apply.

Actual and Proximate Causation

The primary issue in the area of causation is that of *proximate cause*—that is, whether the defendant's negligent act was connected to the plaintiff's harm to such an extent as to be considered the legal cause of the harm. Before any determination of proximate cause, however, the defendant's conduct must be shown to be the actual cause of the plaintiff's harm. If the same harm would have resulted if the negligent act had never occurred, then the act is not the actual cause of the harm. This is sometimes referred to as the "but for" test; the particular harm in question would not have been suffered "but for" the negligent act of the defendant.

After the existence of actual causation between the plaintiff's harm and the defendant's act has been established, recovery requires that it be demonstrated that the latter is also the proximate cause of the former. Proximate cause is tested by determining whether or not the harm which resulted to the plaintiff was a reasonable, foreseeable consequence of the defendant's act. To demonstrate proximate cause, it is sufficient to show that the probable consequence of the defendant's act was harm of the same general character as that which befell the plaintiff. It is not necessary to show that the harm to the plaintiff in its precise form or particular manner should have been foreseen by the defendant. For example, Jerry Janitor, in cleaning a spot off the basketball court, used a cleaning substance that left the floor extremely slippery. During the game later that day, Ralph Rocket slipped on the spot and seriously injured his knee. Jerry's use of the improper cleaning substance was the proximate cause of Ralph's injury.

One last problem of determining causation occurs when there is more than one cause of injury. In some cases, when a combination of causes led to the damage, a defendant can defeat claims of liability by showing that there was an unforeseeable intervening cause. An *intervening cause* is one which comes into existence after the negligent action of the defendant and somehow affects the "result."

Often there may be more than one cause for any given injury. In such cases, no liability will be assigned to individual causes unless the individual cause was a "substantial factor" in the creation of the ultimate result. This substantial factor test precludes liability for inadvertent or minor causational factors. The test is predicated on the theory that any cause should not be held partly or totally liable for the injury unless it substantially causes the harm.

NOTES ——————————————————————————————————

1. For a case involving intervening negligence in which the court did *not* relieve the original wrongdoer of liability, see *Freeman v. U.S.*, 509 F.2d 626 (6th Cir. 1975). Plaintiff brought an action against the United States for wrongful death of parachutists. In affirming judgment for the plaintiff, the court of appeals held that the air controller owed a duty of care to the parachutists, that they were not contributorily negligent in jumping through the cloud cover into Lake Erie, and that the intervening negligence of the pilot and jump master in directing a jump through a cloud cover did not relieve the government of liability.

2. For a case in which the court decided that *no* proximate cause existed, see *Kallish v. American Baseball Club of Philadelphia*, 138 Pa. Super. 602, 10 A.2d 831 (1940). Plaintiff spectator sought recovery for injuries sustained by his four-year-old son when the boy fell from an overcrowded parapet in defendant's ballpark. In ruling in favor of the defendant, the superior court held that there was no circumstance from

which it could be inferred that conduct of other patrons could have been foreseen and controlled by the club or that the club had knowledge or constructive notice that patrons were standing on the parapet or that their conduct was disorderly and that such conduct was the proximate cause of injury to the patron.

3. For a case in which a court decided that proximate cause *did* exist, see *Schofield v. Wood*, 170 Mass. 415, 49 N.E. 636 (1898). Plaintiff spectator sought recovery for injuries sustained when the rail he was leaning on gave way. Plaintiff contended that the rail had been negligently maintained. In affirming a jury verdict for the plaintiff, the supreme judicial court held that the fact that other spectators pushed plaintiff did not relieve defendant of liability for negligent maintenance of the rail.

4. For further information, see the following law review article: Harty, "School Liability for Athletic Injuries: Duty, Causation and Defense," 21 *Washburn Law Journal* 315 (Winter 1982).

Damages

Damages are a pecuniary compensation given by courts to any person who suffers an injury through the unlawful act, omission, or negligence of another. Damages may be either compensatory or punitive. *Compensatory damages* consist of money given to the injured party that is measured by the amount of actual injury incurred. For example, Suzie Slowpitch suffered an injury as a result of the negligence of the school district in not properly maintaining the softball field. She was hospitalized and missed work at her part-time job for three weeks. The court instructed the school district to compensate her for hospital costs and lost wages. In intentional tort actions, when no actual injury has occurred, nominal damages may still be awarded. These damages are a minimum amount given when no real loss or injury can be proved but when a right has been infringed. Generally, they are $1 or less.

Punitive damages are awarded to an injured party as punishment for outrageous conduct inflicted on the party and to deter future transgressions. They are awarded to a plaintiff in an amount over and above the amount given to compensate for the actual loss, where the wrong done was aggravated by violence, oppression, malice, fraud, or excessively wicked conduct. Punitive damages are intended to comfort the plaintiff for mental anguish, shame, or degradation suffered. In addition, punitive damages also serve to punish the defendant and to set an example for other wrongdoers. They are based on entirely different policy considerations than are compensatory damages, which merely reimburse a plaintiff for any actual loss suffered. For example, Kenny Kicker, after failing to successfully complete a football drill in practice, was forced by

Coach Haze to push a football back and forth in front of the school 50 times with his nose during school hours. Kenny sued Coach Haze and the school and was awarded punitive damages for suffering mental anguish, shame, and degradation.

Unlike intentional tort actions in which the plaintiff need not prove actual damages in order to recover, negligence actions require that the plaintiff establish that he or she suffered damage as a result of the defendant's conduct. In a negligence action, the plaintiff may seek recovery of damages in any or all of the following four areas:

1. pain and suffering—past, present, and future
2. medical expenses—past, present, and future
3. diminution of earning capacity—past, present, and future
4. loss of consortium (right to a spouse's companionship)

NOTES _____

1. In *Lynch v. Board of Education of Collingsville Community School District*, 390 N.E.2d 526 (Ill. Ct. App. 1979), the court awarded $600,000 in damages to the plaintiff due to a dramatic personality change caused by injuries received in a powderpuff football game that was authorized by the school. The school had failed to provide adequate protective equipment. (See page 344.)

2. In *Benjamin v. State*, 115 Misc. 2d 71, 453 N.Y.S.2d 329 (Ct. Cl. 1982), the court awarded compensatory damages for reimbursement of medical expenses incurred by the plaintiff spectator due to injuries sustained when a hockey puck left the rink. (See page 376.)

Wrongful Death Statutes

Wrongful death statutes exist in all states. They provide a statutory cause of action in favor of the decedent's (person who died) personal representative for the benefit of certain beneficiaries (e.g., a spouse, parent, or child) against the person who negligently caused the death of the spouse, parent, or child. The provision changes the common law rule that the death of a human being is not a proper civil cause of action. The cause of action is for the wrong to the beneficiaries and for their loss of companionship and suffering—not for the harm done to the decedent.

The majority of the statutes award compensatory damages. These damages attempt to evaluate the monetary worth of the individual and award money based on that determination. In a minority of jurisdictions, the statutes measure damages by the level of culpability shown by the negligent party. The damages awarded are greater for injuries inflicted intentionally than for those inflicted merely negligently. Additionally, a few states employ a combination of the two methods to determine damages.

NOTES ───

1. For a case in which the court decided that a wrongful death statute was not applicable, see *Truelove v. Wilson*, 285 S.E.2d 556 (Ga. Ct. App. 1981). An action was brought for wrongful death of a student who was fatally injured when struck by a metal soccer goalpost during a physical education class. Punitive damages and damages for maintenance of a nuisance were also sought. The DeKalb Supreme Court decided in favor of the defendants and held that (1) punitive damages were not available in wrongful death actions; (2) the county board of education and the county school district were entitled to a defense of sovereign immunity; and (3) individual defendants who were school employees and members of the county board of education were entitled to the defense of sovereign immunity.

2. For cases in which the court decided that a wrongful death statute was applicable, see the following:

(a) *Magabgab v. Orleans Parish School Board*, 239 So. 2d 456 (La. 1970). (See page 349.)

(b) *Woodring v. Board of Education of Manhasset*, 435 N.Y.S.2d 52 (1981). (See page 376.)

Reasonable Person Standard

Even if a particular relationship does not exist between parties, a person owes to others the duty of exercising reasonable care in his or her activities. The courts "measure" the conduct in each negligence case against the "reasonable person" standard—that is, how a person of ordinary sense using ordinary care and skill would react under similar circumstances. It is important to note that the conduct of the "reasonable person" is not necessarily "perfect" conduct but is that of a prudent and careful individual. As employed by the courts, the standard of reasonableness takes into account the risk apparent to an actor, the capacity of the actor to meet the risk, and the circumstances under which the person must act.

The reasonable person is held to possess a minimum level of knowledge common to the community in which the injury occurs. A negligent defendant who possesses superior knowledge, skill, or intelligence, however, will be held to a greater degree of care— that is, conduct which conforms to that of others with similar knowledge and/or skills. For example, a team doctor performing a procedure on an athlete on the playing field would be held to the same standard of skill and conduct exhibited by other team doctors in the same specialty performing a similar procedure. When the reasonable person standard entails a degree of skill or knowledge higher than that of a judge or the lay person sitting on a jury, qualified expert testimony is utilized to establish the proper standard of care for the defendant in question. Again, using the case of a team doctor sued for negligence, both parties would probably call as witnesses other qualified team doctors who would testify as to how the procedure is usually performed and what precautions or steps are taken under normal circumstances. This expert testimony would help establish the standard of care for the situation. The jury would then determine whether the defendant surgeon met the standard of care.

The reasonable person is deemed to possess physical characteristics identical to those of the defendant in question. If the actor is exceptionally strong, for example, the standard of care demands that the person exhibit conduct which parallels that of a reasonably prudent person of like strength under similar circumstances. The reasonable person standard does not take into account the temperament or emotions of the individual actor. The law seeks objectivity and not subjectivity based on a person's mental attributes or states. There are several reasons for this. First, it would be extremely difficult, if not impossible, to prove what was in an individual's mind at the time of the particular conduct. Second, the harm caused by a negligent act is not changed by the actor's particular thoughts or feelings. Finally, the courts have determined that a person must learn to conform to the standards of the community or to pay for violating those standards.

It is argued that in extreme cases of mental deficiency the actor cannot comprehend the danger inherent in certain conduct. The courts, however, have still applied the reasonable person standard when dealing with insane defendants. This is based on the public policy consideration of promoting the responsibility of guardians for those in their care. The sanction for civil liability involves monetary compensation and not personal liberty. Therefore, courts and legislatures have determined that protecting the public from harm, or at least requiring those responsible to pay for their own harm, is a goal of sufficient importance to justify distinguishing between civil liability and moral culpability.

A "greater degree of care" standard may be applicable when dealing with an inherently dangerous object or an activity in which it is reasonably foreseeable that an accident or injury may occur.

NOTE _____

1. The courts found that a reasonable care standard was exercised by a defendant in the following cases:

(a) In *Johnson v. Krueger*, 36 Colo. App. 242, 539 P. 2d 1296 (1975), plaintiff sought recovery in negligence for injuries sustained when, while playing football, he ran onto defendant's land and fell on a stump 10 inches high and 6 inches in diameter. In ruling in favor of the landowner, the court of appeals held that the landowner did not act unreasonably in leaving the stump on his land. It was not reasonably foreseeable that a child would run from a football game onto an adjacent lot, a considerable distance onto landowner's property, and fall on the stump which was clearly visible, even when the owner knew children often played football on the adjacent lot.

(b) In *Rabiner v. Rosenberg*, 176 Misc. 885, 28 N.Y.S.2d 533 (1941), plaintiff spectator sued for damages sustained when a fish slipped off defendant fisherman's hook, causing the hook to snap back and become embedded in the plaintiff's eye. The trial court, in ruling in favor of the defendant, held that the fisherman acted as any prudent fisherman would have and was not liable.

(c) In *Reddick v. Lindquist*, 484 S.W.2d 441 (Tex. Civ. App. 1972), plaintiff widow sued in wrongful death for the loss of her husband, who was killed when defendant's boat ran over him after he fell while water skiing. In ruling in favor of the defendant, the court of civil appeals held that the deceased's negligence in attempting a maneuver which an ordinarily prudent skier would not have tried was the proximate cause of the fatal accident.

(d) In *Smith v. Vernon Parish School Bd.*, 442 So. 2d 1319 (La. Ct. App. 1983), plaintiff sued the school board, the physical education teacher, and the insurer of the teacher for damages suffered in a trampoline activity during a physical education class at a high school. The court held that the teacher exercised reasonable supervision and that the "greater degree of care" standard was not applicable.

Standard of Care for Children

Children as defendants in a negligence case present an important exception to the reasonable person standard. Children are not held to the same objective standard of duty that is applied to adults. The courts recognize that at young age levels there exists a wide range of mental capabilities and experiences. The law attempts to accommodate this variety by viewing the reasonable child as one who exercises in his or her actions a degree of care that is reasonably to be expected of children of like age, intelligence, and experience. For example, in a baseball game an 11-year-old boy swung at a pitched ball and missed it; the bat slipped from his hands and struck his teammate in the head, and caused serious injuries. The court held that there was no negligence because the youngster exercised a reasonable degree of care for a person of his

age, intelligence, and experience. However, under this more subjective standard, it follows that if a 6-year-old boy has intelligence
vastly superior to that of his peers, the child will be held to that
standard of care encompassing his superior knowledge. Several
states have established age brackets which purport to distinguish
childhood from adulthood. This method has been criticized, however, because of the problems inherent in setting an accurate age-
level guideline regarding mental capabilities.

An exception to the application of this subjective standard for
children occurs when a child engages in an activity normally
reserved for adults, such as driving an automobile or hunting with
a gun. In cases such as these, the courts in many jurisdictions will
apply the reasonable standard for adults without any special consideration of the fact that the individual is a child.

Defenses for Negligence

Once the four elements essential to a negligence action have been
presented by the plaintiff, the defendants in such lawsuits can
employ a number of common defenses. The following are the most
common defenses employed by defendants in tort actions for
negligence:

1. no negligence
2. contributory negligence
3. comparative negligence
4. assumption of risk
5. immunity, statute of limitations, and Good Samaritan statutes

No Negligence

The defendant usually attempts to prove first that his behavior did
not constitute negligence. This can be approached in two ways.
The defendant can dispute the negligence claim by either attacking
one or more of the four previously discussed requirements for
negligence or by proving that he exercised reasonable care in his
actions as specified by the reasonable person standard. Thus a
defendant may defend a charge of negligence by asserting that he
had no duty toward the plaintiff. Even if a defendant had a duty
toward the plaintiff, he would not be liable if he did not breach
that duty. Therefore, if the defendant owed the plaintiff a duty of
reasonable care and properly discharged that duty, any harm to
the plaintiff would not be actionable negligence on the part of the
defendant.

NOTE _____

1. For a case in which the plaintiff was precluded from recovery because the defendant was not negligent, see *Cramer v. Hoffman*, 390 F.2d 19 (2d Cir. 1968). The court found, based on New York law, that an institution was not liable for the negligence of a physician who was an independent contractor exercising his own discretion. The court concluded that there was not an automatic agency relationship established between the university and its physician.

Contributory Negligence

Any act of the plaintiff which amounts to a lack of ordinary care and contributes to the proximate cause of the injury is contributory negligence. Contributory negligence is, in essence, a departure from the standard of reasonableness required of all people, including plaintiffs. There does not have to be an actual appreciation of the risk involved. There need only be a risk that is known or would be known and avoided by a reasonable person. A plaintiff also has a duty to exercise ordinary care. Without such care, the plaintiff is at least to some degree contributorily negligent.

In a jurisdiction that recognizes the defense of contributory negligence, a finding of contributory negligence effectively bars the plaintiff from any recovery from the defendant. The success of the defense of contributory negligence rests on the defendant's ability to prove that the plaintiff failed to exercise due care for his own safety and that this lack of due care was the proximate cause of the plaintiff's injury. In contributory negligence theory, as in negligence theory, the standard of care for children is reasonable care. The child's age, intelligence, and experience, however, are relevant to the issue of whether reasonable care was exercised. With respect to both negligence and contributory negligence, there are situations in which the negligent conduct of one party may be imputed to a second party under the doctrine of respondeat superior, which means "look to the man higher up."

NOTES _____

1. In the following cases the plaintiff was precluded from recovery because of a successful contributory negligence defense.

(a) In *Juntila v. Everett School Dist. #24*, 48 P.2d 613 (Wash. 1935), plaintiff spectator sought recovery for injuries sustained when the guard railing on which he was seated while watching a football game collapsed. In ruling for the defendant, the Washington Supreme Court held that the plaintiff, who sat on the railing knowing it was not intended as a seat, was contributorily negligent.

(b) In *Powless v. Milwaukee Co.*, 94 N.W.2d 187 (Wis. 1959), plaintiff spectator sought recovery for injuries suffered because she was struck by a foul ball. In ruling for the defendant, the Wisconsin Supreme Court held that even if owners were negligent under the "safe-place" statute, the plaintiff's choice of seat and failure to react to the noise and excitement around her after hearing the bat hit the ball made her guilty of contributory negligence.

(c) In *Shields v. Van Kelton Amusement Corp.*, 127 N.E. 261 (N.Y. 1920), plaintiff ice skater sought recovery for injuries sustained when she fell as a result of a soft spot on defendant's outdoor skating rink. In ruling against the plaintiff, the court of appeals held that the plaintiff, an experienced skater, was aware that the ice was getting soft and that defendant's placement of benches near the soft spot to prevent access was sufficient to notify patrons of dangerous areas. Therefore, the court found that the plaintiff was contributorily negligent.

(d) In *Pierce v. Murnick*, 145 S.E.2d 11 (N.C. 1965), plaintiff, a ringside spectator at defendant promoter's wrestling match, sought recovery for injuries sustained when a wrestler fell on him from the ring. In ruling for the defendant, the North Carolina Supreme Court held that the promoter was not required to take steps for the safety of invitees which would reasonably impair enjoyment of the exhibition by the usual patrons, and that even if defendant were negligent in failing to take precautions to protect the plaintiff, the plaintiff was barred by contributory negligence in choosing the ringside seat.

(e) In *Polsky v. Levine*, 243 N.W.2d 503 (Wis. 1976), plaintiff, a minor, sought recovery for injuries sustained while water skiing on defendant camp operator's lake. In ruling for the defendant, the Wisconsin Supreme Court held that since plaintiff could have kicked the rope and tow bar free and avoided injury, but did not do so because he would have fallen and received unsuccessful marks, he failed to exercise ordinary care for his own safety and could not recover.

2. For a case in which the defense of contributory negligence was *not* successful, see *Harrison v. Montgomery County Board of Education*, 456 A.2d 894 (Md. Ct. App. 1983). A suit was brought by an eighth grader who was rendered a quadriplegic while attempting a running front flip during a "free exercise" day in the gymnasium. The Maryland court refused to abandon the doctrine of contributory negligence in favor of comparative negligence. The court found dissatisfaction with the doctrine in Maryland case law; however, the court said that a change should be left to the legislature.

Comparative Negligence

Comparative negligence is a statutory rule adopted in many states in an effort to alleviate the harshness of the contributory negligence doctrine. Comparative negligence statutes seek to divide the responsibility between the two negligent parties. Under a comparative negligence statute, the jury or fact finder determines the proportionate degree of negligence that will be attributed to all parties involved. The damages are then assessed pro rata.

In states that have adopted the doctrine of comparative negligence, contributory negligence on the part of the plaintiff is not necessarily a complete bar to recovery. Generally, two rules are applied under the theory of comparative negligence in most states:

1. If the plaintiff's negligence as compared with total negligence of all defendants is greater than 50 percent, plaintiff is totally barred from recovery. For example, a plaintiff who is determined to be 60 percent at fault will not be able to recover against the defendant.

2. If the plaintiff's negligence as compared with the total negligence of all defendants is 50 percent or less, plaintiff's damages are reduced in proportion to his negligence. For example, a plaintiff who suffers $100,000 in damages and whose negligence is determined to be 40 percent recovers $100,000 minus 40 percent of $100,000, or $60,000.

Assumption of Risk

Assumption of risk means that the plaintiff has given prior consent to what would normally be an unpermitted, potentially injury-causing action. This consent effectively relieves a defendant's obligation to a certain standard of conduct toward the plaintiff. There is no longer any legal duty existing between the two. When there is no duty, there is no negligence.

Assumption of risk requires that the plaintiff know and fully appreciate the risks involved in pursuing the course of action to which he is committed. In addition to knowing and appreciating the risk, the plaintiff must also carefully and reasonably agree to assume whatever risk is involved.

The defense of assumption of risk may be utilized in those states that have not passed a comparative negligence statute to supplement the contributory negligence statute. In such states, the defendant may claim that the plaintiff, by assuming the risk of injury, is barred from any recovery. Under the comparative negligence statute, however, partial recovery is allowed in many situations in which the plaintiff's contributory negligence proximately contributed to his injury. This did not reconcile with the previous legal interpretation under which no recovery was allowed to a plaintiff who was found to have assumed the risk, even when such assumption of risk was considered reasonable under the circumstances. In states in which assumption of risk has been abolished as a defense in negligence actions, a plaintiff is entitled to full recovery if his assumption of risk was reasonable; if such assumption of risk was unreasonable, contributory negligence may exist and recovery is therefore governed by the state's comparative negligence statute. In sports cases, assumption of risk is an important concept because its action may negate a plaintiff's case. If the plaintiff is deemed to have assumed the risk, there may be a valid excuse for a tort that may have been committed.

NOTES _____

1. The plaintiff was precluded from recovery because of a successful assumption-of-risk defense in the following cases.

(a) In *Schentzel v. Philadelphia Nat'l League Club*, 96 A.2d 181 (Sup. Ct. Pa. 1953), plaintiff, a women spectator viewing a baseball game for the first time, sought recovery for injuries sustained when she was struck by a foul ball while seated in the upper deck near first base. The court held that the plaintiff knew or should have known that foul balls sometimes go astray, that she had assumed the risk, and that the defendant was not negligent in failing to provide screens for the upper deck.

(b) In *Richmond v. Employers' Fire Insurance Co.*, 298 So. 2d 118 (La. Ct. App. 1974), plaintiff, a college baseball player, sought recovery from the defendant college coach and insurance company for injuries sustained during practice in which the coach was allegedly negligent in allowing a bat to fly from his hands. In ruling for the defendants, the court of appeals held that the coach was not negligent and that the player had assumed the risk of injury inherent in a baseball practice session.

2. The defense of assumption of risk was *not* successful in the following cases.

(a) In *Rutter v. Northeastern Beaver County School District*, 437 A.2d 1198 (Pa. 1981), the plaintiff lost an eye as a result of an injury which occurred during a summer football practice supervised by the high school coaches. The plaintiff was playing a type of touch football known as "jungle football" when he was injured. The court abolished the doctrine of assumption of risk because of the extreme difficulty in applying the doctrine and because the doctrine is duplicative of two other concepts—the scope of the defendant's duty and the plaintiff's contributory negligence.

(b) In *Stevens v. Central School District*, 270 N.Y.S.2d 23 (App. Div. 1966), plaintiff sought recovery for injuries sustained when, while playing basketball in defendant's school building, his momentum carried him through a glass window in a door just behind the basket. In ruling for the plaintiff, the court held the plaintiff had not assumed the risk of the dangerous condition caused by use of ordinary window glass in the door. The court ruled that the defendant was negligent in not using safety glass in the doors.

3. For more information on the *Rutter* decision, see the following law review article: "Note: *Rutter v. Northeastern Beaver County School District*," 21 *Duquesne Law Review* 815 (1983).

Immunity, Statute of Limitations, Good Samaritan Statutes

Other defenses that may be raised when appropriate are those of immunity, expiration of the statute of limitations, and Good Samaritan statutes. The same type of immunity that can be raised in assault and battery cases—that stemming from relationships between the parties or the capacity of the parties—can also be applied to negligence actions.

Individual states establish statutory periods for maintaining a tort action, and a plaintiff filing an action after the expiration of the state's statute of limitations is completely barred from recovery. (See *Hackbart v. Cincinnati Bengals*, 435 F. Supp. 352 [D. Colo. 1977], *rev'd*, 601 F.2d 516 [10th Cir. 1979], on page 294 on the issue of assault and battery.) One last type of statutory defense involves Good Samaritan statutes. The states that have adopted Good Samaritan statutes will impose a lesser standard of care for doctors and other individuals trained in first aid who gratuitously render medical assistance to a sick or injured person. The Good Samaritan statutes may impose a standard of gross negligence or they may hold that medical personnel cannot be held liable at all. For example, a doctor who stops to help someone injured in a car accident cannot be held negligent under Good Samaritan statutes unless the treatment provided is grossly negligent or actually worsens the condition of the person in need of treatment.

NOTES

1. The Good Samaritan doctrine as a matter of law precludes negligence liability for one who sees and attempts to aid another person who has been placed in imminent and serious peril through the negligence of a third person. This exemption exists provided the attempt is not recklessly or rashly made. The negligence of a volunteer must actually worsen the position of a person in distress before liability will be imposed. The exemption is provided by statute in most states.

2. New York has a Good Samaritan statute that applies to dentists:

Notwithstanding any inconsistent provision of any general, special or local law, any licensed dentist who voluntarily and without the expectation of monetary compensation renders first aid or emergency treatment at the scene of an accident or other emergency, outside of a hospital or any other place having proper and necessary medical equipment, to a person who is unconscious, ill or injured shall not be liable for damages for injuries alleged to have been sustained by such person or for damages for the death of such person alleged to have occurred by reason of an act or omission in the rendering of such first aid or emergency treatment unless it is established that such injuries were or such death was caused by gross negligence on the part of such dentist. Nothing in this subdivision shall be deemed or construed to relieve a licensed dentist from liability for damages for injuries or death caused by an act or omission on the part of a dentist while rendering professional services in the normal and ordinary course of practice. [Title 8 Art. 133 Education Law, Section 6611]

3. The following examples of Good Samaritan statutes are from the Massachusetts General Laws.

Ch. 112A Sec. 13. Liability of doctors, nurses, hospitals, ambulance operators and attendants:

No physician duly registered . . . and no hospital shall be liable in a suit for damages as a result of acts or omissions related to advice, consultation or orders given in good faith to ambulance operators and attendants who . . . under emergency conditions and prior to arrival of the patient at the hospital, clinic, office or other health facility from which the emergency communication to the ambulance operators or attendant is made shall be liable in a suit for damages as result of his said acts or omissions based upon said advice, consultations or orders. . . .

Ch. 112, Sec. 54A. Physician or person trained in emergency medical care; assignment to interscholastic football games:

A physician employed by a school committee or a person who has completed a full course in emergency medical care as provided in section six of chapter one hundred and eleven C shall be assigned to every interscholastic football game played by any team representing a public secondary school in the commonwealth, and the expenses of such physician or person shall be paid by the school committee of the city, town or district wherein such football game is played.

Ch. 112. Sec. 851. Emergency care, etc. of injured persons by members of ski patrols; exemption from civil liability:

No member of a ski patrol duly registered in the National Ski Patrol system, who, in good faith, renders emergency care or treatment to a person who has become injured or incapacitated at a place or in an area where an emergency rescue can be best accomplished by the members of such a ski patrol together with their special equipment, shall be liable in a suit for damages as a result of his acts or omissions, either for such care or treatment or as a result of providing emergency transportation to a place of safety, nor shall he be liable to a hospital for its expenses if, under such emergency conditions, he causes the admission of such injured or incapacitated person.

4. See Chapter 7, page 356, for a discussion of sovereign immunity.

THE DOCTRINE OF VICARIOUS LIABILITY

The doctrine of vicarious liability imposes liability for a tortious act upon a person who was not personally negligent, because of the relationship between the parties. The most typical relationships which give rise to vicarious liability are master-servant (employer-employee) and principal-agent. Vicarious liability is also known as the doctrine of respondeat superior.

Vicarious liability imposes liability for a negligent act by A upon C, because of some legal relationship between A and B, such as employer-employee. Under the doctrine of vicarious liability, B is liable to C, the party injured by A, even though B was not himself negligent, did not aid or encourage the negligence of A, and did everything he could to prevent harm to C. For example, if the groundskeeper of a stadium fails to fix a hole on the front of the pitcher's mound and an injury results to a player, the owner of the stadium and the employer of the groundskeeper may be held vicariously liable to the injured player.

The justification for the doctrine of vicarious liability has been a topic of debate since the doctrine first appeared in the mid-1700s. The catalyst for the introduction of vicarious liability was the industrial revolution, which complicated commerce and industry. The rationale behind the doctrine is based on public policy considerations. Since the servant is furthering the master's employment, the master should be responsible for the servant's actions. This places an increased burden on the master, but the master is in a better position to bear the risks of injuries to others. A master is in a better position to cover risks by insuring himself. In addition, this doctrine allows an innocent plaintiff to recover from a "deep pocket."

In sports-related cases under vicarious liability, the employer may be held responsible when the employer exercises control and direction over the employee, and the employee is negligent while acting within the scope of his employment. Vicarious liability is usually imposed when an employee has been involved in unreasonable or grossly negligent conduct. Liability is usually not imposed on the employer for intentional torts committed by the employee. An intentional tort is usually considered beyond the scope of authority of the employee, not under control of the employer, and not in the furtherance of the employer's business. For example, if a coach assaults a bartender after work, the school district will not be held liable under a vicarious liability theory. However, an employer may be held responsible for an intentional tort committed by an employee if the employee was under the authority and control of the employer and the tort was committed in the furtherance of the employer's business purpose. These same general rules apply to principal-agent vicarious liability situations in sports-related cases.

The doctrine of vicarious liability is widely applicable to tort actions for negligence in the sports setting. For example, a coach may be held liable for the actions of his players, a school district may be held liable for the actions of a coach or a teacher, or an athletic administrator may be held liable for the actions of a coach. In order for an employer to be held liable in these situations, the employee must first be found negligent under the primary standard of reasonable care, and then the action must be determined to have been within the scope of the defendant's employment.

In a case (sport or nonsport) involving a monetary award for damages, it is common practice to sue in the alternative—that is, to sue each party involved in the alleged incident of negligence. This practice serves three primary purposes:

1. It allows the plaintiff to determine exactly who is liable for the particular injury.
2. It allows the plaintiff to determine which party involved in the suit has money sufficient to pay the damages award ("deep pocket").
3. It prevents multiple suits on the same cause of action directed against the various defendants.

NOTES _____

1. For a case in which a promoter of athletic events was held liable for negligent actions of his supervisory personnel, see *Rosenberger v. Central La. District Livestock Show, Inc.*, 312 So. 2d 300 (La. 1975). Plaintiff bareback bronco rider sought recovery from defendant rodeo promoters and defendant employees for injuries sustained at the rodeo. In ruling for the plaintiff, the Louisiana Supreme Court held that the negligence of the rodeo supervisor in failing to check whether the gate of the rodeo facility was closed resulted in plaintiff's injuries and that promoters were liable under the doctrine of respondeat superior.

2. For a case in which an owner of a facility could be held liable for the negligence of an employee if the employee is acting within the scope of his job, see *Johnson v. County Arena*, 349 A.2d 643 (Md. Ct. App. 1976). Plaintiff sought recovery in wrongful death for a roller skater who was struck from behind and knocked down by a skating guard while the guards were playing tag. In ruling against the defendant arena owner, the court of special appeals held that the evidence on the issue of whether the guard had exercised the amount of care and prudence in the performance of his duties commensurate with his relationship with the patron required submission to the jury.

3. In *Fustin v. Board of Education of Community Unit Dist. No. 2*, 242 N.E.2d 308 (Ill. App. 1968), plaintiff, a high school basketball player, sought recovery for injuries sustained when struck in the face by the fist of an opposing player. In ruling for the defendant school board, the court of appeals held that the employer's lack of negligence prevented application of respondeat superior and the fact that the board had taken out liability insurance did not in any way make the board liable.

4. In *Hackbart v. Cincinnati Bengals*, 435 F. Supp. 352 (D. Colo.

1977), *rev'd.*, 601 F.2d 516 (10th Cir. 1979), a team was sued under the doctrine of respondeat superior for the alleged reckless misconduct of one of its players.

5. In *Mogabgab v. Orleans Parish School Board*, 239 So. 2d 456 (La. Ct. App. 1970), the school district and principal were held not liable for the death of a football player who died from heat exhaustion, although the coach had actively denied medical assistance to the player for over two hours. (See Note 1b on page 349.)

6. In *Toone v. Adams*, 262 N.C. 403, 137 S.E.2d 132 (1964), a coach was not held responsible for the action of a fan since he had not directly incited the fan to a violent act. (See Note 1 on page 350.)

7. In *Averill v. Luttrell*, 311 S.W.2d 812 (Tenn. Ct. App. 1957), a club was not held liable for an intentional tort committed by its employee since the employee's action was not within the scope of his employment or working to further his employer's business.

8. In *Domino v. Mercurio*, 17 A.D.2d 342, 234 N.Y.S.2d 1011 (1962), *aff'd*, 13 N.Y.2d 922, 193 N.E.2d 893 (1963), a school district was held liable under the doctrine of respondeat superior for the negligence of its employees who allowed spectators at a softball game to push a bench too close to the playing surface. Therefore, the school district was held responsible for the injuries caused to a player who fell over the bench. (See Note 1d on page 345.)

9. In *Rosensweig v. State of New York*, 158 N.E.2d 229 (N.Y. 1959), doctors employed by the state boxing commission were held to be agents and thus servants of the state. (See page 381.)

10. In *Welch v. Dunsmuir Joint Union High School District*, 326 P.2d 633 (Cal. Ct. App. 1958), the doctor was held to be an independent contractor. (See Note 1a on page 348.)

11. In *Morris v. Union High School District A, King County*, 294 P. 998 (Wash. 1931), and *Vargo v. Svitchan*, 301 N.W.2d 1 (Mich. Ct. App. 1980), both school districts were held vicariously liable for the negligence of their employee, the football coach. (See Notes 1a and b on page 344.)

12. In *Tomjanovich v. California Sports*, No. H-78-243 (S.D. Tex. 1979), the defendant basketball team was held vicariously liable for the actions of one of its players.

Exception: Independent Contractors

The problems raised by the existence of independent contractors are important in understanding the scope of the doctrine of vicarious liability. An independent contractor is a person who, although in some way is connected to the employer, is not under the employer's control. Thus, if such a person is determined to be an independent contractor, no vicarious liability may be imposed.

To determine the status of any person, the degree of control that the employer has over the employee's actions must be examined. The person who was hired for a specific, limited purpose, with no direct supervision, and who works without allowing the employer to have control over his actions is most likely an independent contractor. Once a determination has been made that the person is an independent contractor, the employer may not be held liable for negligence committed by that independent contractor. As a general rule, a doctor who is provided by a school that is hosting a football game is considered to be an independent contractor. Here, although paid by the school district, the doctor is not in any way under its control when making medical decisions. Thus, the doctrine of vicarious liability would not be applicable, and the school would not be liable for the doctor's medical negligence.

Another group that is classified as independent contractors are officials and referees. In most cases the referee has been determined by the courts to be an independent contractor. (See Exhibit 3–8 in Chapter 3 and page 382 in Chapter 7.)

NOTES ——

1. A plaintiff's recovery against an employer is based on the defendant being found to be an employee rather than an independent contractor. In *Gross v. Pellicane*, 167 A.2d 838 (N.J. Super. Ct. App. Div. 1961), petitioner, a free-lance jockey, sought workers' compensation for injuries sustained while riding defendant's horse in a race. In affirming the award, the trial court held that petitioner was an employee of the horse trainer, due to the control the trainer exercised over his duties, rather than an independent contractor.

2. In *Cramer v. Hoffman*, 390 F.2d 19 (2d Cir. 1968), the court held that a physician's negligence could not be imputed to the university when the plaintiff first alleged that the doctor was an agent of the hospital and not of the university. By not raising this issue until the trial, plaintiffs unfairly surprised the defendants.

DEFAMATION LAW

Sports are played in public settings and are coached and administered in what often seems like "the heat of battle." As such, amateur athletic administrators have to be extremely cautious that what begins as a sporting event does not erupt into litigation involving defamation—either libel or slander. The passions of the contest should not be allowed to evolve into inappropriate statements about an individual to the media or the general public. Athletic administrators have to always be on guard for such eventualities and must instruct their staff about the potential litigation any such statement could cause for the organization or individuals involved.

Defamation law is concerned with the protection of personal

reputation. The law in most states strongly protects and guards a person's reputation. The focus of a defamation action is on the alleged defamatory statement and its impact on third persons. *The Restatement (Second) of Torts*, section 559, defines a defamatory communication as one which "tends to harm the reputation of another as to lower him in the estimation of the community or to deter third persons from associating or dealing with him."

To establish liability for defamation there must be (1) a false and defamatory statement concerning another, (2) publication to a third person, (3) some degree of fault on the defendant's part, and (4) damages. A defamatory statement is also one that exposes the plaintiff to public hatred, shame, contempt, or ridicule. The reputation that is protected by the law of defamation is the opinion of others. The plaintiff must show that his or her reputation was injured in the eyes of a respectable group of the community.

Defamation is an intentional tort in that the defendant need only intend to make the publication of the statement or material. It matters not that the defendant did not intend to harm the reputation of the plaintiff. He will still be accountable if he intended to make the defamatory statement.

Defamation is divided into libel and slander. *Libel* is the publication of defamatory matter by writing. There are three classes of libel: (1) libel per se, which includes materials that are obviously defamatory; (2) materials that could be taken as defamatory or as not defamatory; and (3) materials that are not by themselves defamatory but when combined with other facts become libelous. *Slander* is the publication of defamatory matter through spoken words.

Libel

The basic elements of libel are a defamatory statement, publication, and damages. Truth is a defense to a libel action; however, it is only a qualified defense—not an absolute defense. The defendant has the burden of proving the truth of the communication if his defense is truth. If the libel is true, the plaintiff has the burden of proving that it was published with malice. The level of malice required to defeat the defendant's proof of truth and to make the defamatory matter actionable in spite of the truth is hatred, ill will, or malevolent intention. The plaintiff must also prove that a third person was exposed to the publication. Finally, the plaintiff must prove actual damages. There are two basic forms of damages in this context—general and special damages. *General damages* include humiliation and mental and physical suffering. *Special damages* are those damages that are the natural but not the necessary result of the alleged wrong. The defendant may be able to mitigate damages by making a retraction or taking some other measure.

Slander

Slander is publication of defamatory matter by spoken words. There must be a publication, and the plaintiff must be held up to scorn and ridicule as a result of the defamatory statement. A statement is slanderous per se if it falls into one of the following categories:

1. Accuses the plaintiff of criminal conduct.
2. Accuses the plaintiff of having a loathsome disease.
3. Accuses the plaintiff of being unchaste.
4. Accuses the plaintiff of misconduct in public office.
5. Tends to injure plaintiff's profession, business, or trade.

Truth is an absolute defense to a slander action. Again, however, the plaintiff must show that the statement was heard and understood by a third person. To show damages, the plaintiff must prove that it was slanderous per se or must prove special damages.

The United States Supreme Court has established standards that apply in libel and slander situations. In these decisions the Court balanced the competing interests of protecting the reputation of an individual against freedom of the press. In the first of these decisions in 1964 the Court held that the constitutional guarantee of a free press requires a public official to prove actual malice in the publication of a defamatory falsehood in order to recover for defamation (*New York Times Company v. Sullivan*, 376 U.S. 254, 84 S. Ct. 710 [1964]). In 1967 the Court extended the constitutional privilege to public figures as well as public officials. Finally in *Gertz v. Robert Welch Inc.*, 418 U.S. 323, 94 S. Ct. 2997 (1974), the Court extended the "actual malice" standard. A public official or public figure who has been defamed must prove that the defendant published the statement with actual malice—that is, knowing that the material was false or in reckless disregard to whether it was false or not.

Defamation should be distinguished from both intentional infliction of emotional distress and invasion of privacy. *Intentional infliction of emotional distress* (see page 327) is classified as an intentional tort and is concerned with the impact on the individual plaintiff without regard to third persons. *Defamation* involves the element of publication to third persons, as well as the requirement that the material be taken by these third persons as damaging. Defamation must also be distinguished from the tort of invasion of privacy. An action for *invasion of privacy* (see page 324) concerns one's right to peace of mind and comfort, while an action for defamation involves the plaintiff's character or reputation. Invasion of privacy can also be distinguished from defamation in that truth is an absolute defense to the defamation action, but truth is not a defense to an invasion-of-privacy action.

A leading sports case in the area of libel and slander law is *Curtis Publishing Co. v. Butts*, 87 S. Ct. 1975 (1967). Curtis Publishing Company had printed an article alleging that Wallace Butts, while the athletic director at the University of Georgia, had supplied to Paul Bryant, the head football coach at Alabama, information concerning Georgia's game plan for an upcoming game against Alabama. The article was based on a phone conversation between Butts and Bryant, supposedly overheard by an insurance salesman. Butts brought action for libel against Curtis in federal court and was awarded compensatory and punitive damages. Curtis appealed the decision to the Supreme Court, arguing that Butts was a public figure and as such needed to prove the article was written with actual malice. The Supreme Court held that a public figure who is not a public official may recover damages for a defamatory falsehood which is obviously damaging to his reputation, on a showing that the conduct of the publisher was highly unreasonable and constituted an extreme departure from the standards of investigation and reporting ordinarily adhered to by responsible publishers.

NOTE ——————————————————————————————————

1. The following cases involve individuals in sports who were sued or brought suit for defamation.

(a) In *Chuy v. Philadelphia Eagles Football Club*, 431 F. Supp. 254 (E.D. Pa., 1977), *aff'd*, 595 F.2d 1265 (3d Cir. 1979), a pro football player brought an action against his team, the Philadelphia Eagles, based on breach of contract, intentional infliction of emotional distress, and defamation. Chuy's defamation claim was founded on an allegedly false statement made by a team physician which was reported to the press. The court found that Chuy was a public figure. He was a prominent starting player on a pro team, and he had voluntarily placed himself in the public eye. Once it was established that Chuy was a public figure, in order to succeed Chuy had to meet the "actual malice" test established in *New York Times Company v. Sullivan*. Although the evidence showed that the doctor knew that the statement was false, Chuy was not allowed to recover.

The court held for the Eagles on the defamation claim because Pennsylvania law provided that the newspaper columnist had to understand the statement as defamatory for there to be liability.

Since Chuy could not show that the reporter took the statement in a defamatory way, Chuy was barred from recovery. In a different case arising out of the same incident, Chuy also sued for intentional infliction of emotional distress. (See page 327.)

(b) Chuy also sued the Philadelphia Eagles and the National Football League on antitrust grounds based on the facts arising out of the same situation. See *Chuy v. Philadelphia Eagles*, 407 F. Supp. 717 (E.D. Pa., 1977).

(c) In *Rutledge v. Arizona Board of Regents*, 660 F.2d 1345 (9th Cir. 1981), a football coach was sued for defamation by one of his players. (See Note 1b on page 347.)

(d) *Paul Hornung v. NCAA, Walter Byers, Tom Hansen, Jim Frank, John Toner, Wiles Hallock and Western Kentucky University*, No. 82 CI-06769 (Jefferson Circuit Court, Kentucky, July 30, 1982), is a pending multimillion dollar action by former Green Bay Packer and Heisman Trophy winner Paul Hornung against officials who represented the NCAA. Since his retirement in 1967, Hornung has had an extensive broadcast career, including coverage of many college games. He was under an agreement in principle with Turner Broadcasting to provide color commentary for 19 college games. However, a representative of the NCAA sent Turner Broadcasting a letter which contained the following statement:

> Paul Hornung was not approved for 1982. The committee believes he is closely identified with professional football, that he had at least one undesirable public situation while a professional player and that the image which he projects or is projected for him does not personify college football.

Hornung claimed the letter was false and was published by the NCAA et al. with actual malice and in reckless disregard of the true facts. Hornung alleged, as the result of said letter, defamation and interference with contractual relationships occurred. In 1985, a jury awarded Hornung zero dollars in actual damages, $160,000 in consequential damages, and $1 million in punitive damages. The NCAA has appealed.

(e) In *Carlen v. University of South Carolina*, No. 83-379-0 (U.S.D.C., Dist. S. Carolina, February 11, 1983), plaintiff, former head football coach at the University of South Carolina, sued the university, in part, under a defamation theory. He alleged that his termination in breach of his contract permanently damaged his reputation as a major college football coach, irreparably impairing his ability to obtain another position. The case was settled.

THE TORT OF INVASION OF PRIVACY

An action for invasion of privacy is designed to protect a person's mental peace and/or comfort. Invasion of privacy is an intentional tort. The laws prohibiting invasion of privacy are intended to protect the purely private matters of a person. Although some intrusions into a person's life are expected and must be tolerated in society, when the intrusions become excessive or unjustified, then a cause of action will exist for invasion of privacy.

The *Restatement (Second) of Torts*, § 652, determines the ways in which one may tortiously invade the privacy of another. That section provides:

> One who gives publicity to a matter concerning the private life of another is subject to liability to the other for invasion of his privacy, if the matter publicized is of a kind that
> (a) would be highly offensive to a reasonable person; and
> (b) is not of legitimate concern to the public.

As set forth in Prosser, *Law of Torts*, § 117 (1971), one can invade the privacy of another in four distinct ways:

1. Intruding upon one's physical solitude.
2. Publicly disclosing private facts.
3. Putting one in a false light in the public eye.
4. Appropriating some element of another's personality for commercial gain.

In an action for invasion of privacy, the intrusion must be substantial and must be into an area for which there is an expectation of privacy. For example, simply staring at a person would not generally amount to an intrusion; wiretapping, on the other hand, would amount to an intrusion.

The plaintiff must also show that the publication of private matters involved a matter which in fact was truly private. Newsworthy, public interest matters or public facts are not considered to be of a purely private nature. Court records, for example, are open to the public and are therefore not viewed as private facts.

The United States Supreme Court in *Time, Inc. v. Hill*, 385 U.S. 374, 87 S. Ct. 534 (1967), held that the First Amendment to the United States Constitution protects reports of newsworthy matters. These matters can be publicized unless, as was discussed in the previous section, actual malice is shown. The actual malice standard may be applied, even though a plaintiff was a private person who did not want the publicity.

In *Bilney v. Evening Star Newspaper Co.*, 406 A.2d 652 (Md. Ct. App. 1979), a leading case in the area, members of the University of Maryland basketball team brought suit against two newspapers. The newspapers published an article concerning certain players whose academic standing was threatening their eligibility. The newspapers printed that the players were in danger of academic dismissal and gave details of their academic records. The players based their action, in part, on the theory of invasion of privacy. The court, basing its decision on the *Restatement (Second) of Torts*, § 652, held that the players were public figures. The court found that there was widespread public interest in Maryland basketball. When the players' academic standing threatened their eligibility, then the privacy of those facts lessened. The court stated that "the publication of their eligibility-threatening status was not unreasonable and did not trample community mores" of what is legitimate public interest.

The court relied primarily on the reasoning of the *Restatement (Second) of Torts*, § 652D. A public figure cannot complain when given publicity that was sought, even though it may be unfavorable. The *Restatement (Second) of Torts* also states that the publicity of public figures "is not limited to the particular events that arouse the interests of the public" (§ 652D, comment). The legitimate public interest of these figures extends into some of their private matters. The court also held that the right to make public the private facts of a public figure is not an unlimited right. The court held that what is allowable is determined by community mores: "The line is to be drawn when the publicity ceases to be the giving of information to which the public is entitled and becomes a morbid and sensational prying into private lives" (§ 652, comment).

The *Bilney* case typifies the difficult burden an athlete has in winning an invasion-of-privacy action. The Maryland players were unsuccessful because the news article did not invade a "private" area. The opinion reflects how difficult it is for a person classified as a public figure to recover for invasion of privacy. Public figures must put up with more publicity concerning their private lives than one who is not a public figure. Since most pro athletes and the majority of big-time college student-athletes would probably be classified as public figures, it would be difficult for them to recover under the theory of invasion of privacy.

NOTES ————————————————————————————

1. In Massachusetts, for example, there is a statute governing invasion of privacy (Mass. G.L.A. 214, § 1B). It provides: "A person shall have a right against unreasonable, substantial or serious interference with his privacy." This section allows for legal as well as equitable relief. It also appears broad enough to cover the four distinct ways to invade the privacy of another as discussed above and mentioned in Prosser, *Law of Torts*.

2. For further information, review the discussion on the Buckley Amendment in Chapter 5, page 273.

THE TORT OF INTENTIONAL INFLICTION OF EMOTIONAL DISTRESS

The tort of intentional infliction of emotional distress is designed to protect a person's emotional tranquility. Simple minor disturbances and infringements are not actionable. The provoking conduct must be outrageous for the plaintiff to have an action for intentional infliction of emotional distress. An increasing number of states are recognizing intentional infliction of emotional distress as an independent tort. The recent trend of states recognizing this tort has been to adopt principles of the *Restatement (Second) of Torts*, § 46. Section 46 sets forth the following four requirements:

1. There must be extreme and outrageous conduct.
2. The conduct must be intentional or reckless.
3. The conduct must cause emotional distress.
4. The distress must be severe.

The intent required under § 46(2) is simply the intent to engage in the conduct; that is what is meant by intentional. Section 46, however, does not require that the defendant have a criminal or tortious intent, or even an intent to cause emotional distress. It is enough if the conduct has

> been so outrageous in character and so extreme in degree as to go beyond all possible bounds of decency and to be regarded as atrocious, and utterly intolerable in a civilized community. [*Restatement (Second) of Torts*, § 46, comment (d)]

Thus, if the defendant is joking and informs the plaintiff that her son has been killed, and the plaintiff suffers emotional distress, the defendant will be liable. Or, if a doctor falsely or recklessly makes it known to a person that he is suffering from a fatal disease, then the doctor will be liable.

The conduct required by § 46 is outrageous and extreme. The plaintiff has an initial burden of showing enough evidence for reasonable persons to find extreme and outrageous conduct. Section 46 also requires that the plaintiff actually suffer severe emotional distress. Comment (j) to § 46 requires that the plaintiff prove that he suffered severe distress and that this distress was not unreasonable, exaggerated, or unjustified.

A leading case in the area of intentional infliction of emotional distress is *Chuy v. Philadelphia Eagles Football Club*, 431 F. Supp. 254 (E.D. Pa. 1977), *aff'd*, 595 F.2d 1265 (3d Cir. 1979). Chuy, a professional football player, brought suit against the Eagles and the National Football League seeking to recover the balance of his salary allegedly due on his contract and for damages for defamation and intentional infliction of emotional distress. Chuy had suffered a serious injury while playing football.

Chuy's claims for emotional distress were based on a statement made by a team physician who was being interviewed by the press. The doctor reported that Chuy had contracted a rare blood disease which would prevent him from ever playing football again. Chuy, having no prior knowledge of the existence of such a condition, claimed that upon hearing the report he was put under incredible emotional anguish and he anticipated death.

The court held that the doctor's conduct was sufficiently outrageous. The court found that the doctor intentionally told news reporters that Chuy was suffering from a blood disease, knowing that this was in fact not true. Chuy recovered $10,000 in compensatory damages for this intentional infliction of emotional distress. Chuy also recovered $60,000 in punitive damages, which was affirmed on appeal as not being excessive.

Amateur athletic administrators must also be on their guard about statements made by members of an organization's staff that could lead to litigation such as that in *Chuy*. The following are examples of potential instances in which such statements to the media could lead to similar litigation:

- A coach's statement about the playing ability of a student-athlete, including professional career aspirations.
- An administration's statement about the employment tenure of a coach.
- A trainer's announcement about the playing ability or injury of a student-athlete.
- A sports information director's comments about student-athletes and coaches.

In any of the above situations, if the statement was "extremely outrageous" and led to some injury to the individual about whom the statement was made, an athletic administrator might anticipate that litigation will be filed.

PRODUCTS LIABILITY LAW

Products liability is an expansive area of tort law which allows a party who has been injured by a product defectively designed, manufactured, or distributed to recover under one of several possible causes of action. The causes of action in products liability cases are negligence, strict liability, and breach of warranty.

The class of possible defendants in a products liability action is broad. Everyone in the chain of distribution of a product is potentially liable, from the manufacturer to the seller or lessor to those who service or install the product. A product is any item of personal property, most commonly consumer goods, and includes the container in which it is sold. Even vacant land that has been altered by earth-moving equipment to be made into a baseball diamond can be a "product," so that the manufacturer (earth mover) could be liable for injuries caused by holes or bumps in the surface.

The plaintiff in a products liability case must show that a defect existed at the time the product left the control of the defendant and that the injury was caused by the defect. Courts have most frequently applied a definition of defect from the *Restatement (Second) of Torts*, § 402A, which says a product is in a defective condition if it is "unreasonably dangerous to the user." Comment (i) of section 401A further defines a defect:

> The article sold must be dangerous to the extent beyond that which would be contemplated by the ordinary consumer who purchases it, with the knowledge common to the community as to its characteristics.

In the amateur sports setting an athletic administrator has to be particularly aware of potential product liability problems. Sports involve the participation of individuals and the use of equipment by those individuals, and both factors are the basis for any product liability lawsuit. Ultimately, such litigation leads to increases in a sports organization's insurance premiums, a subject discussed in Chapter 7.

The Sporting Goods Manufacturers Association has been lobbying for liability relief from Congress and the state legislatures, because it contends that product liability litigation and other tort lawsuits are making sports unaffordable in the United States. The association recently made this statement:

> The sporting goods industry concludes that liability relief is imperative to maintaining affordable and available recreational products and sports programs. For American sports, the two minute warning is sounding. The time for debate and study is over. Public officials need to stop the bleeding if the U.S. sporting goods industry and amateur sports in America are to survive. We have no more "deep pockets."

In reviewing this problem area, the association notes further:

> Sporting goods manufacturers, retailers, schools, amateur sports groups, municipalities, and private providers of recreation services are suffering from:

1. a panoply of frivolous suits;
2. extravagant awards for injury predicated on the "deep pocket" theory;
3. insurance that is either unavailable or unaffordable;
4. erosion of contributory negligence and assumption of risk defenses.

The result:

1. U.S. companies, large and small, are dropping product lines or going bare;
2. U.S. jobs are lost or never created;
3. U.S. sporting goods manufacturers' competitive position is being further eroded;
4. less sporting goods product is available to consumers and at higher cost;
5. injured parties are compensated in some states and victimized in others;
6. schools are dropping their sports programs;
7. amateur sports groups are disbanding leagues or hiking dues to where they may be unaffordable to participants;
8. volunteer coaches, refs, and other league officials are refusing their services out of fear of being sued;
9. municipalities are closing facilities or dropping recreational activities; and
10. private providers of services at campgrounds and marinas, on rivers and at water sports sites, or gymnastic and health clubs are abandoning their services.

While the association's position represents only one side of the situation, there is no doubt that product liability lawsuits remain a big problem for equipment manufacturers and amateur athletic administrators.

NOTES ───

1. For further information, see the following law article: Williamson, "Sports Products Liability: 'It's All Part of the Game—Or Is It?' " 17 *Trial* 58 (1981).

2. To contact the Sporting Goods Manufacturers Association, use the following addresses or phone numbers:

Palm Beach Headquarters:
200 Castlewood Drive
N. Palm Beach, FL 33408
(305) 842-4100

Washington Office:
1625 K Street, N.W., Ste. 900
Washington, DC 20006
(202) 775-1762

Negligence as a Cause of Action

In products liability law, a manufacturer of a product has the duty to meet legal standards of safety and care in the product's design, manufacture, and use. In addition, the supplier of the product and the seller may be liable for negligence if they have not exercised reasonable care. The courts generally balance the probability and gravity of the potential harm against the social value of the product and the inconvenience of taking precautions in determining whether or not a duty of care has been breached.

The standard of care involved in manufacturing is one of reasonable care in both the manufacture and design of the product to ensure that it will be reasonably safe when used in the manner in which it was intended. In addition, when a product may be dangerous even when properly used, a manufacturer may have a duty to warn users of the product about the hazard. However, the manufacturer is not required to make the safest or best possible product, although the product will be compared to similar products. The similar products will be used to help determine what is a "reasonably" safe product.

Sellers, the retailers of a product, are also subject to liability for negligence under some circumstances. A seller of a product which the seller knows to be dangerous has a duty to warn a purchaser who has no knowledge of the dangerous nature of the product. A seller may also have a duty to inspect a product manufactured by another if the seller knows or has reason to know that it is likely to be hazardous.

Advertisers and marketers of a product also have a duty to exercise reasonable care. When a product appears on the market, a warning about the dangers associated with the product must accompany it. This warning must be adequate and disclose the dangers from an improper design as well as dangers that are possible even when the product is properly used. The warning must also be sufficient to protect third parties who might reasonably be expected to come into contact with the product.

Suppliers, the wholesalers of a product, must also exercise reasonable care. First, a supplier has a duty to use reasonable care to make a product safe. In addition, if the supplier knows or has reason to know that the product is dangerous and that the user is not likely to realize the danger, the supplier must exercise reasonable care to notify the user of the potential danger. For example, the Flybynight Company was contracted to replace a drainage system at a high school soccer field. After completion of the job, the ground around one of the drainpipes settled, leaving the pipe exposed. Kenny Keeper dove to make a save; he fell on the pipe and suffered severe injuries. The Flybynight Company was negligent for its failure to insure the safety of the field. The school would also be a potential defendant for failing to hire a competent contractor to install the new drainage system.

Strict Liability as a Cause of Action

The strict liability cause of action requires that one who sells a product which is unreasonably dangerous because of a defect— whether in design or manufacture—be held liable for any physical harm proximately caused by use of the product. The seller will be liable to the ultimate user or customer, provided that the product has not been changed from its initial state or condition. Liability can be found only if the product has been used in the manner and for the purposes intended by the sellers; therefore, a seller will not be liable for harm resulting from unforeseeable, abnormal use of the product. This strict liability standard applies despite the fact that a seller may have exercised all the care necessary in, and appropriate for, the preparation and sale of the product.

The theory behind strict liability is that when the seller markets its product for use and consumption by the public, it assumes a special responsibility to any member of the public for any injury caused by the product. The public has the right to expect that the seller will provide a reasonably safe product. There is a strong public policy supporting the demand that the burden of accidental injuries caused by a seller's products be placed on those who marketed them. The theory is that the cost inherent in the assumption of responsibility can be insured; it will be treated as a cost of production and added to the cost of the item. Therefore, the consumer is given the maximum possible protection from unreasonably dangerous products in that the people in the best position to provide this protection are those who market and profit from the products.

Most courts have applied the *Restatement (Second) of Torts*, §402A definition of strict tort liability, which states:

1. One who sells any product in a defective condition unreasonably dangerous to the user or consumer or to his property is subject to liability for physical harm thereby caused to the ultimate user or consumer, or to his property; if:

(a) the seller is engaged in the business of selling such a product, and

(b) it is expected to and does reach the user or consumer without substantial change in the condition in which it is sold.

2. The rule stated in subsection (1) applies although:

(a) the seller has exercised all possible care in the preparation and sale of his product, and

(b) the user or consumer has not bought the product from or entered into any contractual relation with the seller.

Breach of Warranty as a Cause of Action

A cause of action for products liability may be based on a breach-of-warranty claim against a manufacturer. This is basically an adaption of contract law to torts problems. First, the plaintiff would have to establish that there was an express or implied warranty. Then the plaintiff would have to prove that the warranty was breached by the defendant. The advantage to a claim based on warranty principles is that the plaintiff does not have to prove that the product was defective in its design.

An *express warranty* is an affirmation of material fact concerning the nature and fitness of a particular product upon which the buyer might reasonably rely. An *implied warranty* does not arise from any words of the seller, either oral or in writing, but is a rule of law in every state. The rule is embodied in § 2-314 of the Uniform Commercial Code, which states: "A warranty that the goods shall be merchantable is implied in a contract for their sale if the seller is a merchant with respect to goods of that kind."

Chapter 7

APPLICATION OF
TORT LAW

INTRODUCTION

Chapter 7 is organized according to possible defendants in sports tort cases. The chapter begins with a discussion of the potential liabilities of a participant in a sporting event. It then focuses on the potential liabilities of coaches and teachers in the areas of supervision, instruction and training, medical assistance, and vicarious liability for actions of fans and players. The legal theory most commonly used in this area is negligence. The chapter next covers the potential liabilities of administrators, schools, and universities. Administrators may be found negligent in hiring personnel (an employee such as a coach or teacher) or in supervising personnel. Administrators may also be found vicariously liable for the negligence of an employee in rendering medical assistance. Finally, administrators may be found negligent for not providing equipment, or vicariously liable if an employee did not furnish equipment or furnished ill-fitting or defective equipment. Schools and universities may also be sued under a vicarious liability theory for the negligence of any of their employees in the area of supervision and personnel, medical assistance, and equipment.

A defense for the administrator, school, or university may be the doctrine of sovereign immunity, the next topic presented in Chapter 7. Charitable immunity and civil liability immunity legislation are also discussed in this section. The next sections of Chapter 7 cover the liability of facility owners and possessors, which may include defects in a building or negligent supervision of a crowd, and the liability of medical personnel for negligent treatment of an injured athlete or fan.

The chapter continues with a discussion of a newly developing area of sports torts—the potential liabilities of officials-referees and umpires. Some officials have been sued for injuries to athletes that have allegedly resulted from a failure to take corrective action to remedy the injury-causing situation. Examples include failing to stop a game during inclement weather conditions or allowing objects or spectators to be too close to the playing area. Officials, referees, and umpires have also been sued for the incorrect application of game rules and making incorrect judgment calls. The next section sets forth cases involving defects in equipment.

The final section in Chapter 7 discusses liability insurance and how high school athletic associations and high schools are purchasing insurance to combat the rising number of tort claims being made by those associated with sports activities. The National Collegiate Athletic Association implemented a liability insurance program, which began in the 1985-86 academic year. This last section also includes a discussion on the waiver and release of liability.

LIABILITY OF PARTICIPANTS

The liability stemming most directly from sports activity is that for injuries to participants. Until recently, most sports-related injuries were viewed as a natural outgrowth of the competitive and physical nature of sports. This attitude was supported by the traditional belief that a participant assumes the dangers inherent in the sport and is therefore precluded from recovery for an injury caused by another participant. Although this theory has some merit, it fails to address injuries that occur during a game that are not necessarily an outgrowth of competitive spirit.

This traditional attitude has been strictly scrutinized in recent decisions which clearly establish that a player does not necessarily assume the risk of all injuries resulting from gross recklessness on the part of another player. Nor does the player necessarily consent to intentional attacks falling outside the recognized rules of the sport. Thus, the defenses of assumption of the risk or of consent must be reviewed on a case-by-case basis to determine whether or not they are applicable in a particular instance (see Chapter 6).

This change in attitude has occurred in part because of the increasing number of serious injuries to sports participants. The increased volume of sports participation resulting from the involvement of boys and girls, and men and women, in unprecedented numbers has produced a corresponding increase in the number of sports-related injuries. The NCAA estimates that in a single football season alone there are approximately 1 million injuries at 20,000 high schools (50 per school) and 70,000 injuries at 900 colleges and universities (78 per institution). On the average, there is one injury per player per year in the National Football League (NFL).

A second reason for the change in attitude is that professional sports, and to some extent, intercollegiate and amateur athletics, are now viewed as businesses. Because of this, people are more inclined to see the situation as one in which a lawsuit is a viable option. In addition, amateur athletic associations have increased revenues and may have deep pockets to pay large awards. A third reason is that legal precedents have been established which allow injured athletes to recover. Finally, the rise in sports-related lawsuits is a result of society becoming increasingly reliant on the judicial system for the resolution of disputes.

An increase in charges of negligence and other tortious conduct has paralleled the rising number of sports injuries in recent years. One factor behind the rise in participant-versus-participant lawsuits is the steady erosion of the athlete's traditional reluctance to sue fellow participants. The increasing recognition of the dangers involved in playing a game against an opponent who does not follow an accepted safety rule has increased the likelihood of a lawsuit. Players are refusing to accept injury-provoking actions of opponents when the actions are not sanctioned by the rules of the game. There is some legal precedent which recognizes that each player has a legal duty to refrain from unreasonably dangerous acts (See Notes 1b and c and Note 2.)

Courts have found that many sports, including soccer, softball, and football, have created safety rules to help define the often unclear line between legal and illegal behavior on the field. A safety rule is one that is initiated to protect players and to prevent injuries rather than to make the game more exciting or interesting. The existence of safety rules mandates that in many situations a player be charged with a legal duty to every other player involved in the activity. This legal duty requires the player to refrain from conduct, proscribed by such rules, which is likely to cause harm. In cases involving the alleged violation of a safety rule, the courts have held that a player is liable for tort action if his or her conduct displays deliberate, willful, or reckless disregard for the safety of other participants and results in injury to another participant.

Thus, a participant may recover for either intentional torts or for gross negligence (see Chapter 6). Actions based on ordinary negligence are still difficult to establish in athletic cases. However, case law indicates that there are situations in sports for which the commonly accepted defenses of assumption of risk and contributory negligence are not adequate to bar recovery by the plaintiff (see Chapter 6).

NOTES ⎯⎯⎯⎯⎯⎯⎯⎯⎯⎯⎯⎯⎯⎯⎯⎯⎯⎯⎯⎯⎯⎯⎯⎯⎯⎯⎯⎯⎯⎯⎯

1. The courts discussed the liability of participants in sports in the following cases.

(a) In *Gaspard v. Grain Dealers Mutual Insurance Co.*, 131 So. 2d. 831 (La. 1961), Andrus Gaspard brought suit for damages for personal injuries on behalf of his son Ronnie following an injury to the boy in a playground baseball game. Defendant, Grain Dealers Mutual Insurance Company, had issued a comprehensive liability policy to Alfred Viator, the father of the boy responsible for the plaintiff's injury. At the trial court level, the defendant denied any negligence on the part of Ronald Viator and pleaded assumption of risk as a bar to plaintiff's recovery. In the alternative, the defendant alleged contributory negligence on the part of Ronnie Gaspard.

Following a decision in the defendant's favor, the plaintiff filed this appeal. The appeals court found that young Viator's action did not constitute negligence because he exercised a reasonable degree of care. Gaspard assumed the risk as he "knew of the danger and clearly acquiesced or proceeded in the face of danger by voluntarily playing the game." Accordingly, the court denied Gaspard's appeal.

(b) In *Bourque v. Duplechin*, 331 So. 2d 40 (La. 1976), plaintiff brought suit for injuries he received in a softball game. In 1974, Jerome Bourque played second base on an amateur softball team sponsored by Boo Boo's Lounge. Adrien Duplechin was a member of the opposing team. During the game, Duplechin was on first base when a teammate hit a ground ball. Duplechin started for second base as the shortstop threw the ball to Bourque. Bourque caught the ball, stepped on second base, and then stepped away from second base to throw the ball to first and complete a double play. After Bourque had thrown the ball to first base, Duplechin ran full speed into Bourque and brought his left arm up under Bourque's chin. When Duplechin made contact with Bourque, Bourque was standing 5 feet away from second base. The umpire ejected Duplechin from the game for his conduct.

Bourque brought suit against Duplechin and his liability insurer. The lower court found for Bourque.

The court of appeals rejected Duplechin's argument that when Bourque voluntarily participated in the softball game, he assumed the risk of injury. The court stated that while Bourque did assume the risk of those injuries, which were common incidents of baseball and softball, he did not assume the risk of Duplechin breaching his duty to play softball in the ordinary fashion without unsportsmanlike conduct and inflicting wanton injury to his fellow players.

Allstate Insurance Company claimed on appeal that there was no coverage under its policy because Duplechin's actions were an intentional tort and he should have expected injury to occur. On this issue, the court quoted William Prosser from the *Law of Torts*, 4th edition:

> . . . the mere knowledge and appreciation of a risk, short of substantial certainty, is not the equivalent of intent. The defendant who acts in the belief or consciousness that he is causing an appreciable risk of harm to another may be negligent, and if the risk is great his conduct may be characterized as reckless or wanton, but it is not classed as an intentional wrong.

Thus, in the court's opinion, Duplechin did not commit an intentional tort because he was not motivated by a desire to injure Bourque. Duplechin's conduct was negligent and was thus covered under the Allstate policy. Bourque had suffered a fractured jaw; broken seven teeth, which had to be crowned and one tooth replaced by a bridge; and his chin required plastic surgery. In view of the foregoing, the court of appeals found the award of $12,000 for pain and suffering and $1,496 for special damages not excessive. The judgment of the trial court was affirmed.

(c) In *Griggas v. Clauson,* 128 N.E.2d 363 (Ill. 1955), Griggas, a 19-year-old member of an amateur basketball team, brought suit for injuries received during a game in 1953. During that game he was guarded by La Verne Clauson. While Griggas had his back to Clauson and was about to receive a pass from a teammate, Clauson pushed him and then struck him in the face with his fist. As Griggas fell, Clauson struck him again and knocked him unconscious. Clauson began to swear profusely and made statements to the effect that he was going to teach Griggas a lesson and that one of the two was going to play in the city and the other was not. Griggas was hospitalized for about three weeks. The Appellate Court of Illinois supported a trial court decision for Griggas. It held that the evidence in the record supported the finding that Griggas was subjected to a wanton and unprovoked battery.

(d) In *Nabozny v. Barnhill,* 334 N.E.2d 258 (Ill. App. 1975), plaintiff soccer player filed suit for injuries received when he was kicked in the head by an opponent during an amateur soccer game involving two teams composed of high school age players. The defendant, David Barnhill, was playing a forward position for one team, and the plaintiff, Julian Nabozny, was the goaltender for the other team. Barnhill kicked Nabozny in the head while Nabozny was in possession of the ball. Contact with the goaltender while he is in possession of the ball is a violation of FIFA (International Association Football Federation—soccer's international governing body) rules which governed the contest. The resultant injury left the plaintiff with permanent skull and brain damage. Nabozny brought suit, and the trial court directed a verdict in favor of the defendant.

On appeal, the court noted that it did not wish to "place unreasonable burdens on the free and vigorous participation in sports by our youth," but also stated that "athletic competition does not exist in a vacuum." Therefore, in reversing the trial court decision, the court held that a player is charged with a legal duty to every other player on the field to refrain from conduct proscribed by a safety rule. The court held that when athletes are engaged in athletic competition, all teams involved are trained and coached by knowledgeable personnel; a recognized set of rules governs the conduct of the competition; and a safety rule is contained therein which is primarily designed to protect players from serious injury. Thus, a reckless disregard for the safety of other players cannot be excused.

(e) In *Barrett v. Phillips,* 223 S.E.2d 918 (N.C. 1976), a wrongful death suit against a high school and an athletic association was brought when Barrett's son was killed in a collision during a high school football game with a player over 20 years old. The defendants were in violation of a rule prohibiting players over age 19 from playing. The court reasoned that the purpose of the rule was not for the safety of the players, and there was no actionable negligence because there was no causal connection between the death and the violation of the rule.

(f) In *Osborne v. Sprowls*, 419 N.E.2d (Ill. 1981), a bystander sued a participant for injuries incurred during a "tackle-the-football" game. This game is a combination of football, keep-away, and soccer in which all players chase the person with the football until he is tackled or he kicks or throws the ball away. The Supreme Court of Illinois determined that an ordinary negligence standard would apply because Osborne was neither a participant nor was he located in an area where the game was or could be in progress. The court determined the defendant owed the plaintiff the duty to select an area free from the presence of nonparticipating individuals.

2. The liability of participants has also been a subject of much judicial scrutiny on the professional sports level. The following cases examine this area of sports law.

(a) In *Hackbart v. Cincinnati Bengals*, 435 F. Supp. 352 (D. Colo. 1977), *rev'd*, 601 F.2d 516 (10th Cir. 1979), Charles Clark, a running back with the Cincinnati Bengals, was sued for reckless misconduct by Dale Hackbart, a defensive back for the Denver Broncos. Clark had struck Hackbart in the head, an action outside the rules of the game of football. The trial court had ruled that there was no duty between the players. However, the appeals court found enough justification for a retrial on a reckless misconduct theory before a jury to determine the liability of defendant Charles Clark. The case was settled before trial for a reported $200,000.

(b) In *Manning v. Grimsley*, 643 F.2d 20 (1st Cir. 1981), Ross Grimsley, a pitcher for the Baltimore Orioles, was upset at the heckling fans at Fenway Park and upon finishing his warmups, threw a ball through a protective screen and hit the plaintiff. The plaintiff sued the pitcher and his employer for battery and negligence. The district court ruled for the defendant on both counts. The court of appeals, however, vacated and remanded the decision regarding the battery charge, holding that the jury verdict on the negligence charge did not preclude the plaintiff from maintaining the battery charge.

3. For further information on participant liability in sports, see the following law review articles:

(a) Ranii, "Sports Violence Lawsuits Erupt," *National Law Journal*, February 9, 1981, p. 1.

(b) Carroll, "Torts in Sports—I'll See You in Court," 16 *Akron Law Review* 537 (Winter 1983).

(c) "Comment: A Proposed Legislative Solution to the Problem of Violent Acts by Participants During Professional Sporting Events," 7 *University of Dayton Law Review* 91 (1981).

(d) Hayes, "Professional Sports and Tort Liability: A Victory for the Intentionally Injured Player," *Detroit College of Law Review* 687 (Summer 1980).

(e) Gulotta, "Torts in Sports: Deterring Violence in Professional Athletics," 48 *Fordham Law Review* 764 (April 1980).

LIABILITY OF COACHES AND TEACHERS

Coaches or teachers, as individuals, are always responsible for any intentional torts they commit in their capacity as coaches or physical education teachers. They are generally not shielded by the defenses of consent, privilege, and immunity from liability by virtue of their positions. (See Chapter 6.)

The coach is judged by the standard of a "reasonable coach" and the teacher by the standard of a "reasonable teacher." There are some limited exceptions in which coaches and teachers are held to a lower standard of care and will not be held liable unless they are deemed to be grossly negligent. One situation involves coaches or teachers who are given the status "in loco parentis"—that is, the coach or teacher is placed in the position of the parents of the student-athlete (see Note 1d on page 347). A coach or teacher may, however, have a number of defenses available (see page 310).

Since a minor is often involved in this area, note should be taken that certain defenses such as contributory negligence, comparative negligence, and assumption of the risk may be affected by the different standard of care for children (see page 309). The defense of sovereign immunity is a particularly important one for coaches and teachers. As a general rule, the coach or teacher cannot be sued individually when the school district is protected under sovereign immunity (see page 356). However, this protection is limited and may not cover the coach who is not acting within the scope of employment or who has been misfeasant.

Until recently, very little litigation was brought against coaches and teachers as a result of the sovereign immunity protection and the reluctance by potential plaintiffs to bring lawsuits. This was especially true in the case of coaches and teachers who were often members of the community and highly respected for their work. However, the coach and teacher are increasingly likely to be sued today, since injured student-athletes are more likely to bring suit and the sovereign immunity doctrine is being eroded (discussed later in this chapter on page 356).

In many of the cases, the institution has been sued under the doctrine of respondeat superior (also called the doctrine of vicarious liability) for the coach's or teacher's negligence, and the coach has not been a named defendant. However, the basis for the litigation is the negligence of the coach or teacher, and in future cases the coach or teacher may be sued individually. The areas of responsibility for which a coach or teacher may be sued include supervision, instruction and training, medical assistance, and vicarious liability for actions of fans and players.

Failure to Provide Adequate Supervision

The coach and teacher are responsible for providing reasonable supervision to the student-athletes under their direction. However, they are not insurers of the safety of everyone under their supervision.

Examples of failure to provide adequate supervision include negligent supervision at a football game or failure to provide the proper equipment for the game. It would also include improperly supervising an off-season weight training program or encouraging an injured student-athlete to play. An additional responsibility for the coach and teacher is to check the playing area to make sure it is in proper playing condition and that nothing is on or near the playing area that could cause injury; such obstructions include benches, other students, and spectators.

Finally, the coach and teacher also may be sued for nonplaying field activities, such as supervising student-athletes who are going to or from the playing field. The coach and teacher are responsible for providing reasonable supervision. Any supervisory capacity carries with it the responsibility to exercise due care—that is, the care of a "reasonable supervisor" (see page 307) for the safety of anyone who is likely to or actually does come into contact with the area under supervision. The duty entails using reasonable care in either rectifying dangerous situations or warning those who may encounter them of the possible hazards. A supervisor generally is not liable for any intentional acts of his employees unless it can be proved that he was negligent in choosing or supervising the employee(s) involved. A school district or supervisor is liable in such instances only if the institution, or one to whom the district or supervisor is legally responsible, breaches the requisite standard of reasonable care. If the supervisor is not negligent himself, liability will be assessed only if the employee and the action taken satisfy the requirements of respondeat superior (see page 316). Also, the doctrine of sovereign immunity (discussed later in this chapter on page 356) may bar the action unless the state involved has specifically eliminated its immunity under this doctrine.

A supervisor is not, however, an insurer of everyone's safety; rather, the supervisor needs only to exercise reasonable care. Unless there is information or notice to the contrary, the supervisor is entitled to assume that all under his or her supervision will also be exercising due care. Thus, a spectator who is injured by another spectator may not enforce a claim against a school district or its administrators unless the school district or administrator, having had notice that the other spectator was likely to cause an unreasonably dangerous condition, failed to take steps to prevent the injury. Past experience, moreover, will be considered when assessing liability. For example, if the same spectator appeared at another contest and injured a fellow spectator, the school district might be held liable because the first situation provided warning of the person's potentially dangerous nature. The duty of care required may depend on the type of event. Rock concerts, for instance, may require more security and precautions than do track and field events.

NOTE ——————————————————————————————————————

1. The following cases deal with supervision of student-athletes by the coach or teacher:

(a) *Morris v. Union High School District A, King County,* 294 P. 998 (Wash. 1931), was a suit brought by a high school athlete who injured his back during football practice. The coach, who was well aware of the injury, or should have become aware of it in the exercise of reasonable care, "permitted, persuaded and coerced" the athlete to play in a game. As a result of the athlete's participation, he suffered more serious injuries to his back and spine. The athlete brought suit against the school district alleging that the school district was liable for the negligence of its coach, who negligently coerced him to play. The court ruled in favor of the plaintiff and held that the school district was liable.

(b) *Vargo v. Svitchan,* 301 N.W.2d 1 (Mich. 1980), was a suit brought by a high school athlete who, while participating in a summer weight training program at the high school gymnasium, attempted to lift a 250- to 300-pound weight, fell, and received injuries resulting in paraplegia. The plaintiff's lawsuit charged the school's athletic director, principal, and superintendent with negligent supervision of the football coach. The court of appeals held that the school's principal and athletic director were sued for "personal neglect" in maintaining inadequate school facilities, in allowing an illegal summer weight-lifting program, and providing insufficient supervision. Therefore, they were not entitled to the protection of the governmental immunity statute. The school superintendent was entitled to protection under the governmental immunity standard because there was no "personal neglect" on his part.

(c) In *Lynch v. Board of Education of Collingsville Community School District,* 390 N.E.2d 526 (Ill. 1979), parents of a junior in high school brought a negligence suit on her behalf against the school district for damages she received as a result of an injury suffered in a "powderpuff" intramural football game. Plaintiffs alleged ordinary negligence on the part of the defendant in failing to provide adequate equipment and willful and wanton misconduct in failing to adequately supervise the game. An appeals court, in affirming the trial court's decision for the parents, held that since the teams' coaches were teachers and the field on which the contest was played was fenced and could have been locked to keep students out, there was sufficient evidence for the jury to conclude that the game was authorized by the school. The court also held that the presence of the plaintiff's parents at the game site did not obviate the school's duty to provide adequate equipment.

(d) In *Domino v. Mercurio*, 17 A.D. 2d 342, 234 N.Y.S.2d 1011 (1962), *aff'd*, 13 N.Y.2d 922, 193 N.E.2d 893 (N.Y. 1963), a negligence suit was brought by plaintiff father against the local board of education and playground supervisors who were employees of the board for injuries sustained by his son, who, while playing softball on the school playground, fell over a bench that was too close to the base path. The court held that the board could be held liable for the negligence of the playground supervisors who allowed spectators to congregate too close to the third base line and moved a bench into a dangerous position near that line. It was not necessary that the board itself be found guilty of negligence in selecting playground supervisors.

(e) *Foster v. Houston General Insurance Company*, 407 So. 2d 759 (La. 1981), was a suit for the wrongful death of a mentally retarded student-athlete. A member of his school's Special Olympics basketball team, plaintiff was en route to basketball practice at an off-campus facility when he dashed in front of a car and was struck and killed while under the supervision of one teacher. The teacher had assumed responsibility for 11 players because the other teacher involved was detained in class. The trial and appeals courts ruled that the defendant teachers owed the deceased a legal duty and breached their duty by failing to act reasonably under the circumstances. They did not provide an adequate number of supervisory personnel, and they were negligent in the selection of the safest possible walk route. The defendant school board was not liable for independent negligence.

(f) In *Kersey v. Harbin*, 591 S.W.2d 745 (Mo. 1979), a negligence suit was filed against school officials for fatal injuries sustained by plaintiff's son during gym class. Decedent engaged in a brief scuffle after a fellow student deliberately and persistently stepped on decedent's heels. Decedent sustained a skull fracture during the scuffle, which occurred on the stairway leading from the locker room to the gymnasium. The plaintiff alleged that the school authorities had possessed actual and/or constructive knowledge of quarrelsome propensities on the part of the fellow student and, despite such knowledge, had failed to take "appropriate measures to prevent injury . . . by exercising ordinary care." The appeals court held that "supervisory public school employees and teachers are not immune from tort liability for inadequate supervision of their students but that such liability is highly subjective and the scope of their duties extremely narrow." The case was remanded to the trial court for a factual determination.

Failure to Provide Proper Instruction and Training

The coach and teacher are responsible for providing proper instruction and training to the student-athletes; they should be qualified to teach the particular activity involved. In addition, the coach must properly instruct the student-athletes on the activity, the safety rules, and the proper method of playing. There have been a number of cases involving football-related injuries, in which the injured player alleged that the coach or teacher did not provide proper instruction and training concerning tackling. In addition, a proper preseason conditioning program should be provided, although such programs become an issue where football practice is started in August and some players experience fatal injuries from heat exhaustion.

Coaches and teachers should keep detailed records of their instruction and training sessions. They should also be aware of any new developments in their sport. Some companies have started producing instruction and training films to assist coaches and teachers in preparing their student-athletes.

Another area of potential liability for the coach or teacher is a claim by a student-athlete of assault and battery. Several issues are raised in this area. Is there a defense of privilege? Is the standard of care "reasonable care" or "gross negligence"? Does sovereign immunity protect the coach and teacher? Can force be used to bring about compliance with commands and punishment for prohibited conduct? Can force be used when the player has not performed adequately? There has not been a great deal of litigation in this area, but coaches and teachers should be aware that cases may be brought (see Notes 1b and d).

NOTE

1. The following cases deal with the instruction and training of student-athletes by coaches and teachers.

(a) In *Vendrell v. School District No. 26C, Malheur County,* 233 Or. 1, 376 P.2d 406 (1962), plaintiff, a freshman football player who had played two years of junior high football, brought suit against the school district for damages for the neck injury he sustained while playing in a high school game. The plaintiff suffered a fractured neck when he lowered his head and collided with two opposing players. The plaintiff contended that he was an inexperienced player and had been improperly trained. The court of appeals ruled against the plaintiff, holding that the plaintiff was not inexperienced in that he had played for two years in junior high school and during those years had received substantial football training from competent coaches. The court held that the game of football is an inherently rough sport in which body contact and some degree of injury is inevitable and that no player should need to have this explained.

(b) In *Rutledge v. Arizona Board of Regents*, 660 F.2d 1345 (9th Cir. 1981), *aff'd*, U.S. 719, 103 S. Ct. 148 (1983), plaintiff student-athlete sued his college football coach for assault and battery, demotion, harassment, embarrassment, defamation, and deprivation of his scholarship. Plaintiff claimed that in October 1978, the coach took his helmeted head between his hands, shook it from side to side, yelled obscenities, and then struck his mouth with his fist. Plaintiff filed suit in Arizona state court but was denied relief. He then filed suit in federal district court. The court dismissed the complaint, and Rutledge appealed. On appeal, the 9th Circuit Court of Appeals held that the university, the board of regents, and the athletic director were entitled to at least partial immunity. The coaches were not entitled to immunity, and the athletic director was not immune on the charge he failed to properly supervise the coach. However, the court dismissed Rutledge's assault and battery complaint because it had been previously litigated in state court.

(c) In *Pirkle v. Oakdale Union Grammer School Dist.*, 253 P.2d 1 (Cal. 1953), an eighth grade student brought an action against the school district for injuries received from being blocked during a touch football game that was played without supervision. The court held for the defendant on appeal, ruling that the players had been properly selected and instructed. The court also held that plaintiff's injuries could not have been readily apparent to a lay person and that no further damage resulted from a delay in receiving medical treatment.

(d) In *Hogenson v. Williams*, 542 S.W.2d 456 (Tex. 1976), an action for assault was brought when the coach, displeased with the blocking of a seventh grade player, grabbed him by the face mask and knocked him to the ground. The player received a severe cervical sprain. The jury found for the defendant, but the appeals court held the trial judge had improperly interpreted the rule of "privileged force" granted a teacher when he instructed the jury that "intent to injure is the gist of an assault." Rather, a teacher or coach can use force necessary to invoke compliance with his commands or to punish the child for prohibited conduct. A coach cannot use force merely because the student's performance is inadequate, even though the coach may consider such violence to be constructive. The jury verdict was reversed and remanded.

(e) In *Kluka v. Livingston Parish School District*, 433 So. 2d 302 (La. 1983), a basketball coach was held not liable for injuries to a student who caught his foot between two mats while wrestling the coach in a friendly match. The court held that the student initiated the match and knew that wrestling could lead to injury.

Failure to Provide Prompt and Capable Medical Assistance

A common risk encountered in the area of sports is the risk of serious injury. When an injury to an athlete or spectator appears to be serious, those in charge of the activity are under a duty to use reasonable efforts to obtain reasonably prompt and capable medical assistance. At the same time, there is a duty to refrain from actions that might aggravate an injury, when a reasonable person would know of the risk.

The coach and teacher are held to a standard of "reasonable care" when rendering medical assistance to an injured student-athlete. They are not expected to provide the assistance of a doctor or one with medical training. In fact, some of the obligations of the coach and teacher have been shifted to others. For example, many states have passed statutes requiring that medical personnel be in attendance at games (see page 316). Such laws may reduce the liability exposure for the coach and teacher.

The institution may be the responsible party if medical personnel have not been provided. In addition, the institution may be responsible for having medical personnel "reasonably" available, even when it is not statutorily mandated. With medical personnel available, the care of the injured student-athlete may not have to be undertaken by the coach or teacher.

Therefore, in most situations, the main responsibilities of the coach and teacher are twofold. First, they may have to render assistance before the medical personnel arrive. First-aid training may be helpful to prevent a situation in which, for example, the coach improperly moves an injured student-athlete. The second responsibility is to exercise reasonable care in sending an injured athlete for medical treatment.

NOTE _____

1. The following cases deal with the duties of amateur athletic programs and personnel in regards to medical assistance.

(a) In *Welch v. Dunsmuir Joint Union High School District*, 326 P.2d 633 (Cal. 1958), plaintiff high school football player was injured during a scrimmage between two high school teams and brought suit against the school district. The player was lying on the ground unable to get to his feet. One coach suspected the player might have a serious neck injury and had him take hold of his hands to see if there was any grip in them. The evidence was conflicting as to whether or not the team physician, who was present at the scrimmage, examined the player before he was moved to the sidelines. Evidence indicated, however, that plaintiff was carried from the field without the aid of a stretcher or board or any other solid structure beneath him. Medical testimony established that the plaintiff became a permanent quadriplegic caused by damage to the spinal cord. The jury ruled for the plaintiff, and the appeals court held that from the evidence presented the jury could have reasonably inferred that both the doctor and the coach were negligent in the removal of the plaintiff from the field—the coach for failing to wait for the doctor and allowing the plaintiff to be moved, and the doctor for failing to act promptly after the injury.

(b) *Mogabgab v. Orleans Parish School Board*, 239 So. 2d 456 (La. 1970), was an action brought by parents for the wrongful death of their son, a high school football player who died as a result of heatstroke and exhaustion following a practice. The plaintiffs sued the coach, the school principal, and the school district on the theory that the school was negligent in not making sure the coach was properly trained. They argued also that the school was negligent in making arrangements for the proper care of sick and injured players. The court held that the coach who actively denied the student-athlete access to medical treatment for two hours after symptoms of heatstroke and shock appeared was guilty of negligence. However, the court did not find negligence attributable to the principal or the district because they were unaware of the events.

(c) In *Stineman v. Fontbonne College*, 664 F.2d 1082 (8th Cir. 1981), plaintiff was a deaf student-athlete whose softball coaches were aware of her handicap. Plaintiff had signed an authorization for emergency medical treatment in the event of an injury. During the course of practice plaintiff was struck in the eye with a ball. A coach applied ice and advised her, despite the great amount of pain she was experiencing, to go to her room and rest and she would be all right. Neither coach who was present suggested that she seek medical attention. No immediate professional medical attention was given, even though the school infirmary was across the street. Permanent eye damage resulted from the injury. The trial court found negligence on the part of the college in failing to provide the proper medical assistance. The appeals court affirmed the decision; however, it reduced the damages from $800,000 to $600,000.

Vicarious Liability for Actions of Fans and Players

The coach and teacher may be sued under a vicarious liability theory for either an unintentional or an intentional tort. However, plaintiffs generally have difficulty in winning cases based on a vicarious liability theory. For instance, in *Toone v. Adams*, an umpire was injured by a fan, and the umpire sued, among others, the manager for inciting the fan to act. The court held for the manager and found that the manager's actions were not the proximate cause of the umpire's injuries (see Note 1).

The nexus between the coach and the injury may be more easily established in other fact situations which have occurred but have not resulted in litigation. For example, a coach who orders a player to fight or to attempt to injure an opposing player may be liable under the vicarious liability theory if injuries occur.

NOTE

1. For a case involving coaches' vicarious liability for the actions of fans and players, see *Toone v. Adams*, 262 N.C. 403, 137 S.E.2nd 132 (N.C. 1964). A baseball umpire brought suit against the manager and the owner of the team after being assaulted by a fan after a game. The umpire contended that the conduct of the manager, who had been ejected from the game, and the lack of adequate protection were the proximate causes of his injury. The court found that umpires are used to having their calls disputed and that disagreements, as such, are not a major problem. The plaintiff was well escorted on his way to the dressing room, and though the guards themselves could have been more diligent, lack of protection was not the proximate cause of the plaintiff's injury. The court asserted that the club and its manager did not actually intend or could not have reasonably anticipated that one or more persons would assault the plaintiff as a result of the manager's conduct.

LIABILITY OF ADMINISTRATORS, SCHOOLS, AND UNIVERSITIES

Sports-related injuries that occur within the confines of an educational institution raise the issue of legal accountability of the institution itself. From the perspective of the seriously injured plaintiff, it may be highly desirable to obtain a judgment against an institution rather than an individual coach or instructor because the institution is much more likely to have a "deep-pocket" from which the plaintiff bringing suit can receive monetary damage awards.

If an administrator or institution is subject to liability, the standards to which it will be held are the same as in similar areas of tort law. The administrator and institution are required to exercise reasonable care to prevent reasonably foreseeable risks and to make safe foreseeably dangerous conditions by repairing or warning. If the institution fails to maintain a reasonable standard of care, it may be sued for negligence (see Chapter 6). For example, the administrator or institution should establish rules for the safe use of facilities, provide supervision of athletic activities and hire qualified personnel; provide proper medical assistance; and provide proper equipment. Institutions cannot guarantee the safety of students, but they are subject to liability when the institution or someone for whom the institution is legally responsible does not meet the standard of care required by the law.

The administrator, school, or university may also be sued under the theory of vicarious liability for the alleged negligence of an employee (see Chapter 6). An administrator may be sued in his or her role as the supervisor of a coach or teacher. The institution may also be sued in its role as the employer of the administrator, coach, teacher, referee, doctor, or owner or possessor of a facility.

One roadblock in the path of the potential plaintiff, however, is the sovereign immunity doctrine. This doctrine is a rule of law, which in many states exempts public schools and universities from private suit. Sovereign immunity has been around for centuries, but more recently the doctrine has eroded in fairness to injured plaintiffs, who previously could not collect when injured. In states where sovereign immunity has been partially eliminated, there are usually special rules of procedure which the plaintiff must carefully follow. (See page 356.)

NOTE

1. For further information on liability of sports administrators, see the following law review article: "The Student-Athlete and the NCAA: The Need for a Prima Facie Tort Doctrine," 9 *Suffolk University Law Review* 1340 (1975).

Failure to Provide Supervision of Athletic Activities and to Hire Qualified Personnel

The administrator is the supervisor of the coach or teacher, and as such may be held liable in negligence for failing to exercise reasonable care in fulfilling this responsibility. Many of the administrator's duties and responsibilities are similar to the supervisory duties of the coach or teacher in dealing with student-athletes. In dealing with personnel, administrators may be held liable if they have not exercised reasonable care in hiring coaches and teachers with proper skills and qualifications and in insuring that properly qualified personnel are supervising.

Schools and universities are generally sued on a vicarious liability theory, meaning that the negligence of their employee is imputed to the employer. The negligent individual may be an administrator, a teacher, a coach, a substitute teacher, a student teacher, or a referee. Any of these individuals and the school or university may be immune from lawsuit based on sovereign immunity (discussed later in this section on page 356).

NOTES

1. The following cases discuss the liability of the sports administrator and personnel in the area of supervision.

    (a) In *Carabba v. Anacortes School District No. 103*, 435 P.2d 936 (Wash. 1967), the plaintiff, a high school wrestler, brought suit against the defendant school district to recover injuries sustained in a match. The plaintiff was injured when the referee's attention was diverted and his opponent applied an illegal "full nelson" hold. The plaintiff was paralyzed below the neck due to substantial severance of his spinal cord. The court held that because the referee was an agent for the school district, the school could be held vicariously liable for the referee's negligence.

(b) In *Cook v. Bennett*, 288 N.W.2d 609 (Mich. 1979), plaintiff elementary school student brought suit after being seriously injured while playing "kill" during recess. In the game of "kill" all participants attempt to obtain the ball by tackling the lone participant who has it. In regards to the school's principal, the appeals court reversed the trial court's decision and held that "the extent to which a school principal is protected by immunity is dependent on whether the act complained of falls within the principal's discretionary or ministerial powers." The court held that inadequate supervision is not a discretionary function and is not protected by governmental immunity.

(c) In *DeMauro v. Tusculum College, Inc.*, 603 S.W.2d 115 (Tenn. 1980), plaintiff brought suit for injuries he received in a golf class. Plaintiff was injured when a teaching assistant, an inexperienced golfer who was assigned to supervise plaintiff's class, was attempting to demonstrate how to hit a golf ball. The teaching assistant "shanked" the shot, which struck the plaintiff in the face. The court allowed the plaintiff to sue the college under the doctrine of vicarious liability.

(d) In *Germond v. Board of Education of Central School District No. 1*, 197 N.Y.S.2d 548 (App. Div. 1960), plaintiff student sought recovery from defendant school board and teacher for injuries sustained when struck in the face by a bat swung by an older student during a softball game on the school's playground. A trial court's decision against the board was affirmed by the court of appeals. The court held that the board assumed responsibility for the individual negligence of a teacher. The board's failure to reasonably enforce adequate rules with respect to playing games on the playground and its failure to provide adequate supervision was sufficient evidence to justify a verdict against the board. The evidence presented sustained a finding of no cause of action against the school teacher who had been supervising play. The appellate court ruled that "the mere presence of the older girls would not necessarily alert a reasonable and careful teacher of young children to danger."

(e) *Brahatcek v. Millard School District #17*, N.W.2d 680 (Neb. 1979), was a suit involving an action for the death of a ninth grade student who was accidently struck by a golf club during physical education class. The court held that the school district and instructors were negligent in not providing supervision and that the lack of supervision was the proximate cause of the student's death. It held that the instructors should have foreseen the intervening negligent act of the student who fatally struck the other student. If there had been proper supervision, the death would not have occurred, and therefore intervening negligence of the classmate did not preclude the district from liability for the death.

(f) *Crohn v. Congregation B'nai Zion*, 317 N.E.2d 637 (Ill. 1974), was a negligence suit brought by plaintiff father against defendant summer day camp for injuries sustained when plaintiff's 7-year-old daughter was struck in the face by a baseball bat which was swung by a boy, age 10, during activity supervised by a 15-year-old counselor. The trial court directed a verdict in favor of defendants. On appeal, the court held that the evidence did not overwhelmingly favor the defendants on the question of whether the camp provided a safe place and adequate supervision for children's activities. Judgment was reversed and remanded.

(g) In *Larson v. Independent School District #314*, 289 N.W.2d 112 (Minn. 1979), plaintiff sued the superintendent of the school district, the principal of the high school, a physical education teacher, and the school district, charging them with negligence due to improper teaching and supervision. The plaintiff became a quadriplegic due to an injury suffered while performing a "headspring over a rolled mat" in a physical education class. The court held that the superintendent was not sufficiently involved to be found negligent, but the teacher was personally liable for negligent spotting and teaching of the exercise and the principal was negligent for not supervising the physical education curriculum more closely.

(h) *Lockard v. Leland Stanford Junior University*, No. 774-201, First Amended Complaint (Sup. Ct. Calif. 1980) (settled), was a suit that was eventually settled prior to trial. It was commenced by a student who suffered serious injuries while using a trampoline in the school gymnasium. The defendants were a diverse group that included the university, the manufacturer of the trampoline, and some 50 "John Does" who were in some way connected to the university. The plaintiff's theory was that the defendants were negligent in the operation, maintenance, repair, design, inspection, and servicing of the trampoline. In addition, the complaint cited lack of supervision or training of the plaintiff in his exercises and failure to provide spotters. The plaintiff reportedly received a multimillion dollar settlement.

2. For further information on the liability of sports administrators and personnel in the area of supervision, see the following legal articles:

(a) Cohen, "Gymnastics Litigation: Meeting the Defenses," *Trial* (August 1980).

(b) Greenwald, "Gymnastics Litigation: The Standard of Care," *Trial* (August 1980).

(c) Fidel and Langerman, "Responsibility Is Also a Part of the Game," *Trial* (January 1977).

Failure to Provide Proper Medical Assistance

Administrators, schools, and universities are generally not responsible for providing direct medical treatment to an injured student,

student-athlete, or spectator. However, the administrator, school, or university may be sued on the doctrine of vicarious liability (see page 316) if the coach improperly provided medical treatment. The administrator, school, or university generally will not be held responsible for the medical malpractice of a doctor, since in most cases the doctor is held to be an independent contractor and not an employee. However, the administrator, school, or university may be held responsible for the negligent selection, supervision, or hiring of medical personnel. There may also be potential liability if the administrator, school, or university was negligent in not providing medical personnel at a game or practice. Many schools and universities have rules that require medical personnel at certain events, such as football or basketball games. And finally, the school or university may be held responsible on the theory of vicarious liability if the administrator is found to be negligent.

NOTES

1. The following cases deal with the alleged liability of sports administrators and personnel in the area of medical assistance.
   (a) In *O'Brien v. Township High School District #214*, 392 N.E.2d 615 (Ill. 1979), plaintiff student-athlete brought a suit which alleged negligence by the school district for permitting an incompetent and untrained student to administer medical and surgical treatment, for failing to carry out treatment properly, and for failing to secure parental consent. On appeal, the court found that an educator's immunity under the Illinois School Code should not bar plaintiff's complaint. The court held that the treatment of injuries or medical conditions does not fall into the realm of action "necessary for the orderly conduct of schools and maintenance of a sound learning atmosphere" and as such was subject to ordinary negligence claims: "To hold school districts to an ordinary care standard in this area does not appear unduly burdensome." The court did affirm the trial court's opinion that the facts of the case did not represent a "reckless disregard for the safety of others" and thus did not constitute willful and wanton misconduct.
   (b) In *Cramer v. Hoffman*, 390 F.2d 19 (2nd Cir. 1968), plaintiff brought suit after being seriously injured while making a tackle during football practice. Plaintiff alleged that the cervical injuries and paralysis which he received were a consequence of negligence in moving him and in treatment. The action was brought against the university, the coach, and the treating physician. The plaintiff in his suit sought to hold the university liable for any negligence of the doctor under an agency theory. The trial judge ruled as a matter of law that the alleged negligence of the doctor could not be imputed to the university. The court held that the plaintiff failed to set forth any substantial facts to prove an agency relationship

between the doctor and the university. The court of appeals agreed and noted that under New York law an institution is not responsible for the negligence of physicians who are independent contractors exercising their own discretion.

2. Many states, including Massachusetts, require a physician or person trained in emergency medical care to be assigned to all interscholastic football games. See Mass. Gen. Laws Ann. ch. 112, § 54A and § 10.12-5(e). (See page 316.)

Failure to Provide Safe Equipment

The failure to provide equipment or the failure to provide satisfactory equipment has been the basis for a number of lawsuits brought against administrators, schools, and universities. The individuals who are involved with equipment vary from institution to institution. They include the coach, the teacher, an equipment manager, a business manager who purchases the equipment, an athletic director, and/or other administrators. All of these individuals are employees of the institution, and the institution may be responsible for their negligent acts under the theory of vicarious liability (see page 316).

Although many lawsuits filed against institutions regarding equipment have been unsuccessful, they at least indicate potential liability areas. The first consideration is the purchase of appropriate equipment for the athletic activities offered. The second consideration is the purchase of equipment that is of satisfactory quality. For example, with respect to football helmets, the institution should adhere to guidelines established by the National Operating Committee on Standards for Athletic Equipment (NOCSAE) (see Note 8 on page 394). The third consideration is the provision of equipment for the athletic activities in which equipment is necessary. For example, plaintiffs may allege that a defendant school or a school district was negligent in not providing equipment for a tackle football game. The fourth consideration is the provision of properly fitting equipment. For example, plaintiffs may allege that football equipment did not fit properly and that it was the proximate cause of the resulting injuries. The fifth and last consideration is the periodic inspection of the equipment and reconditioning when necessary. The NOCSAE guidelines will again be useful.

NOTE

1. The following cases deal with the liability of sports administrators and personnel in the area of equipment.

(a) In *Gerrity v. Beatty*, 373 N.E.2d 1323 (Ill. 1978), plaintiff alleged that the school district provided unsatisfactory equipment, which resulted in a severe injury. The plaintiff had complained about the ill-fitting equipment but no replacement equipment was provided. The court held the school district negligent for failing to ensure that equipment provided for student-athletes is fit for the purpose intended.

(b) In *Turner v. Caddo Parish School Board*, 214 So. 2d 153 (La. 1968), plaintiff spectator grandmother sued defendant school authorities for negligence when she was injured by a football player who intentionally ran out of bounds. The Louisiana Supreme Court, in reinstating the trial court's dismissal, held that defendant was not negligent in failing to anticipate spectators who do not know plays are often designed to carry the ball out of bounds. The court also held that defendant was not negligent in its failure to provide a barricade.

THE DEFENSE OF IMMUNITY

An *immunity* is a condition which protects against tort liability regardless of the circumstances. An immunity is to be distinguished from a *privilege,* which operates to excuse the commission of a tort under specific conditions. Sovereign immunity is the type of immunity most often encountered in a sports setting, although charitable immunity may, in some instances, be a consideration.

Sovereign Immunity

Historically, all states had sovereign immunity laws. Recently, however, some state courts and state legislatures have determined that the state can be sued in certain situations for certain activities. To determine if an entity is immune from legal recourse, one must first determine whether it is a governmental entity. Governmental entities may be federal, state, or local governments; municipalities; or any activity that is under the control of any of the aforementioned.

Certain public policy considerations underlie the establishment of sovereign immunity. One rationale is that public agencies have limited funds and should expend them only for public purposes. To allow an individual to sue a public entity unfairly restricts the amount of funds that should be devoted to the public welfare. Another rationale for sovereign immunity is the idea that the state can do no wrong. This is a vestige of the historical policy that a king could do no wrong and was the original basis for the establishment of sovereign immunity. Other reasons include the idea that the public cannot be held responsible for the torts of their government employees and that public bodies themselves have no authority to commit torts. Many believe that the aforementioned policy considerations are not compelling, and the trend in several jurisdictions is to repeal or limit the immunity granted to governments.

Sovereign immunity rests on the concept that a state must give consent to be sued. Most states have given such consent, either in the form of a statute which authorizes an individual to sue or by providing special courts and procedures to be followed when an instrumentality of the state is responsible for an injury (i.e., court of claims). These statutes are generally narrowly interpreted, but they have been extended to agencies related to but not part of the actual state government. Public high schools and high school athletic associations are usually included as part of the list of agencies whose traditional sovereign immunity may be eliminated by statutes of this kind.

In those states governed by a sovereign immunity statute, the distinction between governmental and proprietary activities presents an important legal issue. A *governmental activity* is one that can only be performed by the state and as such is commonly protected from lawsuits on the grounds of sovereign immunity. Education is a governmental activity. A *proprietary activity* is one that is done by the state but could be undertaken by the private sector and is therefore not given the protection of sovereign immunity. An example is when a town leases its facility to an outside organization for a rock concert.

In any lawsuit brought against a government entity, it must first be determined whether the activity on which the plaintiff's case against the state entity is based is a governmental or proprietary activity. If the activity is found to be a governmental one, the action brought by the plaintiff is automatically dismissed based on the sovereign immunity statute that protects the governmental body. A determination that the activity is proprietary in nature, however, permits continuation of the case and possible recovery of damages by the plaintiff. Naturally, then, in the initial stages of a case involving the state, the defendant commonly argues that the activity in question was governmental and the plaintiff claims it was proprietary.

The distinction between governmental and proprietary functions is very difficult to make. A sports facility may be conducting either a proprietary or a governmental function, depending on the circumstances in existence at any given time. In the case of a public school using its own sports facility, the courts have usually found that the holding of athletic contests is part of the educational function of the state and is therefore a governmental function protected by the sovereign immunity doctrine. If the facility is leased for use by the private sector, the courts have concluded that the school will be conducting a proprietary activity (by leasing) and will therefore be liable for injuries sustained as a result of the negligent maintenance or construction of the facility.

NOTES

1. The liability of sports administrators and personnel and the concept of sovereign immunity are discussed in *Cantwell v. University of Massachusetts*, 551 F.2d 879 (1st Cir. 1977). Plaintiff gymnast was hurt due to the negligence of an assistant coach. She sued the coach and the university. The district court dismissed the action against both the coach and university on the basis of sovereign immunity. The court of appeals agreed, except for stating that if the coach's act was misfeasance instead of nonfeasance, he would be subject to personal liability and sovereign immunity would not protect him.

2. Generally, liability of school districts and colleges for tortious acts or omissions of its officers, agents, or servants shall be determined according to the normal rules of tort law. Some states by statute have made their public agencies immune to suits in tort. See, for example, the following cases.

    (a) In *Clary v. Alexander County Board of Education*, 203 S.E.2d 820 (N.C. 1974), a North Carolina student who was injured when he crashed into glass panel doors placed at the end of a basketball court was denied any recovery for his injuries. The doors did not have safety glass, and as evidence of the unsafe structure, there was shown to have been several previous collisions with the doors. However, the court found statutory immunity and stated that the purchase of liability insurance was not enough to abrogate the immunity.

    (b) In *Zawadzki v. Taylor*, 246 N.W.2d 161 (Mich. 1976), the court denied recovery to a student who sustained eye injuries when struck by a tennis ball in physical education class. The court reasoned that the school district was protected by a statute granting immunity from tort liability for government agencies.

    (c) In *Holzer v. Oakland University Academy of Dramatic Arts*, 313 N.W.2d 124 (Mich. 1981), plaintiff brought suit against the university seeking to recover damages based on an injury sustained while attempting to perform an exercise in a "movement" class. The Oakland County Circuit Court entered a summary judgment for the defendant. On appeal it was held that the operation of a state university was a governmental function immune from tort liability.

3. The liability of a school district will not be sustained in the absence of a statute imposing such liability. See, for instance, *Perkins v. Trask*, 23 P.2d 982 (Mont. 1933). Plaintiff parent sued defendant school district for negligence in the drowning of her son in defendant's swimming pool. In affirming the trial court's dismissal, the Montana Supreme Court held

that school districts are not liable for injuries caused by negligence of officers, agents, or employees unless liability is imposed by statute.

4. Sovereign immunity, even if not expressly abrogated, will not protect a state from all liability. See, for instance, *Johnson v. Municipal University of Omaha*, 187 N.W.2d 102 (Neb. 1971). Plaintiff, a pole vaulter, brought this personal injury action against Municipal University of Omaha to recover damages for injuries he sustained while attempting a vault during a track meet in the university's stadium. Plaintiff had landed during a vault on one of the wooden boxes used to support the uprights. The uprights hold the crossbar which measures the height of the vault. The Nebraska Supreme Court affirmed the trial court's decision and held that where a reasonable person would perceive an act to involve risk of harm to another, such risk will be negligent and unreasonable only when the risk is so great it outweighs the utility of the act or the manner in which it is performed. The court found that the wooden boxes used by the university to hold the uprights served a useful purpose in that they expedited the event, made officiating easier, and did not restrict the level of the crossbar to a maximum height of 15 feet.

5. A school will not be liable if its exercise of a governmental function causes any injury. See, for instance, *Rhoades v. School District #9*, 142 P.2d 890 (Mont. 1943). Plaintiff, a visiting spectator at defendant school's basketball game, sought recovery for injuries sustained when an improperly maintained stairway collapsed. In ruling in favor of the school district, the Montana Supreme Court held that the school district was exercising a "government function" so that it could not be held liable. See also, *Fetzer v. Minor Park District*, 138 N.W.2d 601 (N.D. 1965).

6. When a school district is immune as a governmental agency, its employees will avoid liability if they are performing discretionary duties. See, for instance, *Hall v. Columbus Board of Education*, 290 N.E.2d 580 (Ohio App. 1972). Plaintiff elementary school student sought recovery from the board of education and school officials for an injury sustained in a fall from a sliding board on the school playground. In ruling in favor of the board of education, the court of appeals held that the board of education was immune as a governmental agency of the state and that school officials were not liable for torts committed by them in performance of duties involving judgment and discretion.

7. Immunity for a school board will not guarantee immunity for individuals. See, for example, *Short v. Griffiths*, 255 S.E.2d 479 (Va. 1979). Plaintiff sued the school board, athletic director, baseball coach, and buildings and grounds supervisor for injuries sustained by falling on broken glass while running laps around the school's outdoor track facility. The court held that the athletic director and the buildings and grounds supervisor were not entitled to immunity, even though their employer (school board) had immunity. The court reasoned that the employees of a local government agency should be answerable for their own acts of simple negligence, even though they are engaged in working for an immune employer, because to hold otherwise would be to unacceptably widen the role of sovereign immunity.

8. For a case in which the court found no liability for a sports

administrator's discretionary decision, see *Brown v. Wichita State University*, 547 P.2d 1015 (Kan. 1976). Plaintiffs sought to recover as third-party beneficiaries after a charter airplane carrying the school football team crashed. The Kansas Supreme Court made the distinction between a governmental function and proprietary function and held the team a commercial activity. The court found it to be a proprietary function and held the action could be maintained. See also, *Shriver v. Athletic Commission of Kansas State University*, 222 Kan. 216 (1977).

9. The availability of insurance will not eliminate immunity as a defense. See, for example, the following cases.

(a) In *Weinstein v. Evanston Township Community*, 40 Ill. App. 3d 6, 351 N.E.2d 236 (Ill. App. 1976), the court held that the purchase of liability insurance did not waive general immunity of the school district, and no damages were awarded to a junior high school student who was injured while exercising on the parallel bars.

(b) In *Merrill v. Birhanzel*, 310 N.W.2d 522 (S.D. 1981), plaintiff sued the teacher who was in charge of a required wrestling class at the time of plaintiff's injury. During the match, the plaintiff was thrown to the ground and his left ankle was broken. The court failed to find any grounds for the district to be sued given its sovereign immunity. It noted that the "authority to purchase, and the purchase of liability insurance does not provide that permission. . . . We have consistently held that if there is to be a departure from the immunity rule, the policy must be declared and the extent of liability fixed by the legislature."

Charitable Immunity

Charitable immunity was developed to limit the liabilities of charitable organizations. The justifications for applying the charitable immunity laws are based on the following reasons:

1. Donations to charitable organizations constitute a trust fund which may not be used for an unintended purpose.
2. No profits have been accumulated, so the doctrine of vicarious liability cannot apply.
3. Charities perform governmental or public duties and therefore should be immune.
4. The overall good of a charity is protected by not diverting its money to pay damage claims.

The doctrine of charitable immunity, similar to sovereign immunity, has been eliminated in many jurisdictions.

NOTE

1. The following cases discuss the liability of sports administrators and personnel and the concept of charitable immunity.

(a) In *Southern Methodist University v. Clayton*, 142 Tex. 179, 176 S.W.2d 749 (1943), plaintiff spectator sought recovery from Southern Methodist University (SMU) for injuries sustained when a temporary bleacher collapsed during the SMU-Texas A&M football game in 1940. The court held that SMU, a charitable institution, is immune from liability for torts of its agents unless the injured party is an employee of the charity. The Supreme Court of Texas reasoned, in affirming a trial court decision: "It is better for the individual to suffer injury without compensation than for the public to be deprived of the benefit of the charity."

(b) In *Pomeroy v. Little League Baseball of Collingswood*, 362 A.2d 39 (Super. N.J. 1976), plaintiff spectator at a Little League game sought to recover for injuries sustained when a bleacher collapsed. In affirming judgment for the defendant, the court held that the league had been established for purely educational purposes—that is, to build character and sportsmanship—and that the charitable immunity statute prevented the plaintiff from recovery from the defendant.

Civil Liability Immunity Legislation

Increasingly, and for a number of reasons, governmental bodies have seen a need to institute regulations that govern certain aspects of sports. An area that has undergone particular legislative scrutiny is liability for sports coaches, administrators, and officials, especially in regards to youth sports organizations. Legislation has been proposed on both the federal and state levels of government and has been enacted in New Jersey, Pennsylvania, and Delaware.

Proponents of civil liability immunity legislation contend that it is needed because of a proliferation of civil lawsuits that threaten to force many of those involved in sports, especially volunteers, from participating in sports organizations. It is reasoned that coaches and managers of youth sport organizations and other like groups cannot carry out their roles without fear of being sued for damages. For instance, during consideration of the New Jersey legislation, the most frequently cited case involving Little League lawsuits was a complaint filed by a Camden County mother against the Runnemede Youth Athletic Association seeking $750,000 in damages after her son misjudged a fly ball and was struck in the eye. The mother had claimed that her son usually played second base but was put in the outfield, a position for which he was not properly trained. After the case was settled out of court for $25,000, the league encountered problems obtaining insurance.

In response to the liability crisis facing youth sports, a Youth Sports Volunteer Coalition (YSVC) was established. It is composed of some 22 amateur organizations, including Little League Baseball, Pop Warner Football, and the United States Olympic Committee. The coalition notes:

> Each year millions of volunteers, mostly mothers and fathers who consider youth athletic activity as a vehicle for family togetherness and development, give freely of their time to provide wholesome recreational programs for our nation's youth. Much of what is good in our country is the result of volunteerism. To let the volunteer element of our society erode or be eliminated by frivolous lawsuits would be a grave injustice to the present and future generations.

The YSVC particularly favors legislation such as the Nonprofit Sports Liability Limitation Act (H.R. 3756), which was first introduced in Congress on November 13, 1985, by Congressman George Gekas (R. Penn.). The legislation's purpose, as noted in H.R. 3756, is "to limit the civil liability of certain persons associated with nonprofit sports programs." H.R. 3756 specifically proposed:

> Sec. 2. Limitation on Liability of Nonprofit Sports Programs
> (a) Uncompensated Qualified Staff—Any person who renders services without compensation as a member of the qualified staff of a nonprofit sports program shall not be liable under the laws of the United States or of any State for civil damages resulting from any negligent act or omission of such qualified member occurring in the performance of any duty of such qualified member.
> (b) Sponsors and Operators—Any person who sponsors or operates a nonprofit sports program shall not be liable under the laws of the United States or of any State for civil damages resulting from any negligent act or omission—
>> (1) of any person who renders services without compensation as a member of the qualified staff of a nonprofit sports program; and
>> (2) occurring in the performance of any duty of such qualified member.

For the purpose of the legislation, H.R. 3756 defined a "nonprofit sports program" as

> any program (whether or not it is registered with or recognized by any State or any political subdivision of any State)—
> (A) that is in a competitive sport formally recognized as a sport, on the date the cause of action to which this Act applies arises, by the Amateur Athletic Union or the National Collegiate Athletic Association;
> (B) that is organized for recreational purposes and whose activities are substantially for such purposes; and

(C) no part of whose net earnings inures to the benefit of any private person.

The YSVC made these comments about the Gekas bill:

> The Youth Sports Volunteer Coalition, an organization of nonprofit youth sports programs, has come together to focus national attention on this critical liability problem and to generate support for legislative reform as stated in House Bill 3756, the "Nonprofit Sports Liability Limitation Act." For this bill to become law, and allow volunteerism to remain a steady and positive influence on our nation's youth, we need your support. Millions of kids are counting on us.

NOTES _____

1. For further information about government's increasing regulation of sports in the United States, see Johnson and Frey, *Government and Sport: The Public Policy Issues* (Totowa, N.J.: Rowman and Allanheld Publishers, 1985).

2. For further information about civil liability of volunteer coaches, contact the Youth Sports Volunteer Coalition, P.O. Box 3485, Williamsport, Pennsylvania 17701.

3. The following states enacted legislation to deal with the civil liability immunity crisis for those involved in sports:

(a) The State of New Jersey enacted Senate Bill No. 1678 in 1986 to provide immunity for volunteer athletic coaches and officials. The legislation stated in part:

> 1.a. Notwithstanding any provisions of law to the contrary, no person who provides services or assistance free of charge, except for reimbursement of expenses, as an athletic coach, manager, or official for a sports team which is organized or performing pursuant to a nonprofit or similar charter shall be liable in any civil action for damages to a player or participant as a result of his acts of commission or omission arising out of and in the course of his rendering that service or assistance.
>
> b. The provisions of subsection a. of this section shall apply not only to organized sports competitions, but shall also apply to practice and instruction in that sport.
>
> c. Nothing in this section shall be deemed to grant immunity to any person causing damage by his willful, wanton, or grossly negligent act of commission or omission, nor to any coach, manager, or official who has not participated in a safety orientation and training program established by the league or team with which he is affiliated.
>
> d. Nothing in this section shall be deemed to grant immunity to any person causing damage as the result of his negligent operation of a motor vehicle.

(b) The state of Pennsylvania enacted House Bill No. 1625 in 1986. The legislation, which provided a negligence standard in the conduct of certain sports programs, stated in part:

Sec. 8332.1. Manager, Coach, Umpire or Referee and Nonprofit As-
        sociation Negligence Standard
        (a) General rule—Except as provided otherwise in this sec-
        tion, no person who, without compensation and as a volunteer,
        renders services as a manager, coach, instructor, umpire or
        referee or who, without compensation and as a volunteer,
        assists a manager, coach, instructor, umpire or referee in a
        sports program of a nonprofit association, and no nonprofit
        association, or any officer or employee thereof, conducting or
        sponsoring a sports program, shall be liable to any person for
        any civil damages as a result of any acts or omissions in
        rendering such services or in conducting or sponsoring such
        sports program unless the conduct of such person or nonprofit
        association falls substantially below the standards generally
        practiced and accepted in like circumstances by similar persons
        or similar nonprofit associations rendering such services or
        conducting or sponsoring such sports programs and unless it is
        shown that such person or nonprofit association did an act or
        omitted the doing of an act which such person or nonprofit
        association was under a recognized duty to another to do,
        knowing or having reason to know that such act or omission
        created a substantial risk of actual harm to the person or
        property of another. It shall be insufficient to impose liability
        to establish only that the conduct of such person or nonprofit
        association fell below ordinary standards of care.
        (b) Exceptions—
            (1) Nothing in this section shall be construed as affecting
            or modifying the liability of such person or nonprofit asso-
            ciation for any of the following:
                (i) Acts or omissions relating to the transportation of
                participants in a sports program or others to or from a
                game, event or practice.
                (ii) Acts or omissions relating to the care and mainte-
                nance of real estate unrelated to the practice or playing
                areas which such persons or nonprofit associations own,
                possess or control.

(c) The state of Delaware enacted House Bill No. 411 in 1986, which
related to exemptions from civil liability of certain persons associated with nonprofit sports programs. The legislation stated in part:

Sec. 6836. Limitation on Liability of Non-profit Programs
        (a) Uncompensated qualified staff—Any person who renders
        services without compensation as a member of the qualified staff
        of a non-profit sports program shall not be liable under the laws
        of this State for civil damages resulting from any negligent act or
        omission of such qualified member occurring in the performance
        of any duty of such qualified member.
        (b) Sponsors and operators—Any person who sponsors or oper-
        ates a non-profit sports program shall not be liable under the laws
        of this State for civil damages resulting from any negligent act or
        omission:
(1) of any person who renders services without compensation as a
member of the qualified staff of a non-profit sports program; and
(2) occurring in the performance of any duty of such qualified member.

LIABILITY OF FACILITY OWNERS AND POSSESSORS

The duty that the owner or possessor of a facility owes varies, depending on the characterization of the party who was injured while on the premises. To establish a duty for owners, operators, supervisors, or possessors of land, the status of the person injured must be determined. Generally, there are two classes of persons: licensees and invitees. A *licensee* is one who enters the property of another, with the owner's consent, for the licensee's own purposes. The occupier of the property owes only a duty of ordinary care. There is no obligation to inspect the area to discover dangers currently unknown, or to warn of conditions which should be obvious to the licensee. The occupier of the property owes a licensee a duty to warn only when a risk is known or should have been known under the reasonable person standard, which the licensee is unaware of.

An *invitee* is owed a greater degree of care by the owner, operator, supervisor, or occupier of the property. There is an affirmative duty to be free from known defects as well as from defects which should have been discovered by the exercise of reasonable care. The basis of liability is the implied representation at the time of the invitation that the premises are safe to enter. The invitation does not have to be extended personally for an individual to be classified as an invitee. The invitation implies that reasonable care has been exercised for the safety of the invitees. The owner or possessor of the property is not, however, an insurer of the safety of the invitees. That is, the owner does not guarantee safety under all possible circumstances. Instead, the owner or possessor must only exercise reasonable care for the invitees' protection.

The distinction between licensee and invitee is important because the different standards of care that may be applied can be decisive in determining the outcome of a lawsuit. An athlete or a spectator at a sports event is characterized as a business invitee. A *business invitee* is a visitor who brings a monetary benefit to the person in possession of the property. The business invitee is also a person whom the possessor encourages to enter onto the property. By such encouragement the possessor implicitly represents that the premises are safe to enter.

The distinction between patent and latent defects is also important in any discussion of the liability of owners and possessors of sports facilities. Both types of defects are potentially injury causing, but an owner or operator cannot be held liable for undiscovered and undiscoverable defects.

A *patent defect* is one that is plainly visible or that could easily be discovered upon inspection. A facility owner or a lessee is liable for obvious defects, such as old debris on steps that create a hazard, if they cause an injury. A *latent defect* is a hidden or concealed defect that could not be discovered by reasonable inspection. It is a defect of which the owner has no knowledge, or of which, in the exercise of reasonable care, the owner should not have knowledge. Owners and lessees are generally not liable for injuries caused by latent defects.

In the eyes of the law, when a facility is leased, it is, in effect, sold for a period of time. Thus, the lessee—the person taking control of the property—assumes the responsibilities of the lessor—the person giving up control of the property—toward those who enter the property. The lessor still has a duty, however, to disclose any concealed or dangerous conditions—any latent defects—to lessees, their guests, and others reasonably expected to be on the premises. For this duty to attach, the lessor does not have to believe that the condition is dangerous or to have definite knowledge of the defect. Instead, it is sufficient that the lessor be informed of facts from which a reasonable person would conclude that there is a possible danger. The lessor has no duty to warn about patent defects, which are defined as known, open, or obvious conditions. When a property is leased for a purpose that includes admission to the public, the lessor has an affirmative duty to exercise reasonable care to inspect and repair the leased property. This duty is imposed to prevent an unreasonable risk to the public. Liability will extend only to parts of the premises open to the public and to invitees who enter for the purpose for which the place was leased.

Facility owners and possessors have a duty to exercise reasonable care in maintaining the premises and in supervising the conduct of others at the facility. They are, however, entitled to assume that participants will obey the rules and that employees will not be negligent, absent notice to the contrary. Thus, their duty does not include protecting consumers from unreasonable risks. An unreasonable risk is one such that the probability of injury outweighs the burden of taking adequate precautions (see page 298).

The general rule is that facility owners and possessors are liable for conditions on their premises which cause physical harm if they know or should reasonably have known about the existence of the dangerous condition when such a condition poses an unreasonable risk to an invitee. The requirement of reasonable care is supported by the assumption that a spectator or a participant assumes all the ordinary and inherent risks of the particular sport (see page 313). These inherent risks are those commonly associated with the sport in question. The application of this common knowledge rule will depend on the circumstances. No invitee, whether a player or a spectator, assumes the risk that an owner will fail to meet his duty of reasonable care.

A facility owner and possessor's duty of reasonable care can be divided into three areas. First is the duty to protect invitees from injurious or defective products. An owner and possessor must exercise reasonable care in the selection of equipment necessary for the operation of the facility. Second, owners and possessors must exercise reasonable care in the maintenance of the facility itself and any equipment in the facility. Standards of safety, suitability, and sanitation must be maintained. In addition, if an invitee uses any of the equipment and the facility owner or possessor supervises, then the facility owner or possessor is held to a standard of reasonable care. Third, an owner and possessor must guard against foreseeable harmful risks caused by other invitees. A breach of any of these duties may subject a facility owner or operator to liability for negligence.

Promoters and other sports event organizers often use the facility only for a day or a few days. They do not own the facility, and they are not in a long-term lease situation; therefore, they cannot be considered a permanent tenant. Some examples are a boxing match, the Harlem Globetrotters, and the Ice Capades. The promoter owes a duty of reasonable care in the maintenance and supervision of the facility. With respect to maintenance, the owner is more likely to be responsible for patent defects that go uncorrected. With respect to supervision, the promoter is responsible for reasonable care in the running of the event, although the determination of reasonable care may differ depending on the type of event. For example, the amount and type of security may differ for a family event as opposed to a rock concert. The promoter, however, is not responsible for unique or unforeseeable events causing injury in the absence of notice that an injury is apt to occur. Therefore, courts have often refused to find liability for patrons' injuries caused by other spectators. Promoters are only required to exercise reasonable precautions. However, to protect themselves in the event that an invitee is successful in a claim against a promoter, facility owners or possessors may require a promoter to execute a lease agreement (see Exhibit 3–6 on page 78). An agreement will usually require the promoter to obtain general liability insurance and agree to indemnify and hold harmless the facility owner or possessor.

Owners of facilities that allow alcoholic drinks to be consumed at athletic events have instituted some of the following procedures:

- To purchase beer, customers must go to the concession stand. Beer vendors no longer are allowed to sell beer to customers in their seats. In addition, low-alcohol (3.2 beer) and no-alcohol beer are offered for sale.

- At football games, the sale of beer is discontinued at the beginning of the third quarter.
- The largest capacity beer sold is 20 ounces, instead of the 32-ounce "big beers."
- Season ticket holders can lose their ticket rights for subsequent seasons if they become involved in fights or other such rowdy behavior.
- No-alcohol seating sections are designated.

Generally, a facility operator is not responsible for all injuries that occur at its stadium or arena; it only needs to take reasonable precautions. Control of alcoholic beverage sales in the facility, limiting or supervising the practice of tailgating in pregame and postgame situations, and ensuring that security is present inside and outside the facility would seem to address these concerns. At a minimum, sponsored activities require some type of increased safety measures, especially if there have been incidents of rowdiness or other disruptive behavior in the past. If such measures are undertaken, liability should be greatly reduced.

Another potential problem area for facility owners is tailgating, which has become a standard component of the traditional college football weekend. In fact, many colleges and universities have actively promoted the concept, seeking to capitalize on its popularity to market their intercollegiate athletic programs. In most cases, tailgating is a harmless afternoon's pleasure for fans, but on occasion it can lead to excessive drinking and rowdy behavior. It is this aspect of tailgating that must concern facility administrators.

In general, the last few years have seen an increasing concern by society about excessive drinking and its impact on public safety. Some states have acted on these concerns by raising the drinking age and eliminating "happy hours," and in addition there have been toughening attitudes by the judiciary to alcohol-related crimes.

Sports administrators have also been concerned about drinking at intercollegiate events. The National Collegiate Athletic Association has long banned the sale of alcoholic beverages at NCAA tournaments and postseason championship events, and many campuses have policies that limit consumption of alcoholic beverages at on-campus athletic events. The University of Massachusetts at Amherst, for example, banned pregame "keg" parties in the stadium parking lot beginning with the 1984 football season.

As a general summary, the following checklist will help facility owners protect themselves against possible litigation:

1. Anticipate any potentially injurious situations in the facility (stadium, arena, pool, etc.) or event site (baseball field, soccer field, etc.).
2. Insure that the facility is adequately maintained, and perform regular inspections (with written reports) on the condition of the facility.
3. In designing a facility, make safety a top concern of the architects and planning committee. Insure that safe materials are used throughout the facility (glass, padding, mats, etc.).
4. Designate an individual on the staff to serve as the safety expert.
5. Develop a clear, written policy concerning safety in the facility, institute a reporting procedure for potential problems, and document any mishaps in detail.
6. Develop policies for alcoholic consumption at the facility.

NOTES

1. The following lawsuits were brought against facility owners and possessors by participants.

(a) In *Kaiser v. State*, 55 Misc. 2d 576 N.Y.S. (1967), plaintiff bobsledders sought recovery for injuries sustained when their bobsled crashed on the state's bobsled run. In granting summary judgment for the plaintiffs, the court of claims held that evidence established that the state was negligent in failing to close the run, even though it had actual notice of a gash in the wall in sufficient time to suspend operation before bobsledders were injured.

(b) In *Praetorius v. Shell Oil Co.*, 207 So. 2d 872 (La. Ct. App. 1968), plaintiff baseball player sought recovery from a defendant baseball field owner for injuries sustained when he stepped into a hole while running from home to first. In reversing the trial court's judgment for the plaintiff, the court of appeals held that the defendants were not negligent in failing to properly maintain the area in the batter's box where small holes and depressions were dug by batters' cleats during the course of a softball game.

(c) In *Ardoin v. Evangeline Parish School Board*, 376 So. 2d 372 (La. 1979), plaintiff student, while playing softball during a physical education class at his elementary school, tripped over a 12-inch square piece of concrete embedded in the base path between second and third base. His father brought a negligence suit against the school, alleging that the concrete slab, which protruded at least half an inch above ground, constituted such a hazardous condition that it was a breach of the required standard of care on the part of the school board to fail to remove it from the playing field. The school district argued that no evidence had been presented that it had actual knowledge of the concrete slab. In affirming the trial court's finding of negligence on the part of the school authorities, the appeals court held that the school board had constructive knowledge of the hazardous condition since it should have anticipated and discovered the potential danger and eliminated it before allowing students to use the field during physical education classes.

(d) In *Sykes v. Bensinger Recreation Corp.*, 117 F.2d 964 (7th Cir. 1941), plaintiff bowler sought recovery under the Wisconsin "safe place" statute for injuries sustained as a result of catching his foot in a 2-inch space between the floor of the alley and the bottom of a return, through which he slipped and fell on the alley. In reversing judgment for the plaintiff, the court of appeals held that a proprietor is not an insurer of bowlers' safety and that the mere fact that such an accident happened does not prove the place was not safe. "Safe" is a relative term, and what is safe depends on the facts and conditions of each case.

(e) In *Clary v. Alexander County Board of Education*, 199 S.E.2d 738 (N.C. 1973), plaintiff senior student on a high school basketball team brought suit after suffering severe lacerations when he collided with some glass panels along one wall of the gymnasium while running wind sprints. Plaintiff alleged negligence on the part of the school board for permitting breakable glass to be used in the gym and in permitting the coaches to direct the players to run wind sprints toward the glass panels. An appeals court affirmed a trial court decision and held that the evidence indicated the plaintiff was contributorily negligent and affirmed the decision. The court reasoned that the plaintiff had run similar wind sprints in the gym during his three previous years in the basketball program. "Yet he chose to run at the panel at full speed without slowing down until he was within three feet of the glass. Anyone [doing such] . . . would be compelled by his momentum to crash into the wall and suffer injury." Plaintiff contended he was excused from contributory negligence because he was acting under the instructions of his coach. The appeals court disagreed and held that a reasonable person disregards orders when compliance with such orders could result in injury.

(f) In *Friedman v. State*, 282 N.Y.S.2d 858 (Ct. Claims 1967), plaintiff skier sought recovery for injuries sustained in a fall from an aerial ski lift at a ski center owned by the state. In granting judgment for the plaintiff, the court of claims held that the state was negligent in its placement of signs relating to the time of chair lift operation, size of signs, and failure to use a loudspeaker to announce that the lift was closed for the night and that such negligence was the proximate cause of injuries sustained when the plaintiff fell from the lift after it had stopped for the night while she was descending.

(g) In *Ragni v. Lincoln-Devon Bounceland, Inc.*, 234 N.E.2d 168 (Ill. App. 1968), plaintiff trampoline user sought recovery for injuries sustained in landing on the frame of defendant's trampoline. In affirming a lower court verdict, the appellate court held that owner had no duty to warn plaintiff, who had received instruction on indoor trampolines in college, that the mat in the middle of the trampoline was the only safe place to land.

(h) In *Maddox v. City of New York, et al.*, 455 N.Y.S.2d 102 (1982), 467 N.Y.S.2d 972, 121 Misc. 2d 358 (1983), 487 N.Y.S.2d 354 (Sup. Ct. 1985), a former New York Yankee center fielder brought suit against the owner, maintenance company, and designer of Shea Stadium for an injury that occurred when he slipped on the wet field in Shea Stadium. In ruling for the plaintiff on defendant's motion for a summary judgment, the court found that Maddox did not assume the risk of playing on a dangerous field in that, as an employee, he was under the orders of his superiors. The appeals court reversed the lower court decision and held (1) that the doctrine of assumption of risk completely barred recovery; (2) that a professional baseball player did not fall within protected individuals under the statute governing general duty of the employer to protect health and safety of employees; (3) that even if eligible under the statute, the ballplayer failed to allege any fault by employer which resulted in the wet condition of the playing field; and (4) that player was not acting within the confines of the superior's instructions when he was injured.

(i) In *Eddy v. Syracuse University*, 433 N.Y.S.2d 923 (1980), plaintiff sought recovery for injuries he received during a frisbee game. Plaintiff was an "ultimate frisbee" player for a team of college students. In March 1977, the team traveled to Syracuse University to play against a group of Syracuse students, although the latter team was neither officially recognized nor sponsored by the defendant. During the course of an "ultimate frisbee" game played in the basketball gymnasium, the plaintiff crashed through a glass window in one door, severely lacerating his arm. The plaintiff sued the university for negligence in a personal injury action. The defendant argued that since it did not authorize use of the gym, had no foreknowledge of plaintiff's use, could not have foreseen that students would use the basketball courts for an "ultimate frisbee" game, and that the gym was not defective in design or construction for its ordinary purposes, there was lack of evidence to even submit the issue of negligence. The trial court ruled for the plaintiff. In affirming the trial court verdict, the appeals court held: "Surely the jury could have concluded that . . . on the campus of a large university . . . some of its students, and their guests, might use the facility without express permission . . . (in novel games)." Also properly left to the jury were the questions of whether the glass doors, located as they were in a building intended to be used for strenuous physical activity, constituted a dangerous condition and whether the risk presented by the glass doors could have been alleviated without imposing an undue burden on the university.

(j) In *Graver v. State of New York*, 181 N.Y.S.2d 994 (1959), plaintiff sought recovery for personal injuries sustained when the chair he was to sit in on the lift at Belleayre State Park swung or was tipped such that it struck the back of his right leg, fracturing it. The trial court found the evidence sufficient, based on the doctrine of res ipsa loquitur, to establish that the state was negligent in permitting the accident to happen. The court found that the sate was a common carrier in the operation of the chair lift, stating that "the degree of care to be exercised should be commensurate with the danger to be avoided."

2. The following lawsuits involved actions of other spectators, and were brought against facility owners and possessors by spectators.

(a) In *Weldy v. Oakland H.S. District*, 65 P.2d 851 (Cal. App. 1937), plaintiff, a spectator at a football game supervised by agents of defendant school district, sued for negligence for injuries sustained when struck by a bottle thrown by a fellow student. The appeals court held that the plaintiff had failed to state a cause of action. The complaint did not allege that defendant should have foreseen the rowdyism of the student nor that the defendant's servants were responsible for some act or omission amounting to negligence.

(b) In *Porter v. California Jockey Club*, 285 P.2d 60 (Cal. App. 1955), plaintiff, a race track spectator, sought recovery from defendant track operator for injuries sustained when she was violently knocked down by another spectator. The appeals court, in ruling for the defendant, held that in absence of facts which would reasonably put defendant on notice that one spectator would run violently into another so as to put the duty on defendant to guard against it, there was no question of negligence.

(c) In *Townsley v. Cincinnati Gardens, Inc.*, 314 N.E.2d 409 (Ohio App. 1974), plaintiff, a minor, brought suit after being assaulted in a washroom by a group of boys while he was attending a Harlem Globetrotters exhibition at Cincinnati Gardens. The plaintiff, as a business invitee of the facility owner, sought damages for negligence on the part of the facility. The trial court held for the plaintiff, stating that "the defendant either knew, or, in the exercise of ordinary care, should have known of the danger which victimized the plaintiff." On an appeal, the decision of the trial court was reversed. The appeals court ruled that there was no evidence to indicate that the defendant could have anticipated, or reasonably have known of, the danger to the plaintiff.

(d) In *Berman v. University of Notre Dame*, 453 N.E.2d 1196 (Ind. App. 1983), plaintiff sued the University of Notre Dame for injuries she suffered as she left a Notre Dame home football game. The injury occurred in the stadium's parking lot when a third party, who was tailgating and became involved in a fight, fell onto the plaintiff and broke her leg. Plaintiff claimed that the school had "a duty to protect her from injury caused by the acts of other persons on the premises" since she was a business invitee. The university argued that it could not be held liable for the act of a third person since it had no knowledge or notice of any danger to the woman. The Court of Appeals of Indiana, Third District, noted that the issue involved two different factors: An operator of a place of public entertainment generally "owes a duty to keep the premises safe for its invitees";

on the other hand, "an invitor is not the insurer of invitee's safety and before liability may be imposed on invitor, it must have actual or constructive knowledge of the danger." The court reasoned that Notre Dame was aware of the tailgate parties in the parking areas around the stadium and the fact that drinking occurs. It recognized that while Notre Dame did not have particular knowledge of any danger for the plaintiff, it was aware that intoxicated people pose a threat to the safety of patrons at the games. The appeals courts therefore reversed the lower court's decision and held that Notre Dame had a duty to do all it could reasonably do to protect those people who attend the games from injury inflicted by the acts of third parties.

(e) In *Whitfield v. Cox*, 52 S.E.2d 72 (Va. 1949), plaintiff spectator, at defendant promoter's wrestling match, sought recovery in negligence for injuries sustained when she was struck by a whiskey bottle thrown by another spectator. The supreme court of appeals held that defendant was not required to search patrons for objects which could be used to injure other patrons.

(f) In *Philpot v. Brooklyn Nat'l League Baseball Club*, 100 N.E.2d 164 (N.Y. 1951), plaintiff spectator sought recovery for injuries sustained when she was struck by a broken bottle in defendant's ballpark. In reversing judgment for defendants, the court of appeals held that whether defendant provided a sufficient means of protecting plaintiff from reasonably foreseeable risk of harm from a bottle where no waste receptacles were provided and where the park seats were slanted so as to allow bottles to spill, was a question for the jury to decide.

3. The following lawsuits involving actions of participants were brought against facility owners and possessors by spectators.

(a) In *Wiersma v. Long Beach*, 106 P.2d 45 (Cal. App. 1940), plaintiff, who purchased a ticket to watch a wrestling match held in defendant's municipal auditorium, sought recovery for injuries sustained when one of the wrestlers deliberately hit him with a chair. The district court of appeals held that, since the city had leased the auditorium to a promoter, it was not responsible to the plaintiff for the misconduct of its tenant.

(b) In *Silvia v. Woodhouse*, 248 N.E.2d 260 (Mass. 1960), plaintiff wrestling spectator sought recovery for injuries sustained when wrestler, who had been ejected from the ring, was knocked back into him while trying to reenter. The supreme judicial court held that the defendant, who had seen such jostling before, was negligent in either failing to warn patrons or for failing to move seats back to a safer distance.

(c) In *Perry v. Seattle School District*, 405 P.2d 589 (Wash. 1965), plaintiff spectator sued defendant school district for negligence when she was injured by a football player who was pushed out of bounds over her. The Supreme Court of Washington held that, even though defendant did not charge admission and could have roped off the area, it was not negligent; the court believed that reasonable care had been exercised to provide for the safety of spectators.

(d) In *Turner v. Caddo Parish School Board*, 214 So. 2d 153 (La. 1968), plaintiff spectator grandmother sued defendant school authorities in negligence when she was run down on a football play that was intended to carry the ball out of bounds. The Louisiana Supreme Court held that defendant was not negligent in failing to anticipate spectators who did not know that plays are often carried out of bounds or for failing to have a barricade.

(e) In *Rich v. Madison Square Garden*, 266 N.Y.S. 288 (Sup. Ct. 1933), plaintiff spectator sought recovery for injuries sustained when struck by a hockey stick during a game at defendant's rink. The trial court held that the defendant was not required to foresee that a hockey stick would fly into the stands and was therefore not liable for failure to have constructed protective screens.

(f) In *Ramsey v. Kallio*, 62 So. 2d 146 (La. 1952), plaintiff spectators sought recovery from the operator of a wrestling arena for damages incurred when a wrestler jumped out of the ring and assaulted them. The court of appeals held that the operator had no reason to expect that the wrestler would jump from the ring and assault spectators and therefore was not liable.

(g) *Ratcliff v. San Diego Baseball Club of the Pacific Coast League*, 81 P.2d 625 (Cal. App. 1938), was an action for injuries sustained when a bat slipped out of baseball player's hands and flew into the stands. The district court of appeals held that, while screens for all seats are not required, those in charge of professional baseball games are required to exercise ordinary care to protect patrons from injuries, and the question of whether the defendant exercised such care where plaintiff was struck with a bat in the aisle on the way to a seat was for a jury to decide.

(h) In *Iervolino v. Pittsburgh Athletic Co.*, 243 A.2d 490 (Super. Pa. 1968), plaintiff spectator sought recovery for injuries sustained after being struck by a foul ball. In reversing the trial court's judgment for the plaintiff, the superior court held that, in absence of proof that the operator of game had deviated from ordinary standards in erection or maintenance of the ballpark, it was an error to permit a jury to determine what safety measures, if any, the operator should have taken for protection of its customers and that plaintiff assumed the risk of injury from foul balls.

(i) In *Guttenplan v. Boston Professional Hockey Ass'n, Inc.*, No. 80-415 (S.D.N.Y. 1981), four hockey fans sued nine individual Boston Bruin hockey players, the Bruins, the New York Rangers, Madison Square Garden, Inc., the National Hockey League, and the city of New York for $7 million in damages for injuries suffered when a players' brawl on the ice spilled over into the stands in December 1979. The suit charged that the plaintiffs were "stomped" by the Bruins players while league and arena security personnel "merely observed and made no attempt to prevent or stop" the altercation. Criminal charges against individual Bruin players were dropped due to conflicting evidence and testimony that indicated fans had provoked the players. A federal judge dismissed the civil damage suit on jurisdictional grounds.

(j) In *Duffy v. Midlothian Country Club, et al.*, No. 75 L 12096, Cook County Circuit Court (1982), plaintiff spectator sought recovery after being struck by a golf ball at the 1972 Western Open and losing an eye. She was standing in the rough between the first and 18th holes, watching play on the first hole. She was hit by a golfer playing the 18th hole, 200 to 250 yards away. Duffy was found 10 percent at fault when her negligence was compared to the tournament sponsors, but was awarded compensation. The court barred the assumption-of-risk defense.

(k) In *Johnson v. Houston Sports Ass'n*, 615 S.W.2d 781 (Tex. Civ. App. 1980), plaintiff spectator filed a personal injury action after being struck in the face by a baseball during pregame batting practice. In affirming the trial court decision, the court of civil appeals held that it was not an error to give an instruction on an unavoidable accident when there was evidence (1) that the spectator saw the screened area behind home plate even though the seats in that area were not filled, made no attempt to sit in the protected area, (2) that the screened-in seats were visible from all over the field, (3) that the screens were the same or similar to those used in stadiums all over the country, and (4) that the area offered more protection than the same area in other stadiums. The court of civil appeals also held that it was not an error to refuse to submit the spectator's requested special issue on whether the ball was negligently knocked into the stands on the occasion in question when there was no evidence that the batter who struck the ball that hit the spectator committed any negligent act in striking the ball or that the batter conducted himself differently from the practices of other baseball players in the same situation.

(l) In *McNiel v. Fort Worth Baseball Club*, 268 S.W.2d 244 (Tex. Civ. App. 1954), plaintiff spectator brought suit against the baseball club for personal injuries sustained when struck in the eye by a foul ball. The court of civil appeals held that a patron at a baseball park who was familiar with the game and the particular park, by voluntarily selecting a seat in an unscreened portion of the park and remaining there after the batting cage was removed during batting practice prior to the game, assumed the risk, incident to batting practice, of foul balls being deflected into the stands; therefore, plaintiff could not recover from club when he was struck and injured by a ball which he observed.

(m) In *Knebel v. Jones*, 266 S.W.2d 470 (Tex. Civ. App. 1954), plaintiff spectator brought suit against defendant's park for injuries sustained when she was struck by a foul ball. The district court entered judgment for the plaintiff. The court of civil appeals reversed and held that when the patron could have observed, by mere ordinary observation, that she was not sitting in an area protected by a screen, she was negligent in not so observing, and she was not entitled to recover from defendant, as owner of ballpark, for injuries sustained by her when a foul ball struck her in the face.

(n) In *Baker v. Topping*, 222 N.Y.S.2d 658, 15 A.D.2d 193 (Sup. Ct. 1961), the supreme court, appellate division, held that spectator, who was struck by a baseball while being escorted by an usher, through the aisle leading to his reserved seat in an unscreened section of the stadium, was precluded from recovering under the doctrine of assumption of risk.

(o) *Benjamin v. State*, 453 N.Y.S.2d 329 (Ct. Cl. 1982), was an action brought by an 11-year-old spectator, who in November 1979 was injured in a college hockey doubleheader at Romney Arena, a state facility on the campus of the State University of New York at Oswego. Plaintiff was seated behind the protective fence, 10 to 15 feet north of the nearest players' bench. While there, an errant puck found its way through the open area in front of the players' bench, passed behind the protective fence, and struck plaintiff on the left side of the forehead. Plaintiff brought action against the state alleging that the state failed to provide adequate protection for the safety of spectators seated in the arena. At the trial an expert testified that in similar facilities it was the usual and customary practice to protect the area around the players' bench. Absent such protection, it was the usual and customary practice to restrict seating in an arena without protection from the zone of danger. Since neither course of action was chosen, the court held that the state failed to provide plaintiff with adequate protection that evening. The court found that the failure of the state to provide for the safety of its patrons in the protected seating area constituted negligence and that such negligence was a substantial factor in bringing about the injuries.

4. The following lawsuits involving the equipment in facilities and buildings were brought against facility owners and possessors.

(a) In *Taylor v. Hardee*, 232 S.C. 338, 102 S.E.2d 218 (1958), plaintiff spectator sought recovery for injuries sustained when a bleacher, negligently constructed by defendant speedway owner, collapsed under him. The supreme court held that evidence of how the bleachers were constructed was sufficient on the issue of the race track owner's negligence to send the question to the jury.

(b) In *Rockwell v. Hillcrest Country Club*, 181 N.W.2d 290 (Mich. App. 1970), plaintiffs, golf spectators, sought recovery from injuries sustained when, while watching a golf tournament, a suspension bridge collapsed and dropped plaintiffs into the river below. The court of appeals held that plaintiffs had established a prima facie case of negligence because the bridge capacity was 25 people, that 80 to 100 people were on the bridge when it collapsed, and that no warning signs or supervisors were present.

(c) In *Woodring v. Board of Education of Manhasset*, 435 N.Y.S.2d 52 (1981), plaintiff brought a wrongful death suit against the school district after a platform railing in the gymnasium gave way, throwing decedent to his death. In affirming the $1,400,000 award to plaintiff, the appeals court found evidence that the school district (1) lacked a preventive maintenance program, (2) improperly constructed the platforms, (3) failed to inspect its gymnasium facilities regularly, and (4) should have known—given the extensive use of the platforms by students—that injury was foreseeable if the railings were not properly maintained or constructed. The appeals court thus sustained the jury's determination of the defendant's negligence.

(d) In *Novak v. City of Delavan*, 143 N.W.2d 6 (Wis. 1966), plaintiff spectator brought an action against the city and the school district for injuries sustained as a result of a bleacher collapse at an athletic event. The court held that because the only use the school district made of the facility was for seven football games, since the school district did not purport to inspect the bleachers or perform any maintenance services, and because it was the city, not the school employees, who attended to any bleacher problems, the school district could not be held liable when a footboard gave way; the school district had no control or custody and thus no obligation to repair the bleachers. However, the city was found to be negligent for failing to properly maintain its property.

(e) In *Witherspoon v. Haft*, 106 N.E.2d 296 (Ohio 1952), plaintiff spectator sued defendant, who had installed temporary bleachers at a football game, for injuries sustained when the plaintiff fell from the last row of bleachers, which were negligently fastened. The Ohio Supreme Court held that reasonable minds could conclude that failure of defendants to fasten the top plant seat securely resulted in serious hazard to the plaintiff.

(f) In *Williams v. Strickland*, 112 S.E.2d 533 (N.C. 1960), plaintiff race track patron sued defendant race track owner in negligence for injuries sustained when a wheel came off a race car and struck her. The North Carolina Supreme Court held that the operators of the race track could be held liable for failure to exercise care commensurate with known or reasonably foreseeable dangers incident to motor vehicles racing at high speed, because no seats were provided and no ropes strung to indicate where patrons could stand to view the races safely.

(g) In *Thurman v. Clune*, 125 P.2d 59 (Cal. App. 1942), plaintiff spectators sought recovery for injuries sustained when they were hit by a flying puck in defendant's unscreened ice rink. The district court of appeals held that the question of whether the defendant was negligent in failing to warn of the danger of flying pucks or in failing to provide protective screens should be decided by a jury.

(h) In *Parker v. Warren*, 503 S.W.2d 938 (Tenn. App. 1973), plaintiff spectator sued defendant promoter when the bleacher on which she was to view a wrestling match collapsed. In affirming a verdict for the plaintiff, the court of appeals held that the evidence made a submissible case for res ipsa loquitur, that the promoter was required to use ordinary care with respect to the bleacher conditions and had a duty to inspect, and that patrons were entitled to assume that premises were in safe condition.

5. In 1985 New York State Senator Dunne introduced legislation to mandate nonalcohol seating sections for sporting events. The legislation mandated:

> Section 1. The alcoholic beverage control law is amended by adding a new section one hundred six-b to read as follows:
>
> 106-b. Nonalcohol seating section at spectator events. 1.(a) Every person who operates a facility for the performance of spectator events on the premises of which facility alcoholic beverages are sold or otherwise furnished for consumption on such premises shall establish, separate from other seating accommodations, nonalcohol seating accommodations within such premises wherein the possession or consumption of alcoholic beverages shall not be permitted. At least twenty-five per cent of the seating accommodations of each separately designated ticket price at such facilities shall be segregated contiguously to the maximum extent feasible for the purpose of constituting nonalcohol seating accommodations.

The legislation is indicative of the type that governing bodies might begin instituting if sports administrators fail to regulate the problem of alcohol at sporting events. (S. 5690 and A. 7502, New York State Senate Assembly, introduced May 7, 1985.)

6. For further information on facility liability, see the following law review articles:

(a) "Tort Liability and the Recreational Use of Land," 28 *Buffalo Law Review* 767 (Fall 1979).

(b) Note, "Owner Liability for Intentional Torts Committed by Professional Athletes Against Spectators," 30 *Buffalo Law Review* 565 (1981).

(c) Wong and Ensor, "Torts and Tailgates," 9 *Athletic Business* 46 (May 1985).

(d) "Facility Liability: Spotting Danger Before It Strikes," 10 *Athletic Business* 106 (June 1986).

(e) Fisher and Single, "Beer in the Ballpark: Recommendations to the Liquor License Board of Ontario Concerning the Renewal of Beer Sales at Sporting Events," Document No. 39, Alcoholism and Drug Research Foundation, Toronto, Ontario (1983).

(f) "Sports Liability Insurance," 10 *Athletic Business* 12 (May 1986).

(g) "A Payoff for Prevention," 11 *Athletic Business* 36 (March 1987).

LIABILITY OF MEDICAL PERSONNEL

A person or an organization in charge of a sports activity has a duty to provide reasonable medical assistance to participants as well as to spectators. To determine if this duty has been met, both the quality of care and the speed of the treatment must be considered. The quality of the treatment will be assessed by looking at the qualifications of the provider and the type of treatment offered. The speed of the treatment may be determined by the response time and availability of medical personnel.

There are many different levels of health care providers within the American medical system. With respect to athletic events, these providers may be doctors or nurses; more often they are trainers or emergency medical technicians (EMTs). The standard of care required of each medical provider is based on the person's training and qualifications (see page 307). A higher standard of care is established if the class of medical personnel can perform skills and training beyond what is expected of the reasonable lay person. For example, the standard of care imposed on the medical profession is that the doctor must have met the level of skill and knowledge common to the profession in general or common to the profession within the nearby geographical area.

In the case of a specialist, however, the duty has increasingly become more stringent. A specialist must act with the skill and knowledge reasonable within that specialty. Thus, while in the past, little has distinguished medical malpractice cases involving athletes from other cases, the growing ranks of doctors practicing sports medicine will certainly lead to a higher standard of care for doctors specializing in sports injuries in negligence lawsuits brought by injured athletes.

The standard of care is usually established by expert testimony. For example, a doctor may be negligent while others of lesser skill and expertise would not be. The standard for any other member of the medical system would be applied in a similar fashion.

Generally, medical personnel are considered independent contractors rather than employees (see page 319), even though they may be paid by a school district, facility owner, or other supervisory body. As independent contractors, even if they are found to have been negligent, their employers cannot be held liable under the doctrine of vicarious liability (see page 316). To determine if a doctor or other medical person is an independent contractor, the court considers the degree of control exercised by the employee's supervisor over actual medical decisions. Although the general rule is that medical personnel are independent contractors, there have been cases in which the employer has been held liable under the doctrine of vicarious liability. In these cases, courts have found that the employer exercised control and direction over the medical personnel. (See *Chuy*, pages 323 and 327.)

There are some special considerations for a doctor involved in the area of athletics. The first concerns the relationship between a doctor and patient. Typically, the doctor is paid by the patient. However, in sports, the doctor is hired and paid by the amateur athletic organization. Usually, there is a confidential relationship between doctor and patient. When the doctor is employed by a third party, however, the normal relationship is not established.

In effect, then, team doctors have two masters to serve: the athletic organization for which they work and the player they treat. And, while both the organization and player are concerned with restoring the player to full health, there are potential situations in which the team may seek a shorter rehabilitation program while the player may favor a more cautious time frame for recovery. The team doctor is placed in the middle. The doctor's dilemma is highlighted by suits involving the team doctor if the player believes the doctor has not placed his or her long-term recovery before the program's wishes.

In addition to this potential conflict, the normal confidential relationship between a doctor and patient (the athlete) changes when a third party, the athletic organization, pays the doctor. The athletic organization typically has full access to the athlete's medical records and often discusses the appropriate treatment for the injured athlete with the doctor and patient. In some situations, the athletic organization has access to the medical records and the athlete does not. As an example, Rafael Septien, a former place-kicker with the Dallas Cowboys, sued the Cowboys for full access to his medical records. The confidential relationship between a doctor and a patient may also preclude a doctor's release of information to the athletic organization or anyone else without permission from the patient.

Another consideration concerns the prescribing of pain-killing drugs to enable the athlete to continue playing for the benefit of the team but to the potential detriment of the player's career. There have been situations on the professional level in which athletes—for example, Bill Walton and Dick Butkus—have brought lawsuits against their employers and team physicians for prescribing pain-killing drugs that allowed them to play without informing them of the potential harm to their long-term careers. These cases could be applicable at the collegiate level given similar circumstances. Furthermore, they raise the issue of the responsibility a doctor has to his patient—the injured player—and the responsibility the doctor has to his or her employer—the team.

One final consideration is that even though doctors may be negligent in their handling of an injured player, they may not be legally liable under normal tort analysis. When a player is injured through intentional or negligent actions on the part of a coach, referee, player, spectator, or anyone else, subsequent negligent action will not usually relieve the original negligent party from liability created by the original action. Doctors may, however, be liable as an additional defendant if their conduct is found to be a substantial factor in the injury or if additional injuries occurred because of their negligence. Subsequent medical negligence is generally not an unforeseeable, unreasonable cause which would relieve the original party from liability.

NOTES ———————————————————————————————————————

1. For a successful case brought based on medical malpractice, see *Rosensweig v. State of New York*, 158 N.E.2d 229 (N.Y. 1959). Physicians hired by the State Athletic Commission, who were negligent in failing to diagnose a boxer's prefight brain injury, were deemed to be independent contractors. As such, the state was not liable for the injuries caused by the physicians' negligence.

2. For a case in which a team physician was sued for failure to provide good, sound, reasonable medical care, see *Bayless v. Philadelphia National League Club*, 472 F. Supp. 625 (E.D. Pa. 1979). Plaintiff baseball player argued that he had been given pain-killing drugs without knowledge of their potential side effects. The court determined that the plaintiff's exclusive remedy for the action lay under the state workers' compensation act and was not under legal jurisdiction.

3. For a case in which a professional sports team could have been held liable for the negligence of its medical staff and its assistance provided for the spectators, see *Fish v. L.A. Dodgers Baseball Club*, 128 Cal. Rptr. 807 (Cal. App. 1976). Plaintiffs sought recovery from defendant club and defendant physician for the death of their son, who died as a result of an allegedly negligent diagnosis after being struck by a foul ball. In reversing judgment, the court of appeals held for the plaintiffs, finding that negligence of the ballpark doctor in failing to ascertain decedent's symptoms necessitated the emergency surgery which resulted in death. This converted decedent from a patient who probably would have survived without emergency surgery to a patient who had little hope of recovery. The trial court's verdict in favor of the club was also reversed for consideration of the issue of the agency relationship between the parties.

4. For a case in which the court ruled that the school district was immune from tort liability, see *Deaner v. Utica Community School District*, 297 N.W.2d 625 (Mich. App. 1980), an action brought for damages suffered by plaintiff student during wrestling class when a vertebrae injury resulted in his quadriplegia. The appeals court held that summary judgment could not be granted to the doctor who had examined and approved the student's participation because issues of fact had to be decided.

5. For a case in which a professional hockey team was found to be liable for the team doctors' actions, see *Robitaille v. Vancouver Hockey Club*, 3 W.W.R. 481 (Ct. App. B.C. 1981). Plaintiff professional hockey player brought suit against his club for injuries incurred while playing. A shoulder injury caused the plaintiff recurring problems, which the club's management and physicians attributed to mental rather than physical causes. The plaintiff was ordered to play while injured and sustained a minor spinal cord injury during a game. He requested medical attention but was ignored, since he was perceived as having mental problems.

Further play aggravated the minor injury, and the plaintiff suffered a spinal cord injury which left him permanently disabled. The appeals court upheld the award of damages to the plaintiff and held that the club had breached its duty to ensure the fitness, health, and safety of its player. The club was also found to have exercised sufficient control over the doctors to make the doctors employees of the club. Therefore, the club was liable for the acts of the doctors.

6. For a case in which the athletic trainer was found to not be liable for negligent treatment, see *Gillespie v. Southern Utah State College*, 669 P.2d 861 (Utah 1983). Plaintiff sought recovery against the college for its trainer's negligence in treating a sprained ankle. The court held that the trainer is not a "guarantor" of good results because that standard would result in anyone treating an injury to be "strictly" liable for any adverse consequences resulting from the treatment.

7. For further information on liability of medical personnel, see the following law review articles:

   (a) "Malpractice on the Sidelines: Developing a Standard of Care for Team Sports Physicians," 2 *Journal of Communication and Entertainment Law* 579 (Spring 1980).

   (b) King, "Duty and Standard of Care for Team Physicians," 18 *Houston Law Review* 657 (1981).

   (c) Russell, "Legal and Ethical Conflicts Arising from the Team Physician's Dual Obligations to the Athlete and Management," 10 *Seton Hall Legislative Journal* 299 (1987).

8. In *Krueger v. Bert Bell NFL Retirement Plan*, 234 Cal. Rptr. 579 (Cal. App. 1 Dist. 1987), the court ruled in favor of a retired professional football player and held that he may be entitled to damages for fraudulent concealment of medical information by team personnel.

LIABILITY OF OFFICIALS, REFEREES, AND UMPIRES

Officials, referees, and umpires of athletic contests may incur tort liability as a result of their actions or inactions on the playing field. There have been two distinct areas in which suits against officials, referees, and umpires have been filed. The first is the personal injury area in which the official, referee, or umpire is sued for negligence. The second is the judicial review of an official's, referee's, or umpire's decision. There have been few reported cases in either of these areas, since few cases have been filed and many of those have been settled. However, this area has the potential for increased litigation.

In the personal injury area, the official, referee, or umpire may be sued for negligence in a number of different situations. The first is when there has been a failure to inspect the premises. For instance, a plaintiff may contend that a referee should have inspected the field for holes or other dangerous field conditions that could cause injury to players. The second situation is when the official, referee, or umpire fails to keep the playing area free of equipment and/or spectators. For example, a ball or bat may be left on the playing field, and a player trips, falls, and is injured by the equipment. With respect to spectators, an injured spectator might contend that the official, umpire, or referee should have stopped play on the field and warned the spectators to move from the playing area. A player who is injured by running into a spectator might contend that the official, referee, or umpire should have moved the spectator away from the playing area. The third situation involves weather conditions; an injured player may contend that the official, referee, or umpire should not have started the game or that the game should have been stopped. The fourth situation involves equipment which causes injury to a player. It could be argued that the official, referee, or umpire has the responsibility to prevent a player from participating if the player's equipment is obviously ill-fitting. A situation that may be more likely to result in successful litigation is when a referee does not enforce a rule, especially a safety rule such as a "no jewelry" rule in basketball. The fifth and final situation involves a potential claim that the official, referee, or umpire did not properly enforce the rules of the games. For example, the plaintiff may allege that the basketball referees failed to control the game by not calling fouls or technical fouls and that this resulted in a much rougher game, which was the proximate cause of the injuries suffered by the plaintiff.

The area of judicial review of an official's, referee's, or umpire's decision is one that has been infrequently litigated. Generally, courts are reluctant to review playing field decisions, whether they have been judgmental errors or a misapplication of a rule. Plaintiffs have not been successful in this area, and the courts will continue to show their reluctance to become involved in decisions on the playing field unless fraud or corruption can be found.

A problem not related to the liability of referees, officials, and umpires but one that an athletic administrator and the official should be aware of is the type of relationship created by the association of referees, officials, and umpires. The official may be classified as an independent contractor or an employee. This distinction becomes important if an official is injured in the course of performing his or her duties. If acting as an independent contractor, the official will not be eligible for workers' compensation. If classified as an employee, the official would be entitled to receive those benefits (see page 213). In addition, the athletic administrator could be held liable for the actions of the referee under the legal theory of vicarious liability if the referee is deemed to be an employee. The athletic administrator will generally not be held responsible for the actions of the official if he or she is an independent contractor (see page 319). The interpretation of a referee's status differs from state to state, based on state laws and the legal relationship between the referees and the hiring institution. An examination of legal cases involving the question to determine a particular state's interpretation of the relationship is advised (see Note 4).

The following liability checklist will help officials, referees, and umpires protect themselves against possible litigation.

1. Inspect playing surface, including sidelines and endlines, for visible and potential hazards.
2. Determine if weather conditions are appropriate for competition and do not allow coaches or other athletic officials to influence the decision.
3. Inspect game equipment, such as bases and goalposts.
4. Inspect players' equipment for safety and make sure that players are not wearing any potentially dangerous jewelry or accessories.

NOTES

1. The following cases involve intentional and negligent injury of officials.

(a) In *Dillard v. Little League Baseball Inc.*, 390 N.Y.S.2d 735 (1977), plaintiff umpire sued Little League for negligence in failing to provide him with a cup which provides groin protection after he was seriously injured when struck by a pitched ball in the groin area during a game. The court dismissed the case on the grounds that plaintiff had assumed the risks of such injury when he volunteered to umpire the game. The court based its decision on the fact that it was not customary for Little League to provide such equipment, as it is personal to the wearer. Additionally, the plaintiff could have provided it himself at little expense.

(b) In *Carroll v. State of Oklahoma*, 620 P.2d 416 (Okla. Crim. App. 1980), appellant challenged an Arizona statute under which he was convicted for assault. Appellant was an assistant coach for the losing team at a baseball tournament. After the game, the home plate umpire was at the trunk of his car in the parking lot changing uniforms in preparation for the next game. He was surrounded by a group of players from the losing team who were criticizing his calls. The assistant coach approached the group, exchanged words with the umpire, and struck the umpire on the jaw with his fist. The assistant coach was convicted of "assault upon a sports officiary" under Oklahoma law.

The appellant challenged the statute on the grounds of being unconstitutionally vague. The court of criminal appeals, however, held that the statute clearly indicated which persons were covered and also apprised the public of what particular conduct was deemed punishable, for which reasons the court found the statute neither unconstitutionally vague and indefinite, nor void for uncertainty.

(c) In *McGee v. Board of Education of the City of New York*, 226 N.Y.S. 329 (1962), plaintiff sought recovery for injuries suffered while coaching. The plaintiff was a high school teacher employed by defendant, board of education, and was assigned by the school principal to assist the regular coach of the student baseball team. While conducting a practice session on fielding bunts, the plaintiff stood behind the pitcher's mound and advised the pitcher what to do. The practice session was conducted on a temporary diamond, and the bases were only about 80 feet apart instead of the regulation 90 feet. As a result, the pitcher stood on a direct line between first and third bases. McGee was hit in the face by a ball thrown to third base by the first baseman, who made the throw when the head coach called out for him to "get the man at third." The first baseman had not on previous occasions during the practice routine thrown the ball to third base, but rather had returned the ball to home plate for the next bunt. Plaintiff brought suit against the board of education on the grounds that their employee, the head coach, was negligent in conducting the practice session on a diamond of non-regulation size, without making adjusting precautions, and in suddenly directing a departure from the practice routine while plaintiff's attention was distracted, thereby exposing him to the hazard of being hit by a thrown ball. The appeals court held that, generally, players, coaches, managers, referees and others who voluntarily participate in an athletic event must accept the risks to which their roles expose them. Though there may be occasions when a participant's conduct amounts to such careless disregard for the safety of others as to create risks not fairly assumed, what the scorekeeper may regard as an "error" was not, according to the court, the equivalent, in law, of negligence.

(d) In *McHugh v. Hackensack Public Schools*, N.J. Sup. Ct., Mercer Co., Docket No. 1-2542-81 (1983), plaintiff high school basketball referee was attacked by an unknown fan after a state tournament game and sought damages from the public school system because it did not provide a safe place to work, safe entry and exit before and at the conclusion of the game, or proper supervision of the crowd. The trial court granted summary judgment in favor of the school since the school was immune under the New Jersey Tort Claims Act.

(e) For another case involving intentional and negligent injury of officials, see *Toone v. Adams* on page 350, Note 1.

2. The following cases involve liability by an official for player injury.

(a) In *Cap v. Bound Brook Board of Education*, N.J. Sup. Ct., Cape May Co., Somerset City (Settled 1984), New Jersey high school football officials were sued for permitting a game to be played on a field that was in an unsafe and unplayable condition, which allegedly was a factor in a player's becoming paralyzed following an injury suffered during the contest. The case was dismissed against the officials and settled with the other co-defendants.

(b) In *Nash v. Borough of Wildwood Crest*, N.J. Sup. Ct., Cape May Co., Docket No. 1-6624-77 (Settled, 1983), a recreational softball catcher sought recovery for injuries suffered when he was struck in the eye by a softball while catching without wearing a protective mask. In slo-pitch softball, a catcher is not required to wear a mask. The player sued and alleged that the umpire should have given him his mask and then officiated from behind the pitcher's position rather than from behind home plate. The case was settled prior to trial, with the plaintiff receiving $24,000.

(c) In *Pantalowe v. Lenape Valley Regional High School*, N.J. Sup. Ct., Sussex Co., Docket No. L-40828-26 (1976), a New Jersey high school wrestling referee was sued for allegedly allowing a wrestler to continue an illegal hold on his opponent, which resulted in a paralyzing injury. The case was settled by monetary damages.

(d) In *Smith v. National Football League*, U.S. Dist. Ct., Fla., No. 74-418 Civ. T-K, plaintiff, an All-Pro and National Football League (NFL) Lineman-of-the-Year, sued the head linesman and one of the attendants of the down markers, along with the Tampa Bay Sports Authority and the NFL for $2.5 million. The plaintiff alleged that a collision he had with the down marker caused a serious knee injury that ended his career. He claimed that the collision was a result of neglect on the part of the defendants, including the failure of the sports official to properly supervise and move the markers and the use of dangerous equipment. The jury in the case's second trial found no liability on the part of the defendants.

3. Officials' decisions have been reviewed in the following cases:

(a) In *Georgia High School Ass'n v. Waddell*, 285 S.E.2d 7 (Ga. Sup. Ct. 1981), the Georgia Supreme Court ruled that it does not possess authority to review the decision of a high school football referee. The high school referee admitted that he made the error—not awarding an automatic first down on a roughing-the-kicker penalty—which might have been determinative of the final outcome for the game. The trial court had overturned the referee's ruling based on a school's property right in the game of football being played according to the rules. The court ordered the game to be replayed from the point of the referee's error. The Georgia Supreme Court reversed, stating: "We now go further and hold that courts for equality in this state are without authority to review decisions of football referees because those decisions do not present judicial controversies."

(b) In *Tilelli v. Christenbery*, 1 Misc. 139, 120 N.Y.S.2d 697 (Sup. Ct. 1953), a New York court upheld the decision of a boxing referee and a ringside judge. The New York Athletic Commission had ordered that the voting card of the judge, who they suspected was involved in an illegal gambling scheme, be changed. The court overruled the commission and held that the suspicion of illegality was not sufficient enough grounds for the court to intercede in the decision and substitute its judgment for that of the assigned judge.

(c) In *State ex rel. Durando v. State Athletic Commission*, 75 N.W.2d 451 (Wis. 1956), a court upheld the State Athletic Commission's decision that under its rules it had no authority to reverse a boxing referee's alleged failure to properly administer the "knockdown" rule.

(d) In *Wellsville-Middleton School District v. Miles*, (Mo. Cir. Ct., 1982) (unreported), a court dismissed for failure to state a claim a lawsuit filed by the plaintiff school district against the Missouri State High School Activities Association. The plaintiff claimed that the official scorer in a state tournament basketball game had made a scoring mistake which ultimately led to plaintiff's team losing the contest. The plaintiff had challenged the correctness of the final score.

(e) *Wellsville-Middleton School District v. Miles*, Docket No. 406570 (Mo. Cir. Ct., 1982) (unreported), a companion case to the *Wellsville-Middleton* case above, was filed by three student-athletes on the affected high school team. The plaintiffs alleged that the referee negligently failed to follow proper procedures, which ultimately affected their opportunity to secure college athletic scholarships. The plaintiffs dropped their suit after dismissal of the companion suit.

(f) In *Bain v. Gillespie*, 357 N.W.2d 47 (Iowa App. 1984), plaintiff, a Big-10 basketball referee, filed suit for injunctive relief and damages against defendants who produced T-shirts with his likeness in a noose imprinted on them. Defendants had produced the T-shirts following a controversial call by the referee at an intercollegiate basketball game. Injunctive relief was granted to the referee.

4. The following cases involve officials and workers' compensation issues.

(a) In *Gale v. Greater Washington, D.C. Softball Umpires Ass'n*, 311 A.2d 817 (Md. Ct. Spec. App. 1973), the court ruled that an umpire is not an employee of an umpire association, but an "independent contractor," thereby precluding the umpire from receiving workers' compensation under Maryland law.

(b) In *Ehehalt v. Livingston Board of Education*, 371 A.2d 752 (N.J. App. Div. 1977), the court ruled that a basketball official is not an employee of the school for which he or she officiates regularly but an "independent contractor," thereby precluding the official from recovering workers' compensation under New Jersey law.

(c) In *Ford v. Bonner County School District*, 612 P.2d 557 (Idaho Sup. Ct. 1980), the Idaho Supreme Court found that a high school football official injured while officiating is an employee of the school district and entitled to workers' compensation under Idaho law.

(d) In *Daniels v. Gates Rubber Co.*, 479 P.2d 983 (Col. Ct. App. 1970), the court found that a member of the Umpires Association of Colorado, who was struck in the eye by a softball while umpiring a corporate recreational league game, was not an employee of the corporation for purposes of the Colorado workers' compensation statute.

(e) In *Warthen v. Southeast Oklahoma State University*, 641 P.2d 1125 (Okla. Ct. App. 1981), the court ruled that a university drama professor, who was also a licensed basketball referee and was asked by a dean to referee an intramural fraternity game, sustained a compensable injury when he died while officiating the game.

5. For a case in which a court found that an umpire might be liable for allowing a game to proceed on an unfit playing surface, see *Forkash v. New York*, 227 N.Y.S.2d 827 (App. Div. 1966). The plaintiffs sought recovery for injuries sustained in a collision in the outfield during a city-sponsored softball game. In reversing the trial court's dismissal, the appellate court division held that whether the players could recover was a question for a jury to determine. The evidence presented proved that the collision took place after one plaintiff tripped over a piece of glass. The umpire furnished by the city had been advised that the outfield was not in playing condition but had directed that the game proceed.

6. For a case in which a promoter was held not liable for all actions of a referee employed by him, see *Ulrich v. Minneapolis Boxing and Wrestling Club, Inc.*, 129 N.W.2d 288 (Minn. 1964). The plaintiff, a 77-year-old wrestling spectator, sought recovery from defendant promoter for injuries sustained when a referee, hired by the defendant, whirled about, striking him. The Minnesota Supreme Court held that the injury was not proximately caused by the promoter's alleged failure to provide adequate crowd supervision, exposure of the referee to the plaintiff when he left the ring, or employment of a referee with dangerous propensities.

7. The following cases also involve officials, and their duties and liabilities.

(a) *Agnew v. City of Los Angeles*, 82 Cal. App. 2d 616, 186 P.2d 450 (1947), details duties of officials.

(b) *Wilhelm v. San Diego United School Dist.*, No. N29412 (Cal. Super. Ct., filed July, 1985), involves an attack on an official at a high school basketball game.

(c) *Banfield v. George Junior Republic, Inc.*, (N.Y. Sup. Ct., filed 1983), involves a negligence claim by a basketball official against a private school.

(d) *Frazier v. Rutherford Board of Education*, No. L-05689-83 (N.J. Super. Ct. Law Div., filed Jan. 1983), involves a long-jump official and an injury to a high school track athlete.

8. For further information on the subject of sports officiating and the law, see the following law articles:

(a) Dedopoulos and Narol, "A Guide to Referees' Rights and Potential Liability," 16 *Trial* 18 (March 1980).

(b) Dedopoulos and Narol, "Kill the Umpire: A Guide to Referee's Rights," 15 *Trial* (March 1979).

(c) Ranii, "Sports Violence Lawsuits Erupt," *National Law Journal*, February 9, 1981, p. 1.

(d) Narol and Dedopoulos, "The Official's Right to Sue for Game-Related Injuries," *National Law Journal*, June 7, 1982, p. 26.

(e) "A Workers' Compensation Casebook," *Referee*, September 1983.

(f) Narol and Dedopoulos, "The Official's Potential Liability for Injuries in Sporting Events," *National Law Journal*, September 6, 1982, p. 20.

(g) Davis, "Sports Liability: Blowing the Whistle on the Referees," 12 *Pacific Law Journal* 937 (1981).

(h) Narol, "Player Injuries: Baseball Umps' Potential Liability," *Referee*, February 1984.

(i) Supp., "Liability for Injury to or Death of Umpire, Referee, or Judge of Game or Contest," 10 *American Law Reports*, 3d 446.

(j) "Tort Liability of Public Schools and Institutions of Higher Education for Injuries Resulting from Lack or Insufficiency of Supervision," 38 *American Law Reports*, 3d 830.

(k) "Tort Liability of Public Schools and Institutions of Higher Education for Accident Occurring During School Athletic Events," 35 *American Law Reports*, 3d 725.

(l) "Modern Status of Doctrine of Sovereign Immunity as Applied to Public Schools and Institutions of Higher Learning," 33 *American Law Reports*, 3d 703.

(m) Carpenter, "Decreasing Sports Violence Equals Increasing Official's Liability," 3 *Loyola Entertainment Law Journal* 127 (1983).

(n) "Note: Sports Liability: Blowing the Whistle on the Referees," 12 *Pacific Law Journal* 937 (1981).

(o) Narol, "The Legal Chalkboard," 67 *Athletic Journal* 42 (January 1987).

(p) Narol, "Protecting the Rights of Sports Officials," 23 *Trial* 64 (January 1987).

APPLICATION OF LEGAL PRINCIPLES TO DEFECTS IN EQUIPMENT

The "failure to warn" theory is established upon the finding of a manufacturer's duty to warn of known latent and potential injury-causing defects in the design of equipment. The extent of the duty is based on the age and experience of the reasonably foreseeable users of the product.

In order to maintain a suit based on a theory of a "failure to warn," the plaintiff must prove that the product is defective in design. The test used by courts has two distinct prongs. The first prong involves looking at the product to see if it has failed to perform as safely as an ordinary consumer would expect. Whether it was used as intended, or was misused or tampered with, will be considered in making the determination of safety. If the plaintiff cannot directly establish that the product failed to perform adequately, this part of the test may be satisfied by the second prong, which involves proving that the product's defective design proximately caused the injury and that the benefits of the challenged design do not outweigh the inherent risk of danger created by the design. To aid in its determination as to both defectiveness and resultant liability, the court will also consider factors such as the nature of the sport, the type of injury, the amount of use or foreseeable misuse, the degree to which the particular risk is greater due to the defect, and the current state of the art in designing an absolutely safe product. (See also "Products Liability Law" in Chapter 6, page 328.)

NOTES ───

1. The following cases involve the application of legal principles to defects in equipment.

(a) In *Dudley Sports Co. v. Schmitt*, 279 N.E.2d 266 (Ind. 1972), a 16-year-old high school boy sought recovery for injuries received when he was struck in the face by the throwing arm of an automatic baseball pitching machine, which was purchased in March 1965 by Danville High School. Designed and manufactured by Dudley, the machine consisted of a frame and an open extended metal throwing arm. No protective shield guarded the throwing arm. When the arm reached a ten o'clock energized position and it received a ball, energy was released from the coiled spring and transmitted to the arm; the arm passed through a clockwise pitching cycle at a high rate of speed and came to rest in a four o'clock position. The machine was capable of delivering a powerful blow in the ten o'clock position, even if it was unplugged.

When the machine was uncrated, it came with a parts list, assembly instructions, and a tool to deactivate the spring. The only warning instruction contained in the crate was a general warning tag which said: "Warning! *Safety First* STAY CLEAR OF THROWING ARM AT ALL TIMES." No operating instructions were included in the crate. The machine was stored, unplugged, behind locked doors in locker room no. 2. However, the two adjoining locker rooms, with inside entrances to locker room no. 2, were not locked from the outside hallway entrance. On the day he was injured, plaintiff student was sweeping in locker room no. 2, as he had done in the past at the request of the coaching staff. He said that as he approached the front of the machine he heard a whistling noise and a pop. He was hit in the face by the throwing arm and received extensive facial injuries.

Plaintiff brought this action alleging negligence against the high school, the sporting goods company, and Dudley. The appeals court held that Dudley was negligent in the design, manufacture, and sale of the machine. The ability of the machine to operate while unplugged as a result of even a slight vibration was considered a latent danger, which could only be discovered through an examination of the machine combined with knowledge of the engineering principles which produce the action of the machine. Such knowledge is not ordinarily possessed by a 16-year-old high school boy who had never seen the machine before.

(b) In *Heldman v. Uniroyal, Inc.*, 371 N.E.2d 557 (Ohio App. 1977), a professional tennis player injured her knee during a tennis championship and brought suit for damages against Uniroyal, Inc., which supplied the tennis court surface for the matches. Plaintiff claimed that the defendant made certain representations and warranties, both expressed and implied, concerning its court surface. An appeals court ruled that there was sufficient evidence to raise a jury question as to whether plaintiff assumed the risk by playing in the match. The court reached its conclusion based on the reasons that the plaintiff told all the members of her team that the court was in a dangerous condition, that she was a professional tennis player and is presumed to know the various risks attendant with playing on different types of surfaces, and that a higher degree of knowledge and awareness is imputed to professional tennis players than to average nonprofessional tennis players as to the dangers of playing on a synthetic tennis court having obvious bubbles on the playing surface.

(c) In *Byrns v. Riddell, Inc.*, 550 P.2d 1065 (Ariz. 1976), plaintiff student-athlete brought a products liability action against Riddell, Inc., a manufacturer of football helmets, after he had sustained a head injury in an interscholastic football contest in October 1970. Plaintiff was injured in a play in which he received an "on-side" kick. The supreme court examined evidence relating to proof of strict liability in tort to determine whether the trial court properly found for Riddell. The supreme court reversed based on doubts raised as to the possibility of a defect in the design of the helmet, the place of impact, and the presence of the defect at the time the helmet left the seller's hands. The case was remanded to the trial court to make these determinations.

(d) In *Everett v. Bucky Warren, Inc.*, 380 N.E.2d 653 (Mass. 1978), plaintiff hockey player claimed that his serious head injury resulted from the defective design of the helmet he wore. The team's hockey coach distributed to the team helmets which were of a three-piece design, consisting of three plastic pieces. One piece covered the back of the head, one the forehead, and one the top of the head. The pieces were attached to each other by elastic straps. The straps expanded, depending on the size of the wearer's head, leaving gaps as large as three-fourths of an inch. This design was somewhat unique; however, there were also available on the market helmets which were of a one-piece design with no gaps.

During a game with the Brown University freshman team, plaintiff threw himself in front of a Brown player's shot in an attempt to block it. The puck struck Warren above the right ear, penetrating a gap in the helmet and causing a skull fracture. The injury required that a steel plate be inserted in his skull and caused recurring

headaches. Warren then brought suit against the school, the manufacturer, and the retailer on the grounds of strict liability.

The appeals court held that the manufacturer could be found
strictly liable for producing a helmet with an "unreasonably dangerous design." Factors that the court weighed when determining
whether a particular design is reasonably safe included "the gravity
of the danger posed by the challenged design, the likelihood that
such danger would occur, the mechanical feasibility of a safer
alternative design, the . . . cost of an improved design, and the
adverse consequences to the product and the consumer that would
result from an alternative design." The court held that the gravity
of the danger was demonstrated by the injuries, that helmets of the
one-piece design were safer than the model used and were in
manufacture prior to the injury, and that, while more expensive
than the helmets used, the one-piece helmets were not economically unfeasible.

(e) *Halbrook v. Oregon State University*, Case No. 16-83-04631,
Circuit, Court of the State of Oregon for Lane County, (1983)
(pending), was an action brought by the family of a boy who died
from injuries received during baseball practice. In March 1982, the
student-athlete was participating in an Oregon State University
baseball practice on an Astroturf field when he collided with another
player, fell to the ground, and struck his head. As a result of the
injuries, Halbrook died. Plaintiff-estate alleges that the university
and the Oregon State Board of Higher Education were responsible
for the proper selection, installation, maintenance, and repair of the
athletic field surface. More specifically, the university and state
board of higher education failed to hire a competent and qualified
installer for the Astroturf, they failed to adequately supervise the
activities of the installer they had hired, and they failed to perform
adequate shock absorbency tests upon the Astroturf when they
knew or should have known that continued use would diminish its
shock absorbency characteristics. Plaintiff alleged that the Astroturf
sold by defendant Monsanto was in a defective condition, was
unreasonably dangerous, and created an unreasonable risk of harm
because it was too hard and without adequate cushioning. In
addition, plaintiff claims that Monsanto marketed the Astroturf
without adequate warnings to the average user. Plaintiff also sued
Matrecon, the company which sold the asphalt that was placed
under the Astroturf, under many of the same theories that were
alleged against Monsanto.

2. For a case in which liability for failure to warn was based on
constructive knowledge, see *Filler v. Rayex Corp.*, 435 F.2d 336 (7th Cir.
1970). Plaintiff baseball player sued defendant sunglass manufacturer for
negligence, strict liability, and breach of implied warranty of fitness for a
particular purpose when the glasses shattered into his eye. The court of
appeals, in affirming the district court in favor of the plaintiff, held that
defendant, which advertised the glasses as providing protection against
baseballs, had constructive knowledge of the danger and was liable for

failure to warn and liable for breach of warranty of fitness for a particular purpose.

3. For a case in which the court held there is no duty to warn of known dangers, see *Garrett v. Nissen Corp.*, 498 P.2d 1359 (N.M. 1972). Plaintiff, an experienced trampoline user, sued defendant trampoline manufacturer for negligence for failure to warn of the danger involved in landing incorrectly. The supreme court held there is no duty to warn of dangers known to user of product, either under strict liability or negligence theories.

4. For a case in which the court warned that there was a duty to warn of known dangerous conditions, see *Pleasant v. Blue Mound Swim Club*, 128 Ill. App. 2d 277, 262 N.E.2d 107 (1970). Plaintiff diver sought recovery from defendant pool owner for injuries sustained when he hit the pool bottom after diving off the board. The appellate court held for the plaintiff and found that the evidence would support a finding that the water level of the pool had been lowered to the extent that it constituted a dangerous condition, which was brought about by defendant by a back flushing process, and that the manager and lifeguards were negligent for failure to warn swimmers of the danger.

5. The following cases involve negligent design.

(a) In *Standard v. Meadors*, 347 F. Supp. 908 (N.D. Ga. 1972), plaintiff water skier sought recovery from defendant designer and manufacturer of a speed boat for injuries sustained when the boat propeller severed her leg while she was in the water waiting to be towed. The district court held that the allegation that the boat was negligently designed so that the prow (front of the boat) obscured the forward view of the operator and that the propeller was manufactured so that it would not stop upon contacting a person in water, stated a claim upon which relief could be granted under Georgia law.

(b) In *Hauter v. Zogarts*, 120 Cal. Rptr. 681 (1975), plaintiff sought recovery for injuries sustained when he was hit on the head by a golf ball following a practice swing with a golf training device that was described by manufacturer as "completely safe, ball will not hit player." The California Supreme Court held that the plaintiff was entitled to recover on the theories of false representation, breach of express and implied warranties, and strict liability in tort based on defective design.

6. For a case that held that a mere change in design is not sufficient to establish the existence of a defect and that misuse of a product may preclude liability, see *Gentemen v. Saunders Archery Co.*, 355 N.E.2d 647 (Ill. App. 1976). Plaintiff archer sought recovery in strict products liability against the manufacturer of "string silencers," which broke when he used them and injured him. In affirming a jury verdict for the defendant, the appellate court held that the evidence was sufficient to warrant a reasonable belief that the change in design did not establish the existence of a defect in the product and that the plaintiff had misused it.

7. For a case in which it was held that a breach of warranty will cause

liability, see *Salk v. Alpine Ski Shop*, 115 R.I. 309, 342 A.2d 622 (1975). Plaintiff skier sought recovery from defendant ski manufacturers for injuries sustained in a fall. The Rhode Island Supreme Court held that there was no jury question presented as to the negligence of the ski manufacturer in that there was no competent evidence that the failure of the bindings to release actually caused the injury. Furthermore, the plaintiff failed to show a breach of express warranty in that the skier did not establish that the advertisement of the manufacturer warranted that the bindings would release in every situation presenting a danger to the user's limbs.

8. The National Operating Committee on Standards for Athletic Equipment (NOCSAE) was organized to research and test equipment to develop new standards and improve existing ones. NOCSAE was founded in 1969 in an effort to reduce death and injuries through the adoption of standards and certification for athletic equipment. Fatalities decreased by more than 50 percent by 1977, after a 37-year high of 36 deaths in 1968. The number of cases of permanent quadriplegia from neck injuries in the early 1970s averaged 35 per year; these were reduced to 7 in 1977, 9 in 1978, and 7 in 1979. NOCSAE published helmet standards in 1973, and manufacturers and reconditioners have improved their equipment to meet those standards. An area of recent study was face masks for ice hockey helmets. Research in the future may result in helmets for lacrosse and equestrian competition.

9. For further information on the application of legal principles to defects in equipment, see the following law articles:

(a) Levin and Bortz, "Torts on the Courts," *Trial* 28 (June 1978).

(b) Williamson, "It's All Part of the Game—Or Is It?" *Trial* 58 (November 1981).

LIABILITY INSURANCE

Liability insurance is a form of indemnity whereby the insurer undertakes to indemnify or pay the insured for a loss resulting from legal liability to a third person. It is based on contract law principles. Liability insurance protects an insured against financial loss resulting from lawsuits brought against him or her for negligent behavior. Common subjects for liability insurance in athletics are risks from use of the premises, from faulty products, from use of vehicles, and from the practice of professions.

Insurance is effective even if the insured has committed a minor violation of the criminal law. A minor violation will not invalidate the insurance or deprive the defendant of protection. An insurance policy may be invalidated, however, if the insured's conduct was so outrageous that it would be against public policy to indemnify it. The policy may also be invalidated if the insured misrepresented a material fact at the time of the application for the policy.

One of the standard provisions in any insurance policy requires the insured to cooperate fully with the insurance company by providing full and accurate information about the accident. It may also require the insured to attend the trial, to take part in it if required, and to do nothing for the injured party that would harm the insurance company. A violation of any of the above requirements would relieve the insurance company of liability to the injured third party.

The term "subrogation" is often times found in tort cases involving insurance claims. *Subrogation* is the right of a party who has paid the legal obligation of a third party to recover payment from the third party who has benefited. For example, a fan is injured at a baseball stadium by a foul ball that passed through a hole in the netting behind home plate, and that the hole was there because of the negligence of a third-party contractor who damaged the screen during installation. If the liability insurer for the stadium pays the injured fan, it has a right, under subrogation, to sue the installer for negligence, just as its insured, the stadium owner, had.

Typically, insurance policies contain a clause which entitles the insurer to be subrogated to his insured cause of action against any party who caused a loss which the insurer paid. The insurer can also be entitled to subrogation in the absence of an express contractual provision. This is called *equitable subrogation*. In some states, however, an insurance company must prove it was not a gratuitous payment in order to recover under equitable subrogation.

One response by institutions and sports associations to the increasing number of lawsuits brought under a tort liability theory is to use insurance. The National Federation of High School Associations and many state high school athletic associations and their member schools have adopted a liability/lifetime catastrophe medical plan. The plan covers the National Federation of State High School Associations, the state high school athletic/activity association, their member schools and school districts, and member school administrators, athletic directors, coaches, and trainers. This type of insurance allows the student-athlete who suffers a catastrophic injury to waive suit and opt for medical, rehabilitation, and work-loss benefits for the rest of his or her life. The philosophy behind the insurance plan is to provide needed benefits to the injured student-athlete, without the time, costs, and risks involved in litigation. If the injured student-athlete opts for the benefits provided by the insurance policy, the institution saves time, expense, and a possible award in favor of the plaintiff.

The NCAA has instituted a similar catastrophic injury protection plan. The NCAA's plan, which can be adopted by institutions on an individual basis, should accomplish two important objectives. First, by having this type of plan, it should reduce—if not eliminate—the number of workers' compensation cases filed against NCAA member institutions. The NCAA policy is similar to workers' compensation in that it provides benefits to catastrophically injured student-athletes regardless of fault. And the benefits offered by the NCAA program may be more attractive than a successful workers' compensation claim. For instance, a student-athlete's claim for workers' compensation benefits may have to be litigated. Second, the NCAA insurance policy assists the catastrophically injured student-athlete by providing benefits immediately, without time delays, without the costs of litigation, and without the uncertainties involved in litigation. The benefits are provided for the lifetime of the student-athlete, and the plan is extremely helpful to the student-athlete who is injured without fault. The student-athlete who is catastrophically injured as a result of negligence of an institution or one of its employees still has the alternative of litigating the case and not collecting the benefits provided by the NCAA policy.

NOTES

1. For a case involving liability insurance and sports, see *Strong v. Curators of University of Missouri*, 575 S.W.2d 812 (Mo. 1979). Plaintiffs sued for the death of their 6-year-old child in a swimming pool run by defendant university. The defense of sovereign immunity was raised, and the plaintiffs countered with the argument that insurance precluded the necessity for and therefore abrogated the doctrine of sovereign immunity. The court held that the purchase of liability insurance will not, by itself, abrogate the doctrine.

2. For further information on liability insurance, see the following articles:

(a) Quinn, "Litigating Youth Sports Injuries," 22 *Trial* 76 (March 1986).

(b) "Sports Liability Insurance," 10 *Athletic Business* 12 (May 1986).

(c) "Cancelling the Quality of Life," 10 *Athletic Business* 12 (June 1986).

WAIVER AND RELEASE OF LIABILITY

In the law, there are often competing legal theories in a given situation. The resolution of this type of situation is usually based on the preeminent public policies existing at the time the conflict arises. In the area of waivers and releases of liability, the underlying principles of tort law and contract law conflict. *Waivers* or *exculpatory agreements* are contracts that alter the ordinary negligence principles of tort law. *Contract law* is based on the idea that any competent party should have the absolute right to make a binding agreement with any other competent party. The only limit to this right to make such agreements is that a contract is invalid if it violates public policy. For example, a contract in which the parties agree to commit a crime would violate an important public policy of preventing crime.

Tort law, on the other hand, is based on the idea that a party should be responsible for negligent or intentional actions that cause injury to another person. Waivers, then, create a conflict between the right to enter into contracts and the policy that one should be held responsible for injury-causing negligent actions. The conflict between contract and tort law principles has been resolved in favor of the general rule that waivers and releases of liability will be enforceable unless they frustrate an important public policy or unless the party getting the waiver is unfairly dominant in the bargaining process. This resolution is based on the general contract law principle that a party is bound by the signing of a contract unless there is evidence of fraud, misrepresentation, or duress.

In order to determine if fraud, misrepresentation, or duress exists, a court will consider whether the party waiving its rights knew or had an opportunity to know the terms. This does not mean that merely failing to read or to understand a waiver and release of liability will invalidate it. It must be conspicuous and not be hidden in fine print so that a careful reader is unlikely to see it. The waiver and release of liability must also result from a free and open bargaining process. If one party forces the other to agree to a waiver, it may not be enforceable. The last consideration is whether the express terms of the waiver and release of liability are applicable to the particular conduct of the party whose potential liability is being waived. In other words, the language of the waiver must be clear, detailed, and specific. A waiver and release of liability will not be enforceable if it attempts to insulate one party from wanton, intentional, or reckless misconduct. Therefore, only liability for negligent actions can be waived.

If the person signing the waiver and release of liability is a minor, other issues are raised. Under basic contract principles, a minor may repudiate any otherwise valid contract. A problem may also arise when parents sign waivers for their children. Courts are struggling with the issue of the rights of minors that may be waived by their parents.

For competent adult participants in sports activities, waivers and releases of liability are generally upheld. However, questions are frequently litigated in the area of auto racing. Courts have reasoned that a driver is under no compulsion to race; therefore, a driver has the ability to make a decision whether to race and to assume all the risks inherent in auto racing. This may include risks that arise as a result of negligence on the part of the event's promoters. Courts are generally more reluctant to enforce a waiver and release of liability signed by spectators based on the theory that they may not be as familiar with the risks of auto racing or that they are entitled to assume that the premises are reasonably safe. (See Exhibit 7–1.)

NOTES ————————————————————————————————

1. The following cases involve waiver and release of liability in sports.
   (a) *Doyle v. Bowdoin College v. Cooper International, Inc.*, 403 A.2d 1206 (Me. 1979), was an action brought by plaintiffs on behalf of their son Brian, who was injured while playing floor hockey at a clinic sponsored by defendant college and directed by the school's agents. Plaintiffs alleged that the defendant's negligence resulted in their son's injury when a plastic hockey blade flew off the end of another boy's stick, hitting Brian in the eye, shattering his glasses, and damaging his retina so as to leave him partially blind.

   The case was tried before a jury which concluded that the negligent conduct of defendants Bowdoin College and its agents proximately caused plaintiffs' son's injuries. The defendants appealed this judgment, contending that the trial court erred in holding (1) that certain documents were *not* releases relieving defendants of all liability for future injuries Brian might suffer as a result of defendants' negligent conduct and (2) that another document was not a contract of indemnification obligating the injured child's mother to reimburse defendants for any liability they might incur regarding injuries sustained by him at the clinic.

   The appeals court denied the defendants' appeal. It noted that courts have traditionally disfavored contractual exclusions of negligence liability. The court found that the documents executed by the child's parents contained no express reference to defendants' liability for their own negligence: "Though the documents state that Bowdoin College will not 'assume' or 'accept' any 'responsibility' for injuries sustained by Brian . . . whether 'assumed' or 'accepted,' or not, Bowdoin College has such responsibility in any event because the *law* had imposed it."

   (b) In *Williams v. Cox Enterprises, Inc.*, 283 S.E.2d 367 (Ga. App. 1981), plaintiff, who had participated in the 10,000-meter Georgia Peachtree Road Race, brought a class action lawsuit charging sponsors of the event with negligence in failing to adequately warn participants of the inherent dangers involved in running the race. In the 1977 race, plaintiff suffered heat stroke, heat prostration, renal failure, and other disorders, which resulted in the permanent impairment of some motor functions. Cox Enterprises argued in the trial court that plaintiff had assumed the risk of injury and that he had signed a required waiver-of-liability form. Plaintiff argued that the waiver was invalid because given the size of the event and the fact that the race was so well publicized, it was the public duty of the sponsor to provide and ensure the safety of the participants. Plaintiff also contended that the waiver was invalid due to the disparity in bargaining positions between the runners and the race officials. Plaintiff claimed that because running had become so popular and because the Peachtree Road Race was "the only road race of its kind in the Atlanta area," he and other athletes were under "enormous pressure to enter it on whatever terms were offered to them."

An appeals ocurt held that the contractual waiver of liability is valid unless the waiver violates public policy. The court held that the contract signed by the plaintiff was valid. It also held that plaintiff signed the waiver without duress; thus his claim of disparity in bargaining positions was not valid. The court further held that the application signed by plaintiff described the race as "grueling" due to heat and humidity. Since plaintiff admitted having read the warning and being aware of the danger, recovery was precluded under the assumption-of-risk doctrine.

(c) In *Garretson v. United States*, 456 F.2d 1017 (9th Cir. 1972), a federal court held that a release was valid when plaintiffs had read conspicuous language and previously signed similar forms.

(d) In *Winterstein v. Wilcom*, 16 Md. App. 130, 293 A.2d 821 (1972), a release was held valid because it had been freely entered into and bargained for by two equal parties.

2. Releases are not valid if they are not clearly stated. For example, in *Hertzog v. Harrison Island Shores Inc.*, 21 App. Div. 2d 859, 251 N.Y.S.2d 164 (1964), plaintiff beach and yacht club member sought recovery for injuries received in a fall from the gangplank leading to the dock on club premises. The court held for the plaintiff, despite the fact that the plaintiff signed a release of liability. The court reasoned that a provision of the membership application, providing that, if accepted as a member, plaintiff would waive his claim for any loss to personality or for personal injury while a member of club, was not sufficiently clear or explicit to absolve club of its own negligence in regard to the plaintiff's fall.

3. See Appendix D for additional examples of waiver and release of liability forms.

SEATTLE PUBLIC SCHOOLS

1982–83 STUDENT INFORMATION AND PARENTAL APPROVAL FORM

A. STUDENT INFORMATION

1. Student's Name _____ Birth Date _____ Age _____

2. Name of Parent(s) _____

3. Address of Parent(s) _____

4. Name of Person(s) with whom Student Resides _____

5. Address of Person(s) with whom Student Resides _____

6. If this student does not reside with a parent, supply the following information:

   (a) How long has the student resided with this person(s)? _____

   (b) Has a legal guardianship been appointed by the courts? Yes ____ No ____
   (If the answer is "yes", submit a certified copy of the court order or letter of guardianship.)

7. School attended last year _____ City _____

8. Grade level completed last June _____

9. Did student pass in at least four (4) full-time subjects in the immediately preceding semester/trimester and receive the maximum credit given? Yes ____ No ____

10. Describe any physical limitations or problems that should be known by the coach:

    _____

    _____

B. STUDENT RIGHTS

Students participating in the Interscholastic Athletic program are governed by the rights, protection and responsibilities as prescribed by the Washington Interscholastic Activities Association Handbook, the Metropolitan League By-Laws, and their respective schools.

Students and/or their parent(s)/guardians may make application for exceptions to League and WIAA eligibility regulations and may appeal any decisions relative to such request through their school principal.

C. STUDENT RESPONSIBILITIES

Participants are required to conform to the rules and regulations of their school, Metropolitan League, and the WIAA, and to conduct themselves in a safe and sportsmanlike manner. Violators are subject to probation, suspension or expulsion.

D. STUDENT ELIGIBILITY REQUIREMENTS

1. Prior to participation in practice of athletic contests a student must:

   (a) PHYSICAL EXAMINATION—During the 12-month period prior to first participation in interscholastic athletics in a middle school, a junior high school, and prior to participation in a high school, a student shall undergo a medical examination and be approved for interscholastic athletic competition by a medical authority licensed to perform a physical examination. Prior to each subsequent year of participation, a student shall furnish a statement, signed by a medical authority licensed to perform a physical examination, which provides clearance for continued athletic participation.

   The school in which this student is enrolled must have on file a statement (or prepared form) from a medical authority licensed to give a physical examination, certifying that his/her physical condition is adequate for the activity or activities in which he/she participates.

Exhibit 7-1 Waiver and Release of Liability Form

To resume participation following an illness and/or injury serious enough to require medical care, a participating student must present to the school officials a physican's written release.

(b) be covered by the school's athletic injury insurance or have on file in the school office a properly signed League Insurance Waiver form.

(c) Seattle school students must have paid for the school's Catastrophic Insurance coverage.

(d) have on file in the school office a signed Student Information and Parental Approval form.

2. To be eligible to participate in an Interscholastic contest a student must:

(a) be under twenty (20) years of age on September 1 for the Fall sport season; on December 1 for the Winter sport season; and March 1 for the Spring sport season.

(b) have passed in at least four (4) full-time subjects in the immediately preceding semester/trimester and earned the maximum credit given for each subject.

(c) be enrolled in and currently passing at least four full credit subjects.

(d) reside with their parents, the parent with legal custody, or a court appointed guardian who has acted in such a capacity for a period of one year or more.

(e) not miss practices or games for the purpose of participating in non-school athletic activities.

(f) not accept cash awards in any amount or merchandise of more than $100.00 in value, or have ever signed a contract with or played for a professional athletic organization.

3. Students shall be entitled to four consecutive years of participation after entering the ninth (9th) grade.

4. A student completing the highest grade offered in an elementary or middle-school is eligible for athletic participation upon entering a public or non-public high school. After starting his/her attendance in a high school, a student who transfers voluntarily or involuntarily to another high school shall become ineligible unless he/she obtains a signed Transfer Form from the principal of the high school from which he/she transfers, indicating that the transfer was not for athletic or disciplinary reasons.

5. Be in attendance a full day of school on any game date which falls on a school day.

6. Your athletic eligibility can be adversely affected by:

(a) Providing misleading or false information relative to factors which affect your eligibility. (Loss of minimum of one year of eligibility.)

(b) Missing a game or practice to participate in an out-of-school athletic activity.

(c) Participating in an athletic activity under a false name.

(d) Disruptive behavior during practice and/or contests.

(e) Irregular attendance at school or practice.

(f) Committing and/or aiding or abetting in the commission of any physical abuse or attack upon any person associated with athletic practices or contests.

(g) Using a school uniform in a non-school athletic event or failure to maintain proper care or return of athletic equipment.

Exhibit 7-1 Continued

We have read, understand, and agree to abide by the Student Rights and Responsibilities and Student Eligibility listed in this form.

Date: _____ , 19_____   Signed _____
                                                       Parent or Guadian

                                      Signed _____
                                                       Student

WARNING, AGREEMENT TO OBEY INSTRUCTIONS, RELEASE, ASSUMPTION OF RISK, AND AGREEMENT TO HOLD HARMLESS

(Both the applicant student and a parent or guardian must read carefully and sign.)

SPORT (check applicable box):

☐ Football   ☐ Basketball   ☐ Track
☐ Volleyball   ☐ Wrestling   ☐ Baseball
☐ Cross-Country   ☐ Gymnastics   ☐ Softball
☐ Soccer   ☐ Swimming   ☐ Tennis
☐ Golf

STUDENT

I am aware playing or practicing to play/participate in any sport can be a dangerous activity involving MANY RISKS OF INJURY. I understand that the dangers and risks of playing or practicing to play/participate in the above sport include, but are not limited to, death, serious neck and spinal injuries which may result in complete or partial paralysis, brain damage, serious injury to virtually all internal organs, serious injury to virtually all bones, joints, ligaments, muscles, tendons, and other aspects of the muscular skeletal system, and serious injury or impairment to other aspects of my body, general health and well-being. I understand that the dangers and risks of playing or practicing to play/participate in the above sport may result not only in serious injury, but in a serious impairment of my future abilities to earn a living, to engage in other business, social and recreational activities, and generally to enjoy life.

Because of the dangers of participating in the above sport, I recognize the importance of following coaches' instructions regarding playing techniques, training and other team rules, etc., and to agree to obey such instructions.

In consideration of the Seattle School District permitting me to try out for the _____ High School _____ team and to engage in all activities
                                              (indicate sport)
related to the team, including, but not limited to, trying out, practicing or playing/participating in that sport, I hereby assume all the risks associated with participation and agree to hold the Seattle School District, its employees, agents, representatives, coaches, and volunteers harmless from any and all liability, actions, causes of action, debts, claims, or demands of any kind and nature whatsoever which may arise by or in connection with my participation in any activities related to the _____ High School _____ team. The terms hereof shall serve as a release and
                 (indicate sport)
assumption of risk for my heirs, estate, executor, administrator, assignees, and for all members of my family.

> The following to be completed only if sport is *football, wrestling, gymnastics,* or *baseball*:
>
> I specifically acknowledge that _____ is a VIOLENT CONTACT SPORT involving even greater risk of injury than other sports. _____
>   (initial)

Date: _____ , 19 _____   _____
                                                 Signature of Student

Exhibit 7-1 Continued

PARENT/GUARDIAN

I, _____, am the parent/legal guardian of _____ (student). I have read the above warning and release and understand its terms. I understand that all sports can involve many RISKS OF INJURY, including, but not limited to, those risks outlined above.

In consideration of the Seattle School District permitting my child/ward to try out for the _____ High School _____ team and to engage in all ac-

(indicate sport)
tivities related to the team, including, but not limited to, trying out, practicing, or play-ing/participating in _____ I hereby agree to hold the Seattle School District,

(indicate sport)
its employees, agents, representatives, coaches, and volunteers harmless from any and all liability, actions, causes of action, debts, claims, or demands of every kind and na-ture whatsoever which may arise by or in connection with participation of my child/ward in any activities related to the _____ High School _____

(indicate sport)
team. The terms hereof shall serve as a release for my heirs, estate, executor, adminis-trator, assignees, and for all members of my family.

The following to be completed only if sport is *football, wrestling, gymnastics,* or *baseball:*

I specifically acknowledge that _____ is a VIOLENT CONTACT SPORT involving even greater risk of injury than other sports. _____

(initial)

Date: _____, 19 _____

_____
Signature of Parent or Legal Guardian

10/82

Exhibit 7-1 Continued

Chapter 8

SEX DISCRIMINATION ISSUES

INTRODUCTION

As women's athletics enters into a mid-life growth pattern following the initial explosion in women's intercollegiate programs in the
1970s and early 1980s, it faces great uncertainties. The absorption
of the now defunct Association of Intercollegiate Athletics for
Women (AIAW) by the NCAA, the effects of the Supreme Court's
Grove City College decision on enforcement of Title IX in athletics,
the loss of football television revenues by the NCAA and its
potential effect on the funding of nonrevenue-producing sports
championships, and the failure of the Equal Rights Amendment to
be ratified as a federal constitutional amendment pose serious
issues for those individuals concerned with the continued development of women's athletic programs. With scarcely enough time
to reflect on how far and how fast they have come with their
programs, women's athletic program administrators at the high
school and college level face new and increasingly difficult problems to solve.

Many indicators, including increases in participation, spectators,
and local and national media coverage, point to the growth in
women's athletics. The development of athletic opportunity for
women may be attributed, to some extent, to Title IX of the
Education Amendments of 1972, a federal statute that prohibits
sex discrimination. Before Title IX, women comprised only 5
percent of the total number of athletic participants in high school
and 15 percent in college. By 1984, 30.8 percent of all participants
in NCAA intercollegiate athletics were women.

As compiled by the NCAA, the average number of women's
varsity sports in the association has risen from 5.61 in 1977 to 7.1
in 1986–87, and the aggregate expenditures for women's intercollegiate athletics have increased from $24.7 million in 1977 to $116
million in 1981. The AIAW studied the relative amounts of financial
aid given to male and female athletes from 1973 to 1982. The
AIAW estimated that for 1973–74, NCAA Division I schools spent
an average of $1.2 million on men's athletic programs but only
$27,000 on women's programs. By the 1981–82 academic year,
however, the institutions expended an average of $1.7 million on
men and $400,000 on women. The result was contrary to the
predictions made by many opponents of Title IX who thought the
increased money spent on women's programs would decrease the
amount of money available for men's programs.

This point is again demonstrated in that the average NCAA
Division I school spent $1.65 million on men's athletics in 1978—
an increase from the $1.2 million spent in 1973. Expenditures
during that time for women's athletics increased from a low of

$27,000 in 1973 to $276,000 in 1978. Between 1973 and 1978, the amount of money spent on scholarships for men increased 35 percent. At the same time, NCAA Division I operations budgets increased by 40 percent, and salaries for coaches went up 56 percent. Thus, while funding for women's sports increased dramatically, funding for men's athletics increased as well.

The growth of women's sports has been impressive, as evidenced, for example, by the dramatic increase in women's overall participation. Since 1972, the number of women participating in athletics has more than doubled. By 1980, women comprised slightly less than one-third of all athletic participants (see Note 3). Athletic budgets for women's athletics have also increased. The average women's athletic budget for a Big-Ten school in 1974 was $3,500. In 1977–78, it had increased to anywhere from $250,000 to $750,000. In 1974, 60 U.S. colleges offered athletic scholarships for women. In 1981, 500 colleges were offering scholarships to women in such diverse sports as track, tennis, basketball, and volleyball. One example of this extensive growth is the University of Oklahoma women's athletic program budget for 1980, which was $700,000—a 600 percent increase from the same budget in 1974. Women's athletics has also developed quickly on the conference level. In the 1983–84 academic year, 28 Division I, 15 Division II, and 17 Division III conferences sponsored women's competition.

Since the adoption in 1981 of the NCAA governance plan for women's athletics, the association has opened its committees and services to reflect the change in its structure. In 1984, 187 women occupied 230 different positions on NCAA committees. In 1981–82, during its first year of operating women's championships, the NCAA sponsored 29 championships in 13 sports. By 1984–85, the NCAA offered 33 women's championships in 15 sports. In 1982–83, the NCAA's subsidy of 30 women's championships was $2.2 million and exceeded its support of 289 men's championships that were nonrevenue-producing by 8.4 percent. In 1983–84, women's athletics received 49 percent of the total $709,200 NCAA promotional budget.

Participation in and funding of women's athletics have increased for many reasons. A major factor is the drastic change in society's attitudes toward women, including a perception by women themselves about their own athletic capabilities and participation. According to a 1985 comprehensive survey commissioned by Lite Beer from Miller Brewing Company in cooperation with the Women's Sports Foundation, the transformation of attitudes is due to three developments in the opinions of women:

1. Women believe they have something to teach men about humane competition.

2. Women are seeking sports partners of equal skill, regardless of gender.

3. Women have strong self-confidence and a clear conviction that sports participation does not diminish femininity (see Note 2).

These attitudinal changes have helped increase athletic opportunities for women.

The NCAA has repeatedly stated that it is committed to equal athletic opportunity without regard to sex. Despite its late entry into providing athletic opportunities for women, the NCAA has made significant strides in doing so since 1981. Within the ranks of the NCAA, however, there were disagreements concerning the direction the association should take following the dissolution of the AIAW and the NCAA's assumption of control over women's intercollegiate athletics. For instance, at a May 1984 meeting of administrators of NCAA women's athletic programs, the representatives present requested that a show of support be indicated in the minutes of the meeting for H.R. 5490, a civil rights legislative proposal in the United States Congress.

House bill 5490 and Senate bill 2568 were proposed as a response to the Supreme Court's *Grove City College v. Bell* decision, which ruled that Title IX only applies to the individual programs receiving federal funding at an institution of higher education and not to the entire institution. The proposed bills would ensure that athletic programs would still fall within the parameters of Title IX. Despite the concerns of its women's athletic program administrators, the NCAA filed a statement with the chair of the U.S. House of Representatives Subcommittee on Postsecondary Education supporting the objectives of H.R. 5490 but objecting to the bill's construction. In general, the NCAA believed that the impact of the *Grove City College* decision on women's athletics was overstated, that the bill's authority would be overinclusive, and that the demands of inspection and enforcement would be too burdensome and costly.

Beyond Title IX concerns, high school and college athletic administrators are increasingly worried about the funding of women's intercollegiate programs. Some worry that the NCAA made commitments to attract women's athletic programs into the association in the early 1980s that it will find hard to continue. This is especially true in light of the reduced funding that the NCAA will receive from college football television contracts due to the U.S. Supreme Court's decision in *National Collegiate Athletic Ass'n v. Board of Regents of University of Oklahoma* (see Chapter 9, page 502).

At the May 1984 meeting of administrators of NCAA women's athletic programs, John Toner, chair of the session, stated:

> It seems to many who are responsible for generating the dollars to pay intercollegiate athletics costs that there must be some correlation between added program costs and increased revenues to support those costs. It seems to me that it is time for women leaders to concentrate on how they can stimulate and enlarge the income from women's programs.

As women reach the competitive level of men's athletics, they also begin to face the same pressures to succeed, market, and control corruption in their programs. Merrily Dean Baker, University of Minnesota women's athletic director, notes: "The potential for corruption is there and may already be employed in some places. I think our greatest challenge will be to avoid the pitfalls of the men." The NCAA's director of enforcement David Berst noted further: "We already have the worst example in men's programs. We hope that women conclude it's intolerable to end up in this same situation." Berst added that cheating has not reached the proportions of men's basketball and football, "but there are apparently some abuses that are intentional in nature."

The statistics seem to substantiate these opinions. Since the NCAA took over women's athletics in 1982, 3 schools in the sport of basketball have been placed on probation for recruiting violations, and 12 other schools have received reprimands. The violations range from having the athlete try out before an offer of a scholarship is made to entertaining family members. With increased interest, increased media exposure, increased popularity and prestige, and increased money, administrators and coaches are feeling more pressure to do what is necessary to win. (See Becker, "Crucial Time for Women's Basketball," *USA Today*, March 26, 1986, p. C1.)

Another concern is that while participants' and fans' interest in women's intercollegiate athletics continues to grow in the 1980s, the number of women holding positions as administrators and especially coaches has eroded. From 1973 to 1984 the percentage of men coaching women's sports on the NCAA's division I level rose from 10 to 50 percent. While this problem may be in part a reflection of the limited experience of women in the coaching ranks, some also claim it is because women have a limited role in the governing procedures of the NCAA.

In the face of these challenges, women's athletics may no longer rely on once available legal options. Initially, Title IX and other legislation were vanguards of changed societal attitudes, as well as legal factors that helped bring about substantial change in sex discrimination in the United States. The availability of legal options brought about an increased reliance on the legal system to redress sex discrimination. Women brought complaints about unequal treatment to court and, even more importantly, were often successful in their litigation. Recently, however, a trend of setbacks has besieged the women's movement. The failure to enact the Equal Rights Amendment and limitations imposed on Title IX enforcement by the U.S. Supreme Court have caused concern among promoters of women's athletics. A direct result of the *Grove City College* decision on intercollegiate athletics was the immediate dropping of 23 Title IX investigations. The retrenchment of programs that were so instrumental in the progress achieved in women's athletics, the absence of an organization such as the AIAW to champion the movement's specific issues, and potential funding problems are at the forefront of concerns facing women's athletics in the late 1980s.

When charges of sex discrimination are filed, the plaintiffs usually base their arguments on the equal protection laws, Title IX, and/or state equal rights amendments. Therefore, Chapter 8 begins with a discussion of the various legal theories and principles utilized in sex discrimination cases in high school and intercollegiate athletics. The chapter next focuses on the legality of and the scope and applicability of Title IX. How the Office of Civil Rights conducts compliance reviews of alleged Title IX violations follows. The chapter then discusses sex discrimination cases involving individual athletes. The cases have been grouped according to the presence or absence of teams available to either sex and according to whether the sport involved is a contact or noncontact sport. The final section of Chapter 8 focuses on sex discrimination in the area of athletic employment. The Equal Pay Act and Title VII, federal statutes that specifically pertain to discrimination in employment, are discussed. Employment discrimination in the area of coaching, officiating, refereeing, and media coverage is also examined.

NOTES _____

1. For further information on sex discrimination in women's athletics, see Tokarz, *Women, Sports and the Law: A Comprehensive Research Guide to Sex Discrimination in Sports* (Buffalo: William S. Hein Company, 1987).

2. For further information on the survey by Miller Lite and the Women's Sports Foundation, see "Miller Lite Report on Women in Sports: Summary," copyright 1985 by Miller Brewing Company, 3939 West Highland Boulevard, Milwaukee, Wisconsin 53208.

3. For further information on sex discrimination in athletics, see the following law review articles:

(a) "Sex Discrimination in High School Athletics: An Examination of Applicable Legal Doctrines," 66 *Minnesota Law Review* 1115 (1982).

(b) "Title IX: Women's Collegiate Athletics in Limbo," 40 *Washington and Lee Law Review* (1983).

(c) "Case for Equality in Athletics," 22 *Cleveland State Law Review* 570 (Fall 1973).

(d) "Legal Problems of Sex Discrimination," 15 *Alberta Law Review* 122 (1977).

(e) "Sex Discrimination and Intercollegiate Athletics," 61 *Iowa Law Review* 420 (December 1975).

(f) "Sex Discrimination and Intercollegiate Athletics: Putting Some Muscle on Title IX," 88 *Yale Law Journal* 1254 (May 1979).

(g) "Emergent Law of Women and Amateur Sports: Recent Developments," 28 *Wayne Law Review* 1701 (1982).

(h) "Equality in Athletics: The Cheerleader v. The Athlete," 19 *San Diego Law Review* 428 (1974).

(i) "Sex Discrimination in High School Athletics," 47 *University of Missouri at Kansas City Law Review* 109 (Fall 1978).

(j) "Sex Discrimination in Interscholastic High School Athletics," 25 *Syracuse Law Review* 525 (Spring 1974).

(k) "Sex Discrimination in Park District Athletic Programs," 64 *Women's Law Journal* 33 (Winter 1978).

(l) "Sex Discrimination in Athletics: A Review of Two Decades of Accomplishments and Defeats," 21 *Gonzaga Law Review* 345 (1985/86).

4. At NCAA member institutions, the number of female participants in intercollegiate athletics increased from 32,000 in 1971–72 to 64,000 in 1976–77, and rose to 80,000 by 1982–83—a 150 percent increase in 12 years. During that period, 1971–1983, the number of NCAA member institutions that sponsored women's intercollegiate sports increased as follows:

	1971 *(663 schools)*	*1982* *(753 schools)*
Basketball	307	705
Cross Country	10	417
Softball	147	416
Swimming	140	348
Tennis	243	610
Track and Field	78	427
Volleyball	208	603

5. On the high school level, prior to the enactment of Title IX in 1972, fewer than 300,000 girls took part in high school athletics. In 1986, this figure rose to 1.8 million (compared with 3.3 million boys participating).

6. Administrators and coaches will find the following organizations useful resources:

(a) Women's Sports Foundation, 195 Moulton Street, San Francisco, Ca 94123. This organization publishes *Women's Sports and Fitness*, a monthly magazine. The foundation also created the Women's Sports Hall of Fame, a traveling exhibit.

(b) Women's Equity Action League, 805 Fifteenth Street, N.W., Washington, D.C. 20005. This organization established the project SPRINT, whose major purpose is to promote equal opportunity for women in sports. The organization also publishes *In the Running*.

(c) National Association for Girls and Women in Sport, 1201 Sixteenth Street, N.W., Washington, D.C. 20036. The association regularly publishes official rule books for many women's sports.

(d) Center for Women and Sport, White Building, Pennsylvania State University, University Park, PA 16802.

(e) Association for Intercollegiate Athletics for Women, 1201 Sixteenth Street, N.W., Washington, D.C. 20036.

(f) NOW Task Force on Women Sports, National NOW Action Center, 425 Thirteenth Street, N.W., Suite 1001, Washington, D.C. 20004.

LEGAL PRINCIPLES UTILIZED IN
SEX DISCRIMINATION CASES

Sex discrimination in high school and intercollegiate athletics has been challenged using a variety of legal arguments, including equal protection laws, Title IX of the Education Amendment of 1972, state equal rights amendments, and the Equal Pay Act. Most challenges have been based on either the equal protection laws or Title IX, or both. For example, in *Pavey v. University of Alaska v. National Collegiate Athletic Ass'n*, 490 F. Supp. 1011 (D. Alaska 1980), an action was brought against the University of Alaska charging it with discrimination against female student-athletes in the operation of its athletic program in violation of Title IX and the Fourteenth Amendment's due process and equal protection clauses. The university filed a third-party suit against the NCAA and the AIAW, which charged that the two associations' inconsistent rules required the university to discriminate in its athletic program in violation of federal laws. The NCAA and AIAW made motions for dismissal of the suit. In denying the motions, the district court held that the university's suit stated a valid claim, that the university was reasonably trying to avoid a confrontation with the two associations' rules that could cause a disruption in the participation of student-athletes in intercollegiate athletics, and that the facial neutrality of the associations' rules did not negate the university's claim that those rules, in combined effect, forced the university to discriminate in its athletic programs.

Equal protection arguments are based on the Fifth Amendment of the U.S. Constitution, which guarantees equal protection of the law to all persons found within the United States. (See Chapter 4, page 158, for a further discussion of equal protection.)

Title IX is a relatively recent method of attacking sex discrimination. Although the original legislation was passed in 1972, implementation was delayed for the promulgation of regulations and policy interpretations. Even with the delay, many have claimed that the rise in participation by women in athletics was directly related to the passage of Title IX. A state equal rights amendment can also be used to attack alleged sex discrimination; however, not all states have passed such legislation. The fourth argument concerns two separate statutes: the Equal Pay Act and Title VII of the Civil Rights Act of 1964. Although neither statute was passed to deal specifically with sex discrimination, both have been used to challenge employment-related discrimination.

In a sex discrimination case, the plaintiff usually contends that there is a fundamental inequality, regardless of whether a plaintiff employs an equal protection or Title IX approach. In attempting to deal with these claims, the court considers three factors. The first is whether or not the sport from which women are excluded is one involving physical contact. Total exclusion from all sports or from any noncontact sport is considered a violation of equal educational opportunity. The second factor is the quality and quantity of opportunities available to each sex. The courts compare the number of athletic opportunities available to each sex as well as the amount of money spent on equipment, the type of coaches provided, and the access to school-owned facilities. The third factor the courts consider is age and level of competition involved in the dispute. The younger the athletes involved, the fewer the actual physiological differences that exist. Without demonstrable physiological differences, the justification of inherent biological differences as a rational basis for the exclusion of one sex from athletic participation is negated.

Equal Protection Laws

The basic analysis utilized for equal protection questions was discussed in Chapter 4, page 158. Here we examine more closely the effects of using gender to classify persons for different athletic opportunities.

Historically, sex has been an acceptable category for classifying persons for different benefits and burdens under any given law. In 1872 the Supreme Court, in *Bradwell v. State*, 83 U.S. (16 Wall) 130 (1873), opened with the statement that a woman's place was in the home. The Court went on to say that this was part of a "divinely ordained law of nature." In 1908, the Court stated in *Muller v. Oregon,* 208 U.S. 412, 28 S. Ct. 324, 52 L.Ed. 551 (1908), that a classification based on gender was a valid constitutional classification. Such a classification was not considered to be a violation of equal protection, regardless of whether it was based on actual or imagined physical differences between men and women. Modern equal protection theories have now gained preeminence, and the use of gender to classify persons is considered less acceptable.

A school's, conference's, or athletic association's rules prohibiting mixed-gender competition have typically been challenged on equal protection grounds. As women's rights have been gaining importance and attracting attention in all areas, so too have women begun to assert their right to participate in athletics free from sex discrimination. In a number of cases, women have been successful in asserting their right to participate on an equal basis with men, and one legal theory they have utilized on these occasions has been the equal protection clause.

Under traditional equal protection analysis, the legislative gender-based classification must be sustained unless it is found to be patently arbitrary and/or if it bears absolutely no rational relationship to a legitimate governmental interest. Under this traditional rational basis analysis, overturning discriminatory laws is extremely difficult. The implication for sex discrimination sports litigation in high schools and colleges is such that women may be excluded from athletic participation upon a showing of a rational reason for their exclusion and by providing comparable options for those who are excluded. The rational reason must be factually supported and may not be based on mere presumptions about the relative physical and athletic capabilities of women and men. It remains, however, a relatively easy standard for the defendant to meet, as it invokes only the lowest standard of scrutiny by the court.

The court will apply its highest standard, that of strict scrutiny, if it finds that the classification restricts a "fundamental right" or if the rule involves a "suspect" classification. Under the standard of strict scrutiny, the party seeking to enforce the regulation must show that the rule's classification is necessary to promote a compelling governmental purpose or interest. To date the courts have not found sex to be a suspect class, which would elevate it to the status held by race, national origin, and alienage. Sex and other classifications may, however, be deemed "suspect" under a state equal protection clause. In addition, the courts have generally ruled that participation in interscholastic and intercollegiate sports is not a fundamental right under the equal protection clause. Consequently, this participation interest alone does not warrant the application of strict scrutiny in evaluating a classification.

If the courts were, however, to decide that sex is a suspect class or athletic participation is a fundamental right, all rules that classify on the basis of gender would become subject to strict scrutiny analysis. If this were the standard, the rule makers would have to prove that there are compelling reasons for the classification and that there is no less restrictive alternative. They would also have to prove that the classification was directly related to the constitutional purpose of the legislation and that this purpose could not have been achieved by any less objectionable means. Many rules and laws would fail to meet this high standard, and hence would be judged to be discriminatory.

Some courts have moved away from the broad interpretation of the rational relationship test by increasing the burden on the defendant. This intermediate test, between the rational basis and strict scrutiny test, was first established by the Supreme Court in *Reed v. Reed*, 404 U.S. 71, 30 L.Ed. 2d 225, 92 S. Ct. 251 (1971). The Supreme Court established therein that sex-based classifications must be "reasonable, not arbitrary, and must rest upon some ground of difference having a fair and substantial relation to the object of the legislation, so that all persons similarly circumstanced shall be treated alike." The Supreme Court again addressed this issue in *Frontiero v. Richardson*, 411 U.S. 677, 36 L.Ed. 2d 538, 93 S. Ct. 1764 (1973); in a plurality opinion, Justice Brennan reasoned that sex-based classifications "serve important governmental objectives and must be substantially related to the achievement of those objectives."

A factual basis for any gender classification must exist. Mere preferences or assumptions concerning the ability of one sex to perform adequately are not acceptable bases for a discriminatory classification. This intermediate test is still one step away from a declaration by the courts that sex is an inherently suspect class.

Because a Supreme Court majority opinion to apply a strict scrutiny analysis in gender-based cases does not yet exist, courts may opt to apply either a rational basis test or the intermediate standard of review. The intermediate standard requires more than an easily achieved rational relationship but less than a strict scrutiny standard would demand. The class must bear a substantial relationship to an important but not compelling governmental interest. Also, the relationship between a classification and a law's purpose must now be founded on fact, not on general legislative views of the relative strengths and/or abilities of the two sexes.

Three key factors commonly are considered in an equal protection analysis of athletic discrimination cases. The first factor is state action. Before any claim can be successfully litigated, a sufficient amount of state action must be present. Without state action, an equal protection argument under the U.S. Constitution is not applicable. This factor has significant ramifications in cases in which the athletic activity is conducted outside the auspices of a state or municipal entity or a public educational institution. Examples include youth sport leagues such as Little League Baseball, Pop Warner Football, and the YMCA's Youth Basketball Association.

The second factor is whether the sport involves physical contact. In contact sports the courts have allowed separate men's and women's teams. This "separate but equal" doctrine is based on considerations of the physical health and safety of the participants. When separate teams do not exist, however, both sexes may have an opportunity to try out and to meet the necessary physical requirements on an individual basis. A complete ban on the participation of one sex will not be upheld if it is based on generalizations about characteristics of an entire sex rather than on a reasonable consideration of individual characteristics. (See *Clinton v. Nagy* on page 443.)

The third factor to be considered is whether both sexes have equal opportunities to participate. This "equal opportunity" usually requires the existence of completely separate teams or an opportunity to try out for the one available team. If there are separate teams, however, it is permissible for the governing organization to prohibit co-ed participation. Unlike classifications based on race, when gender is a determining factor, "separate but equal" doctrines may be acceptable. The issue then often becomes whether the teams are indeed equal (see *O'Connor v. Board of Education of School District No. 23* on page 456 and *Ritacco v. Norwin School District* on page 458). Other factors that have been taken into consideration are the age of the participant and the level of the competition. Physical differences between boys and girls below the age of 12 are minimal. Therefore, health and safety considerations that might be applicable to older athletes have not constituted legitimate reasons for restricting young athletes' access to participation (see *Bednar v. Nebraska School Activities Ass'n* on page 449.)

The legal analysis of any particular case, however, will depend on the philosophy of the court and the particular factual circumstances presented (see *Brenden v. Independent School District 742* on page 447). Some courts are reluctant to intervene in discretionary decisions made by an association governing athletic events unless there are obvious abuses. (See Chapter 4 for a discussion of judicial review.) Other courts have been reluctant to intervene in discretionary decisions because they do not believe they are equipped with the administrative knowledge or time necessary to oversee the administration of sport programs effectively.

Historically, challenging sex discrimination based on the equal protection laws has not been totally effective. The constitutional standard of rational relationship has been a very difficult one for a plaintiff to challenge alleged sex discrimination successfully. The use of the intermediate standard, a more stringent test, is partly attributable to some of the recent successful challenges of alleged sex discrimination. However, the plurality decision of the Supreme Court in *Frontiero v. Richardson* lessens the impact of the intermediate standard. A strong decision by the court with respect to the intermediate standard or a finding that sex should be included as a suspect category would greatly assist plaintiffs in attacking alleged sex discrimination.

Another disadvantage of the equal protection laws is that they constitute a private remedy. Therefore, the plaintiff must be in a position to absorb the costs of litigation. This reduces the number of complaints filed and encourages settlement before final resolution of a number of equal protection claims.

NOTES

1. In *Ridgefield Women's Political Caucus, Inc. v. Fossi*, 458 F. Supp. 117 (D. Conn. 1978), girls and taxpayer parents brought claims against town selectmen seeking to prohibit the town from offering public property at a nominal price to a private organization that restricted membership to boys. The district court found for the girls and parents, ruling that the town selectmen had no right to offer land at less than fair value to the private organization in question as long as this organization restricted membership and the town failed to offer to girls comparable recreational opportunities equivalent to those provided by the organization in question. Until such services are offered, any conveyance of the property at a nominal fee would constitute governmental support of sex discrimination in violation of the equal protection clause of the Fourteenth Amendment.

2. In *Kelly v. Wisconsin Interscholastic Athletic Ass'n*, 367 F. Supp. 1388 (E.D. Wis. 1973), the court held that the claim of female students excluded from participation on the male varsity swimming teams because of an association rule stated a constitutional claim under the Fourteenth Amendment against the high school association officials who, either directly or in their official capacities, allowed enforcement of such rule. The court held that the female students failed to state a cause of action on which relief could be granted (a) against the association because they failed to allege the necessary "state action"; (b) against the state superintenent of schools because they failed to allege any facts to support failure

to provide due process; or (c) against the board of school directors because actions may not be maintained against municipal corporations.

3. The California Supreme Court ruled in October 1985 that "Ladies Night" discounts must be banned because they discriminate against men. The state's high court unanimously found that sex-based price discounts violate "clear and unambiguous" language of the state's civil rights act. One chief justice believed that the discount, designed to attract more female patrons, may in fact hurt both men and women, "because it reinforces harmful stereotypes ("California Bans Sex-Based Discounts," *Boston Globe*, October 18, 1985, p. 18, col. 6).

4. For further information on athletic participation and equal protection, see "Sex Discrimination in Secondary School Athletics," 46 *Tennessee Law Review* 222 (Fall 1978).

5. In *Richards v. United States Tennis Ass'n*, 400 N.Y.S. 2d 267 (Sup. Ct. N.Y. County 1977), an action was brought by a professional tennis player, who had undergone a sex-change operation, against a professional tennis association which sought a preliminary injunction against the organization to prevent it from requiring the tennis player to undergo a sex-chromatin test to prove she was a female and eligible to participate in a women's tournament. The court granted the injunction and held the test was grossly unfair, discriminatory, and inequitable, and violated the tennis player's rights under the New York Human Rights Law.

Title IX

Section 901 (a) of Title IX of the Education Amendments of 1972 contains the following language:

> No person in the United States shall, on the basis of sex, be excluded from participation in, be denied the benefits of, or be subjected to discrimination under any education program or activity receiving Federal financial assistance.

Title IX became law on July 1, 1972, as Public Law 92-318. It specifically and clearly recognizes the problems of sex discrimination and forbids such discrimination in any program, organization, or agency that receives federal funds. A long process of citizen involvement preceded the first set of regulations. In July 1975, the Department of Health, Education and Welfare (HEW) issued the regulations designed to implement Title IX.

These regulations are found in Title 45, Code of Federal Regulations (C.F.R.), section 86 A-F. The regulations were criticized by many as being vague and inadequate. In December 1978, HEW attempted to alleviate the criticism by releasing a proposed policy interpretation, which attempted to explain but did not change the 1975 requirements. However, not until December 1979, seven years after the original passage of Title IX, did the Office of Civil Rights (OCR), the successor to HEW, release the policy interpretation for Title IX. These final guidelines specifically included interscholastic and intercollegiate athletics. Developed after numerous meetings and countless revisions, they reflected comments from universities, legislative sources, and the public.

The policy interpretation focused on three areas which the OCR evaluates to determine whether an institution is in compliance with Title IX regulations with regards to athletics. First, the OCR assesses whether an institution's athletic scholarships are awarded on a "substantially proportional" basis. To determine this, the amount of scholarship money available for each sex is divided by the number of male or female participants in the athletic program and results are compared. If comparison shows "substantially equal amounts" of money spent per athlete, or if a disparity is explained by legitimate and nondiscriminatory factors, the OCR will find compliance.

The second area of assessment under the policy interpretation is the degree to which the institution provides equal treatment, benefits, and opportunities in certain program areas. The areas considered by the OCR in evaluating equal treatment include equipment, coaching, and facilities. (See page 421 for a complete list of factors.)

The final area the OCR assesses is the extent to which the institution has met the interests and abilities of male and female students. The policy interpretation requires that the school "equally and effectively" accommodate the athletic interest and abilities of both men and women. This determination requires an examination of the institution's assessment of the athletic interest and abilities of its students, its selection of offered sports, and its available competitive opportunities. The OCR evaluates the level of competitive opportunities in one of three ways:

1. Are intercollegiate competitive opportunities provided in numbers substantially proportionate to the respective enrollments of each sex?

2. Is the institution's current and historical practice of program expansion responsive to the athletic interests of the underrepresented sex?

3. Does the institution accommodate the abilities and the interests of the underrepresented sex in the current program?

If the OCR determines that an institution complies with any one of these tests, the institution is judged to have effectively accommodated the interest and the abilities of its student-athletes.

The policy interpretation developed by the OCR contained some strict guidelines for assessing Title IX compliance, including the following:

1. The inclusion of football and other revenue-providing sports.
2. "Sport-specifics" comparisons as the basis for assessing compliance.
3. "Team-based" comparisons (grouping sports by levels of development) as the basis for compliance assessments.
4. Institutional planning that does not meet the provisions of the policy interpretation as applied by the OCR.

The policy interpretation also outlined certain "nondiscriminatory factors" to be considered when assessing Title IX compliance. These factors include differences that may result from the unique nature of particular sports, special circumstances of a temporary nature, the need for greater funding for crowd control at more popular athletic events, and differences that have not yet been remedied but which an institution is voluntarily working to correct. In the area of compensation for men's and women's coaches, HEW assessed rates of compensation, length of contracts, experience, and other factors, while taking into account mitigating conditions such as nature of duties, number of assistants to be supervised, number of participants, and level of competition.

The major issues raised regarding Title IX revolve around the scope of the legislation and the programs to which it is applicable. The July 1975 policy regulations issued by HEW covered three areas of activity within educational institutions: employment, treatment of students, and admissions. Several sections of the regulations concerned with the treatment of students included specific requirements for interscholastic, intercollegiate, intramural, and club athletic programs.

One important issue is whether Title IX applies to an entire institution or only to the programs within that institution which receive direct federal assistance. The Supreme Court ruled in *Grove City College v. Bell* (see page 435) that only those programs within an institution that receive direct financial assistance from the federal government should be subject to Title IX strictures. This interpretation is often referred to as the "programmatic approach" to the Title IX statute (see *Othen v. Ann Arbor School Board* on page 432). Others have reached the opposite conclusion—that the receipt of any federal aid to an institution, whether it be limited to only certain programs or indirect (for example, student loans) programs, should place the entire institution under the jurisdiction of Title IX (see the *Haffer v. Temple University* U.S. Court of Appeals decision on page 434). This interpretation is called the "institutional approach" to Title IX.

While Title IX does not require the creation of athletic programs or the same sport offerings to both sexes—for example, a football program for women or a volleyball program for men—it does require equality of opportunity in accommodation of interests and abilities, in athletic scholarships, and in other benefits and opportunities (see *Othen v. Ann Arbor School Board* on page 432).

Athletics and athletics programs were not specifically mentioned in Title IX when it first became law in 1972. Congress was generally opposed to placing athletics programs under the realm of Title IX. However, HEW, taking the position that sports and physical education are an integral part of education, specifically included athletics, despite strong lobbying efforts to exempt revenue-producing intercollegiate sports from the Title IX requirements. This specific inclusion of athletics occurred in 1974 and extended from general athletic opportunities to athletic scholarships. The principles governing athletic scholarships included the idea that all recipients of federal aid must provide *"reasonable opportunities"* for both sexes to receive scholarship aid. The existence of *"reasonable opportunities"* is determined by examining the ratio of male to female participants. Scholarship aid must then be distributed according to this participation ratio (see Title 45, *Code of Federal Regulations*, Section 86.13[c]).

Another section of the HEW Title IX regulations specifies requirements for athletic programs (see 45 C.F.R. sec. 86.41[c]). Contact sports are subject to regulations distinct from those governing noncontact sports. The regulations in this section state that separate teams are acceptable for contact sports and for teams in either contact or noncontact sports in which selection is based on competitive skill. There is one exception to the rule forbidding separate teams when selection is based on competitive skill: If a school sponsors a team in a particular sport for one sex but not for the other, and if athletic opportunities for the excluded sex have been historically more restricted than athletic opportunities for the other sex, members of the excluded sex must be allowed to try out for the team. The exception does not apply if the sport is a contact sport. For noncontact sports, if only one team exists, both sexes must be allowed to compete for positions on the team. The Office of Civil Rights, which monitors compliance of Title IX, considers many factors in determining the equality of opportunity, including the following:

1. Selection of sports and the level of competition offered
2. Facilities available (medical, training, locker rooms, practice, competitive)
3. Equipment and supplies available
4. Games and practice schedules

5. Methods of travel and per diem allowances
6. Coaching and academic tutoring (including assignment and amount of compensation)
7. Housing and dining facilities
8. Publicity

Athletic expenditures need not be equal, but the pattern of expenditures must not result in a disparate effect on opportunity. Institutions may not discriminate in the provision of necessary equipment, supplies, facilities, and publicity for sports programs.

The OCR may use additional factors in determining whether an institution is providing equal opportunity for members of both sexes in its sports program. However, some of the factors listed (publicity, academic tutoring, housing, and dining services) are relevant in intercollegiate programs but are not generally relevant in assessing a sports program in a secondary school.

The procedures for Title IX analysis are established in special administrative guidelines, which list specific factors that should be examined in determining whether or not equality in athletics exists. The number of sports, the type of arrangements, and benefits offered to women competing in athletics are reviewed. When teams of one sex are favored in such areas as funding, coaching, and facilities, resulting in severely reduced opportunities for the other sex to compete, the courts will closely examine program expenditures, number of teams, and access to facilities to determine if the school is fulfilling the requirements of Title IX. As a general rule, although Title IX does not require the adoption of programs or equivalent funding, increases in either or both may be necessary to redress past discrimination.

The final area of coverage in the regulations is the method of enforcement of Title IX. Compliance with the dictates of the law is monitored by the OCR in the Department of Education (formerly part of the Department of Health, Education and Welfare). The procedure to be followed is initiated by the OCR, which makes random compliance reviews and also investigates complaints submitted by individuals. The first step in the process is to examine the records kept by the institution under investigation to review its attempted compliance with Title IX. Each institution must adopt and publish complaint procedures and designate one employee to carry out its Title IX responsibilities, including investigation of complaints. The institution must notify all students and employees of the designated employee's name, office address, and telephone number. Following a preliminary review, the OCR has the option to conduct a full hearing or to drop the case.

If the OCR calls a full hearing, the institution has the right to have counsel present and to appeal an adverse decision; the complainant has neither of these rights. The affected individual is not a party involved in the hearing. Instead, the OCR becomes the complainant and pursues the claim. If the OCR finds that there has not been substantial compliance, it may turn its finding over to federal or local authorities for prosecution under the appropriate statutes (see page 436).

A number of attempts to lessen the impact of Title IX have been made since 1979. One of these proposed changes was introduced on June 11, 1981, by Senator Orrin G. Hatch of Utah. His amendment (S. 1361) would have specifically restricted the scope of Title IX to those programs that receive direct funding from the federal government. The amendment was also designed to specify that money received by students in the form of scholarships, grants, or loans does not constitute federal aid for Title IX purposes. Passage of this amendment would have effectively eliminated claims by women in the areas of athletics and other extracurricular activities, health care, guidance counseling, and residential housing, since these programs do not generally receive direct federal funding. It would have also restricted the application of Title IX with respect to employment discrimination claims, therefore relegating employment discrimination problems to the less inclusive legislation of Title VII of the Civil Rights Act of 1964.

Supporters of the amendment found merit in the proposal in that it advocated the lessening of federal involvement in education. Furthermore, some educators argued that the slackening of governmental restraint would not necessarily create a situation in which women's athletic programs would suffer. Instead, they claimed, administrators would become more innovative in terms of women's programs once they were freed of the threat of legal action if these programs did not immediately meet the standards of men's programs. Senator Hatch's proposal was not passed, and he subsequently withdrew the legislation.

Another proposed amendment, commonly referred to as the Family Protection Act, advocated the repeal of Title IX. Its provisions would remove from the jurisdiction of federal courts the right to determine whether the sexes should be allowed to intermingle in athletics or in any other school activity. A third effort to restrict the power of Title IX involved a bill (S. 1091) introduced by Senators Hatch and Edward Zorinsky of Nebraska. It proposed that institutions be reimbursed by the OCR for expenses incurred during any investigation the OCR conducts of institutional programs or activities. Opponents of this bill argued that should the OCR be required to reimburse schools without a corresponding increase in its own budget, the total budget actually available for enforcement would diminish. They argued that less money for enforcement would restrict the number of investigations initiated by the OCR, thereby limiting the potential deterrent value of the threat of such an investigation.

NOTES _____

1. In *Lieberman v. University of Chicago*, 660 F.2d 1185 (7th Cir. 1981), *cert. denied*, 456 U.S. 937 (1982), the court held that Title IX does not provide a damages remedy, citing *Pennhurst State School and Hospital v. Halderman*, 451 U.S. 1 (1981), a case in which the Court had declined to impose upon the states as a condition of receiving federal funding the obligation to comply with the "bill of rights" section of the Developmentally Disabled Assistance and Bill of Rights Act. An individual Title IX plaintiff is entitled only to injunctive and declaratory relief. The court reasoned that the imposition of a damages remedy might give rise to "a potentially massive financial liability" upon an institution, which could theoretically exceed the amount of the federal funds received. (Compare *Guardians Association v. Civil Service Commissioner of the City of New York*, 103 S. Ct. 3221, 3232 n.23 [1983], which cited *Lieberman* with approval and concluded compensatory relief is not available as a private remedy for Title VI violations not involving intentional discrimination.)

2. In *Alexander v. Yale University*, 631 F.2d 178 (2d Cir. 1978), the court held that a party seeking relief under Title IX must demonstrate a personal "distinct and palpable injury," and the relief requested must "redound to that party's personal benefit." Former students lacked standing to get any relief from sexual harassment charges.

3. For further information concerning the institutional and programmatic approaches to Title IX application, see the following law review articles:

(a) "The Application of Title IX to School Athletic Programs," 68 *Cornell Law Review* 222 (1983).

(b) "The Program-Specific Reach of Title IX," 83 *Columbia Law Review* 1210 (1983).

4. For an examination of the legislative history of Title IX in respect to athletics, see the following law review articles:

(a) Johnson, "The Evolution of Title IX: Prospects for Equality in Intercollegiate Athletics," 11 *Golden Gate University Law Review* 759 (1981).

(b) "Title IX and Intercollegiate Athletics: Adducing Congressional Intent," 24 *Boston College Law Review* 1243 (1983).

5. For an examination of judicial interpretation of Title IX and athletics, see "Judicial Deference to Legislative Reality: The Interpretation of Title IX in the Context of Collegiate Athletics," 14 *North Carolina Central Law Journal* 601.

6. For further general information on Title IX, see the following law review articles:

(a) "Half-Court Girls" Basketball Rules: An Application of the Equal Protection Clause and Title IX," 65 *Iowa Law Review* 766 (1980).

(b) "HEW's Final 'Policy Interpretation' of Title IX and Intercollegiate Athletics," 6 *Journal of College and University Law* 345 (1980).

(c) "Implementing Title IX: The HEW Regulations," 124 *Pennsylvania Law Review* 806 (1976).

(d) "Intercollegiate Athletics and Title IX," 46 *George Washington Law Review* 34 (1977).

(e) "The Legality and Requirements of HEW's Proposed Policy Interpretation of Title IX and Intercollegiate Athletics," 6 *Journal of College and University Law* 161 (1980).

(f) "Postsecondary Athletics in an Era of Equality: An Appraisal of the Effect of Title IX," 5 *Journal of College and University Law* 123 (1978–79).

(g) "Sex Discrimination in Athletics," 21 *Villanova Law Review* 876 (October 1976).

(h) "Sex Discrimination in Athletics: Conflicting Legislative and Judicial Approaches," 29 *Alabama Law Review* 390 (Winter 1978).

(i) "Title IX and the NCAA," 3 *Western State University Law Review* 185 (Spring 1976).

(j) "Title IX and Intercollegiate Athletics: Scoring Points for Women," 8 *Ohio Northern University Law Review* 481 (July 1981).

(k) "Title IX of the Education Amendments of 1972: Change or Continuity?" 6 *Journal of Law and Education* 183 (April 1977).

(l) "Title IX's Promise of Equality of Opportunity in Athletics: Does It Cover the Bases," 64 *Kentucky Law Journal* 432 (1975–76).

(m) "Sex Discrimination in Athletics: A Review of Two Decades of Accomplishments and Defeats," 21 *Gonzaga Law Review* 345 (1985/86).

7. A number of states throughout the United States have adopted Title IX as state legislation.

The ERA and State Equal Rights Amendments

Although there are many legal alternatives to allegations of sex discrimination, to date there has been no nationwide comprehensive prohibition of sex discrimination. Supporters of the Equal Rights Amendment (ERA) argued that passage of a constitutional amendment would remedy the lack of such a general prohibition. In order to amend the United States Constitution, the proposed amendment must first be passed by a three-fourths vote of both the United States Senate and the House of Representatives. Then it must be ratified by at least 38 state legislatures. The ERA was passed in both Houses of Congress in 1972, but it did not receive the necessary 38 ratifications from state legislatures by the required deadline of July 1, 1982.

In some instances, individual states have passed their own equal rights amendments. A state court may apply its equal rights or equal protection clause to extend greater protection against sex-based classifications than that available under federal equal protection of the Fourteenth Amendment. For example, some state courts have held that their state equal protection clauses render any classification based on sex suspect. A stricter standard of scrutiny is then applied, and the court is more likely to find the classification unconstitutional than are federal courts, which apply the lower standard of the federal equal protection clause. The federal equal protection clause does not prevent state courts from affording broader rights under their state constitutions. Thus, equal rights amendments have impacted on athletics at the state level but not at the federal level. Several cases have been decided in favor of the complainant on the basis of a state ERA. All of these cases, however, could have been decided on other arguments in states without ERAs.

In general, the proposed federal ERA absolutely prohibited discrimination based on gender and required that any law using gender as a basis for classification be subject to a strict scrutiny analysis by the courts. Opponents of the ERA claimed that this prohibition was an unnecessary step. They believed that women's rights are sufficiently protected by the U.S. Constitution, state equal protection laws, and other federal legislation such as the Equal Pay Act, Title VII, and Title IX.

Supporters of the ERA argued that without proper enforcement, neither Title IX nor Title VII can alleviate the basic problems of sex discrimination. The weakness of Title IX in particular is dependent on federal funding, since a reduction in funding can effectively diminish the OCR's enforcement capabilities. In addition to this financial vulnerability, sex discrimination statutes are also subject to congressional revisions, which may lessen or even negate much of the available protection. It has been argued that a constitutional amendment would be more sheltered from fluctuating political interests.

Supporters of a constitutional amendment continue to argue that the effectiveness and importance of an equal rights amendment can be demonstrated in *Darrin v. Gould* (see Note 1). In *Darrin*, the lower court considered the equal protection argument and ruled in favor of the defendant. The Washington Supreme Court, however, reversed the decision in favor of the plaintiffs, based on the state's equal rights argument. As such, the court's decision may be effectively downgraded with the subsequent passage of limiting legislation to the state ERA. Regardless of the precarious position in which protection against sex discrimination exists, the existence of an equal rights amendment on the state level is often helpful and may even be crucial to the success of sex discrimination cases.

NOTES ───

1. In *Darrin v. Gould*, 85 Wash. 2d 859, 540 P.2d 882 (1975), an action was brought by the parents of high school students Carol and Delores Darrin, who appealed a Washington Superior Court decision denying them relief in their class action claim of illegal discrimination against females in interscholastic football competition. The Washington Supreme Court found that the school board's denial of permission for the girls to compete on the boys' interscholastic contact football team constituted "a discrimination by state action based on ability to play." Under the due process clause of the Fourteenth Amendment, "performers are entitled to an individualized determination of their qualifications, not a determination based on the qualifications of a majority of the broader class of which the individual is a member." The Supreme Court decided that the Darrin girls could participate, based on the provision of Washington's Equal Rights Amendment, which stated: "Equality of rights and responsibility under the law shall not be denied or abridged on account of sex."

2. In *MacLean v. First Northwest Industries of America, Inc.*, 600 P.2d 1027 (Wash. Ct. App. 1979), a class action was brought against the city of Seattle and the corporation operating a professional basketball team that alleged "Ladies Night" price-ticketing policies were violative of the state's equal rights amendment that prohibited sex discrimination. The court of appeals reversed a lower court decision and found the ticket practice a violation of the amendment.

3. In *Commonwealth, Packal v. Pennsylvania Interscholastic Athletic Ass'n*, 18 Pa. Commw. Ct. 45, 334 A.2d 839 (1975), the state of Pennsylvania, acting through its attorney general, filed suit against the Pennsylvania Interscholastic Athletic Association (PIAA), charging that Article XIX, Section 38 of the PIAA bylaws, which states that "girls shall not compete or practice against boys in any athletic contest," was in violation of both the Fourteenth Amendment of the U.S. Constitution and Pennsylvania's equal rights amendment. Plaintiff claimed that the association's rule denied to female athletes the same opportunities to practice and compete in interscholastic sports that were afforded male athletes. Pennsylvania's ERA provides that "equality of rights under law shall not be denied or abridged in the Commonwealth of Pennsylvania because of the sex of the individual." The court found the association's rule to be "unconstitutional on its face under the ERA" and proclaimed that "none of the justifications for it offered by the PIAA, even if proved, could sustain its legality." The court found it unnecessary to consider whether or not the rule also violated the Fourteenth Amendment.

4. Four states responded to Title IX by opening all teams to both sexes. The results were that boys dominated all the teams, and fewer girls than ever could compete. In Indiana, the first- and second-place volleyball teams (previously all female) had one and three boys, respec-

tively. In West Virginia, the first-place girls' bowling team was composed of five boys. Michigan was forced to change its rule so that boys could not compete on a statewide level on girls' teams. This information came from reports sent to member organizations by the National Federation of State High School Athletic Associations.

5. As of 1986, the following 19 states had enacted their own individual equal rights amendments: Alaska, Arizona, California, Colorado, Connecticut, Hawaii, Illinois, Louisiana, Maryland, Massachusetts, Montana, New Hampshire, New Mexico, Pennsylvania, Texas, Utah, Virginia, Washington, and Wyoming.

6. As of 1986, the following 23 states and the District of Columbia had enacted their own statutes prohibiting sex discrimination in educational sports programs: Alaska, California, Colorado, Connecticut, Florida, Hawaii, Idaho, Illinois, Iowa, Louisiana, Maine, Massachusetts, Michigan, Minnesota, Montana, Nebraska, New York, North Carolina, Oregon, Rhode Island, South Dakota, Washington, Wisconsin.

7. For further information on individual states' ERAs, see the following law review articles:

(a) "Hawaii's Equal Rights Amendment: Its Impact on Athletic Opportunities and Competition for Women," 2 *University of Hawaii Law Review* 97 (1979).

(b) "Sexual Equality in High School Athletics: The Approach of *Darrin v. Gould*," 12 *Gonzaga Law Review* 691 (Summer 1977).

LEGAL CHALLENGES TO TITLE IX

Legality of Title IX

The Title IX regulations and accompanying policy interpretations were promulgated by the Department of Health, Education and Welfare (HEW) and were not finalized until July 1979 after many revisions and in spite of remaining ambiguities. Many of the remaining questions may eventually be decided by the courts in any future interpretations of Title IX.

The first legal challenge to Title IX was brought by the NCAA. The NCAA sought declaratory and injunctive relief for the invalidation of the Title IX regulations promulgated by HEW in *National Collegiate Athletic Ass'n v. Califano*, 444 F. Supp. 425 (D. Kan. 1978), *rev'd*, 622 F.2d 1382 (10th Cir. 1980). The NCAA specifically sought relief for the invalidation of the Title IX regulations promulgated by HEW with respect to sex discrimination in athletics. Summary judgment was granted to HEW, as the district court held that the NCAA did not have standing as an association representing its member schools to pursue the suit. The NCAA appealed the district court decision. The appeals court reversed the lower court ruling and held that while the NCAA does not have standing to sue in its own right, it does have standing to sue on behalf of its members. (See Chapter 4, page 96, for a discussion of standing.)

NOTE _____

1. For further information, see the following law review articles:
   (a) Cox, "Intercollegiate Athletics and Title IX," 46 *George Washington Law Review* 34 (November 1977).
   (b) "Sex Discrimination in High School Athletics," 47 *University of Missouri at Kansas City Law Review* 109 (Fall 1978).
   (c) "Sex Discrimination and Intercollegiate Athletics: Putting Some Muscle in Title IX," 88 *Yale Law Journal* 1254 (May 1979).

Scope and Applicability of Title IX

A major issue involved in Title IX litigation centers on arguments concerning the scope of Title IX. The question is whether Title IX applies only to the specific departments receiving direct funding (commonly referred to as the "programmatic approach") or extends to any department within an institution that benefits from federal assistance (commonly referred to as the "institutional approach"). The dilemma is often expressed as whether Title IX is, or is not, program-specific. An integral factor in the resultant litigation has been the determination of what constitutes qualifying federal assistance. In some cases, it has been argued that federal student loan programs constitute federal aid to an institution, while other interpretations define federal aid as only those funds specifically earmarked or directly given to a particular program. Therefore, in terms of the scope of Title IX, the questions become very complex: What constitutes federal aid? Is indirect aid or direct aid required by the statute? Once federal assistance is found, is only the particular program that benefits from the aid or the entire institution subject to Title IX regulation?

The decision in *Grove City College v. Bell* has answered some of these questions, but other issues remain to be clarified through further litigation or legislation. Many of the cases preceding *Grove City College v. Bell* deal with the "programmatic" versus "institutional" issue. A programmatic approach was taken by the district courts in *Othen v. Ann Arbor School Board, Bennett v. West Texas State University, Hillsdale College v. Department of Health, Education and Welfare*, and *University of Richmond v. Bell*. An institutional approach was taken by the court in *Haffer v. Temple University* and the court of appeals in *Grove City College v. Bell*. The resolution of certain issues was extremely important, not only in terms of the potential ramifications for hundreds of schools whose only federal assistance existed in the form of indirect aid or student participation in loan programs, but also in terms of the establishment of a precedent and subsequent settling of contradictory approaches and decisions among the circuit courts.

The decision in *North Haven Board of Education v. Bell* had particularly important ramifications for Title IX litigation. While the case did not specifically deal with athletics, the Supreme Court resolved two fundamental questions about the scope of Title IX, which were applicable to athletics. First, it decided that Title IX prohibited discrimination against employees as well as against students. Second, it determined that both the power to regulate and to terminate federal assistance are program-specific. Thus, Title IX sanctions are limited to particular programs receiving federal financial assistance.

The issue of "programmatic" versus "institutional" was ultimately decided by the Supreme Court in *Grove City v. Bell*. This 1984 decision had an immediate and dramatic impact on then-pending litigation initiated by the Department of Education (successor to HEW and responsible for Title IX enforcement) against colleges and school systems alleged to be in violation of Title IX. The Department of Education had to drop cases in which policies in an athletic department were being challenged if it could not be established that the athletic departments or programs were direct recipients of federal funds. Cases against the University of Alabama, University of Maryland, Penn State University, the New York City school system, and at least 19 other institutions were discontinued or severely narrowed when no such connection could be found.

The Office of Civil Rights (OCR) commenced a proceeding in March 1984, which may be indicative of the strategy the OCR will employ in the future. The OCR informed Auburn University that an investigation had revealed Title IX violations in the Auburn athletics department. The OCR conceded that it no longer had jurisdiction over the athletics department, but charged that its investigation also revealed Title IX violations in the awarding of financial aid. The OCR therefore commenced proceedings to terminate all federal funding for the Auburn financial aid program. Concentration on athletic scholarship policies may be the most effective legal tool remaining for the OCR unless and until federal legislation reaffirming Title IX's applicability to all of a school's or college's programs is passed.

Such legislation was introduced by a bipartisan coalition of U.S. senators and representatives in April 1984. The legislation proposed to change the wording in Title IV, Title IX, the Rehabilitation Act (rights of the handicapped), and the Age Discrimination Act to state that discrimination was prohibited in the programs and

activities of any "recipient" of federal funds. The bill further
defined "recipient" as "any state or political subdivision thereof,
. . . or any public or private agency, institution or organization, or
other entity . . . to which federal financial assistance is extended
(directly or through another entity or a person)." As of 1987,
however, no legislation has been enacted to reverse the Supreme
Court's decision.

The Supreme Court addressed two issues in arriving at its
decision in the *Grove City* case: the question of direct versus
indirect funding, and also the question of "program-specific" versus "institutionwide enforcement." Obviously, if a specific department received direct federal funding, the Title IX jurisdiction
would apply. However, the *institution* of Grove City College never
directly received federal funds; only a few of its students did.
Hence, without first determining whether this type of funding
marked Grove City College as a "recipient" of federal funds, it
would be impossible to reach the more critical question of the
meaning of "program."

The unanimous decision of the Court on the first issue was that
federal funding, even as indirect as the basic education opportunity
grants (BEOGs) of the college's students, was sufficient to make
the institution a "recipient" within the meaning of Title IX. On
the second question, the meaning of "program," the Court adopted
the narrow interpretation that Title IX enforcement is limited to
the specific program actually touched by financial aid. The Court,
however, did not offer a definition of "program." Nevertheless, the
decision made it no longer possible to interpret "program" as
"institution."

The significance of the *Grove City* case for high school and
college athletic administrators is that since federal funding does
not enter the program areas of physical education and sports, in
many cases, not even indirectly, Title IX cannot be enforced in
those areas.

Those disappointed by the *Grove City* decision have suggested
that because federal funding often forms a portion of the money to
construct gymnasiums and stadiums on school grounds and campuses, the activities held within such facilities should be sufficiently touched by federal assistance to be under the Title IX
jurisdiction. Yet, it appears that tying facilities to programs carried
on within them is too tenuous to find Title IX jurisdiction. The
rapid and massive cancellation of Title IX investigations by the
OCR following the *Grove City* decision made it apparent that
jurisdiction over sex discrimination in athletic programs cannot be
as broadly pursued by the OCR.

Others who view the *Grove City* case as a setback have expressed hope that scholarship disbursements to athletes, some of which include federal funds administered by the college's financial aid office, would be sufficient to invoke Title IX antidiscrimination sanctions to entire athletic programs. Yet, in light of the Auburn University situation, it seems unlikely that anything beyond the scholarships themselves would be subject to Title IX enforcement. Prior to the *Grove City* decision, the OCR found discriminatory activities in the athletic program at Auburn. Within a few days after the *Grove City* decision, the OCR dropped its case, except that portion concerning scholarships. Consequently, it appears that the OCR will not attempt to use scholarships as a means to trigger Title IX enforcement.

The future of Title IX is difficult to predict, but in the absence of clarifying legislation, Title IX may be of limited use in fighting discrimination in athletic programs. It is likely that opportunities for women will be reduced as a result of the *Grove City* decision, as is evidenced by the rapid reduction of scholarships for women at some colleges following the *Grove City* case.

NOTES

1. In *Yellow Springs Exempted Village School District Board of Education v. Ohio High School Athletic Ass'n*, 443 F. Supp. 753 (S.D. Ohio 1978), *aff'd*, 647 F.2d 651 (6th Cir. 1981), a suit was brought against the Ohio High School Athletic Association (OHSAA) and the Ohio Board of Education challenging the association's rule excluding girls from participation in contact sports. In 1974, two female students competed for and earned positions on the Morgan Middle School's interscholastic basketball team. The board excluded them from the team and then created a separate girls' basketball team. This action was taken to comply with OHSAA Rule 1, section 6, which prohibited mixed-gender interscholastic athletic competition in contact sports such as basketball. Failure to exclude the girls from the team would have jeopardized the school district's membership in the association. The district court held that the "Association's exclusionary rule deprives school girls of liberty without due process of law. Freedom of personal choice in matters of 'education and acquisition of knowledge' is a liberty interest protected by the due process clause of the Fourteenth Amendment." The appeals court upheld portions of the district court's decision and ruled that Title IX focuses on "recipients" of federal aid. Since OHSAA was not itself a recipient of federal aid and does not bear the burden of noncompliance, it may not adopt a rule that limits the abilities of recipient schools to furnish equal athletic opportunities for girls and boys.

2. In *Othen v. Ann Arbor School Board*, 507 F. Supp. 1376 (E.D. Mich., 1981), 699 F.2d 309 (6th Cir. 1983), a complaint was filed on behalf of female student-athletes charging the Ann Arbor school board and its golf coach with sex discrimination in violation of Title IX. The

father of the girls sought a temporary restraining order immediately restoring his daughter to the 1979 golf team and prohibiting discrimination "against women who want to play on the Pioneer golf team." The district court denied the motion for an injunction and found the father/daughter failed to demonstrate a likelihood of success on the merits.

The school board responded to the amended complaint with a motion for summary judgment, stating that none of the athletic programs at Pioneer received federal financial assistance and therefore were not covered by the provisions of Title IX. A school official testified that the only federal financial aid that the board received was "impact aid" in the form of payments to the school systems to compensate for increased enrollments caused by the proximity of federal facilities and the loss of tax revenue resulting from these tax-exempt federal properties. This money was channeled through the Ann Arbor school system's general fund and indirectly aided athletic programs. The school board also asserted that the golf team had always been open to both men and women, and students were accepted "as their abilities warranted."

The district court found the athletic programs at Pioneer received no direct federal assistance and the indirect federal assistance from "impact aid" was "de minimus." The court's finding that "the clear language of Title IX and the intent of Congress requires that the Act [Title IX] be applied programmatically" had important ramifications in the case. Since it was determined that the athletic programs and activities under the jurisdiction of the Ann Arbor School Board received no direct federal financial assistance, the school board was not obligated under the law to establish a golf team for girls. Therefore, the daughters were not excluded from participation, denied, or discriminated against in violation of Title IX.

3. In *Bennett v. West Texas State University*, 525 F. Supp. 77 (N.D. Tex. 1981), plaintiffs, six female athletes, filed a class action suit charging West Texas State University (WTSU) with sex discrimination, based on their denial of equal opportunity in the institution's intercollegiate athletic program. The athletes contended that WTSU had intentionally discriminated against female athletes in the following areas:

    (a) The allocation of athletic scholarship money
    (b) Travel allowances, allocations, and expenditures
    (c) Scheduling of games and practice times
    (d) The compensation and treatment of coaches
    (e) The provision of supplies, equipment, and laundry facilities
    (f) The provision of support staff
    (g) The provision of locker room, practice, and office facilities
    (h) Authority to spend in excess of budget allocations
    (i) The provision of publicity, promotion, and awards
    (j) Perpetuating and aiding assistance to organizations and persons who discriminate on the basis of sex in providing aid, benefit, and service to students and employees

The athletes stated that the effect of these policies has been to exclude them from full participation and benefits thereof and subject them to sex discrimination in violation of Title IX. The district court rejected the

athletes' contentions, finding that the athletic department of WTSU was
not subject to Title IX regulation. The court ruled that the language of
Title IX showed "the clear intent of Congress" in that the terms "recipient" and "programs" limited Title IX application to only specific programs
or activities that receive direct financial assistance.

This decision was reversed without opinion after the *Grove City
College* decision (see 698 F.2d 1215 [5th Cir. 1983]).

4. *Haffer v. Temple University*, 524 F. Supp. 531 (E.D. Pa. 1981),
aff'd, 688 F.2d 14 (3rd Cir. 1982), was an appeal of the district court
decision denying summary judgment to Temple University on the basis
that its athletic department was not exempt from Title IX regulation.
Eight women undergraduates had filed a class action suit charging Temple
University with sex discrimination in its intercollegiate athletic program
in violation of Title IX. Temple had requested summary judgment arguing
that Title IX applied only to those educational programs or activities
which received direct federal funding and that the athletic department at
Temple had received no such assistance.

After an extensive examination of the federal funding received by the
institution, the district court rejected Temple's request for summary
judgment. The court held that "Title IX coverage is not limited to
educational programs and activities that receive *earmarked* federal dollars, but also includes any program that *indirectly* benefits from the
receipt of federal funds; because Temple's athletic program indirectly
benefits from the large amounts of federal financial assistance furnished
to the University in the form of grants and contracts, Title IX is applicable
to Temple's athletic program." In addition, the court held that "even if
Title IX is construed to require direct federal financing, the Temple
athletic program receives and benefits from several hundred thousand
dollars worth of annual federal aid, and therefore is covered under Title
IX."

Temple appealed the decision, questioning whether the court's inclusion of the athletic program under Title IX jurisdiction was consistent
with the wording of the statute, which required that the education
program or activity receive "federal financial assistance" as a prerequisite
for its inclusion in the realm of Title IX authority. The appeals court
affirmed the lower court's opinion. The appeals court rejected the "program-specific" interpretation put forth by Temple, claiming that the
entire institution should be considered the "program." In referring to
Grove City College (appellate court decision), the court suggested that
"the legislators (who enacted Title IX) did not contemplate that separate,
discrete and distinct components or functions of an integrated educational
institution would be regarded as the individual program to which section
901 . . . refer(s)." The court added that "if Temple University as a whole
is to be considered the program or activity" for Title IX purposes, it
follows that because the university as a whole receives federal monies, its
intercollegiate athletic department is governed by Title IX. The court
held that the district court's theory that federal monies received by the
institution benefited the athletic program because it freed other univer-

sity money for athletic program-related purposes was consistent with its finding that Title IX was applicable.

5. In *Hillsdale College v. Department of Health, Education and Welfare*, 696 F.2d 418 (6th Cir. 1982), HEW issued an order disqualifying students from participation in federal aid programs in response to the refusal of Hillsdale's officials to sign an "assurance of compliance" with Title IX. Hillsdale appealed the HEW order. The court reversed and held for Hillsdale, reasoning that because Congress failed to adopt proposals that would have prohibited all discriminatory practices of an institution that receives federal funds, it was clear that, as enacted, Title IX adopts a "programmatic as opposed to institutional approach to discrimination on the basis of sex in education." Even though the court found that Hillsdale was subject to Title IX regulations in those programs receiving federal financial assistance, the court believed that while HEW had been given the authority to promulgate regulations for Title IX enforcement, in this case, the order imposed was in excess of statutory authority in that it would subject the entire college, rather than any one program, to the strictures of Title IX.

6. In *North Haven Board of Education v. Bell*, 102 S. Ct. 1912, 456 U.S. 512, 72 L.Ed.2d 299 (1982), a tenured teacher in the North Haven public school system filed a complaint on her behalf and others with HEW and its secretary, Bell, alleging that North Haven had violated Title IX by refusing to rehire her after a one-year maternity leave. The U.S. Supreme Court held that ". . . petitioners [North Haven] disputed the Department's authority to regulate any employment practices whatsoever, and the District Court adopted that view, which we find to be in error."

7. In *Brief of the Council of Collegiate Women Athletic Administrators (CCWAA) as Amicus Curiae in Support of Respondent: Grove City College, Petitioner, v. T. H. Bell, Secretary of the United States Department of Education, Respondent, No. 82–792 (October Term, 1983, August 5, 1983)*, the CCWAA presented its arguments in support of the Department of Education in *Grove City College v. Bell*. The CCWAA was concerned that a narrow interpretation (programmatic) of Title IX in *Grove City College* by the U.S. Supreme Court would have an adverse impact on women's intercollegiate athletic progams:

> If the ruling of the Court in this case is interpreted to mean that Title IX does not apply to athletics, the discrimination claims of women athletes will have to be litigated under the broad mandate of the Equal Protection Clause, thus making every such discrimination claim a cumbersome Constitutional law case. . . . If the decision of this Court is interpreted to mean that Title IX does not apply to athletics, the regulations will have no force as law at all.

8. In *Grove City College v. Bell*, 465 U.S. 555, 104 S. Ct. 1211, 79 L.Ed.2d 516 (1984), a private, liberal arts college refused to execute an "assurance of compliance" with Title IX. The Department of Education initiated proceedings to declare the college and its students ineligible to receive basic educational opportunity grants (BEOGs), and the college and four of its students filed suit after an administrative law judge ordered

federal financial assistance terminated until Grove City met the requirements of Title IX. The U.S. Supreme Court ruled that the language of Title IX made it program-specific, that only those programs directly receiving federal funds were subject to the regulations of Title IX. This ruling applies to schools that participate in the BEOG program. Otherwise, one student receiving federal aid would trigger Title IX coverage of the entire institution. This does not square with the program-specific language of the legislation.

9. Immediately following the *Grove City College* decision, the OCR dropped its efforts to cut off federal aid to the University of Maryland and Auburn University for Title IX violations in their athletic departments. The OCR decided it did not have jurisdiction to investigate the departments because they received no direct federal funding. However, in the case of Auburn University, the OCR decided it would still seek to pursue enforcement on the student financial aid program at Auburn since the program received federal aid. Financial aid was involved because the OCR charged that the institution had failed "to award athletics scholarships and grants-in-aid so as to provide reasonable opportunities for such awards for students of each sex in proportion to the number of students of each sex participating in intercollegiate athletics." For further information, see "Grove City Decision Spurs OCR Actions," *NCAA News*, March 21, 1984, pp. 1, 16.

OCR TITLE IX COMPLIANCE REVIEWS
AND ENFORCEMENT

The Office of Civil Rights is responsible for conducting compliance reviews of Title IX. The OCR selects schools at random to review for Title IX compliance and also reviews schools based on complaints brought by individuals. Educational institutions are required to keep and submit to the Department of Education accurate compliance reports to enable it to determine whether Title IX requirements have been satisfied. The educational institution is also required to permit access by the Department of Education to its books, records, accounts, and other sources of information, and its facilities, that may be pertinent to ascertaining compliance. Considerations of privacy or confidentiality will not restrict access. The OCR, in regards to Title IX violations in athletics, begins its investigations by notifying the schools and then collecting data on the overall athletic program. The information may include the number of teams, scheduling of games and practice times, travel and per diem allowances, compensation of coaches, provision of facilities, and amount of publicity (press releases and media guides, etc.). Aggrieved individuals may also sue an institution directly, without being required to rely on the enforcement mechanism of the Department of Education (see Note

2). Based on a review of the data, the OCR will determine whether or not equivalent treatment, benefits, and opportunities as mandated by Title IX have been afforded to both sexes.

A finding of inequality in a single component of the progam is not a basis in and of itself for the OCR to find a school in noncompliance with Title IX. The OCR's approach in investigating and determining compliance with Title IX has been to focus on the overall provision of equivalent opportunities in the athletic program. Therefore, the OCR will look to other components of the athletic program before it finds the school to be in noncompliance. In addition, Secretary Terrel H. Bell of the Department of Education adopted a nonconfrontation approach in 1981. Under this policy, the OCR may find schools in compliance with Title IX if the schools agree to rectify any violations of Title IX found through the OCR's investigation.

OCR officials will meet with the administrators of an investigated institution and review the OCR's proposed findings before a letter of noncompliance is issued. If the institution voluntarily forms a committee to adopt a plan to rectify its violations within a reasonable period of time, the institution will be granted a letter of compliance because it is implementing a corrective plan. The Department of Education is then responsible for monitoring the progress of the plan. If the plan is not implemented within the time specified or proves to be an inadequate remedy, the institution will be found in noncompliance and further legal action against the school could be taken.

If there is a failure to comply with Title IX, or a voluntary compliance agreement cannot be reached, or the violations cannot be corrected by informal means, compliance may be effected by the suspension or termination of, or refusal to grant or to continue, federal financial assistance. Additionally, the Department of Education may refer the matter to the Department of Justice, with a recommendation that appropriate proceedings be brought to enforce any rights of the United States.

Prior to suspending, terminating, or refusing to grant or continue federal financial assistance, an institution must be afforded the opportunity to a hearing before an administrative law judge. If the educational institution does not request a hearing within the time allowed, the right to the hearing is waived and a decision will be made on the basis of the information then on file.

After a hearing is held, the hearing judge will either make an initial decision on the institution's compliance, or certify the entire record, including his or her recommended findings and proposed decision, to the appropriate reviewing authority for a final decision. Both the Department of Education and the institution may appeal that determination to the department's reviewing authority. If the reviewing authority affirms the administrative law judge's decision, the institution may request a review by the secretary of education.

If the Department of Education decides to withdraw funding, it must report that decision to the appropriate congressional committees 30 days prior to the termination of funds. Having exhausted its administrative remedies, the institution could then seek judicial review of the department's actions.

In the area of athletics, the Department of Education rarely applies the formal administrative process to terminate funds to enforce Title IX regulations. The formal enforcement process is usually avoided because institutions have typically developed voluntary compliance plans acceptable to the OCR.

NOTES

1. In *Office of Civil Rights Title IX Compliance Review of the University of Akron*, the OCR selected the University of Akron for a Title IX compliance review of the university's intercollegiate athletics program. Various complaints alleged that the university discriminated against female athletes in selection of sports and levels of competition. For example, the school had no varsity track team for women, and it offered no scholarships for women athletes.

The OCR found that the University of Akron provided men and women equivalent treatment in five areas: (1) provision and maintenance of equipment and supplies, (2) travel and per-diem allowances, (3) provision of housing and dining services and facilities, (4) publicity, and (5) support services.

The OCR found that benefits, opportunities, and treatment were not equivalent in the areas of (1) scheduling of games and practice times, (2) opportunity to receive coaching, (3) provision of locker rooms, practice, and competitive facilities, (4) provision of medical and training facilities and services, (5) recruitment of student-athletes, and (6) the accommodation of student interests and abilities. The OCR concluded that these disparities violated Title IX. However, the University of Akron was implementing a plan that would remedy the disparities within a reasonable period of time. Therefore, the university was found to be in compliance with Title IX.

2. In *Office of Civil Rights Title IX Compliance Review of University of Iowa*, the OCR investigated the women's athletic program at the University of Iowa. The sports information director's (SID) staff for the University of Iowa's women's program consisted of a full-time director, a quarter-time graduate assistant, two part-time assistants, and a student volunteer. It was determined that the provisions of publicity personnel were not equivalent because the lack of professional, travel, and clerical support severely limited the ability of the women's sports information director to perform tasks critical to her job function.

The following problem areas in the Iowa SID operation also were addressed by the OCR:

(a) Men's basketball, football, and wrestling received radio and TV coverage. Women's team events were broadcast occasionally on local radio.

(b) A newsletter that provided information about men's programs was sent to local high schools from six to eight times a year. No such service was rendered for the women's program.

(c) All media guides for the women's programs were mimeographed on plain paper and contained limited data. No recruitment brochures were provided. Three of the media guides for the men's programs were printed books that contained color photographs. All guides contained a great variety of data on the individual players, the coaches, and the facilities. The disparity present in the provision of publications was found to be of concern because of the impact they have on recruiting and attendance figures.

The following remedial actions were taken by the University of Iowa:

(a) A commitment was made to provide equivalent services and publications.

(b) A centrally located SID office encompassing a women's SID, a men's SID, and a pooled staff of assistants was established.

(c) A marketing assistant for men's minor sports and women's athletics was hired.

3. In *Office of Civil Rights Title IX Compliance Review of Central Michigan University*, the OCR examined the athletic publicity operation at Central Michigan University. The university sports information director (SID) had concentrated on those events that attracted the greatest spectator and media attention. Public relations luncheons were held only for football and men's basketball. Generally, football and men's basketball were the events that received television broadcasting, although some of the women's basketball tournament also received television coverage.

The SID office produced game programs, season brochures, fact books, and press releases for the football, men's basketball, and baseball teams. Recruitment brochures and player profiles for all other teams (except women's basketball) were inserted in the men's game programs and received additional coverage through press releases only.

The following remedial actions were taken by Central Michigan University to correct deficiencies noted by the OCR review of its athletic publicity operation:

(a) SID coverage of away games was increased for all teams.

(b) Game programs were provided for women's athletics home events.

(c) A fact book was produced for the women's basketball team. (Fact sheets were developed for those women's sports that do not generate sufficient fan and media interest to warrant fact-book production.)

(d) Radio and television coverage of women's athletic events was expanded.

4. In *Cannon v. University of Chicago*, 406 F. Supp. 1257 (N.D. Ill.

1976), *aff'd on rehearing*, 559 F.2d 1077 (7th Cir. 1979), *rev'd*, 441 U.S. 677 (1979), *cert. denied*, 460 U.S. 1013 (1983), the Supreme Court reversed the lower courts and held that a private right of action will be implied under Title IX. Also, the Court said that administrative remedies need not be exhausted before filing suit in federal court.

5. See Exhibit 8–1 for a Title IX compliance checklist from the perspective of the educational institutions.

SEX DISCRIMINATION CASES INVOLVING INDIVIDUAL ATHLETES

The subsections and cases that follow are discussed in terms of the presence or absence of teams available to either sex. Within each category, the subsections and cases are further divided into those dealing with contact and those dealing with noncontact sports. This was done because the approach taken—and sometimes the results reached—by the courts is different because of the type of sports involved.

The division of subsections and cases is not by legal theory, since very often the litigation makes use of one, two, or even three prominent theories—for example, equal protection, Title IX, and state equal rights amendments (in certain states). To distinguish between the cases would therefore entail too much repetition without sufficiently differentiating the decisions.

The courts view contact sports and noncontact sports differently. Thus, in cases involving sex discrimination in athletics, the arguments used will vary depending on whether or not the particular sport is designated a contact sport. Under Title IX, contact sports include boxing, wrestling, rugby, ice hockey, football, basketball, and other sports in which the purpose or major activity involves bodily contact. In some jurisdictions, baseball and soccer have also been labeled contact sports.

In a sport designated "contact," certain arguments are commonly propounded. The most frequent argument raised by defendants is that women, as a group, lack the physical qualifications necessary for safe and reasonable competition against men in a sport in which bodily contact is expected to occur. It is argued that women are more susceptible to injury because they have a higher percentage of adipose (fatty) tissues and a lighter bone structure. Because of these physiological differences, the argument goes, contact sports are dangerous for all women.

Plaintiffs counter this argument by insisting that determinations of physical capability should be made on a case-by-case basis. When there is no other opportunity for participation in a certain

- Determine whether Title IX applies to the educational institution.
- If Title IX is applicable to the educational institution, determine the specific programs or activities (including athletics) which must be conformed to Title IX requirements.
- Evaluate, from time to time, the athletic department's policies and practices and their effects concerning treatment of student-athletes, and employment of both athletic and non-athletic personnel working in connection with its program or activity.
- Modify any policies and practices of the athletic department which do not or may not meet the requirements of Title IX.
- Take appropriate remedial steps to eliminate the effects of any discrimination which may have resulted from adherence to policies and practices which did not conform to Title IX.
- When applying for federal financial assistance for any athletic program or activity, execute and deliver an assurance that each athletic program or activity to which Title IX applies will be operated in compliance with its requirements.
- Designate at least one employee to coordinate the athletic department's efforts to comply with and carry out its responsibilities under Title IX, including investigation of any complaint communicated to the department alleging noncompliance with Title IX.
- Adopt and publish grievance procedures providing for prompt and equitable resolution of student-athlete and employee complaints alleging any action which does not conform to Title IX.
- Implement specific and continuing steps to notify applicants for employment, student-athletes and parents of student-athletes, employees, sources of referral of applicants for employment, and all unions or professional organizations holding collective bargaining or professional agreements with the athletic department, that it does not discriminate contrary to Title IX.
- Prominently include a statement of the athletic department's non-discrimination policy in each announcement, bulletin, catalog, or application.
- Comply with Title IX in programs subject to its application, unless an exemption applies.
- Keep such compliance reports as required by the Department of Education, including data showing the extent to which members of each sex are beneficiaries of and participants in federally-assisted programs and activities of the athletic department.
- Recognize that a claim of sex discrimination may be based on grounds other than Title IX, including the equal protection clause of the Fourteenth Amendment to the United States Constitution.

Exhibit 8-1 Title IX Compliance Checklist *Source*: Adapted from Rapp, *Education Law*, Vol. I, pp. 10–103–10–105.

sport, a blanket prohibition is overinclusive and violates equal protection by assuming that all women have identical physical structures and that all men are stronger and more athletically capable than women. Indeed, the health and safety rationale behind such total exclusion may fail a court challenge, as has been demonstrated in some cases. In one case, a woman who was 5'9" tall and weighed over 200 pounds was denied a chance to play football because her supposedly lighter bone structure would render her more susceptible to injury. There was, however, no height or weight requirements for men, and the court thus found exclusion from participation to be unacceptable. (See *Clinton v. Nagy* on page 443.)

Although the most important consideration used to substantiate separate teams for contact sports is the health and safety of the participants, this argument does not apply to noncontact sports. Since there is no legitimate and important state interest for allowing exclusion from noncontact sports, citing sex as the sole exclusionary factor would constitute a violation of the U.S. constitutional guarantees of the equal protection clause. Thus, the arguments made by defendants in noncontact sports sex discrimination cases are different.

The most common argument is that if men and women are allowed to compete together and/or against each other, the psychological development of both would be impaired. This stance is generally based on a variation of the "tradition" argument, which says that allowing men and women to compete as equals will irreparably disturb the innate nature of relationships between the sexes.

Another commonly made argument is that if men and women are allowed to compete together, men will dominate the co-ed teams. The underlying rationale here is that since men are inherently stronger and more physically capable than women, co-ed teams will actually limit opportunities for women. Plaintiffs argue that a justification of this sort does not take into account individual differences among participants. It also does not recognize the argument that if women are given opportunities to compete against men from the beginning of their athletic careers, their capabilities would improve and men might not be able to totally dominate the athletic field.

Men's Team, No Women's Team

The general rule in both contact and noncontact sports is that when only one team is available, both sexes must be allowed to try out for and play on that team. Determinations as to the student-athlete's capability and risk of injury must be made on an individual basis, with the recognition that the contact or noncontact sports designations only make a difference if there is opportunity for athletes of both sexes to compete. If there is ample opportunity for women to compete on their own, courts appear to be less apt to allow women to compete with men in contact sports.

NOTE _____

1. For further information, see the following law review articles:
   (a) "The Case for Equality in Athletics," 22 *Cleveland State Law Review* 570 (1973).
   (b) "Female High School Athlete and Interscholastic Sports," *Journal of Law and Education* 185 (April 1975).
   (c) "The Emergent Law of Women and Amateur Sports: Recent Developments," 28 *Wayne Law Review* 1701 (Summer 1982).

Contact Sports

In cases in which contact sports are involved and there is no women's team, there is a split in decisions as to whether to allow a female to play on the men's team. In some cases, as represented by *Clinton v. Nagy* (see Note 1), the courts uphold the women's sex discrimination claim and allow participation on the men's team. In other cases, the plaintiff female was not successful because of the lack of state action or because there was no violation of the sex discrimination laws (see Notes 2 and 5).

NOTES _____

1. In *Clinton v. Nagy*, 411 F. Supp. 1396 (N.D. Ohio 1974), a 12-year-old girl alleged that recreation and city officials deprived her of equal recreational opportunities in refusing to allow her the opportunity to qualify to play recreational league football because of her sex. Pursuant to 42 U.S.C. § 1983, the girl sought to prohibit the officials from denying her equal recreational opportunities on the basis of sex and to receive a declaratory judgment that "the policies, customs, and practices of the defendants are in violation of the Constitution." The court held that when a regulation is based on a sex-based classification, "the classification is subject to scrutiny under the Equal Protection Clause of the Fourteenth Amendment to ascertain whether there is a rational relationship to a valid stated purpose." The court therefore decided the case for the girl.

The court stated that organized contact sports are considered an opportunity and means of developing strength of character, leadership qualities, etc., "yet, although these are presumably qualities to which we desire all of the young to aspire, the opportunity to qualify to engage in sports activities through which such qualities may be developed has been granted to one class of the young and summarily denied to the other."

2. In *Junior Football Ass'n of Orange County, Texas v. Gaudet*, 546 S.W. 2d 70 (Tex. Civ. App. 1976), the trial court granted a temporary injunction allowing a girl to play football in the Junior Football Association until she reached puberty. This decision was based on Article 1, Section 3a of the Texas Constitution, which provides: "Equality under the law shall not be denied or abridged because of sex, race, color, creed or national origin."

The association appealed on the basis that there was no state action sufficient to authorize the injunction. The association complained that there was insufficient evidence of state involvement to authorize the temporary injunction and the court agreed. On appeal, the temporary injunction order was reversed and dissolved. Even though the association was chartered by the state of Texas as a nonprofit corporation, the players usually practiced on school grounds, and games were played in a park owned by the City of Orange, the court of appeals did not find state action or private conduct closely interrelated in function with state action.

3. In *Lavin v. Chicago Board of Education*, 73 F.R.D. 438 (1975), *Lavin v. Illinois High School Ass'n*, 527 F.2d 58 (7th Cir. 1977), a class action lawsuit for declaratory, injunctive, and monetary relief against the Chicago Board of Education was instituted because plaintiff Lavin was denied participation in interscholastic athletics based on her sex. Lavin and another classmate tried out for the varsity basketball team at their high school and were denied positions on the squad because of the Illinois State High School Association rules. Lavin contended that the Fourteenth Amendment guarantee of equal protection had been violated. The appeals court reversed and remanded the trial court's summary judgment for the board of education and awarded monetary damages to the athletes. On remand, the trial court denied the class action claim because Lavin was no longer a member of the "class" because of graduation. In addition, the trial court reasoned that she did not present an argument that showed she was qualified enough to make the boys' squad, and therefore was not a member of that particular "class" of girls either. The trial court allowed Lavin's individual claim for damages.

4. In *Muscare v. O'Malley*, Civil No. 76-C-3729 (N.D. Ill. 1977), an action was brought by a 12-year-old girl who wanted to play *tackle* football in Chicago Park District football games. There was a *touch* football program available for girls. In ruling for the girl, the court reasoned that offering a sport for males, yet not to females, is a violation of equal opportunity rights under the Fourteenth Amendment.

5. In *Lincoln v. Mid-Cities Pee Wee Football Ass'n*, 576 S.W.2d 922 (Tex. Civ. App. 1979), an action was brought by an 8-year-old female, who had played on the Pirates, a Mid-City Pee Wee Football team, in 1977. After the season ended, a decision was made to provide a separate league for girls. Because very little interest was shown at registration for the 1978 season, the girls' league was dropped and the girl was told she could not play again on a boys' team. The girl then brought an action under the Texas Equal Rights Amendment (ERA) for a permanent injunction preventing the association from enforcing its decision. The appeals court affirmed the trial court's decision to deny the injunction. The court

stated that the discrimination complained of must be state action or private conduct that was encouraged, or closely interrelated in function with state action. The court found neither and held that the Texas ERA does not cover purely private conduct.

6. In *Hoover v. Meiklejohn*, 430 F. Supp. 164 (D. Colo. 1977), an action was brought by plaintiff Hoover, who wanted to play on her high school soccer team. The Colorado High School Athletic Association limited interscholastic soccer team membership to boys. The district court held for Hoover, based on an equal protection analysis. The court held that the appropriate analysis requires a triangular balancing of the importance of the opportunities being unequally burdened or denied against the strength of the state's interests and the character of the group being denied the opportunity. The court found that a complete denial, as in this case, violated Hoover's rights to equal protection.

The court determined that the school had three options. It could allow co-ed teams, it could discontinue the sport for males, or it could field a second all-female team.

7. In *Leffel v. Wisconsin Interscholastic Athletic Ass'n*, 444 F. Supp. 1117 (E.D. Wis. 1978), plaintiff brought a class action suit charging that an interscholastic athletic association's rule limiting co-educational athletics violated her civil rights as guaranteed under the equal protection clause. The court granted summary judgment for the plaintiff, finding that

> exclusion of girls from all contact sports in order to protect female high school athletes from unreasonable risk of injury was not fairly or substantially related to a justifiable government objective in the context of the Fourteenth Amendment, where demand for relief by plaintiffs would be met by establishing separate girls' teams with comparable programs.

The plaintiffs were granted the right to participate in a varsity interscholastic program in any sport in which only a boys' team was provided.

8. In *Simpson v. Boston Area Youth Soccer, Inc.*, Case No. 83-2681 (Super. Ct. Mass. 1983) (settled), an action was brought by a sixth-grade female soccer player. Defendant soccer association excluded the girl from the all-male soccer team in her town. The girl had played for three years on co-educational teams, and many of her former teammates were on the team. Although the soccer association also maintained a girls' league, no team in that league was readily accessible to the girl. The girl was also considered an above-average soccer player and maintained that the girls' league would present inferior competition. The case was settled when defendant soccer league agreed to change its constitution and bylaws to allow females to play on male teams, with such teams being entered in the boys' league.

9. In *Force v. Pierce City R-VI School District*, 570 F. Supp. 1020 (W.D. Mo., 1983), a 13-year-old female plaintiff sought injunctive relief to allow her to play on the interscholastic football team. The court granted injunctive relief for the girl and held that

> (1) no sufficiently substantial relationship was shown between blanket prohibition against female participation on a high school football team and Title IX of the Educational Amendments of 1972, the high school activities

association rules and regulations, and maintaining athletic educational programs which are as safe for participants as possible, or administrative ease, and (2) under the circumstances, rules and regulations of high school activities association and manner of promulgation and enforcement thereof constituted "state action," thus subjecting association's actions to equal protection clause requirements and, as such, enforcement of a rule which effectively prohibited members of the opposite sex from competing on the same team in interscholastic football was enjoined.

10. In *Lantz v. Ambach*, 620 F. Supp. 663 (S.D.N.Y. 1985), the court prohibited enforcement of a New York public high school regulation that prohibited mixed sex competition in football, as a violation of the Fourteenth Amendment, and permitted a 16-year-old healthy female student to try out for junior varsity football. Although the court acknowledged an important governmental objective in protecting the health and safety of female high school students, it found the regulation was overbroad and lacked reasonable relation to the objective.

11. In *Opinion of the Justices to the House of Representatives*, 274 Mass. 836, 371 N.E.2d 426 (1977), the Supreme Judicial Court of Massachusetts rendered an opinion that proposed legislation which would have disallowed participation of girls with boys on the following contact sports teams—football and wrestling—would be unconstitutional under the state's equal rights amendment. The court specifically reserved the question whether a statute "more limited in its impact" would serve a compelling state interest—for example, whether females could be constitutionally excluded from male teams in a particular sport if they were provided with an equal team.

12. For further information, see the following law review articles:
   (a) "Irrebuttable Presumption Doctrine: Applied to State and Federal Regulations Excluding Females from Contact Sports," 4 *Dayton Law Review* 197 (1979).
   (b) "Title IX of the Education Amendment of 1972 Prohibits All-Female Teams in Sports Not Previously Dominated by Males," 14 *Suffolk University Law Review* 1471 (Fall 1980).
   (c) "Girls' High School Basketball Rules Held Unconstitutional," 16 *Journal of Family Law* 345 (Fall 1978).
   (d) "Sexual Equality in High School Athletics: The Approach of *Darrin v. Gould*," 12 *Gonzaga Law Review* 691 (Summer 1977).

13. Review *Yellow Springs Exempted Village School District Board of Education v. Ohio High School Athletic Ass'n* on page 432 concerning the scope and applicability of Title IX, and *Darrin v. Gould* on page 427 concerning the legality of a state equal rights amendment.

14. See Chapter 4, page 98, for an explanation of the standards required for an injunction.

15. See Chapter 7, page 396, for a discussion of waivers and releases of liability. The plaintiff in *Clinton v. Nagy* signed one before being allowed to participate.

Noncontact Sports

In cases in which noncontact sports are involved and there is no women's team, the trend and majority of cases allow the women to participate on the men's team. Some cases (see Notes 1 and 2) allowed women to participate on men's cross-country and tennis teams where there were no women's teams. Some courts have prevented females from participating on the men's teams (see Notes 7 and 8). In cases where private organizations are involved, the plaintiff women also must prove state action (see Notes 11b, c, and d).

NOTES _____

1. In *Gilpin v. Kansas State High School Activities Ass'n*, 377 F. Supp. 1233 (D. Kan. 1974), Gilpin, a junior at Southeast High School in Wichita, Kansas, brought a civil rights suit against the Kansas State High School Activities Association (KSHSAA). Gilpin claimed she was deprived of equal protection by a KSHSAA rule that prevented her from participating in interscholastic cross-country competition solely on the basis of her sex.

The court held that because Southeast High School offered no cross-country program for girls, the KSHSAA rule effectively deprived Gilpin of an opportunity to compete at all. The court held:

> Thus, although the Association's overall objective is commendable and legitimate, the method employed to accomplish that objective is simply overbroad in its reach. It is precisely this sort of overinclusiveness which the Equal Protection Clause disdains.

The district court determined that the KSHSAA rule prohibiting mixed competition was unconstitutional as applied to Gilpin and accordingly granted her the requested injunctive relief.

2. In *Brenden v. Independent School District 742*, 342 F. Supp. 1224 (D. Minn. 1972), *aff'd*, 477 F.2d 1292 (8th Cir. 1973), plaintiff high school student-athletes brought an action against Independent School District 742, alleging violation of their constitutional rights under the Fourteenth Amendment and Civil Rights Act (42 U.S.C. § 1983). The plaintiffs contended that the Minnesota State High School League (MSHSL) rule prohibiting girls from participating in boys' interscholastic athletic competition was arbitrary and unreasonable as applied to their particular situations and thus, constituted a violation of their rights under the equal protection clause of the Fourteenth Amendment.

Because of the circumstances—that is, the girls were capable of competing on the boys' team, that no girls' team existed at their respective schools in the sports in which they wished to participate, and that Brenden and St. Pierre were kept from participation solely on the basis of sex—the court found the application of the rule to be arbitrary and unreasonable. Since the classification by sex had no fair or substantial relation to the objective of the interscholastic league rule, its application to Brenden and St. Pierre was in violation of the equal protection clause of the Fourteenth Amendment. The district court granted the requested injunctive relief and prohibited the MSHSL from imposing sanctions on the schools or any of their opponents stemming from plaintiffs' participation on boys' interscholastic athletic teams.

3. In *Reed v. Nebraska School Activities Ass'n*, 341 F. Supp. 258 (D. Neb. 1972), plaintiff Reed, a student-athlete at Norfolk High School in Nebraska, brought an action which challenged a state high school athletic association's practice of providing a public school golf program for boys, while providing none for girls and prohibiting girls from interscholastic participation with or against boys. Reed sought a preliminary injunction prohibiting the Nebraska School Activities Association and school officials from denying her membership on the boys' golf team. The court held for Reed and stated:

> For Debbie Reed, her benefits are fixed in time to the present golf season and when it ends, so will its benefits to her. The loss, whatever its nature or dimensions, will be irretrievable. It is true that defendant's interest in enforcement of the rules . . . will be similarly lost . . . however, that interest is less weighty than those of Debbie Reed in the context of this case.

4. In *Carnes v. Tennessee Secondary School Athletic Ass'n*, 415 F. Supp. 569 (E.D. Tenn. 1976), an action was brought by an 18-year-old girl who wanted to play on the boys' high school baseball team. Plaintiff Carnes sought a preliminary injunction from the court against the Tennessee Secondary Athletic Association rule barring mixed competition in contact sports. Baseball in this case was considered a contact sport.

In granting the preliminary injunction, the district court held that there was a likelihood that Carnes would prevail on the merits of the claim of invalidity of the association's rule and that a denial of injunction would result in irreparable harm to Carnes, whose last opportunity to play high school baseball was drawing to an end.

5. In *Morris v. Michigan State Board of Education*, 472 F.2d 1207 (6th Cir. 1973), plaintiff Morris brought an action against a state high school athletic association rule barring mixed competition in interscholastic sports. Morris and a female friend wanted to play on the high school boys' tennis team. There was no girls' team.

Morris contended a violation of equal protection under the Fourteenth Amendment. The lower court ruled for Morris. The appeals court affirmed the decision but remanded the suit to the lower court to have noncontact sports added to the wording of the order granting the injunction. As a result of the case, Michigan Laws Act 183 were enacted, which permitted women to participate with men on noncontact sports teams.

6. In *Haas v. South Bend Community School Corporation*, 259 Ind. 515, 289 N.E.2d 495 (1972), a suit was brought by a female who was seeking injunctive relief from a state high school athletic association rule barring mixed competition on sports teams. Plaintiff Haas had made the "B" golf team but was denied the opportunity to play with the "A" team because of the association's rule. The lower court held for the association. The decision was later reversed by the appellate court, which held that the rule was a violation of equal protection under the Fourteenth Amendment and the Civil Rights Act. The court found the association's arguments to be insufficient justification for barring girls from noncompetitive sports or from denying girls the chance to qualify.

7. In *Harris v. Illinois High School Ass'n*, No. S-Civ. 72–75 (S.D. Ill. 1972) (unreported), an action was brought by plaintiff Harris, who wanted to play on her high school boys' tennis team. There was no girls' team. The court ruled for the defendant and held that gender classifications were rational. Harris's claim that she had a "right" to participate in interscholastic sports was denied.

8. In *Gregoria v. Board of Educ. of Asbury Park*, Case No. A-1277-70 (N.J. Super. Ct. App. Div. 1971) (unreported), an action was brought by plaintiff Gregoria, who wanted to play on the high school boys' tennis team. There was no girls' team. The board of education would not permit her to play. The trial court ruled in favor of the board of education. The appeals court affirmed the lower court's ruling that the "psychological well-being of girls is a rational reason for exclusion."

9. In *Hollander v. Connecticut Interscholastic Athletic Conf., Inc.*, Civil No. 12-49-27 (Conn. Super. Ct., New Haven County, 1972), *appeal dismissed*, mem., 164 Conn. 658, 295 A.2d 671 (1972), an action was brought by plaintiff Hollander, who wanted to run on the boys' cross-country team at her high school. The Connecticut Intercollegiate Athletic Association barred mixed competition. The court worked out an agreement with the association to allow girls to compete on boys' teams in noncontact sports. Despite that, the court held for defendant association based on Fourteenth Amendment equal protection arguments. The court expressed the opinion that allowing girls to compete on the same teams with boys would bring into question the physical safeguard for girls and the "removal of challenge and incentive for boys to win."

10. In *Bednar v. Nebraska School Activities Ass'n*, 531 F.2d 922 (8th Cir. 1976), the mother of a high school student brought a civil rights action on behalf of her daughter, who had been denied the opportunity to participate on the boys' cross-country team because of her sex. There was no girls' team. The district court issued a preliminary injunction prohibiting the school from excluding Bednar from competition. The school association appealed the decision, but the court of appeals affirmed, finding that as Bednar was one of the top competitors in her event and her qualification for higher levels of competition was likely, she would be subject to irreparable harm if she were not allowed to compete.

11. The following cases involve suits against Little League Baseball:

(a) In *Rappaport v. Little League Baseball, Inc.*, 65 F.R.D. 545 (1975), a group of parents and plaintiff girl filed suit against the Little League because of its policy of excluding girls from participation. The Little League changed its policy after the complaint was filed. The court ruled the case moot.

(b) In *King v. Little League Baseball, Inc.*, 505 F.2d 264 (6th Cir. 1974), an action was brought by a 12-year-old girl who wanted to play on a Little League team. The national Little League Baseball rules excluded girls from competing. However, the Little League Regional Board permitted plaintiff King to try out, and she made the team on the basis of her ability. The team was notified by the National Little League Association that if King continued to play or practice with the team, the team would lose its charter. King was dropped from the roster, which resulted in the town revoking the team's privilege to use the municipal field for games. King was then put back on the roster, and the team lost its charter.

The case was dismissed and affirmed on appeal. The courts held that there was not sufficient state action involved in the defendants' enforcement of the "no girls" rule to bring it under the color of state law. The courts agreed that they did not have jurisdiction over the subject matter in the case.

(c) In *McGill v. Avonworth Baseball Conference*, 364 F. Supp. 1212 (W.D. Pa. 1973), an action was brought by a 10-year-old girl against a nonprofit corporation operating a baseball conference, claiming that she was unconstitutionally discriminated against on the basis of sex when the conference refused to permit her to play Little League baseball. The team used public fields, and plaintiff McGill sought an injunction against their use. The district court held for the conference, stating that the actions of the conference could not be considered state action for purposes of the Civil Rights Act, that the conference's decision was not unreasonable or discriminatory in light of the circumstances, and that the classification was rational where any contact sport was involved.

(d) In *McGill v. Avonworth Baseball Conference*, 516 F.2d 1328 (3rd Cir. 1975), the court of appeals affirmed the trial court's decision for the conference because the girl had failed to show significant state involvement in the league's discrimination. The court reasoned that the waiver of a $25 fee for use of the public playing field was de minimus, that analysis of nature, value, and proportion of state aid to the conference did not end the court's inquiry, and that nexus between the state's and the conference's allegedly offensive policy was not sufficiently close so that the conference's action could be fairly treated as state action in that the conference was granted nonexclusive, scheduled use of four public playing fields, school buildings were used only for once-a-year registration purposes, and no government officials were involved in determining eligibility requirements.

(e) In *Fortin v. Darlington Little League, Inc.*, 376 F. Supp. 473 (D.R.I. 1974), *rev'd*, 514 F.2d 344 (1st Cir. 1975), an action was brought by a 10-year-old girl who was denied the opportunity to try out for Little League baseball solely because of her sex. Plaintiff Fortin argued that the baseball park where the team played was public property, a fact that supplied sufficient proof to find the required state action. The appeals court ruled for the girl, reversing the lower court's decision. The appeals court found that the league's preferred dependency on city baseball diamonds introduced signif-icant state involvement to find state action. The appeals court also rejected the league's argument that the discrimination was appro-priate because females would injure more easily than males, be-cause it was not supported by the facts.

(f) In *National Organization for Women, Essex County Chapter v. Little League Baseball, Inc.*, 127 N.J. Super 522, 318 A. 2d 33 (Ct.

App. Div. 1974), the Essex County chapter of the National Organization for Women (NOW) filed suit on behalf of 8- to 12-year-old girls who wanted to play Little League baseball. NOW contended this discrimination against girls was a violation of New Jersey's antidiscrimination laws. In affirming a lower court order for the girls, the superior court held that the evidence permitted the finding that girls of the particular age concerned were not subject to greater hazard of injury while playing baseball than boys of the same age group and that the Little League did not fall within any statutory exemptions.

12. In August 1983, Mary Decker, Grete Waitz, and 50 other leading female runners filed a sex discrimination suit against the International Olympic Committee (IOC), the Los Angeles Olympic Organizing Committee, the International Amateur Athletic Federation, The Athletics Congress, and others. The suit was filed in Los Angeles Superior Court and sought an order that would force the defendants to include 5,000- and 10,000-meter runs for women at the 1984 Olympic Games in Los Angeles. These events were part of the men's events and were historically excluded from the women's program because of the belief that women could not physically handle the distances. (See *Martin v. International Olympic Committee* on page 105 and "Female Runners Sue to Add Long Events," *New York Times*, August 12, 1983, p. A18, Col. 1.) The request for injunctive relief was denied by the court. The IOC later added these events to the women's program for the 1988 Olympic Games in Seoul, S. Korea.

Women's Team, No Men's Team

The all-women-no-men-type of case has arisen only with noncontact sports. Unlike the converse situations just covered, men are generally not allowed to play on all-female teams. To support this conclusion, courts often cite the theory that male participation would destroy any attempt to redress past discrimination.

Noncontact Sports

In cases in which there is a women's team and no men's team for noncontact sports, there is a split in decisions as to whether to allow a male to play on the women's team. In *Gomes v. Rhode Island Interscholastic League* (see Note 1), the court upheld the male's sex discrimination claim and allowed him to play on the women's volleyball team. In *Clark v. Arizona Interscholastic Ass'n* (see Note 2), the court refused to allow boys to compete on the girls' volleyball team. The plaintiff male may not be successful for a variety of reasons, including lack of state action when a private organization is involved (see Note 3), prohibition of males on women's teams to redress disparate treatment of females in scholastic athletic programs (see Note 4), promotion of athletic opportunities for females (see Note 5), and the fact that males already have more athletic opportunities than females (see Note 6).

NOTES _____

1. In *Gomes v. Rhode Island Interscholastic League*, 469 F. Supp. 659 (D.R.I. 1979), *vacated as moot*, 604 F.2d 733 (1st Cir. 1979), plaintiff Gomes, a senior at Rogers High School in Newport, Rhode Island, brought an action under the federal civil rights statute. He sought preliminary injunctive relief prohibiting school officials from preventing his participation on the girls' volleyball team since the school offered no separate male squad in this sport. Rogers High allowed Gomes to join the all-female team but did not use him in Rhode Island Interscholastic League competition for fear of league disqualification.

Consequently, Gomes brought suit against the league at the start of the volleyball season. He alleged that the rule against male participation in volleyball competition violated both the Fourteenth Amendment and Title IX. Without reaching the constitutional issues, the district court ruled in Gomes's favor. The district court found that the exception for separate-sex teams under Title IX was not applicable since defendants sponsored no men's volleyball teams and opportunities for boys to play the sport previously had been nonexistent. Since the district court decision was rendered in the middle of the volleyball season, the league persuaded the appeals court that implementation of the district court's order would disrupt the remainder of the season. The appeals court stopped the implementation of the order pending review. The merits of the case were never reached on appeal since the case was dismissed as moot (the season had ended and Gomes was graduating), the judgment vacated, and the case remanded for dismissal.

2. In *Clark v. Arizona Interscholastic Ass'n*, 695 F.2d 1126 (9th Cir. 1982), *cert. denied*, 104 S. Ct. 79 (1983), plaintiffs were Arizona high school students who demonstrated their prowess in volleyball by participating on national championship teams sponsored by the Amateur Athletic Union. The student-athletes were not, however, able to participate on their high school volleyball teams. Their schools only sponsored interscholastic volleyball teams for girls, and a policy of the Arizona Interscholastic Association (AIA) had been interpreted to preclude boys from playing on girls' teams, even though girls are permitted to participate on boys' athletic teams.

The trial court found that the rules and regulations of the AIA do not violate the equal protection clause of the Fourteenth Amendment. It held that the maintenance of a girls only volleyball team "is substantially related to and serves the achievement of the important governmental objective" of (1) promoting equal athletic opportunities for females in interscholastic sports, and (2) redressing the effects of past discrimination. On appeal, the trial court decision was affirmed, upholding the rule prohibiting boys from playing on the girls' volleyball team. The appeals court noted that in this case, the alternative chosen may not maximize equality, and may represent trade-offs between equality and practicality. But since absolute necessity is not the standard, and absolute equality of opportunity in every sport is not the mandate, even the existence of wiser alternatives than the one chosen does not serve to invalidate the policy here since it is substantially related to the goal. That is all the standard demands. . . . While equality in specific sports is a worthwhile ideal, it should not be purchased at the expense of ultimate equality of opportunity to participate in sports. As common sense would advise against this, neither does the Constitution demand it.

For further information on *Clark v. Arizona Interscholastic Ass'n* see the following law review articles:

(a) "Constitutional Law—Equal Protection—Sex Discrimination Against Males in Athletics—Physiological Differences Are Valid Reasons to Exclude Boys From Girls' Athletic Teams" (*Clark v. Arizona Interscholastic Ass'n*, 695 F.2d 1126 [9th Cir. 1982], *cert. denied*, 104 S. Ct. 79 [1983]), 6 *Whittier Law Review* 151 (1984).

(b) "Equal Protection Scrutiny of High School Athletics" *Clark v. Arizona Interscholastic Ass'n*, 695 F.2d 1126 [9th Cir. 1982] *cert. denied*, 104 S. Ct. 79 [1983]), 72 *Kentucky Law Journal* 935 (1983–84).

3. In *White v. Corpus Christi Little Misses Kickball Ass'n*, 526 S.W.2d 766 (Tex. Civ. App. 1975), an action was brought by plaintiff White, a 10-year-old boy who was not allowed to register to play in the girls' kickball association, because of his sex. The district court held for the association, and the boy appealed. On appeal, the boy argued that denial of right to play because of his sex was a denial of equal protection under both federal and state constitutions. The appeals court denied his claim because he had failed to establish the requisite state action. His participation was denied by a private organization acting without any connection to government except that the games were played in a public park.

4. In *Forte v. Board of Education, North Babylon Union Free School District*, 431 N.Y.S.2d 321 (1980), an action was brought by plaintiff Forte on behalf of his son, a 17-year-old high school student who wanted to play on the North Babylon High School volleyball team, which was all female. The court held for the school district. The court reasoned that the rule the school district had enacted was a discernible and permissible means of redressing disparate treatment of females in interscholastic athletic programs.

5. In *Petrie v. Illinois High School Ass'n*, 75 Ill. App. 3d 980, 31 Ill. Dec., 653, 394 N.E.2d 855 (1979), an action was brought by plaintiff Petrie, who wanted to play on the girls' high school volleyball team since the school had no boys' team. The Illinois High School Association would not allow Petrie to play on the girls' team. The appeals court affirmed a lower court decision which upheld the association's rule. The court found no violation of state law and reasoned that the association's rule "substantially related to and served the achievement of the governmental objective of maintaining, fostering, and promoting athletic opportunities for girls."

6. In *Mularadelis v. Haldane Central School Board*, 74 A.D.2d 248,

427 N.Y.S.2d 458 (1980), an action was brought by plaintiff Mularadelis, a member of his high school's girls' tennis team, who was told by the school board that he could no longer play on the team. The appeals court reversed a lower court decision and held for the school board on the basis that Title IX allowed for the exclusion of boys from the girls' team when there were, overall, more athletic opportunities for boys in the community.

7. In *Atty. Gen v. Massachusetts Interscholastic Athletic Ass'n Inc.*, 378 Mass. 342, 393 N.E.2d 284 (1979), an action was brought by the state attorney general, who claimed that an athletic association rule excluding boys from competing on a girls' team, even though a girl could play on a boys' team if that sport was not offered for girls, was discriminatory. Injunctive relief was sought.

The Massachusetts Supreme Judicial Court held that the discriminatory classification could not be justified by (1) the theory that the classification was based on inherent biological differences rather than sex, (2) the theory that absolute exclusion on the basis of gender was necessary to protect player's safety, and (3) the theory that such a discriminatory classification would protect "emergent girls' programs from inundation of male athletes." The court found that more of the above were applicable and held that any "rule prohibiting any boy from playing on a girls' team was invalid under the state equal rights amendment and statute barring sex discrimination in the educational sphere." The case was remitted for declaration that the rule was invalid and an issuance of an injunction prohibiting its application.

Women's Teams and Men's Teams

Four different types of legal arguments are raised in cases in which there are teams for both sexes. The first type is in cases in which the plaintiff women argue that "separate but equal is not equal." In these situations the women sue to participate on the men's team because the competition may be better and the women are far superior to the participants on the women's teams. As *O'Connor v. Board of Education of School District 23* (see Note 1 on page 411) illustrates, the court will generally approve "separate but equal" teams and rule against plaintiff females who want to play on boys' teams based on playing ability arguments.

The second type of argument is that the separate teams are not equal, especially with respect to the benefits and opportunities provided to the teams. In *Aiken v. Lieuallen* (see Note 2 on page 411), plaintiff female athletes contended that they were discriminated against in the areas of transportation, officiating, coaching, and the school's commitment to competitive programs. In a similar situation, *Blair v. Washington State University* (see Note 3 on page 411), the court awarded damages to plaintiff female athletes and ordered equivalent funding for men's and women's athletic programs.

The third type of case occurs when two teams exist, but the women compete under different rules than the men (see page 459). These situations, challenged on equal protection grounds, have produced mixed results. The trend seems to be away from allowing different rules to exist when those rules are based purely on the gender of the athletes, especially when those rules place those who play under a disadvantage if they want to continue in the sport.

The fourth type of case involves different seasons for the same men's and women's sport (see page 462). The courts have generally held that separate seasons of play are not a denial of equal protection of the law.

Separate But Equal

The sexes are generally separated when it comes to participation in sports, and the challenges to this practice have been largely unavailing. The doctrine of "separate but equal" remains applicable to sex distinctions, even though it has been rejected for distinctions based on race. Thus, if separate teams exist for men and women, there may be a prohibition against co-ed teams or against women competing against men. The doctrine of "separate but equal" raises the critical question of whether or not such separate teams are substantially equal. The fact that two teams exist does not necessarily satisfy the doctrine. "Separate but equal" is based on the concept that the exclusion of a group is not unconstitutional if the excluded group is provided with comparable opportunities. If women are excluded from the men's basketball team but are provided with an equal one of their own, the school district will not be in violation of Title IX under the "separate but equal" theory. When the sexes are segregated in athletics, there must be an overall equality of expenditures, coaching, and access to facilities. Without this substantial equality, the existence of separate teams and the prohibition of women competing with men may be unconstitutional.

Apart from these circumstances, the segregation of the sexes in athletics is generally upheld, although the court is careful to examine the specific circumstances in each case before making a determination. The court usually considers whether or not the particular sport in question is considered to be a contact or a noncontact sport. Physiological differences between the sexes have been found to be a valid reason for the exclusion of one sex from a contact sport. Contact sports include boxing, wrestling, rugby, ice hockey, football, basketball, and other sports in which the major activity involves bodily contact.

When dealing with noncontact sports, the courts have allowed co-educational participation when only one team is sponsored and athletic opportunities for the excluded sex have previously been limited.

Contact Sports

In cases in which there are both women's and men's teams in contact sports, the courts have generally not allowed a female to participate on the men's team. In *O'Connor v. Board of Education of School District No. 23* (Note 1), the court denied the sex discrimination allegation of a female who wanted to participate in better competition by playing on the men's team. The other issue which may be raised is whether the separate men's and women's teams are in fact equal. Both *Aiken v. Lieuallen* (Note 2) and *Blair v. Washington State University* (Note 3) deal with this issue.

NOTES _____

1. In *O'Connor v. Board of Education of School District No. 23*, 645 F.2d 578 (7th Cir. 1981), *cert. denied*, 454 U.S. 1084, 102 S. Ct. 641, 70 L.Ed2d 619 (1981), an appeal was instituted in response to a district court order granting a preliminary injunction to restrain defendant school board from refusing to permit female plaintiff to try out for the boy's sixth grade basketball team. The plaintiff argued that the school board's policy of maximizing participation in sports by providing for separate but equal boys' and girls' interscholastic sports teams violated Title IX. The appellate court held that the trial court abused its discretion in granting a preliminary injunction restraining the school board because the plaintiff failed to show a reasonable likelihood of success on the merits.

2. In *Aiken v. Lieuallen*, 39 Or. App. 779, 593 P.2d 1243 (1979), an action was brought by plaintiff taxpayers and parents of student-athletes on the University of Oregon's women's varsity basketball team who appealed a determination by the chancellor of the State Board of Higher Education that the university was not violating state statute ORS 659.150, which prohibited discrimination on the basis of sex in state-financed educational programs. The plaintiffs filed a complaint in March 1977, alleging that the following four areas of Oregon's athletic program were in violation of ORS 659.150: transportation, officiating, coaching, and commitment to competitive programs. A contested case hearing was held in October 1977, in which the hearing officer determined that the university was in violation of ORS 659.150.

The findings and recommendations were issued in March 1978 and were submitted to the Oregon chancellor of higher education for review and entry of an order. The chancellor reversed the hearing officer's decision and found that the university was not in violation of the statute. The appeals court reversed the chancellor's order and sent the case back for further proceedings. The court, after reviewing the plaintiffs' allegations of discrimination in the areas of transportation, officiating, coaching, and university commitment, stated that upon the second hearing, the chancellor should address these allegations to determine whether the university's actions have led to "unreasonable differentiation of treatment" under ORS 659.150. Determinations of the unreasonableness of actions should include evaluations of whether or not the action by the university had a disparate effect on the opportunity for women to participate in athletics.

3. In *Blair v. Washington State University*, No. 28816 (Super. Ct. Wash.) (unreported), a class action suit was brought by present and former female student-athletes at Washington State University, which alleged sex discrimination in its athletic programs. The plaintiffs based their claim on the state of Washington's equal rights amendment. The court held for the female student-athletes and ordered, in part, increased financial support for women's athletics.

4. In *Hutchins v. Board of Trustees of Michigan State University*, C.A. No. G79–87 (W.D. Mich. 1979) (unreported), the women's basketball team from the East Lansing campus of Michigan State brought a Title IX complaint against Michigan State University and the board of trustees, alleging that the men's team was receiving better treatment. The alleged better treatment included more money for traveling and better facilities. The court held for the women's basketball team and issued a temporary restraining order barring the better treatment of the men's team.

5. In *Petersen v. Oregon State University* (settled 1980), two student-athletes filed a complaint with the Board of Education of the State of Oregon, alleging that Oregon State University (OSU) offered athletic programs of lesser quality to female student-athletes than were offered to their male counterparts. A settlement reached in July 1980, entitled "OSU Conciliation Agreement for Sex Equality in Intercollegiate Athletics," implemented a five-year plan at OSU designed to put the men's and women's athletic programs on an equal competitive basis.

6. For further information on *Aiken* and *Petersen*, see "*Aiken v. Lieuallen* and *Petersen v. Oregon State University:* Defining Equity in Athletics," 8 *Journal of College and University Law* 369 (1981–82).

7. In *Michigan Department of Civil Rights, ex rel. Forton v. Waterford Township Department of Parks and Recreation*, 335 N.W.2d 305 (Mich. Ct. App. 1983), plaintiff brought a Civil Rights Act claim based on defendant's policy of maintaining a gender-based elementary-level basketball program. The appeals court reversed the district court's decision and ruled in favor of the plaintiff. The court reasoned that (1) separate leagues involved were not equal and could not withstand equal protection analysis, and consequently violated the Civil Rights Act, and (2) subsequent modification of policy to allow up to two girls to participate on each boys' basketball team and two boys on each girls' basketball team did not cure the statutory violation.

8. In *Lafler v. Athletic Board of Control*, 536 F. Supp. 104 (W.D. Mich. 1982), the court upheld the denial of a woman's application to box in the flyweight division of the Golden Gloves boxing competition under the Fourteenth Amendment, the state public accommodation statute,

and the state equal rights amendment. The court cited Title IX regulations permitting establishment of separate male-female teams in contact sports and the Amateur Sports Act provisions providing for separate programs for females and males.

Noncontact Sports

In cases in which there are both women's and men's teams in noncontact sports, the courts have generally not allowed the female to participate on the men's team. The rationale is that separate but equal is equal, since this enhances athletic opportunities for females.

NOTES _____

1. In *Ritacco v. Norwin School District*, 361 F. Supp. 930 (W.D. Pa. 1973), a high school graduate and her mother filed a class action challenging the Pennsylvania Interscholastic Athletic Association (PIAA) rule, which in effect required separate girls' and boys' teams for interscholastic noncontact sports. The district court ruled in favor of the defendant school district. It held that since the school district had not deprived Ritacco of her constitutional rights in violation of the Civil Rights statute, 42 U.S.C. § 1983, she was entitled to neither the declaratory judgment nor the injunctive relief. The court held that "separate but equal" in the realm of athletic competition is justifiable and permissible when a rational basis for the rule exists, and that sex, unlike race, is not an inherently suspect classification for purposes of determining a denial of equal protection. The court concluded that the PIAA rule forbidding co-educational noncontact sports teams did not invalidly and unfairly discriminate against females. In fact, the court observed that this rule had produced positive effects on girls' interscholastic athletics in Pennsylvania since its adoption in 1970. The court was convinced that "the prime purpose behind the no-mixed-sex competition rule is a valid one seeking to enhance the quality, quantity, and calibre of interscholastic sports opportunities for girls and boys in Pennsylvania."

2. In *Ruman v. Eskew*, 343 N.E.2d 806 (Ind. Ct. App. 1975), an action was brought by plaintiff Ruman, who wanted to play on the high school boys' tennis team, even though there was a girls' team at her school. The Indiana High School Athletic Association prohibited girls from playing on boys' teams if girls' teams in the same sport exist. The court held for the defendant, and relying on *Haas v. South Bend Community School Corporation* (see page 448), upheld the rule, since it was reasonably related to the objective of providing athletic opportunities for both males and females. The court of appeals further stated that "until girls' programs comparable to those established for boys exist, the rule cannot be justified." However, in this case, since the trial court had already decided the issue of "whether the tennis program for girls at Munster High School during the school year 1974–75 was and is comparable to that for boys,"

the appellate court believed it was in no position to "review the eviden-
tiary basis upon which the facts rest."

3. In *Gregoria v. Board of Education of Asbury Park*, Case No. A-
1277-70 (N.J. Super. Ct. App. Div. 1971), the trial court refused to
prohibit enforcement of the New Jersey Athletic Association rule prohibiting co-ed interscholastic sports, including noncontact sports such as
tennis. Among the rational bases for the policy, the court cited the
psychological impact on males, the need for additional female trainers,
and the possibility of insufficient bathroom facilities. The appeals court
affirmed the lower court's ruling that the "psychological well-being of
girls is a rational reason for exclusion."

4. Deb Schiff, a 16-year-old student at West Essex Regional High
School in New York, was initially barred from participating on the boys'
fencing team because state regulations said she could not compete
because the school offered a separate girls' division. Sabers were allowed
in the boys' division, but they were not used by the girls' team. Schiff
objected to the ban on the grounds that a nearby female high school
student was allowed to play on the football team, while she was denied
an opportunity to participate in a less violent sport.

The executive committee of the New York Interscholastic Athletic
Association later granted Schiff a waiver of the rules in her favor. The
decree may open the door to any other girl in the state who is deprived
of competing on a boys' team. ("Schoolgirl Fencer to Duel with Boys,"
N.Y. Times, February 19, 1986, p. 16, col. 5.)

Same Sport, Different Rules

Cases and issues in this section have traditionally arisen in basketball because of women's playing rules being different from men's
rules. As evidenced by *Bucha v. Illinois High School Ass'n* (see
page 461), the cases have also evolved from generally disparate
treatment of student-athletes rather than from different rules of a
sport.

Contact Sports

In cases in which there are different playing rules for women's and
men's teams in contact sports, there is a split in decisions as to
whether the women's rules should be changed to conform with the
men's. The plaintiff women in these cases generally have alleged
sex discrimination based on the rule differences with men's sports
and also the reduced opportunity to compete against other women
(who had the advantage of playing under men's rules) for college
scholarships. In *Dodson v. Arkansas Activities Ass'n* (Note 1), the
court ruled for the plaintiff, while in *Jones v. Oklahoma Secondary
School Activities Ass'n* (Note 2) and *Cape v. Tennessee Secondary
School Athletic Ass'n* (Note 3), the courts ruled for the defendant
athletic associations.

NOTES _____

1. In *Dodson v. Arkansas Activities Ass'n*, 468 F. Supp. 394 (E.D. Ark. 1979), plaintiff Dodson, a junior high school basketball player in the Arkadelphia, Arkansas, public school system, brought an action in January 1977 against three defendants: the school district, the superintendent, and the Arkansas Activities Association (AAA). Her suit challenged the constitutionality of rules for girls' junior and senior high school basketball, which in Arkansas differed from those under which boys played. The court held that, "none of the reasons proffered [for the rule differentiation] is at all relevant to a gender-based classification." The defendant stated that "no physiological differences between males and females . . . prohibit females from playing five-on-five basketball," and the primary justification given for the sex-based distinction between rules was simply that of tradition. The court ordered that the defendants be permanently prohibited and restrained from enforcing different rules for girls and boys playing junior and senior high school basketball in Arkansas. However, after stating that the case was not about male-female competition or discrimination between programs, the court stated:

> The point here is that Arkansas boys are in a position to compete on an equal footing with boys elsewhere, while Arkansas girls, merely because they are girls, are not. . . . Arkansas schools have chosen to offer basketball. Having taken that step, they may not limit the game's full benefits to one sex without substantial justification.

2. In *Jones v. Oklahoma Secondary School Activities Ass'n*, 453 F. Supp. 150 (W.D. Okla. 1977), plaintiff Jones sought an injunction to suspend the association's split-court basketball rules, arguing that they created an arbitrary and unreasonable distinction between boys and girls that violated her right to equal protection. The court held for the athletic association. Jones's Title IX arguments were dismissed because she did not follow administrative procedures. Her Fourteenth Amendment argument was seen as faulty because her allegations concerning her reduced opportunity to compete in the future and a reduced likelihood for college scholarships did not rise to the level of an equal protection interest. Her claims that such rules interfered with her enjoyment of the game as well as her physical development also did not establish a cognizable equal protection claim.

3. In *Cape v. Tennessee Secondary School Athletic Ass'n*, 424 F. Supp. 732 (E.D. Tenn. 1976), *rev'd per curiam*, 563 F.2d 793 (6th Cir. 1977), plaintiff Cape, a high school student, challenged the "split-court" rules used in women's basketball. These rules, she claimed, denied her the full benefits of the game as well as an athletic scholarship to college. The court held for the athletic association and dismissed Cape's arguments, which were based on a private right of action under Title IX and the Fourteenth Amendment. The court held that Cape, who sought to challenge the regulations, must first exhaust all administrative remedies within the Department of Health, Education and Welfare under Title IX before her suit could be addressed in federal court.

4. For further information, see Johnson, "Half Court Girls' Basketball

Rules: An Application of the Equal Protection Clause and Title IX," 65 *Iowa Law Review* 766 (March 1980).

Noncontact Sports

The courts have allowed different rules for men's and women's noncontact sports. The courts can apply a rational relationship test and find that the physical and psychological differences between male and female athletes justify different rules.

NOTE ───

1. In *Bucha v. Illinois High School Ass'n*, 351 F. Supp. 69 (N.D. Ill. 1972), plaintiffs, two female students at Hinsdale Center Township High School, brought a class action challenging the Illinois High School Association (IHSA) bylaws placing limitations on girls' athletic contests that were not applicable to boys' athletics. The girls sought to have the court declare the IHSA rules in violation of the equal protection clause of the Fourteenth Amendment and to prohibit the enforcement of the bylaws. They also sought a judgment against all defendants in the amount of $25,000.

The court first determined that the named plaintiffs in this cause adequately represented all the members of their class and thus, their standing to bring a class action was affirmed. It stated:

> Although these two girls might have an interest in becoming members of presently all-boy teams, they also have an interest in seeking the development of a "separate but equal" program. . . . The fact that the named plaintiffs have interests which exceed those of some class members will not defeat the class action, so long as they possess interests which are coextensive with those of the class.

The defendants—IHSA, its directors, and the board of education of Hinsdale Township—based their motions to dismiss on three arguments:

1. The IHSA and the board of education were not persons within the meaning of 42 USC § 1983 (1970).
2. The challenged discrimination was not an action under color of state statute, ordinance, regulation, custom or usage.
3. The challenged discrimination did not constitute a deprivation of a right guaranteed by the U.S. Constitution and laws.

Concerning the defendants' first argument, the court held that "all defendants may properly be prohibited as persons under § 1983, but only the individual defendants can be liable for the damages sought." On the second argument, the court rejected defendants' contention that the acts of the IHSA did not amount to state action and therefore could not be reached under § 1983.

On the third and final argument, the court reviewed the girls' complaint that the athletic association had denied them equal protection, stating that the relevant inquiry was whether the challenged classification based on sex was rational. Because participation in interscholastic athletics is not a constitutionally guaranteed right and the Illinois courts do not interfere with the policies of a voluntary association such as the IHSA unless it acts "unreasonably, arbitrarily, or capriciously," the girls had asserted their claims based on an equal educational opportunity argument and not the right to interscholastic athletic participation.

The court analyzed the alleged denial of equal protection in this case using the traditional test that identifies the purposes or objective of a legislative scheme and then asks whether the challenged discrimination bears a rational relationship to one of those purposes.

The court found a factual basis for defendants' claims that the physical and psychological differences between male and female student-athletes would lead to male domination of co-ed interscholastic sports and result in decreased female athletic participation should unrestricted competition between the sexes be permitted. It held that

> the uncontroverted existence of a bona fide athletic program for girls coupled with the physical and psychological differences . . . also support the rationality of the IHSA's decision to conduct girls' interscholastic sports programs different from boys'.

The district court entered summary judgment in favor of all defendants on the basis that the traditional equal protection standard

> requires this court to defer to the judgment of the physical educators of the IHSA once a rational relationship has been shown to exist between their actions and the goals of interscholastic athletic competition.

Same Sport, Different Seasons

The courts have allowed different seasons for men and women in the same sport as long as there is a rational basis for the difference. In one case, an athletic association scheduled men's swimming in a different season (e.g., fall) than the women's season (e.g., winter) and was challenged on sex discrimination grounds. The athletic association's decision was upheld. The court reasoned that there was a reasonable basis for the decision: the lack of available pool time for both women's and men's teams to practice during the same seasons.

NOTE ───

1. In *Striebel v. Minnesota State High School League*, 321 N.W.2d 400 (Minn. 1982), an action was brought by plaintiff female student-athlete against the Minnesota State High School League (MSHSL), challenging the constitutionality of a MSHSL rule which authorized "separate seasons of play for high school athletic teams separated or substantially separated according to sex." The MSHSL had established separate seasons for boys and girls in tennis and swimming. The district court held that the league's policy of establishing separate seasons for boys and girls was constitutional and in compliance with the statute. The court found that under the circumstances presented, separating teams by season was a "reasonable means of achieving maximum participation by both sexes in the high

school athletic program." On appeal, the Minnesota Supreme Court held that "where limited athletic facilities made it necessary to schedule high school boys' and girls' athletic teams in two separate seasons, and neither was substantially better than the other, that scheduling decision was not a denial of equal protection of the law."

SEX DISCRIMINATION CASES INVOLVING ATHLETIC EMPLOYMENT

The following sections and cases focus on sex discrimination in the area of athletic employment. Sex discrimination in this context can best be defined as the imposition of any barrier to employment which affects one gender but not the other. The plaintiff is generally an employee who serves as a coach or physical education teacher. The courts favor coaches or instructors who can prove that school districts or universities have discriminated against them on the basis of sex. The rulings in these cases favoring coaches and teachers post a warning to school officials that the rights of coaches must be understood and considered.

Equal Pay Act and Title VII

Two separate statutes specifically pertain to discrimination in employment. The first is the Equal Pay Act, which was passed in 1963 (effective date was June 10, 1964). The second is Title VII of the Civil Rights Act of 1964. While the Equal Pay Act deals solely with wages paid to women and men within the same company, Title VII focuses on discriminatory hiring/firing practices and advancement policies within companies. Neither is specific to the issue of sex discrimination; however, they both encompass discrimination on the basis of race, religion, or national origin. Both of these statutes have been applied to interscholastic and intercollegiate athletics, primarily in suits brought by female coaches claiming sex discrimination.

The Equal Pay Act stipulates that an employer must pay equal salaries to men and women holding jobs that require equal skill, effort, and responsibility and that are performed under similar working conditions. The Equal Pay Act, 29 U.S.C. § 206(d)(1) (1982), provides that:

> No employer having employees subject to any provision of this section shall discriminate, within any establishment in which such employees are employed, between employees on the basis of sex by paying wages to employees in such establishment at a rate less than the rate at which he pays wages to employees of the opposite sex in

such establishment for equal work on jobs the performance of which requires equal skill, effort, and responsibility, and which are performed under similar working conditions. . . .

The basic theme underlying the act is "equal pay for equal work." The courts apply a "substantially equal test" for judging the equality of jobs under the Equal Pay Act. The courts interpret this standard as consistent with the middle course intended by Congress between a requirement that the jobs in question be exactly alike and a requirement that they merely be comparable. In conducting its inquiry, the court looks at overall job content. The plaintiff must show that any job differences are so insignificant that they do not contribute to the differences in pay. The courts will look behind job classifications to the substance of the work. Any differences in job duties and responsibilities must be real and not just indicated by a nominal title or designation. Consequently, the Equal Pay Act addresses only the most overt wage discrimination cases and does not apply to problems created by prior discrimination in the workplace.

The Labor Department's Division of Wages and Hours was initially responsible for enforcing the Equal Pay Act under the Fair Labor Standards Acts (29 U.S.C. § 201 et seq). In 1979, enforcement was moved to the Equal Employment Opportunity Commission (EEOC). By statute, the EEOC consists of five members and is empowered to receive complaints, intervene in certain civil actions, and otherwise administer the Equal Pay Act and Title VII. Enforcement procedures consist of routine checks as well as investigations in response to specific complaints. If an employer is discriminating and the EEOC determines that this cannot be corrected informally, the Department of Labor may file suit to enforce the law.

An individual party bringing a discrimination complaint must establish that his or her job is substantially equal to that of another employee of the opposite sex who is being paid more for performing similar services and tasks. The party must file the suit within two years of the alleged discrimination, or within three years if the discrimination is found to be willful. If a claim is substantiated and a violation is found, the complaining party may receive the differences between the wages paid to men and women for a maximum two-year period or three years plus a penalty if the discrimination is found to be willful.

The other statute available to combat employment discrimination is Title VII of the Civil Rights Act of 1964 (42 U.S.C. § 2000e-2[a] 1976), which states that

[i]t shall be an unlawful employment practice for any employer to fail or refuse to hire or to discharge any individual, or otherwise

discriminate against any individual with respect to his compensation, terms, conditions, or privileges of employment, because of such individual's race, color, religion, sex, or national origin. . . .

Title VII was enacted as a comprehensive prohibition on private acts of employment discrimination. It forbids discriminatory employment practices based on the race, color, religion, sex, or national origin of the applicant. These categories may, however, be used to differentiate between applicants when sex, religion, or national origin is a bona fide occupational qualification (BFOQ). A BFOQ is very narrowly defined as an actual job requirement, not merely a customer or employer preference. For example, race is never considered a BFOQ.

Title VII also contains a "nonretaliation" provision which prohibits all employers defined in the act from discriminating against any employee or job applicant who has invoked his or her rights under Title VII or who has assisted with or participated in any proceeding brought by someone else.

In the analysis of the courts, the alleged sex discrimination action need not only be based upon a consideration of an unalterable characteristic (like gender) possessed by the discriminatee but which is not possessed by the discriminator. Thus, not only are acts such as terminating female employees when they marry or refusing to accept employment applications from any female actionable, but also acts taken by a member of one sex against a member of the same sex can be actionable. A demand for sexual favors directed by one male to another as a condition of employment can be just as discriminatory as a similar demand directed by a male to a female.

Title VII is applicable to all employers of more than 15 persons, and it specifically covers almost all state and local government employees as well as employees of most educational institutions. It is enforced by the EEOC, which has the authority to process and investigate any complaints. The EEOC may also bring suits in federal court if necessary. A charge brought by the EEOC is based on what the EEOC perceives to be a pattern or practice of unlawful discrimination which adversely affects an entire class of individuals. The EEOC may also conduct industrywide compliance reviews. If the discrimination found by the EEOC in state or local government cannot be corrected informally, the EEOC may refer the matter to the U.S. Attorney General. In all other cases, the EEOC may go to federal court to enforce the law.

Enforcement of Title VII is not limited to EEOC actions, however, because the legislation also has individual and class causes of action. This type of charge originates from an individual or group of individuals who allege that they were adversely affected by some act of unlawful discrimination. Organizations can bring discrimination claims on behalf of their members if the alleged discriminatory action injured its members, if the claim can proceed without the participation of those injured members, and if the claim is relevant to the organization's purposes.

The requirements for filing a charge include the following:

1. The person filing the charge must be or represent an aggrieved person (must have a personal stake in the outcome of the controversy and must have suffered a personal injury), except in cases in which the charge is filed by the EEOC itself.
2. The charge must be directed against an "employer" as defined by Title VII.
3. The charge must be filed within the specified time limits.
4. The form of the charge must comply with certain procedural requirements.

Once these requirements are met, the EEOC will proceed with the charge.

The remedies of both injunctive and affirmative relief are available to the winning party in an employment discrimination suit. The prevailing party may be awarded back pay and attorney's fees as well as an injunction prohibiting the employer's unlawful action. In addition, the court may order the employer to cease its discriminatory practices, to reinstate employees, and to implement an appropriate affirmative action plan to eliminate existing discrimination and prevent its recurrence. These remedies are guided by the two goals of the act: (1) to achieve equality of employment opportunity by removing barriers based on race, color, religion, sex, or natural origin, and (2) to make the victim of unlawful discrimination whole—to put the victim in the position he or she would have been in had the discrimination not occurred.

Both of these approaches have limitations. Even taken together, they are not sufficient to enforce a prohibition against sex discrimination. Although the Equal Pay Act applies to all employers, Title VII has been limited to employers of more than 15 people. Thus, many smaller businesses are not subject to the mandates of Title VII. The Equal Pay Act is limited in other ways. For example, it is directed only to discrepancies in pay levels once on a job. It does not address the problem of discriminatory hiring or advancement policies. The basic weakness of these acts is that neither is all-encompassing. They fail to address the overall problems of sex discrimination that exist outside of the workplace. Thus, very few of the problems of discrimination encountered in athletics are addressed by either act. This legislation provides potential relief only in athletic employment.

Another major problem in pursuing litigation under these statutes is the cost. Neither statute provides any guaranteed basis for the eventual recovery of attorney's fees and/or double or triple damages. Thus, litigation is not an option for many of those who might wish to file claims. Cases are seldom pursued, and the effectiveness of the legislation diminishes as the chance that an employer will be punished lessens. One last problem is that until recently, courts have been reluctant to interpret the statutes broadly. This reluctance stems from the fact that hiring and salary decisions are well within the area of management prerogatives allotted to employers. The court is reluctant to interfere in any discretionary decision unless there has been a clear abuse of that discretion. Thus, it is very difficult to establish a case based on a complaint regarding practices in either of these areas. Usually, the evidence is open to a variety of interpretations. Such circumstances can make it difficult or even impossible for a plaintiff to prevail in a sex discrimination case under application of the aforementioned statutes.

NOTES

1. In *Kunda v. Muhlenberg College*, 621 F.2d 532 (3rd Cir. 1980), an action was brought which involved an employment discrimination case based on sex. The plaintiff was a female physical education instructor at a private college. She was denied tenure because she lacked a master's degree, whereas three male members of the physical education department who lacked master's degrees were promoted. The court issued an injunction requiring the college to promote the female instructor with tenure and back pay. The court of appeals affirmed the decision, stating that "Academic institutions' decisions are not *ipso facto* entitled to special treatment under federal laws prohibiting discrimination." The court noted that although the interests of an educational institution in academic freedom are important, academic freedom is not implicated in every academic employment decision.

2. In *Caulfield v. Board of Education of City of New York*, 632 F.2d 999 (2d Cir. 1980), the court upheld a decision that Title IX applies to athletic hiring practices because discrimination against women's access to supervisory positions has a discriminating effect on the institution's students, the direct beneficiaries of federal financial aid. Coaching and other supervisory positions in athletic programs must be assigned without discrimination, even if the program receives no direct federal aid for funding the positions.

3. In *Cannon v. University of Chicago*, 60 L.Ed.2d 560, 99 S. Ct. 1946, 441 U.S. 677 (1979), the Supreme Court held that Title IX should be interpreted as being similar in intent to Title VI of the Civil Rights

Act of 1964. The court cited cases in which plaintiffs suing officials of the
federal government under Title VI secured orders requiring those officials
either to aid recipients of federal funds in devising nondiscriminatory
alternatives to presently discriminatory programs or to cut aid to those
programs. The court held that these rulings applied to Title IX situations
as well.

4. In *Shenefield v. Sheridan County School District No. 1*, 544 P.2d
870 (Wyo. 1976), plaintiff Shenefield, a female teacher in Wyoming, was
passed over for a teaching position by the principal in favor of a man who
could coach as well as teach and be hired for $2,600 less than Shenefield.
The Wyoming Fair Employment Commission agreed that sex discrimination had taken place. The district court reversed the commission's decision, and the teacher appealed to the state supreme court.

The court, which analyzed the case under the State Fair Employment
Practices Act, reasoned that a school board does not give up its freedom
to choose the teacher (coach) it wants just because it advertises such a
position. The court, in favoring the hiring of the male teacher, stated:

> If it turns out for reasons of economy, one applicant can fulfill the needs of a
> district at a cost substantially less than another applicant, even though the
> rejected applicant may on paper possess the greater qualifications, a selec-
> tion of the less expensive teacher cannot be said by any board or court to
> have been the result of discrimination on the basis of sex.

The court concluded that a school board has the discretion of hiring a
teacher who can also coach and should be able to select a teacher who is
personally attractive to it without the threat of discrimination.

5. In *Civil Rights Division of Arizona Department of Law v. Amphi-
theater Unified School District No. 10*, 680 P.2d 517 (Ariz. App. 1983),
defendant school district combined two positions, biology teacher and
football coach, and advertised them as a single position. One of the
female applicants filed this lawsuit under the Arizona Civil Rights Act,
contending that this practice of coupling academic contracts with added
contracts to coach football had a disparate impact on women applicants
for academic teaching positions. The trial court, which examined the case
under Title VII due to its similarity to the Arizona Civil Rights Act, ruled
in favor of the school district on the theory that it had established the
defense of business necessity in filling the positions together. The court
of appeals disagreed and held that this method of filling the dual teaching-
coaching position had a disparate impact on females. The court held that
the school district in this instance failed to prove that a business necessity
existed which required them to couple the contracts.

6. In *Anderson v. City of Bessemer City, North Carolina*, 557 F. Supp.
412 (W.D.N.C.), *rev'd*, 717 F.2d 149 (4th Cir. 1983), *rev'd*, 470 U.S. 564,
105 S. Ct. 1504, 84 L.Ed. 518 (1985), the Supreme Court upheld a claim
of sex discrimination by a female applicant for position of city recreation
director under Title VII. The Court agreed with the district court, which
found that the female was more qualified than the male applicant who
was offered the position and that the selection committee was biased.

7. In *Harrington v. Vandalia-Butler Board of Education*, 418 F. Supp.
603 (S.D. Ohio 1976), *rev'd*, 585 F.2d 192 (6th Cir. 1978), *cert. denied*,

441 U.S. 932 (1979), the court upheld a female retired physical education teacher's claim that unequal working conditions violated Title VII, but ruled that compensatory damages, except for back pay awards, were unavailable under Title VII. Because the teacher had been unable to recover damages, the court ruled that she was not a "prevailing party" and that she therefore was not entitled to attorney's fees.

8. Title VI of the Civil Rights Act of 1964, U.S.C. § 2000d, et. seq., prohibits discrimination on the basis of race, color, or national origin in connection with any program or activity which receives federal financial assistance. Title VI was designed to prevent the use of federal funds to promote discrimination and has been construed as protecting individual rights to be free from discrimination. Title IX was closely modeled after Title VI and adopts the same prohibitory language and procedural regulations of Title VI.

Coaching

Allegations of discrimination based on sex have often been made in the area of coaching. Many of the claims are based on a lack of pay parity between the coaches of male and female teams. Often coaches of women's teams—women, usually—are paid less than coaches of men's teams. According to the National Education Association, in the 1977–78 school year, only 28 percent of high school districts paid coaches equally. The justification most often made by school districts for the pay differential is that coaches of men's teams and coaches of women's teams do not perform equivalent work. In order to redress the inequality in salary, women must prove they perform substantially equivalent work. Some factors that courts consider in making determinations are the nature of the game, the number of the players being supervised, the length of the playing season, the time taken up in practices, the amount of travel required, and any other responsibilities undertaken by the coach—for example, recruiting, scouting, academic counseling, and so forth.

In cases in which it is difficult for the coach of a women's team to meet the standard of "equivalent work," the argument has been made that the work is more difficult. Plaintiff coaches of women's teams have argued that girls have not been as exposed to sports as boys; therefore, coaches of women's teams often spend much more time actually teaching their players. They do not have the luxury of merely retraining skills to a player who has participated in that sport for a number of years. Instead, they often coach women who have had little experience in the particular sport at all. However, as women's athletic programs proliferate at the youth levels, this argument is becoming less effective.

1. In *Burkey v. Marshall County Board of Education*, 513 F. Supp. 1084 (N.D. W. Va. 1981), plaintiff Burkey instituted a girls' basketball program at a junior high school in West Virginia during the 1971–72 school year. She posted a career mark of 31–5 in the four years she coached the team. In the 1973–74 season, Burkey received nominal remuneration for coaching. In keeping with school board policies, Burkey was paid one-half of the amount given to the coach of the junior high boys' team. Additionally, she was prevented from coaching the boys' team, solely on the basis of her sex. In 1977, HEW issued a finding that the school district's operation of the girls' athletic program violated the rights of women coaches and female student-athletes as protected under Title IX. The Equal Employment Opportunity Commission also found reasonable cause to believe the board's policies constituted unlawful sex discrimination against Burkey. She was removed as coach and transferred from the junior high to an elementary school after she filed a complaint with the West Virginia Human Rights Commission.

Burkey brought suit against the school board, alleging sexual discrimination in violation of rights granted to her by Title VII, the Civil Rights Act of 1971, and the Equal Pay Act. The court found for Burkey and awarded her $1,260 in lost back pay. It also ordered the school board to offer Burkey the next available vacant physical education teaching position in either the junior or senior high school, and to offer her the head coach's position for girls' basketball at that school.

2. In *California Women's Coaches Academy v. California Interscholastic Federation*, Case No. 77-1270 LEW (C.D. Cal. 1980) (settled), the California Women's Coaches Academy and three individual members of the academy filed a class action on behalf of themselves and certain other female coaches and officials for girls' high school interscholastic athletic contests.

The plaintiffs made certain allegations of unlawful sex discrimination, including charges that the defendants (education officials):

(1) Excluded women from participating in the Federated Council.
(2) Established fewer interscholastic sports for girls than for boys.
(3) Established shorter seasons for girls than for boys.
(4) Discriminated on the basis of sex in the hiring of persons to appoint officials for girls' contests.
(5) Discriminated on the basis of sex in the hiring of officials for girls' contests.
(6) Established lower rates of pay for officials of girls' interscholastic athletics.

The plaintiffs reached out-of-court settlements with each group of defendants.

The following is a summary of the terms and conditions that were common in all parts of the settlement:

(1) The number of sports available to female athletes will equal approximately the same number of those available to male athletes.
(2) Levels of competition and scheduling will be determined without regard to the sex of the athlete.

(3) Facilities will be made available without regard to the sex of the athlete.
(4) The length of the season in identical sports will consist of an equal number of weeks.
(5) Appointments to officiate and rates of officials' pay for identical sports will be determined without regard to the sex of the athletes or the officials.
(6) Plaintiffs and class members will relinquish any claims they had for lost wages and lost employment opportunities due to past discrimination by defendants.
(7) Defendants need not schedule identical sports during the same season as long as it is not to the detriment of one sex over another.

3. In *Jackson v. Armstrong School District*, 430 F. Supp. 1050 (W.D. Pa. 1977), an action was brought by plaintiffs Jackson and Pollick, who were women's basketball coaches. They claimed the school district had violated Title VII and the Pennsylvania Human Relations Act by paying them significantly less than the male coaches of the men's basketball team. There were four men and four women within the district coaching women's basketball who were all paid equally. The court ruled in favor of the school district, finding that it lacked jurisdiction under the State Human Relations Act and that the coaches' claim was not valid.

4. In *Kenneweg v. Hampton Township School District*, 438 F. Supp. 575 (W.D. Pa. 1977), plaintiffs Kenneweg and Love sued the Armstrong School District on grounds of sex discrimination. They were both coaches and claimed they were paid less because of their sex. The court held that because the charge filed with the Equal Employment Opportunity Commission had dealt only with the question of pay, the complaint could not be amended to allege discrimination with respect to working conditions. The court also held that the actions of the school district in paying female coaches of female sports less than male coaches of male sports did not constitute discrimination based on sex. The court decided for the school district, stating that the claim was based on a Title VII argument and that "disparity in treatment not based on plaintiffs' sex was not a valid claim under Title VII."

5. In *State Division of Human Rights v. Syracuse City Teachers Ass'n*, 412 N.Y.S.2d 711 (App. Div. 1979), an action was brought by two female coaches who had filed a complaint with the State Division of Human Rights. The women had agreed to coach the junior high girls' basketball team as volunteers and were not paid. The women later found that the male basketball coach was receiving $308 to coach the boys' team. The commissioner of the Human Rights Division found that the board of education had discriminated against the women and ordered equal payment. The appeals board affirmed the decision.

The court overturned the commissioner's decision and held for the teachers association. It found no discrimination in employment by the board. The court reasoned that both the male and female coaches were treated equally and that the unequal pay schedule was reasonable because the job responsibilities and time commitment differed.

6. In *United Teachers of Seaford v. New York State Human Rights Appeal Board*, 414 N.Y.S.2d 207 (App. Div. 1979), the court held that a union has the obligation to represent its member coaches fairly and impartially and may not discriminate on the basis of race or sex. The fundamental purpose of a union is to provide for its members the bargaining power that unity creates; when a union fails to exercise that power in the bargaining process and permits an employer to discriminate against union members, it discriminates against them as surely as if it proposed the inequitable agreement. Evidence proved that the union was aware of the unduly low salaries and that the union had settled for an agreement that grossly discriminated against female coaches.

7. In *Kings Park Central School District No. 5 v. State Division of Human Rights*, 424 N.Y.S.2d 293 (App. Div. 1980), the petitioners asked the court to review a decision of the State Division of Human Rights finding unlawful discrimination by the petitioner in paying coaches of boys' teams more than those of girls' teams. The court granted the petition and found no discrimination by the school district. Although the skill, effort, and responsibility were equal, coaching boys' teams required greater coaching time and travel.

8. In *Brennan v. Woodbridge School District*, 8 Empl. Prac. Dec. 9640 (D. Del. 1974), the court held that lower pay to a female coach of a girls' softball team constituted a violation of the Equal Pay Act, since she performed work equal to that of the male coach of the boys' hardball team.

9. In *Erickson v. Board of Education, Provise Township High School*, 120 Ill. App. 3d 264, 458 N.E.2d 84 (1983), the court held that the Equal Pay Act was not violated when compensation for coaches was set in accordance with the sex of the players rather than the sex of the coaches. The court ruled that no sex discrimination had taken place since the difference was explained by the application of a higher pay rate to all coaches who worked in male sports than to those coaches who worked in female sports.

10. In *Countiss v. Trenton State College*, 77 N.J. 590, 392 A.2d 1205 (1978), the court held that the fact that 11 of 13 male coaches and 4 of 7 female coaches were tenured failed to establish that the university had demonstrated sex bias in awarding tenure to physical education instructors. However, the court held that the fact that female coaches received only 4 hours per year release time credit while male coaches received 10 hours did constitute sex discrimination.

11. In *Pennsylvania Human Relations Comm'n v. School District of Township of Millcreek*, 28 Pa. Commw. 255, 368 A.2d 901 (1977), *rev'd*, 474 Pa. 146, 377 A.2d 156 (1977), the court held that failure to pay equal supplemental wages to the coach of the girls' varsity tennis team (as opposed to the boys' team) constituted discrimination in violation of the state human relations statute.

12. For further information, see "Equal Pay for Coaches of Female Teams: Finding a Cause of Action under Federal Law," 55 *Notre Dame Law Review* 751 (June 1980).

Sports-Related Employment Discrimination

While Title IX has been available as a basis to contest sex discrimination in coaching, attacks on perceived inequalities in other sports-related employment have largely consisted of allegations of the denial of equal protection rights. Cases regarding discrimination in officiating, refereeing, and media coverage have stemmed from charges that employment practices, and specifically exclusionary rules, are arbitrary, are related to no legitimate purpose, and are, therefore, violations of the plaintiff's constitutional rights.

Officiating

Arbitrary height and weight requirements for umpires and referees may act unlawfully to discriminate against women. When such requirements are not sufficiently related to the job, they may be deemed to be arbitrary and thus impose unconstitutional restrictions.

One issue in particular—women athletes who wish to compete in professional wrestling—has produced a series of decisions in which state athletic commissions were named defendants. The courts, in most cases, have granted the commissions great latitude in granting licenses and have generally upheld their decisions.

NOTES ————————————————————————————————

1. In *New York State Division of Human Rights v. New York-Pennsylvania Professional Baseball League*, 36 App. Div. 2d 364, 320 N.Y.S.2d 788 (1971), *aff'd*, 29 N.Y.2d 921, 279 N.E.2d 856, 329 N.Y.S.2d 920 (1972), the plaintiff Human Rights Division brought an action upon a complaint by a female umpire charging the defendant baseball league with a violation of a state statute (Sec. 296, Executive Law) prohibiting employment discrimination. The New York Supreme Court, Appellate Division, held that league rules requiring an umpire to stand at least 5'10" tall and weight at least 170 pounds "were not justified by the claim that umpires must command respect of big men or by factors relating to increased size of professional catchers, physical strain, travel conditions and length of games, and that the standards were inherently discriminatory against women." The league was ordered to cease and desist such discrimination.

2. In *State Division of Human Rights v. New York City Dep't of Parks and Recreation*, 3 A.D.2d 25, 326 N.Y.S.2d 178 (1971), the court invalidated the height requirement of 5'6" and the weight requirement of 125 lbs. for lifeguards because of the discriminatory impact on women and the lack of proof of job relatedness.

Participation in Professional Sports

Although females have competed with males on all levels of amateur athletics, relatively few women have entered as participants into professional sports. Sex discrimination cases litigated in regard to female participation in professional sports have largely concerned professional wrestling. These cases have not centered on the right to participate with men but rather on the constitutionality of rules that refuse women the right to petition for and receive a professional wrestling license. Plaintiffs have relied on equal protection claims to challenge these exclusionary rules.

NOTES

1. In *Calzadilla v. Dooley*, 29 A.D.2d 152, 286 N.Y.S.2d 510 (1968), a discrimination suit was brought by a woman wrestler who alleged the refusal by the state's athletic commission to grant her a professional wrestling license constituted a violation of the Fourteenth Amendment's equal protection clause. In arguing that "a great deal of latitude and discretion must be accorded the State Athletic Commission," the court held that the commission's rule against granting wrestling licenses to women was not "an unjust and unconstitutional discrimination against women." The court reasoned that no one had an inherent right to participate in public wrestling exhibitions.

2. In *Hesseltine v. State Athletic Comm'n*, 126 N.E.2d 631 (Ill. 1955), plaintiff Hesseltine (also known as Rose Roman) applied through normal procedures for a permit to wrestle. The Illinois State Athletic Commission rejected her application. She appealed to the circuit court and won. The commission appealed. The appeals court affirmed the decision. The defendant's adoption of a rule excluding women from wrestling within the state was seen as arbitrary and therefore invalid.

3. In *State v. Hunter*, 208 Ore. 282, 300 P.2d 455 (1956), defendant Hunter, a female wrestler, was prosecuted for competing in a wrestling match that was held in violation of a statutory ban on women's wrestling. The court ruled in favor of the plaintiff, holding that the ban on women's participation in wrestling was not unconstitutional.

4. In *Whitehead v. Krulewitch*, 25 A.D.2d 956, 271 N.Y.S.2d 565 (1966), plantiff Whitehead appealed a ruling of the New York Special Term Court denying her a professional wrestling license. The New York Supreme Court, Appellate Division, affirmed the decision.

5. In *Garrett v. New York State Athletic Comm'n*, 82 Misc. 2d 524, 370 N.Y.S.2d 795 (1975), the court held that a claim by a woman boxer of wrongful denial of a professional boxing license stated a cause of action under the Fourteenth Amendment. Thus, the athletic commission's motion to dismiss the case was denied. The court directed the woman to resubmit her application, and the commission would have to provide her with its answer.

6. In *Rubin v. Florida State Racing Comm'n*, Civil No. 6819113 (11th Cir Dade County, Fla., 1968), the court upheld the claim of a female plaintiff for an apprentice jockey license.

7. In *Kusner v. Maryland Racing Comm'n.*, Civil No. 37044 (Civil Ct.-

Prince George's County, Md. 1968), the court upheld the claim of a female plaintiff for a jockey license.

8. For further information, see the following law review articles: "Employment and Athletics Are Outside HEW's Jurisdiction," 65 *Georgetown Law Journal* 49 (October 1976).

The Media

Barring members of the news media from locker rooms has been an area of concern for many sports organizations. If a barred reporter is female (see Note 1, *Ludtke v. Kuhn*), and male members of the news media are not similarly restricted, she may allege a violation of equal protection of the laws under the Fourteenth Amendment. In all Fourteenth Amendment cases, the plaintiff must demonstrate that state action is involved before relief under the Fourteenth Amendment can be considered (see page 140). The court in *Ludtke* found such state action because the New York Yankees had leased their stadium from the city of New York, a subdivision of the state. Private universities that lease stadiums from the state, municipal, or local governments could face a similar result. When public institutions such as state universities are involved, a court is likely to find state action without the need for such a relationship with a facility. A court is likely to have difficulty finding state action when a private institution (for example, the Boston Red Sox) does not lease from a governmental entity but instead owns its playing facility.

The *Ludtke* decision is the only reported case involving a rule barring female reporters from a male locker room. One important issue—the players' right to privacy—remains unanswered after *Ludtke*. In *Ludtke*, the court found that the players' right to privacy had been negated by the presence of television cameras in the locker room. If the right of privacy is not negated in a future case, the court will have to strike a balance between the players' right to privacy and the female reporters' right not to be discriminated against.

NOTES ───

1. In *Ludtke v. Kuhn*, 461 F. Supp. 86 (S.D.N.Y. 1978), a civil rights action suit was brought by plaintiff female reporter for *Sports Illustrated* magazine. The female reporter sought an order "enjoining defendants, the New York Yankees, from enforcing a policy determination made by Baseball Commissioner Kuhn, and approved by American League President MacPhail, which required that accredited female sports reporters be excluded from the locker room of the Yankee clubhouse in Yankee Stadium." Defendants admitted that accredited male sports reporters

could enter the locker room after a ball game for the purpose of interviewing ballplayers and that such fresh-off-the-field interviews were important to the work of sports reporters. The defendants argued that women reporters were excluded from the locker rooms "in order (1) to protect the privacy of those players who are undressed or in various stages of undressing and getting ready to shower; (2) to protect the image of baseball as a family sport; and, (3) preservation of the traditional notions of decency and propriety."

The court held "that defendants' policy of total exclusion of women sports reporters from the locker room at Yankee Stadium is not substantially related to the privacy protection objective and thus deprives plaintiff Ludtke of that equal protection of the law which is guaranteed her by the Fourteenth Amendment."

The court stated:

> The undisputed facts show that the Yankees' interest in protecting ballplayer privacy may be fully served by much less sweeping means than that implemented here. The court holds that the state action complained of unreasonably interferes with plaintiff Ludtke's fundamental right to pursue her profession in violation of the due process clause of the Fourteenth Amendment.

2. Counsel for Kuhn and Major League Baseball decided not to appeal *Ludtke v. Kuhn*, since they believed that the decision was not a damaging precedent. (See *NCAA Public Relations and Promotions Manual*, NCAA publication, Mission, Kansas, 1985, Appendix C.)

3. The NCAA requires that its championship teams open locker rooms to all certified members of the media after a 10-minute cooling-off period. See, for instance, *1983 Men's and Women's Soccer National Collegiate Championships Handbook*, NCAA publication, Mission, Kansas, 1983, p. 49.

4. For further information on media access to locker rooms, see "Civil Rights in the Locker Room," 2 *Journal of Communication and Entertainment Law*, 645 (Summer 1980).

Chapter 9

TELEVISION AND MEDIA BROADCASTING

INTRODUCTION

Amateur athletic associations, conferences, and individual schools have a property right in the accounts and descriptions of their games, whether the event broadcast is on the radio, television, or cable television. This property right has numerous legal ramifications and involves copyright, antitrust, and contract law. It is important for athletic administrators to be aware of these legal considerations when entering into contract negotiations for the broadcast rights to their organization's sporting events.

In order to detail these legal considerations some basic terminology relating to the broadcasting industry must be reviewed:

- *Standard Broadcast Television.* What most individuals consider "television." Local television stations broadcast programming which is received by local home television when the antenna picks up air transmission signals. Standard broadcast television is broadcast on channels 2–69, with channels 2–13 known as very high frequency (VHF) and channels 14–69 known as ultra high frequency (UHF).
- *Cable Television* (formerly known as CATV [community antenna television]). A service provided to consumers by which traditional television programming and/or other broadcast signals (e.g., pay cable) are brought into the home of the subscriber by way of cable transmission (as opposed to over-the-air transmission), usually for an initial installation charge and a monthly subscription fee.
- *Pay Cable.* Refers to a premium cable television service, by which special channels are provided to subscribers for an additional cost that provides unique programming such as sports. Examples of special channels would be Sports Channel or HBO, among others. Standard broadcast stations can be brought into a subscriber's home or business by cable to give a better signal. In addition, cable can provide subscribers with stations which regular antennas would not be able to pick up.
- *Superstations.* Refers to a local independent distant signal television station whose programs, including sports, are carried via satellite to cable systems outside the station's local broadcast range. Distant signals are television stations outside a viewer's ordinary viewing area. Examples would be WTBS in Atlanta, WWOR in New Jersey, and WPIX in New York.
- *Satellites.* Serve as a space-based distribution system of program services for standard broadcast and cable television. Satellites relay television signals across the world.
- *Earth Station, Uplink, Downlink,* and *Transponder.* All are

terms used in satellite transmissions of broadcast signals. The uplink is the ground-to-satellite transmission of a broadcast signal; a downlink is a satellite-to-earth-station transmission of a broadcast signal; and an earth station is a ground antenna designed to communicate with a satellite. A transponder is the part of the satellite that consists of the receiver to pick up the signals from the uplink, a processor to convert the signal's frequency and amplify its strength, and a transmitter to re-broadcast the signal on the downlink.

• *Fixation*. Recording all or parts of a broadcast on film, video-tape, or replay tape for purposes of protecting the copyright and the manner in which it was recorded.

Chapter 9 begins with an explanation of why sports broadcasts are a protectable property right of the athletic organization spon-soring the event. Congress further strengthened this legal right with the passage of the Copyright Act of 1976, the topic of the next section. The chapter goes on to discuss issues and clauses that are unique to sports broadcast contracts.

In addition to the impact of the copyright laws on broadcast contracts, the antitrust laws have also had a major impact. In 1984, the Supreme Court declared that the NCAA 1982–85 football television plan violated the Sherman Antitrust Act. This ruling, which affected networks, producers, syndicators, advertisers, and NCAA member institutions, is examined next in Chapter 9. The final section of the chapter presents a broadcasting checklist for athletic administrators so that some of the legal problems sur-rounding television and media broadcasting can be avoided.

SPORTS BROADCASTS: A PROTECTABLE PROPERTY RIGHT

Since 1921 it has been held that an athletic organization has the right to control the dissemination of the accounts of its games. The early cases in this area dealt with unauthorized radio broadcasts of professional sports contests. In cases of unauthorized use, the courts held that such use was a misappropriation of a club's property right to control "descriptions or accounts" of games, and to allow broadcast stations to do so would be an "unjust enrich-ment" to a station. *Property* is generally defined as

that which belongs exclusively to one . . . the unrestricted and exclusive right to a thing; the right to dispose of a thing in every legal way, to possess it, to use it, and to exclude everyone else from interfering with it. [*Black's Law Dictionary*]

This legal right was further strengthened when Congress enacted the Copyright Act of 1976. In enacting that law Congress extended copyright protection to live sports broadcasts. Copyright grants the owners of a copyrightable work the exclusive right to "perform the copyrighted work publicly." Since the enactment of copyright law, legal issues have arisen over who owns the copyright for a broadcast.

It was widely believed by broadcast networks that the copyright belonged to them. However, in 1978 the Copyright Royalty Tribunal concluded that, based on the legislative history of the 1976 legislation, the copyright belonged to the sports entity whose game or event is being telecast. This view was upheld by the courts.

For the sports administrator the importance of the above holding is that (1) the amateur sports organization or its parent institution has the ultimate right to decide whether it wants to have its sporting events (property) broadcast on one of the electronic media, and (2) for any subsequent rebroadcast of the sports entity's game the organization can expect to receive compensation.

Another interesting property issue raised in broadcasting revolves around who owns the rights to a game—the home team or the away team? Generally, this issue is resolved in the game contract, and such agreements usually give the property right to the home team or host sports entity. At least one court has ruled that, based on common law principles of misappropriation and contractual interference, a visiting team controls the right to broadcast a game back to its "home" city and surrounding area (see *Wichita State University Intercollegiate Athletic Ass'n v. Swanson Broadcasting Co.*, Case No. 81C130 [Sedgwick City, Kan. Dist. Ct., Jan. 3, 1981]).

COPYRIGHT LAWS

As noted previously, the Copyright Act of 1976 gave sports organizations a right to copyright the broadcast of their games or contests, insuring a statutory property right. Amateur athletic organizations are most often impacted by the copyright laws in regards to retransmission of a broadcast of the organization's games or contests. This rebroadcasting most frequently occurs with cable television—for instance, when a local cable system broadcasts a game from a distant signal television station. Under the 1976 law, cable television companies were granted a compulsory license that exempts them from having to seek permission to retransmit any programming that a standard broadcasting television station is originating. This means that if a local television station is broadcasting a school's basketball game and if a cable system has the capability to pick up that transmission, the cable company can also broadcast it over its cable system without the permission of the school.

Cable systems do have to pay a royalty commission for telecasting the contest to a central fund. To distribute these royalty payments to deserving sports entities (and nonsports copyright holders), the 1976 Copyright Act established the Copyright Royalty Tribunal. The Tribunal was established so that each cable network and each rights holder would not have to negotiate for the rights to each game. The Tribunal is a governmental agency that must decide who gets royalties and how much they receive in the way of payments. With sports the Tribunal has devised a distribution formula that weighs relative marketplace values of the programming retransmitted against the value to the cable system for using the broadcast and the harm inflicted by its broadcast to the copyright holder. The cable companies pay a royalty fee that is based on a sliding scale relative to their overall revenues. When the first royalty fees were divided for the year 1978, it was determined that sports would receive 12 percent of the total pool, which amounted to $15 million. In 1979 and 1980 the split was 15 percent of the pool to sports.

In intercollegiate athletics, the NCAA represents its membership collectively before the Copyright Royalty Tribunal. The association has filed a joint claim for cable royalty fees on behalf of its interested member institutions since the Tribunal was first convened in 1978. One member of the NCAA's legal counsel noted in 1983 that "the only way to guarantee that sports teams will receive all of the royalty fees for sports programs is for each allied conference and member institution to have a written contractual provision reserving its copyright ownership." To ensure that such contractual language is included in all broadcast contracts, the NCAA recommends that the following clauses be considered for use by the membership:

1. *Reserving Copyright Ownership.* _____
   [name of institution or conference] shall own the copyright in all broadcasts (live or delayed,) films, videotapes and recordings of events telecast pursuant to this agreement. Notice of the _____ [name of institution or conference] copyright shall be included as part of every _____ [name of institution or conference] sports event telecast made pursuant to this agreement. The notice shall consist of the symbol © or the word "Copyright," followed by the year that the event

is first telecast and the name "_____"
[name of institution or conference], and shall appear in the
opening and closing credits.

2. *Reserving Right to Receive Statutory Cable Royalty Fees.*
_____ [broadcasting station] and _____
[institution or conference] agree that _____
[institution or conference] shall be entitled to receive all copyright royalty fees attributable to use of the broadcasts, films,
videotapes and recordings of _____[insti-
tution or conference] sports events, including all copyright royalty fees paid by cable systems pursuant to Section 111 of the
Copyright Revision Act.

3. *Inclusion in Contracts to Assure "Fixation" of Telecasts of Events.*
(a) _____ [broadcasting station] shall film
or videotape each event broadcast pursuant to this agreement
and shall make and preserve such copies of the film or tape and
evidence of fixation of the broadcast as may be requested by
_____[institution or conference] for copy-
right purposes. A copyright notice, consisting of the symbol © or
the word "Copyright," followed by the year that the event is first
telecast and the name "_____" [institution
or conference], shall be placed on both the actual videotapes or
tape cassettes of the telecasts, and the cases or containers in
which the videotapes or cassettes are kept. (b) _____
[broadcasting station] shall provide _____
[institution or conference] with a written statement that each
broadcast made pursuant to this agreement was recorded and the
manner in which it was recorded (by videotape of entire broadcast, replay tape or audiovisual logger).

The NCAA also has an elaborate annual system for collecting
data from its membership concerning retransmissions of broadcasts. In June 1985 the NCAA distributed its data collection form
for the 1984 calendar year, which noted in part the following:

It now is time to collect information regarding 1984 telecasts that
may qualify for cable copyright fees from all institutions and conferences that want the NCAA to file a joint claim in their behalf for a
share of the 1984 fees. As in the past, this office will undertake the
responsibility for initial data collection and organization, and the
Association's Washington, D.C., legal counsel will file the formal
claim with the Copyright Royalty Tribunal.

In order to participate, please complete the enclosed form . . .
relating to your nonnetwork telecasts during calendar year 1984 and
the authorization letter . . . typed on your own stationery. These

documents, completed, should be returned to . . . the NCAA national office, for receipt not later than July 5, 1985. When compiling your list, please keep in mind the following points:

1. This request concerns copyright ownership or "right," *not* "rights to telecast." The transfer or sale to a station or production company of the rights (including exclusive rights) to telecast your games does not automatically affect copyright ownership. . . .

2. Only *nonnetwork* (local or regional) over-the-air television broadcasts (of any sport) qualify for statutory copyright royalty fees. Any games broadcast as national network programs by NBC, ABC, or CBS (or cablecast by ESPN or USA, or shown *only* on a local cable company) should not be listed. NBC/TV's regional basketball telecasts should be noted separately. A local telecast by a station affiliated with a network *should be listed*. Games broadcast by public broadcasting stations may qualify and should be reported.

3. Please list the *call letters* of *all* stations on which each game was telecast. We will conduct the necessary research to determine whether the stations listed were carried by cable systems on a distant-signal basis. It is *important* that you identify every station that broadcast by its call letters. *We cannot process a claimed telecast that does not include the call letters of the station*.

4. Please identify whether the contest was telecast live or on a delayed basis.

5. Please indicate whether the broadcast was preserved or "fixed" in some manner (i.e., all or parts of the broadcast were recorded on film, videotape, replay tape or audiovisual logger). It is *not* necessary that copies of the film or tape be available.

6. If an event was broadcast more than once, either by the same or different stations, please list each broadcast separately.

7. Information is needed concerning broadcasts from January 1 through December 31, 1984 (calendar year, not playing season). Please be sure to check records for *both* the 1983–84 seasons for the 1984 information.

All copyright fees are paid by cable systems. These proceedings place no liability whatsoever upon local broadcast stations, and you simply are claiming compensation for use by cable systems of telecasts of your events that originally were licensed only for local or regional broadcast television coverage. Understandably, you may not be aware that cable retransmission has taken place. If we do not receive information about your telecasts, however, it will not be possible for the NCAA to secure fees for which you are eligible.

BROADCAST CONTRACTS

Copyright protection is just one area of contract language that must be scrutinized by amateur athletic administrators in order to ensure that all the broadcast rights of an athletic organization are protected. The basics of contract law, which were covered in Chapter 3, are just as important. Here, we will focus on contract issues and clauses that are unique to the broadcast business.

Rights Granted

In a broadcast contract, the sports organization grants the rights to broadcast the game in exchange for some specified benefit, generally a rights fee from the broadcast organization. The broadcast organization might be only one station, or it might consist of a number of stations that form a network. Usually, a broadcast organization seeks exclusive rights to telecast a game. *Exclusive rights* are defined as rights granted by the sports organization to one broadcaster for the purpose of setting up a single-station broadcast or an exclusive network, and such rights do not permit any other broadcast organization the right to broadcast the event. Exclusive rights are the opposite of *multi-originations*—that is, when many broadcast organizations are given the right to telecast the same event.

Exclusive rights may be granted for different technologies. Therefore, an organization might negotiate exclusive rights contracts for live standard broadcast television, delayed standard broadcast television, cable television, and/or radio. Often, in intercollegiate athletic broadcast contracts, exceptions are included, even in exclusive arrangements, to allow for an origination by a student radio or television station of a sports broadcast so that the students can gain experience in sports broadcasting. A contract clause with a broadcasting organization might specify as follows: "The parties acknowledge that notwithstanding this agreement, [name] University may grant to University's student-run radio station the right to broadcast any game."

In general, any broadcast contract would include at a minimum the following clauses:

1. Term and scope of contract, including event(s) to be broadcast
2. Definitions
3. Access and admission to events
4. Facilities furnished
5. Stipulations, requirements, and reservations
6. Rights fee and schedule of payments

Exhibit 9–1 is a typical radio contact, and Exhibit 9–2 is a typical television or cable television contract.

Broadcast Rights of a League or Conference

Beyond contractual matters with broadcasters, an amateur athletic administrator must also be concerned about the property rights to a broadcast between competing clubs, institutions, and within a league or conference arrangement. For instance, with any championship sponsored by the NCAA, the association "owns all rights to each and all of its championships. . . . These rights include . . . rights to television (live and delayed), radio broadcasting, filming and commercial photography" (*1987–88 NCAA Manual*, Exec. Reg. 1–18, Media and Film Rights). The NCAA grants rights to telecast its championships on a sliding scale that represents in part the attractiveness and marketability of the event. For instance, for the 1984 Division II and Division III Football Championships, the policy was as follows:

Television

The sale of all television rights to NCAA championship competition shall be handled by the Association's executive director. Requests for film rights should be forwarded to the executive director with the committee chair's recommendations.

Championship competition may be televised without geographical restriction over transmitters located more than 120 miles from the competition site. Any competition that is declared a sellout at least 24 hours in advance may be televised without restriction.

Rights for these telecasts will be awarded on a bid basis in which the NCAA shall have the right to accept any one bid on its merit or reject any or all bids.

Delayed Television

Delayed television (for showing after 10:30 p.m. local time) will be awarded on a bid basis, with the Association reserving the same rights to accept or deny the bid or bids.

In all cases the NCAA sponsor restriction policy . . . shall be followed to the letter.

Television News

The games committee may permit any individual television station and/or cable network to broadcast on a live or delayed basis on its regular television news programs not to exceed two minutes of action footage of the championship competition without securing the rights from the NCAA and payment of a rights fee. Such a "news

AGREEMENT made as of this _____ day of (month), 19____ by and between CORPORATION on behalf of Radio Station WXXX-AM, (address) (Station) and _____ (Sports Organization).

The parties hereby agree as follows:

1.(a) Except as otherwise specified, (Sports Organization) grants (Station) the sole and exclusive right to broadcast and rebroadcast over the facilities of (Station), and to authorize the radio broadcast of, all (Sports Organization)'s games, including regular season and any post-season games to which (Sports Organization) has broadcast rights, (hereinafter the "Games") during the (name years) seasons. The parties acknowledge that notwithstanding this Agreement, (Sports Organization) may grant (i) to (Sports Organization's) student-run radio station the right to broadcast any Game and (ii) to any opponent of (Sports Organization) in any Game the right to broadcast or grant broadcast rights with respect to that Game to another radio station or cable radio station.

(b) Broadcasting may commence hereunder from the point of origin of a Game up to thirty (30) minutes prior to the scheduled commencement of a Game and continue up to thirty (30) minutes simultaneously with its playing. (Station) may in its discretion broadcast a pre-Game and post-Game show in connection with the broadcast of the Games. (Unless otherwise indicated, reference to "Game(s)" herein shall be deemed to include any post-Game or pre-Game show.) (Station) shall have the sole and exclusive right to sell or otherwise use all of the commercial time in the adjacencies prior to the pre-Game and subsequent to the post-Game Shows, together with all commercial time during the broadcast of each Game, and to retain all revenue derived therefrom.

(c) (Station) may terminate this Agreement effective (date) of any year while this Agreement is in effect upon prior written notice to (Sports Organization).

(d) (Station) and (Sports Organization) shall negotiate in good faith during the period beginning on (date) and ending on (date) (the "Negotiating Period") with respect to the possible renewal of this Agreement.

2. For all rights granted by (Sports Organization) herein and for the performance of all the terms and provisions of this Agreement on the part of (Sports Organization) to be performed, (Station) agrees to pay and agrees to accept the annual license fee as follows:

(Station) shall pay (Sports Organization) fifty percent (50%) of the "adjusted net profits" made by (Station) in selling commercial availabilities in and adjacent to broadcasts of the Games. As used herein "net profits" shall mean the (Station's) revenues (net of agency commissions) derived from said commercial availabilities for each Game less all of (Station's) reasonable and necessary costs attendant to producing and promoting the availabilities for each Game less all of (Station's) reasonable and necessary costs attendant to producing and promoting the broadcast of the Games and selling the said availabilities, including, without limiting the generality of the foregoing, out-of-pocket advertising and promotion costs, talent and announcer fees, production and technical costs, transmission costs to (Station's) facilities, travel costs for talent, production and technical personnel, rights fees, merchandising costs, coaches' show production costs including coaches' talent fee, Game statistical costs, and account executive commissions. (Station) shall retain the first five thousand dollars ($5,000) of net profits, for each Game, and the balance remaining shall be deemed to be "adjusted net profits."

(Station) shall pay (Sports Organization) each year's license fee in one payment on or before the date following thirty (30) days after the last Game played by (Sports Organization) team during that year's season. (Station) shall provide (Sports Organization) with a statement of revenues and costs at that time. At (Sports Organization's) request, (Station) shall produce supporting documentation for the figures set forth in the statement of revenues and costs provided to (Sports Organization).

3. The rights granted (Station) in subparagraph 1(a) are confined to radio and do not include motion picture or television broadcasting rights, all of which are reserved to (Sports Organization) for its sole use and benefit at any time. In the event (Station) is unable to obtain facilities to broadcast a Game through circumstances beyond its

Exhibit 9-1 Radio License Agreement

control, it may produce and broadcast transcriptions, recordings and recreations of any such Game.

4.(a) (Station) shall have complete control over the production (including pre- and post-production) and format of its broadcasts hereunder, including, without limitation, length of coverage. (Station) shall select and employ the "play-by-play" and "color analyst" announcers; provided, however, that (Sports Organization) shall have the right to require the selection of different announcers if (Station's) selection is unacceptable to (Sports Organization).

(b) (Sports Organization) shall make available to (Station) without charge at all home Games held at (sites) and shall take all reasonable steps at all away Games, which for purposes of this Agreement shall include (Sports Organization) home Games played at the Byrne Meadowlands Arena or Madison Square Garden, to make available to (Station) suitable space for (Station's) equipment and broadcasting and technical personnel, including access, provision for electrical power lines, cable lines and such other equipment and facilities as (Station) deems necessary or desirable. (Sports Organization) shall use its best efforts to obtain such away Game facilities without charge to (Station). (Station) shall have the right to display its name and trademark on any broadcasting booth and shall have the right to display the initials "WXXX-AM", and its frequency and trademark, on all equipment used in connection with broadcast of the Games; provided, however, (Sports Organization) cannot guarantee the foregoing with respect to the broadcast of away Games, as defined above.

(c) (Sports Organization) will and will cause its employees, and its head coach to cooperate with (Station) in all reasonable respects in all phases of the preparation, production and broadcast of the Games and attendant activities, including pre-Game and post-Game shows and at no additional charge; provided, however, that the head coach shall be paid reasonable compensation of $_____ per game by (Station) for appearances of any coach's show.

(d) So far as it is authorized to do, (Sports Organization) hereby grants to (Station), and (Station) may grant to others, the right to disseminate, reproduce, print and publish the names "(Sports Organization) Name" and the names, likenesses, voices and biographical material of (Sports Organization's) players and coaches, and of all persons connected with the attendant activities, as news or informative matter for publicity and/or advertising purposes in connection with any Game, but not for any direct endorsement of any commercial product or service without (Sports Organization's) and any such person's written consent.

5. (Sports Organization) shall provide the following, at its own expense:

(a) A (Station) dinner, at a (Sports Organization) or other suitable facility, [ ] prior to commencement of each season listed in paragraph 1(a) above, arranged in consultation with (Station).

(b) A full page in each Game program which (Sports Organization) is responsible for producing to promote (Station)'s broadcast. (Station) shall provide (Sports Organization) printed copy for such ad.

(c) Four (4) public address announcements promoting (Station's) broadcast and acknowledging (Station's) sponsors at every home Game held at Arena. (Sports Organization) shall use its best efforts to have such public address announcements promoting (Station's) broadcast and acknowledging sponsors at each home game of (Sports Organization) held at the Byrne Meadowlands Arena and Madison Square Garden.

(d) Fifty (50) tickets to each (Sports Organization) home Game held at Arena. (Sports Organization) shall use its best efforts to provide such tickets at each home Game of (Sports Organization) held at the Byrne Meadowlands Arena and Madison Square Garden.

6.(a) (Station) has the right to preempt any Game, in whole or in part, and (Station) shall have fully discharged its obligations to (Sports Organization) with respect to the Games by payment of the applicable compensation set forth in paragraph 2 hereunder. If (Station) preempts any Game(s), (Station) shall either: (i) broadcast said Game(s) on another radio station at its expense; (ii) tape delay broadcast the Game(s); or (iii) broadcast a "split-feed" (as that term is commonly understood in the broadcast industry) of the Game(s).

(b) In the event that the broadcasting of any Game is prevented or omitted because of: suspension or disruption or termination of a Game for any reason, Act of God; inevitable accident; fire; lockout, strike or other labor dispute; riot or civil commotion; act of public enemy; enactment, rule, order or act of any government or gov-

Exhibit 9-1 Continued

ernmental instrumentality (whether federal, state, local or foreign); failure of technical facilities; failure or delay of transportation facilities; or any other cause of a similar or different nature; the revenues derived from the sale of availabilities for the broadcast of said Game shall not be included in computing the net profits, and the total number of Games shall be reduced.

7. (Sports Organization) warrants that, to the best of its knowledge and ability:

(a) It has the full right and power to grant (Station) the rights hereby granted and to enter into and fully perform this Agreement; and that the exercise by (Station) of the rights herein granted as contemplated by this Agreement will not violate any rights of any person, firm or corporation.

(b) The Games are sanctioned by the National Governing Body and that the Games will be conducted in accordance with applicable National Governing Body rules. The Games shall be subject to and conducted in accordance with applicable National Governing Body rules. The Games shall be subject to and conducted in accordance with all applicable federal, state and local laws.

(c) All representations to (Station) by (Sports Organization) and all representations made by (Sports Organization) to third parties about any and all elements of the Games including without limitation, format, record of the participants, etc., are and shall be accurate and true in all material respects. (Sports Organization) further warrants that it has made and will make full disclosure to (Station) with respect to all such elements of the Games as soon as practicable after (Sports Organization) has knowledge thereof.

(d) All publicity which it issues or disseminates or otherwise makes available concerning all elements of the Games will be accurate and true in all material respects.

(e) All rights herein granted to (Station) in and to the Games are and will be free and clear of liens and encumbrances of every kind and character which are the result of actions by (Sports Organization)

(f) None of the Games will contain any defamatory, scandalous or obscene matter contrary to law or to the generally accepted standards of the radio broadcast standards or of the Federal Communications Commission.

(g) There is no outstanding contract, commitment or arrangement, and no pending or threatened claim or litigation which is or may be in conflict with this agreement or which may in any way limit, restrict, impair or interfere with either party's rights hereunder.

(h) No part or any of the Games will violate or infringe the copyright, trademark, performing patent, literary, intellectual, artistic or dramatic right, the right of privacy, or any other right or privilege or any third person or party.

8.(a) (Sports Organization) shall indemnify and hold harmless (Station) and any person, firm or corporation deriving rights from (Station) from all claims, damages, liabilities, costs and expenses (including reasonable counsel fees), arising out of or caused by, (i) any breach by (Sports Organization) of any warranty or agreement made by (Sports Organization) herein, (ii) any act or omission by (Sports Organization), or persons whose services are furnished by (Sports Organization) with regard to any Game or element furnished by (Sports Organization) to (Station) hereunder, or (iii) the use of any materials, persons or services furnished by (Sports Organization) in connection with (Station)'s production or broadcast of the Games.

(b) (Station) shall indemnify and hold harmless (Sports Organization) from and against any and all suits, claims, damages, liabilities, costs and expenses, including reasonable counsel fees, arising out of any breach by (Station) of any agreement made by it herein or out of the use of any materials or services furnished by (Station) or by any advertiser, if any, for and in connection with the broadcast of the Games.

(c) The indemnitee hereunder shall promptly notify the indemnitor of any claim, demand or litigation, and the indemnitor shall be solely responsible for the defense, settlement or payment thereof; provided that the indemnitee may, if it so desires, at its own cost and expense and by its own counsel, participate in any such defense, and in such event its counsel will cooperate with counsel for the indemnitor. Any settlement by an indemnitor under this Agreement which derogates from the rights of the indemnitee hereunder may be concluded only with the express approval of the indemnitee, which will not be unreasonably withheld. Indemnitor's liability hereunder shall be limited to any judgment or settlement approved by indemnitor. The foregoing indemnities shall survive this Agreement.

9.(a) (Sports Organization) will comply with the requirements of Section 507 of the Federal Communications Act of 1934, as amended, concerning broadcast matter and

Exhibit 9-1 Continued

disclosures required thereunder, insofar as that Section applies to persons furnishing program material for radio broadcasting. (Sports Organization) warrants and represents that none of the Games or related activities include or shall include any matter for which any money, service or other valuable consideration is directly or indirectly paid, promised to, or charged or accepted by (Sports Organization). (Sports Organization) shall exercise reasonable diligence to inform its employees, players and other persons with whom (Sports Organization) deals directly in connection with the Games and related activities, of the requirements of the said Section 507; provided, however, that no act of any such employee, player or of any independent contractor connected with any of the Games or related activities shall constitute a breach of the provisions of this paragraph unless (Sports Organization) has actual notice thereof. As used in this paragraph, the term "service or other valuable consideration" shall not include any service or property furnished without charge or at a nominal charge for use in or in connection with the Games or related activities unless it is so furnished in consideration for an identification in such broadcast . . . of any person, product, service, trademark or brand name beyond and identification which is reasonably related to the use of such "service or property in such broadcast," as such terms are used in the said Section 507.

(b) (Station's) Program Practices Department policies and standards shall apply to the Games and to the sites of the Games; (Station) agrees to provide (Sports Organization) with a copy of its program policies and standards. (Sports Organization) shall comply with and shall use its best efforts to cause those persons controlling each site to comply with all such policies and standards.

10. Each party acknowledges that the rights and privileges granted to the other pursuant to this Agreement are special, unique, extraordinary and unusual in character, and that the breach by either party of any of the provisions contained in this Agreement will cause the other party irreparable injury. In the event of any such breach by either party, the non-breaching party will be entitled to injunctive relief or other equitable relief to enjoin and restrain such violation for a period ending not less than one (1) year after the expiration or any termination of this Agreement.

11.(a) Except as otherwise specifically provided herein, all notices hereunder shall be in writing and shall be given by personal delivery, registered or certified mail or telegraph (prepaid), at the respective addresses hereinabove set forth, or such other address or addresses as may be designated by either party. Such notices shall be deemed given when mailed or delivered into a telegraph office, except that notice of change of address shall be effective only from the date of its receipt.

(b) Nothing herein shall create any association, partnership, joint venture, or the relation of principal and agent between the parties hereto, it being understood that neither party shall have the authority to bind the other or the other's representatives in any way.

(c) This Agreement shall be construed in accordance with the laws of the State of _____ applicable to contracts made and fully performed therein.

(d) Neither party may assign, license or sublicense this Agreement or any of its rights hereunder to any person, firm or corporation, or any parent, subsidiary or affiliated corporation without the prior written consent of the other party. Any permitted assignment shall not relieve the assigning party of any of its obligations hereunder.

(e) If any provision of this Agreement, as applied to either party or to any circumstance, shall be adjudged to be void or unenforceable, the same shall in no way affect any other provision of this Agreement, the application of such provision in any other circumstance, or the validity or enforceability of this Agreement.

(f) No waiver by either party of the breach of any term or provision of this Agreement shall be construed to be a waiver of any prior or subsequent breach of the same or any other term or provision.

(g) This Agreement contains the entire understanding of the parties hereto relating to the subject matter herein contained, and this Agreement cannot be changed, rescinded or terminated orally.

IN WITNESS WHEREOF, the parties hereto have executed this Agreement as of the day and year first above written.

SPORT ORGANIZATION   STATION

By _____   By _____

Exhibit 9-1   Continued

This Contract made as of this _____ day of _____, 19 _____, between

_____, with its

principal address at _____

_____ (hereinafter "Institution") and

the _____

(hereinafter "Station,") a ___(state)___ corporation with executive offices at
(address) _____

WITNESSETH:

1. (Institution) hereby grants to (Station) exclusive television rights (except as expressly hereinafter otherwise provided) to produce and to cablecast for distribution to subscription cable television systems, throughout the United States of America, each athletic event described in paragraph 2, below, subject to the terms and conditions of this Contract.

2. Each athletic event subject to this Contract (hereinafter "the event"), the participants in the event, the date or dates of the event, and the consideration payable within 15 days following the occurrence of the event by (Station) to (Institution) for all rights granted herein with respect to the event (hereinafter "rights fee") are as follows:

EVENT	DATE(S)	RIGHTS FEE

3. All arrangements with other participants in the event related to the cablecasting of the event, including but not limited to any required consent of an opponent or participant and any compensation to be paid to an opponent or participant therefor, will be made by (Institution).

4. (Institution) will make available to (Station) and any sponsors suitable space, as specified to (Institution) at the time of (Station's) advance technical survey of the site of the event, as shall be necessary for their participation in the production of the cablecast of the event. (Station) will have the right to install, maintain in, and remove from each site and the surrounding premises such wires, cables and apparatus as may be necessary for (Station's) participation in the production of the cablecast of the event and to use power at the site without additional charge; provided, however, that such facilities shall not substantially interfere with the use of the site or with any of the means of ingress or egress. Employees and agents of (Station) and of sponsors will be admitted to the site free of charge to the extent necessary to accomplish the pick up and cablecast of each event and of the commercial announcements, and (Institution) will provide to (Station) the credentials necessary for such purposes.

5. At least three (3) days prior to the date of the event, (Institution) will furnish to (Station) a list of all musical compositions to be played before, during and after the event and during any intermissions. If (Station) is unable to clear any musical composition for performance, (Station) will so notify the (Institution) and each composition which cannot be cleared will not be played.

6. (Station), each sponsor, its advertising agencies, and affiliated cable systems shall have the right and may grant to others the right to make appropriate references, including but not limited to the use of pictures, to (Institution), any opponent, and their respective teams, athletic personnel, and any and all other persons connected with the event, in promoting, advertising and cablecasting the event and the sponsorship of such cablecast by the sponsors.

7. Except as expressly limited by this Contract, the (National Governing Body), and (Station), with the (National Governing Body's) approval, may at any time use and

Exhibit 9-2 Cable Television Agreement (Institutional Contract)

reuse portions of films, tapes or other recordings of the event on news, documentry and other sports programs, highlights programs, anthologies, pre-event and post-event programs. The rights granted herein include such usage without additional charge or compensation to (Institution).

8. All rights granted to (Station) pursuant to this Contract, and all rights to be exercised by (Station) pursuant to this Contract, will be used only in connection with cablecasting by subscription cable television systems. Nothing herein contained shall be construed as granting to (Station) any right to produce, to broadcast, to cablecast, or to transmit television programs for presentation by broadcast television stations, subscription broadcast television stations, or pay-per-program cable television systems, and (Station) agrees to take reasonable and adequate security measures to prevent such presentations. Except as specifically required or authorized in this Contract, (Station) shall not use (present, exhibit, perform, exploit, lease, sell, license, or otherwise use by any means, method or process, now or hereinafter known), or authorize any other person to so use, any right herein granted to (Station).

9. (a) Except as expressly limited by this Contract, the television rights granted to (Station) hereunder shall be exclusive (limited, however, to use in cablecasting for distribution to subscription cable television systems), for the duration of the periods of exclusivity specified in this Contract, and, without limiting the generality of the foregoing, (Institution) shall not grant the right to produce or televise, whether for presentation by broadcast television stations, subscription broadcast television stations, pay-per-program cable television systems or otherwise, the event during such periods.

(b) In the event that a television broadcast station or a cable television system should fail to respect (Station's) program exclusivity or other rights hereunder pursuant to the rules of the Federal Communications Commission or other applicable law or regulation, (Station) shall notify (Institution) and the (National Governing Body) promptly of such fact and may institute such actions and proceedings as are proper under the rules of the Federal Communications Commission or any other applicable law or regulation in order to enforce its program exclusivity and other rights hereunder and to recover damages for the violation thereof. (Institution) or the (National Governing Body) may, but shall not be obligated to, join (Station) in such actions and proceedings and, if it so elects, (Institution) or the (National Governing Body) may institute and prosecute such actions and proceedings in its own name.

(c) Notwithstanding the foregoing or any other provision of this Contract, (Station) may use, and (Station) or (Institution) may permit any television broadcaster or cablecaster to use extracts of programs of events of the broadcast, or to televise extracts of such events by whomsoever produced, not to exceed two (2) minutes in running time, at any time (but not on a live basis) for telecasts or cablecasts within the framework of general newscasts and sports newscasts and such use shall not be a violation of (Station's) right of exclusivity or any other right of (Station) or (Institution) under this Contract.

10. (Institution) and (Station) hereby assign to the (National Governing Body) all copyright interest in all programs comprised of or relating to broadcast. (Station) will take all necessary steps to prevent all such copyright of all material from falling into the public domain. (Station) will fix all such television programs in a tangible form, affix appropriate notice of the copyright interest on all tape cassettes or film reels of such programs, and include in each cablecast, video tape, film, or other copy thereof an appropriate notice of copyright.

11. (Station) will not simultaneously cablecast and distribute any event of the broadcast to a cable television system, any part of the subscribers to which are located in the television market area of the site of the event, if, in (Institution's) opinion after consulting with (Station), such release of the cablecast would materially reduce attendance at such event. If simultaneous release of the cablecast of such event is not permitted at the site of the event, any delayed release of the cablecast of the event in such television market shall not be made until at least twenty-four (24) hours have elapsed after the conclusion of the event, unless (Institution) in writing authorizes earlier releases.

Exhibit 9-2 Continued

12. All rights granted to (Station) pursuant to this Contract shall be limited in territorial scope to the United States of America.

13. Neither this Contract, nor any license or right herein granted by (Institution) to (Station) may be assigned by (Station), either voluntarily or by operation of law, without the written consent of (Institution) and the (National Governing Body) provided, however, that (Station) may assign to the (National Governing Body) or to any other person the right to produce any television program subject to this Contract. This Contract may not be assigned by (Institution).

14. Nothing herein contained shall in any way create any association, partnership, joint venture, or the relation of principal and agent between (Station) and (Institution), or be construed to evidence an intention to constitute such. Neither of the parties hereto shall represent that any such relationship exists contrary to the terms of this paragraph, by advertising or otherwise.

15. (Institution) warrants and represents that it has the authority to enter into this Contract and to grant the rights granted to (Station) hereunder, and that all required consents and authorizations of all opponents and other entities or persons having an interest herein have been obtained.

16. All notices hereunder shall be in writing and shall be by personal delivery, by registered or certified mail, or by telegraph, at the respective addresses of the parties.

17. This Contract constitutes the entire agreement of the parties hereto, and, except as herein otherwise specifically provided, may not be changed except by an agreement in writing signed by an officer or other authorized representative of the party against whom enforcement is sought.

18. The following attached provisions supplement, or if they contradict the foregoing shall supercede, the foregoing terms and conditions of this Contract (list attachments):

IN WITNESS WHEREOF, the parties have executed this Contract as of the day and year first above written.

STATION	INSTITUTION
By: _____	By: _____
Date: _____	Date: _____
Title: _____	Title: _____

Exhibit 9-2   Continued

program" must be a regularly scheduled program devoted exclusively to general news and/or sports news. Sports entertainment programs do not qualify under this provision.

An allied conference within the NCAA may also have its own policies for broadcasting. In part, this will reflect how much power the individual conference member institutions have granted the conference to act as an agent for them in seeking broadcasting possibilities. An athletic administrator must always be aware of what rights have been granted to a conference and what rights an institution retains. At a minimum, most allied conferences have the rights to conference championship event broadcasts.

An example of an allied conference's television policy for NCAA Division IA football and Division I basketball would be that called for by the Big-10 Conference in 1986, a portion of which is reprinted here:

Television Policies

A. Football
  1. The conditions of the Conference Football Television Plan shall be followed.
  2. The fee for filming of a game to be used for a commercial highlights show shall be negotiated by each Conference member.
  3. A fee shall not be assessed for the filming of a game to be used for a coach's television show and/or school highlights show.
  4. A fee shall not be assessed for the filming of game action to be used on a regularly scheduled news program, with the footage used not to exceed two minutes in length.
  5. The fee for a live or delayed telecast shall be negotiated by each Conference member.
  6. A cablecast shall be assessed at least the minimum fee of a TV station broadcasting less than the complete schedule of a Conference member.
  7. Each member university may sponsor a weekly delayed telecast beginning at 10:30 P.M. local time.
B. Basketball
  1. The fee for a live or delayed telecast by the visiting Conference member involving a game from the host university's local package shall be $1,000, or as mutually agreed between the two competing universities.
  2. A fee shall not be assessed for the filming of game action to be used on a regularly scheduled news program, with the footage used not to exceed two minutes in length.
  3. The fee for filming of a game to be used for a commercial highlights program shall be negotiated by each Conference member.
  4. The minimum fee for a basketball telecast shall be established at one-half the highest hourly rate for the originating station.
  5. A fee shall not be assessed for the filming of a game to be used for a coach's television show and/or school highlights show. [*Handbook of the Big-10 Conference*, Appendix xi-3-A & B]

A typical allied conference agreement for delayed broadcast rights within the conference is that used by the Southwest Athletic Conference in 1987–88. It noted the following:

Delayed Football and Basketball Television Rights and Basketball Radio Rights

The following policy regarding delayed telecasts of football and basketball games and radio broadcasts of basketball games is in effect.

a. Delayed television rights for both football and basketball games will be disposed of by individual Conference members and funds derived from the sale of these rights shall be retained by the home institution. This policy is subject to the additional restriction that films, coaches' shows excepted, shall not be released for television purposes in the home area of the visiting institution without first obtaining the approval of such release from the visiting institution.

b. Each member institution shall be permitted to dispose of its basketball radio rights and retain the fees therefrom. Exception to this regulation is the Conference Basketball Tournament.

   By agreement of both institutions, radio rights as stated in (b) may be waived.

c. The post-game film rights for the football season may be disposed of by individual Conference members and funds derived from the sale of these rights be retained by the home institution. This policy is subject to additional restriction that films shall not be released for television purposes in the home area of the visiting institution without first obtaining the approval of such release from the visiting institution.

   Particular attention is called to the fact that before a film or tape of a game can be released in the home area of the visiting institution permission for such release must be obtained from the visiting institution. Also, in accordance with NCAA Rules post-game films or tape cannot be shown on television earlier than 10:30 P.M. (local time) the night of the game.

To ensure that the above policy was followed, the Southwest Athletic Conference included the following clause in its conference football contracts:

1. Live telecasting of the game shall be only with consent of both parties. Receipts from Conference radio broadcasting and live television shall be divided according to Southwest Athletic Conference rules and regulations which are in effect at the date of the game. Proceeds from Home Team radio, delayed television, movie rights and all sums derived therefrom shall belong to the Home Team. The Visiting Team will be given an outlet and space in the press box, free of charge, for radio, delayed television and movie coverage to the Visiting Team's own locale, and all sums received by the Visiting Team from these rights shall belong to the Visiting Team.

Allied conferences also need a policy for distribution of revenues, including broadcast revenue, among member institutions. In 1986–87, the Pacific-10 Conference used the following system:

Financial Distribution

1. Football Ticket Settlement. Financial settlement of traditional rival football games shall consist of a 50-50 split of the net receipts with no minimum guarantee or maximum payout. Financial settlement of all other Conference football games shall consist of a 50-50 split of the net receipts, with a minimum guarantee of $125,000 and a maximum payout of $200,000.

   a. Net Receipts. Net receipts shall be defined as gross receipts less deductible game expenses.

   b. Gross Receipts. Gross receipts shall be defined as the amount realized from the sale of tickets for the contest, except tickets sold to faculty and fulltime employees and their spouses and to students of the host institution, for which accounting must be made.

   c. Game Expenses. The host institution shall retain 15 percent of the gross revenue to cover game expenses after admission taxes and the game officials have been paid.

   d. Settlement Deadline. The deadline for the final financial settlement for all Conference football games shall be February 1 following the season.

   e. Conference Television. Revenue for appearances on the Conference's football television package (other than local game telecasts) shall be distributed according to the Conference formulae set forth in AR 1-3-e.

2. Basketball Ticket Settlement. Financial settlement of traditional rival basketball games shall consist of a 50-50 split of the net receipts with no minimum guarantee or maximum payout. Financial settlement of all other Conference basketball games shall consist of a 50-50 split of the net receipts with a minimum guarantee of $12,500 and a maximum payout of $20,000.

   a. Net Receipts. Net receipts shall be defined as gross receipts less deductible game expenses.

   b. Gross Receipts. Gross receipts shall be the amount realized for the sale of tickets for the contest, except tickets sold to faculty and fulltime employees and their spouses and to students of the host institution, for which accounting must be made.

   c. Game Expenses. The host institution shall retain 15 percent of the gross receipts after admission taxes and game officials have been paid to cover game expenses.

   d. Settlement Deadline. The deadline for the final financial settlement for all Conference basketball games shall be May 1 following the season.

e. Complimentary Tickets. Complimentary tickets shall be accounted for at the top reserved seat price. No complimentary tickets shall be provided for the visiting team in basketball.

f. Returned Tickets. There shall be no credit given by the host institution for any tickets left at will call by the opponent which remain unclaimed at the conclusion of the game. These tickets, along with the will call envelopes, will be returned to the opponent by the host institution on the first working day after the game. All claimed will call envelopes also should be returned at the same time.

Up to 10 tickets may be returned 1½ hours prior to game time. All other unsold tickets must be returned to the home institution no later than 48 hours prior to tip off or the tickets shall become the responsibility of the visiting institution.

g. Will Call Tickets. No "collect" will call tickets will be accepted from the visiting institution. Will call tickets from the visiting institution must be presented to the host institution for pickup 1½ hours prior to game time.

3. Football Television Income

a. Live Telecast. Television income resulting from an appearance by a member institution in a live telecast (other than home area telecasts), after deduction of any applicable NCAA assessment, will be divided according to the following formula:

55% to Pacific-10 participant(s)

45% to Pacific-10 members (divided 10 ways)

b. Home Area Telecast:

(1) Conference Game. Television income resulting from an appearance on a live home area telecast of a Conference game that is shown only in the home areas of the competing teams shall be divided according to the following formula:

50% to each Pacific-10 Conference participant

(2) Non-Conference Game. Television income resulting from an appearance on a live home area telecast of a non-conference game that is shown only in the home areas of the competing teams shall be divided between the competing institutions per the provisions of their game contract.

c. Incentive Fees. Incentive fees paid by the television networks for moving a site and/or date of a football game for television purposes shall be retained by the participating institution(s) and not included within the Conference's distribution of television revenue. Incentive fees may be approved by the Administrative Committee for a team which moves a game to accommodate television if the move adds to out-of-pocket costs.

d. Lighting Expenses. The cost for providing necessary lighting to make an appearance on the Conference's football television series shall be deducted from the television revenue as an expense item and the remainder of the television revenues shall be distributed as per the formula set forth in this regulation.

e. Distribution of Receipts. Television income resulting from an appearance by a member institution in a telecast, the income from which is subject to one of the above formulae (other than local area telecasts), shall be sent to the Commissioner by the participating or host member institution. The Commissioner shall invest the pooled monies and the accrued interest shall be used to decrease the assessment for Pacific-10 membership. The Commissioner then shall distribute the original monies as per the formula set forth in this regulation to the member institutions.

4. Basketball Television Income. Television income resulting from an appearance by a member institution in the Conference's basketball television packages shall be shared, with 50% of the appearance fee going to the participant and the remaining 50% being divided equally among the ten members.

a. Extra Expenses. A member institution shall be compensated for the full cost of extra expenses it incurs in making adjustments for the Conference basketball television packages.

5. Football Postseason Income. A member institution which participates in a postseason football game shall choose between the following alternatives:

a. Non-January 1 Game.
(1) The participating institution will be provided a travel allowance equal to the cost of round trip air coach fares for 150 persons. The remaining revenue will be divided into 11 equal shares, with the participating institution receiving two shares and the other nine members receiving one share each; or
(2) The participating institution may elect to receive actual gross receipts from the bowl to a maximum of $500,000, and may appeal through a detailed budget process for additional expenses, not to exceed the Conference's share of the bowl game receipts. The remaining revenue shall be divided equally among the Conference's ten members.

b. January 1 Game. A member institution which participates in a postseason football bowl game on January 1 shall submit a detailed budget for approval by the Men's Administrative

Committee and Council in accordance with budget procedures developed by the Conference. The Conference will consider payments for expenses for a party of 500 to be acceptable. The party would consist of the official party (President-Chancellor, trustees/regents, governor, faculty representative, etc.), the team party (players, coaches, manager, trainers, secretaries, etc.), athletic department staff, dependents and band members.

6. NACDA Kickoff Classic Income. A member institution which participates in the NACDA Kickoff Classic shall receive actual gross receipts from the game to a maximum of $450,000, with the remaining revenue being divided equally among the Conference's ten members.

7. Basketball Postseason Income:

a. NCAA Tournament. A member institution which participates in the NCAA basketball tournament shall submit detailed expenses on the Conference's approved budget form to receive reimbursement for those expenses not covered by its NCAA reimbursement. The remaining revenue will be divided equally among the Conference's ten members. The participating institution may retain all expense monies provided by the NCAA.

b. NIT Tournament. All revenue derived from the NIT preseason or postseason basketball tournaments shall be retained by the participating institution. [*1986–87 Pacific-10 Conference Handbook*, Administrative Rules, Chapter 1, secs. 1–7]

In representing the members of an athletic conference, the conference administration must grant many of the same rights to a broadcast company that an individual institution would usually grant. For example, in 1980 the Eastern College Athletic Conference (ECAC) sent a memo to conference members on its television contract with TVS Television Network (TVS) that noted in part (this contract is no longer in effect):

. . . [T]he Conference has granted to TVS "the exclusive worldwide rights to telecast (commercial, noncommercial, pay or cable) live or on tape (including rights to retelecast in whole or in part any game which had been televised live as one of the games to be provided to TVS under Section 3 and/or Section 4 hereinafter set forth), all Conference basketball games to be played on Saturday or Sunday between 11:00 a.m. and 7:00 p.m. (local time) for the following basketball seasons: 1979–80 and 1980–81, and if TVS exercises its option as provided in Section 2 hereof, 1981–82 and 1982–83."

In addition, the Conference has granted TVS the exclusive right of first negotiation for the 1983–84 season (assuming TVS has exercised its option for the 1981–82 and 1982–83 seasons). However, this right of first negotiation does not include any right of first refusal on the part of TVS.

Paragraph 8 of the Agreement further provides as follows:

> 8. *Exclusivity*. Conference agrees that its member schools' basketball teams will not appear or play on any other live or taped telecast (commercial, noncommercial, pay or cable) on any Saturday or Sunday (11 a.m. to 7 p.m., local time) during each basketball season. The Conference will be subject to a penalty of $50,000 for each such violation, to be deducted from the rights fees otherwise payable to Conference hereunder. The foregoing exclusivity requirements shall not apply to games in which the Conference team is not designated as the host institution if in conflict with existing contracts, it being understood that Conference will use its best efforts to amend any such existing contracts to conform with such exclusivity requirements. Conference will notify its members of this exclusivity provision and assure that future commitments will comply therewith.

In view of these contractual obligations Conference members may not appear or play on any other live or taped telecast (commercial, noncommercial, pay or cable) on any Saturday or Sunday (11 a.m. to 7 p.m., local time) during each basketball season as defined above with the sole exception of those games in which the Conference team is *not* designated as the host institution *and* there is in existence a contract for such game entered into prior to October 31, 1979 (the date of the ECAC-TVS Agreement) which contract entitles the non-Conference host team to televise that game on a Saturday or Sunday between the hours of 11:00 a.m. and 7:00 p.m. Furthermore, even where such a contract should exist, the Conference team is requested to use its best efforts to rearrange the time of such telecast so as to avoid conflict with the exclusivity period set forth in paragraph 8 of the ECAC-TVS Agreement.

Conference members were also advised that any agreement entered into by them after October 31, 1979 with a non-Conference team in which the non-Conference team is designated as the host institution *must* contain the following provision in order for the Conference to avoid the penalty set forth in paragraph 8 quoted above: "The parties hereto agree that there will be no live or taped telecast (commercial, noncommercial, pay or cable) of this game on any Saturday or Sunday from 11:00 a.m. to 7:00 p.m. between January 1, and the day after the final game of the NCAA Division I Championship Tournament."

Broadcast Rights of an Individual Institution

The *NCAA Radio Network Manual* noted in its 1984 edition that provisions should be made in contracts between individual institutions for radio broadcasts and suggested the following clause be included in game contracts:

D. *Contracts Between Universities*—Radio language differs between institutions in terms of what radio broadcast rights are and what they should be. A suggested sample section concerning radio broadcasts in contracts between institutions could be as follows:

> The Radio Broadcast of the home game shall be under the control of the HOME TEAM. The rights of each team are as follows:
>
> The Visiting Team shall be allowed one free radio outlet for its official station or network. All other stations shall pay the established fee set by the Home Team. All stations from the Visiting Team's territory must be certified to the Home Team by the Visiting Team. The Visiting Team shall control radio rights and income in its home normal market area only.

In a nonconference game, an institution must also protect its broadcast rights. A typical contract clause would be like the one the University of Kentucky used in 1979:

> 10. The University of Kentucky Athletics Association shall have full control of all radio and television rights and income derived therefrom. Each competing team shall be allowed one free radio outlet for a station in its home state, with all other visiting stations paying the established fee as set forth by the University of Kentucky. All visiting radio and television stations in the home state of the visiting schools must be certified by the officials of the visiting schools.

Broadcast Rights of a Facility Owner

A facility owner may also have to specify broadcast rights for a contest held within a facility. For instance, for the 1985 Kickoff Classic held at Giants Stadium in East Rutherford, New Jersey, the New Jersey Sports and Exposition Authority used the following clause in its contract with Brigham Young University:

> *Communication Rights*
>
> (a) The parties agree that Katz Sports, Inc., a division of Katz Communications, Inc., shall have exclusive, world-wide television rights to broadcast the Game.
> (b) The parties agree that CBS Radio, Inc. shall have exclusive radio rights to broadcast the Game.
>
> Notwithstanding the above, BYU may designate a commercial radio station and/or network which originates its broadcast signal within the State of Utah to broadcast a live report of the Game, and for this privilege the designated stations and/or network shall pay to the Authority a radio broadcast rights fee of $1,750.00.

Restrictions on the Use of Advertising

Finally, in any broadcast there may be restrictions placed on the use of certain types of advertising. An athletic administrator must be aware of any governing body's or institution's restrictions. For instance, the NCAA has the following regulation regarding advertisements:

> *Section 19. Advertising.* (a) Advertising policies of the NCAA are designed to exclude those advertisements that do not appear to be in the best interests of higher education. The executive director shall have the authority to rule in cases where doubt exists concerning acceptable advertisers and advertising copy of game programs, broadcasts and telecasts of NCAA championships; however, the following expressly are prohibited: alcoholic beverages (except malt beverages, beer and wine as limited hereafter), cigarettes and other tobacco products, professional sports organizations or personnel (except as specified hereafter), and organizations promoting gambling.
>
> (1) Advertising of malt beverages, beer and wine may be used in game programs if consistent with the policy of the host institution. Such advertisements, however, shall not comprise more than 14 percent of the space in the program devoted to advertising or not more than 90 seconds per hour of any telecast or broadcast (either a single 60-second commercial and one 30-second commercial or three 30-second commercials).
>
> (2) Advertisements featuring active professional athletes from the sport for which an NCAA telecast, broadcast or game program is being produced shall be prohibited. Advertisements featuring active professional athletes in other sports may not comprise more than seven percent of the space devoted to advertising in a game program or 30 seconds per hour of any telecast or broadcast. Parties representing the NCAA in advertising sales or involved in advertising sales for NCAA telecasts, broadcasts or game programs shall take every reasonable step to discourage the use by advertisers of active professional athletes from sports regulated by the NCAA, informing the advertisers of the NCAA's desire that such professional athletes not be used. Every potential sponsor shall be advised of the terms of this provision prior to contracting with such sponsor. Advertisements in telecasts, broadcasts or programs are not acceptable that contain reference to or photographs of the games, personnel (except as noted above), broadcasts, telecasts or other activities of professional sports organizations. Advertising content in a game program shall

not exceed 40 percent of the total pages in the program, including the cover pages.

(b) Nontherapeutic drugs and, generally, other drugs and patent medicine advertisements are excluded; however, analgesics, cold remedies, antacids and athletics training aids that are in general use are acceptable. Institutional advertising by pharmaceutical firms also is acceptable.

(c) No commercial advertisement may relate, directly or indirectly, the advertising company or the advertised product to the participating institutions or their athletes, or the Association itself, unless prior written approval has been granted by the NCAA executive director.

(d) The NCAA reserves the right of final approval for all advertising in any championship. [*1987–88 NCAA Manual*, Exec. Reg. 1-19]

APPLICATION OF ANTITRUST LAW TO
SPORTS BROADCASTING

Basic antitrust law principles are discussed in Chapter 13. In this section we discuss the basic application of antitrust law to sports broadcasting. For amateur athletic administrators that means being careful not to try to control the overall flow of their sports broadcasts, in a concerted action, such that a monopoly or other antitrust violations develop. It is always important to remember that the antitrust laws were designed to encourage the easy flow of any business activity into the general stream of commerce. In drafting such laws, legislators reasoned that it was important to have open and free market competition.

The major antitrust decision involving broadcasting and amateur athletics occurred on June 27, 1984. On that date, the Supreme Court of the United States, in a 7–2 decision (*NCAA v. Board of Regents of University of Oklahoma*), struck down the NCAA's 1982–85 football television plan because it violated federal antitrust law. The ruling immediately impacted networks, producers, syndicators, advertisers, and NCAA member institutions, all of which had to scramble to implement broadcast schedules for the 1984 season. This decision, and its ramifications, continues to be a major factor today in the broadcast industry. (See Note 5a.)

The reactions to the decision were predictably and decidedly mixed: "It's the worst possible thing that could have happened," said University of Michigan athletic director Don Canham. Pennsylvania State University athletic director Jim Tarmon reacted to the decision with concern, stating: "The worst scenario is that everyone is on their own. We don't feel that scenario is in Penn

State's best interest or the best interest of college football." Other parties were delighted by the Supreme Court's decision: "The position of the universities has been vindicated. The property right theory has been upheld," said Chuck Neinas, executive director of the College Football Association (CFA).

The lawsuit brought by the University of Oklahoma and the University of Georgia against the NCAA is likely to have long-term repercussions within amateur athletic governance. Here we focus on the impact that the Supreme Court's decision will have on how amateur athletic organizations will meet their new responsibility to provide competition in broadcasting of their events.

An important group in the area of television and intercollegiate athletics is the College Football Association of America. The CFA is composed of 63 NCAA Division I-A member institutions and includes 5 of the major football-playing conferences: the Big 8, Southeast, Southwest, Atlantic Coast Conference, Western Athletic Conference, and major independents such as Notre Dame, Pittsburgh, Penn State, and Boston College. The only major football-playing schools which are not CFA members are the Pacific-10 and Big-Ten Conferences. The CFA was formed to promote the interests of its Division I-A member schools within the National Collegiate Athletic Association structure. Beginning in 1979, the CFA started to believe that its voice in the formulation of football television policy was diluted in the 800-plus institutions of the NCAA membership, and was not reflective of its own members' importance in obtaining a national television contract.

The CFA negotiated a contract of its own with the National Broadcasting Company (NBC) for the 1982 and 1983 football seasons. The NBC contract was more attractive to CFA members in terms of rights, fees, and appearances than the 1982–85 agreements that the NCAA had with ABC and CBS. While CFA member institutions were considering whether to accept the NBC pact, the NCAA indicated that doing so would be in violation of NCAA rules and that disciplinary sanctions would result. This caused many CFA members that originally had approved the CFA-NBC contract to vote against accepting it. As a result of the CFA's failure to contract with NBC and continued dissatisfaction with the NCAA's television policy, the University of Georgia Athletic Association and the University of Oklahoma brought suit in November of 1981. They challenged the NCAA's exclusive control over televised football games and contended that the NCAA was violating the Sherman Antitrust Act by its exclusive television contracts with two major networks—ABC and CBS. The NCAA, since it was given authority by a vote of its membership at its annual convention in January of 1952, had administered the live telecasting of games for its member institutions. The details of the television plan have varied through the years. The plans have, however, consistently limited the number of live television appearances an NCAA member institution could make in a year; prevented individual member institutions from contracting on an individual basis with national, local, and cable television companies; fixed revenue amounts for rights fees allocated by the NCAA to member institutions whose teams appeared as part of the network television contract; and allocated a percentage of the total television contract for the NCAA's operating budget.

The NCAA argued that the television package was beneficial to its membership as a whole and accomplished two important purposes. First, it protected the live gate of college and high school football games, which resulted in higher attendance at games. In support of this argument, the NCAA pointed to an increase in total attendance for NCAA football games in all but one year during the period of 1953–1983.

Second, the NCAA contended that its plan had the positive effect of spreading television revenues and exposure to a greater number of member institutions. The NCAA also contended that limitations on the number of television appearances a member institution could make allowed a greater number of institutions to appear on television, which resulted in the schools receiving substantially higher rights fees. In addition to the revenues, these institutions received invaluable television exposure and extensive media attention. As a result, the recruitment efforts of these institutions were enhanced.

The NCAA maintained that uncontrolled televising of football games would result in the creation of a football *super* power group, since a limited number of institutions would be attractive to television broadcasters. With increased revenues and media attention to the super power group, the NCAA predicted that the disparity among the member institutions would be increased. This would be contrary to the policies and purposes of the NCAA, since it would place irresistible temptations for the development of winning teams, thereby threatening the future of the sport.

Judge Burciaga, a federal district court judge, ruled in favor of the University of Oklahoma and the Georgia Athletic Association on September 15, 1982, reasoning that the television contracts between the NCAA and ABC, CBS, and the Turner Broadcast System were in violation of the Sherman Antitrust Act and therefore void. The court held that "[t]he right to telecast college football games is the property of the institutions participating in the games, and that right may be sold or assigned by those institutions to any entity at their discretion." Judge Burciaga found

that the NCAA's television football controls constituted price fixing, output restriction, a group boycott, and an exercise of monopoly power over the market of college football television. The court
found that the membership of the NCAA agreed to limit production to a level far below that which would occur in a free market
situation. In addition, Judge Burciaga was not persuaded that the
televising of college football games would have any negative impact
on game attendance at nontelevised games.

Judge Burciaga disagreed with the NCAA that the television
controls helped maintain competitive balance among the football
programs of various schools. In his reasoning, he compared the
telecasting policies of NCAA football to NCAA basketball. The
NCAA does not control the televising of regular season basketball
games. The arrangements are left to the individual member institutions and conferences which have contracted with various national and local television and cable companies. Judge Burciaga
rejected the NCAA's contention that televising football was distin-
guishable from televising basketball; in fact, he held "the market
in television basketball to be persuasive evidence of how a free
market in television football would operate." Judge Burciaga's
decision rendered illegal the NCAA's television contracts with ABC
and CBS for $131.75 million each and Turner Broadcasting System
for $18 million. His decision voided a total of $281.5 million in
television contracts.

The NCAA appealed the decision to the Court of Appeals for the
Tenth Circuit, arguing that Judge Burciaga incorrectly concluded
that there was price fixing in the awarding of television contracts,
since there was vigorous competition among the networks in
bidding for the national television contracts. The NCAA further
argued that the court erred in its conclusion that the NCAA was
not a voluntary association. In May 1983, the court of appeals
upheld the district court's ruling.

As noted previously, in *NCAA v. Board of Regents of University
of Oklahoma*, the U.S. Supreme Court upheld the decisions of the
district court and court of appeals. The Supreme Court summarized its decision by noting:

> The NCAA plays a critical role in the maintenance of a revered
> tradition of amateurism in college sports. There can be no question
> but that it needs ample latitude to play that role, or that the
> preservation of the student-athlete in higher education adds richness
> and diversity to intercollegiate athletics and is entirely consistent
> with the goals of the Sherman Act. But consistent with the Sherman
> Act, the role of the NCAA must be to *preserve* a tradition that might
> otherwise die; rules that restrict output are hardly consistent with

this role. Today we hold only that the record supports the District Court's conclusion that by curtailing output and blunting the ability of member institutions to respond to consumer preference, the NCAA has restricted rather than enhanced the place of intercollegiate athletics in the Nation's life.

In the wake of the Court's ruling a number of lawsuits related to the decision were filed. Unsatisfied with the CFA agreement, which forbid national appearances by member association teams or networks other than ABC or Entertainment and Sports Programming Network (ESPN), the University of Southern California (USC), the University of California at Los Angeles (UCLA), along with the Pacific-10 and Big-Ten Conferences, brought suit against the ABC-CFA agreement which prevented two games—UCLA against Nebraska and USC against Notre Dame—from being telecast. The suit sought preliminary and permanent injunctions against the defendants because the ABC-CFA exclusive agreement, it was charged, prevented *crossover* games, which are games between CFA member schools and non-CFA member schools. In granting the injunction for UCLA and USC, a federal district court sitting in Los Angeles noted that if the exclusion was allowed to stand, the schools would be harmed by loss of revenue. "By issuance of this order, ABC and ESPN are not measurably harmed, other than by some perceived diminution of their ability quickly to dispatch CBS from the market for nationwide football telecasts." Soon afterwards, the parties to the suit settled their differences and dropped any further litigation involving this situation. In general, such questions of property broadcast ownership are now determined in the game contracts, as was discussed earlier. (See Note 5b.)

Soon after the decision, the Association of Independent Television Stations (INTV) filed two suits in federal district court aimed at opening the college telecast market further to local broadcast stations. INTV is a coalition of stations not affiliated with the major networks (ABC, CBS, and NBC). The suits sought on antitrust grounds to open *protected* time frames that the major networks have arranged with the different football governing bodies, such as the CFA. INTV's first suit was filed in Los Angeles against CBS and the Big-Ten and Pacific-10 Conferences. The second suit was filed in Oklahoma City against ABC, ESPN, the CFA, and the Big Eight Conference.

In March 1986, Judge Burciaga rejected the arguments of INTV and ruled that CFA's plan granting some networks exclusivity in two time periods was allowable under the antitrust laws. Judge Burciaga noted:

The CFA is a powerful entity. . . . Nonetheless, it remains to be demonstrated beyond reasonable factual dispute that the CFA can both control price and restrict entry to the college football television market. The market is a different one than the court analyzed in 1982. Unlike the NCAA, the CFA . . . have their rivals.

In establishing that the NCAA had a public responsibility to provide a free and open market for college football telecasts, the above court decisions have raised a number of questions for all amateur athletic administrators. Important questions remain concerning the legality of any national or regional television plan that seeks to place controls and limitations on the marketplace.

NOTES

1. For further information on federal government regulation of television, see 47 C.F.R. § 1 et seq., which deals with the Federal Communications Commission.

2. For further information on cable television, see "Coping with the Complexity of Cable in the 80's," *Nielsen Station Index*, A.C. Nielson Co. (1979), which gives the reader an overview of the cable television industry and its technology; covers basic terminology, language, and legal issues involving rights and liabilities of individuals establishing a cable operation.

3. For further information on the legal aspects of telecasting sporting events, see the following law review articles:

(a) Hochberg and Horowitz, "Broadcasting and CATV: The Beauty and Bane of Major College Football," *Law and Contemporary Problems* 112 (Winter–Spring, 1973). Reviews the legal concerns surrounding the broadcasting of sporting events and other issues, such as the pirating of broadcast signals.

(b) Hochberg and Garrett, "Sports Broadcasting and the Law," 59 *Indiana Law Journal* 155 (1984). Reviews the legal issues raised by the broadcasting of sports on the so called "Superstations"; details some of the economic concerns this poses to sports organizations.

(c) Cryan and Crane, "Sports on the Superstations: The Legal and Economic Effects," 3 *Entertainment and Sports Law Journal* 35 (Spring 1986). Reviews the effect the Supreme Court's ruling had on the televising of intercollegiate football on the television and cable television broadcast media. It places particular emphasis on the public policy concerns of the Supreme Court, that such broadcasts should not be artificially restrained by sports organizations.

(d) Wong and Ensor, "The Impact of the U.S. Supreme Court's Antitrust Ruling on College Football," 3 *Entertainment and Sport Lawyer* 3 (1985).

4. For further information on the NCAA and the broadcast industries, see:

(a) *Cable Television and Other Alternatives to Conventional Televi-*

sion, Briefing Book, NCAA Subcommittee on Non-network Television, NCAA Publications (Mission, Kan., 1981). Gives the reader an overview of cable television applications to intercollegiate athletics. The material is somewhat dated but does contain a good historical perspective of the NCAA relationship with the broadcast industries and the association's initial reaction to this new broadcast medium.

(b) Host, *NCAA Radio Network Manual*, NCAA Publications (Mission, Kan., 1984). Gives the reader an overview of how to establish and operate an intercollegiate football or basketball radio network. This is a comprehensive study which includes sample contracts and other documents.

(c) *NCAA Public Relations and Promotions Manual*, NCAA Publications (Mission, Kan., 1985). Gives the reader a comprehensive overview of the operation of a public relations office for intercollegiate athletics. It contains chapters on the broadcast industry.

5. The following major court cases involve amateur athletics and broadcasting.

(a) In *National Collegiate Athletic Ass'n. v. Board of Regents of University of Oklahoma*, 468 U.S. 85, 104 S. Ct. 2948, 82 L.Ed.2d 70 (1984), two members of a college athletic association successfully brought an antitrust challenge to the association's plan for televising the college football games of member institutions for the 1981–1985 seasons.

(b) In *Regents of University of California v. ABC*, 747 F.2d 511 (9th Cir. 1984), the court upheld a preliminary injunction to bar Nebraska and Notre Dame, members of the College Football Association, which had an agreement with ABC, from refusing to allow games with non-CFA members to be televised on CBS.

(c) In *Cox Broadcasting Corp. v. National Collegiate Athletic Ass'n*, 297 S.E.2d 733 (Ga. 1982), broadcasting companies filed action seeking to restrain athletic associations from alleged breach of contract concerning broadcasts of college football games.

(d) In *Colorado High School Activities Ass'n v. NFL*, 711 F.2d 943 (10th Cir. 1983), it was alleged that the telecast of professional football games within 75 miles of a "protected" high school game violated federal and state antitrust laws. The court ruled against the association because the association did not identify the specific stadium where the game was to be played. The association only identified the metropolitan area where the high school game was to be played, which was not sufficient to invoke the statute.

(e) In *Warner Amex Cable v. American Broadcasting Companies, Inc.*, 499 F. Supp. 537 (S.D. Ohio 1980), Warner Amex Cable sought a preliminary injunction against the NCAA and ABC which would have stopped the defendants from preventing the televising of football games which were not otherwise televised by commercial networks. The court denied the injunction, stating that the issuance of an injunction would potentially threaten the NCAA and its member institutions.

6. For further information on the Copyright Act of 1976, see 17 U.S.C. 101 *et seq*.

A BROADCASTING CHECKLIST

In addition to achieving a basic understanding of sports broadcasting rights, how sports broadcast contracts are written, and how the antitrust laws affect sports broadcasting, amateur athletic administrators can minimize legal problems that often accompany television and media broadcasts of athletic events by referring to the following broadcasting checklist:

1. Establish who has the property right in a broadcast.
2. Make sure the requirements of the 1976 Copyright Act are being followed, especially in regards to "fixing" the broadcast and in filing for any royalty fees due with the Copyright Royalty Tribunal.
3. Include proper broadcast rights clauses in any game or contest contract, including rights of opponents regarding broadcasts into their "home" territory.
4. Review conference or league rights to broadcast of applicable championships or individual games or contests.
5. Review all facility lease or rental contracts and facility third-party contracts for possible broadcast rights problems.
6. Review all contracts with television, cable, or radio broadcast stations to ensure proper clauses are included to protect sports entity's property right in a broadcast.
7. Review all conference or league broadcast contracts for possible antitrust monopoly problems.

Chapter 10

TRADEMARK LAW

INTRODUCTION

Trademarks on manufactured items for sale extend to various major intercollegiate programs and other amateur sports organizations such as the United States Olympic Committee and the United States Tennis Association, as well as to professional sports leagues and teams. As a result of the growth in the use of sports trademarks, there has been an increasing amount of litigation in this area, and the guidelines governing the use of sports trademarks are still being established in the courts. With the increase in the consumer demand for sports-related items and the intensifying competition among manufacturers to cash in on this lucrative business, the courts' decisions and interpretations of the laws governing the use of trademarks have become of paramount importance to the sports industries.

Chapter 10 first presents the principles of trademark law. The chapter next ties trademark law to intercollegiate athletics. Some of the recent cases that have defined the crucial issues involved in the use of sports trademarks are discussed. The last section of Chapter 10 focuses on licensing programs and the increasing use of licensing agents by colleges and universities for the sale of products bearing school logos. Such items account for millions of dollars of sales. Therefore, controlling the school or organization trademarks can have favorable economic results.

PRINCIPLES OF TRADEMARK LAW

The Federal Trademark Act of 1946, Lanham Act § 45, 15 U.S.C. §§ 1051–1127 (1946), commonly known as the Lanham Act, governs the law of trademarks, the registration of trademarks, and remedies for the infringement of registered trademarks. Many common law principles governing this area have also been incorporated into the act. The Lanham Act was passed to "simplify trademark practice, secure trademark owners in their goodwill which they have built up, and to protect the public from imposition by the use of counterfeit and imitated marks and false descriptions." The Lanham Act's definition of "trademark" was distilled from, and is consistent with, definitions appearing in court decisions both under prior trademark laws and common law.

A *trademark* is defined in the federal Lanham Act as "any word, name, symbol, or device or any combination thereof adopted and used by a manufacturer or merchant to identify his goods and distinguish them from those manufactured or sold by others." Trademarks refer to goods and can be distinguished from service marks and collective marks. The Lanham Act defines a *service mark* as "a mark used in the sale or advertising of services to identify the services of one person and distinguish them from the services of others." While a trademark identifies and distinguishes the source and quality of a tangible product, a service mark identifies and distinguishes the source and quality of an intangible service. The term *collective mark*, as defined in the Lanham Act, means a trademark or service mark used by the "members of a cooperative, an association, or other collective group or organization and includes marks used to indicate membership in a union, an association or other organization." League and sports teams' names and logos are, when used to identify the activities of the leagues and teams, service marks (see Exhibit 10–1). A league name or logo may even be considered a collective membership mark.

A trademark serves the following functions:

1. It designates the source or origin of a particular product or service, even though the source is unknown to the consumer.
2. It denotes a particular standard of quality which is embodied in the product or services.
3. It identifies a product or service and distinguishes it from the products or services of others.
4. It symbolizes the goodwill of its owner and motivates consumers to purchase the trademarked product or service.
5. It represents a substantial advertising investment and is treated as a species of property.
6. It protects the public from confusion and deception, ensures that consumers are able to purchase the products and services they want, and enables the courts to fashion a standard of acceptable business conduct.

Identification Function of a Trademark

Although the trademark does not necessarily disclose on its face the origin of the goods, it does provide the purchaser with a way of recognizing the goods of a particular seller or manufacturer. When the seller or manufacturer has conveyed desirability of the goods to the purchaser through the trademark, the seller or manufacturer has something of value. This identification function of the trademark also serves as a symbol of the goodwill a business has built up. Trademarks, therefore, "are the symbols by which goodwill is advertised and buying habits established." *Goodwill* is a business value, which arises from the reputation of a business and its relations with its customers. It is unique to the particular

Int. Cl.: 41

Prior U.S. Cl.: 107
United States Patent and   Reg. No. 1,234,940
Trademark Office   Registered Apr. 12, 1983

SERVICE MARK
Principal Register

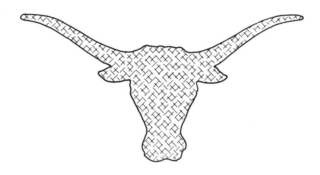

Board of Regents, The University of
  Texas System (Texas agency)
201 W. 7th St.
Austin, Tex. 78701

For: ENTERTAINMENT SERVICES—
NAMELY, COLLEGE SPORT GAMES
AND EVENTS RENDERED LIVE AND
THROUGH THE MEDIA OF RADIO
AND TELEVISION, in CLASS 41 (U.S.
Cl. 107).

First use 1958, in another form 1914;
in commerce 1960, in another form,
1914.

The drawing is lined for the color
orange.

Ser. No. 322,001, filed Aug. 3, 1981.

KIMBERLY KREHELY, Examining Attorney

Exhibit 10-1 Example of a Service Mark

business. Goodwill has also been defined as "buyer momentum" and "the lure to return." Goodwill is an intangible asset of a business. An *intangible asset* exists only in connection with something else. A patent is an intangible asset. It is an idea or formula, not something that can be touched. A *tangible asset*, on the other hand, is something that can be touched. A car or truck is a tangible asset of a business.

Legal Protection and Registration of a Trademark

If a "word, name, symbol, or device, or any combination thereof" qualifies for trademark protection, its owner can register that trademark or service mark in any state in which the product or service is used (see Exhibit 10–2). A trademark can also be registered in the U.S. Patent and Trademark Office in Washington, D.C.

In order to qualify for trademark protection, a "word, name, symbol, or device, or any combination thereof" must be distinctive—that is, able to be distinguished from the "word, name, symbol, or device" of other owners or manufacturers. Generic names of products and services do not qualify for trademark protection. Words such as "cola," "table tennis," and "photocopier" are examples of nondistinctive, or generic, terms. They represent the actual product and are not associated with the source or manufacturer of the product. Terms such as "Coca-Cola," "Ping-Pong," and "Xerox," however, are protected by the trademark laws. They clearly are identified with the manufacturer and qualify as being distinctive terms.

Certain nondistinctive words can qualify for trademark protection under the Lanham Act if they become distinctive—in other words, if they become associated with a single source. "Mc-Donalds" is an example of a nondistinctive name that has become synonymous with fast-food restaurants. When nondistinctive words become distinctive and qualify for trademark protection, they are said to have acquired secondary meaning.

Secondary Meaning

Secondary meaning is a mental recognition in the buyer's mind, associating symbols, words, colors, and designs with goods from a single source. Secondary meaning "tests the connection in the buyer's mind between the product bearing the mark and its source." Secondary meaning in a commercial sense is buyer association, mental association, drawing power, or commercial magnetism. Secondary meaning is important when the trademark is nondistinctive. Nondistinctive marks may not be registered and protected under the Lanham Act as trademarks until they have become distinctive of the goods in commerce.

An example of a nondistinctive mark is a descriptive mark. Descriptive marks, which are considered weak marks, are, at most, given narrow trademark protection. A mark is descriptive if it describes the intended purpose, function, or use of the goods, the size of the goods, the class of users of the goods, a desirable

The State of Texas

SECRETARY OF STATE

Date of Registration <u>July 31, 1981</u>

Registration No. <u>36975</u>

CERTIFICATE OF REGISTRATION

I, GEORGE W. STRAKE, JR., Secretary of State of the State of Texas, hereby certify:

That the attached is the duplicate APPLICATION FOR REGISTRATION.

That in accordance with the provisions of CHAPTER 16, TEXAS BUSINESS AND COMMERCE CODE and the application filed in this office the MARK described below has been duly registered in this office on behalf of:

Name of Applicant ___ Board of Regents, The University of Texas System

Address of Applicant ___ 201 West 7th Street

Austin Texas 78701

Description of Mark ___ Texas

Class Number ___ Intl. 41 Education & Entertainment

Dates of First Use: Anywhere <u>1914</u>   In Texas <u>1914</u>

The Term of Registration is for Ten Years and Extends to and

Includes ___ July 31, 1991

IN TESTIMONY WHEREOF, I have hereunto signed my name officially and caused to be impressed hereon the Seal of State at my office in the City of Austin, this

<u>31st</u> *day of* <u>July</u>, *A.D. 19* <u>81</u>

_____
Secretary of State

Exhibit 10-2   Example of a Certificate of Trademark Registration

characteristic of the goods, or the end effect upon the user. Some examples of descriptive marks are "Beer Nuts" for salted nuts, "Holiday Inn" motel, and "Raisin Bran" cereal made with raisins and bran. Secondary meaning of nondistinctive marks must be demonstrated in order to ensure maximum legal protection.

Secondary meaning does not have to be demonstrated when the trademark is distinctive. Distinctive marks may be registered and protected under the Lanham Act as trademarks. Some examples of distinctive marks are arbitrary and fanciful or suggestive marks, which are considered strong marks, and these are given strong trademark protection. *Arbitrary marks* are those "words, names, symbols, or devices" that are in common linguistic use but which, when used with the goods or services in issue, neither suggest nor describe any ingredient, quality, or characteristic of those goods or services. Some examples of arbitrary marks are "V-8" juice, "Stork Club," "Ivory" soap, and "Old Crow" whiskey. *Fanciful marks* are coined words that have been invented for the sole purpose of functioning as a trademark. Such marks comprise words that are either totally unknown in the language or are completely out of common usage at the time, as with obsolete or scientific terms. Some examples of fanciful marks are "Clorox" bleach, "Kodak" photographic supplies, and "Polaroid" cameras. Suggestive marks are legally indistinguishable from arbitrary marks. An example of a suggestive mark would be "Greyhound" for a bus line, a name that suggests speed and sleekness.

Infringement of a Trademark

The Lanham Act defines *trademark infringement* as the reproduction, counterfeiting, copying, or imitation, in commerce, of a registered mark "in connection with the sale, offering for sale, distribution, or advertising of any goods or services on or in connection with which such use is likely to cause confusion, or to cause mistake or to deceive without consent of the registrant." The "likely to cause confusion" element, which has proven to be the key factor in the majority of sports trademark cases, has been particularly important in trademark infringement cases involving professional sports leagues and sporting goods manufacturers and sellers.

When a manufacturer imprints the team name or nickname, city or regional area of the team, team player name or number on retail sporting apparel, issues may arise as to whether the names, symbols, and descriptive terms are trademarks. Of paramount concern is whether there is a likelihood of confusion such that the public believes the manufacturer's goods are endorsed or authorized by the professional sports league. In the important sports trademark case of *National Football League Properties, Inc. v. Wichita Falls Sportswear, Inc.*, 532 F. Supp. 651 (W.D. Wash. 1982), it was the court's scrutiny of the consumer confusion issue that led to the plaintiff's success in preventing a defendant sportswear company from selling and manufacturing NFL football jersey replicas which created the likelihood of confusion. NFL Properties alleged that its trademark rights were violated when Wichita Falls manufactured jerseys in the blue and green colors of the Seattle Seahawk players. The court stated that NFL Properties had the burden of proving (1) the secondary meaning of the descriptive term (e.g., Seattle) which relates the jersey to the NFL team and (2) that Wichita Falls' activities created a likelihood of confusion.

NOTES ──────────────────────────────────────

1. NFL Properties, the NFL's licensing operation, has successfully gained similar relief as granted in the *Wichita Falls* case in a number of state and federal courts. See also:

(a) *National Football League Properties, Inc. v. Dallas Cap & Emblem Manufacturing Company*, 327 N.E.2d 247 (Ill. App. Ct. 1975).

(b) *National Football League Properties, Inc. v. Consumer Enterprises, Inc.*, 327 N.E.2d 242 (Ill. App. Ct. 1975).

(c) *National Football League Properties, Inc. v. James Gang Silk Screen Works, et al.*, Case No. 80-1929T (S.D. Cal. 1980).

(d) *National Football League Properties, Inc. v. Motwani and Various John Does, Jane Does, and XYZ Corporations*, Case No. 81-293 (E.D. La. 1981).

(e) *National Football League Properties, Inc. and Los Angeles Raiders v. Richard Lieber, et al., and Does One through One Hundred*, Case No. 424283 (Super. Ct. Cal., L.A. Co. 1982).

(f) *National Football League Properties, Inc. v. Eugene Robinson et al., and Does One through Four Hundred*, Case No. C 440022 (Super. Ct. Cal., L.A. Co. 1983).

(g) *National Football League Properties, Inc. and Miami Dolphins Ltd. v. Various John and Jane Does and ABC Companies*, Case No. 83-2830 (Cir. Ct. Dade Co. 1983).

(h) *National Football League Properties, Inc. v. Michael Yingling, Elliot Johnson, Nobuko Hamshalter and Various John and Jane Does and ABC Companies*, Case No. 84-839 (Cir. Ct. Hillsborough Co. 1983).

2. For further information on trademark law, see the following:

(a) Gilson, *Trademark Protection and Practice* (New York: Matthew Bender, 1982).

(b) McCarthy, *Trademarks and Unfair Competition* (New York: The Lawyers Cooperative Publishing Company, 1973).

(c) Callman, *Unfair Competition, Trade-Marks, and Monopolies*, 4th ed. (Wilmette, Ill.: Callaghan & Co., 1981).
(d) "Trademarks: Protection of Merchandising Properties in Professional Sports," 21 *Duquesne Law Review* 927 (Summer 1983).

TRADEMARK LAW AND INTERCOLLEGIATE ATHLETICS

The need for trademark protection in intercollegiate athletics is a relatively recent occurrence that reflects the growing popularity of intercollegiate athletics as a consumer product. Consumers purchase the intercollegiate sports product, for example, when they buy admission tickets to intercollegiate events, view commercial television, purchase periodicals and books relating to intercollegiate athletics, or subscribe to cable television channels devoted to sports. A by-product of the increased purchasing of intercollegiate athletic products is a desire by the consumer to be identified with an athletic program. This identification process often entails purchases of products with the consumer's favorite athletic team's logo or mascot printed on them. The dramatic increase in the purchases of such products over the past decade has led to an increased awareness of the need for trademark protection in intercollegiate athletics.

In *University of Pittsburgh v. Champion Products, Inc.*, 686 F.2d 1040 (3d Cir. 1982), *cert. denied*, 459 U.S. 1087, 103 S. Ct. 571, 74 L.Ed2d 933, 51 U.S.L.W. 3460 (1982), the United States District Court declined to extend the *Wichita Falls* holding to intercollegiate athletics, reversing on remand an appeals court decision that had applied the professional sports-related *Wichita Falls* rationale. The court of appeals had extended the *Wichita Falls* decision by holding that the University of Pittsburgh had a right of prospective injunctive relief against a manufacturer that allegedly infringed the university's trademark. This was seen as an especially important development in sports trademark law, given the previously unrestricted use of educational institutions' symbols, which manufacturers/sellers had enjoyed for years. Furthermore, the right to control a particular symbol would have allowed the institution not only to gain financial benefits but also to protect and cultivate its own reputation and good name.

However, the district court on remand from its original decision that dealt with an unrelated question found that "there is no likelihood of confusion, whether of source, origin, sponsorship, endorsement, or any other nature, between the soft goods of . . . Champion Products, Inc., emblazoned with Pitt insignia, and with . . . Pitt." The court declined to apply the *Wichita Falls* rationale which the appeals court had suggested might govern.

Since the 1930s, the school had goods with its insignia manufactured and sold by one company, initially for the school's athletic department, somewhat later for retail sales in the local area, and eventually for national distribution. In the mid-1970s the school registered its marks under state and federal trademark laws in order to protect what it believed were valuable rights. This was due to the increasing popularity and national prominence of Pitt's football team. School officials sought to enter into a licensing agreement with Champion for continued use of the insignia. Champion was the premier manufacturer of "soft goods" imprinted with the insignia of educational institutions and was reproducing emblems of more than 10,000 schools, colleges, and universities. The company was reporting annual sales in excess of $100 million. It had no such licensing agreement with any other schools, and it refused to enter into an agreement with Pitt.

Pitt went to court to stop Champion's unauthorized use of the school's insignia. The district court denied Pitt's request for a temporary injunction pending trial due to the doctrine of laches (neglect for an unreasonable time to take lawful action). The court of appeals, however, ruled that Pitt's delay in bringing infringement action did not prevent its right to future injunctive relief. The case was remanded to the district court.

In ruling against Pitt, the district court noted that Pitt as the plaintiff in this case had to prove four elements to be successful in its litigation. These elements, considered essential for success in any trademark case based on unfair competition, were likelihood of confusion, nonfunctionality, secondary meaning, and priority of use. In the opinion of the district court, Pittsburgh did not "provide any real evidence of confusion." The court held that the university's presentation was very weak, and instead of showing a likelihood of confusion, the university showed little chance of any confusion whatsoever. The district court, in discussing the functionality aspect of the case, noted: "The insignia on these soft goods serves a real, albeit aesthetic function for the wearers." Similarly, the court found no likelihood that in regards to secondary meaning the university was being associated with the manufacture of the product.

Finally, as to priority of use, Pitt had to show that it had priority "of trademark use in commerce." The district court ruled that the Pitt insignia was an ornament and not eligible for trademark protection. The court noted that Pittsburgh had failed to prove any of the elements necessary to make its case.

Other issues in the intercollegiate athletics area are raised in *Texas A&M University System v. University Book Store, Inc.*, Court of Appeals for the Tenth Supreme Judicial District of Texas at Waco,

No. 10-84-088-CV, (1984) (unreported decision). University Book Store, Inc. (UBC) and four other retail book stores filed suit against Texas A&M in August 1981. UBC operated stores near the university's campus in College Station and wanted to sell goods with the Texas A&M marks on them. Texas A&M refused to allow UBC to do so.

The case was tried without a jury, and a judgment was rendered for UBC; the trial court canceled Texas A&M's marks. The judgment was based on the trial court's finding that Texas A&M "is not the owner of the described marks" because it has not used the marks, and the conclusion that "the certificates of registration should be canceled pursuant to Art. 16.16(a)(4)(B), Tex. Bus. & C. Code."

Texas A&M appealed on two grounds, asserting that (1) the trial court erred in failing to dismiss this suit on their plea of sovereign immunity, and (2) the trial court's finding that Texas A&M does not own the service marks because of lack of use is not supported by any evidence.

The court of appeals reversed the district court's decision. It based its decision on sovereign immunity and also held:

> We disagree with appellees' contentions that the University is not the owner of the service marks and that the registrations are unlawful or invalid acts. The service marks carried rebuttable presumptions of the validity of the registrations, of the University ownership of the service marks, and of the University's exclusive right to use the mark in connection with higher education services.

The court of appeals reasoned that "there is no evidence rebutting the University's use of the marks in connection with its higher educational services."

A number of different considerations are raised in the *Texas A&M University System* case, in contrast to the *University of Pittsburgh* case. First, a retailer was involved instead of a manufacturer. Second, the plaintiff in *Texas A&M University System* challenged the marks and, as a plaintiff, could not successfully raise a laches argument, since laches is generally viewed to be a defense. And third, *Texas A&M University System* involved state institutions, which consequently raised sovereign immunity arguments.

While this chapter has focused on the legal issues involved, litigation may well be obviated by purely business considerations. On the intercollegiate level, despite its success on the merits in the *University of Pittsburgh* case, Champion Products settled the case and executed a licensing agreement with the university. There is clearly a trend for manufacturers to execute licensing arrangements with mark owners, despite the possibility of success on the merits in a trademark case on the intercollegiate level. There are a couple of reasons for the move to licensing agreements and away from litigation. First, the manufacturer that challenges the university faces litigation expenses. Second, a manufacturer may have other business dealings with a university which may be adversely affected by litigation. For example, Champion Products supplies uniforms for intercollegiate athletic programs at many universities, and the loss of this business would be costly.

When Champion settled the *University of Pittsburgh* case by executing a licensing agreement with Pittsburgh, many other major manufacturers decided to do the same as well. As a result, mark holders and manufacturers are presently on good terms (at least temporarily). However, this does not foreclose the possibility of future litigation, and there may be a licensee or a nonlicensed manufacturer waiting for the right time and fact situation to challenge the universities.

NOTES ──

1. In *University of Georgia Athletic Ass'n v. Latte*, 756 F.2d 1535 (11th Cir. 1985), a federal appeals court held that a beverage distributor could not sell "Battlin' Bulldog Beer" because the University of Georgia had the exclusive right to market and control Georgia Bulldog merchandise.

2. For further information, see Wong, "Recent Trademark Law Cases Involving Professional and Intercollegiate Sports," *Detroit College of Law Review*, Issue I (Spring, 1986), pp. 87–119.

LICENSING PROGRAMS FOR INTERCOLLEGIATE ATHLETICS

As of 1985, nearly 80 universities had instituted licensing programs, and what may be developing is a situation analogous to the professional leagues. A number of licensing agents handle licensing programs for a university's athletic department or school store. One of them, International Collegiate Enterprises of Northridge, California, represents over 50 universities and bowl games. There are several reasons why a university or bowl game might use a licensing agent. For example, a university may not have the expertise or time to register the marks, negotiate licensing agreements with manufacturers, police licensed manufacturers for quality control, police for mark infringers, and litigate when necessary. Also, a licensing agent often packages marks to manufacturers on a state, regional, or conference basis.

Along with the advantages of using a licensing agent are several potential disadvantages. One is that the university may prefer to control the selection of manufacturers and the quality of products.

The university may also prefer to maintain flexibility in arranging licensing agreements. For example, universities that handle their own licensing programs may vary fees according to the type of product, the sales volume, whether the item is academically oriented, and other factors. A university that contracts with a licensing agent pays 40 to 50 percent of the royalty revenues generated, which reduces the university's net royalty revenues to 3 or 4 percent (instead of 6 to 8 percent). Another disadvantage is that the university may prefer to retain control of decision-making authority with respect to enforcement of mark infringement cases.

Economies of scale are linked with licensing agents who represent numerous clients. For example, the agents can negotiate with one manufacturer on behalf of all the schools they represent. A college athletic conference could, for instance, decide to arrange for all its member institutions to contract with one licensing agent and distribute revenues equally within the conference. Another advantage to using a licensing agent for all conference members and the conference itself is that it allows the licensing agent to market individual member institutions and the conference merchandise together.

Universities face a number of decisions and challenges in the area of trademarks and service marks. Initially, there is the decision of whether to begin a licensing program. If the answer is affirmative, the university must register the existing marks both on the state and federal level. The university may later be faced with the decision of whether to register a new mark, such as "Phi Slamma Jamma" at the University of Houston. The university must weigh the advantages and disadvantages of handling the licensing program itself or contracting with a licensing agent. In either situation, the university must establish public association with the mark, as used on various products, with the university's sponsorship. The university must decide whether and what collateral marks and products will be sold. Finally, the university must be able to enforce the marks. If the university undertakes its own licensing program, it must police the mark wherever the products are sold. This may be only on a local basis in the state or region of the university, or it may be on a national basis if the school has a national reputation and sells its products nationwide.

Policing marks against infringers is one of the key determinants of long-term success for intercollegiate licensing programs. This is a costly and timely consideration, and one that may well reduce the profitability of a licensing program for universities that do not realize great royalty revenues. It remains to be seen whether universities will be able to establish the expertise and spend the manpower and dollars necessary for effective enforcement of their marks. This issue alone may be the compelling reason for many universities to contract with a licensing agent, who, with tremendous economies of scale, can police and enforce marks (see Exhibit 10–3).

Regardless of whether the university decides to handle the licensing program by itself or to contract with a licensing agent, it must make some decisions regarding the distribution of royalty revenues. Among the alternatives to be considered in distributing royalty revenues are appropriating money for athletic scholarships, the general scholarship fund, or a general university fund, or returning the money to the campus bookstore.

There are other issues involving campus bookstores, such as whether the campus bookstore should receive a most favored status and be allowed to carry items that do not require royalty payments, since if the bookstore did not have a priority status, it would pass these additional costs to students at the university who purchase items at the bookstore and effectively increase the cost of going to school. There are also several compelling reasons against granting bookstores a most favored status. First, this would place outside competitors at a distinct disadvantage. The off-campus bookstores would have the increased overhead cost of royalty payments. Second, granting most favored status is economically inequitable to some university students. Those who benefit from the exemption are individuals who purchase items at the campus bookstore, which include some of the students but also nonstudents. A far more equitable and efficient economic model would require royalty payments from the goods sold at campus bookstores, which the consumers, the purchasers of the goods, would pay. This, in effect, would be a user tax, which is a far more efficient tax in that those who use the product pay the tax. The royalty revenues obtained from a licensing program that includes campus bookstores could then be distributed to a general university fund that would benefit all students at the university. Third, many purchasers are not university students, and if campus bookstores receive most favored status, then this group of purchasers would, in effect, be subsidized. The alumni of the university are probably the majority of these purchasers, and they may not need the subsidy. And fourth, potential antitrust issues are raised by giving campus bookstores the competitive advantage of selling items not requiring royalty fees.

NOTE ──

1. In the fall of 1983, Mr. Finus Gaston of the University of Alabama did a survey of collegiate licensing programs. His report, "Administrative

Decision Making: A Study of Collegiate Trademark Licensing Programs"
(May 1984), contained the following conclusions:

1. Significant differences exist in the perceptions of college and university administrators on important issues associated with collegiate trademark licensing:
   a. All royalty income from the collegiate licensing program should be deposited into the university's general fund to be used as deemed appropriate by the university board of trustees.
   b. Colleges and universities that operate licensing programs should charge the same royalty fee for all license agreements.
   c. As the collegiate licensing movement develops there will emerge a need for all colleges and universities to standardize their license agreements and operating procedures.
   d. Colleges and universities that operate licensing programs should closely examine each product prior to licensing.
   e. Colleges and universities that operate licensing programs should actively promote the sale of their licensed products.
2. Agreement on the concept of collegiate trademark licensing exists among institutional leaders by their endorsement of the following principles:
   a. Collegiate licensing is a legitimate activity for institutions of higher education.
   b. Colleges and universities have a legal right to protect the use of their institutional names, logos, and insignia on commercial products.
   c. The payment of royalty fees to colleges and universities by product manufacturers will not unreasonably increase the cost of merchandise to consumers.
   d. The primary purpose for establishing a collegiate licensing program should not be to create a source of unrestricted income for the institution.
   e. Colleges and universities that operate licensing programs should be willing to engage in litigation to enforce their trademark rights.
3. Despite diversity in administrative structures and practices, the development of licensing consortia such as Collegiate Concepts, Incorporated, will force standardization of operating procedures and, possibly, organizational structures.
4. There is a need for more expertise in trademark law among university counsel, for more support of the licensing program from the university administration, for better enforcement procedures to prevent trademark infringement, and for more coordinated efforts among licensing professionals in program standardization and the promotion of collegiate licensing.

CCI/ICE REVOCABLE NONEXCLUSIVE LICENSE TO USE CERTAIN INDICIA OF UNIVERSITIES

This is an Agreement between _____ _____ , a corporation of the State of _____ , having its principal place of business at _____ _____ (hereafter called "Licensee"), and International Collegiate Enterprises, Incorporated, a corporation of the State of California, whose address is 6312 Variel Avenue, Suite 205, Woodland Hills, CA 91367-2574 (hereafter called "ICE"), and Collegiate Concepts, Incorporated, a corporation of the State of Delaware, whose address is 4501 Circle 75 Parkway, Suite E-5180, Atlanta, GA 30339 (hereafter called "CCI"), a joint venture (hereafter called "CCI/ICE").

Whereas CCI/ICE represents certain licensing interests of the various universities listed in Appendix A attached hereto, pursuant to which, it has to the extent referred to in this agreement the exclusive right to license within the United States for commercial purposes the use of certain University designations, comprising designs, trademarks, service marks, logographics and/or symbols, and

Whereas Licensee desires to be licensed to utilize Licensed Indicia, as hereinafter defined in connection with the manufacture, sale, and/or distribution of certain articles of merchandise;

Now, therefore, in consideration of the premises and the mutual promises and covenants herein contained, the parties hereto agree as follows:

1. DEFINITION

For the purposes hereof:

(a) "Member Universities" or "Universities" means the universities listed on Appendix A attached hereto.

(b) "Indicia" means the designs, trademarks, service marks, logographics, and symbols which have come to be associated with the respective Member University.

(c) "Licensed Indicia" means Indicia which are set forth in Appendix B attached hereto.

(d) "Licensed Articles" means the articles of merchandise or products listed in Appendix C attached hereto and bearing one or more Licensed Indicia.

(e) "Retail Sales" means the sale of Licensed Articles directed to the ultimate consumer at retail outlets or through mail order, catalogs or any other forms of direct response.

(f) "Net Sales" means the amount of gross sales of Licensed Articles after deducting any credits for returns actually made and allowed as such. In computing Net Sales there shall be no deduction for costs incurred in manufacturing, selling, advertising (including without limitation cooperative or other advertising or promotional allowances) or distributing the articles covered by this agreement, nor shall any indirect expenses be deducted, nor shall any deductions be made for uncollectable accounts.

(g) "Premium" means any article given free or sold at less than the usual selling price for the purpose of increasing the sale, promoting, or publicizing any other product or any service, including incentives for sales force, trade or consumer.

2. GRANT OF LICENSE

(a) Grant: Subject to the limitations set forth in paragraph 2(e) below and other conditions of this agreement, CCI/ICE hereby grants to Licensee the nonexclusive right to utilize the Licensed Indicia on the Licensed Articles. This license applies only to indicia of the Universities listed in Appendix A which Licensee has selected pursuant to paragraph 4(a) hereof.

Exhibit 10-3 Example of a Licensing Agent's Contract with a University

(b) Territory: The license hereby granted extends to the United States of America, its territories and possessions, and the Commonwealth of Puerto Rico, as well as to United States military bases abroad.

(c) Term: This agreement shall begin effective the last date of signature below and shall continue for twelve (12) months, unless terminated sooner in accordance with the provisions of this agreement.

(d) Renewal: Provided that net royalties from the sale of Licensed Articles during the term of this agreement exceed the level required for payment of the advance fee prescribed in section 7(c) hereof, and set forth in Appendix C, Licensee shall be considered for renewal of this agreement for a period of one year, subject to a satisfactory performance of the requirements of Section 9(a). Such determination is at the sole discretion of CCI/ICE.

(e) Limitation on License: No license is granted hereunder for the use of Licensed Indicia for any purpose other than upon or in connection with the Licensed Articles. No license is granted to Licensee hereunder for the manufacture, sale or distribution of Licensed Articles to be used as premiums, for publicity purposes, for fund raising, as give aways, in combination sales, or to be disposed of under similar methods of merchandising. Licensee shall not use any of the Licensed Indicia in connection with any sweepstake, lottery, game of chance of any similar promotional or sales device, scheme, or program. In the event Licensee desires to sell Licensed Articles for such purposes, Licensee agrees to obtain written approval therefor from CCI/ICE.

(f) Licensee recognizes that any person who has collegiate athletic eligibility cannot have his or her name and/or facsimile utilized on any commercial product. Therefore, in conducting licensed activity under this agreement, Licensee shall not encourage or participate in any activity that would cause an athlete or a University to violate any rule of the National Collegiate Athletic Association (NCAA).

3. PROMOTIONAL PROGRAMS

(a) General: Licensee recognizes that promotions are inherent to the success of any licensing program and as such will assist CCI/ICE with such promotional efforts by its participation.

(b) Merchandising Catalog: CCI/ICE plans to produce annually, a merchandising catalog, in which participation by Licensee is anticipated. Licensee will provide all necessary Licensed Articles for display therein upon request of CCI/ICE. The display of Licensee's products and the cost of the development and promotion of such catalog and for periodic changes therein, presently contemplated to be annual, shall be agreed upon in advance by CCI/ICE and Licensee.

4. SELECTION OF MEMBER UNIVERSITIES AND PERFORMANCE GUARANTEE

(a) Selections: Prior to contract execution hereof, Licensee may select, by check marks to the list of Appendix A, those Member Universities, and the Licensed Indicia of Appendix B, which Licensee desires to utilize on Licensed Articles.

(b) Performance: With respect to each of the Member Universities selected by Licensee, Licensee undertakes to make and maintain adequate arrangements for the broadest possible distribution of Licensed Articles throughout the territory, consistent with its current marketing and distribution plans and objectives. Licensee agrees to maintain what it normally considers to be adequate inventories of Licensed Articles as an essential part of the distribution program.

5. NONEXCLUSIVITY

The license or licenses granted to Licensee by this Agreement are nonexclusive. Nothing in this Agreement shall be construed to prevent CCI/ICE or any Member University from licensing the use of any of the Licensed Marks to any party for any purpose including, without limitation, the grant of other licenses to other manufacturers during the term of this agreement for the use of the Licensed Marks upon the articles described in Appendix C, either within or outside the territory.

Exhibit 10-3 Continued

6. MODIFICATION BY CCI/ICE OF LISTS OF UNIVERSITIES, INDICIA AND PRODUCTS

(a) The list of Universities in Appendix A hereto, the list of Indicia in Appendix B hereto, the list of University policies in Appendix B-1 hereto, and the list of products or goods in Appendix C hereto, may be changed by CCI/ICE when and if such changes are made necessary by changes in the contracts between the Universities and CCI/ICE. CCI/ICE shall give prompt written notice to Licensee of any additions to, deletions from, or changes in Appendices A, B, or C.

(b) By way of monthly advisory bulletins, CCI/ICE will inform Licensee of any new Member Universities for Appendix A, or changes in Indicia as set forth in Appendix B-1, or changes in policies by Member Universities as set forth in Appendix B-1. Such bulletins will constitute official notice. Licensee agrees to acknowledge all new Member Universities by written response indicating its desire to add or not add such Member University within 30 days of receipt of bulletin. Licensee further agrees that failure to respond will constitute a breach of Section 9(a).

(c) If there is any deletion from Appendices A, B, or C, Licensee agrees that it's permission to use the affected Indicia or to manufacture, distribute, or sell the affected products pursuant to this Agreement will cease on the effective date of the deletion. In such event those provisions of paragraph 20 relating to disposal of inventory will become effective for the affected Indicia or products unless Licensee obtains written permission from the University concerned, to continue to use the Indicia, or to sell the products directly or indirectly, as of the effective date of deletion.

7. RATE, ADVANCE, AND ADMINISTRATIVE FEES

(a) Rate: Licensee agrees that it will pay to CCI/ICE a royalty of _____ of Net Sales of all Licensed Articles sold during the term of this Agreement and during the period allowed pursuant to paragraph 20 hereof (said payments hereinafter called "Royalty Payments").

(b) For purposes of determining the Royalty Payments, sales shall be deemed to have been made at the time of invoicing or billing for said Licensed Articles or at the time of delivery thereof, whichever is earlier.

(c) Initial Advance Payment: Upon execution of this Agreement by CCI/ICE, Licensee will pay CCI/ICE, as a nonrefundable payment, the Initial Advance Payment under this Agreement, set opposite the Licensed Articles in Appendix C. Licensee may deduct this Initial Advance Payment from payments due under the terms of this Agreement.

(d) Administrative Fee: Upon execution of this Agreement by CCI/ICE, Licensee will pay CCI/ICE, as a nonrefundable payment, the Administrative Fee set opposite the Licensed Articles in Appendix C.

8. MULTIPLE ROYALTIES

CCI/ICE recognizes that Licensee may be subject to other License Agreements, which together with this License Agreement, would subject certain Licensed Articles to one or more additional Royalty Payments. CCI/ICE agrees that the Royalty Payments required to be paid to CCI/ICE hereunder for Licensed Articles, which are subject to other License agreements and additional Royalty Payments, may be reduced by the amount that the other Licensor or Licensors reduces its or their standard royalty, up to a total maximum reduction of three percent (3%) of Net Sales.

9. STATEMENT AND PAYMENTS

(a) On or before the twentieth (20) day of each month, Licensee shall submit to CCI/ICE full and accurate statements showing the quantity, description, and Net Sales of the Licensed Articles distributed and/or sold during the preceding calendar month, listed (1) by category or article and (2) by Member Universities and showing

Exhibit 10-3 Continued

any additional information kept in the normal course of business by the Licensee, which is appropriate to enable an independent determination of the amount due hereunder with respect to the Licensed Indicia of each Member University. All payments then due CCI/ICE shall be made simultaneously with the submission of the statements. Such monthly statements shall be submitted whether or not they reflect any sales.

(b) Licensee shall, unless otherwise directed in writing by CCI/ICE send all royalty payments and accounting reports to

_____

10. EXEMPT AREA

On or around each Member University campus, certain accounts or areas may be exempt from the obligations to pay any Royalty Payments required under paragraph 7(a) for sales made and delivered by Licensee to customers located within said identified exempt area. Appendix B-1 denotes those accounts or areas which are exempt from Royalty Payments. CCI/ICE reserves the right to add or to delete from Appendix B-1, by notification to Licensee in writing.

11. OWNERSHIP OF INDICIA AND PROTECTION OF RIGHTS

(a) Licensee acknowledges and agrees that each University owns each of its Indicia identified in Appendix B, and that each of said Indicia is valid, and that each University has the exclusive right to use each of its Indicia subject only to limited, nonexclusive, revocable permission granted to Licensee to use the Indicia pursuant to this Agreement. Licensee further acknowledges the validity of each state and federal registration, which each University may own for each Licensed Indicia as of the date of this Agreement or which each University may thereafter obtain or acquire. Licensee further undertakes that it shall not, at any time, file any application in the United States Patent and Trademark Office, or in any state, or in Puerto Rico, or in any territory or possession of the United States, or in any foreign country for the trademark or service mark registration of any mark or other Indicia of any of the Universities, whether or not such mark or Indicia is or are identified in Appendix B, and Licensee further undertakes that it shall not register or deposit any of the Universities' Indicia as, or as part of, a trademark, service mark, trade name, fictitious name, or company or corporate name anywhere in the world. Any trademark or service mark registration obtained or applied for, or obtained during this Agreement, affecting the Licensed Indicia, will be transferred to the Member University.

(b) Licensee undertakes and agrees that it will not, on the basis of any use by Licensee of any of the Licensed Indicia, oppose or seek to cancel, in any court or state or federal agency, including, but not limited to, the United States Patent and Trademark Office, any registration for any mark for which any of the Universities files an application or obtains a registration for any goods or services, and Licensee further undertakes and agrees not to object to, or file any action or lawsuit because of any use by any of the Universities of any Indicia of any of the Universities for any goods or services, whether such use be by any of the Universities directly or through different Licensees or authorized users.

(c) Licensee agrees to assist CCI/ICE in the protection of the several and joint rights of the Member Universities and CCI/ICE, in and to the Licensed Marks and shall provide, at reasonable cost to be borne by CCI/ICE, any evidence, documents, and testimony, concerning the use by Licensee of any one or more of the Licensed Indicia, which CCI/ICE may request for use in obtaining, defending, or enforcing any Licensed Indicia or its registration.

(d) Licensee agrees that nothing in this Agreement shall give to Licensee any right, title, or interest in any Licensed Indicia (except the right to use in accordance with the terms of this Agreement) greater than Licensee already has and all uses by Licensee of any Licensed Indicia associated with each Member University. The Licensee, upon specific request from CCI/ICE, shall provide the following to CCI/ICE for each Licensed Indicia and for each Licensed Article to the extent reasonably available to Licensee:

Exhibit 10-3 Continued

(1) The date of first sale of each Licensed Article, description of the Licensed Article and Licensed Indicia thereon and name and address of the recipient of the initial distribution of the Licensed Article within the home state of the respective Member University.

(2) The date of the first sale of each Licensed Article, description of the Licensed Article and Licensed Indicia thereon and name and address of recipient of the initial distribution of the Licensed Article outside the home state of the respective Member University.

12. DISPLAY AND APPROVAL OF INDICIA

(a) Licensee shall use the Licensed Indicia properly on all labels, containers, packages, products, tags, and displays, in all print advertisements and literature, and in all television and radio commercials. On all visible material, the Indicia shall be emphasized in relation to surrounding material by using a distinctive type face, or color, or underlining, or other technique approved by the Universities. Any use of any Indicia shall conform to the requirements as specified on the Appendix B. Wherever appropriate, the Licensed Indicia shall be used as a proper adjective and the common noun for the product shall be used in conjunction with the Licensed Indicia and the proper symbol to identify the Indicia as a trademark, (viz, the circled "R" symbol if the Indicia is registered in the United States Patent and Trademark Office or the "TM" symbol if not so registered), shall be placed adjacent to each Indicia. Except when otherwise expressly authorized in writing by CCI/ICE, Licensee shall not use on any one product the Indicia of more than one University.

(b) CCI/ICE will provide to Licensee guidance on the proper use of the Licensed Indicia. A true representation or example of any proposed use by Licensee of any of the Indicia listed in Appendix B, in any visible or audible medium, and all proposed advertisements and promotional materials depicting any Indicia or referring thereto, shall be submitted at Licensee's expense to CCI/ICE for approval prior to such use. CCI/ICE shall have thirty (30) days from its receipt of the proposed material within which to approve or disapprove the proposed use. If CCI/ICE fails to disapprove the use within thirty (30) days, Licensee may use the Indicia in the form and on the material sent to CCI/ICE subject to the conditions of this Agreement. Licensee shall not use any Indicia in any form or in any material disapproved by CCI/ICE.

(c) Licensee shall display on each product or its container the trademark and license notices required by CCI/ICE's written instructions in effect as of the date of manufacture.

13. DISPLAY OF OFFICIAL TAG

Licensee agrees and undertakes to attach to each product or its container an "Officially Licensed Collegiate Product" tag or label in the form prescribed by CCI/ICE.

14. PROCEDURE FOR PRODUCT APPROVAL

(a) Licensee understands and agrees that it is an essential condition of this Agreement to protect the high reputation enjoyed by the Universities, and that the goods sold, promoted, or advertised in association with any of the Licensed Indicia shall be of high and consistent quality, subject to the approval and continuing supervision and control of the Universities.

(b) The standards, specifications, and characteristics of each product to be sold under each of the Licensed Indicia are set out in Appendix C annexed hereto, or in an attachment to Appendix C. Licensee agrees to adhere strictly to the agreed standards, specifications, and characteristics for each product sold under each of the Licensed Indicia.

(c) Prior to the production or sale of any product of which a physical sample has not already been inspected and approved by CCI/ICE, Licensee shall submit to CCI/ICE, at Licensee's expense, one sample of the product for each University

Exhibit 10-3 Continued

checked in Appendix A and one sample of CCI/ICE files, as it would be produced for sale. CCI/ICE shall have thirty (30) days from the receipt of a sample within which to approve or disapprove the product or obtain additional time, up to thirty (30) days, by written notice thereof within the first thirty (30) day period. If CCI/ICE approves the product or fails to disapprove the product within thirty (30) days from the receipt thereof, or during said additional time, the product shall be accepted to serve as an example of quality for that item, and production quantities may be manufactured by Licensee in strict conformity with the sample that was submitted. Only items manufactured in accordance with the corresponding sample accepted hereunder, and which have substantially the same relative quality position in the marketplace as do the sample thereof, may be manufactured.

(d) At least thirty (30) days prior to renewal in accordance with paragraph 2(d), in addition to any other requirement, Licensee shall submit to CCI/ICE such number of each product sold under the Licensed Indicia as may be necessary for CCI/ICE to examine and test to assure compliance with the quality and standard requirements for products bearing licensed Indicia, as set forth in Appendix D attached hereto. Each product shall be shipped in its usual container or wrapper, together with all labels, tags, and other material which usually accompany the product. Licensees shall bear the expense of manufacturing and shipping the required number of products to the destination designated by CCI/ICE. CCI/ICE shall have thirty (30) days from the receipt of each sample to approve or disapprove the product. Failure to approve by the end of said thirty (30) day period shall be deemed to be an approval.

(e) If CCI/ICE notifies Licensee of any defect in any product, or of any deviation from the approved use of any of the Indicia, Licensee shall have thirty (30) days from the date of notification from CCI/ICE within which to correct every noted defect or deviation. Defective products in Licensee's inventory shall not be sold under, or in association with, any of the Licensed Indicia, but if it is possible to correct all defects in the goods in Licensee's inventory, such goods may be sold under one or more of the Licensed Indicia after all defects are corrected.

(f) A product and the manner of use of Indicia on the product and on materials associated with the products shall be deemed to be approved for the purposes of paragraphs 12(b) and 14(c) and (d), with respect to any University, when Licensee regularly sells or supplies that product bearing the Indicia to the bookstore or any department of that University, so long as Licensee is not notified of any disapproval of a product or manner of use of Indicia by the University or by CCI/ICE. CCI/ICE shall have the right to require the submission of samples for inspection or testing at any time and Licensee shall promptly comply, at its expense, with such requirement, as provided in paragraph 14(d).

15. NO JOINT VENTURE OR ENDORSEMENT OF LICENSEE

Nothing in this Agreement shall be construed to place the parties in the relationship of partners or joint venturers or agents and neither Licensee nor CCI/ICE shall have the power to obligate or bind each other in any manner whatsoever. CCI/ICE is in no way a guarantor of the quality of any product produced by Licensee. Licensee agrees that it will neither state nor imply, either directly or indirectly, that the Licensee, or its activities, other than pursuant to exercise of the license herein, are supported, endorsed or sponsored by CCI/ICE or by any Member University and, upon the direction of CCI/ICE, shall issue express disclaimers to that effect.

16. INFRINGEMENT

Neither CCI/ICE nor any Member University shall be liable as the result of activities by Licensee under this agreement for infringement of any patent, copyright, or trademark belonging to any third party, or for damages or costs involved in any proceeding based upon any such infringement, or for any royalty or obligation incurred by Licensee because of any patent, copyright, or trademark held by a third party.

Exhibit 10-3 Continued

17. INDEMNIFICATION AND INSURANCE

Licensee hereby agrees to be solely responsible for, to defend, and indemnify CCI/ICE, the Member Universities, and their respective officers, agents, and employees, and to hold each of them harmless from all liability claims, demands, causes of actions or damages, including reasonable attorney's fees caused by or arising from workmanship, material, or design of any Licensed Article or out of any action by the Licensee in using the Licensed Marks in connection with the manufacture, sale, distribution, or any other use of the Licensed Articles. Licensee will obtain, prior to the first sale of any Licensed Article, product liability insurance providing protection for CCI/ICE, Member Universities, and their respective officers, agents, and employees as insureds in amounts of coverage specified below, against any claims, demands, or causes of action and damages, including reasonable attorney's fees arising out of any alleged defects in such articles, or any manufacture or use thereof. Such insurance policy shall not be cancelled without at least thirty (30) days written notice to CCI/ICE. CCI/ICE shall be furnished with a certificate of such insurance. Licensee agrees that such insurance policy or policies shall provide coverage of One Million Dollars ($1,000,000) for personal injuries arising out of each occurrence and coverage of Three Hundred Thousand Dollars ($300,000) for property damage arising out of each occurrence. However, recognizing that the aforesaid amounts may be inappropriate with regard to specific classes of goods, it is contemplated that CCI/ICE and Licensee may agree upon reasonable adjustment to the foregoing amounts.

18. RECORDS AND RIGHT TO AUDIT

Licensee agrees to keep all books and accounts and records covering all transactions relating to the license herein in a manner such that the information contained in the statements referred to in Paragraph 9 can be readily determined. CCI/ICE and/or its duly authorized representatives shall have the right to examine such books of account and records and all other documents and material in Licensee's possession or under it's control, with respect to the subject matter and terms of this Agreement, and shall have a reasonable amount of freedom and access thereto for such purposes and for the purpose of making copies and/or abstracts therefrom. Should an audit indicate an underpayment of 10% or more of the royalties due in terms of the contract, the cost of audit will be paid by Licensee, along with the full amount of underpay, within fifteen (15) days from receipt of a memorandum of charge from CCI/ICE. All such books of account and records shall be kept available for at least four (4) years after the termination of this agreement.

19. CANCELLATION

(a) To the extent then permitted by law, this Agreement shall be deemed cancelled automatically, effective immediately, should any of the following occur:

(1) Any voluntary or involuntary act of insolvency on the part of Licensee, including, but not limited to, an adjudication of insolvency, any filing under any provision of the Bankruptcy Act, the appointment of a receiver or trustee, an assignment for the benefit of creditors, or any bulk sale by Licensee for the payment of debts; or

(2) Any attempt by Licensee to grant a sublicense or any attempt by Licensee to assign any right or duty under this Agreement to any person, corporation, partnership, association, or any other third party, without the prior written consent of CCI/ICE.

(b) CCI/ICE may cancel this Agreement, effective thirty (30) days from the date of written notice to Licensee, should any of the following occur.

(1) Any failure by Licensee to account for and to pay to CCI/ICE within twenty (20) days of the due date, the royalties due for the period prior to the date when such accounting and payment are due; or

(2) Any act or omission by Licensee for which any Clause or Paragraph of this Agreement provides for cancellation or termination; or

Exhibit 10-3 Continued

(3) Any other breach by Licensee of any Clause or Paragraph of this Agreement for which cancellation or termination is not otherwise provided, unless, within thirty (30) days, Licensee fully remedies such omission or breach.

(4) Any act or omission by Licensee which should reflect unfavorably or embarrass or otherwise detract from the high reputation of any Member University.

20. EFFECT OF TERMINATION AND DISPOSAL OF INVENTORY

After termination of this Agreement, Licensee shall have no further right to manufacture, advertise, distribute, sell, or otherwise deal in any Licensed Articles, and Licensee shall not use any Licensed Indicia or any derivation thereof of any Indicia confusingly similar thereto, unless expressly authorized by a Member University or except as elsewhere herein provided. Upon such termination, unless the same shall occur pursuant to paragraph 14, hereof, Licensee may dispose of Licensed Articles which are on hand or in process at the time of such termination, for a period of one hundred eighty (180) days thereafter provided all payments then due are first made to CCI/ICE and statement of payments with respect to that one hundred eighty (180) day period are thereafter made in accordance with paragraph 9 hereof.

21. FINAL STATEMENT

If the Agreement is terminated by CCI/ICE pursuant to paragraph 19, Licensee will furnish to CCI/ICE a statement showing the number and description of Licensed Articles on hand or in process within thirty (30) days after notice of termination is given.

22. SURVIVAL OF RIGHTS

(a) The terms and provisions of this Agreement necessary to protect the rights and interest of the Universities in their marks, Indicia, copyrights, names, reputations, and goodwill shall survive the cancellation or termination of this Agreement for any reason, including licensee's obligation under paragraph 17.

(b) The terms and conditions of this Agreement providing for the furnishing to CCI/ICE of any reports, statements, or accounts and payment of monies due to CCI/ICE, and the right to examine and make copies of Licensee's books and records to determine or verify the correctness and accuracy of Licensee's reports, statements, accounts, or payments shall survive the cancellation of termination of this Agreement for any reason.

(c) All of the terms and conditions of this Agreement which provide for any activity following the effective date of cancellation or termination of this Agreement shall survive until such time as those terms and conditions will have been fulfilled or satisfied.

23. NOTICES

All notices and statements to be given and all payments to be made hereunder, shall be given or made to the parties at their respective addresses set forth above, Attention: President, unless notification of a change of address is given in writing. Any notice shall be sent by first class mail, or by mailgram, telex, TWX, or telegram, and shall be deemed to have been given at the time it is mailed or sent.

24. CONFORMITY TO LAW

(a) Licensee undertakes and agrees that the manufacturing and sale of all of the products described in Appendix C hereto shall be in conformity with all federal, state, and local laws, ordinances, regulations, and rules.

(b) Licensee undertakes and agrees to obtain and maintain all required permits and licenses at Licensee's expense.

(c) Licensee undertakes and agrees to pay all federal, state, and local taxes which may be due on or by reason of the sale of any products described in Appendix C.

Exhibit 10-3 Continued

25. SEVERABILITY

In the event any portion of this Agreement is declared invalid or unenforceable for any reason, such portion is deemed severable herefrom and the remainder of this Agreement shall be deemed to be, and shall remain, fully valid and enforceable unless such validity or unenforceability tends to deprive either party of the benefits to be provided it by this Agreement, in which case said deprived party shall have the option of keeping this Agreement in effect or terminating.

26. MISCELLANEOUS

This Agreement and any rights herein granted are personal to Licensee and shall not be assigned, sublicensed, or encumbered without CCI/ICE's written consent. This Agreement constitutes the entire Agreement and understanding between the parties hereto and cancels, terminates, and supersedes any prior Agreement or understanding relating the subject matter hereof between Licensee and CCI/ICE and Member Universities. There are no representations, promises, agreements, warranties, covenants or understandings other than those contained herein. None of the provisions of this Agreement may be waived or modified, except expressly in writing signed by both parties. However, failure of either party to require the performance of any term in this Agreement or the waiver by either party of any breach thereof shall not prevent subsequent enforcement of such term nor be deemed a waiver of any subsequent breach. When necessary for appropriate meaning, a plural shall be deemed to be the singular and a singular shall be deemed to be the plural. The attached appendices are an integral part of this Agreement. Paragraph headings are for convenience only and shall not add to or detract from any of the terms or provisions of this Agreement. This Agreement shall be construed in accordance with the laws of the State of California, and shall not be binding on CCI/ICE until signed by an officer of CCI/ICE.

Licensee:

by: _____

title: _____

date: _____

Collegiate Concepts, Inc.
International Collegiate Enterprises, Inc.
A Joint Venture

by: _____

title: _____

date: _____

Exhibit 10-3 Continued

Chapter 11

PROFESSIONAL CAREERS
AND PLAYER AGENTS

INTRODUCTION

One of the most important responsibilities of athletic administrators at both the high school and college level is to provide guidance to student-athletes who are dealing with possible professional career opportunities. The performance of this duty serves a dual purpose: It ensures the continued eligibility of the player and it prepares the athlete to deal with the sometimes unsavory business of professional sports.

Chapter 11 begins with the question of eligibility and how contact with agents can affect the athlete's status. The chapter next addresses the structure and function of the professional leagues' drafts and collective bargaining agreements. In addition, salary and contract information is provided. The chapter then looks at player agents—their functions and how and by whom they are regulated. The information contained in this section will help the athletic administrator to understand the issues which may face the student-athlete in the selection of a player agent. Chapter 11 concludes with two brief sections on individual performer sports and the opportunities available to U.S. athletes who want to play in foreign leagues.

AMATEUR ELIGIBILITY ISSUES

The athletic administrator who deals with the college student-athlete must be aware of certain issues that might have an effect on the eligibility of the athlete. The issues that will most likely affect the amateur status of a student-athlete are the payment or employment of an athlete. These areas have already been addressed in Chapter 5; here we focus on how important it is that the athletic administrator understand why athletes are sometimes willing to sacrifice their eligibility for the opportunity to become a professional.

An athlete faces many pressures when deciding whether or not to turn pro. Peer pressure is often a factor in that the athlete thinks he must prove his worth to others who play at the same level. The signing of a professional contract may put to rest any questions his peers have as to his ability. The money an athlete can earn as a professional also makes becoming a professional seem a very attractive proposition. The money may be viewed by the athlete as a way of becoming self-supportive and/or helping the family. He may feel the pressure to secure these outstanding amounts before his amateur eligibility is up so that he can avoid the risk of a career-threatening injury during his amateur career limiting his chances of ever earning the large salary.

Player agents themselves may put pressure on an athlete to turn pro. These agents will try to recruit using various methods, both legal and illegal, and the athlete may have a hard time retaining amateur status in the face of attractive offers of a professional contract. From the agent's standpoint recruiting is a very competitive business, and signing a hot prospect before someone else can be most rewarding. A final source of pressure on an athlete may come directly from the professional teams. They may try to lure the athlete into special deals with bonus money and high salary offers, although this has usually occurred only when there were competing leagues.

It is the athletes themselves who must ultimately make the critical decisions which will impact many areas of interest. They first must decide if they are ready to compete at the professional level. They then must try to establish which round they will be drafted in and, if drafted, whether or not it is the right team for them. In professional basketball and football, the athletes usually do not have the luxury of picking a desired team, but they may have more flexibility in professional baseball. They must also decide whether they are physically and mentally prepared for the rigors of the game, both on and off the court or field. Another question is what will happen if they wait to turn pro. By waiting, will they sacrifice a large contract, or will they maybe attract an even larger contract?

Other issues also face student-athletes. Whether or not they can talk to an attorney or player agent must be considered. If they are able to talk to a player agent, they must decide if it is possible for the agent to be a part of the marketing of their abilities. Athletes who are drafted must realize that they may lose their amateur eligibility by being drafted. And, if drafted, how long will the drafting team keep their rights?

Student-athletes who do not want to take the step of employing an agent need to know to whom they can turn for assistance. Will the league office give them some direction? Will the club that is interested in drafting them be helpful in giving some direction? And who from the club is best to talk to? Upon being drafted, the athletes will also want to talk with a representative of the players' union to obtain salary information and to find out about the procedures and applications of membership.

We will attempt to address several of these questions in this chapter. However, there is neither the time nor the space to address all of these issues, mainly because the rules and regulations differ for each professional league, for each sport (e.g., track and basketball differ), and for each amateur association (e.g., the NCAA and the USOC have different interpretations of "amateur"). In addition, the practices of the leagues and unions differ for each sport. Because there are so many combinations of rules, regulations, and league practices, to which are added the student-athlete's on-the-field accomplishments, potential, and maturity levels, each student-athlete's case should be handled individually. Another reason for individual treatment according to many general managers of professional teams is that both the draft and player evaluations are inexact sciences.

This chapter may raise more questions than it answers. What is important, however, is that it raise the level of awareness for athletic administrators and student-athletes in terms of their options and the information they should be striving to obtain so that they can make informed decisions. From the perspective of the athletic director, this area is often ignored; yet the negative ramifications for an athletic program can be tremendous. Several programs, including Villanova's, Iona's, and Alabama's basketball programs, have been penalized because a student-athlete entered into a professional contract or agreed to be represented by an agent before the expiration of his collegiate eligibility. Such a step can result in the forfeiture of victories, finishes in a tournament, and the recall of television and/or tournament participation monies. From the student-athlete's perspective, the decisions concerning a professional career and representation are extremely important, because one mistake can bring about severe consequences. In pursuit of information about a professional career, student-athletes should be concerned about maintaining their eligibility. They should also be aware of the dire consequences to themselves and their institution of an incorrect decision.

PROFESSIONAL CAREERS

Professional careers can be very lucrative for an athlete. The status of being a "professional" represents a very high level of achievement. It also represents a challenge, for the athlete must maintain this status and avoid the premature dissolution of his or her professional career. The average time span of a professional career is short, and many athletes achieve their highest skill level only to fall from the professional ranks within a short period. Before entering the professional ranks the amateur athlete must become knowledgeable about the draft, player contracts, and the collective bargaining agreement for the sport in question.

Beginning with the draft, amateur athletes should know their options relative to the draft. After the draft, the two key legal documents are the standard player contract and the collective bargaining agreement. The end product of negotiations between an agent and the player's club will be the player's salary. Athletic administrators should have an understanding of these basic elements so that they are prepared to advise the student-athlete in the event that their advice is sought.

Professional Drafts

The draft is used by each sport as a means of distributing young talent among the various teams in the league. Generally, each team will make a selection in reverse order of finish from the previous season and can trade to improve its draft position. Another important purpose of the draft is to reduce to one the number of teams with which an incoming player can negotiate. This, in theory, has the effect of minimizing players' negotiating leverage and thereby reducing player salaries, but also equalizing talent among teams.

Each of the four major professional leagues holds an annual draft. The eligibility, duration of eligibility, and signing rules for the draft vary from one sport to another.

Major League Baseball

Major League Baseball has the most complicated rules of any of the professional drafts. Each year Major League Baseball conducts one amateur free agent selection meeting on or about June 10th (a January amateur free agent draft, as well as "secondary phases" of drafts, for previously selected players, was eliminated in 1986). The players eligible for the summer amateur free agent selection meeting consist of high school graduating seniors (or those without remaining eligibility); certain four-year college players; junior college (JUCO) players; and all other amateur players not previously selected.

A high school player who is drafted may sign with the professional club. If he decides not to sign and instead enrolls in a four-year college, he becomes selectable at the next summer selection meeting at which he becomes eligible according to the Professional and College Players Rules of Major League Baseball. There are, however, five exceptions:

1. The player who has reached age 21 and is currently between school years.
2. The player who has completed his junior year and is currently between school years.
3. The player who has completed the full period of eligibility for intercollegiate baseball.
4. The player whose association with the college has been terminated by reason of scholastic deficiency.
5. The player who withdraws from college and remains out for at least 120 days (including the date of withdrawal).

A junior college player is eligible for selection at any summer selection meeting. However, upon reentering junior college, such players cannot be signed until the completion of the college baseball season (signings during tournament time were allowed beginning in 1987).

Once a player is drafted, the onus is on the team to begin negotiations within 15 days and offer the player a contract. Since initial minor league salaries have maximum ceilings of $700 per month at all class levels (AAA, AA, A, Rookie Leagues), the signing bonus is one of the major items of negotiation for selected players, especially those chosen in the earlier rounds.

Other relevant considerations include the following:

1. The summer amateur free agent selection meeting is not open to the press. The names of selected players are released alphabetically rather than by round of selection, and they are not released to the media until seven days following the selection meeting. The exception is Round 1 selections; those names and the order of selection are immediately released.
2. Each draft consists only of a regular phase (the "secondary phase" draft for previously selected but unsigned players was eliminated in 1986). Each club other than Rookie League clubs is entitled to select, at each selection meeting, the following number of players:
     Major League Club: one
     Class AAA Club: one
     Class AA Club: one
     Class A Club: no limit
   A club's right to select shall be terminated when (a) it has

selected its limit of players as set forth above, (b) it has announced a "pass," or (c) it has failed to respond to a call.

3. The draft is conducted in reverse order of *league* finish.
4. Selected players are placed on a club's Negotiation List until the start of the next Closed Period (seven days preceding June selection meeting) unless, at an earlier date:
   (a) The player signs.
   (b) The player is found to be not eligible.
   (c) The player enters or returns to college.
   (d) The club's negotiation rights are revoked (failure to tender contract within 15 days).
5. A club cannot transfer its negotiation rights to another club.
6. A college or JC player selected at the preceding June draft whose team's intercollegiate schedule (including regional or national tournaments) extends past the start of the Closed Period, may be signed during the Closed Period, during the interim starting day after the team's last intercollegiate game and ending at 12:01 A.M. of the day on which the June draft commences.
7. An amateur player who is eligible for the summer free agent selection meeting but is not selected may be signed by *any* club from the conclusion of the summer selection meeting until the start of the next Closed Period, in compliance with the Professional and College Players Rules. However, a college player eligible solely because of age or completion of his junior year, but not selected, may be signed by *any* club *only* during summer recess between school years. If he returns to college, he becomes subject to the next summer's free agent selection.
8. A player who was not previously contracted with a Major League or National Association club, *who is not a United States resident*, and who is not subject to high school, college, JUCO, or American Legion draft eligibility rules may be signed by any club if (a) he is 17 years old at the time of signing, or (b) if he is 16 years old upon signing and will reach 17 prior to either the conclusion of the effective season he signed for, or September 1 of the effective season, whichever date is later. An amateur player shall be considered a U.S. resident, for draft purposes, if he is enrolled in a U.S. high school or college or has been a resident of the United States for at least one year.
9. No player in high school may sign a contract during his period of eligibility for participation in high school athletics

(there are exceptions for dropouts, Canadian, and Latin American students).
10. Clubs and club representatives are prohibited from suggesting or influencing players to withdraw from high school or college, or to transfer.

A player's NCAA eligibility is not affected when he is drafted by a club.

National Basketball Association

The NBA holds its annual draft in June, after the completion of the playoffs. The draft consists of seven rounds, with teams selecting in reverse order of finish for the previous year. The NBA developed a lottery in response to critics who claimed some teams were dumping games in order to gain a higher draft pick. All seven teams who do not make the playoffs participate to determine their draft order. However, the team with the worst record in the league is guaranteed a pick no worse than the fourth overall to try to ensure the availability of a quality player for the team that needs a player most. In addition, no team that acquires a lottery pick by trade can select higher than fourth if that team participated in the playoffs during the preceding season. All players whose college eligibility has expired are automatically included in the draft pool.

The notification and participation in the draft effectively renounces the athlete's remaining or future intercollegiate eligibility. If a player changes his mind, he must rescind his notification before the aforementioned deadline passes in order to maintain intercollegiate eligibility. Any college undergraduate may ask to be drafted by submitting his name to the NBA at least 45 days prior to the draft. High school seniors can also be declared eligible for the draft by notifying the NBA. Once drafted, the player loses NCAA eligibility.

Once drafted, the NBA team must offer the athlete at least a minimum contract by September 5. The minimum salary for an NBA rookie is $75,000 per season. If the player declines the offer, his rights are held by the team until the next draft. If a player signs a professional contract with another league (such as the Continental Basketball Association or European league) after being drafted by an NBA team, the NBA team retains the right to negotiate with the player within the period ending one year from the earlier of the following two dates: (1) the date the player notifies the NBA team that he is immediately ready to sign a contract or (2) the date of the college draft occurring in the 12-month period from September 1 to August 30 in which the player notifies the NBA team of his availability and intention to play in the NBA during the season immediately following the stated 12-month period.

National Football League

The NFL has perhaps the strictest and narrowest eligibility rules of the four major professional leagues. Only college players who have completed their eligibility may be drafted. A player who graduates before his eligibility expires must submit a letter stating his intention to be graduated before the fall semester if he wants to be drafted. In this case, the team which selects this player cannot offer the athlete a contract until it receives word from the NFL office that he has in fact graduated. If the player fails to graduate, the club loses the selection and the player forfeits his college eligibility. The timing of the NFL draft fluctuated in response to the now defunct USFL, but it usually falls between March and May and lasts 12 rounds.

The NFL also has a supplemental draft for players who become eligible after the draft but before the start of the NFL season. Cleveland Browns quarterback Bernie Kosar took this route. Cleveland had to give up its first-round selection in the next NFL draft in this situation.

Players who have lost their intercollegiate eligibility due to improper conduct may request special permission from the commissioner to be included in the draft pool. This has become a concern for college administrators, because of players who have forfeited their eligibility due to receipt of payments from agents in violation of NCAA rules.

Any NFL draftee must be offered a minimum contract by June 7, or he is free to negotiate with any team. If he chooses not to sign, he is eligible for the next NFL draft, but once again is limited to one club in negotiations. However, if a drafted player does not play professional football for two years, he may then sign with any team. A player who plays professionally in the Canadian Football League or any other professional football league and whose rights are held by an NFL club can only negotiate with that club for two years. After that point the player may negotiate with any NFL team, but the team which held his original rights can match the offer and thereby retain the player. Exhibit 11–1 expands on the basic eligibility rules that are enforced by the NFL.

National Hockey League

The NHL holds its annual draft on the Saturday of the second full

ELIGIBILITY OF NEW PLAYERS

A member club cannot sign a player to an NFL Player Contract or select a player in a draft (principal or supplemental) until such player meets one of the following requirements:

COLLEGE ELIGIBILITY. All college football eligibility of such player has expired through participation in college football (expiration does not include a loss of college football eligibility through withdrawal from school, dismissal or signing of a professional contract in another football league). Or,

GRADUATION. Such player has been graduated and received a diploma from a recognized college or university prior to the beginning of the League's next regular season ("recognized college or university" means any institution listed in the Blue Book of College Athletics published by the Rohrich Corporation, 903 E. Tallmadge Avenue, Akron, Ohio 44310 and/or the *Education Directory, Colleges and Universities*, U.S. Dept. of Education, Washington, D.C.). A diploma of graduation issued by a recognized college or university to a student under an accelerated course or program is acceptable for eligibility purposes despite the fact that the student actually attended such institution for a period of less than four years. Or,

FIVE-YEAR RULE. Five League seasons have elapsed since such player first entered, attended, practiced football at, or participated in football games for a recognized junior college, college, or university ("recognized junior college, college, or university" means any institution listed in appropriate publications by the publishers cited in the above section). Special consideration is granted to those players whose college and/or conference allow five years of football eligibility, during all of which a player may participate full-time, as distinguished from those who "red-shirt," *i.e.*, do not participate during one particular year. If a player under such circumstances has completed four years of participating football eligibility and elects not to avail himself of the fifth year, such player is eligible for selection in the League. Or,

NON-FOOTBALL COLLEGIANS. Such player did not play or otherwise participate in college football, and four League seasons have elapsed since the player first entered or attended college. Or,

SPECIAL ELIGIBILITY. Such player has been granted eligibility through special permission of the Commissioner.

OTHER ELIGIBILITY RULES

The following additional rules have bearing on the basic requirements listed above:

ANOTHER SPORT. The fact that a player has college athletic eligibility remaining in a sport other than football does not affect his eligibility for the League, provided such player meets all other applicable League eligibility requirements.

COMPLETION OF COLLEGE GAMES. Despite the fact that player may meet other League eligibility requirements stated here, a member club cannot sign a player to a player contract, select a player in a draft (principal or supplemental), or in any manner, directly or indirectly, engage the services of a player until completion of all football games, including postseason bowl games, in which the team of the school or college of such player is to participate and in which the player is to participate. If a club violates this section, it is subject to disciplinary action by the Commissioner.

COLLEGE AND NFL IN SAME SEASON. No person who plays college football after the opening date of the NFL training season in any year may be under

Exhibit 11-1 NFL Rules: Eligibility for the Player Draft

contract to, practice with, or play games for a club in the League during the balance of that same football season.

REPEATED ELIGIBILITY. No person who has never been drafted in the League and who has a college *football* eligibility remaining and who registers at a college for the fall term or semester may be signed to a contract by a club in the League until the close of the next succeeding principal draft of the League, at which time he would be eligible for selection regardless of how many seasons in excess of five have elapsed since he first registered at a college and regardless of how many drafts for which he was eligible have transpired.

EARLY SIGNINGS. No person eligible for a draft (principal or supplemental) may be signed to a contract with a club in the League until completion of the draft for which he is eligible.

EARLY GRADUATION. Any player who expects to graduate before his college football eligibility expires may become conditionally eligible for the League's principal draft (i.e., the 12-round annual draft that includes approximately 336 choices) by declaring to the Commissioner in writing his intention to graduate before the League's next succeeding regular season, which declaration must be in the Commissioner's office no later than 15 days before the date of the opening of the principal draft (for 1987, the deadline is Monday, April 13). The Commissioner has the authority to change the receipt date of the written declaration if he deems such change appropriate. If a player's written declaration is received in timely fashion and the League Office determines that he has a reasonable opportunity to graduate before the next succeeding regular season of the League, all member clubs will be advised of his conditional eligibility for the principal draft. Any player so designated cannot be signed to an NFL Player Contract, regardless of whether he is selected in the draft, until the League office is advised by an appropriate authority at the player's college that he has graduated. Any player who makes such a declaration to graduate and who does not graduate before the next succeeding regular season of the League will be ineligible in the League for that season and postseason; and, if such player has been selected in the principal draft, the selecting club will forfeit its selection choice. Any player who fails to make a timely written declaration of his intent to graduate but does graduate before his college football eligibility expires and before the beginning of the next succeeding regular season of the League will be eligible for a supplemental draft.

ELIGIBLE PLAYER NOT SELECTED. A player eligible for a draft (principal or supplemental) who is not selected is a free agent and may be signed by any club in the League, provided, however, that if such player returns to college *to play football*, he is subject to the provisions of *REPEATED ELIGIBILITY* and/or *COLLEGE AND NFL IN SAME SEASON* above.

SUPPLEMENTAL SELECTION. Any player who is ineligible for the principal draft but who becomes eligible after such draft and prior to the beginning of the League's next regular season is not eligible to be signed as a free agent but is eligible for a supplemental selection procedure conducted by the Commissioner. The order of selection in any supplemental draft will be established by a weighted lottery (the weakest club will have its name in the drawing 28 times, the next weakest 27 times, etc., until the Super Bowl winner will have its name in once). The procedure proceeds by rounds, and any club selecting a player forfeits a selection choice in the next succeeding principal draft equal to that exercised in the supplemental draft.

Exhibit 11-1 Continued

week in June. Any amateur player who will turn 18 by September 15 is eligible. Any player who has gone undrafted previously may be selected until he is 20 as of the next September 15, after which he becomes a free agent able to negotiate with any team.

A drafted player must receive a bonafide offer by the next draft or he is eligible to be drafted again, or if he doesn't meet the age requirement, he becomes a free agent. There is no maximum age requirement for European players, who must be drafted before they can sign. Finally, any drafted player who enters college remains the property of the drafting team until 180 days after he graduates or leaves school.

Unlike football and basketball, and similar to baseball, participation in the NHL draft is not detrimental to collegiate or high school eligibility. If a player is selected but decides not to sign, he can still participate on the amateur level.

The Standard Player Contract

Once an agent representing the player and management reach an agreement, it is then usually up to the athlete to give his approval to the agent, at which point the contract is formed. After consumation of the contract, the player is legally bound to perform to the best of his abilities during the term of the contract, and management must perform its part by remunerating the athlete as expressed in the agreement. Appendix E contains an example of a standard player contract, also called a uniform player contract, for the National Basketball Association.

Although both sides are committed to the agreement legally, a recent trend in pro sports, particularly baseball, has been renegotiation of contracts. Renegotiation is almost always initiated by the athlete after a season in which he performed well beyond all expectations at the time of the original agreement. Management is in no way forced to even consider the athlete's request; however, teams are often compelled to do so in order to keep the player happy and motivated. Most clubs have established policies regarding renegotiation, which vary from firm nonrenegotiation to frequent renegotiation. One of the most common alternatives used by many teams is to reward players by adding on years at the end of the contract at an increased salary.

It should also be pointed out that attorneys who represent players often face ethical concerns with respect to renegotiation. Many of these agents may advise a client not to renegotiate a contract because they believe in the sanctity of contracts. One way to circumvent this problem is to include a "reopener clause" in the

---

SIGNING BONUS

Between _____ and _____
                    (Club)   (Player)

As additional consideration for the execution of NFL Player Contract(s) for the year(s) _____, and for the Player's adherence to all provisions of said contract(s), Club agrees to pay Player the sum of $ _____.

The above sum is payable as follows:

$ _____ upon execution of this rider (Player acknowledges receipt of said sum); and

$ _____ on _____ 19____ ; and

$ _____ on _____ 19____ ; and

$ _____ on _____ 19____ .

It is expressly understood that no part of the bonus herein provided is part of any salary in the contract(s) specified above, that said bonus will not be deemed part of any salary in the contract(s) specified above if Club exercises an option for Player's services in a season subsequent to the final contract year, and that such obligations of Club are not terminable if such contract(s) is (are) terminated via the NFL waiver system.

In the event Player, in any of the years specified above or an option year, fails or refuses to report to Club, fails or refuses to practice or play with Club, or leaves Club without its consent, then, upon demand by Club, Player will return to Club the proportionate amount of the total bonus not having been earned at the time of Player's default.

Date: _____

Club: _____   Player: _____

By: _____

Exhibit 11-2   A Signing Bonus Used by the NFL

original contract, which would allow renegotiation to take place if certain stated situations came about.

Another important aspect of the player contract for both the player and the club is the bonus clause. It is often the desire of both parties to include a bonus clause in the player's contract because it can provide for the contingency that the player will be worth more than current accomplishments or prospects indicate. In some instances, a bonus clause may be given to lure a player to sign. This signing bonus can serve more than one purpose. It can also provide up-front money that may be the only reward a marginal player receives under the contract. If the player is released before the regular season begins because of failure to make the team, he at least gets to keep the signing bonus, even though the rest of the contract becomes null and void. Exhibit 11–2 is an example of a signing bonus that the NFL uses.

FOOTBALL

Quarterback:
250 passing attempts .... $
150 completions .... $
Pass 1,000 yards .... $
Pass 1,500 yards .... $
Pass 2,000 yards .... $
Pass 5 touchdowns .... $
Pass 10 touchdowns .... $

Running Back: Rushes for 400 yards .... $
Catches over 40 passes .... $
Scores 6 touchdowns .... $
Scores 5 touchdowns rushing .... $
Scores 3 touchdowns rushing .... $
Leads NFC or AFC in scoring .... $

Defense:
Leads team in total tackles .... $
Leads team in assists .... $
Leads NFL in tackles .... $
Leads NFC in tackles .... $
Leads or ties linebackers in interceptions .... $
Returns interception for touchdown (each) ... $
Leads or ties team in tackles for loss .... $
Fumble recoveries (each recovery) .... $
Ties or leads team in interceptions .... $
Leads NFL in interceptions .... $
Leads NFC in interceptions .... $
Leads or ties team linebackers for quarterback
sacks .... $
Quarterback sacks (each sack) .... $

BASKETBALL

In addition to other monies Player shall receive the following, if such are attained in any year under this contract:
For averaging over 20 points per game, the sum of $_____ .
For leading the team in scoring, the sum of $_____ .
For leading the NBA in assists or steals, the sum of $_____ .
For being in the top five in the NBA in scoring, the sum of $_____ .

HOCKEY

30 goals or 65 points .... $_____ , and
35 goals or 75 points .... $_____ , and
40 goals or 85 points .... $_____ , and
45 goals or 95 points .... $_____ , and
50 goals or 105 points .... $_____ .

Exhibit 11-3 Examples of Statistical Bonus Provisions in Football, Basketball, and Hockey

Bonus clauses are also used to compensate a player who has exceeded expectations. It is important to structure the bonus so that the proper salary escalation is allowed if the player fulfills or exceeds current prospects. Different leagues attach different names to the same types of bonus clauses. Generally, however, bonuses can be broken down based on status (the signing bonus), statistical performance, volume of play, awards and honors, and other contingencies. Exhibit 11–3 contains examples from actual statistical bonus provisions in those sports that allow them.

Collective Bargaining Agreements

The players' union, an integral part of the professional athlete's career concerns, has a wide variety of functions. The union helps the players when grievances are filed against management, it provides information to player agents to aid in negotiations with individual teams, and it generally looks out for the collective best interests of the players, including the generation of revenues for the association through licensing and marketing programs using the particular association's logo. The primary function of the players' union, however, is to negotiate the collective bargaining agreements, which are the bread and butter behind the maintenance of players' salaries and the other benefits that have been negotiated. An example of what the union can do for an individual player is highlighted by comparing the average salary for an NFL player before 1982 ($81,000) and after the collective bargaining agreement was negotiated ($200,000 by 1986).

The collective bargaining agreement (CBA), which is determined by the negotiation between the players' union and the league, is valuable to professional athletes. They must learn to recognize the importance of this agreement with the help of the player agent and team representative.

The categories negotiated in the CBA between the two parties include economic, benefit, and noneconomic concerns. Severance pay, which is awarded to athletes who have finished their careers, minimum wage scales, minimum rookie salaries, playoff money, all-star allotments, and preseason pay are all chiefly economic concerns. Disability compensation in the line of duty, permanent disability, widows' and survivors' compensation, life insurance, major medical insurance, injury protection (in the NFL a player who is injured during one season and is waived the next season receives an amount equal to half of his salary for that next season up to a maximum of $65,000), dental coverage, and joint control of insurance are concerns that are presented in the bargaining ses-

National Football League

1. Jim Kelly, quarterback, Buffalo Bills, $1,100,000
2. Joe Montana, quarterback, San Francisco 49ers, $1,000,000
3. Marc Wilson, quarterback, Los Angeles Raiders, $1,000,000
4. John Elway, quarterback, Denver Broncos, $1,000,000
5. Lawrence Taylor, linebacker, New York Giants, $900,000
6. Marcus Allen, runningback, Los Angeles Raiders, $900,000
7. Neil Lomax, quarterback, St. Louis Cardinals, $875,000
8. Raymond Clayborn, defensive back, New England Patriots, $825,000
9. Joe Klecko, defensive line, New York Jets, $812,000
10. Bernie Kosar, Quarterback, Cleveland Browns, $800,000

Source: The Sporting News, March 16, 1987.

Major League Baseball

1. Eddie Murray, first baseman, Baltimore Orioles, $2,460,000
2. Jim Rice, outfielder, Boston Red Sox, $2,412,000
3. Mike Schmidt, third baseman, Philadelphia Phillies, $2,127,333
4. Don Mattingly, first baseman, New York Yankees, $1,975,000
5. Ozzie Smith, shortstop, St. Louis Cardinals, $1,940,000
6. Gary Carter, catcher, New York Mets, $1,925,571
7. Dale Murphy, outfielder, Atlanta Braves, $1,900,000
8. Dave Winfield, outfielder, New York Yankees, $1,861,460
9. Jack Morris, pitcher, Detroit Tigers, $1,850,000
10. Fernando Valenzuela, pitcher, Los Angeles Dodgers, $1,850,000

Source: Sports Illustrated, April 20, 1987.

Exhibit 11-4   Base Salaries of Highest Salaried Players in Football, Major League Baseball, Basketball, and Hockey

sions that outline general benefits. There are also noneconomic concerns that the players' union will make known when negotiating a CBA. These include player contracts, regulation of player agents, players' medical rights, noninjury grievance procedures, rules impact, joint counseling programs, and drug-testing policies.

Salary Information

Base salaries that are negotiated by the agent for the client are often just a part of the total package of benefits outlined in the contract. However, the base salary is often the means by which an athlete weighs his or her net worth in comparison to other athletes in the sport. The following exhibits show a variety of salary information for the four major sports. Exhibit 11–4 details the salaries of the ten highest salaried players in each of the four major

National Basketball Association*

1. Larry Bird, forward, Boston Celtics, $1,800,000
2. Moses Malone, center, Philadelphia 76ers, $1,600,000
3. Jack Sikma center, Seattle Sonics, $1,600,000
4. Kareem Abdul Jabbar, center, Los Angeles Lakers, $1,500,000
5. Julius Erving, forward, Philadelphia 76ers, $1,250,000
6. Ralph Sampson, forward, Houston Rockets, $1,200,000
7. Otis Birdsong, guard, New Jersey Nets, $1,075,000
8. Seven tied at $1,000,000
   (Earvin Johnson, Los Angeles Lakers; Kevin McHale, Boston Celtics; Jim Paxon, Portland Trail Blazers; Mychal Thompson, Portland Trail Blazers; Wayne Rollins, Atlanta Hawks; Marques Johnson, Los Angeles Clipper; Isiah Thomas, Detroit Pistons)

National Hockey League*

1. Wayne Gretzky, forward, Edmonton Oilers, $825,000
2. Mike Bossy, forward, New York Islanders, $610,000
3. Marcel Dionne, forward, Los Angeles Kings, $475,000
4. Dave Taylor, forward, Los Angeles Kings, $450,000
5. Bryan Trottier, forward, New York Islanders, $450,000
6. Denis Potvin, defenseman, New York Islanders, $425,000
7. Mike Liut, goalie, St. Louis Blues, $400,000
8. Barry Beck, defenseman, New York Rangers, $385,000
9. Gil Perreault, forward, Buffalo Sabres, $375,000
10. Kent Nilsson, forward, Calgary Flames, $360,000

*(As of 1985)

Exhibit 11-4 Continued

professional sports. Exhibit 11–5 shows how the average and minimum salaries of Major League Baseball players have increased over the period from 1967 to 1987. Exhibit 11–6 examines the number of years that a player has served in Major League Baseball and compares this to the average salary at each experience level. Exhibit 11–7 shows a salary survey of the National Hockey League players. Exhibit 11–8 gives the average salaries earned by National Football League players during the 1986 season, and Exhibit 11–9 details the compensation that was awarded to players who were drafted in the first five rounds of the 1986 NFL draft.

Major League Baseball has the most extensive minor league system, and because the players in the minors are not represented by a union, the parent teams exercise strict control over salaries. In fact, the contract salary is set by the Major League Rules and published in the *Baseball Blue Book*. According to the *1987 Blue*

Year	Minimum Salary	Average Salary
1967	$ 6,000	$ 19,000
1968[a]	10,000	N.A.
1969	10,000	24,909
1970	12,000	29,303
1971	12,750	31,543
1972	13,500	34,092
1973	15,000	36,566
1974	15,000	40,839
1975	16,000	44,676
1976	19,000	51,501
1977	19,000	76,066
1978	21,000	99,876
1979	21,000	113,558[b]
1980	30,000	143,756[b]
1981	32,500	185,651[b]
1982	33,500	241,497[b]
1983	35,000	289,194[b]
1984	40,000	329,408[b]
1985	60,000	340,000
1986	62,000	N.A.
1987	62,500	410,732

[a]First basic agreement between clubs and Major League Players Association.

[b]Salary figures have been discounted for salary deferrals without interest at a rate of 9% per year for the period of delayed payments.

Exhibit 11-5 Average Salaries, Major League Baseball, 1967–1987 *Source*: Major League Baseball Players Association.

Book, players in the minor leagues at all levels in their first contract season are paid $700 per month, and those at the AA or AAA level may be increased up to $850 per month at the discretion of the team if the player is retained on the active list for a minimum of 30 days. The teams compensate for the inflexible salary by enticing the athlete with signing and incentive bonuses and a college scholarship plan that the club agrees to provide for the athlete's schooling at an accredited college or university (subject to certain restrictions regarding cost and time).

Service (through 1983)

At Least	But Less Than	No. of Players	Mean Salary*
15		22	705,352
14	15	6	674,573
13	14	15	625,435
12	13	22	512,591
11	12	25	618,793
10	11	27	570,518
9	10	31	607,672
8	9	37	472,929
7	8	37	562,126
6	7	44	536,722
5	6	45	422,540
4	5	51	412,050
3	4	57	310,054
2	3	69	200,251
1	2	83	103,234
0	1	158	51,908

*Salary figures have been discounted for salary deferrals without interest at a rate of 9 percent per year for the period of delayed payments.

Exhibit 11-6 Average Salary vs. Years of Service, Major League Baseball, 1984 *Source*: Major League Baseball Players Association.

PLAYER AGENTS

A player agent, also called a player representative, is a person authorized by another person to act in his or her name. The promise of compensation is not required to establish the relationship, although such compensation is usually presumed. The NCAA constitution prohibits college student-athletes from using player agents, stating:

Any individual who contracts or who has ever contracted orally or in writing to be represented by an agent in the marketing of the individual's athletic ability or reputation in a sport no longer shall be eligible for intercollegiate athletics in that sport. An agency contract not specifically limited in writing to a particular sport or particular sports shall be deemed applicable to all sports. Securing advice from a lawyer concerning a proposed professional sports

Salary Range (000's)	Forwards (No. Players)	Defensemen (No. Players)	Goalies (No. Players)	Total (No. Players)	Percent
Under 50					
51– 60	—	1	—	1	0.2%
61– 70	5	4	—	9	2.0%
71– 80	19	9	4	32	7.0%
81– 90	41	21	3	65	14.3%
91–100	32	16	7	55	12.1%
101–110	28	10	1	39	8.6%
111–120	21	5	2	28	6.2%
121–130	15	13	3	31	6.8%
131–140	11	12	5	28	6.2%
141–150	15	12	6	33	7.2%
151–160	9	5	—	14	3.1%
161–170	16	7	—	23	5.1%
171–180	11	5	2	18	4.0%
181–190	3	—	1	4	0.9%
191–200	11	1	4	16	3.5%
201–300	23	14	3	40	8.8%
Over 300	11	5	1	17	4.0%
Total	271	140	42	453	100.0%
Median Salary	$114,700	$123,500	$132,000	$120,000	
Average Age	24.7	24.9	26.2	25.0	
Average Yrs. Pro	4.6	4.7	6.2	4.8	
Nos. in Option Yr.	34.0	20.0	6.0	60.0	13.2

Note: 352 players from 21 clubs responded to this survey by the NHL Players' Association.

Exhibit 11-7   Salary Survey, National Hockey League Players Association, October 1984

contract shall not be considered contracting for representation by an agent under this rule unless the lawyer also represents the student-athlete in negotiations for such a contract. . . . [*1987–88 NCAA Manual*, Constitution 3-1-(c)]

Because several player agents have represented student-athletes in contract negotiations under the guise of supplying legal advice, the NCAA Council issued a clarification concerning the use of legal counsel by student-athletes. The council asserted that any student-athlete may retain counsel for the purpose of reviewing a contract offered by a professional team. However, the student-athlete who decides to have legal counsel contact a professional team concerning the contract offer has effectively hired counsel as an agent and is no longer eligible. Additionally, the NCAA specifies that a contract which is executed and does not specifically refer to a particular sport will be considered applicable to all sports. Also, any type of agency contract is prohibited, including present contracts for provision of future services. This rule applies at all times, and therefore includes those contracts made prior to matriculation at college.

At its 1984 convention, the NCAA approved a plan, recommended by its Special Committee on Player Agents, under which athletics career counseling panels would be established to assist student-athletes who are contemplating foregoing their remaining college eligibility to pursue a career in professional sports (*1987–88 NCAA Manual*, Constitution 3-1-[h]-[4]). In addition, should the athlete opt for a professional career, the panel would assist in the selection of a competent representative or agent. Representatives would be selected from a list of player agents who have registered with the NCAA. The player-agent registration materials were approved by the NCAA Special Committee on Player Agents in May 1984 (see Exhibits 11–10 and 11–11). The committee has also considered a program of sanctions against registered agents who violate their agreement with the NCAA.

Player representatives are a relatively recent phenomenon in collegiate sports. The growth of professional leagues, teams, and salaries since the late 1960s has made athlete representation a very lucrative and extremely competitive business. Agents use a variety of methods to charge their clients for services rendered. The most common is for an agent to take a percentage of the total value of the player contract—anywhere from 3 to 10 percent. Some agents will represent a player in a contract negotiation for a predetermined fee, regardless of the time spent or the amount of the contract. Agents may also elect to charge an hourly rate for each hour spent working for the athlete—usually between $100 and

1986 Average Salaries

Team (No.)	Salary	Base
N.Y. Jets (51)	$260,000	$239,000
San Francisco (56)	259,709	229,196
San Diego (50)	243,455	198,670
L.A. Raiders (56)	239,169	228,223
Dallas (57)	231,052	180,026
Kansas City (56)	228,664	174,182
Seattle (51)	226,006	193,617
N.Y. Giants (51)	225,856	186,274
Washington (59)	214,974	178,194
New England (59)	214,899	205,855
Miami (54)	213,277	195,972
Cincinnati (50)	209,285	165,985
L.A. Rams (53)	203,839	175,594
St. Louis (54)	200,006	175,181
Chicago (56)	200,955	199,722
Atlanta (58)	198,380	160,297
Tampa Bay (54)	195,588	169,549
Cleveland (58)	195,051	197,465
Green Bay (55)	186,845	157,445
Indianapolis (52)	185,942	153,730
New Orleans (62)	185,387	161,798
Detroit (50)	184,215	160,645
Buffalo (62)	176,110	165,731
Minnesota (52)	175,326	154,096
Philadelphia (51)	169,242	162,867
Pittsburgh (61)	165,409	146,331
Houston (51)	159,812	151,627
Denver (53)	145,097	196,330

(The averages as of October 2 were compiled in by the NFLPA and published in Lawdible, a sports law reporting service. Denver was 28th in average salary and eighth in base because the NFLPA doesn't count deferred income in the average salary. Denver has a lot of deferred income in its contracts including John Elway's entire $900,000 base salary in 1986.)

Average Salary Leaguewide
1532 players: $203,565

Average Base Salary
$180,818

Average Salary for Starters
$256,153

Average Base for Starters
$239,759

Average Salary for Non-Starters
$163,015

Average Base for Non-Starters
$135,369

Average Salary by Position

Player (No.)	Salary	Base
Quarterback (79)	$333,591	$327,088
Running back (162)	229,304	185,379
Wide receiver (166)	197,173	174,203
Tight end (94)	164,609	156,156
Off. linemen (289)	194,706	171,060
Def. linemen (201)	225,584	189,942
Linebacker (230)	197,818	177,262
Def. back (255)	177,981	164,113
Punter (27)	107,366	109,401
Kicker (27)	166,262	151,646

Top Salary per Year

1976
O. J. Simpson, Buffalo, $733,358

1977
O. J. Simpson, Buffalo, $733,358

1978
O. J. Simpson, San Francisco, $733,358

1979
O. J. Simpson, San Francisco, $806,668

1980
Walter Payton, Chicago, $475,000

1981
Archie Manning, New Orleans, $600,000

1982
Archie Manning, New Orleans, $600,000

1983
Dan Fouts, San Diego, $750,000

1984
Joe Montana, San Francisco, $800,000

1985
Joe Montana, San Francisco, $900,000

1986
Jim Kelly, Buffalo, $1,000,000

(The figures since 1983 are for the top base salary. The previous figures included a pro-rated share of the signing bonus.)

Exhibit 11-8   Average Salaries Earned During 1986 NFL Season *Source: The Sporting News,* March 16, 1987.

	First	*Second*	*Third*	*Fourth*	*Fifth*
Average Base Salary	$161,292	$125,357	$111,731	$79,074	$71,259
Average Signing Bonuses	578,365	240,000	121,154	71,157	41,704
Average Reporting Bonuses	50,000	0	0	36,250	36,250
Average Roster Bonuses	22,500	11,000	9,333	13,000	11,167
Average Contract Length	4.1 years	3.9	3.6	3.7	3.2

Exhibit 11-9 Compensation Awarded to Players in First Five Rounds of **1986 Player Draft**

$200. The other alternative is a combination of a stated percentage (usually less than 7 percent), plus a predetermined or hourly fee, whichever is less.

The disadvantage for the athlete in agreeing to pay an hourly fee to the agent is that the athlete is obligated to that agent if he doesn't make the team. However, if the athlete makes the team, the fee based on an hourly rate may be less than the contingency fee rate. If the athlete and agent have agreed to a contingency fee, however, there is no obligation to pay the agent if the athlete does make the team. On the other hand, the athlete may find paying an hourly fee to the agent a disadvantage if the agent extends the contract negotiations ad infinitum.

These agent fees can become enormous in view of the salaries paid to some of today's superstar athletes (see Exhibit 11–4). The escalation of player salaries has made the percentage method very popular among agents (see Exhibits 11–5, 11–6, 11–7, 11–8, and 11–9). Because of the tremendous amount of money available, some agents are tempted to lure top athletes, even while they are still in school. In order to build or protect their own personal interests, some agents will contact, offer inducements to, and attempt to sign student-athletes with remaining college eligibility. They may also entice athletes to leave college early to join professional teams. Inducements may take the form of cash, "loans," and/or the use of a car or other benefits. This transfer and acceptance of money or other benefits by student-athletes is in direct conflict with the principles of amateurism and specifically violates rules related to receiving compensation or pay and limits on the amount and type of acceptable remuneration (*1987–88 NCAA Manual*, Constitution 3–1).

The offer sheet is one method by which agents may attempt to circumvent NCAA rules. An offer sheet is presented by the player agent to the student-athlete, who often mistakes it for a contract. The student-athlete signs this form prior to the expiration of college eligibility, but the agent will not sign it until after the student-athlete's eligibility has expired. Since most student-athletes are not versed in the technicalities of the requirements for a binding contract, they often believe they have a contract with the agent and will discontinue dealing with other agents. Agents who use this tactic to reserve players claim the offer sheet is not an agency contract until the representative executes the document at the close of the student-athlete's playing season. Since no contract exists, there can be no violation of NCAA rules. The NCAA, however, disagrees, believing that the substance of its rules clearly prohibits any agreements to provide future services, even if the agreement does not constitute an enforceable contract.

NOTES ───

1. Some agents in the past have argued that because the NCAA does not govern player agents, members of the profession are not subject to the association's rules. Furthermore, some agents have gone as far as to publicly acknowledge that their business conduct as an agent is often in "constant and conscious violation of NCAA rules." (See "Some Offers They Couldn't Refuse," *Sports Illustrated*, May 21, 1979, p. 28.)

2. The player's responsibility to the agent upon signing an offer sheet may be an area of contention. In 1979, a suit was filed against O. J. Anderson, a former University of Miami football player. The suit alleged breach of contract and damages in the amount of $52,000. Anderson had signed an offer sheet with an agent before his eligibility had expired. Immediately upon Anderson's expiration of eligibility, the agent signed the offer sheet and had it notarized. Subsequently, Anderson decided that he did not want the agent to represent him, and the agent filed the suit in an attempt to enforce the offer sheet agreement. The suit was settled before trial.

3. When a coach acts as an adviser concerning a student-athlete's professional prospects, does this make the coach an agent? Is the coach's role thus incompatible with NCAA rules? Technically, any person who agrees to help a student-athlete deal with professional offers is an agent. Therefore, a coach who acts as a buffer between a student-athlete and agents or professional teams, when such action is done with the consent and knowledge of the student-athlete, is arguably an agent, even if no compensation or promise of compensation is involved.

This problem was the focus of an NCAA investigation involving George Rogers, a star running back at the University of South Carolina, and his coach, Jim Carlen. The NCAA decided that Carlen was not acting as Rogers's agent, even though the coach admitted acting as a buffer for

Rogers. Carlen had done so to protect Rogers from tempting offers that might affect his playing eligibility. The NCAA did not further clarify the basis for the agent-buffer distinction.

4. Former Iona College (New York) basketball player Jeff Ruland lost his eligibility for his senior year of competition when it was discovered that he had signed a personal management contract with a professional agent. Although both Ruland and his agent initially repudiated the arrangement, the agent later divulged that under the terms of their agreement he was to receive 10 percent of Ruland's gross earnings for the next four years. He also asserted that he had given the basketball player both cash and gifts and had provided financial management services. While Ruland stated publicly that he considered any arrangement with the agent to be null and void, the representative made it clear that any attempt to replace him would be dealt with in court.

During the controversy, Iona College maintained the position that Ruland had been "sweet-talked" into the agreement in violation of NCAA rules. Ruland, who went on to play professional basketball, acknowledged his relationship with the agent a year later. While admitting that his actions had been in violation of NCAA standards, Ruland commented that the practice of dealing with professional agents was commonplace among college student-athletes.

5. In October 1984, Mike Rozier, former University of Nebraska star running back and 1983 Heisman Trophy winner, revealed that while still under NCAA eligibility regulations, he accepted money from an agent and negotiated a professional football contract with the USFL's Pittsburgh Maulers. Both acts were violations of NCAA regulations. Rozier accepted a total of $2,400 during his last intercollegiate season. His contract with the Maulers was finalized a few days before the Orange Bowl in Miami, and was signed hours after the completion of the game. Rozier claimed that he made his revelations because he was ashamed and hoped that young athletes could learn from his mistakes. For further details of this incident, see "The Year the Heisman Went to a Pro," *Sports Illustrated*, October 22, 1984, p. 21.

6. Leigh Steinberg, a leading sports agent and head of the Ethics Committee of the Association of Representatives of Professional Agents, in October 1984, alleged that "At least one third of the top athletes in college football and basketball are signing early every year. It is usually done in return for money payments. It is an open secret that no one wants to talk about. It is unconscionable." Steinberg suggested that increasing scholarship monies awarded by the schools might take some of the pressure off the student-athletes to sign early with agents. For further information, see the following articles:

(a) "Steinberg: Early Signings Are Common Practice," UPI Wireservice, *Newark Star Ledger*, November 1, 1984, p. 58.

(b) "Agents Have Upper Hand with Top College Players," AP Wireservice, *Newark Star Ledger*, November 1, 1984, p. 109.

7. The following sections of "Athletic Agencies," California Labor Code, Section 1500, enacted first in 1981, are applicable to amateur athletics:

Section 1530.5. Contents of Contract; Notice Concerning Amateur Status

The contract shall contain in close proximity to the signature of the athlete a notice in at least 10-point type stating that the athlete may jeopardize his or her standing as an amateur athlete by entering into the contract.

Section 1545. Students; Filing Copies of Certificates and Contracts with Secondary or Postsecondary Educational Institutions

(a) An athlete agency shall, prior to communicating with or contacting in any manner any student concerning an agency contract or a professional sport services contract, file with the secondary or postsecondary educational institution at which the student is enrolled a copy of the registration certificate of the athlete agency.

(b) An athlete agency shall file a copy of each agency contract made with any student, with the secondary or postsecondary educational institution at which the student is enrolled, within five days after such contract is signed by the student party thereto.

(c) Filing of the copies required by subdivisions (a) and (b) shall be made with the president or chief administrative officer of the secondary or postsecondary educational institution, or the secretary of such officer, or by registered or certified mail, return receipt requested, directed to such officer.

For further information on agent registration in California, see page 567 and Sobel, "The Regulation of Player Agents: State of California, NFL Players Association, and NCAA Adopt Rules to Regulate Athletes' Agents," 5 *Entertainment Law Reporter* 10 (March 1984).

8. In 1984, the NCAA Council approved a voluntary player-agent registration program to begin in the 1984–85 academic year. The NCAA's purpose was to provide its member institutions and their student-athletes with a reliable system of gathering information on player agents so they could make decisions concerning representation. In registering with the NCAA, an agent agrees to notify (as opposed to seek permission from) directors of athletics prior to contacts with enrolled student-athletes.

In conjunction with the registration program, the NCAA also suggested that the member institutions implement counseling panels to help their student-athletes make career decisions (*1987–88 NCAA Manual*, Constitution 3-1-[h]-[4]). The NCAA makes available to member institutions a booklet, "A Career in Professional Sports: Guidelines That Make Dollars and Sense," which the association recommends be used as background information for student-athletes.

9. The University of Illinois has the following policy concerning player agents:

> In recent years player agents, with or without knowledge of the NCAA rules and regulations, have prematurely talked with, advised, and signed athletes with remaining eligibility to professional contracts, thus ending a player's collegiate eligibility. Therefore, it is essential that all coaching and administrative personnel be aware of and knowledgeable about NCAA rules and regulations relating to player agents. [*Policy and Procedure Manual*, The Athletic Association of the University of Illinois, 1984, section 1, p. 24 (e)]

10. Leo Zinn, the agent for Cincinnati Bengals' cornerback Lemar Parrish, was successful in recovering after Parrish terminated him in 1974 shortly after Zinn negotiated a four-year contract for Parrish. Zinn sought to recover his 10 percent commission on the 1974–1977 Bengals' contracts

and did so. The court ruled that Zinn fulfilled the terms of the contract to use reasonable efforts to procure professional football employment, despite failing to obtain jobs or contracts in many cases; it was not a failure to perform. See *Zinn v. Parrish*, 644 F.2d 360 (7th Cir. 1981).

11. Some agents have been accused of going far beyond the activities which resulted in the defenses raised by Lemar Parrish against Leo Zinn. Charges of outright fraud or embezzlement have been made and, at least in one instance, have been substantiated. Consider the following: Richard Sorkin's 1978 conviction for grand larceny represents an example of an agent misappropriating client funds. Sorkin allegedly misappropriated money from approximately 50 professional athletes he was representing, totaling more than $1.2 million. Acting as their agent and handling their funds, Sorkin had easy access to the athletes' monies and squandered their funds for his own uses, either through mob gambling or bad personal investments. See *People v. Sorkin*, No. 46429 (Nassau County, N.Y., Nov. 28, 1977), *sentence aff'd*, 407 N.Y.S.2d 772 (App. Div. 2d Dept., July 24, 1978). See also, "The Spectacular Rise and Ignoble Fall of Richard Sorkin, Pros' Agent," *New York Times*, October 9, 1977, Sec. 5, p. 1; *New York Times*, February 2, 1978, Sec. 4, p. 15.

12. Detroit Lions free agent running back Billy Sims, under the guidance of his agent Jerry Argovitz, signed a contract with the Houston Gamblers on July 1, 1983. On December 16, 1983, Sims signed a second contract with Detroit, and filed a complaint in Oakland County Circuit Court seeking a determination that the July 1, 1983 contract between Sims and the Houston Gamblers was invalid because the defendant, Jerry Argovitz, breached his fiduciary duty when negotiating the Gamblers' contract. The court concluded that Argovitz breached his duty to Sims by having significant ownership interest in the Houston franchise, and not representing him properly in contract negotiations with Detroit. The contract between Sims and Houston was rescinded by the court. See *Detroit Lions, Inc. and Sims v. Argovitz*, 580 F. Supp. 542 (E.D. Mich. 1984).

13. Los Angeles Raiders running back Greg Pruitt filed a $2.4 million lawsuit in July 1984, charging his former investment adviser with securities fraud, racketeering, and embezzlement. Pruitt claimed that the adviser embezzled about $150,000 by forging Pruitt's name on checks and withdrawing money from Pruitt's account. Pruitt charged that some 156 checks were forged over a three-year period and that the adviser had made investments of Pruitt's money that yielded exceedingly low returns. The company for whom the adviser worked settled with Pruitt in late November 1984, and the suit was dropped. See *San Francisco Chronicle*, November 30, 1984, p. 87.

14. For further information on player agents, see the following:

(a) "The Offer Sheet: An Attempt to Circumvent NCAA Prohibition of Representation Contracts," 14 *Loyola University Law Review* 187 (December 1980).

(b) Ruxin, *An Athlete's Guide to Agents* (Bloomington, Indiana University Press, 1982).

(c) "Agent-Athlete Relationship in Professional and Amateur Sports:

The Inherent Potential for Abuse and the Need for Regulation," 30 *Buffalo Law Review* 815 (1981).

(d) Ruxin, "Unsportsmanlike Conduct: The Student-Athlete, the NCAA, and Agents," 8 *Journal of College and University Law* 347 (1982).

(e) "Athletics Career Counseling Panels," Legislative Assistance (column), *NCAA News*, May 30, 1984, p. 3.

(f) "Attorneys and Professional Contracts," Legislative Assistance (column), *NCAA News*, May 9, 1984, p. 7.

(g) Fox, "Regulating the Professional Sport Agent: Is California in the Right Ballpark?" 15 *Pacific Law Review* 1231 (July 1984).

(h) Massey, "The Crystal Cruise Cut Short: A Survey of the Increasing Regulatory Influence over the Athlete-Agent in the National Football League," 1 *Entertainment Sports Law Journal* 53 (1984). "Agents of Turmoil," *Sports Illustrated*, August 3, 1987, p. 34.

Functions of the Player Agent

Attorneys and agents who represent professional athletes are called on to render a wide variety of services for their clients. The diversity of services, in fact, is such that it is unreasonable to expect one individual to master all the knowledge and skills necessary to accomplish the tasks demanded. Among other realities, this has led to a separation of the law and management functions, and player representatives are examining a number of devices that would allow them to use full-service operations.

The traditional role of the player agent has been to negotiate the player's contract and represent the athlete on any other legally related issues with the club. Representation today may also include marketing of the player's name; soliciting personal appearances; and offering financial and investment advice, tax planning and tax return preparation, and personal, legal, and financial counseling. An athlete must consider either retaining independent advisers for legal, financial, and investment advice or a multifaceted management group that can provide all of these services. With demands for the full range of services coming to the fore, pressures are mounting to set up a business organization that will respond to the plethora of needs. The point to remember is that the player representative is in a business that demands a number of services. Before proceeding with other considerations, such as the legal and ethical constraints placed on player representatives, the functions themselves must be considered.

Negotiating

The player agent must be able to obtain the necessary background information, map the appropriate strategies, and have the flexibility to counter alternatives in order to represent the client effectively. When entering into a negotiation session, the agent must be prepared, not only in terms of the issues to be brought up, but also in regard to refuting or responding to management's claims. A good agent will know the market value of his client, based on salaries of comparable players (same position, ability). The agent should also have detailed information about the team with respect to his client's likelihood to succeed, chances of starting, depth at client's position, and historic negotiation outcomes. This type of preparation is of paramount importance to the agent if an optimal contract is to be negotiated.

One important point to remember in the sports context is that, in a sense, one rarely stops negotiating. The signed contract is usually only the first step. A number of occurrences during the term of the contract may call for even greater skill on the part of the negotiator, a point emphasized later in this chapter.

A second important point is the interconnections between the negotiating function and the functions described below. One cannot, and should not, attempt to isolate completely one from the others. As noted earlier, a single individual cannot effectively handle all functions, at least not in the great majority of situations. So, knowing how to deal with the overlaps while dividing the functions efficiently calls for careful thought, planning, and organizational structure.

Counseling

Counseling is an often overlooked function of vital importance, both during negotiations and after the contract is signed. Making certain the client understands what is at stake in a professional sports contract may prevent later disillusionments.

For the nonsuperstar, the contract may be largely illusory, in that it exists only if the player makes the team. There are no guarantees. Such rudimentary facts are not always grasped by the client. Making the team and contract rights are not always paired in the client's mind. Such information must be conveyed.

After the contract is signed, other problems call for counseling. For example, the player makes the team but is sitting on the bench. Personal frustrations become predominant. In this and many other contexts, the counseling function is crucial.

Managing

Many athletes come out of college with little self-discipline and an almost total lack of knowledge about financial matters. The money soon disappears if the client is left unsupervised.

Not all player representatives get into money management, and those who do not should advise the client as to where such assistance can be obtained. An ongoing relationship between the representative and a firm that deals in management and investments should be explored.

Marketing

There is a prevailing attitude, although a mistaken one, that most professional athletes do well because of lucrative endorsements and other types of outside income. In truth, such wealth is largely reserved for the top stars. Other athletes do what they can to supplement their income with personal appearances at local clubs, dinners, commercial establishments, and other less-than-top-dollar affairs. Even so, the possibilities for some types of outside income do exist. How aggressively they are sought on behalf of the client varies with the representative, but some willingness on the part of the representative to assist the client in seeking supplementary income is demanded. With that in mind, a few rules and regulations should be noted.

First, chances are that either the player's contract with the club or the league's collective bargaining agreement will have some provisions regarding endorsements. These should be reviewed before any action is taken. Second, the other side of the marketing issue is being vigilant about protecting the player's name and image. These are property rights capable of protection under a variety of legal theories, including rights of privacy and publicity. Instances in which athletes have had to resort to the courts over alleged infringements are many, although in more than one case the player was held to have signed away his rights through the broad grant contained in an earlier contract. Noting these should be fair warning to the player agent about the careless granting of rights.

Cases in this area continue to appear, as athletes are more and more often viewed as celebrities whose names and images have commercial potential. Together with the ever-growing number of cases dealing with the rights of celebrities in other entertainment areas, these cases have brought about a substantial body of law revolving around rights or privacy and publicity.

Resolving Disputes

When things have gone awry under an existing contract, and the other side is believed to have done something that must be redressed legally, the player's representative basically has two possibilities for action: arbitration and litigation. Arbitration has preempted litigation in many situations in professional sports. A player agent must thus be aware of these instances because the time period in which complaints under arbitration must be filed is often short. Rights are easily waived. The arbitration process, which is usually initiated through the players' association, is specified in the collective bargaining agreement between the association and the league. This document has become indispensable in the player agent's library. Litigation is a feasible alternative in some situations. Alleged antitrust violations by a league or a club, for example, are still the province of the courts, although the leagues have become increasingly insulated from attacks by the labor exemption existing under the Sherman and Clayton acts. Even so, the cases still come up.

Planning

An athlete's career lasts but a short time. The average career for professional athletes, assuming they make the team in the first place, is in the four- to five-year range, varying only slightly by the sport played. Thus, for many, there is never anything beyond the first contract. For this reason, the player agent must prepare the client for what will occur in the not-too-distant future. Such a task is easy to describe but hard to carry out.

Athletes may claim that they realize theirs will not be a long career, but it is hard to grasp just how short a career can be. Most players are not really prepared for the end. Their attitude is invariable—"next year, perhaps, but not now."

The player agent may be unable to cushion the psychological blow completely. The hope is that the client has had sufficient time to produce enough income so that at least some preparations can be made for the financial transition. Achieving this goal relates to the managing function, but it adds the future ingredient of careful planning. The player agent needs to obtain professional assistance in order to maximize the client's financial resources so that a bridge can be built to span the time period needed to get the athlete into a new career. A player agent in this business for any period of time will have to confront this problem.

NOTE _____

1. The following excerpts are from an information pamphlet that was sent to prospective professional athletes by a sports consulting firm that was attempting to establish itself.

What We Do

Contract negotiation: We deal directly with management to obtain the maximum commitment regarding salary, benefits and contract provisions.

Endorsements and appearances: We will seek to supplement our client's regular income by promoting product endorsements and personal appearances. We will both pursue appearance possibilities and negotiate on our client's behalf for endorsement fees.

Investments: We will review investment recommendations and proposals with our Investment Consultants. In addition, we will draw upon investment research from several investment banking and brokerage firms to augment our investment consultants.

Financial planning, insurance, legal and tax matters. We will also:
1. Evaluate our client's financial condition and establish a proper plan to insure maximum use of present and future earnings.
2. Have outside insurance consultants analyze our client's insurance programs and make recommendations as to adequacy of individual and group life, health and accident and disability insurance programs. We will make recommendations to our clients according to their needs after reviewing our consultants' proposals.
3. Provide complete legal advice in all areas of general law as they may affect our clients' needs.
4. Prepare personal Federal, State and other necessary tax returns—and—provide complete professional advice on Foreign Tax Matters, Tax-Sheltered Investments and other areas of tax specialization.

Our policy will be to care for the normal needs of the client and this effort will be incorporated into the negotiation fee.

Our clientele will be normally drawn from those who are not superstars and it is our feeling that we should not charge them excessively. We are sure that our fees are at least ½ to ⅓ of those fees charged by other people in the athletic representative field.

We want to establish a feeling of honesty and fairness with our clients. We are sure that from our clients will come superstars with whom we will become more involved. But, we will always maintain a policy of providing low cost and honest service to the average professional athlete.

In most cases, our advice to the athletes will be to let their money grow in savings or in AAA bonds. Then, when they have reached superstar status and/or have a large enough cash base, we will have them diversify their investments.

Outside Consultants

Investment advisers. We will receive investment advice from professional investment counselors and investment banking and brokerage firms. Our investment counselors include:

Investment Banking and Brokerage Houses.

We work closely with several brokerage houses including [names of firms]. Investment research and recommendations which are acted upon by us will realize brokerage commissions to those firms. Therefore, there will be no outside fee expense in conjunction with such investments.

Attorneys and tax specialists. We receive legal and tax advice from several major law firms.

Insurance, pensions, profit sharing, etc. Our insurance consultants include representatives and managers of several major Insurance Companies—to include: [names of firms].

Advertising consultants. Our Advertising Consultants are creative directors, artists and copy writers at several Advertising Agencies and provide leads of client firms seeking professional athletes as well as advice on public relations, fee schedules and promotions.

Regulation of Player Agents

A good deal of notoriety has surrounded the relationship between player agents and their athlete clients. The publicity concerning those who represent players has been far from favorable. As a result, increasing scrutiny is being directed toward the player representative, leading in some instances to legal and other constraints being placed on the agent, obviously having an effect on the client relationship.

Government Regulation

California is one state that has enacted legislation directed at so-called "athlete agencies." Under Sec. 1500, et seq., of the California Labor Code, registration, bonding, and other requirements are imposed. However, the code's description of an athlete agency "does not include any employee of a professional sports team, and does not include any member of the State Bar of California when acting as legal counsel for any person." Just who constitutes "legal counsel" can obviously be tricky, particularly for the sports attorney who wishes to go beyond contract negotiation into some of the other activities discussed earlier. Clearly, at least for some activities, the attorney would be moving into nonlegal functions that would qualify the attorney as an "athlete agency."

Player agents have also been questioned about their activities in connection with other legal restrictions. *Zinn v. Parrish*, 644 F.2d 360 (7th Cir. 1981), raises the possibility of an agent being in violation of federal securities laws. Though the issue was ultimately resolved in favor of the agent, the message of the case sounds a warning (see Note 10 on page 560). (Also see *Detroit Lions and Sims v. Argovitz*, Note 12 on page 561.) Clearly, legislatures and courts are placing increased scrutiny on the actions of player agents.

NOTES ————————————————————

1. In 1981–82 the California Legislature enacted a bill which prevented any person from engaging in an "athlete agency" without first registering with the state's labor commissioner. The bill stipulated that agents must submit to the labor commissioner a schedule of fees to be charged and also put up a $10,000 surety bond. An agent must also file certification with a postsecondary institution prior to contacting or com-

municating with a student-athlete regarding agency. Also, any contract made with any student must be filed with the postsecondary institution within five days after the agreement is signed.

2. The senate of the California Legislature has a Select Committee on Licensed and Designated Sports, whose staff has been active in assessing the impact of the foregoing California legislation. Many are of the opinion that the statute, as originally passed, suffered from ambiguity and arguable underinclusion. Thus, the committee in 1984 proposed amendments to the California law that would change the current registration system to a licensing system. The most significant change would seem to be in defining which "agents" must be licensed—in particular, the new category characterized as "attorney agent." Though the amendments were not approved in 1984, their chances of eventual passage are strong. Accordingly, the definitional language is included here for analysis. Proposed new language appears in italics.

SEC. 2. Section 1500 of the Labor Code is amended to read:

1500. The following definitions shall govern the construction of this chapter:

(a) "Person" means any individual, company, corporation, association, partnership, or their agents or employees.

(b) "Athlete agency" *"agent"* means any person who, as an independent contractor, directly or indirectly, recruits or solicits any person to enter into any agency *agent* contract or professional sport services contract, or for a fee procures, offers, promises, or attempts to obtain employment for any person with a professional sport team.

"Athlete agency" *"agent"* does not include any employee of a professional sport team, and does not include any member of the State Bar of California when acting as legal counsel for any person.

(b) *"Attorney agent" means any member of the State Bar of California who, as an independent contractor, or in conjunction with a firm, directly or indirectly recruits or solicits any person to enter into an agent contract or professional sport services contract, or for a fee procures, offers, promises, or attempts to obtain employment for any person with a professional sport team.*

(c) *"Agent" means both athlete agent and attorney agent.*

(d) *"Agent"* contract" means any contract or agreement pursuant to which a person authorizes or empowers an athlete agency *agent* to negotiate or solicit on behalf of such *the* person with one or more professional sport teams for the employment of such *the* person by one or more professional sport teams.

(e) "Professional sport services contract" means any contract or agreement pursuant to which a person is employed or agrees to render services as a participant or player on a professional sport team.

3. Discussion of the California legislation, as originally enacted, can be found in the following articles:

(a) Fox, "Regulating the Professional Sports Agent: Is California in the Right Ballpark?" 15 *Pacific Law Journal* 1231 (1984).

(b) Sobel, "The Regulation of Player Agents," *Entertainment Law Reporter* (March 1984), p. 3.

4. The state of Oklahoma was one of the early states to pass legislation specifically aimed at controlling player representatives in their dealings

with NCAA student-athletes in Oklahoma. The following excerpts are from the *Oklahoma Statutes,* title 70, section 821.61–70:

Athlete Agents [New]

§ 821.61. Definitions

A. As used in Sections 5 through 14 of this act:[1]

1. "Person" means an individual, company, corporation, association, partnership or other legal entity;

2. "Athlete agent" means a person who, directly or indirectly, recruits or solicits an athlete to enter into an agent contract or professional sport services contract with that person, or who for a fee procures, offers, promises or attempts to obtain employment for an athlete with a professional sports team;

3. "Agent contract" means any contract or agreement under which an athlete authorizes an athlete agent to negotiate or solicit on behalf of the athlete with one or more professional sports teams for the employment of the athlete by one or more professional sports teams;

4. "Oklahoma NCAA athlete" means any athlete who is eligible to participate in intercollegiate sports contests as a member of a sports team at an institution of higher education that is located in this state and that is a member of the National Collegiate Athletic Association; and

5. "Oklahoma non-NCAA athlete" means an athlete in a team sport who resides in this state who is not an Oklahoma NCAA athlete.

B. For purposes of Sections 5 through 14 of this act, execution by an athlete of a personal service contract with the owner or prospective owner of a professional sports team for the purpose of future athletic services is equivalent to employment with a professional sports team.

Added by Laws 1985, c. 354, § 5, emerg. eff. July 30, 1985.

§ 821.62. Registration of agents

A. Unless an athlete agent is registered with the Secretary of State as provided in subsection C of this section, an athlete agent may not:

1. Contact, directly or indirectly, an Oklahoma NCAA athlete while the athlete is located in this state; or

2. Contact, directly or indirectly, an Oklahoma non-NCAA athlete who has never signed a contract of employment with a professional sports team while the athlete is located in this state.

B. A registered athlete agent may make those contacts only in accordance with Sections 5 through 14 of this act.[1]

C. A written application for registration or renewal must be made to the Secretary of State on a form prescribed by the Secretary of State and must state:

1. The name of the applicant and the address of the applicant's principal place of business;

2. The business or occupation engaged in by the applicant for the five (5) years immediately preceding the date of application;

3. The applicant's formal training, practical experience and educational background in the subjects of contracts, contract negotiation, complaint resolution, arbitration or civil resolution of contract disputes, federal income taxation and federal estate planning;

4. The names and addresses of five (5) professional references;

---

[1] Sections 821.61 to 821.70 of this title.

5. The names and addresses of all athletes for whom the athlete agent is currently performing professional services;

6. The names and addresses of all athletes for whom the athlete agent has previously performed professional services, accompanied by a brief explanation of the reason the athlete agent is not currently performing professional services for the athletes; and

7. The names and addresses of all persons, except bona fide employees on stated salaries, who are financially interested as partners, associates or profit sharers in the operation of the business of the athlete agent, except that an application for registration or renewal by any member of the Oklahoma Bar Association must state only the names and addresses of those persons who are involved in the activities of the athlete agent and is not required to state the names and addresses of all persons who may be financially interested as members of a law firm or professional corporation but who do not become involved in the business of the athlete agent.

D. The registration is valid from July 1 of one year through June 30 of the following year. An initial registration is valid until the first June 30 following the date of the registration. Renewal of the registration may be made by the filing of an application for renewal and a renewal bond as provided in subsection G of this section.

E. To produce sufficient revenue to offset the expenses incurred by the Secretary of State in administering Sections 5 through 14 of this act, an annual filing fee of One Thousand Dollars ($1,000.00) shall be paid by the athlete agent.

F. When an application for registration or renewal is made and the registration process has not been completed, the Secretary of State may issue a temporary or provisional registration certificate that is valid for a period not to exceed ninety (90) days and that is subject in appropriate circumstances to the automatic and summary revocation by the Secretary of State.

G. An athlete agent must deposit with the Secretary of State, before the issuance or renewal of a registration certificate, a surety bond in the sum of One Hundred Thousand Dollars ($100,000.00). If the applicant is a member in good standing of the Oklahoma Bar Association, proof of an equivalent amount of professional liability insurance may be provided in lieu of a surety bond. The surety bonds must be payable to the state and must be conditioned that the person applying for the registration will comply with Sections 5 through 14 of this act, will pay all amounts due any individual or group of individuals when the person or the person's representative or agent has received those amounts, and will pay all damages caused to any person by reason of the intentional or unintentional misstatement, misrepresentation, fraud, deceit or any unlawful or negligent acts or omission by the registered athlete agent or the agent's representative or employee while acting within the scope of his employment. This subsection shall not limit the recovery of damages to the amount of the surety bond or the professional liability insurance.

H. If a registrant fails to file a new bond or new proof of professional liability insurance with the Secretary of State before the expiration of the thirtieth day after the date of receipt of notice of cancellation by the surety of the bond or the issuer of the insurance, the registration issued to the athlete agent under the bond or insurance is suspended until the time that a new surety bond or proof of insurance is filed.

I. The Secretary of State may suspend or revoke a registration for a violation of Sections 5 through 14 of this act or a rule adopted under Sections 5 through 14 of this act.

J. Fees and other funds received under Sections 5 through 14 of this act by the Secretary of State shall be deposited in the State Treasury to the credit of the General Revenue Fund.

Added by Laws 1985, c. 354, § 6, emerg. eff. July 30, 1985.

§ 821.63. Agent's contract—Schedule of fees—Maximum fee

A. Any agent contract to be used by a registered athlete agent with an Oklahoma non-NCAA athlete who has never before signed a contract of employment with a professional sports team must be on a form approved by the Secretary of State. This approval may not be withheld unless the proposed form of agent contract is unfair, unjust and oppressive to the athlete.

B. The following provision must be printed on the face of the agent contract in prominent type: "This athlete agent is registered with the Secretary of State of the State of Oklahoma. Registration does not imply approval or endorsement by the Secretary of State of the specific terms and conditions of this contract or the competence of the athlete agent."

C. A registered athlete agent must file with the Secretary of State a schedule of fees that the agent may charge to and collect from an Oklahoma non-NCAA athlete who has never before signed a contract of employment with a professional sports team and must file a description of the various professional services to be rendered in return for each fee. The athlete agent may impose charges only in accordance with the fee schedule. Changes in the fee schedule may be made from time to time, but a change does not become effective until the seventh day after the date the change is filed with the Secretary of State.

D. If a multiyear professional sport services contract is negotiated by a registered athlete agent for an Oklahoma non-NCAA athlete who has never before signed a contract of employment with a professional sports team, the athlete agent may not collect, in any twelve-month period, for the services of the agent in negotiating the contract, a fee that exceeds the amount the athlete will receive under the contract in that twelve-month period.

E. A registered athlete agent shall file with the Secretary of State a copy of an agent contract made with an Oklahoma non-NCAA athlete who has never before signed a contract of employment with a professional sports team. If the Oklahoma non-NCAA athlete is a student at an institution of higher education located in this state, the athlete agent also shall file the contract with the athletic director of the institution. The contract must be filed not later than the fifth day after the date the contract is signed by the athlete. An agent contract may be terminated by the athlete before the expiration of the tenth day after the date the contract has been filed as provided by this section.

Added by Laws 1985, c. 354, § 7, emerg. eff. July 30, 1985.

§ 821.64. Prohibited activities

A registered athlete agent may not:

1. Sell, transfer or give away any interest in or the right to participate in the profits of the athlete agent without the prior written consent of the Secretary of State;

2. Publish or cause to be published any false, fraudulent or misleading information, representation, notice or advertisement;

3. Advertise by means of cards, circulars or signs, or in newspapers and other publications, or use letterheads, receipts or blanks unless the adver-

tisement, letterhead, receipt or blank is printed and contains the registered name and address of the athlete agent;

4. Give any false information or make any false promises or representations concerning any employment to any person;

5. Divide fees with or receive compensation from a professional sports league or franchise, or its representative or employee;

6. Enter into any agreement, written or oral, by which the athlete agent offers anything of value, including the rendition of free or reduced-price legal services, to any employee of an institution of higher education located in this state in return for the referral of any clients by that employee;

7. Offer anything of value, excluding reasonable entertainment expenses and transportation expenses to and from the athlete agent's registered principal place of business, to induce an Oklahoma non-NCAA athlete who has never before signed a contract of employment with a professional sports team, to enter into an agreement, written or oral, by which the athlete agent will represent the athlete; or

8. Except as provided in Section 9 of this act,[1] contact, directly or indirectly, an Oklahoma NCAA athlete to discuss the athlete agent's representation of the athlete in the marketing of the athlete's athletic ability or reputation or enter into any agreement, written or oral, by which the athlete agent will represent the athlete, until after completion of the athlete's last intercollegiate contest, including postseason games, and may not enter an agreement before the athlete's last intercollegiate contest that purports to take effect at a time after that contest is completed.

Added by Laws 1985, c. 354, § 8, emerg. eff. July 30, 1985.

§ 821.65. On-campus agent interviews

If an institution of higher education located in this state elects to sponsor athlete agent interviews on its campus before the Oklahoma NCAA athlete's final year of NCAA eligibility, a registered athlete agent may interview with the athlete to discuss the athlete agent's representation of the athlete in the marketing of the athlete's athletic ability or reputation. The athlete agent shall strictly adhere to the specific rules of each separate electing institution with regard to the time, place and duration of the athlete agent interviews. The interviews must be conducted in that final year during a period not to exceed ten (10) consecutive days.

Added by Laws 1985, c. 354, § 9, emerg. eff. July 30, 1985.

§ 821.66. Violations—Penalties

A. A registered athlete agent who violates the provisions of subsections A or B of Section 6 of this act[2] or the provisions of Section 8 of this act[3] is subject to:

1. Payment of a civil penalty not to exceed Ten Thousand Dollars ($10,000.00) to be determined by the seriousness of the violation;

2. Forfeiture of any right of repayment of anything of value either received by an Oklahoma NCAA athlete as an inducement to enter into any agent contract or received by an athlete before completion of the athlete's last intercollegiate contest;

3. Payment of a refund of any consideration paid to the athlete agent on an athlete's behalf; and

---

[1]Section 821.65 of this title.
[2]Section 821.62 of this title.
[3]Section 821.64 of this title.

4. Payment of reasonable attorney's fees and court costs incurred by an athlete in suing an athlete agent for a violation of this act.

B. Any agent contract that is negotiated by an athlete agent who has failed to comply with this act is void.

C. An athlete agent commits an offense if the agent knowingly or intentionally violates the provisions of subsection A of Section 6 of this act or the provisions of Section 8 of this act. An offense under this subsection is a misdemeanor and shall be punishable by a fine of not more than Five Hundred Dollars ($500.00), or by imprisonment of not to exceed one (1) year, or by both such fine and imprisonment.

Added by Laws 1985, c. 354, § 10, emerg. eff. July 30, 1985.

§ 821.67. Records to be kept by athletic agent

A. An athlete agent shall keep records approved by and filed annually with the Secretary of State. The records must contain:

1. The name and address of each person employing the athlete agent, the amount of fee received from the person and the specific services performed on behalf of the person; and

2. All travel and entertainment expenditures incurred by the athlete agent, including food, beverages, maintenance of a hospitality room, sporting events, theatrical and musical events and any transportation, lodging or admission expenses incurred in connection with the entertainment.

B. The records kept by the athlete agent under paragraph 2 of subsection A of this section must adequately describe the:

1. Nature of the expenditure;
2. Dollar amount of the expenditure;
3. Purpose of the expenditure;
4. Date and place of the expenditure; and
5. Person or persons in whose behalf the expenditure was made.

Added by Laws 1985, c. 354, § 11, emerg. eff. July 30, 1985.

§ 821.68. Implementing rules and regulations

The Secretary of State may adopt rules necessary to carry out Sections 5 through 14 of this act.[1]

Added by Laws 1985, c. 354, § 12, emerg. eff. July 30, 1985.

§ 821.69. Application of act

Sections 5 through 14 of this act[1] apply only to actions performed on or after the effective date of this act.

Added by Laws 1985, c. 354, § 13, emerg. eff. July 30, 1985.

§ 821.70. Time for registration and compliance with act

An athlete agent is not required to be registered and is not required to comply with this Sections 5 through 14 of[1] act[2] until October 1, 1985.

Added by Laws 1985, c. 354, § 14, emerg. eff. July 30, 1985.

5. In addition to California and Oklahoma, the following states passed legislation in 1987 dealing with agents: Louisiana (*Revised Statutes*, Title 4, Chapter 7, secs. 421–430); Alabama (Alabama Athlete Agents Regulatory Act of 1987, House bill 667); and Texas.

6. For further information on the regulation of agents, see the following articles:

---

[1]Sections 821.61 to 821.70 of this title.
[2]So in enrolled bill. Probably should read "Sections 5 through 14 of this act."

(a) Ruschmann, "Are Sports Agents Racing a Regulatory Blitz?" *Michigan Bar Journal* 1124 (November 1986).

(b) Nimoy and Hamilton, "Attorneys and the California Athlete Agencies Act: The Toll of the Bill," *Commercial/Entertainment Law Journal* 551 (Summer 1985).

(c) "Agent-Athlete Relationship in Professional and Amateur Sports: The Inherent Potential for Abuse and the Need for Regulation," 30 *Buffalo Law Review* 815 (Fall 1981).

Ethical Constraints

The player representative who is also an attorney faces the constraints imposed by the canons of ethics. This can be particularly troublesome when competing with nonlawyers who do not face similar requirements. Issues relating to solicitation are foremost among these concerns.

Another ethical area is somewhat more subtle. This relates to dealing with student-athletes who still have remaining college athletic eligibility. Under the NCAA rules, any number of activities involving the athlete with a prospective representative may cause forfeiture of the athlete's remaining eligibility. While these regulations do not impose restrictions directly on the player representative, they do raise ethical issues for that person. It is also possible that a court might view a representative's activities, whereby the representative causes an athlete to lose eligibility, as constituting "unclean hands." This could affect the representative's legal remedies in certain situations.

NOTE ───

1. The American Bar Association's Ethical Code (EC) of Professional Responsibility states:

[A] lawyer should maintain high standards of professional conduct and should encourage fellow lawyers to do likewise. He should be temperate and dignified, and he should refrain from all illegal and morally reprehensible conduct. . . .

EC 2–3 Advice is proper only if motivated by a desire to protect one who does not recognize that he may have legal problems or who is ignorant of his legal rights or obligations. Hence the advice is improper if motivated by a desire to obtain personal benefit, secure personal publicity, or cause litigation to be brought merely to harass or injure another.

EC 2–4 A lawyer who volunteers advice that one should obtain the services of a lawyer generally should not himself accept employment, compensation or other benefit in connection with that matter.

These considerations should be followed by all American Bar Association members. Nevertheless, the position of player representative allows for opportunities to violate some of these recommendations.

NCAA Regulations

The NCAA has recently become more concerned with the actions of player agents, particularly as they relate to on-campus solicitation of student-athletes. Accounts of former college athletes stating that they had received illegal payments from agents while still in school have caused the NCAA to crack down in this area (see Chapter 5).

In 1982 the NCAA prepared a manual called "A Career in Professional Sports: Guidelines That Make Dollars and Sense." This booklet was designed to help students obtain competent representation. It provides a more general discussion of the NCAA's athlete-representation regulations, which are found in Article 3 of the NCAA Constitution. The following excerpts are from Article 3:

Section I. Principle of Amateurism and Student Participation
An amateur student-athlete is one who engages in a particular sport for the educational, physical, mental and social benefits derived therefrom and to whom participation in that sport is an avocation. . . .

(a) An individual shall not be eligible for participation in an intercollegiate sport if the individual:

(1) Takes or has taken pay, or has accepted the promise of pay, in any form, for participation in that sport, including the promise of pay when such pay is to be received following completion of the intercollegiate career; or

(2) Has entered into an agreement of any kind to compete in professional athletics in that sport or to negotiate a professional contract in the sport; or

(3) Has directly or indirectly used athletic skill for pay in any form in that sport; however, a student-athlete may accept or have accepted scholarships or educational grants-in-aid administered by an educational institution which do not conflict with the governing legislation of this Association, and may receive compensation authorized by the United States Olympic Committee to cover financial loss occurring as a result of absence from employment to prepare for or participate in the Olympic Games . . . and may borrow against his or her future earnings potential from an established, accredited commercial lending institution exclusively for the purpose of purchasing insurance (with no cash surrender value) against a disabling injury that would prevent the individual from pursuing his or her chosen career, provided no third party is involved in arrangements for securing the loan. . . .

(b) Any individual who signs or who has ever signed a contract or commitment of any kind to play professional athletics in a sport, regardless of its legal enforceability or the consideration (if any) received; plays or has ever played on any professional athletic team in a sport, or receives or has ever received, directly or indirectly, a salary, reimbursement of expenses or any other form of financial assistance from a professional organization in a sport based upon athletic skill or participation, except as permitted by the governing legislation of this Association, no longer shall be eligible for inter-collegiate athletics in that sport.

(1) A student-athlete shall be eligible although, prior to en-rollment in a collegiate institution, the student-athlete may have tried out at his or her own expense with a professional athletic team in a sport or received not more than one expense-paid visit from any one professional organization in a sport, provided such a visit did not exceed 48 hours and any payment or compensation in connection with the visit was not in excess of actual and necessary expenses.

(2) A student-athlete shall not try out with a professional athletic team in a sport during any part of the academic year (i.e., from the beginning of the fall term through completion of the spring term, including any intervening vacation period) while enrolled in a collegiate institution as a regular student in at least a minimum full-time academic load, unless the student-athlete may try out with a professional organization in a sport during the summer or during the academic year while not a full-time student, provided the student-athlete does not receive any form of expenses or other compensation from the professional organization.

(c) Any individual who contracts or who has ever contracted orally or in writing to be represented by an agent in the marketing of the individual's athletic ability or reputation in a sport no longer shall be eligible for intercollegiate athletics in that sport. An agency contract not specifically limited in writing to a particular sport or particular sports shall be deemed applicable to all sports. Securing advice from a lawyer concerning a proposed professional sports contract shall not be considered contracting for representation by an agent under this rule unless the lawyer also represents the student-athlete in negotiations for such a contract. Any individual agency or organization representing a prospective student-athlete for compensation in placing the prospect in a collegiate institution as a recipient of athletically related financial aid shall be considered an agent or organization marketing the athletic ability or reputation of the individual.

(d) An individual may participate singly or as a member of a team against professional athletes; but if the individual participates or has ever participated on a team known to the individual or which reasonably should have been known to the individual to be a professional team in that sport, that individual no longer shall be eligible for intercollegiate athletics in that sport. . . .

0.1.3. A professional team shall be any organized team which is a member of a recognized professional sports organization, which is directly supported or sponsored by a professional team or professional sports organization, which is a member of a playing league that is directly supported or sponsored by a professional team or professional sports organization or on which there is an athlete receiving directly or indirectly payment of any kind from a professional team or professional sports organization for the athlete's participation.

0.1.4. A noncollegiate amateur team or playing league which receives financial support from a national amateur sports administrative organization or an administrative equivalent, either of which receives developmental funds from a professional team or professional sports organization, shall not be considered a professional team or league.

0.1.5. An individual may compete on tennis or golf teams with persons who are competing for cash or a comparable prize, provided the individual does not receive payment of any kind for such participation.

(e) Subsequent to becoming a student-athlete . . . an individual shall not be eligible for participation in intercollegiate athletics if the individual accepts any remuneration for or permits the use of his or her name or picture to directly advertise, recommend or promote the sale or use of a commercial product or service of any kind or receives remuneration for endorsing a commercial product or service through the individual's use of such product or service.

(1) If a student-athlete's appearance on radio or television is related in any way to athletic ability or prestige, the student-athlete shall not receive under any circumstances remuneration for that appearance; nor shall the student-athlete make any endorsement, expressed or implied, of any commercial product or service. The student-athlete may, however, receive legitimate and normal expenses directly related to such an appearance.

(2) It is permissible for a student-athlete's name or picture or the group picture of an institution's athletic squad to appear in an advertisement of a particular business, commercial product or service provided the advertisement does not include a reproduction of the product with which the business is associated or any other item or description identifying the business or service other than its name or trademark; there is no indication in the makeup or wording of the advertisement that the squad members, individually or collectively, or the institution endorse the product or service of the advertiser, and the student-athlete has not signed a consent or

release granting permission to use the student-athlete's name or picture in a manner inconsistent with the requirements of this paragraph.

(3) It is permissible for a student-athlete's name or picture to appear in books, articles or other publications, films, videotapes or other types of electronic reproduction related to sport skill demonstration, analysis or instruction provided such print and electronic media productions are for educational purposes, there is no indication that the student-athlete expressly or implicitly endorses a commercial product or service, the student-athlete shall not receive under any circumstances any remuneration or expenses for such participation, and the student-athlete has signed a release statement that conditions the use of the student-athlete's name or image in a manner consistent with the requirements of this subparagraph and has filed a copy of the statement with the member institution in which the student is enrolled.

(f) Compensation may be paid to a student-athlete only for work actually performed and at a rate commensurate with the going rate in that locality for services of like character. Such compensation may not include any remuneration for value or utility which the student-athlete may have for the employer because of the publicity, reputation, fame or personal following the student-athlete has obtained because of athletic ability. A student-athlete who receives compensation prohibited under this legislation no longer shall be eligible for participation in intercollegiate athletics, unless the compensation is authorized by the United States Olympic Committee to cover financial loss occurring as a result of absence from employment to prepare for or participate in the Olympic Games.

(1) A student-athlete may serve as a coach or an instructor for compensation in a physical education class outside of the student-athlete's institution in which the student-athlete teaches sports techniques or skills or both, but a student-athlete shall not be so employed if the employment is arranged by the student-athlete's institution or a representative of its athletic interests.

(2) A student-athlete may not receive compensation for teaching or coaching sports skills or techniques in the student-athlete's sport on a fee-for-lesson basis.

(3) A student-athlete may be employed by his or her institution to work in the institution's summer camp unless otherwise restricted by the provisions of the bylaws and interpretations relating to playing and practice seasons and summer camps.

(4) A student-athlete may officiate games or contests for compensation except those involving teams which are members of or affiliated with a recognized professional sports organization. . . .

The NCAA has implemented two programs which it believes will improve the agent–student-athlete relationship. First, it now permits institutions to provide counseling for student-athletes regarding a professional sports career. The goal of the counseling is to present the athlete with information and expertise from a variety of sources in an effort to allow the athlete to better evaluate the various services provided by the payer agents.

The counseling panels are organized by the institution. The panel consists of three people from the institution who will advise the student-athlete. The guidelines by which the three-member panel are selected are left to the discretion of the university. For the most part, it is suggested that the panel consist of employees from the institution. The committee can consist of a member of the bar, a law professor, or a teacher of business law; someone who deals with financial matters; and a person chosen at random. During the actual advising and counseling sessions, no agent or prospective agent may be present. The NCAA has also recently allowed one full-time member of the athletic department staff to serve as a panel member.

The institution decides whether or not to organize these panels; they are not required by the NCAA. In institutions that have set up counseling panels, the student-athletes are able to utilize the panel's services at any time. They do not have to wait for their eligibility to expire.

Some of the responsibilities of the panel are to establish policies that indicate the manner by which an agent can contact a student-athlete, to provide support and guidance during interviews with prospective agents, and to coordinate presentations by speakers for the benefit of the student-athlete.

The second program which the NCAA has implemented is a voluntary agent registration program that is intended to foster communication between the NCAA and player agents. Exhibit 11–10 is a copy of the memorandum that the NCAA sent to player agents on September 1, 1986, outlining the two programs: student-athlete counseling and registration of player agents. Exhibit 11–11 is a player-agent registration form.

College or University Regulations

A number of NCAA members have taken their own steps to ensure that student-athletes do not lose their eligibility as a result of infractions relating to agent representation. Duke University, for example, asks all agents to register prior to visiting any athlete. The university intends to monitor the agents closely under its counseling committee (see Exhibit 11–12).

MEMORANDUM

September 1, 1986

TO: Individuals Acting in the Capacity of Player Agents.

SUBJECT: 1986–87 Player Agent Registration Program.

During the 1984–85 academic year, the NCAA initiated two programs designed to increase the information available to student-athletes concerning player agents and the transition from collegiate to professional athletics.

The first, a revision of NCAA Constitution 3-1-(h), permits an institution to provide counseling to student-athletes regarding professional careers through a panel appointed by the institution's chief executive officer consisting of institutional employees outside the athletics department. Each institution's panel will obtain information and expertise from a variety of sources (e.g., lawyers, financial consultants, professional sports teams, player associations and player agents) in an effort to provide objective information about professional career opportunities and evaluate the various services and proposals extended by player agents.

The second means for generating accurate information is through an annual registration of player agents. This voluntary program, which more than 400 agents participated in last year, is intended to foster communication between the Association and player agents. An individual registers by supplying requested educational and professional information, and returning the signed form to this office. In signing the form, you agree to notify the director of athletics (or his or her designated representative) before the first contact with an enrolled student-athlete with remaining eligibility or with the student-athlete's coach.

It is also understood that your name may be removed from the registration list if you: (a) engage in any activity prior to a student-athlete's agreement to be represented that would jeopardize the student-athlete's eligibility, or (b) fail to contact the appropriate individual prior to the first contact with enrolled student-athlete or the student-athlete's coach. A sanctioning body has been established to consider both the circumstances related to an inquiry and the agent's response in each case.

Participation in the registration program will work significantly to your advantage. Individuals on campus who strongly influence student-athletes (i.e., coaches and directors of athletics) are being urged to advise student-athletes to give consideration only to those individuals who have taken the time to complete a registration form. In addition, the list of registered agents and their affiliation with a particular agency or firm will be a primary reference for member institutions' counseling panels. Panel members will make every effort to recommend registered agents while assisting student-athletes with the selection of competent representation. Counseling panel members also are being forwarded information concerning the basic requirements for certification by the National Football League Players Association as a means for providing student-athletes additional points of reference in the selection of competent representation.

Enclosed is a registration form the Council encourages you to complete and return to this office. Registration lists will be made available to NCAA member institutions, career counseling panels and conference commissioners beginning this fall with updates throughout the academic year. The registration program is an annual procedure, and your participation is applicable to activities and contacts made during the 1986–87 academic year and ensuing summer. *Failure to complete the registration form in its entirety will result in your name not being included on the list of registered player agents.*

Exhibit 11-10   NCAA Memorandum Announcing the Player-Agent Registration Program

None of the information you provide will be released to any individual organization outside the Association (e.g., in response to media inquiries) except for a listing of registered agents and addresses. Member institutions will be provided answers to specific questions concerning information reported on the registration forms; however, duplicate copies of the completed forms will not be circulated to any institution, organization or individual. Overall statistical profiles applicable to the body of registered agents (e.g., the percentage of registered agents who currently represent athletes in the National Football League) may be generally available to you at some future point.

Finally, a copy of NCAA legislation relating to player agents accompanies the registration form. Please review these rules and regulations carefully and feel free to contact this office concerning questions you may have. You may also be interested in obtaining a copy of the NCAA Manual, which contains NCAA rules and regulations, and the NCAA Directory, which lists all NCAA member institutions, as well as the address and telephone number of each institution's director of athletics. Copies of both the NCAA Manual (available for $8) and the NCAA Directory (available for $6) may be ordered by contacting the NCAA publishing department at the address appearing on this letterhead.

If you have questions about the information provided or the registration process in general, please contact this office.

L. DOUGLAS JOHNSON
Director of Legislative Services

LDJ:lab
Enclosures

Exhibit 11-10 Continued

Players Association Certification

Largely through the impetus of player unions, various sports leagues are moving to control the player-representative relationship. Baseball has for some time required that a signed authorization by the player be filed with a club before the club will deal with that player's chosen representative.

The National Football League, as a result of provisions inserted into the 1982 collective bargaining agreement, set a precedent for all professional sports leagues. The NFL Players Association, pursuant to those provisions, has imposed registration and other requirements, including maximum fee schedules, on all who wish to act as contract advisers for NFL players.

Other professional sports unions have followed the NFLPA's lead and established guidelines for the registration and regulation of agents. The National Basketball Players Association, in March 1986, issued a directive to each NBA team, which stated in part:

> . . . (a) The club shall not enter into any negotiations for Player Contracts, unless (i) the player is represented by an agent whose name appears on a list of certified agents furnished by such club, the Players Association, or (ii) the player is acting on his own behalf; and (b) each club, when submitting individual Player Contracts for approval by the NBA, shall provide the name of the player agent

NOTE: Failure to complete this form **in its entirety** will result in the form being returned to you, delaying the processing of your application.

I. **General** (Please print or type)

Name _____ Date of Birth _____ Social Security No. _____

Home Address _____

Home Phone (   )_____

If affiliated with a particular firm or agency as a player agent, please indicate:

Name of Firm or Agency _____

Business Address _____

Business Phone (   )_____

II. **Education**

High School

                                School Name _____

                   Month/Year Graduated _____

College (undergraduate)

                                School Name _____

                     Location (City, State) _____

            Degree(s) and Year Graduated _____

Graduate/Legal

                     College or University _____

                     Location (City, State) _____

           Degree(s) Awarded and Year _____

Admitted to Bar? Yes _____ No _____

            If yes, when and what state(s) _____

III. **Experience**

Number of years' experience as a player agent _____

Sports in which you **currently** represent athletes _____

For each sport noted above, the total number of athletes you **currently** represent:

Names of at least 10 athletes (or all clients, if fewer than 10) you **currently** represent and, in team sports, the team/league to which each athlete is currently under contract and name of team representative with whom you negotiated this contract. If you represent athletes in more than one sport, please provide this information for at least five clients (athletes) in each sport. Use additional sheets if necessary.

Player Name	**Team**	**League**	**Team Representative**

Exhibit 11-11 NCAA Player-Agent Annual Registration Form, 1986–87

List at least five (or all, if fewer than five) past clients (athletes) and their professional teams/leagues:

Do you earn income from work performed in some capacity other than as a player agent? Yes _____ No _____
If yes, describe other occupation(s) or service(s) for which you are paid:

What approximate percentage of your **total** work time is consumed as a player agent?

IV. **Other Qualifications**
Current membership in professional organizations _____

Occupational or professional licenses (e.g., certified public accountant, chartered life underwriter) and date obtained:

Are you currently certified by the NFLPA? Yes _____ No _____ Permanent or Provisional
(circle one)
Are you currently certified by the NBAPA? Yes _____ No _____
General services performed for client athletes (check those that apply and indicate fee charged):
Playing contract negotiations _____ Hourly fee or percentage? _____
Endorsement contract negotiations _____ Hourly fee or percentage? _____
Legal Assistance _____ Tax Consulting _____
Financial Planning _____ Money Management _____

In receiving compensation for contract negotiation services, do you receive payment "up front" or are your payments received as the player is compensated?

If you offer financial planning among your services, names and addresses of individuals, firms or agencies who assist in providing this service:
Name _____ Address _____
Name _____ Address _____
Name _____ Address _____

V. **Previous Employment** (last three positions)
Firm _____ Position _____
Address _____
Firm _____ Position _____
Address _____

Exhibit 11-11 Continued

Firm _____ Position _____

Address _____

VI.   References

Name _____ Position _____

Address _____

Name _____ Position _____

Address _____

Name _____ Position _____

Address _____

I certify that the above information is true, correct and complete to the best of my knowledge. Further, I certify that I will notify the director of athletics (or his or her designated representative) before the first contact with a student-athlete who has eligibility remaining in any sport and is enrolled in an NCAA member institution or before the first contact with the student-athlete's coach and that I have reviewed the NCAA rules and regulations (excerpts from the Association's constitution and selected numbered official interpretations) that accompany this form and will engage in no activity prior to a student-athlete's agreement to be represented that would otherwise jeopardize the student-athlete's eligibility. **I also understand that failure to comply with the terms of this certification may result in removal of my name from the list of registered player agents.**

Signature _____

Date _____

Exhibit 11-11   Continued

who negotiated the contract, or state that the player acted on his own behalf in the negotiations.

If notwithstanding the foregoing, negotiations involving any team and a noncertified player agent take place and a contract is executed, that contract shall be deemed to be void.

The NBPA plan includes a provision for the requirement of certification by player representatives, standards of conduct for player agents in providing services for players, maximum fee schedules, and arbitration procedures for resolving any disputes that arise.

NOTE _____

1. The following are the addresses and telephone numbers of the players union offices and the various league offices.

   (a)   *Union Offices:*
         National Basketball Players Association
         15 Columbus Circle, 4th Floor
         New York, NY 10023
         (212) 541-6608

PLEASE ANSWER ALL QUESTIONS THOROUGHLY

1. General

   a. Full name of applicant: _____

   b. Have you ever been known by any other name or surname (including a maiden name)?

      _____

      (Yes or No)

      If so, state all names used and when used:

      _____

      _____

   c. Date of birth ___/___/___   d. Birthplace _____

2. Education

   a. Law or other graduate school attended:

      _____

      (School)   (City & State)

      Dates of Attendance: From: _____ To: _____

                           Month/Year   Month/Year

      Degree: _____ Date Awarded: _____

   b. Colleges or Universities attended:

      _____

      (Name)   (City & State)   (Dates Attended)   (Degree)

      _____

      (Name)   (City & State)   (Dates Attended)   (Degree)

      _____

      (Name)   (City & State)   (Dates Attended)   (Degree)

   c. High School Attended:

      _____

      (Name)   (City & State)   (Date Degree Received)

3. Current Occupation/Employment

   a. I am currently: (Check One)

      ____ Employed by:

                                     (   )

      _____

      (Name of Employer)   (Address)   (Telephone)

      _____

      (Dates of Employment)

      _____

      (Nature of Employment)

      ____ Self-Employed

   b. If self-employed, please state nature and location of business:

      _____

      _____

      _____

   c. Please list below the names of employers, addresses, positions held, and dates of all employment you have had for the past five years:

      _____

      _____

      _____

Exhibit 11-12 Questionnaire for Registration as a Player Agent Representing Duke University Student-Athletes

_____

_____

_____

4.   **Lawyers and Law Graduates**

a.   Have you been admitted to the Bar in any jurisdiction? _____ **If so, please list**
(Yes or No)
jurisdictions and dates of admission:

_____
(Jurisdiction)   **(Date of Admission)**

_____
(Jurisdiction)   **(Date of Admission)**

_____
(Jurisdiction)   **(Date of Admission)**

b.   Do you have any applications for Bar admission currently pending? _____ **If yes,**
(Yes or No)
please state where you have applied and the status of that application:

_____

_____

c.   Have you ever been disbarred, suspended, reprimanded, censured, or otherwise disciplined or disqualified as an attorney, as a member of any other profession, or as a
holder of any public office? _____ If yes, please describe each such action, the
(Yes or No)
dates of occurrence, and the name and address of the authority imposing the action
in question:

_____

_____

_____

_____

d.   Are any charges or complaints currently pending against you regarding your conduct
as an attorney, as a member of any profession, or as a holder of public office?

_____ If yes, please indicate the nature of the charge or complaint and the name
(Yes or No)
and address of the authority considering it:

_____

_____

_____

_____

e.   Has your right to practice before any governmental office, bureau, agency, commission,
etc. ever been disqualified, suspended, withdrawn, denied, or terminated? _____
(Yes or No)
If yes, please explain fully:

_____

_____

_____

_____

_____

Exhibit 11-12   Continued

5. **Other (Than Legal) Occupations**

a. Are you a member of any business or professional organizations which directly relate to your occupation or profession? _____ If so, please list:
(Yes or No)

_____

_____

_____

_____

b. Please list any occupational or professional licenses or other similar credentials (i.e., Certified Public Accountant, Chartered Life Underwriter, Registered Investment Advisor, etc.) you have obtained other than college or graduate school degrees, including dates obtained:

_____

_____

_____

c. Have you ever been denied an occupational or professional license, franchise or other similar credentials for which you applied? _____ If yes, please explain fully:
(Yes or No)

_____

_____

_____

d. Do you have currently pending any application for an occupational or professional license, franchise or other similar credentials? _____ If yes, please describe and
(Yes or No)
indicate status of each such application:

_____

_____

_____

e. Have you ever been suspended, reprimanded, censured, or otherwise disciplined or disqualified as a member of any profession, or as a holder of any public office?

_____ If yes, please describe each such action, the date(s) of occurrence, and the
(Yes or No)
name and address of the authority imposing the action in question:

_____

_____

_____

_____

f. Are any charges or complaints currently pending against you regarding your conduct as a member of any profession, or as a holder of public office? _____ If yes,
(Yes or No)
please indicate the nature of the charge or complaint and the name and address of the authority considering it:

_____

_____

_____

Exhibit 11-12 Continued

g. Has your right to engage in any profession or occupation ever been disqualified, suspended, withdrawn, or terminated? _____ If yes, please explain fully:
(Yes or No)

_____

_____

_____

_____

6. All Applicants

a. Have you ever been convicted of or pled guilty to a criminal charge, other than minor traffic violations? _____ If yes, please indicate nature of offense, date of convic-
(Yes or No)
tion, criminal authority involved, and punishment assessed:

_____

_____

b. Have you ever been a defendant in any civil proceedings, including bankruptcy pro-ceedings, in which allegations of fraud, misrepresentation, embezzlement, misappro-priation of funds, conversion, breach of fiduciary duty, forgery, or legal malpractice were made against you? _____ If yes, please describe fully and indicate results
(Yes or No)
of the civil proceeding(s) in question:

_____

_____

_____

_____

c. Have you ever been adjudicated insane or legally incompetent by any court?

_____ If yes, please provide details:
(Yes or No)

_____

_____

d. Were you ever suspended or expelled from any college, university, law school, or graduate school? _____ If so, please explain fully:
(Yes or No)

_____

_____

e. Has any surety or any bond on which you were covered been required to pay any money on your behalf? _____ If so, please describe circumstances:
(Yes or No)

_____

_____

_____

f. Are there unsatisfied judgments of continuing effect against you (other than alimony or child support)? _____ If yes, provide full details:
(Yes or No)

_____

_____

Exhibit 11-12 Continued

7. **References**

   a. Please list below the names, addresses, and telephone numbers of three persons, not related to you and not engaged in business with you, who have known you for at least the last three years and who can attest to your character.

_____

_____

_____

_____

_____

   b. Please list below the names, addresses, and telephone numbers of at least two entities which can attest to your financial credit:

_____

_____

_____

8. **Other Services**

   a. Please indicate what services you offer to athletes, in addition to contract negotiation services.

_____

_____

_____

_____

_____

   b. Do you handle players' funds? _____
                                   (Yes or No)

     If so, are you bonded? _____ If yes, please provide details as to the amount of
                             (Yes or No)
     the bond, the name and address of the surety or bonding company, etc.:

_____

_____

_____

DUKE UNIVERSITY AGENT REGISTRATION

   DUKE UNIVERSITY, relying upon an Application for Registration previously filed, hereby grants Registration to _____
_____ to act as an agent pursuant to the Duke University Policy Concerning Student-Athletes of Duke University and Agents adopted September 1, 1985, and amended from time to time thereafter. This Registration is effective beginning as of the date hereof, and shall continue in full force and effect until and unless suspended, revoked, or terminated in accordance with this Policy.

Dated at Durham, N.C. this _____ day of _____, 19____.

                                     DUKE UNIVERSITY

                                      BY: _____
                                           Chairman, Student-Athlete
                                           Counseling Committee

Exhibit 11-12 Continued

Major League Baseball Players Association
805 3rd Avenue, 11th Floor
New York, NY 10022
(212) 826-0808

National Hockey League Players Association
65 Queen Street, West
Suite 210
Toronto, Ontario, Canada M5H 2M5
(416) 868-6574

Major Indoor Soccer League Players Association
2021 L Street, N.W.
Washington, D.C. 20036
(202) 463-2200

National Football League Players Association
2021 L Street, N.W.
Washington, D.C. 20036
(202) 463-2200

Canadian Football Players Association
1919 Scarth Street
Regina Saskatchewan, Canada S4P 2H1
(306) 525-2158

(b) *Professional League Offices:*
National Football League
410 Park Avenue
New York, NY 10022
(212) 758-1500

Canadian Football League
1200 Bay Street
Suite 1800
Toronto, Ontario, Canada M5R 2A5
(416) 928-1200

National Hockey League—New York
500 Fifth Avenue
New York, N.Y. 10110
(212) 398-1100

National Basketball Association
Olympic Tower
645 Fifth Avenue
New York, N.Y. 10022
(212) 826-7000

The National League of Professional Baseball Clubs
350 Park Avenue
New York, NY 10022
(212) 371-7300

Major Indoor Soccer League
757 Third Avenue
Suite 2305
New York, N.Y. 10017
(212) 486-7070

The American League of Professional Baseball Clubs
350 Park Avenue
New York, N.Y. 10022
(212) 371-7600

Baseball Commissioner's Office
350 Park Avenue
New York, N.Y. 10022
(212) 371-7800

Representative-Player Agreements

The relationship established between the player representative and the client has traditionally varied greatly in terms of the formality of any agreement effectuated between the parties. The agreement has ranged from a handshake to a letter of understanding to a detailed contract. Increasingly, interested parties within professional sports are urging that greater formality and detail be introduced into the relationship in order to safeguard the rights of both parties. For example, the NFLPA has suggested a contract form that might be used (Exhibit 11–13). The NBPA Standard Player Agent Contract is similar to the NFLPA model.

NOTE _____

1. For further information on the problems of those who represent the professional athlete, see the following articles and books:
   (a) Garvey, *The Agent Game* (Washington, D.C.: Federation of Professional Athletes, AFL-CIO, 1984).
   (b) Ruxin, *An Athlete's Guide to Agents* (Bloomington, Ind.: Indiana University Press, 1983).
   (c) "Agents of Professional Athletes," 15 *New England Law Review* 545 (1980).
   (d) Hearings Before the House Select Committee on Professional Sports, 94th Cong., 2d Sess. (1976).
   (e) Weistart and Lowell, *The Law of Sports* (Indianapolis: Bobbs-Merrill, 1979). Note particularly, pp. 319–333.
   (f) Gallner, *Pro Sports: The Contract Game*, 1975.
   (g) Woolf, *Behind Closed Doors* (New York: Atheneum, 1976).
   (h) Jones, ed., *Current Issues in Professional Sports* (Durham, N.H.: University of New Hampshire, 1980). Note particularly Shepherd, "Establishing the Contractual Relationship Between the Representative and the Athlete," pp. 13–29.

This Agreement is made this _____ day of _____ , 19___ by and between
_____ , hereinafter "Player," and _____
(name of player)   (name of Contract Advisor)
hereinafter "Contract Advisor," pursuant to and in accordance with the NFLPA Regulations
Governing Contract Advisors, as adopted May 5, 1983 and amended from time to time thereafter. In consideration of the promises made by each to the other, Player and Contract Advisor agree as follows:

1. CONTRACT NEGOTIATION SERVICES   Contract Advisor hereby warrants and represents that he has been duly certified as an NFLPA Contract Advisor pursuant to the NFLPA
Regulations Governing Contract Advisors. Player hereby retains Contract Advisor to represent, advise, counsel, and assist Player in the negotiation, execution, and enforcement of his
playing contract(s) in the National Football League. Such services are to be rendered by Contract Advisor pursuant to and in full compliance with the NFLPA Regulations Governing Contract Advisors. Contract Advisor, serving in a fiduciary capacity, shall act in such manner as to
protect the best interests of Player and assure effective representation of Player in individual
contract negotiations with NFL clubs. Contract Advisor shall not have the authority to bind or
commit Player to enter into any contract without actual execution thereof by the Player.

2. CONTRACT ADVISOR'S COMPENSATION   If Contract Advisor succeeds in negotiating
an NFL Player Contract or contracts acceptable to Player and signed by Player during the
term hereof, Contract Advisor shall be paid a fee equal to the following:

NOTE! Such fee may be less than but may not exceed the maximum fee for Contract Advisors provided in Section 4 of the NFLPA Regulations Governing Contract Advisors, and, in
accordance with that Section, such fee shall not be due and payable to Contract Advisor
unless and until Player receives the compensation provided for in the player contract(s) negotiated by Contract Advisor.

3. EXPENSES   Player shall reimburse Contract Advisor for all reasonable and necessary
communication expenses (i.e., telephone and postage) actually incurred by Player's NFL Con-
tract(s). Player shall also reimburse Contract Advisor for all reasonable and necessary travel
expenses actually incurred by Contract Advisor during the term hereof in the negotiation of
Player's NFL Contract(s), but only if such expenses and the approximate amounts thereof are
approved in advance by Player. Player shall promptly pay all such expenses upon receipt of
an itemized, written statement therefore from Contract Advisor.

4. DISPUTES   Any disputes between Player and Contract Advisor involving the interpretation or application of this Agreement or the obligations of the parties hereunder shall be
resolved exclusively through the Arbitration Procedures set forth in Section 7 of the NFLPA
Regulations Governing Contract Advisors. If Contract Advisor constitutes or represents an
"athlete agency" governed by the Labor Code of the State of California, Contract Advisor
shall provide reasonable notice to the Labor Committee of the State of California of the time
and place of any arbitration hearing to be held under said Arbitration Procedures, and said
Labor Commissioner or his authorized representative shall have the right to attend all arbitration hearings thereunder.

5. DISCLAIMER OF LIABILITY   Player and Contract Advisor, by virtue of entry into this
Agreement, agree that they are not subject to the control or direction of any other person
with respect to the timing, place, manner or fashion in which individual negotiations are to
be conducted (except to the extent that Contract Advisor shall comply with NFLPA Regulations) and that they will save and hold harmless NFLPA, its officers, employees and representatives from any liability whatsoever with respect to their conduct and activities relating to or
in connection with such individual negotiations.

6. TERM   Except as provided otherwise in this Paragraph, the term of this Agreement
shall begin on the date hereof and continue for the term of any player contract or series of

Exhibit 11-13 Standard Representation Agreement Between NFLPA Contract Advisor and Player

contracts negotiated by Contract Advisor on Player's behalf and signed by Player within one year of the date of this Agreement. Player may terminate this Agreement at any time if:

a. Contract Advisor fails to disclose in writing to Player, prior to accepting representation of Player hereunder or continuing to represent Player hereunder, as the case may be, the names and positions of any NFL management personnel whom Contract Advisor has represented or is representing in matters pertaining to their employment by any NFL club; or

b. Contract Advisor substantially fails or refuses to negotiate in good faith on Player's behalf in individual contract negotiations with the NFL club(s) desiring Player's services.

Such termination shall be effective upon the Player's giving written notice to such effect, either personally delivered or sent by prepaid mail to Contract Advisor's business address.

In the event that Contract Advisor fails to negotiate an NFL Player Contract acceptable to Player and signed by him on or before the date which is one year after the date Player signs this Agreement, this Agreement shall automatically terminate as of such later date.

The revocation or suspension of Contract Advisor's Certification as an NFLPA Contract Advisor pursuant to the NFLPA Regulations Governing Contract Advisors shall automatically terminate this Agreement.

In the event that Player has an opportunity to negotiate a new player contract in the NFL at any time prior to the termination of the contract or series of contracts negotiated by Contract Advisor hereunder, Player shall not be obligated to retain Contract Advisor or use Contract Advisor's services for such negotiation, and Contract Advisor shall not be entitled to any fee for such negotiation unless Player retains Contract Advisor through the signing of a new Representative Agreement.

7. FILING   A copy of this Agreement shall be filed by Contract Advisor with the NFLPA within ten days of execution. Any deviation, deletion, or addition in this form shall not be valid until and unless approved by the NFLPA. Approval shall be automatic unless, within ten days after receipt of this Agreement by the NFLPA, the NFLPA notifies the parties either of disapproval or of extension of this ten-day period for investigation or clarification.

8. ENTIRE AGREEMENT; GOVERNING LAW   This Agreement, along with the NFLPA Regulations Governing Contract Advisors, governs the relationship between the parties hereto and can not be modified or supplemented orally. This Agreement supercedes all prior agreements between the parties on the same subject matter.

This Agreement shall be interpreted in accordance with the laws of the State of _____

EXAMINE THIS CONTRACT CAREFULLY
BEFORE SIGNING IT

IN WITNESS WHEREOF, the parties hereto have hereunder signed their names as hereinafter set forth.

_____

Contract Advisor

_____

Player   Date

_____

Parent or Guardian if Player is under 21 years of age

Exhibit 11-13   Continued

(i) Blackman and Gershon, chr., *Counseling Professional Athletes and Entertainers* (New York: Practicing Law Institute, 1970).

(j) Needham, ed., *Counseling Professional Athletes and Entertainers*, 3rd ed. (New York: Practicing Law Institute, 1971).

(k) Gershon and Blackman, chr., *Counseling Professional Athletes and Entertainers* (New York: Practicing Law Institute, 1972).

(l) Blackman and Gershon, chr., *Counseling Professional Athletes and Entertainers* (New York: Practicing Law Institute, 1974).

(m) Blackman, chr., *Representing the Professional Athlete* (New York: Practicing Law Institute, 1976).

(n) "Do Agents Exploit Athletes?" *Professional Sports Journal*, Nov.–Dec. 1979, p. 20.

(o) Blackman and Hochberg, *Representing Professional Athletes and Teams* (New York: Practicing Law Institute, 1980).

(p) Trope, *Necessary Roughness: The Other Game of Football Exposed by Its Most Controversial Super Agent* (Chicago: Contemporary Books, 1987).

(q) Fishoff, *Putting It on the Line* (New York: W. Morrow, 1983).

INDIVIDUAL PERFORMER SPORTS

The sports worlds of tennis, golf, boxing, track, horse and auto racing, and other events that largely have the athlete competing as an individual rather than on a team in a league, present far different vistas than those that have been considered to this point. The possibilities for exploration of issues are so great, in fact, that no attempt is made in this brief aside other than to suggest a few of the important considerations.

Obviously, the basic contract starting points differ. Gone, for example, is the uniform player contract. Even so, its influences are not missing. After all, in tennis and golf, there are players' associations—perhaps not unions in the full sense as in the league sports but important in terms of giving their blessings to certain activities, including the types of contracts tendered players. Thus, when it comes to tennis and golf tournaments, the Sponsor-Player Contract assumes great uniformity as to many of the terms.

Endorsement contracts are staples in individual performer sports. These are not discussed here, except to note their prevalence and importance. But they can comfortably be considered in tandem with league player endorsements.

Finally, for many of the individual performer sports, there are clubs or resorts that wish to have a player's name associated with the facility. Any of a number of deals are possible, ranging from straight money payments to trade-outs and other enticements.

A legal inquiry that is raised but not pursued in this part of the book is whether individual performer sports require variant legal standards in some instances. For example, is injunctory relief available when the athlete fails to honor a contract? When the specific situation is relevant in a court fashioning the relief to be awarded, it may be that a performer in individual sports stands in a position that is different from that of a team player. If so, that must be anticipated in the drafting of the initial agreements.

FOREIGN LEAGUES

Limited alternatives are available to U.S. athletes to play "professionally" in foreign countries. In football, there is the Canadian Football League, where salaries are much less than those in the NFL. For baseball players, Japan offers opportunities, generally for former major leaguers. In basketball and hockey, leagues exist across Europe, with the quality of play varying substantially from country to country, and usually below the quality in the United States.

All foreign leagues limit the number of noncitizens who can play on any one team. This makes the scramble for spots by U.S. players an intense one, particularly in the better leagues. For example, the Italian basketball league is considered the strongest outside the United States. Top players can earn as much as $150,000 a year, even though the league is classified as amateur under international rules. Each Italian team is severely limited as to how many foreign players can make a squad. It takes a top U.S. player, one just below the NBA level, to secure a contract, unless the player can claim Italian citizenship, and not count against the team's foreign quota.

Chapter 12

DRUG TESTING IN AMATEUR ATHLETICS

INTRODUCTION

The drug abuse issue, one of the most emotionally charged and important issues facing athletics and society today, defies easy solutions. The problem of drug abuse has grown at all levels of athletic competition over the last 20 years at a frightening speed, from the interscholastic to the Olympic and intercollegiate levels of competition. In the United States, the increased instance of drug abuse in athletics reflects a like increase and, to a degree, acceptance of drugs among the general populace. It is a serious issue that includes health considerations, law enforcement problems, and moral/ethical questions for athletes, coaches, and athletic administrators.

In June 1984, U.S. Attorney General William French Smith announced a drug abuse prevention program designed to reach 5.5 million interscholastic athletes. According to the attorney general, athletes "can provide the leadership needed to create a peer-pressure strongly against drug use. They can help cut the demands in our society for illicit drugs." The recognition by the nation's highest law enforcement official of this problem at the high school level of athletics underscores the degree to which drug abuse has become a concern in American society.

The plan announced by Attorney General Smith was essentially a drug abuse education program in which prevention materials were provided by the Drug Enforcement Administration (DEA) to participating schools. It was developed as a joint project of the National High School Athletic Coaches Association (48,000 members in 20,000 schools) and the DEA. Its focus was on the special bond of trust and mutual respect that exists between young student-athletes and their coaches.

Jack Lawn, deputy director of the Drug Enforcement Administration, testified about the program before the U.S. Senate Subcommittee on Alcoholism and Drug Abuse on September 25, 1984. He noted:

> The Sports Drug Abuse Awareness Program we have recently launched is designed to do exactly that—to focus on the demand for drugs. What is probably most important about this program is that it is a joint undertaking involving the teamwork of DEA and the National High School Athletic Coaches Association, with support and participation from the IACP, the NFL and the NFL Players Association, and the Office of Juvenile Justice and Delinquency Prevention—and this teamwork is what will make this new initiative successful.
>
> Our goal is to prevent drug abuse among school-age youth, with a

special emphasis on the role of the coach and the student-athlete. We want to reach, and intend to reach, the 48,000 men and women coaches in 20,000 high schools across the country who can, in turn, help us reach five and one-half million student-athletes. And then we hope there will be a snow-balling effect to reach millions of other students who look up to our athletes.

Senator Paula Hawkins of Florida, the subcommittee chair, at the time of the testimony, noted:

Today we examine the impact of illegal drugs on sports and the national efforts of sports figures to fight youth and drug abuse.

Almost every kind of professional sports, and amateur athletics, can be exciting for the spectator, though punishing for the participant. Until recently, however, it was not thought that the tragedy of drug abuse had entered the game, but more and more disturbing information is emerging of the tragic correlation between the pressures of play, both physical and emotional, and resulting drug use.

While there is no reliable scientific data available detailing the amount of drug use by athletes, all indications are that a larger proportion of athletes than non-athletes, both amateur and professional, are abusing drugs and/or alcohol.

One of the most tragic aspects of this situation is, as one sports figure poignantly states: ". . . the saddest thing about an athlete having a drug problem is that the kids see it." We Americans take our sports, and our sports figures, seriously, and expect those involved to be above suspicion, not only of bribery and manipulation, but also of such aberrational behavior as drug abuse. When a major sports figure is found to be drug dependent, even though he may be an involuntary role model, he disappoints and hurts many more people than just himself. It can be devastating not only for the athlete, who throws away the precious gifts of supreme athletic ability and achievement, but also for the young person who idolizes and often emulates him.

Organized sports, both amateur and professional, should be alert to the potential for the corruption that exists in drug use, most importantly because no antidrug program can be successful, whether it stresses education, prevention or treatment, unless it commands the support and participation of the players.

The growing awareness of the presence of drug use in the world of athletics has produced drug and alcohol awareness programs such as the DEA program just described. Another outcome has been drug testing of athletes, a topic surrounded by controversy and more recently by litigation. Extensive drug testing was implemented at the 1984 Summer Olympic Games in Los Angeles. Drug testing was also approved by the NCAA for its championship events. Although the NCAA to date has not required its member schools to implement drug-testing programs, several colleges and universities have done so. Drug testing has not yet been instituted at the interscholastic level, where the emphasis remains on drug education rather than drug testing.

Amateur athletic organizations at all levels—interscholastic, intercollegiate, and Olympic—are struggling to find answers to the many questions the drug-testing issue raises. For example:

- Should the school implement a drug education program, and if so, what type of program?
- Should the school implement a drug-testing program, and if so, what type of program?
- If the school has a drug-testing policy, is it clearly defined and in writing?
- Does the school's drug-testing policy conform to conference and association rules and regulations?
- Does the school have the latest information and technology concerning drug testing?
- Who will conduct the tests?
- Who will be tested?
- Who will pay for the tests?
- Will the tests be random and mandatory or for probable cause only?
- What constitutes probable cause?
- How much notice should be given before testing begins?
- What types of drugs are to be tested for and how frequently?
- Should testing include "street drugs" such as marijuana and cocaine or just performance-enhancing drugs such as steroids?
- What actions will be taken when a student-athlete tests positive?
- Will there be an appeal process for a positive test?
- Is there a method for retesting when the initial results are positive?
- What confidentiality and constitutional law issues does drug testing raise?
- Do the sanctions to be imposed adhere to federal and/or state constitutional law and statutes?

Chapter 12, in examining the drug-testing policies and procedures of the NCAA, NCAA member institutions, interscholastic organizations, and the International Olympic Committee, explores all of these issues. The last section of the chapter discusses the litigation which is beginning to emerge as a result of the drug-testing controversy.

NOTE _____

1. For further information about the legal aspects concerning drug testing of student-athletes, see the following articles:

(a) "Drugs, Athletes and the NCAA: A Proposed Rule for Mandatory Drug Testing in College Athletics," 18 *John Marshall Law Review* 205 (Fall 1984).

(b) Judge, "NCAA Drug Testing: Finding a Constitutional Balance," *Academic Athletic Journal* 39 (Spring 1986).

(c) Zirkel and Kilcoyne, "Drug Testing of Public School Employees or Students," *Inquiry and Analysis* (March 1987).

(d) Lock and Jennings, "The Constitutionality of Mandatory Student-Athlete Drug Testing Programs: The Bounds of Privacy," 38 *University of Florida Law Review* 581 (Fall 1986).

(e) "An Analysis of Public College Athlete Drug Testing Programs Through the Unconstitutional Condition Doctrine and the 4th Amendment," 60 *Southern California Law Review* 815 (March 1987).

(f) "Random Urinalysis: Violating the Athlete's Individual Rights," 30 *Howard Law Journal* 93 (1987).

THE NCAA DRUG-TESTING PROGRAM

In January 1986, the NCAA membership at its annual convention agreed to begin a drug-testing program for NCAA-sanctioned championships and other events like football bowl games. The program, implemented with the fall championship events of 1986, has created a wave of controversy and litigation.

The decision to implement a drug-testing policy was not easily reached. Chief among the dissenting views of the policy is that it singles out the student-athlete, who may or may not be a scholarship athlete, to undergo urine testing that is not required of any other student who lives on campus and participates in student activities. In other words, why should an athlete be treated any differently from a member of the band, drama society, or glee club? However, by passage of the drug-testing policy, the NCAA has made acceptance of a possible postseason mandatory urine test a requirement before a student-athlete can compete in his or her sport on an intercollegiate level. In fact, each year the student-athlete is required to sign a student consent form agreeing to this policy (see Exhibit 12–1).

In the preface to its *1986–87 NCAA Drug Testing Program*, the NCAA stated its rationale for developing the drug-testing program:

With their approval of Proposal No. 30 at the January 1986 Convention, the NCAA member institutions reaffirmed their dedication to

---

DRUG-TESTING CONSENT

In the event I participate in any NCAA championship event or in any NCAA certified postseason football contest in behalf of an NCAA member institution during the current academic year, I hereby consent to be tested in accordance with procedures adopted by the NCAA to determine if I have utilized, in preparation for or participation in such event or contest, a substance on the list of banned drugs set forth in Executive Regulation 1-7-(b). I have reviewed the rules and procedures for NCAA drug testing and I understand that if I test "positive" I shall be ineligible for postseason competition for a minimum period of 90 days and may be charged thereafter upon further testing with the loss of postseason eligibility in all sports for the current and succeeding academic year. I further understand that this consent and my test results will become a part of my educational records subject to disclosure only in accordance with my written Buckley Amendment consent and the Family Education Rights and Privacy Act of 1974.

Signature of Student-Athlete / Date

Signature of Parent or Guardian/Date (required only if student-athlete is a minor)

Exhibit 12-1 NCAA Student-Athlete Drug-Testing Consent Form *Source*: National Collegiate Athletic Association.

the ideal of fair and equitable competition at their championship events. So that no one participant might have an artificially-induced advantage and so that no one participant might be pressured to use chemical substances in order to remain competitive, this NCAA drug-testing program has been enjoined.

The NCAA has long championed that drug education programs be developed by its membership for each of their athletic programs. In its 1985 booklet, "Drugs—The Coach and the Athlete," the NCAA explained the need for drug education:

A major concern in contemporary society involves the problems associated with the misuse and abuse of drugs and medicines. This misuse exists in all segments of society and among all age groups. The problems associated with inappropriate drug use are complex in nature. Therefore, to aid in understanding these problems, the appropriate use of drugs deserves to be incorporated to a greater degree into the basic education of the general public.

Citing Dr. Kenneth Clarke, director of the Sports Medicine Division of the U.S. Olympic Training Center, the NCAA noted that athletes use drugs for a number of reasons:

There are no specific drug problems especially unique to sports, but there are genuine drug problems in our society. (1) Some take drugs in an attempt to improve performance. (2) Some take drugs in an attempt to cope with the grind. (3) Some injudiciously use or are subjected to injudicious use of clinical drugs during treatment for disease or injury. (4) Some take drugs for recreational purposes, either by will or by peer influence. (5) Some possess drugs for illegal sale or distribution. All these different types of problems warrant attention, but on an individual basis.

The NCAA has recommended that a minimum drug education program for student-athletes at member schools should include the following:

1. A drug and alcohol awareness course to be conducted at the beginning of each school year, directed in particular to new student-athletes and emphasizing the adverse effects of drug use on athletic performance as well as on other areas of the student-athlete's academic and personal life.
2. A treatment plan in place for student-athletes who are identified as having a drug-use problem, with the emphasis on rehabilitation rather than on punishment.
3. A training session for coaches, trainers, and team physicians for recognizing and handling drug and alcohol problems, with an emphasis on the support they can provide to the student-athlete with a problem.

The NCAA drug-testing plan is expensive. In 1986–87 the testing program cost $950,000 for approximately 3,000 tests. In addition, $430,000 was budgeted for drug education programs for NCAA athletes. For the 1987–88 testing program, $1,965,000 was budgeted by the NCAA for drug testing and education, 2.5 percent of the NCAA's overall budget. Additional costs accrue to individual schools that choose to implement their own programs.

Critics of the NCAA's drug-testing program claim that it does not:

1. Safeguard student-athletes' procedural rights, especially in regard to the appeal process for a positive test.
2. Safeguard the student's privacy rights, especially when the media become aware of a test result.
3. Give the student-athletes sufficient information before they sign the mandatory consent form.
4. Insure that the school will represent the student-athlete's interests and rights when an athlete tests positive.

In addition, many coaches have criticized the plan for the effect it has on a team when team members must participate in drug testing following an NCAA tournament or a championship victory. John Chaney, basketball coach at Temple University, noted that the NCAA drug-testing program is "just another example of their [NCAA] imposing themselves into becoming Big Brother." Chaney noted further:

> What they're trying to do is overcome something that is already inherent in our society, and there's no way they can do that. They are applying a tourniquet to a wound that requires a much greater covering.
>
> You can't take the evils of society at large and solve them through sports. The education has to come at a much lower level, in the grade schools. Drug testing here just diverts attention from the areas where we should be concentrating. We're dibbling and dabbling here. And what are we going to find? The majority of players are clean livers.

The NCAA drug-testing plan is constantly evolving and being modified, but as offered presents the athletic administrator with the basic materials needed to make an informed decision when dealing with coaches, medical staff, student-athletes, and the NCAA about the plan. Remember, these policies apply only to the NCAA championships and sanctioned events.

Drugs Banned by the NCAA

The NCAA provides a list of banned substances to its membership. More than 90 drugs in 7 different categories are included in this list. These are drugs that the NCAA considers to be "performance-enhancing and/or potentially harmful to the health and safety of the student-athlete." The NCAA refers to the use of any of the banned substances as "doping." Any student-athlete who tests positively will be subject to disciplinary action. A brief description of the seven categories follows. Examples of specific drugs in each of these categories are listed in Exhibit 12–2.

1. *Psychomotor stimulants*. These drugs prevent or delay fatigue, mask pain, and increase self-confidence and aggressiveness. The danger in masking pain is that serious injury can actually have occurred. Preventing or delaying fatigue can lead to heat exhaustion, heat stroke, and even death. These drugs can also give the student-athlete a sense of well-being and euphoria.
2. *Sympathomimetic amines*. These substances are contained in many prescription and over-the-counter decongestants and asthma aids. They are used in the sports setting to increase

1. Psychomotor stimulants

amphetamine	ethylamphetamine	pemoline
benzphetamine	fencamfamine	phendimetrazine
chlorphentermine	meclofenoxate	phenmetrazine
cocaine	methylamphetamine	phentermine
diethylpropeon	methylphenidate	pipradol
dimethylamphetamine	norpseudoephedrine	prolintane

2. Sympathomimetic amines

chlorprenaline	isoetharine	methylephedrine
ephedrine	isoprenaline	phenylpropanolamine
etafedreine	methoxyphenamine	

3. Miscellaneous central nervous system stimulants

amiphenazole	crolethamide	nikethamide
bemigride	doxapram	picrotoxine
caffeine	ethamivan	strychnine
cropropamide	leptazol	

4. Anabolic steroids

clostebol	methenolone	oxymesterone
dehydrochlormethyl-testosterone	methandienone	oxymetholone
	nandrolone	stanozolol
fluoxymesterone	norethandrolone	testosterone
mesterolone	oxandrolone	

5. Substances banned for specific sports: rifle

atenolol	nadolol	timolol
alcohol	pindolol	
metoprolol	propranolol	

6. Diuretics

bendroflumethiazide	ethacrynic acid	metolazone
benzthiazide	flumethiazide	polythiazide
bumetanide	furosemide	quinethazone
chlorothiazide	hydrochlorothiazide	spironolactone
chlorthalidone	hydroflumethiazide	triamterene
cyclothiazide	methyclothiazide	trichlormethiazide

7. Street drugs

amphetamine	marijuana	THC (tetrahydro-cannabinol)
cocaine	methamphetamine	
heroin		

Exhibit 12-2 Categories of NCAA Banned Drugs with Examples *Source: 1986–87 Drug-Testing Program,* National Collegiate Athletic Association.

heart rate, improve breathing efficiency, and increase endurance. Their overuse or misuse could have an adverse effect on the student-athlete's cardiovascular and nervous systems.

3. *Miscellaneous CNS stimulants.* CNS stimulants increase endurance because they stimulate respiration and heart rate. The danger associated with their use in sports is that by

increasing heart rate they also increase blood pressure and
can cause dehydration, cerebral hemorrhage, stroke, and
other cardiac irregularities that could lead to heart arrest or
even death.
4. *Anabolic steroids.* It has long been believed that anabolic
steroids increase muscle mass. They are a derivative of the
male hormone testosterone. Some serious side effects have
been attributed to their use, among them baldness, signs of
virilization in women (sometimes irreversible), testicular at-
rophy to the liver, cardiac disorders, and bone growth damage in children.
5. *Substances banned for specific sports: rifle.* Alcohol is sometimes used in rifle competitions to minimize tremor in the
shooter's arms. Beta blockers are sometimes used to decrease
the heart rate and lower the blood pressure so that the
shooter can get off a shot between heart contractions and
pulsations in the arm. Both are banned by the NCAA. Beta
blockers are known to adversely affect the functioning of the
cardiovascular system.
6. *Diuretics.* Diuretics remove body fluids quickly and thus
body weight. They are used by athletes who need to make
weight classifications. They are also used to flush out other
drugs that an athlete might have been taking prior to competition. The problem with their use is that electrolytes are
removed along with the body fluids and an upset electrolyte
balance can lead to cardiac arrest.
7. *Street drugs.* Drugs such as cocaine, marijuana, heroin, and
amphetamines are used widely outside the sports setting.
They bring about a sense of euphoria and relaxed inhibition.
In the sports setting, they prevent or delay fatigue and mask
pain. In or out of sports, the use of these substances can
cause memory impairment, respiratory distress, convulsions,
coma, and even death.

The point to remember about all of these drugs is that the NCAA
bans them for two reasons—because they illegally enhance performance and because they are potentially harmful to the student-
athlete's health. A practice, rather than a substance, that the
NCAA bans for these same two reasons is blood doping, which is
the intravenous injection of whole blood, packed red blood cells,
or blood substitutes. Blood doping is supposed to enhance performance by virtue of the fact that it increases the ability of the
blood to transport oxygen. If done incorrectly, it could impair the
student-athlete's cardiovascular system. Growth hormones are also
banned by the NCAA for the same reasons.

There are two general exceptions to the NCAA's ban on drugs. One is local anesthetics. As long as they are administered using local or topical injections and are medically justified, the NCAA will approve their limited use. The other exception is asthma or exercise-induced bronchospasm medications. Again, as long as their use is medically justified and the NCAA is notified as to their use, they are permitted; however, only three medications are approved: terbutaline, salbuterol, and biltolterol.

Implementation of the NCAA Drug-Testing Program

The NCAA Executive Committee established a drug-testing committee to oversee the implementation of its drug-testing program. The committee conducts drug education programs for its member schools as was mentioned earlier. It also trains crew chiefs to conduct the actual tests at selected championship events. At these events, student-athletes may be chosen for drug testing in accordance with the following NCAA selection criteria:

4.0. *Athlete Selection*
4.1. The method for selecting student-athletes will be recommended by the NCAA drug-testing committee, approved by the Executive Committee, and implemented by the NCAA staff and assigned principal crew chiefs, in advance of the testing occasion. All student-athletes entered in the event are subject to testing.
4.2. At NCAA individual/team championship events, the top place finishers and a random sample of other student-athletes may be selected for drug-testing. All student-athletes participating in the event are subject to testing.
4.3. In team championships and certified football bowl games student-athletes may be selected on the basis of playing time, positions, or random selection. The selection will be determined prior to or during the competition. During the competition includes up to one hour following the conclusion of an individual's last participation on any particular day.
4.4. If doping is suspected, the crew chief will have the authority to select specific additional student-athletes to be tested.
4.5. Student-athletes may be tested on more than one occasion.
     [1986–87 NCAA Drug-Testing Program]

A student-athlete who has been selected for drug testing must undergo the following specimen-collection procedures as specified by the NCAA:

5.0. *Specimen-Collection Procedures*
5.1. At NCAA championship events, immediately following the final

participation of the student-athlete selected for drug-testing, the student-athlete will be handed a completed Student-Athlete Notification Card by an official courier that informs the student-athlete to accompany the courier to the collection station within one hour, unless otherwise directed, or be subject to a penalty for noncompliance.

5.1.1. The time of notification will be recorded by the courier. The student-athlete will sign the form and will be given a copy of the form.

5.1.2. The courier will give the crew chief the original of the form upon return to the testing station.

5.1.3. During an NCAA competition, if the student-athlete must compete in another event that day, the student-athlete may be excused from reporting to the collection station within the one hour time limit; however, the student-athlete must report to the collection station within one hour following completion of his or her last event of that day.

5.1.4. The student-athlete may have a witness accompany him or her to the station to certify identification of the student-athlete and to monitor the ensuing procedures.

5.2. Only those persons authorized by the crew chief will be in the testing station.

5.2.1. Upon entering the collection station, the student-athlete will provide adequate identification to the crew chief or a designate. The time of arrival is recorded on the Student-Athlete Signature Form and a crew member (Urine Donor Validator) will be assigned to the student-athlete for continuous observation within the station.

5.2.2. The student-athlete will select a new beaker that is sealed in a plastic bag from a supply of such and will be accompanied by the crew member until a specimen of at least 100ml, preferably 200ml, is provided.

5.2.3. Fluids given student-athletes who have difficulty voiding must be in unopened containers (certified by the crew chief) that are opened and consumed in the station.

5.2.4. If the specimen is incomplete or inadequate, the student-athlete must remain in the collection area under observation of the validator until the sample is completed. During this period, the collection beaker must be kept covered and controlled by the student-athlete being tested.

5.2.5. The student-athlete will select a pair of new specimen bottles that are sealed in a plastic bag from a supply of such and will pour approximately two-thirds of the specimen into the bottle marked "A" and the remaining one-third into bottle "B," leaving a small amount (approximately 5ml) of the sample remaining in the beaker.

5.2.6. The crew member will then stopper, cap, crimp and seal each bottle in the required manner under the observation of the student-athlete and the witness.

5.2.7. The student-athlete will select a personal code number from a list provided. This is recorded on the Student-Athlete Signature Form and on the bottles.

5.2.7.1. A crew member will check the specific gravity of the specimen and the pH of the urine remaining in the beaker. If the urine has a specific gravity below 1.004 or is alkaline, the student-athlete will be detained until an appropriate specimen is provided. This finding is recorded on the Manifest and Student-Athlete Signature Form.

5.2.7.2. A new student-athlete code number, selected by the student-athlete, will be applied to the new set of bottles. Both sets of specimens provided by the student-athlete will be sent to the laboratory appropriately identified.

5.3. The crew member will apply the student-athlete's code number in a secure manner to each bottle under the observation of the student-athlete and witness.

5.4. The student-athlete and witness will sign the Student-Athlete Signature Form, certifying that there were no irregularities in the entire process. Any perceived irregularity must be characterized and recorded on the Student-Athlete Signature Form at that time.

5.4.1. Failure to sign without justification is cause for the same action(s) as evidence of use of a banned substance. The crew chief will inform the student-athlete of these implications in the presence of witnesses and record such on the Student-Athlete Signature Form if the student-athlete still will not sign.

5.4.2. The crew member will sign the Student-Athlete Signature Form, give the student-athlete a copy and secure all remaining copies. The compiled Student-Athlete Signature Forms constitute the "Master Code" for that testing occasion.

5.4.3. If the student-athlete refuses to provide urine or fails to appear, the crew chief will inform the student-athlete, if he or she is available, of the implications in the presence of witnesses and record such on the Student-Athlete Form if the student-athlete still will not cooperate.

5.5. All sealed bottles will be secured in an NCAA shipping case.

When the case is full or completed, the crew chief will sign the manifest, put the original and one copy in the case, prepare the case for forwarding and apply the official seal, having recorded its number on the manifest.

5.6. After the last student-athlete has been processed, the cases will be forwarded to the laboratory in the required manner, the remaining supplies kept or returned, and all copies of all forms mailed to the designated persons. *[1986–87 NCAA Drug-Testing Program]*

Once the testing has been completed and the urine samples have been sealed, they are shipped to the UCLA Drug-Testing Laboratory or the National Institute for Scientific Research at the University of Quebec, Montreal, for analysis. These two laboratories were selected by the NCAA and are approved by the International Olympic Committee. The laboratories adhere to the following strict NCAA procedures regarding notification of results:

7.0. *Notification of Results*

7.1. The laboratory will use specimen A for its initial analysis.

    7.1.1. Positives for a banned substance will be reconfirmed with another sample from specimen A before it is determined to be a positive.

    7.1.2. The laboratory director will review any positive results from specimen A and determine if the results should be presented to the laboratory advisory board.

        7.1.2.1. If the results are to be reviewed by the laboratory advisory board, the laboratory director will make appropriate arrangements for review of all information pertaining to the sample by the members of the board.

        7.1.2.2. The deliberations and findings of the laboratory advisory board will be summarized in a confidential report by the laboratory director.

    7.1.3. By telephone, the laboratory will inform the NCAA of the results by each respective code number. Subsequently, the laboratory will mail to the NCAA director of research and sports sciences the original manifest with the respective finding recorded for each code number.

7.2. Upon receipt of the original manifest, and the laboratory findings, the NCAA director of research and sports sciences or her designate will break the number code to identify any individuals with positive findings.

    7.2.1. If a member institution has not heard from the NCAA within 30 days after the specimen was provided, the test results will be assumed to be negative.

    7.2.2. For student-athletes who have a positive finding, that information will be sent by the NCAA to the chief executive officer and the director of athletics immediately by "overnight/signature-required" letter. Concurrently, the student-athlete's director of athletics will be contacted by telephone if possible.

7.2.2.1. Accompanying the notice of the positive finding will be the option to have specimen B tested. Whether or not the institution chooses to have specimen B tested, written notice of the decision must be received by the NCAA within 24 hours of receipt of the notice described in 7.2.2. The institution will be given the option to be represented at the laboratory for the testing of specimen B.

7.2.2.2. If the institution does not choose to have specimen B analyzed, the specimen becomes the property of the laboratory. The NCAA will compile all written laboratory and any laboratory advisory board reports for confidential distribution to the enforcement department for consideration.

7.2.2.3. If the institution cannot arrange for representation or cannot be reached in 24 hours, the NCAA will arrange for a surrogate to represent the institution at the analysis of specimen B. For this purpose, the NCAA Postseason Drug-Testing Committee will develop a list of surrogate witnesses residing in the city where the laboratory is located.

7.2.2.4. The institution's representative or the surrogate will attest by signature as to the code number on the bottle of specimen B, that the bottle's seal has not been broken and that there is no evidence of tampering or contamination.

7.3. Specimen B will be analyzed by a technician other than the technician who analyzed the student-athlete's specimen A.

7.3.1. Specimen B findings will be final. By telephone, the laboratory will inform the NCAA of the findings. The laboratory will send the completed Specimen B Result Form to the NCAA which will be responsible for confidential distribution of this material along with laboratory reports for specimen A and any written findings of the laboratory advisory board.

7.4. The NCAA will notify the institution's chief executive officer and director of athletics of the findings. It is the institution's responsibility to inform the student-athlete. At this point, normal NCAA eligibility procedures will apply. This notification will be initiated by telephone to the athletics director.

This will be followed by another "over-night/signature required" letter to the chief executive officer and the director of athletics.

7.5. The NCAA director of research and sports sciences will send a confidential report of the aggregate findings for that drug testing occasion to the NCAA executive director for reporting to the Executive Committee. No report of aggregate data will be otherwise released without the approval of the NCAA Executive Committee.

7.6. The following is a recommended statement concerning a positive testing that results in a student-athlete's declaration of ineligibility (following the conclusion of the appeals process) both before and following an NCAA championship event.

If inquiries are received, this statement could be released:

"That the student-athlete in question was found in violation of the NCAA eligibility rules and has been declared ineligible for post-season competition." *[1986–87 NCAA Drug-Testing Program]*

NOTE ————————————————————————————————

1. Many allied athletic conferences have taken positions on the drug-testing issue. The *1986–87 Pacific-10 Conference Handbook* includes the following drug abuse resolution:

Whereas, athletes and coaches condition and train for optimal normal performance of the human body, and

Whereas, this is done without artificial manipulation of function, such as by drugs, either in preparation for or in the act of athletic performance,

Be It Resolved, the member institutions of the Pacific-10 Conference shall prohibit the use by any student-athlete of amphetamines and anabolic steroids,

Further Resolved, the member institutions of the Pacific-10 Conference shall prohibit the use by any student-athlete of illegal drugs,

Further Resolved, that appropriate disciplinary measures shall be adopted and vigorously applied at each member institution of the Pacific-10 Conference in cases of such violations of their athletic training rules.

INTERCOLLEGIATE DRUG-TESTING PROGRAMS

The NCAA, as previously discussed, passed legislation which allows it to test for drugs at events over which it has jurisdiction. This includes all NCAA-sponsored championships, such as the NCAA basketball tournament and the NCAA track and field championships. It also covers football bowl games which the NCAA is responsible for sanctioning. The NCAA, however, has not taken jurisdiction for drug testing of its member institutions for non-NCAA championship events, primarily the regular season events.

The NCAA has encouraged, but not mandated, that member institutions implement some type of drug-testing program. For example, the NCAA has suggested that in the future, if one participant tests positive for drugs, then the entire athletic team would be suspended from competition. The implications of such a policy are profound. The team would be disqualified from participating in the championships; the school would suffer a potential financial loss of forfeited tournament proceeds and a possible loss of prestige due to adverse publicity; and even more tragic, the whole team would be penalized for the actions of one of its members. If such a policy were to be implemented (and it has not at this writing), it would place tremendous pressure on a member institution to ensure, before going to a postseason event, that its student-athletes were drug-free. One way to do this would be to implement a drug-testing program which would test the student-athletes on a random basis prior to and during the regular season.

NCAA member institutions have taken a varied approach to the issue of drug testing. These approaches can be categorized as follows:

1. No drug-testing or drug education programs.
2. An educational program on the drug issue, but no drug testing.
3. Mandatory random drug testing.
4. Testing only for street drugs such as marijuana and cocaine.
5. Testing only for performance-enhancing drugs such as steroids.

Colleges and universities that are considering implementing a drug-testing program have to plan carefully. Testing student-athletes for drug use can be a risky business if the policy or procedures intrude on a student's right to privacy or if the tests are inaccurate and produce false results. Both instances can lead to litigation. A meaningful drug-testing program should at the very least contain the following components:

1. *A policy statement.* The reason why the drug education and/or testing program is being implemented should be clearly stated. The reasons generally are to ensure the health and safety of the student-athletes, including the rehabilitation of those who are involved with drugs, and to provide a fair competitive environment for all student-athletes.

2. *An educational component.* The school should make it evident that it is in the business of educating students and that the

drug-testing program tries to inform student-athletes of the dangers of substance abuse.

3. *Identification of Banned Drugs*. What kind of drugs are included in the drug-testing program? Do they include the performance-enhancing drugs such as steroids; street drugs such as marijuana and cocaine; and perhaps even alcohol and tobacco?

4. *A testing component*. The institution must decide whether the tests should be conducted on a random mandatory basis, or for "probable cause." If the testing is done for "probable cause," then the guidelines should indicate what constitutes "probable cause" and who makes that determination. If the testing is done on a mandatory random basis, then the procedure for selecting student-athletes for testing must be determined, as well as when to test and how many times. It is important to determine who conducts the tests and how accurate the tests are.

5. *Sanctions*. An institution must decide what action to take when student-athletes test positive. For example, it must determine who will be notified—coaches, parents, media, etc. It must determine whether the student-athlete will still be allowed to participate. The program should set forth what happens for a first-time offense, second-time offense, and third-time offense. The school may also have to make a decision as to whether the student-athlete continues to receive scholarship or financial aid. And finally, the institution may have to consider what happens when an athlete does not test positive but is found to be involved in drugs as a result of a criminal charge being brought against the student-athlete.

6. *Due process considerations*. The college or university must decide whether to allow a second review if the test is positive, who can conduct the second review, and who will pay for that review. It must determine whether there will be a hearing on the positive result and/or hearings for challenging the penalties that have been recommended. It also must be determined who will hear those appeals, the time period within which these appeals should be brought, whether the student-athlete should be allowed to be represented, whether there is a transcript produced from the hearing, and whether the decision should be made in writing.

7. *Confidentiality issues*. The college or university must be sure that its procedures will not violate the privacy of the student-athlete.

Any institution considering implementing a drug-testing program should adopt a program based on its own internal funding, institutional policies, and staffing. We include here two models as guides for athletic administrators. One is the drug-testing program at UCLA, and the other is the program at Rutgers. These programs were implemented in 1985 and 1986 and may have been modified or updated since that time. Both are presented as a framework from which an athletic administrator or institution could plan its own program.

POLICY STATEMENT: DRUG EDUCATION AND TESTING PROGRAM FOR UCLA STUDENT-ATHLETES*

The goal of the drug education and testing program (hereinafter "program") for UCLA student-athletes will be to promote a drug-free environment for the competitive program. Its purposes are to prevent an unfair competitive edge by those who abuse certain chemical substances (hereinafter "substances" or "substance"), to protect the health and safety of all competitors, to provide assistance for those who are found to engage in substance abuse, to contribute to the education of student-athletes and the public, and to maintain appropriate standards of behavior in intercollegiate sports.

Education and counseling will be cornerstones of the program. These program components will be designed to alert student-athletes and their coaches to the potential harm from substance abuse.

A systematic method for the testing of student-athletes shall constitute a phase of the program. Procedures shall be developed to implement this portion of the program which are fair, assure reliability of the tests, and protect the privacy of the participants.

Prior to implementation of the program, student-athletes and coaches shall be notified in writing. In addition, prospective student-athletes shall similarly be notified.

The program shall provide for appropriate sanctions for those who are not in compliance with the terms and conditions set forth.

To the extent permitted by law, information obtained in the operation of the program shall be confidential.

The UCLA program shall be consistent with applicable NCAA and conference regulations. UCLA shall provide its student-athletes and coaches with information with respect to any NCAA and conference program.

Framework for the Drug Education and Testing Program

I. EDUCATIONAL COMPONENT
    A. Each team and coaching staff shall meet as often as deemed necessary with a qualified member of the University staff to discuss the dangers of substance abuse. These sessions shall

---

*Source: University of California, Los Angeles, Department of Intercollegiate Athletics, 1986.

include information regarding the use of illegal substances, misuse of alcohol and the dangers of using reputedly performance enhancing substances such as anabolic steroids and amphetamines.

B. The program shall draw upon the unique and specialized skills of University personnel. Members of the faculty of the School of Medicine, staff of the Student Psychological Services and staff of the Student Health Service, as well as others, should serve as discussion group leaders, as sources of information about substance abuse and in appropriate cases, as therapists.

II. COUNSELING COMPONENT

A. The University shall identify properly trained counselors to assist in this Program. The services of these counselors shall be made available to student-athletes and coaches if further information or treatment is required.

In addition to counseling by trained specialists available on the campus, informal counseling shall be carried out by members of the Department of Athletics for further assistance in this effort.

B. To the extent permitted by law, all counseling shall be confidential. A system of referral to professionals in Student Health, Neuropsychiatric Institute, and other appropriate University departments shall be developed. Student-athletes and coaches shall be informed of the availability of these resources and methods of entering these programs.

C. Consistent with California law, individual counseling with licensed medical or psychological personnel would be privileged under the patient/physician and/or patient/therapist privilege. With the reality that some student-athletes are minors, parental consent and knowledge may be necessary in some instances. In other appropriate cases, attempts should be made to encourage the student-athlete to permit involvement of parents and spouses in the treatment program.

III. TESTING COMPONENT

A. The testing program shall be confidential and utilize methodology with appropriate sensitivity to minimize the likelihood of inaccuracy.

B. The substances for which tests shall be made include anabolic steroids, central nervous system stimulants, narcotic analgesics, and psychomotor stimulants, all of which are listed in Appendix A (attached). This list is subject to amendment from time to time. Because testing of each individual for all substances that are listed is cost prohibitive, selective tests for substances on the list will be made at reasonable times and places.

C. The program shall contain these major requirements:

1. Notification
   a. A statement of UCLA's policy with respect to substance abuse shall be provided to each student-athlete and all members of the coaching staff on an annual basis. This statement shall provide information on education and counseling programs as well as the protocol for the conduct of tests.
   b. A list of substances for which tests may be conducted and their generic names would be included.
2. Consent
   a. A consent form for student-athletes indicating that he/she had received the information described in #1 above and that the student-athlete agreed to participate in the program would be returned to the team physician at the time of the pre-participation physical examination.

   In addition, the consent form will require the student-athlete to submit information that he/she is taking one or more of the substances under medical supervision. This signed consent form would be a precondition for participation.
3. Testing Protocol
   a. In conjunction with any pre-season medical evaluation, an initial urine specimen shall be collected from each participant for each intercollegiate sport and shall be coded for identification and submitted to the Laboratory. The results of this initial screen shall be provided to the team physician who in turn would notify the individual of positive test results. The Head Coach of each sport would receive information consisting of the number of specimens tested and the number of positive samples. Names of the student-athletes would not be divulged to the Head Coach at this time.
   b. At this point any student-athlete who tested positive would be offered the services of the counseling program on a voluntary basis.
   c. All individuals with positive first samples, plus several other team members selected on a random basis, would be retested.
   d. If an individual was positive again on the second test, a retest of that specimen or of another specimen, at the individual's request, would be carried out. At this point the individual would be referred for mandatory counseling.
   e. Refusal to participate in the counseling program would result in immediate suspension from intercollegiate athletic participation, including practice.

    f. Following the second positive result the Head Coach shall be notified. Parents, spouses, or guardians may be notified with the consent of the student-athlete or as otherwise permitted by law.

    g. Those who participate in the counseling program who do not represent an unreasonable hazard to themselves or other competitors may be allowed to continue participation until a third specimen is obtained.

    h. A third positive test result would incur an immediate suspension from participation. Non renewal of any athletic grant-in-aid may follow such a suspension.

4. Hearings, Appeals and Reinstatement

    a. Hearings

      (1) Student-athletes subject to a sanction under the terms of this program shall be entitled to a hearing before the Senior Associate Athletic Director or his/her designee prior to imposition of the sanction. A request for such a hearing must be made within 24 hours of notification that a sanction is being considered. The hearing shall be held no later than 24 hours after the student-athlete so requests. An extension of time for the hearing may be granted upon a showing of good cause. A student-athlete requesting such an extension may be placed on interim suspension during the extension.

    b. Appeals

      (1) Determinations made under section 4a(1) may be appealed to a committee appointed by the Director of Athletics. Such appeals must be made within five business days of the determination in question.

    c. Reinstatement

      (1) An individual sanctioned as described in No. 3 above may be reinstated on recommendation of medical personnel and the team physician with the concurrence of the Head Coach. Such reinstatement may be subject to specific conditions, including periodic testing to ensure compliance.

5. The student-athlete will not be subject to student disciplinary action as a result of a positive drug test(s). The University will not voluntarily supply personally identifiable test data or results of a test to any law enforcement agency and shall develop procedures to assure that only information necessary to the purposes of this program is retained and all other information concerning the test results is destroyed.

DRUG EDUCATION, TESTING, AND ASSISTANCE PROGRAM: RUTGERS*

Recognizing that the excessive use of alcohol and drugs is a problem in society, which includes the collegiate community, and therefore could be a problem for some student-athletes, thus endangering the health and safety not only of themselves but often of their teammates as well, the Rutgers Division of Intercollegiate Athletics has developed this policy of drug testing, education, and counseling.

01. *PURPOSES*

    01.01. To help educate student-athletes on the harmful effects of the excessive use of drugs (or any use of certain drugs) on their personality, physical and mental development, and performance.

    01.02. To identify users and to help them to be rehabilitated so that they may develop to their full potential in all areas of living, including sports competition.

02. *NOTIFICATION*

This policy statement shall be widely distributed to all coaches and present student-athletes and their parents, and to other selected organizations and personnel.

03. *GENERAL EDUCATION PROGRAM*

A program will be developed for all student-athletes to discuss the drug situation in society generally, the various kinds of drugs and harmful effects of each on their and their teammates' health and safety, and how each student-athlete may best resist the temptation to experiment with or start using harmful drugs.

04. *DRUGS INCLUDED*

With the approval of the Director, any head coach may arrange for testing for the presence of any or all of the following substances:

    04.01. *Alcohol* (in any amount)

    04.02. *Selected drugs* (in any amount): barbiturates (nembutal, phenobarbital, amytal), chlorpromazine (thorazine), cocaine, codeine, D-amphetamine dexadrine, obetrol, glutethimide (doriden), marijuana, meperidine, demeral, mepergan, methadone (dolophine), morphine (roxanol, RMS), propoxyphene (darvon, wygesil, SR-65), and quinine (quinamm, guihdan).

    04.03. *Steroids:* Testosterone and epitestosterone (in amounts above normal range).

    The Director may add other drugs at his option.

*Source: Rutgers—The State University of New Jersey, New Brunswick Area Campuses, Division of Intercollegiate Athletics, 1985.

05. *FREQUENCY OF TESTING*
At any time during the season of practice and regular and post-season competition, unannounced tests may be made of all or a random sample of the squad members, except as set forth in those parts of Section 10, which provide for a student-athlete who has had a positive test, at any time during the academic year, to be tested again at an unannounced time.
06. *TESTING METHODS*
The Breathalizer shall be used for the alcohol test.
For all other substances, urine samples will be collected and analyzed in accordance with generally accepted medical procedures.
07. *PLACE OF TESTING*
The Breathalizer test will be given, and the urine sample collected, in the assigned training or locker room for the sport involved.
08. *TEST RESULTS*
The results of all tests will be immediately communicated to the Director, Assistant Director, head coach, team physician, athletic trainer, student-athlete, and, except for emancipated students, to the parents or guardians. For these purposes, an emancipated student is one with an independent source of income, who is factually and financially independent of his/her parents/guardians, and who has not been claimed by parents/guardians as a dependent on their U.S. Individual Income Tax Return.

Other Intercollegiate Athletic and University personnel may be informed of positive test results as needed in order to support the education and rehabilitation efforts specified in this policy statement.
09. *STATEMENT OF INFORMED CONSENT*
This program is elective for the academic year 1985–1986, but may become mandatory for subsequent years. After the start of the academic year, any head coach who wishes to test the members of the squad may request them to sign, on a voluntary basis, a Statement of Informed Consent, (copy attached), certifying that he/she has read and understands the University's drug program and voluntarily agrees to its application in his/her case. For those under 18 years of age, the co-signature of a parent (or guardian) is required. The Consent shall apply for their entire athletic career at Rutgers except when there is a major substantive change in the policy, at which time a new Consent statement shall be signed.
10. *SANCTIONS, REHABILITATION, AND REINSTATEMENT*
For violations over the course of the student-athlete's career at Rutgers, sanctions in the form of suspension from practice and contests, or ultimately dismissal from the team, will be imposed by the head coach within the minimum and maximum periods shown below. Also shown below are the rehabilitation efforts and conditions for reinstatement for each offense.

10.01. *First Offense*

    10.01.01. *Medical Prescriptions*

        Determine if the test is positive because of a prescription by a qualified physician to treat a specific medical condition; if so, a new prescription should be obtained that does not contain the banned drug(s) (if medically feasible), and no further testing will be done. If the positive test is not caused by a medical prescription, the program described in 10.01.03 and .04 will be started.

    10.01.02. *Sanctions:* From none, to suspension up to two weeks.

    10.01.03. *Rehabilitation:* Counseling by team physician, head coach, athletic trainer, and athletic administrator (if appropriate).

    10.01.04. *Further Testing:* After an appropriate period of time, another unannounced test may be made; a positive result will be considered a second offense.

10.02. *Second Offense*

    10.02.01. *Sanctions:* Suspension for a minimum of two weeks to a maximum of six weeks.

    10.02.02. *Rehabilitation*

        a. Further counseling by coaching staff and team physician.

        b. Referral to the University's Student Health Service for participation in the Alcohol (and Drug) Assistance Program for Students. The director of the program is to certify to the team physician that the student-athlete has or has not completed the program.

    10.02.03. *Reinstatement:* Negative test at the end of the sanction period. A positive test will be considered a third offense.

10.03. *Third Offense*

    10.03.01. *Sanctions, Rehabilitation, and Reinstatement*

        a. Recommendation by the head coach to the Director for dismissal from the team. If the Director approves, the student-athlete shall have the right of due process in accordance with regular division policy. In addition, the Director will recommend to the University Financial Aid Committee that any athletic grant-in-aid not be renewed for any subsequent year.

        b. If the Director does not approve the recommendation for dismissal, the student-athlete shall be suspended for a minimum of six weeks to a maximum of one year.

        (1) Rehabilitation: Referral to the appropriate social agency for rehabilitation.

        (2) Reinstatement: Receipt by the head coach of a written opinion from the social agency that the student-athlete

has been rehabilitated and is ready to assume his/her responsibilities to the program.

11. *RECORD KEEPING*

    11.01. A complete summary record of the results of all tests will be maintained within the Division of Intercollegiate Athletics.

    11.02. All records shall be confidential within the limits of Section 08 and maintained in secure locations within the Division of Intercollegiate Athletics.

    11.03 *Retention periods*

        11.03.01. For student-athletes with negative test results—during their athletic careers at Rutgers.

        11.03.02. For student-athletes with positive test results—six years after they have completed their athletic careers at Rutgers.

    11.04. Access to the records shall be limited to those who are authorized to receive the test results as listed in Section 08.

Statement of Informed Consent

I certify that I have read and fully understand the Division's foregoing drug program policy and agree to participate in the program during my entire athletic career at Rutgers. Specifically, I agree, if requested, to submit voluntarily a urine sample for drug testing, and to take a Breathalizer test for alcohol, at times determined under the policy; to abide by the sanctions imposed; and to cooperate in the counseling and rehabilitation programs recommended. I further agree to the notification of my parents (or guardians) of any positive test results, (not applicable for emancipated students).

SIGNED _____   WITNESSED _____
                    Student-Athlete

_____
                Parent or Guardian
    (If student-athlete is under 18 years old)

DATE _____

INTERSCHOLASTIC DRUG-TESTING PROGRAMS

Drug testing at the interscholastic level is almost nonexistent. The National Federation of State High School Associations (NFSHSA) has recommended against drug testing at the high school level. In 1986, the NFSHSA's TARGET Program, "Helping Students Cope with Alcohol and Drugs," conducted a national survey of high school drug-testing programs and attitudes toward such programs. Although questionnaries were sent to all 50 State High School Interscholastic Athletic and/or Activities Association Headquarters for distribution to member schools in each state, some associations chose not to distribute the questionnaire out of concern that member schools might interpret the questionnaire as reflecting an "in favor of drug testing" position by the association. Thus, 1,209 questionnaires came back from 36 states. The schools ranged in enrollment from 200 to 3,000. The highlights of the tabulation of these questionnaires follow. They were prepared by Charles A. Stebbins.

- One hundred percent of the State Interscholastic Athletics and/or Activities Associations responded in support of the National Federation's position that drug testing not be recommended at the high school level.
- Ninety-four percent of the high schools reported having *no current* drug testing program. Less than 1 percent reported having such a program. Between 5 and 6 percent of the 1,209 reporting schools did not respond to this question.
- Ninety-four percent of the respondents indicated having *no previous involvement* in a drug-testing program. Less than 1 percent responded having a prior testing program, (with some, but not all, still in existence). Between 5 and 6 percent of the schools did not respond to this question.
- Fifty-five percent of the respondents stated they did not favor any type of drug-testing program at the high school level. However, 27 percent were in favor of some type of program, with the majority qualifying their response. Eighteen percent did not respond to this question.
- Problems noted by schools having implemented a testing program included such items as:
  1. Parents denying the existence of a problem.
  2. Parents are resistant to school efforts.
  3. Claims of violation of student rights.
  4. Student participation in athletics dropped noticeably from fall to spring (but questioned whether it was actually due to drug testing).
  5. Difficulty implementing testing procedures for *other* activities and the *entire* student body.
- Positive results noted from implementing a testing program included such items as:
  1. Students needing help were identified and placed in treatment.
  2. Parents were grateful and cooperative when realizing the school was doing something.

3. School-related parent groups gave their approval.
- Of the 25 percent of the schools stating they provided an alcohol/ drug education program in their school, most cited these programs as being utilized:
  1. How to Say No.
  2. Chemical People.
  3. SAP (Student Assistance Program).
  4. National Federation of State High School Association's TARGET Program, Helping Students Cope with Alcohol and Drugs in cooperation with the Hazelden-Cork Sports Education Program.
  5. Quest.
  6. SAPE (Student Assistance Prevention Education).
  7. I–CARE.
  8. K-12 Curriculum Program.
  9. SADD (Students Against Driving Drunk).
  10. Operation Prom/Graduation.
  11. Operation Snowball.
  12. SHOP (Students Helping Other People).
  13. Education provided in classes such as: Health, Science, Drivers Education, Biology, etc.
- Reasons given for not implementing a testing program were: legal ramifications, cost, quality control and recourses to be taken with individuals testing positive.
- Of the 27 percent of the schools stating they favored drug testing (the majority of which qualified their answers), some specified these qualifications to such a program:
  1. Only if mandated.
  2. Only if there was a program established to deal with those who tested positive.
  3. Only to confirm suspicion of student use.
  4. Only if all students were tested and not only those involved in athletics.
  5. Only if research shows a need.
  6. Only if all students and staff are tested.
  7. Only if it is a part of comprehensive prevention education program.
  8. Depends on the community.
  9. Only as it relates to court order.
  10. Only if it were a part of a state or national program.

In summary, the majority of respondents support the National Federation's position that drug testing not be recommended for high schools, and that schools place more emphasis on the development of alcohol/drug prevention and education programs. Those responding in favor of drug testing for the most part were less than decisive, having no firm position on the matter.

Although the results of this NFSHSA questionnaire point out the overwhelming attitude against drug testing at the interscholastic level, a few schools have instituted drug education programs for their high school student-athletes. One such program, in place at Metamora High School in Metamora, Illinois, is presented below, again as a model rather than an ideal, for the benefit of high school athletic directors and administrators who might be planning their own sports-related drug education policies and programs.

A BETTER WAY TO WIN*

Purpose

We, the coaches of Metamora, are committed to providing the students with an environment where they can pursue athletic endeavors that enhance their emotional and physical and spiritual growth. We further contend that drug and alcohol use among our athletes prohibits their holistic growth, and we are obligated to provide possible solutions.

In doing so we, therefore, propose the following program:

Goals

1. Provide factual drug and alcohol information to the students.
2. To create an awareness among parents regarding the effects of drug and alcohol use upon athletes.
3. To avoid injuries to an individual due to the influence of a chemical substance.
4. To avoid dissension which is the result of conflicting values concerning drugs and alcohol use.
5. To provide factual information to the coaching staff regarding effective methods of dealing with athletes who use chemical substances.

Program Components

I. *Education for Coaching Staff*
   All presentations will be available to the teaching faculty of Metamora High School.
   a. *Legal*—This section will provide coaches with practical information pertaining to legal questions and concerns.
   b. *Recognizing symptoms of drug and alcohol use*—This section will discuss behavioral and medical symptoms that are character-

---

*Source: Metamora High School, Metamora, Illinois.

istic of drug using individuals. In addition, coaches will receive an orientation pertaining to paraphernalia of drugs of abuse.

   c. *Creating effective communication with the drug abusing athletes and their parents*—This portion of the program will provide the coaches with practical methods of intervention that enhances communication between the coaches, athletes and their parents.

   d. *Orientation of resources*—The various resources that provide services that may assist the coaching staff will be reviewed, and the process for referring an individual explained.

II. *Education for student athletes*

   a. *Orientation to inform students of the athletic code and consequences of drug and alcohol use*—A contractual form stating the athletic codes and consequences will be reviewed and signed by all athletes. See Appendix A.

   b. *Special educational endeavors*—These endeavors would include speakers from an assortment of resources pertaining to drug and alcohol use. This will be organized and implemented by the "M" Club.

   c. *Orientation of community resources*—This would include a review of social service organizations, clergy, etc. where they can obtain confidential, affordable services.

   d. Physical and medical complications resulting from drug and alcohol use.

III. *Parental Orientation*

During an evening in August parents will be invited to attend a program that (1) reviews the athletic code; (2) provides information regarding this proposed program; (3) a panel of professionals will provide an informative presentation pertaining to drug/alcohol use among athletes; to be sponsored by the Mother's Club.

IV. *Procedures for assisting athletes and their parents when drug and alcohol use is suspected*

   a. *Suspension*

When any one of the symptoms from Column A (Appendix C) occurs the athlete shall be suspended as dictated in the Metamora Athletic Code.

   b. *Coach-athlete conference*

When the coach has observed behavior exhibited from an athlete that is unusual or the athlete displays 3 or more symptoms from Column B (Appendix C), the coach will coordinate a conference between himself and the athlete and inform the Athletic Director.

   c. *Coach-parent conference*

If the symptoms from Column B (Appendix C) observed by the coach persist, the coach will consult with the Dean of Students, a Guidance Counselor and the Athletic Director.

The purpose of this consultation is to provide comprehensive information pertaining to the behaviors of the particular athlete. In addition, this consultation serves as a check and balance system that insures that the decision to contact the parent or parents is based upon objective criteria. The coach who presents the questioned behaviors before the cited consultants is required to review the final outcome of the review with the Director of Athletics prior to telephoning parents.

Upon requesting a conference with the parent or parents, a blood test may be required by either party to determine possible substance use. Secondly, counseling may be recommended and the coach will make such arrangements if desired by the parents.

Contract for Informing Parents

We/I, the parents or parent, or legal guardian of _____
_____ hereby authorize Coach
_____ to inform us/me of any unusual behavior or suspect drug or alcohol use.

DATE: _____

SIGNED: _____

COACH'S SIGNATURE: _____

OLYMPIC DRUG-TESTING PROGRAM

At the 1984 Summer Olympic Games in Los Angeles, the most intensive program (at the time) of drug testing of athletes was developed and implemented. Dr. Anthony F. Daly, Jr., an orthopedist and sports medicine specialist, and vice president and medical director of the Los Angeles Olympic Organizing Committee, noted:

> There's no way to mask the drugs. The testing equipment is so sensitive that it can pick up one part in a billion. It's more sensitive than the equipment used last summer in the Pan American Games in Caracas. Our goal is to protect the athlete from himself and from gaining an unfair advantage. We want a drug-free Olympics where the athlete relies on his natural ability.

The International Olympic Committee and the international federations that govern each Olympic sport ban more than 60 generic drugs in the following five classes:

1. Psychomotor stimulants, including amphetamines and co-caine.
2. Central nervous system stimulants, including caffeine.
3. Sympathomimetic amines, including ephedrine.
4. Narcotic analgesics, including codeine and heroin.
5. Anabolic steroids, including testosterone.

Many over-the-counter remedies for colds, congestion, hay fever, and allergies contain drugs on the list.

Only about 1,500 of the roughly 8,500 Olympic competitors in 1984 were required to submit to drug tests. The selected athletes included the four top performers (or teams) in each event, plus others selected at random. The Olympic drug-testing program, however, was not fool-proof. For example, athletes who used steroids could possibly have escaped detection. An athlete's urine usually is free of steroids if the oral doses are stopped three to four weeks before testing or if injectable steroids are halted three to four months beforehand.

Testosterone, which, like a steroid, speeds muscle regeneration in injured people, was added to the banned list for the first time at the Los Angeles Olympic Games. Because the hormone occurs in the body naturally, Olympic officials tested for excessive levels. Although the definition of excessive levels is high enough to allow some suspected illicit users to escape disqualification, it was established at that level to protect innocent athletes. "It's possible that someone could go around the drug testing system," medical director Daly said. "But we keep closing loopholes, as we have with stimulant drugs. . . . If we keep closing every little loophole that develops, then pretty soon we'll reach the ultimate goal, which is a drug-free Olympics."

Although estimates vary considerably, there was little disagreement that use of anabolic steroids has been extensive among Olympic athletes, at least in certain sports. "In the weightlifting events and probably in track and field, it's a fairly high percentage," Daly said, acknowledging some estimates that up to 95 percent of weightlifters use the drugs. "It's probably a relatively low percentage—lower than people think—in the other events," he added.

Different tests were used to detect various drugs, but the major testing devices at Los Angeles were eight gas chromatograph-mass spectrometers. These machines break down a substance into its component parts, which show up on a graph as a unique chemical "fingerprint," even if the concentration of a drug in urine is as little as one part per billion.

The tests were conducted so that after a competition ended, the athletes to be tested reported to the testing facility. There, they chose a code number and beaker for their urine specimen. Under observation, they produced a sample, a process that sometimes took an hour or two because of dehydration. The athlete then poured equal amounts of the sample into two bottles. As the athlete watched, the crew chief capped the bottles, sealed them with wax and labeled them "A" and "B."

Both bottles were then taken to the testing laboratory at UCLA. Specimen B was set aside, and Specimen A was tested. If no banned substance was found, the test was over. If a banned substance turned up, another sample from Specimen A was checked. If that also tested positive, the athlete and the head of the athlete's national delegation were notified. In that event, Specimen B was tested within ten days in the presence of the athlete and medical representatives from the delegation. The result of the Specimen B test was final. An athlete whose final test was positive was disqualified, lost his or her medal, and faced suspension by the sport's international federation.

Of all the athletes tested at the Olympic Games in 1984, only five were found to be using drugs and disqualified.

DRUG-TESTING LITIGATION

There are important legal issues about drug testing in amateur sports organizations, including issues about the constitutional right of athletes to privacy, illegal search and seizure, and confidentiality. Much of the established case law in this area deals with criminal sanctions imposed by the courts on professional athletes and is not a concern of this book. Four cases, however, are very timely. One is a challenge brought by a Stanford University student against the NCAA (*LeVant v. National Collegiate Athletic Ass'n*, No. 619209 [Cal. Sup. Ct. 1987]). The second is *O'Halloran v. University of Washington*, No. 87-2-08775-1 (Wash. Sup. Ct., 1987). The third is a challenge brought by a student against Northeastern University in Boston (*Bally v. Northeastern University*, Mass. Sup. Ct., 87-1178, 1987). And the fourth involves *Derdyn v. University of Colorado*.

In the *LeVant* case, a senior member of the Stanford University women's diving team, Simone LeVant, challenged the NCAA's requirement that she submit to drug testing to participate in the NCAA Swimming and Diving Championship. Judge Peter G. Stone of the Santa Clara (California) Superior Court granted LeVant a preliminary injunction that barred the NCAA from testing her at the competition. Judge Stone noted in his decision that "the tests appear to the court not to accomplish the goals, the laudable goals set forth by the NCAA in any particularly carefully or well crafted manner. There appears to be very little reasonable relationship to the performance or the general health given the broad application of three thousand substances to all twenty-eight sports."

The court in *LeVant* was particularly concerned about the process by which the NCAA had implemented the drug-testing program. Judge Stone stated:

> The least physically, emotionally or constitutionally intrusive methods to accomplish those laudable goals have barely been considered, much less proposed and implemented. The voluntariness of the athlete's efforts to compete does not necessarily vitiate the reasonable expectation of privacy. The NCAA is and perhaps should be the only game in town. I don't know that. But it cannot require an athlete under these particular circumstances—I should say this athlete—under these particular circumstances to give up that very valuable constitutional right, the right of privacy.

Judge Stone reasoned that "it appears to the court that the testing for certain of the substances under certain narrow circumstances, under certain narrow conditions may indeed pass constitutional muster, but unfortunately that is not what the court is here presented with." According to Judge Stone:

> It seems to the court that honoring the Constitution is the test. The court has no trouble with the fact that the NCAA regulations are pervasive, are manifold, and I think that's all laudable. But giving up the right to play poker for money does not seem to me to equate with giving up the right to urinate in private, the tests from which may reveal lifestyle, or other irrelevant but deeply personal matters.

Judge Stone further stated that "given this program, I do not believe that the defendant meets any of the tests, whether the stringent compelling interest test, or other less stringent tests, even the minimum. The balancing test, probable cause, reasonable suspicion, none of that appears here." Therefore, the court in *LeVant* handed down the following ruling:

> The defendant, NCAA, is prohibited from prohibiting the plaintiff from competing in NCAA events; in forcing the testing procedures of the NCAA drug testing policy as to this plaintiff; requiring the plaintiff to submit to any form of mandatory drug testing; conditioning the right to participate in intercollegiate diving competition on submission to mandatory drug testing; and maintaining any files and records documenting the results of drug tests and/or refusals to submit to same as to this plaintiff . . . or from taking any steps as

against Stanford University or any athletes competing for or on behalf of Stanford University or within the Stanford University Program.

After Judge Stone's preliminary injunction decision in January, 1987, Simone LeVant graduated from Stanford in June 1987. Jennifer Hill and J. Barry McKeever were substituted as plaintiffs in the case when LeVant's ineligibility rendered her case moot. In addition, Stanford University was allowed to intervene so as to raise questions concerning its duties. Stanford University argued that it did not want to enforce an unlawful program. Stanford found itself caught between students challenging the drug-testing program and the NCAA, which required the drug-testing program. Subsequently, a two-week trial of the preliminary injunction issue was held. Judge Conrad L. Rushing ruled that the NCAA's drug-testing program was unconstitutionally void and overbroad. Rushing issued a preliminary injunction to prevent drug testing in all sports, except football and men's basketball. For football and men's basketball, Rushing reduced the NCAA list of substances for testing. Judge Rushing found that there was an invasion of privacy based on Article I, Section 7 of the California Constitution. The NCAA sought a full trial, which was scheduled for February 1988.

In *O'Halloran v. University of Washington*, student-athletes challenged the university's drug-testing program when the student-athletes were ruled ineligible to compete when they refused to participate in the school's drug-testing program.

In July 1987, Superior Court Judge George Mattson ruled that there was an invasion of privacy based on both the U.S. and state constitutions. Mattson also ruled that the NCAA should be brought into the case as a codefendant. The NCAA then successfully moved the case to federal district court. The case is pending; however, it will be an important one to follow since it is in federal district court. U.S. constitutional law arguments are being made, and the NCAA is a defendant.

In *Bally v. Northeastern University*, the plaintiff, a member of the men's cross-country and track teams, challenged the university's random mandatory drug-testing policy. Judge Paul K. Connolly ruled in favor of the plaintiff and found that there was an unreasonable search and seizure and an invasion of privacy, based on Massachusetts state law.

In *Derdyn v. University of Colorado*, a cross-country runner brought the first case concerning a drug-testing program when he challenged the university's program. His case relies on both state and federal constitutional law arguments. It is still pending at this time.

Chapter 13

ADDITIONAL LEGAL CONCERNS IN AMATEUR ATHLETICS

INTRODUCTION

Amateur athletic administrators should be aware of and concerned about three additional legal areas: the antitrust laws, the tax laws, and illegal gambling. These topics are not related. They are given brief mention in Chapter 13 for the purpose of providing an overview and some background information on potential legal problems in these areas.

THE ANTITRUST LAWS

Antitrust laws are designed to promote competition in the business sector through regulation "designed to control the exercise of private economic power" (Gellhorn, *Antitrust Law and Economics*, 1977). In athletics, antitrust law concerns have primarily involved professional sports, which are private economic business entities operated theoretically to make a profit. Increasingly, however, amateur athletic organizations have come under the scrutiny of antitrust laws, partly because of the transformation of many areas of amateur athletics into "big business." This is particularly true of intercollegiate athletics, primarily football and men's basketball. For example, the NCAA's Football Television Plan for 1984–85 was declared to be in violation of the antitrust laws because it prevented the free flow of televised intercollegiate football (see Chapter 9, pages 502–507). The decision, upheld by the U.S. Supreme Court in 1984, disrupted the entire sports telecasting industry by allowing a glut of televised intercollegiate football to flood the market. The decision caused the financial rights fees for these televised games to drop significantly, causing many institutions to experience a shortfall in their annual budgets.

Two major antitrust laws form the underlying basis for court decisions: the Sherman Antitrust Act and the Clayton Act.

The Sherman Antitrust Act

The Sherman Antitrust Act was passed in 1890 during a period of U.S. history when business had gained domination over the delivery of goods and services to the detriment of the average citizen. Therefore, the law was passed with the purpose of encouraging free and open competition in business. The ultimate beneficiary was the consumer, who would not have to pay above-market prices for goods and services. The law was neither detailed nor overly focused. It had two major sections. Section I, which is sometimes referred to as Sherman I, stated: "Every contract, combination in the form of trust or otherwise, or conspiracy in restraint of trade or commerce among the several states or foreign nations is declared to be illegal." Section II, or Sherman II, stated: "Every person who shall monopolize, or attempt to monopolize or combine or conspire with any other person or persons, to monopolize any part of the trade or commerce among the several states, or with foreign nations, shall be deemed guilty of a felony. . . ."

Federal antitrust laws seek to regulate competitive conduct involving interstate commerce. The Sherman Antitrust Act specifically covers transactions in goods, land, or services. Section I of the Sherman Act concerns agreements that restrain trade, such as a group of businesses attempting to fix prices among themselves. In determining what constitutes an impermissible restraint of trade, the courts use a rule-of-reason test, which weighs the alleged illegal practice against the anticompetitive effect it has on business to see if in balance the practice should be deemed improper and unlawful. Some conduct, such as price fixing, is by its nature deemed illegal and does not require a rule-of-reason analysis.

Section II of the Sherman Act attempts to prevent monopolistic action by a business or businesses, such as attempting to control all televised football so as to prevent another school or league from being telecast. It is all right for a monopoly to exist for natural reasons, as long as the monopoly then does not attempt to drive out competition through illegal means.

The Clayton Act

The Clayton Act was enacted in 1914 to tighten up some of the generalities of the Sherman Act. It was specifically designed to prevent certain practices in the sale of goods in interstate commerce. Specific sections of the Clayton Act deal with subjects involving corporate mergers, price discrimination, and other matters.

Antitrust Liabilities of Amateur Athletic Associations

In the past, amateur athletic organizations have not been subject to the antitrust litigation that the professional sports industry has faced. However, with the increased prominence associated with amateur athletics and the money now involved, organizations such as the NCAA are increasingly subject to antitrust litigation.

Historically, defendant amateur athletic associations had been successful in arguing that the antitrust laws were not applicable to them since amateur athletics are not "trade" or "commerce" as

defined by the Sherman Act. Amateur organizations have traditionally argued that since their athletic associations are nonprofit
organizations, their primary purpose is educational and noncommercial in nature, and hence cannot be defined as trade or
commerce. However, in the cases discussed here, the courts seem
to be defining amateur athletics, and especially the NCAA, as
"trade" or "commerce," and therefore are declaring them subject
to the antitrust laws.

In 1972, the federal antitrust laws were first applied to amateur
athletics in *Amateur Softball Ass'n of America v. United States*,
467 F.2d 312 (10th Cir. 1972). In that case, the governing organization for softball in the United States was deemed not exempt
from antitrust laws. The court reasoned that even though the
primary purpose of the association was noncommercial, subsequent actions or operations of an amateur athletic association could
trigger application of the Sherman Act.

A similar result was determined in *Tondas v. Amateur Hockey
Ass'n of the United States*, 438 F. Supp. 310 (W.D.N.Y. 1977). The
court held that the amateur hockey association had significant
market and economic power to trigger possible antitrust law applications. However, in *Ass'n for Intercollegiate Athletics for Women
v. National Collegiate Athletic Ass'n*, 558 F. Supp. 487 (D.D.C.
1983), 735 F.2d 577 (D.C. Cir. 1984), the courts held that the
NCAA's dominance of the amateur sports television market does
not by itself create a monopolistic practice against a rival association, since no illegal tying arrangement existed.

In considering whether the antitrust laws apply to amateur
athletic organizations, athletic administrators should ask the following questions:

1. Is the primary purpose of the amateur association commercial
   or noncommercial?
2. If the primary purpose is noncommercial, do certain aspects
   of the association's activities constitute commercial economic
   enterprises (e.g., radio/television telecasts, sales of goods or
   services, facility rentals, etc.)?
3. Does the association enjoy a dominant position in the marketplace or is it employing practices designed to drive all
   competition from the marketplace using undue influence
   derived from its dominant position?

NOTES _____

   1. The following cases involve unsuccessful attempts at showing antitrust law violations by amateur athletic associations:

(a) *Board of Regents, University of Oklahoma v. National Collegiate Athletic Ass'n*, 561 P.2d 449 (Okla. 1977).

(b) *Jones v. National Collegiate Athletic Ass'n*, 392 F. Supp. 295 (D. Mass. 1975).

(c) *Hennessey v. National Collegiate Athletic Ass'n*, No. CA 76-P-0799-W (N.D. Ala. 1976), *aff'd per curiam*, 564 F.2d 1136 (5th Cir. 1977).

2. For further information, see "Antitrust Issues in Amateur Sports," 61 *Indiana Law Journal* 1 (Winter 1985).

THE TAX LAWS

Several of the tax issues facing the college and high school athletic administrator revolve around the status of most amateur organizations as tax-exempt organizations. These organizations are also commonly referred to as nonprofit or not-for-profit organizations.

Internal Revenue Service Code section 501(a) governs organizations that seek to obtain an exemption from federal income tax. To qualify for the exemption, the athletic endeavor must be organized for one or more of the purposes set forth in section 501. Section 501(c)(3) of the code designates those organizations, which include religious, charitable, educational, scientific, literary, testing for public safety, fostering national or international amateur sports competition, or the prevention of cruelty to children or animals. State or municipal instrumentalities also fall under 501(c)(3), and these may include high schools and state universities. Therefore, activities such as the Olympics, national sports festivals, and state games may fall under the "national or international amateur sports competition" area. Athletic departments may fall under "educational institutions" or "municipal instrumentalities." Booster clubs, Little Leagues, and Pop Warner Football may fall under "charitable organizations."

Nonprofit Organizations

An organization seeking nonprofit status must file an application with the Internal Revenue Service. The purposes and proposed activities of the organization must be set forth in the corporate papers. In addition, a classified statement of receipts and expenditures, and a balance sheet for the current year and the three immediate prior years are needed for existing organizations. If a new organization is applying, a proposed budget for two full accounting periods and a current statement of assets and liabilities must be filed. After receipt of the necessary application materials, the IRS will issue a decision in a determination letter.

There are three main advantages to an organization which attains nonprofit status. The first and major advantage is the exemption from federal income tax liability. The organization is not subject to any tax on the income it generates as long as it is related to the organization's exempt purpose. The second advantage is that services performed in the employ of a nonprofit organization may be exempted from liability for the social security (FICA) taxes. This exemption could provide for lower operating costs for the organization. The third advantage is that contributions by an individual taxpayer or business qualify as charitable contributions and are deductible by the donor for income tax purposes. This is an obvious incentive for individuals and businesses to contribute to a particular organization.

However, obtaining nonprofit status also has its disadvantages. The first is the amount of paper work that must be filed. The second is that the application for exemption and the supporting documentation are available for public scrutiny. However, there are procedures for withholding the information from the public if the IRS determines that the disclosure would adversely affect the organization.

A variety of other restrictions placed on nonprofit organizations should be considered before applying for the favorable tax treatment. For example, the assets of an organization must be permanently dedicated to the exempt purpose. This means that if the organization is dissolved, the assets must be distributed to another exempt purpose, or to the federal, state, or local government for a public purpose. Therefore, one cannot build profits through a nonprofit organization, then dissolve the business and take the profits. In addition, although employees of a nonprofit organization may be paid a salary, the salary cannot be tied to the profitability of the organization.

A not-for-profit organization is often incorrectly interpreted as a business that cannot make money in any tax year. This is untrue; the bottom line for a nonprofit organization may be in the black. However, the profits may not be used to benefit the organizers or employees.

NOTE

1. For further details on nonprofit organizations, see the booklet "How to Apply for and Retain Exempt Status for Your Organization," Internal Revenue Service Publication 557.

Unrelated Business Income

The tax on unrelated business income has become a major issue for athletic organizations. A tax-exempt organization may be held liable for taxes on unrelated business income, which is income from a trade or business, regularly carried on, that is not substantially related to the charitable, educational, or other purpose constituting the basis for its exemption.

It is important for the college athletics administrator to understand how the structure and function of a college athletics department or program relates to the IRS rules and regulations pertaining to unrelated business income and subsequent taxation. The unrelated business income tax was enacted to accomplish two objectives: (1) to eliminate unfair competition between charitable organizations and the taxed private sector and (2) to increase federal tax revenues.

Intercollegiate athletics today are characterized by schools with multimillion dollar athletic budgets, the desire to win and produce revenue to perpetuate those budgets, and an increasing gap between the goals of the educational institution and the goals of the athletic department. Because of this climate in intercollegiate athletics today, there is an increasing need for athletic administrators to deal intelligently with conflicts that arise from activities that, while within an educational and tax-exempt institution, take on the characteristics and function of an "unrelated business."

The IRS language relating to educational organizations, and specifically athletic organizations, reads as follows (Pub. 557, 1985, "Tax-Exempt Status for Your Organization"):

> The term *educational* relates to the instruction or training of individuals for the purpose of improving or developing their capabilities, or the instruction of the public on subjects useful to individuals and beneficial to the community. . . .
>
> An athletic organization must submit evidence that it is engaged in activities such as directing and controlling interscholastic athletic competitions, conducting tournaments, and prescribing eligibility rules for contestants. If not, your organization may be exempt as a social club. . . . Raising funds to be used for travel and other activities to interview and persuade prospective students with outstanding athletic ability to attend a particular university does not evidence an exempt purpose. . . .

The issues surrounding the unrelated business income tax affect the following categories of income:

- Income from rental/admission fees for use of college athletic facilities for profit-making entertainment aimed primarily or solely at the general public (e.g., big-time football and basket-ball games, rock concerts, renting to professional franchises).

- Income from rental/admission fees for use of college athletics facilities by the general public, in which an admission or usage fee is charged.
- Income from tuition for summer camps and clinics on campus (sports camps).
- Income from rental and user fees charged to private companies (e.g., health clubs) that operate on campus and under the auspices of the college athletic department.

The extent to which the above income will be subject to the unrelated business income tax is subject to many conflicting interests. The fact that some university athletic departments operate independently of the rest of the university, both financially and administratively, only adds to the debate over what activities are to be classified as unrelated business activities separate and apart from the charitable, tax-exempt function of the educational institution.

Before looking more closely at what constitutes unrelated business income, according to IRS definition, it is helpful to provide a general overview on the topic. The IRS, in its 1978 decision, created a de facto exemption for college/university athletic programs—a decision that has since raised a few eyebrows from those who perceive university athletic programs largely as a profit-motivated entertainment industry subject to taxation. These critics contend that, by and large, intercollegiate athletic programs are, both financially and philosophically, too far removed from the educational function of the institution to justify charitable, tax-exempt status.

The critical question is whether the operation that produces money, whether it be a big-time college football game, an on-campus health club, or a summer sports camp, meets the three characteristics of unrelated business income within a charitable institution. Generally, an unrelated business is not taxable when (1) it fails to meet all three criteria outlined below, (2) is operated entirely by volunteers, or (3) the business carried on is "primarily for the convenience of the college's members, students, patients, officers, or employees." One also must consider whether the business is "in serious competition" with the private sector. For instance, if a university athletic department conducted a money-making tennis facility that competed with a local, privately operated tennis facility, the income from the university tennis facility may be taxable according to IRS rules.

An institution's "unrelated business taxable income" is defined by the IRS as the net income of any:

1. trade or business that is
2. "regularly carried on" *and* is
3. "not substantially related (aside from the need of such organization for income or funds or the use it makes of the profits derived) to the exercise or performance" of the college's educational function.

Any activity having these three characteristics is an "unrelated business," the income from which, after customary business deductions are taken, is taxed at the regular corporate rates, without regard to whether the entity actually carrying on the business is a charitable corporation. In short, the test of whether an unrelated business is taxable looks to the *source* of the income, irrespective of its use. Proof of the funds' proper use is now irrelevant to the questions of their taxability; instead, the critical question is whether the operation that produces those funds is an "unrelated business." In addition, any organization whose "unrelated" activities become predominant to the overall charitable function and goals of the institution risks losing its basic tax exemption. An organization's activities must still be primarily charitable in nature for it to qualify as a tax-exempt organization in the first place. It is only the problem of primarily charitable entities (e.g., educational institutions) engaging in some noncharitable activity that the unrelated business income tax addresses.

In order to better assess whether an athletic department activity is subject to unrelated business income taxation, it is important for the high school and college athletic administrator to understand the general principles and issues in determining whether the activity constitutes a trade or business regularly carried on and not substantially related to the exercise and performance of the institution's educational function. An activity will be classified as a trade or business if it "is carried on for the production of income from the sale of goods or the performance of services." The activity does not lose identity as a trade or business merely because it is carried on within the larger aggregate of similar activities. In other words, a business activity is not made otherwise by association with charitable (e.g., educational) operations. Additionally, the absence of profits does not necessarily eliminate the possibility of taxation. Instead, it is the *quest for profit* that is decisive.

The key considerations in an inquiry are the (1) existence of profits, (2) the activity's source of funding, and (3) other factors that give the activity a commercial flavor, including broadcast receipts (which alone may show athletic programs to be undertaken for profit purposes) and recruiting intensity. In general, the activity is a trade or business if it is *expected* to make money, even if it also has certain nonfinancial objectives, such as promoting the school's image, or pleasing alumni and state legislators.

Section 512 (a)(1) of the IRS manual lists the key factors in determining if an activity is "regularly carried on" as "the frequency and continuity with which the activities . . . are conducted" and whether they "are pursued in a manner generally similar to comparable commercial activities." For seasonal activities, the operation is regularly carried on if conducted "during a significant portion of the season."

Determining whether or not the activity is "substantially related" is the most difficult to analyze because of the broad definition of "education." Hence, the issue of substantial relatedness usually focuses on a second, more restrictive question: What is the activity's relationship to the exempt purpose? More specifically, does the activity *contribute importantly* to the accomplishment of the exempt purpose of the institution? These judgments are made on a case-by-case basis. Conversely, an activity is substantially related if it "contributes importantly" to the university's educational mission, even if the activity's principal purpose is financial or is otherwise unrelated to education. Under this analysis, university-operated summer sports camps and health clubs will generally fall into the tax-exempt category. How one measures an activity's contribution to education, and thus the contribution's importance, has not yet been clarified by the courts.

In addition to the "important contribution" yardstick, a second consideration is whether the size and extent of the activity is proportional to the nature and extent of the exempt function which it purports to serve.

The question of whether intercollegiate athletics, in general, contributes importantly to the institution's educational mission is problematic at best. Until the courts decide otherwise, intercollegiate athletic programs will remain shrouded in philosophical debate over the word "education" and will remain exempt from taxation as an unrelated business, despite the search-for-profits analysis and the commercial aspects of these activities (including broadcast receipts, independent funding, and the resulting pressures on athletic recruiting). In large part, this is because of legislative sympathy toward the educational institution and a hesitancy to tax college sports.

However, recent protests from the business community may pressure legislators to reconsider their attitude toward taxing these enterprises. As of February 1987, 18 states had enacted or had pending legislation to curb what many consider an unfair competitive advantage available to educational institutions. In addition, action from federal agencies and Congress appears imminent. The legislation which emerges may very well have important ramifications for athletic administrators at the collegiate and high school level.

A university's rental income from professional sports teams is not tax exempt simply because the university uses the same facility itself at other times.

Charitable Contributions

In April 1986 the IRS revised its ruling on the issue of whether payments to athletic scholarship programs qualify as deductions for charitable contributions when the payments afford the right to purchase preferred seating at athletic events. Under the new ruling, payments to athletic scholarship programs qualify for deductions as charitable contributions to the extent that they exceed the fair market value of any substantial benefits received in return. The ruling acknowledges that the institution may place a reasonable fair market value on the preferred-seating privilege, thereby allowing taxpayers to determine what portion of the payment will be tax deductible as a charitable contribution. Additionally, even when the institution fails to place a value on the preferred-seating privilege, it is still possible for the taxpayer to establish that value by other means, however difficult this task may prove given that there is no "market" for ticket-buying privileges.

Basic federal tax principles provide that when a charitable organization confers some substantial benefit in exchange for a contribution, a presumption arises that no part of the contribution is deductible as a gift. The new ruling allows the taxpayer to overcome this by establishing the fair market value of the benefit received and deducting that portion of the contribution that exceeds that value.

The new ruling sets forth four fact situations and conclusions:

Facts

Situation 1. Taxpayer A, an individual, made a payment of $300 to a particular athletic scholarship program maintained by a university. A minimum payment of $300 is required to become a "member" of the program. The only benefit afforded members is that they are permitted to purchase, by paying the stated price of $120, a season ticket to the university's home football games in a designated area in the stadium. Because the games are regularly sold out well in advance, tickets to the games covered by the season ticket would not have been readily available to A if A had not made the payment to the program. The $300 membership fee is paid annually, and a member is required to make a separate $120 payment for each season ticket the member purchases. The university did not inform its donors of the fair market value of the right to purchase a season ticket in the designated area.

Situation 2. The facts are the same as in *Situation 1* except that taxpayer B, an individual, made a payment of $500 to the program, even though only a $300 payment is required to become a "member" of the program. The additional $200 did not result in any benefit to B other than that afforded members who paid $300.

Situation 3. Taxpayer C, an individual, made a payment of $300 to an athletic scholarship program of a university. This payment entitled C to become a "member" of the program and, as a member, to purchase a season ticket, for an additional payment of the stated price, in a designated area in the stadium. Tickets are offered to members before season tickets go on sale to the public. Seating reasonably comparable to that available to C as a result of membership in the program would have been readily available to C even if C had not made the payment to the program.

Situation 4. Taxpayer D, an individual, made a payment of $300 to an athletic scholarship program of a university. This payment entitled D to become a "member" of the program and, as a member, to purchase a season ticket to the university's home football games, for an additional payment of the stated price, in a designated area of the stadium. The membership fee is paid annually, and a member is required to make a separate $300 payment for each season ticket the member purchases. Although the games are not regularly sold out, seating reasonably comparable to that available to D as a result of membership in the program would not have been readily available to D if D had not made the payment to the program. The university reasonably estimated that the fair market value of the right to purchase a season ticket in the designated area of the stadium would be x dollars, and advised prospective members that the additional ($300 − x dollars) was being solicited as a contribution. In making the estimate, the university considered the level of demand for tickets, the general availability of seats, the relative desirability of seats based on their types, locations, and views, and other relevant factors.

Conclusions

In *Situations 1* and *2*, because tickets to the games covered by the season ticket would not otherwise have been readily available to A and B, the right to purchase a season ticket in a designated area in the stadium was a substantial benefit. This substantial benefit was afforded to A and B because each paid the minimum membership fee of $300. Accordingly, a presumption arises that the $300 reflects the value of the benefit received. Unless the taxpayer can establish

that $300 exceeded the value of the benefit received, no part of the
$300 payment is a charitable contribution under section 170 of the
Code.

In *Situation 2*, however, the additional $200 contributed by *B*
resulted in no additional substantial benefit and thus, is a charitable
contribution.

In *Situation 3*, although the taxpayer was entitled to purchase a
ticket before tickets went on sale to the public, and although the
ticket was for seating in a designated area, reasonably comparable
seating would have been readily available to *C* even if *C* had not
made a payment to the program. Although *C* received the benefit of
obtaining a ticket early and of sitting with other program members,
the benefit was not substantial. Accordingly, the entire $300 is a
charitable contribution.

In *Situation 4*, because reasonably comparable seating would not
otherwise have been readily available to *D*, the right to purchase a
season ticket in a designated area in the stadium was a substantial
benefit. This substantial benefit was afforded to *D* because *D* paid
the minimum membership fee of $300. Accordingly, a presumption
arises that the $300 reflects the value of the benefit received. The
university, however, after taking all relevant facts and circumstances
into account, reasonably estimated the fair market value of the
benefit as x dollars. Because the university solicited the other ($300
− x dollars) as a contribution and the x dollar figure reflected the
fair market value of the benefit provided, ($300 − x dollars) of *D*'s
$300 payment is a charitable contribution. [I.R.S., Rev. Rul. 86-63]

If payments solicited for a charitable fund-raising activity are
designed to be partly a gift and partly the purchase price of certain
privileges or benefits, the organization conducting the activity
should employ procedures that clearly establish that not only is a
gift being solicited in connection with the activity, but also the
amount of the gift being solicited. To do this, the amount properly
attributable to the purchase of privileges or benefits and the
amount solicited as a gift should be determined prior to solicitation. After making this determination of the fair market value of
any substantial privilege or benefit, the charitable organization
should notify its donors of the amounts allocable to each component of the payment.

The ruling provides only limited guidance on factors to be taken
into account by the institution in valuing a privilege or benefit. In
the specific case of ticket-purchase privileges, these guiding factors
include "the level of demand for tickets, the general availability of
seats, the relative desirability of seats based on their types, locations, and views, and other relevant factors."

The Tax Reform Act of 1986

The Tax Reform Act of 1986 was the most comprehensive and significant tax legislation passed by Congress since the beginning of World War II. The provisions included in this legislation will have a considerable effect on every individual and business in this country for many years to come. Organizations involved with amateur athletics did not escape the effect of this legislation.

While most of these organizations pay no income taxes, the law has indirectly affected the way they operate. The changes in the rates, the 80 percent limitation on entertainment expenses, and the luxury box restrictions all have potentially negative results for fund raising and ticket selling programs at educational institutions. Also, new rules regarding the treatment of scholarships have imposed additional administrative burdens.

The reduction in individual tax rates from a maximum rate of 50 percent in 1986 to 28 percent in 1988 and additional restrictions on itemized deductions make charitable contributions less palatable. A taxpayer in 1986 who was in the 50 percent bracket and made a $1,000 contribution saved $500 in taxes. In 1988 that $1,000 contribution will only save $280. Also, the restrictions on certain deductions, such as sales taxes and miscellaneous deductions, will reduce the number of people who have enough deductions to itemize. In this situation, no deduction for any contribution will be allowed, as the new law also eliminates the nonitemizer charitable contribution deduction.

In addition, the new limitations on entertainment expenses and luxury box rentals may cause businesses to look elsewhere to spend their money. Starting in 1987, only 80 percent of business meal and entertainment expenses are deductible by the entity that incurs them. This could have an effect on the purchase of tickets for athletic events by businesses. For years this has been an important source of revenue for many athletic endeavors.

Another potentially damaging change in the law relates to the new rules regarding the deduction of the cost of the rental of a luxury skybox. If a business or individual rents a luxury box for more than one event during a year, the deductible amount is subject to certain limitations which began in 1987. The actual cost of the tickets themselves will be deductible, but this cost is tied to the value of the highest priced nonskybox ticket generally available to the public. Any excess over this amount was reduced by 33.33 percent in 1987 and 66.66 percent in 1988, and in 1989 none of the excess will be deductible. The impact of this change on universities that have constructed skyboxes in their stadiums could be substantial. Depending on the reaction of the business community to these changes, these boxes could go unused, and large capital investments on the part of the university could be wasted.

Athletic administrators must also be concerned with the new law's impact on scholarships and grants. In the past, all funds provided to a student as scholarships or grants were not included in the student's gross income. However, under the new law, scholarships and grants awarded after August 16, 1986, for taxable years beginning after December 31, 1986, may contain certain amounts that must be included in the recipient's gross income.

The new law defines qualified tuition and related expenses as tuition and fees required for enrollment, fees, books, supplies, and equipment required for courses of instruction. Scholarships and grants for these expenses are excluded from the recipient's gross income. However, amounts for room and board are not excludable. In addition, any portion of a scholarship or grant representing payment for teaching, research, or other services required as a condition for receiving the qualified scholarship is also included in the recipient's gross income. This would require the grantor to file wage information returns regarding these amounts and also face the possibility of paying social security and employment taxes. In addition, IRS notice 87-31 urges the grantor to supply the recipient with a calculation of the appropriate amount to be included in his or her gross income.

The tax law is a constantly changing body of rules which seem to change without much publicity in some cases. Athletic administrators need to be aware of what effects the new law will have on their organizations so as to properly react and attempt to maintain the support they currently enjoy.

NOTE

1. For further information, see the following law review articles:
   (a) Jensen, "Taxation, the Student-Athlete, and the Professionalization of College Athletics," *Utah Law Review* 35 (1987).
   (b) Judge, "Student-Athletes As Employees: Income Tax Consequences," 13 *Journal of College and University Law* 285 (Winter 1986).

INTERCOLLEGIATE ATHLETICS AND GAMBLING

The problems associated with illegal gambling and the influence it may exert on intercollegiate athletics are of special concern to athletic administrators and others, since gambling affects the integrity of the games, the games themselves, and the public confidence in athletes and sports. Some argue that betting on games is encouraged by the press, which prints the "spread" on games in its sports pages, as well as advertisements on weekly tip sheets and betting aids. Although some contend that betting on athletics is enjoyable and is a form of entertainment, others contend that illegal gambling has a negative impact on society and sports. Many athletic managers have taken steps to combat the dangers of illegal gambling in an effort to preserve the integrity of their schools, conferences, and leagues.

Estimates are that gambling on college athletics is a $1 billion a year industry. Problems associated with and arising from wagering have continually plagued college athletics. In 1945, five Brooklyn College basketball players were expelled from school after they admitted to accepting bribes to lose a game. In 1951, 37 players at 22 schools were caught shaving points (trying to win by fewer points than bookmakers predict) in 44 games. Recently, a gambling scandal at Boston College during the 1978–79 season led to the conviction of basketball player Rick Kuhn, who was sentenced to 10 years in prison on federal gaming charges (see Notes 5–11). More recently, in 1985, a gambling and drug scandal was uncovered at Tulane University. That incident, which involved a number of basketball players, led to the institution's dropping basketball (see Notes 12–14).

The NCAA's disapproval of illegal gambling in intercollegiate athletics is clearly spelled out in the following policy statement:

Policy 8: Gambling and Bribery

Section 1. College administrators should redouble their efforts in counseling the student body at large and athletes in particular as to the seriousness of the gambling problem. This is an unending and continual challenge and one to which college athletics administrators must constantly rededicate themselves.

Section 2. All institutions should warn their athletics squads regularly against the threat and corruption attached to the activities of gamblers; cite existing and applicable Federal, state and local laws; review the tragedy that has struck some students; and post pertinent messages on this subject to remind the student-athletes of these facts.

Section 3. Institutional rules should provide that any student (athlete or nonathlete) shall be expelled from college and any staff member shall be terminated as an employee for failure to report a solicitation to be a party to sports bribery; further, institutional regulations should provide that a student shall be expelled or a staff member shall be terminated if the individual becomes an agent of the gambling industry through the process of distributing handicap information or handling bets. (Note: Institutions should encourage local authorities to enact and enforce laws prohibiting this type of activity on the part of any citizen.)

Section 4. Institutional rules should provide for the termination of employment for life of any staff member who knowingly continues association with known gamblers or bookmakers after being advised by the institution's chief executive officer to discontinue such association.

Section 5. Any additional steps that can be taken to make it more difficult for the briber to gain information or to make contact at the campus level should be undertaken.

Section 6. In those states that do not have antibribery laws or where existing laws are inadequate, member institutions should take the leadership in petitioning state legislatures to pass strong legislation to deal with this subject.

Section 7. No press credentials should be issued to representatives of any organization that regularly publishes, or otherwise promotes the advertising of, "tout sheets" or "tip sheets" or other advertising designed to encourage gambling on college sports events. [*1987–88 NCAA Manual*, Policy 8]

The NCAA has continued to add to its investigating staff to keep up with the gambling problem. Many NCAA investigators are former FBI agents who attempt to maintain contacts with bookmakers, both in Nevada where sports gambling is legal and in other states where it is not. This unorthodox relationship between bookmakers and NCAA investigators is based on mutual concern that sporting events not be rigged to reach a predetermined outcome. The bookmakers cannot afford a rigged game for economic reasons, because their winning percentages and profit margins are based on a "point spread," which they formulate on the theory that the game is not rigged. The NCAA and the individual school's concerns are based on the integrity of the game and on their reputation.

The bookmakers usually alert investigators if there is a sizable change in the point spread on a particular game. Such a change is suspicious and may indicate that bettors have placed large wagers on a team. Of course, heavy betting may occur for other reasons, such as a coach's announcement of an injury to a key player. If no legitimate reasons are found, however, it increases the possibility that gamblers have "fixed" the game by bribing a coach, player, or official. Remember, bribes are not necessarily made to ensure that a team loses—just that it wins by fewer points than the predicted point spread. Once suspicions are aroused, college officials such as the president and athletic director are then informed by the NCAA. They may also be notified if investigators hear "street talk" about "something funny" going on somewhere in the institution's athletic program.

NOTES ——

1. John Thompson, basketball coach of the 1984 NCAA champion Georgetown University team, made the following remarks during an appearance before the District of Columbia Citizen's Gambling Study Commission:

> My opinion then, as now, is that it's not a question of whether gambling should be legal or not, but of being consistent. To legalize some forms of gambling, like lotteries, and to run betting lines in newspapers and broadcast them on television, is a kind of "entrapment."
>
> It's like putting heroin all over the street and advertising it in the newspapers, then arresting somebody for using it. By creating an atmosphere of permissiveness, it tells a kid it's okay to gamble because we've gone public with it.

2. Tony Vaccarino, an agent in the FBI's Criminal Investigations Division, says that coaches should study tapes of all games and talk with players to make sure they are all performing properly. He thinks a coach should get in touch with the FBI "if he feels his team is not performing the way it should." Vaccarino claims the FBI is opposed to legalizing sports gambling of any sort: "We say it would create situations where people get involved in gambling who would normally not get involved. It exposes them to involvement with organized-crime figures—with loan sharks, for instance, to pay off gambling debts."

3. In June 1985, at hearing held by the President's Commission on Organized Crime, John R. Davis, president of the NCAA, testified that the association would be in favor of a law that prohibited the printing of "point spreads" in newspapers, "were it not for apparent constitutional limitations." Davis also called for a federal law banning gambling on amateur sports. At the same hearings, Vince Doria, assistant managing editor for sports at the *Boston Globe*, testified:

> I think most newspapers have come to the conclusion that gamblers are readers too. . . . In fact, they are extremely avid readers of the sports pages.
> I think most of us believe that those readers deserve to be serviced.

See "Davis Gives Views at U.S. Hearing," *NCAA News*, July 3, 1985, pp. 1, 12.

4. For more information on gambling in intercollegiate athletics, see "Gambling on College Games Said to Be Up Dramatically," *Chronicle of Higher Education*, March 2, 1983, pp. 1, 16–18. The following excerpt is from that article:

> The Commission on the Review of the National Policy Toward Gambling recommended in its 1976 report, *Gambling in America*, "that there be an absolute prohibition against the inclusion of wagering on amateur sporting events [if betting on professional sports is legalized]. While the commission recognizes that some amateur events already are the objects of illegal wagering nationwide, it cannot condone the utilization for wagering purposes of educational institutions and similar organizations dedicated to the improvement of youth.

This opinion is in part predicated on the fact that young athletes of high school and college age are far more impressionable and therefore are in greater danger of being subjected to the temptations of player corruption. Additionally, unlike professional sports leagues, particularly the [National Football League], amateur athletic associations do not have enforcement or investigative capabilities which would enable them to maintain sufficient safeguards.

5. Billy Packer and Al McGuire, TV broadcast personalities, have produced a film called *Sell Out*, which warns athletes of the dangers associated with gambling. The film was produced by TPC Communication and financed by Nike, Inc.

6. Nevada, the only state in the nation to allow legal sports gambling, does not permit betting on college games involving public or private institutions, whether the contest is being played inside or outside the state borders. The regulation was enacted in 1972 by the Nevada Gambling Control Board.

7. Most athletic conferences, if they address the problem of gambling at all, do so in a manner to disclaim responsibility. The following excerpt is from the *1986–87 Pacific-10 Conference Handbook*, p. 32.

> Instructions Re: Gambling, Pro Contracts. Each member institution shall carry out its own procedures to inform and instruct its student-athletes on their responsibilities in protecting themselves and their sports from gambling interests. . . .

8. In *United States v. Burke*, 700 F.2d 70 (2d Cir. 1983), Rick Kuhn, a former Boston College basketball player, was charged (along with four co-defendants) and convicted of racketeering by conspiring to fix at least six games, of sports bribery, and of violation of the Interstate Travel and Aid to Racketeering statutes. In sentencing Kuhn to a 10-year sentence, the court noted:

> The crimes in this case are especially significant in view of the ramifications which they have had on the world of sports, college basketball in particular. A group of gamblers and career criminals were able to band together and successfully bribe and influence college athletes. Their motivation was simple and clear—financial gain. The crime, however, reminds millions of sports fans that athletics can be compromised and are not always merely honest competition among dedicated athletes.
>
> While it is true that only one or possibly two athletes were compromised, the effect remains basically the same. Every college athlete may now come under suspicion by fans and coaches. This suspicion has existed previously due to earlier scandals dating back several years, and it is now renewed as a result of this offense.
>
> This 26-year-old defendant undoubtedly assumed one of the more essential roles in this offense. While it may be true that his performance during games was not particularly pivotal, his actions away from the basketball court are of significant importance. He was a member of the 1978–79 Boston College team who initially agreed to participate and thereafter recruited other players, maintained contact with the gamblers and accepted their payments.
>
> It is interesting to note that there was not testimony introduced at the trial which indicated a reluctance on the part of the defendant to participate (in point shaving) or a desire to terminate his involvement. Rather, he

emerges as somewhat of a greedy individual who was more interested in collecting money from his criminal associates than he was in winning basketball games.

The defendant is a product of a stable and supporting working-class family. From a young age, he developed natural abilities in athletics and was essentially successful in signing a professional baseball contract in 1973 and in attending college on a basketball scholarship three years later. Various individuals who have been (associated) with the defendant in his home town of Swissville, Pennsylvania, have described him in very positive terms. The reasons therefore as to why he became involved in this offense remain unclear.

On final analysis, deterrence emerges as the most important sentencing objective. A strong argument can be offered that the substantial term of incarceration imposed on this defendant will be recalled in the future by another college athlete who may be tempted to compromise his performance.

9. The NCAA followed the Kuhn case with great interest and followed up the conviction with the account below, which was published in the *NCAA News*. It shows the interesting sequence of events and the interaction with organized crime that led to Kuhn's 10-year sentence.

The government's case on the Boston College point-shaving case sought to prove that the scandal was a calculated and prolonged undertaking. The following picture of what occurred emerged from the trial.

The investigation began when Henry Hill, who was cooperating with prosecuting authorities and was a participant in the Federal Witness Protection Program, outlined the scheme to the Federal Bureau of Investigation.

Hill, an acknowledged narcotics dealer and truck hijacker, told FBI agents that he and several of his associates had given money and drugs to various members of the Boston College basketball team during the 1978–79 season. In return, the players agreed to "shave points" or deliberately lose games so that Hill and his associates would win large amounts of money by wagering on the games.

The government alleged the plan took shape in the summer of 1978 when Anthony Perla, his brother, Rocco, and Paul Mazzei met with Rick Kuhn, a member of the Boston College basketball team. During these early discussions, Anthony Perla told Kuhn he could earn substantial sums of money if he agreed to participate in a "point-shaving" scheme. After indicating an interest in cooperating, Kuhn was given drugs and other items by the Perla brothers and Mazzei for the rest of the summer.

In September, realizing the group could not handle the plan alone, Mazzei approached Hill. Hill was valuable in that he would be able to contact Jimmy Burke, an organized crime figure with the necessary influence to make the plan succeed. Burke would be able to provide protection from disgruntled bookmakers who might discover the "fix" and lose large sums of money, and he also would be able to arrange for those involved in the scheme to maximize the amount of money that could be wagered and therefore won.

In October, Hill proposed the plan to Burke, who was enthusiastic about it. Burke expressed a desire to meet Mazzei and said he would use only his most trusted bookmakers.

During the first week of November, Mazzei traveled to New York to meet with Burke. Burke reiterated his interest in the plan, but now he said he would like to meet Anthony Perla, who was the principal contact with Kuhn.

Mazzei and Perla came to New York November 16 and met with Burke, who then directed Hill to Boston to meet with the players.

About this time, Kuhn proposed the plan to Boston College captain Jim Sweeney. Sweeney and Kuhn met with Hill, Mazzei and Anthony Perla November 16, with Mazzei telling the players they would have to lose games directly if instructed to do so and that influential people from New York were backing up the scheme.

Shortly thereafter, Kuhn was given $500 and some cocaine, and it was agreed that the team's December 6 game against Providence would be a "trial run."

The test did not go well. Boston College was favored by six to eight points, but it won by 19. Since the group was wagering against Boston College, the group lost. The large margin of victory resulted from the refusal of Sweeney to go along with the plan and from an excellent game by Ernie Cobb, the star of the team.

Hill described Burke as being furious. Rather than abandon the plan, however, the group instructed Kuhn to recruit Cobb. Kuhn and Sweeney later told FBI agents that Cobb was in fact recruited, but Cobb denied receiving any money and never was indicted.

The next significant game was against Harvard December 16. Burke told Hill to go to Boston for the game and tell the players that the group was not going to tolerate the "foolishness" that was exhibited in the Providence game.

By now, Kuhn had attempted to recruit starting center Joe Beaulieu. Beaulieu, however, refused to go along.

Hill, Anthony Perla, Rocco Perla, Paul Mazzei and Judy Wicks (Hill's girlfriend) attended the Harvard game. They saw Boston College win by three points, well under the gambling line of 12. Having bet against Boston College, the group won. After the game, Hill paid Kuhn $3,000 and told him there was more to come in a few days. Another $2,000 was sent to Kuhn by Rocco Perla via Western Union several days later.

The next game that was "fixed" was the December 23 UCLA game. UCLA was a 15-point favorite, and Kuhn told the Perla brothers that Boston College was incapable of winning the game. When Boston College lost by 22 points, the group had won again and on January 8, Kuhn received a Western Union money order for $2,000.

During the next week, Boston College traveled to Honolulu for a holiday tournament. Although no proof exists that the BC games in the event were fixed, gambling lines did shift dramatically (reflecting heavy betting). Also, telephone records show that Burke contacted both Henry Hill and Anthony Perla during the tournament.

The group won again with the January 10 game against Rhode Island, but by the time a January 17 rematch against Rhode Island arrived, the group realized that bookmakers were becoming suspicious. To allay those concerns, the group bet heavily on Boston College to win. The Eagles won the contest, the members of the group won their bets and Kuhn collected another $2,000 from Rocco Perla.

By late January, Kuhn—according to his former girlfriend—was in constant telephone contact with Rocco and Anthony Perla discussing games that were to be fixed.

Boston College played Fordham February 3. It was an important game to the group because it involved a New York team, which meant that large amounts of money could be wagered without raising suspicion. BC was favored by 13 but won by only seven. Rocco Perla attended in place of his brother and provided Kuhn with $1,000 and a stereo system.

Three nights later, Boston College visited New York for a game against St. John's. The Eagles were a nine point underdog, and they lost by nine, resulting in a "push" (a tie). Afterwards, Kuhn's girlfriend said Kuhn was concerned that Cobb was unreliable, but the group wanted his cooperation more than ever.

The next game, a February 10 contest against Holy Cross, was important because it was regionally televised, which again meant that large amounts of money could be wagered without causing concern. Kuhn told the group he would make up for the St. John's game, and Anthony Perla traveled to Las Vegas to bet with legal bookmakers. Hill, who claimed that Burke wagered between $30,000 and $50,000 on the game, watched the contest with Burke. The point spread had Holy Cross by seven, but Boston College lost by only two. The group lost as well. Kuhn himself reportedly lost $10,000 on the game.

The entire series of events might have gone undetected had not Hill come under suspicion in a 1978 robbery of $5.8 million from the Lufthansa Airlines freight terminal at New York's Kennedy International Airport. A Federal attorney asked Hill where he was on a certain date, and Hill said he had been in Boston. When the attorney asked Hill what he had been doing there, Hill said, "Fixing some Boston College basketball games."

On September 8, 1980, the FBI interviewed Kuhn. He admitted he was recruited to shave points, lose games and recruit others to go along. He is thought to have received about $10,500. Another $10,000 was promised to him, but he never received it because he bet it on the Holy Cross game and lost. ["Boston College: A Gamble That Didn't Pay Off," *NCAA News,* February 15, 1982, p. 3.]

10. In 1984, a federal court acquitted Ernie Cobb, a teammate of Kuhn's, of charges arising out of the same violations as those which convicted Kuhn. Cobb admitted accepting $1,000 in 1979 from one of the men convicted but claimed it was not for fixing games but only for giving advice as to which teams Boston College was likely to beat. See "Former College Players Acquitted on Basketball Gambling Charge," *Chronicle of Higher Education,* April 4, 1984, p. 28.

11. In January 1983, the Second U.S. Circuit Court of Appeals unanimously upheld the Kuhn case convictions. In making its ruling, the court upheld the right of news reporters to keep confidential their information and sources in criminal cases. In the appeal, the defense had contended the convictions should be overturned because the trial court would not allow access to press information that was considered vital in cross-examining Henry Hill, the key prosecution witness. The defendants wanted the documents and tapes that were used by *Sports Illustrated,* in a February 1981 article, and were purported to be Hill's first-hand account of the point-shaving scheme. The appeals court concluded that interest did not outweigh the public interest in preserving the confidentiality of journalists' sources. "Reporters," the appeals court said, "are to be encouraged to investigate and expose—free from unnecessary government intrusion—evidence of criminal wrongdoing."

The appeals court in its review said that trial evidence showed the point-shaving scheme was the brainchild of the Perla brothers, who were described as "small-time gamblers with big-time ideas." See *United States v. Burke*, 700 F.2d 70 (2d Cir. 1983).

12. In October 1983, the U.S. Supreme Court upheld the Kuhn case convictions. It rejected the appeal without comment. See *Burke v. United States*, 104 S. Ct. 72, 464 U.S. 816, 78 L. Ed. 2d 85 (1983).

13. In May 1983, in the wake of disclosures made to the FBI by Baltimore Colts quarterback Art Schlichter that while at Baltimore he had run up in four months gambling debts of $389,000, his alma mater, Ohio State, began an investigation into his alleged gambling while a student-athlete. "It would only be prudent administration for us to know what took place," said Ohio State associate athletic director James Jones. See "Collegiate Gambling," *Boston Globe*, May 6, 1983.

14. Schlichter later admitted he had been gambling for years, in high school, at Ohio State, and while with the Colts. See "Schlichter Enters the Next Phase Along the Way Back," *New York Times*, July 23, 1984, p. C1.

15. See also: "Rick Kuhn Sentenced to 10 Years," *New York Times*, February 6, 1982, p. 17.

16. In March 1985, three Tulane University basketball players were arrested and charged with fixing the outcome of games, the first point-shaving scandal to involve intercollegiate athletics since the Boston College incident during the 1978–79 season. It was alleged that the point-shaving scheme involved cocaine purchases for the athletes. In the wake of the scandal, all basketball coaches resigned, the basketball program was terminated, and the athletic director resigned. For further information, see the following articles:

(a) "2 More at Tulane Charged in Fix," *New York Times*, March 28, 1985, p. B11.

(b) "2 at Tulane Held in Basketball Fix," *New York Times*, March 27, 1985, p. B11.

(c) "5th Tulane Student Arrested," *New York Times*, March 29, 1985, p. A27.

(d) "The Darkest Blot," *New York Times*, March 29, 1985, p. A27.

(e) "DA Terms Cocaine Point-Shaving Lure," *New York Daily News*, March 29, 1985, p. 93.

(f) "Cops: Tulane Fixed at Least Two Games," *New York Daily News*, March 27, 1985, p. 53.

(g) "Tulane Ends Basketball," *New York Times*, February 19, 1985, p. A26.

(h) "Tulane Student Pleads Not Guilty," *New York Times*, February 11, 1985, p. B15.

(i) "Two Plead Guilty in Point-Shaving Investigation at Tulane," *NCAA News*, April 10, 1985, p. 3.

(j) "Tulane U., Beset By Recruiting Violations, Gambling Allegations, To Drop Basketball," *Chronicle of Higher Education*, April 10, 1985, p. 31.

(k) "Blowing the Whistle on Men's Basketball at Tulane U.," *Chronicle of Higher Education*, April 17, 1985, pp. 27, 28.

17. In August 1985, the first of the Tulane basketball players to go on

trial, John "Hot Rod" Williams, had a mistrial called after a few days of testimony when the judge ruled that the state's prosecutor had withheld valuable evidence from the defendant's attorney during pretrial discovery. Williams was eventually acquitted. For further information, see the following articles:

(a) "Trial Starts Today for Tulane Star," *New York Times*, August 12, 1985, p. C8.

(b) "Tulane Fix Meeting Recalled," *New York Times*, August 13, 1985, p. A19.

(c) "Tulane Trial Is Halted by Judge," *New York Times*, August 14, 1985, p. B9.

(d) "Williams' Defense Wins a Key Issue," *New York Times*, August 15, 1985, p. B11.

(e) "Mistrial Declared for Ex-Tulane Star," *New York Times*, August 16, 1985, p. A19.

(f) "Mistrial Order Opposed," *New York Times*, August 17, 1985, p. 12.

18. The Tulane basketball players were charged under Louisiana's Bribery of Sports Participants law (L.S.A.—R.S. 14:118.1) which states:

A. Bribing of sports participants is the giving or offering to give, directly or indirectly, anything of apparent present or prospective value to any professional or amateur baseball, football, hockey, polo, tennis or basketball player or boxer or any person or player who participates or expects to participate in any professional or amateur game or sport or any contest of skill, speed, strength or endurance of man or beast or any jockey, driver, groom or any person participating or expecting to participate in any horse race, including owners of race tracks and their employees, stewards, trainers, judges, starters or special policemen, or to any owner, manager, coach or trainer of any team or participant in any such game, contest or sport, with the intent to influence him to lose or cause to be lost, or corruptly to affect or influence the result thereof, or to limit his or his team's or his mount or beast's margin of victory in any baseball, football, hockey or basketball game, boxing, tennis or polo match or horse race or any professional or amateur sport or game in which such player or participant or jockey or driver is taking part or expects to take part, or has any duty in connection therewith.

The acceptance of, or the offer to accept directly or indirectly anything of apparent present or prospective value under such circumstances by any of the above named persons shall also constitute bribery of sports participants.

Whoever commits the crime of bribery of sports participants is guilty of a felony and shall be punished by a fine of not more than ten thousand dollars and imprisoned for not less than one year nor more than five years, with or without hard labor, or both.

B. The offender under this Section, who states the facts under oath to the district attorney charged with the prosecution of the offense, and who gives evidence tending to convict any other offender under that Section, may, in the discretion of such district attorney be granted full immunity from prosecution in respect to the offense reported, except for perjury in giving such testimony.

19. See also, *Louisiana v. Angelo Trosclair, III*, 443 So.2d 1098 (La. 1984) for a Louisiana Supreme Court decision which examined the Louisiana Bribery Sports Participant law in relation to horse racing.

Appendix A

TACTRUST AGREEMENT
Revised January 1, 1985

The Athletics Congress/USA
P.O. Box 120
Indianapolis, IN 46206

TRUST AGREEMENT to establish a trust to be known as TACTRUST by and among the bank, trust company or other fiduciary whose name and address is indicated on Schedule "A" hereof, the individual athletes whose name or names and addresses are set forth on Schedule "B" hereof, and The Athletics Congress of the USA, Inc. whose address is 200 South Capitol Avenue, Suite 140, Indianapolis, Indiana 46225.

1.0   PREAMBLE.   The individual athletes may receive (a) athletic funds by virtue of and as a result of athletic activity or (b) sponsorship payments and benefits as a result of sponsorship activity. The individual athletes wish to be eligible under IAAF rules to enter and compete in international amateur athletic competition notwithstanding their receipt of such funds, payments and benefits. The Athletics Congress of the USA, Inc., as the national governing body in the United States for Athletics, pursuant to the Amateur Sports Act of 1978 (36 USC 371) has obtained the approval of the International Amateur Athletic Federation of the trust to be created hereby as a method of protecting the eligibility of the athletes of the United States.

2.0   DEFINITIONS.   As used in this trust agreement, the following terms shall have the meanings set forth herein:

2.1   "TACTRUST" shall mean the trust fund created by this trust agreement the full name of which shall be "TAC/USA Athletes' Trust."

2.2   "TAC/USA" shall mean The Athletics Congress of the USA, Inc.

2.3   "Athlete beneficiary" or "athlete beneficiaries" shall mean any and all individual athletes party to this trust agreement and any corporate party to this trust agreement identified as an athlete beneficiary on either the signature page of this trust agreement or any amendments thereto provided said corporate party has fully complied with paragraph "20" hereof.

2.4   "IAAF" shall mean the International Amateur Athletic Federation.

2.5 "Trustee" shall mean the bank, trust company, or other fiduciary named on Schedule "A" hereof.

2.6 "Eligibility" shall mean the right under applicable TAC/USA and IAAF rules of an athlete to represent and compete on behalf of the United States of America in the Olympic Games, the Pan-American Games, IAAF World Championships and to compete in other international athletic meetings involving the athletes of two or more countries.

2.7 "Pro-rata" shall mean the equal allocation among the athlete beneficiaries of TACTRUST of the expenses and income of TACTRUST which allocation shall be apportioned among all athlete beneficiaries of TACTRUST based on the average monthly balance (that is to say, the balance at the beginning of each month plus the balance at the end of each month divided by two) in each athlete beneficiary's account in TACTRUST calculated on a calendar year basis.

2.8 "Domestic Competition" shall mean an athletic competition in which all of the participating athletes are citizens of the United States or if citizens of countries other than the United States participate, such athletes are bona fide registered athletes of TAC/USA.

2.9 "International Competition" shall mean an athletic competition in which citizens from more than one country participate and all non-U.S. citizens are not bona fide, registered athletes of TAC/USA.

2.10 "Athletic Funds" shall mean money or other property or benefits received by an athlete in connection with entering, appearing or competing in a domestic or international competition.

2.11 "Sponsorship payments or benefits" shall mean money, property or other benefits received by an athlete pursuant to the TAC/USA Athlete Sponsorship Program.

2.12 Except for the foregoing definitions, any term, word, or phrase used in this trust agreement which is defined in Article 2 of the TAC/USA By-Laws shall have the same definition as provided therein. Any such definition shall and may continue to be amended as, if and when, any amendment is effected in the definitions contained in the said By-Laws.

3.0 PURPOSE. The purposes of this trust agreement are to:

3.1 create a trust fund under IAAF and TAC/USA · rules which provides for (a) the deposit of (i) athletic funds and sponsorship payments or benefits by an athlete beneficiary and (ii) other monies the deposit of which is provided for herein or approved by TAC/USA and (b) a method of withdrawals of principal and income therefrom so that for so long as the athlete beneficiary is a party to this trust agreement, the athlete's eligibility shall not be impaired solely by virtue of payments into or withdrawals from TACTRUST by the athlete; and

3.2 furnish a model private trust agreement for any athlete who does not wish to become an athlete beneficiary of TACTRUST (or who might wish to be an athlete beneficiary thereof for only a part of the funds and payments received by such athlete) but who nevertheless does wish to establish a private trust agreement for all or part of such funds and payments to be received, which private trust agreement will protect the eligibility of such athlete to the same extent and in the same manner as such protection is afforded by TACTRUST.

4.0 CREATION OF TACTRUST. The parties hereto hereby establish TACTRUST and the trustee hereby accepts a trust consisting solely of such property as shall be paid or delivered to the trustee by or on behalf of each athlete beneficiary. The trustee shall hold the trust fund in trust and manage and administer it in accordance with the terms and provisions of this trust agreement. The trustee shall accept no property other than that paid or delivered to it pursuant to paragraph 5.0 et seq. hereof.

5.0 ATHLETE BENEFICIARIES AND PAYMENTS INTO TAC-TRUST. The following provisions describe who may be an athlete beneficiary of TACTRUST and the athletic funds, sponsorship payments and other property which may be accepted into or be subject to TACTRUST.

5.1 Any athlete in whose name a validly issued current TAC/USA registration card has been issued may, while a TAC/USA registered athlete in good standing, become an athlete beneficiary of TACTRUST. No person attending an NCAA school may become a TACTRUST athlete beneficiary until the college or university class of which he or she is a member is graduated unless such person has not competed in a varsity sports program for a period of 12 consecutive months and has declared that he or she will not compete in future in such program.

5.2 Only the following property shall be paid or delivered to the trustee by or for an athlete beneficiary and the trustee shall not accept any other property in TACTRUST.

(i) Athletic funds received by an athlete beneficiary for participating in a domestic competition sanctioned by TAC/USA;

(ii) Athletic funds received by an athlete beneficiary for participating in an international competition sanctioned by either TAC/USA or the national governing body having jurisdiction in the venue of such competition;

(iii) Athletic funds received by an athlete beneficiary prior to January 1, 1982 for participating in a domestic or international competition subject to the approval of TAC/USA;

(iv) Property or funds received by an athlete beneficiary as a donation, provided such donations are permissible under IAAF rules and are approved by TAC/USA;

(v) Payments or benefits received by an athlete beneficiary resulting from an Athlete Sponsorship Program arrangement approved by TAC/USA;

(vi) Property received by an athlete registered or wishing to be registered with TAC/USA from any source whatsoever which if not deposited into TACTRUST would give rise to an impairment of such athlete's eligibility provided, however, that TAC/USA first approves the use of TACTRUST for such purposes.

5.3 All monies paid or delivered to the trustee pursuant to paragraph 5.2 shall be paid and delivered by good check to the trustee and shall represent the entire sum of money payable to the athlete beneficiary with respect to the transaction involved.

5.4 The athlete beneficiary shall give TAC/USA prompt notice of any proposed payment into TACTRUST. TAC/USA may object to such payment by notifying the athlete beneficiary and the trust of its objections within thirty (30) days of its actual receipt of such notice. In the event TAC/USA objects to a payment the trustee shall not accept it into TACTRUST.

5.5 As to any payments which are accepted by the trustee into TACTRUST, the athlete beneficiary for whose account said payment is accepted herein assigns, conveys, transfers, and delivers to the trustee said funds to be administered pursuant to TACTRUST for the purposes herein stated.

6.0 ATHLETE BENEFICIARY ACCOUNT. The trustee shall administer the payments received into TACTRUST as follows:

6.1 The trustee (and not TAC/USA) shall administer TACTRUST.

6.2 Each athlete beneficiary shall be assigned by the trustee a TACTRUST account number. All payments received by the trustee for the benefit of the athlete beneficiary will be credited to such an account. Any income of TACTRUST allocated to the athlete beneficiary shall also be credited hereto. All withdrawals by the athlete beneficiary of funds from TACTRUST and the pro-rata share of the administrative expenses of TACTRUST shall be deducted therefrom.

6.3 The trustee shall not be required to segregate the funds allocable to each athlete beneficiary's account from the funds of other athlete beneficiaries. The trustee may commingle the entire funds paid into TACTRUST and exercise the investment and the other powers conferred upon the trustee on the entire corpus of TACTRUST or such part of it as it deems appropriate.

6.4 All earnings, income, gains, expenses, losses, fees, and other costs allocable to TACTRUST shall be shared on a pro-rata basis by all the athlete beneficiaries.

6.5 The trustee shall have the right to cause the retention in each athlete beneficiary's account of such sums as it deems appropriate to enable the athlete beneficiary to meet his or her pro-rata share of the expenses and costs of the administration of TACTRUST.

6.6 Unless a different time period is otherwise agreed to between the Trustee and TAC/USA, the athlete beneficiary and TAC/USA shall be sent monthly reports by the trustee of transaction activity in the account of each athlete beneficiary not later than ten (10) days after the close of each calendar month.

7.0 WITHDRAWALS OF PRINCIPAL, TRANSFERS, AND DISTRI-

BUTION OF INCOME. The trustee and each athlete beneficiary may deal with the account standing in the name of the athlete beneficiary in the following manner:

7.1 Amounts due for income taxes which arise out of a payment into or out of TACTRUST for the account or the benefit or an athlete beneficiary may be withdrawn from the principal of the TACTRUST allocated to the account of the affected athlete beneficiary.

7.2 The income of TACTRUST shall be computed on an accrual basis. Within 105 days after the close of each calendar year, the trustee shall allocate the income of TACTRUST to the athlete beneficiaries on a pro-rata basis. The trustee shall apportion the income of TACTRUST on the basis of income received and accrued to that date. The income to be allocated to any athlete beneficiary of TACTRUST shall be the income from the last income allocation made before the death of the athlete beneficiary. The trustee shall not be required to prorate any income payment to the date of the athlete beneficiary's death.

7.3 The athlete beneficiary may withdraw all or any part of the principal sum and any interest or income thereto applicable to the account of the athlete beneficiary by requesting the trustee to pay the same in accordance with Schedule "C" hereof. No withdrawal pursuant to this paragraph 7.3 shall be made prior to obtaining the written consent of TAC/USA to said withdrawal, which consent shall be given or withheld by TAC/USA in its sole discretion applied consistently under TAC/USA and IAAF rules. The trustee shall pay the requested sum only after TAC/USA's consent thereto is given.

7.4 The athlete beneficiary may withdraw all or any part of the principal sum standing in his or her account by requesting the trustee to pay all or part of said principal sum to the athlete beneficiary or his or her designee without the written consent of TAC/USA for said withdrawal. The trustee shall make such payments only if the athlete beneficiary states in the written request therefor that "This withdrawal is made without the consent of TAC/USA, and that it is understood that the withdrawal will result in proceedings to impair his or her eligibility." It shall be a rebuttable presumption that a withdrawal without TAC/USA consent was for a purpose not in conformity with applicable rules and regulations of TAC/USA and IAAF subject to review of the reasons for said withdrawal at a hearing which TAC/USA institutes to review the athlete beneficiary's eligibility. The trustee shall forthwith notify TAC/USA of any withdrawal at the time thereof by an athlete beneficiary pursuant to this paragraph 7.4.

7.5 The athlete beneficiary initially may establish or may transfer all or any part of the principal in his or her account to a private trust created for a purpose similar to TACTRUST (the "private trust") in which TAC/USA is also a "notify and consent" party as provided in TACTRUST. A copy of such proposed private trust agreement shall be sent to TAC/USA.

Upon the consent of TAC/USA to such private trust and the actual deposit therein or transfer thereto of all or part of the principal hereof, there shall be no impairment of the athlete's eligibility. All private trusts shall have as one of the trustees thereof a bank, trust company or other institution customarily acting in such capacity. This requirement may be waived by TAC/USA on good cause shown. The name of all private trusts shall be substantially as follows: "TAC/USA and (name of trustee of athlete beneficiary), Athlete's Private Trust" and no acronym thereof shall be utilized by any party thereto.

8.0   ACTS OF REVOCATION AND TERMINATION.   The interest of an athlete beneficiary shall be revoked or terminated in the account standing in his or her name in TACTRUST (or any private trust) upon the happening of any one of the following:

8.1 Upon the death of an athlete beneficiary the interest of said athlete beneficiary shall terminate in TACTRUST and the then entire account standing in the name of the deceased athlete beneficiary shall be paid to the person named in Schedule "D" hereof, and if no person is named therein then to the legal representative of such athlete beneficiary. Any private trust may contain provisions in its initial form or by subsequent amendment which in the event of the death of the athlete beneficiary (a) allows the trust to continue, (b) names successor beneficiaries therein, and (c) terminates the role of TAC/USA in such trust.

8.2 If an athlete beneficiary (a) declares himself of herself in writing to be (i) a professional athlete, (ii) an athlete not wishing to retain eligibility, or (iii) an athlete no longer interested in competing; (b) surrenders for life his or her membership in TAC/USA; (c) is suspended for life as a TAC/USA athlete member; (d) makes any withdrawal of principal pursuant to paragraph 7.4 hereof; (e) accepts athletic funds unless the same are contributed to a trust as provided hereunder; or (f) after January 1, 1983, knowingly competes in an international athletic competition held within the United States not sanctioned by TAC/USA, the interest of the athlete beneficiary in TACTRUST shall be deemed to have been revoked and the trust terminated with respect to said athlete beneficiary. Upon certification to the trustee by TAC/USA of the happening of any one of such events all monies then in the account of such athlete beneficiary shall be paid by the trustee to the athlete beneficiary. The trustee shall have no responsibility under this paragraph except to act in accordance with the certificate of TAC/USA.

8.3 The entire right to receive all monies in the account of the athlete beneficiary shall be vested in the athlete beneficiary of a TACTRUST account subject only to the provisions of this trust agreement and nothing contained herein shall give TAC/USA or the trustee or either of them any right to any part of TACTRUST, the income or increase thereof, or any residuary rights therein, except that nothing contained herein shall be deemed to prohibit the trustee from receiving its compensation from the corpus of TACTRUST as provided in this trust agreement.

8.4 It is the intent of TAC/USA to create TACTRUST and to provide for payments into and out of TACTRUST (and any private trust) which will permit the most favorable incidents of income taxation permissible under existing law and regulations. To the extent that this instrument requires amendment or to the extent any private trust requires provisions more suitable to the needs of any particular beneficiary thereof, TAC/USA will effect said amendment or permit the creation of a private trust provided said amendment or private trust provisions are allowed by IAAF. TAC/USA makes no representation as to the tax consequences of any payment into or out of TACTRUST or any private trust.

9.0 TAC/USA AND THE ATHLETE BENEFICIARIES OF TAC-TRUST. The following provisions are applicable to the relationship of TAC/USA and the TACTRUST athlete beneficiaries:

9.1 TAC/USA shall have no role in the administration of TACTRUST or any private trust except to certify that payments into or out of the particular trust involved are permitted by IAAF and TAC/USA rules.

9.2 TAC/USA shall receive no compensation for its services to or in connection with TACTRUST either directly or indirectly from TACTRUST, the trustee or any athlete beneficiary nor shall any employee, agent, attorney, division or subsidiary of TAC/USA receive direct or indirect compensation therefor from TACTRUST, the trustee or any athlete beneficiary.

9.3 TAC/USA shall not be liable to the trustee or the athlete beneficiary for any loss suffered by TACTRUST or of any impairment of eligibility of an athlete beneficiary resulting from its consent to any payment made into or out of TACTRUST for the account of the athlete beneficiary. Such consent by TAC/USA shall merely signify that based upon the facts certified to TAC/USA at the time of said consent, the payment was in conformity with applicable TAC/USA, IAAF, or TAC-TRUST rules, regulations or provisions. If the facts certified to TAC/USA are found to be true by TAC/USA after investigation, TAC/USA shall use its best efforts to protect the athlete beneficiary's eligibility before any international body.

9.4 Any withdrawal by an athlete beneficiary not approved by TAC/USA pursuant to 7.4 hereof may result in the loss of eligibility of the said athlete beneficiary under applicable TAC/USA or IAAF rules, but nothing contained herein shall be deemed to deprive an athlete beneficiary of his or her rights pursuant to the By-Laws of TAC/USA.

10.0 INVESTMENT POWERS OF TRUSTEE. In addition to any powers which the trustee may have under applicable law, the trustee shall have and in its sole and absolute discretion may exercise from time to time and at any time the following powers and authority with respect to TACTRUST:

10.1 To invest and reinvest trust funds, together with any other assets held by the trustee for the benefit of TACTRUST and its athlete beneficiaries, in shares of stock (whether common or preferred), money market funds, mutual funds, certificates of deposit, IRA funds or other evidences of indebtedness, unsecured or secured by mortgages on real or personal property wheresoever situated (including any part interest in a bond and mortgage or note and mortgage, whether insured or uninsured), and any other property, or part interest in property, real or personal, foreign or domestic, without any duty to diversify and without regard to any restriction placed upon fiduciaries by any present or future applicable law, administrative regulation, rule of court or court decision;

10.2 To sell, convey, redeem, exchange, grant options for the purchase or exchange of, or otherwise dispose of, any real or personal property, at public or private sale, for cash or upon credit, with or without security, without obligation on the part of any person dealing with the trustee to see to the application of the proceeds of or to inquire into the validity, expediency, or propriety of any such disposition;

10.3 To borrow from any lender (including the trustee in its individual capacity) money, in any amount and upon any terms and conditions, for purposes of this agreement, and to pledge or mortgage any property held in TACTRUST to secure the repayment of any such loan;

10.4 To employ in the management of TACTRUST suitable agents, without liability for any loss occasioned by any such agents selected by the trustee with reasonable care, and to compensate any such agent from TACTRUST funds without diminution of or charging against the commissions or compensation due the trustee hereunder;

10.5 To consult with counsel, who may be counsel to TAC/USA, on matters relating to the management of the TACTRUST, without liability for taking or refraining from taking action in accordance with the opinion of such counsel; and

10.6 To do all other acts that the trustee may deem necessary or proper to carry out any of the powers or duties set forth herein or otherwise in the best interests of TACTRUST.

11.0   TAXES, EXPENSES, AND COMPENSATION OF TRUSTEE.

11.1 The trustee, without direction from any party hereto, shall pay out of the principal of TACTRUST all taxes imposed or levied with respect to TACTRUST and, in its discretion, may contest the validity or amount of any tax, assessment, claim, or demand respecting TACTRUST or any part thereof.

11.2 The trustee, without direction from any party hereto, shall pay from TACTRUST the reasonable expenses and compensation of counsel and all other expenses of managing and administering TACTRUST, provided that no compensation to or expense of counsel for TAC/USA shall be paid by the trustee from TACTRUST. All expenses paid pursuant to this paragraph "11.0" hereof shall be paid from the principal of TAC-

TRUST except to the extent that the trustee in its discretion shall determine otherwise. The trustee shall receive such compensation for its services as from time to time shall be agreed upon, without necessity of application to or approval by any court. Until otherwise determined by the trustee and TAC/USA, such compensation shall be as set forth in Schedule "E" hereof. All compensation payable to the trustee shall be paid from the principal of TACTRUST unless the trustee in its discretion shall determine otherwise.

12.0 PRINCIPAL AND INCOME ALLOCATION. Allocation as between principal and income accounts shall be as follows: There shall be credited to principal, to the extent that the same shall constitute principal, all funds received by the trustee from an athlete beneficiary, profits realized on the sale or exchange of investments, and stock dividends or other distributions. There shall be charged against income all expenses properly chargeable to income, including any taxes and assessments chargeable to the income of TACTRUST pursuant to any statute or regulation.

12.1 Dividends or other corporate distributions payable in the stock of the corporation authorizing and declaring the same, however, shall constitute principal and the trustee may apportion extraordinary dividends or other corporate distribution payable in cash or property other than the stock of the corporation authorizing and declaring the same, liquidating dividends, arrears of dividends on preferred stocks, property received in reorganization and other like receipts not constituting ordinary income to principal or income or in part to both in the sole judgment and discretion of the trustee. Premiums paid for the purchase of investments for TACTRUST shall not be amortized.

13.0 TRUSTEE'S LIABILITY. The trustee shall not be liable for the making, retention, or sale of any investment or reinvestment made by it as herein provided nor for any loss to or diminution of TACTRUST, except due to its own negligence, willful misconduct, or lack of good faith. The trustee shall have no liability or responsibility to investigate the truth or falsity of any certificate, content, approval or request received by it from TAC/USA or an athlete beneficiary.

14.0 ACCOUNTS. The trustee shall keep accurate and detailed accounts of all its receipts, investments and disbursements under this agreement. Such person or persons as TAC/USA shall designate shall be allowed to inspect the trustee's account relating to the TACTRUST upon request at any reasonable time during the business hours of the trustee. Within 90 days after the close of the fiscal year of TACTRUST or of the removal or resignation of the trustee as provided by this agreement, the trustee shall file with TAC/USA a written account of its transactions relating to TACTRUST during the period from the submission of its last such account to the close of the fiscal year or the date of the trustee's resignation or removal. Unless TAC/USA shall have filed with the trustee written exceptions or objections to any such account within 60 days after receipt thereof, TAC/USA shall be deemed to have approved such account; and in such case, the trustee shall be forever released and discharged with respect to all matters and things embraced in such account as though such account had been settled by a court of competent jurisdiction in an action or proceeding to which all persons having a beneficial interest in TACTRUST were parties. However, should any question be raised at any time by any athlete beneficiary regarding his or her proper share of the income from TACTRUST, the trustee will use its best efforts to supply TAC/USA with the information necessary to resolve the inquiry. Nothing contained in this agreement shall deprive the trustee of the right to have a judicial settlement of its accounts.

15.0   RESIGNATION OR REMOVAL OF TRUSTEE.

15.1 The trustee may resign at any time upon 90 days' written notice to TAC/USA, or upon shorter notice if acceptable to TAC/USA. TAC/USA, by action of its Board of Directors, may remove the trustee at any time upon 120 days written notice to the trustee, or upon shorter notice if acceptable to the trustee. In the event it resigns or is removed, the trustee shall have its accounts settled as provided in this agreement.

15.2 Upon the resignation or removal of the trustee, TAC/USA, by action of its Board of Directors, shall appoint a successor trustee to act hereunder after the effective date of such removal or resignation. However, TAC/USA shall not appoint as successor trustee either itself or any athlete beneficiary of TACTRUST. Each successor trustee shall have the powers and duties conferred upon the trustee in this agreement, and the term "trustee" as used in this agreement shall be deemed to include any successor trustee. Upon designation or appointment of a successor trustee, the trustee shall transfer and deliver all trust funds to the successor trustee, reserving such sums as the trustee shall deem necessary to defray its expenses in settling its accounts, to pay any of its compensation due and unpaid, and to discharge any obligation of TACTRUST for which the trustee may be liable; but if the sums so reserved are not sufficient for these purposes, the trustee shall be entitled to recover the amount of any deficiency from a successor trustee. When all TACTRUST funds shall have been transferred and delivered to the successor trustee and the accounts of the trustee have been settled as provided in this agreement, the trustee shall be released and discharged from all further accountability or liability for TACTRUST and shall not be responsible in any way for the further disposition of TACTRUST or any part thereof.

16.0   COMMUNICATIONS.

16.1 Any action required by any provision of this agreement to be taken by TAC/USA may be evidenced by a resolution of its Board of Directors certified to the trustee by the secretary or an assistant secretary or equivalent officer of TAC/USA and the trustees shall be fully protected in relying on any resolution so certified to it. Any action of TAC/USA including any approval of or exception to the trustee's accounts with respect to TACTRUST, may be evidenced by a certificate signed by the officer of TAC/USA authorized to do so by resolution by its Board of Directors and the trustee shall be fully protected in relying upon such certificate. The trustee may accept any writing signed by an officer of TAC/USA as proof of any fact or matter that it deems necessary or desirable to have established in the administration of TACTRUST and the trustee shall be fully protected in relying upon the statements in writing. The trustee shall be entitled conclusively to rely upon any written notice, instruction, direction, certificate, or other communication believed by it to be genuine and to be signed by the proper person or persons, and the trustee shall be under no duty to make investigation or inquiry as to the truth or accuracy of any statement contained therein.

16.2 Until notice be given to the contrary, communications to the trustee shall be sent to it at its office designated on Schedule "A" hereof; communications to athlete beneficiaries or their legal representatives shall be sent to the addresses furnished to the trustee by the athlete beneficiary and communications to TAC/USA shall be sent to it at the address set forth in this agreement.

17.0 AMENDMENT. TAC/USA expressly reserves the right at any time and from time to time to amend this agreement and the trust created thereby to any extent that it may deem advisable, provided, however, that such amendment shall not increase the duties or responsibilities of the trustee without its consent thereto in writing, and provided further that no such amendment shall be made which retroactively entitles TAC/USA to earn a fee or other compensation out of the funds constituting TACTRUST or otherwise retroactively reduces the share of any athlete beneficiary to the principal or income of TACTRUST. Such amendment shall become effective upon delivery to the trustee of a written instrument of amendment, duly executed and acknowledged by TAC/USA, and accompanied by a certified copy of a resolution of its Board of Directors authorizing such amendment. An athlete beneficiary of TACTRUST or any private trust pursuant thereto may object to any amendment of the bylaws of TAC/USA (as they affect TACTRUST) or any amendment to TACTRUST by notifying TAC/USA within 30 days of such amendment. If the athlete beneficiary does not waive such objection, the following rules shall apply:

17.1 For so long as the athlete remains eligible, there shall be no further payments into or out of the trust for the account of said athlete beneficiary and the amendment shall be ineffective with respect to the funds in the account of said athlete beneficiary;

17.2 Any funds thereafter received by the athlete may be placed by him or her in a new TACTRUST account which shall be governed by the amendment, and payments into and out of said account shall be permitted in accordance therewith.

17.3 Upon the cessation of the athlete beneficiary's eligibility or any act of revocation or termination pursuant to paragraph "8.0" hereof, the entire balance, without penalty, standing in the account of the athlete beneficiary in the "frozen" TACTRUST and any other TACTRUST in which said athlete has an interest shall be paid to such athlete in accordance with the terms of the trust involved.

18.0 PROHIBITION OF ASSIGNMENT OF INTEREST. Without the consent of TAC/USA the funds of any athlete beneficiary in his or her account and any interest, right, or claim in or to any part of TACTRUST or any payment therefrom shall not be assignable, transferable, or subject to sale, mortgage, pledge, hypothecation, commutation, anticipation, garnishment, attachment, execution, or levy of any kind, and the trustee shall not recognize any attempt to assign, transfer, sell, mortgage, pledge, hypothecate, commute, or anticipate the same, except to the extent required by law.

19.0 MISCELLANEOUS.

19.1 This agreement shall be interpreted, construed, and enforced, and the trust thereby created shall be administered, in accordance with the laws of the state where the trustee is located.

19.2 The captions of the Articles of this trust agreement are placed herein for convenience only and the agreement is not to be construed by reference thereto.

19.3 This agreement shall bind and inure to the benefit of the successors and assigns of TAC/USA, the trustee, and each athlete beneficiary, respectively.

19.4 This agreement may be executed in any number of counterparts, each of which shall be deemed to be an original, but all of which together shall constitute but one instrument, which may be sufficiently evidenced by counterpart.

19.5 The effective date of this trust agreement shall be as to TAC/USA and the trustee the date set forth next to their signatures and as to each athlete beneficiary, the date said athlete beneficiary causes funds to be paid into TACTRUST for his or her account.

20.0 ATHLETE CORPORATIONS. The athlete beneficiary may enter into an agreement with a corporation to receive all or some of the funds described in paragraphs "1.0" and "5.2" of TACTRUST (the "athlete's corporation.") The following provisions shall apply with respect thereto:

20.1 The relationship of the athlete to the athlete's corporation shall not modify or diminish the jurisdiction over the athlete of either The Athletic Congress of the USA, Inc. or the International Amateur Athletic Federation. The athlete shall be fully responsible for all acts of the athlete's corporation as a party to TACTRUST the same as if all such acts were the personal acts of the athlete and the athlete shall be chargeable with knowledge of all such acts without regard to the fact that the person or persons performing such acts for the athlete's corporation are persons other than the athlete.

20.2 Any athlete's corporation wishing to become an "athlete bene-ficiary" as defined in TACTRUST shall, as a condition of maintaining such status, provide to TAC/USA, upon its incorporation or as soon thereafter as possible, a copy of any service or employment agreement with an individual athlete and a copy of any stockholders' agreement. The athlete corporation shall also agree that, during the term of TACTRUST it will report to TAC/USA any material change in any of the above-described documents or in its structure and organization.

20.3 No person declared to be ineligible to compete as an athlete under any applicable TAC/USA or IAAF rule shall be entitled to be a shareholder, officer, or director of an athlete's corporation.

20.4 With respect to an athlete's corporation, TAC/USA makes no representation as to either the tax consequences of its being a party to TACTRUST or any deposits or withdrawals made by it into or out of TACTRUST. TAC/USA shall have no responsibility to any athlete by virtue of any acts, omissions, or defalcations of any person acting for an athlete's corporation it being understood that consent of TAC/USA to an athlete's corporation being an athlete beneficiary of TACTRUST is solely for the benefit of the individual athlete and shall not be deemed to enlarge TAC/USA responsibilities in any manner whatsoever.

IN WITNESS WHEREOF, the corporate parties hereto have caused this agreement to be executed in their respective names by their duly authorized officers under their corporate seals and the individual parties hereto have executed this agreement and affixed their seals.

The Athletics Congress of the U.S.A., Inc.

by _____
The Trustee

(Signing on Schedule "A" hereof)

by _____
The Athlete Beneficiary

(Signing on Schedule "B" hereof)

_____

SCHEDULE A

The Trustee's Signature Page

SCHEDULE B

Athlete Beneficiary Signature Page

SCHEDULE C

1. All requests by athlete beneficiaries for withdrawal of principal from TACTRUST shall be made in writing in the form of a certification to TAC/USA stating that the request is made for the purposes set forth therein and for no other purposes and that the facts contained therein are true and correct.

2. TAC/USA shall approve any request for a withdrawal of principal which is certified to be required to meet an emergency which is of such a nature that failure to have use of TACTRUST funds would have life-changing consequences and TAC/USA after investigation agrees with such conclusion.

3. TAC/USA shall approve a request for a withdrawal of principal which is certified to conform to IAAF Rule 14, Rule 15 or Rule 16.

4. Any request for withdrawal under "2" or "3" hereof shall state the amount of such withdrawal in total and shall include a breakdown thereof and an identification of the use to be made or to have been made of the funds requested to have been withdrawn. In the event a withdrawal is requested for a purpose or use to occur after the receipt of funds by the athlete beneficiary, whether said withdrawal is a withdrawal for a specific purpose or in the nature of a periodic stipend, the athlete beneficiary shall report to TAC/USA in writing on the 10th day of each month the actual uses and expenditures incurred by said athlete beneficiary with respect to the funds withdrawn by said athlete beneficiary during the month preceding.

5. TAC/USA shall have the right to require the athlete beneficiary to furnish supporting documents and other satisfactory evidence of the purpose and use of any funds received by the athlete beneficiary from TACTRUST. Each athlete beneficiary agrees to cooperate with TAC/USA in establishing that all withdrawals from TACTRUST by that athlete beneficiary have been for the purposes certified in requesting said withdrawal and a failure to so cooperate shall constitute an act of revocation of TACTRUST by said athlete beneficiary.

SCHEDULE D

Name of Person Entitled to Funds in the Event of Beneficiary's Death

ACL CONSENT FORM/AUTOMATIC COST OF LIVING WITHDRAWAL TACTRUST PROGRAMS—1987

To: _____ Name of Athlete _____
Athlete's Social Security Number: _____

You are entitled to an Automatic Cost of Living withdrawal (ACL) as explained in the TACTRUST HANDBOOK for 1986 in the following amount:

Dependents, including athlete (Circle One)

	Annual ACL	Quarterly ACL	Monthly ACL
1	11,423.	2,856.	952.
2	18,919.	4,730.	1,577.
3	21,936.	5,484.	1,828.
4	24,674.	6,169.	2,056.
5	26,884.	6,721.	2,240.

Withdrawals pursuant to ACL need to be explained or substantiated by the athlete.

Withdrawals other than ACL must be explained, substantiated and approved in accordance with TAC/USA and IAAF rules.

ACL withdrawals should be taken pro-rata as the year progresses. Since ACL does not accumulate from one year to the next, please use your ACL first each year before using any other entitlements, and let TAC/USA know if you have unused ACL remaining at year's end.

You are asked (a) to inform the undersigned as to the amount of any ACL withdrawal made by you, so that your account may be kept up to date, and (b) to sign a copy of this notice and return it to the undersigned.

The Internal Revenue Code requires that we report to them any payments to you that exceed $600.00. In order to facilitate year-end filings, you must complete and return the W-9 form enclosed with this package in order to establish a TACTRUST account.

Please be mindful that this ACL consent does not relieve you of the requirement to deposit Athletic Funds and Sponsorship Payments into TACTRUST before withdrawing any part thereof. A failure to do so may impair eligibility even though there is an entitlement to funds.

_____
Athlete Beneficiary Signature & Address
TAC/USA BY:

_____   Dated: _____

_____

_____
TAC/USA Athlete's Card Number

_____

Please reply to:
THE ATHLETICS CONGRESS/USA
P.O. Box 120
Indianapolis, Indiana 46206-0120

Appendix B

SAMPLE ATHLETIC CONTRACTS
SERVICE AGREEMENT

I THIS AGREEMENT, made in duplicate and entered into this _____ day of _____, 19_____ A.D.

—BETWEEN— (Printer)

Hereinafter referred to as the PRODUCER of the FIRST PART

—AND— (University)

Hereinafter referred to as the SPONSOR of the SECOND PART.

II. NOW THEREFORE this agreement witnesseth that in consideration of the mutual covenants and undertakings here it is hereby agreed as follows:

THE PRODUCER agrees to supply 5500 copies of Basketball Program size 8-½ × 11 for the SPONSOR on a good quality 70-pound coated stock paper, with covers to the SPONSORS choosing but not to exceed .9 points in weight, on or before _____.

THE PRODUCER agrees to hold the SPONSOR free from any liability other than the terms of this agreement.

THE PRODUCER will supply an advance PROMOTIONAL DIRECTOR to sell advertising to local commercial outlets usually by telephone on behalf of the SPONSOR.

THE PRODUCER will retain a special bank account called University Basketball Program into which all advertising money will be deposited.

THE PRODUCER will retain the balance as consideration for producing the program.

THE CHOICE of editorial content is up to the SPONSOR. It must be provided by the SPONSOR at no expense to the PRODUCER and must reach the PRODUCER no later than six (6) weeks before the publishing deadline of the Program. Editorial material must be typewritten.

    *SPONSOR will have the option to use a 4-page, 4-color insert at SPONSOR's expense.

    *Cover and opponent information shall be sent to printer in groupings of 4.

THE PRODUCER will allow the SPONSOR 12 pages of editorial regardless of advertising sales, plus the space on the front cover. The PRODUCER will sell no more than 12 pages of advertising plus the space on the remaining three covers.

III   IT IS the sole responsibility of the SPONSOR to provide the editorial content as per contract, and if the editorial content is late the _____ week delivery will not necessarily apply. It is understood that the liability for publishing the publication as per contract does not take effect with the PRODUCER until the PRODUCER has received the editorial content from the SPONSOR.

IN WITNESS WHEREOF the parties hereto have hereunto set their hands and seals, the day hereinbefore mentioned.

SIGNED, SEALED and DELIVERED

In the presence of:

PRODUCER: Printer

SPONSOR: University

PROMOTIONAL CONTRACT

THE AGREEMENT is entered into on this _____ day of _____ by and between The Promotion, a __(state)__ Corporation, located at __(address)__   __(telephone number)__ , hereinafter referred to as "Corporation," or "University," and "Client," whose name, address and telephone number are:

WHEREAS, Corporation owns the exclusive rights to The Promotion, an artistic sculpture; and

WHEREAS, the Corporation has received Certificates of Copyright, Service Mark, and Trademark registering The Promotion as the exclusive property of the Corporation; and

WHEREAS, Client is desirous of contracting for the appearance and performance of The Promotion at the time, date and place specified below; and

WHEREAS, the parties are desirous of setting forth the terms and conditions of their agreement.

NOW, THEREFORE, for good and valuable consideration, it is hereby agreed as follows:

1. PERFORMANCE

A. Client hereby contracts for the appearance and a performance by The Promotion, the date, time and place set forth below:

Client recognizes The Promotion may be in town just on the day of the performance and the presence of The Promotion at any time other than at the time of the performance must be arranged separately.

B. Client recognizes the production and performance to be provided by The Promotion, its comic abilities, skits and activities shall be under the exclusive direction and control of Corporation.

C. Unless otherwise mutually agreed, it is expressly understood The Promotion shall not be required to appear at a sponsor's place of business or at any other location except as set forth in paragraph A above.

D. Client recognizes The Promotion is an identifiable entertainment character which has been developed and created by the Corporation. Accordingly, no logo, emblem, advertising symbol, or other similar items shall be placed on the costume of The Promotion to wear.

E. Corporation shall use reasonable efforts to have The Promotion available for media related appearances which help promote the event scheduled in paragraph A above. In addition, Corporation shall make The Promotion available for the signing of autographs immediately after the performance.

F. Although ___(name)___ may perform as The Promotion, Corporation hereby expressly reserves the right to have any employee of Corporation perform as The Promotion. Client hereby acknowledges and agrees that it has no rights, either express or implied, for _____ to personally perform as The Promotion and the selection of the personnel to perform as The Promotion is within the sole and absolute discretion of Corporation.

G. If Client chooses to advertise the event in its own magazine/ program, then no color photographs of The Promotion may be used larger than a total half-page, or color flyers or color posters that would otherwise conflict with sales of The Promotion's souvenir items, unless agreed to in writing. Any size black and white photos are permissible, however.

2. FEES AND RELATED EXPENSES.

A. Corporation shall cause The Promotion to appear and perform a production at the date, time and place set forth above. Client agrees to pay Corporation a fee in the sum of $_____ for the appearance and performance of The Promotion. A deposit of $_____ shall be paid by Client upon executing and returning this Agreement to Corporation. The balance of the fee, namely, $_____, shall be paid to Corporation by a cashier's check on or before the date and time of the performance set forth above. Payment shall be made solely to "The Promotion."

B. Client shall arrange for and provide two (2) hotel rooms for the night of the performance. It is expressly understood the charges for the hotel accommodations will be billed directly to Client and shall include a reasonable allowance for meals. Client agrees to provide local ground transportation to and from the airport, hotel and the place of the performance for employee(s) of Corporation performing as The Promotion. Should the employee(s) of Corporation arrange for and pay for hotel accommodations, and local ground transportation, then such expenses shall be reimbursed to Corporation by Client upon presentation of receipts.

3.   CANCELLATION OF PERFORMANCE.

A. If the event at which The Promotion is to perform be cancelled for any reason other than labor strike or natural catastrophe, e.g., flood, blizzard, etc., then twenty-five percent (25%) of the fee shall be paid to Corporation as a guaranteed fee. Any deposit in excess of the 25% guarantee shall be returned and a full refund issued in the exempt circumstances.

B. Once The Promotion's performance starts, the entire fee shall be deemed fully earned and there shall be no refunds for fees and expenses set forth in paragraph 2 above if the event at which The Promotion is performing is prematurely terminated, e.g., a game called for rain.

C. Client recognizes and acknowledges the Corporation schedules other performances of The Promotion in various geographic locations which require employee(s) of the Corporation who perform as The Promotion to travel by conventional means of commercial transportation, e.g., regularly scheduled airlines, railroads, buses, etc. Corporation hereby represents that it will use good faith, due diligence and its best efforts to provide The Promotion at the event set forth in paragraph 1 above on a timely basis. However, Client hereby releases Corporation from any and all liability and/or damages which may result should the Corporation be unable to provide The Promotion at the performance set forth in paragraph 1 above if the cause of such missed performance is due to a cause outside the control of Corporation. Should The Promotion miss the appearance, Corporation shall return Client's deposit in full, or reschedule the date.

4.   MISCELLANEOUS.

A. As a professional consideration, the parties agree to hold in confidence the contents of this Agreement and not to publicly disclose its details, please.

B. Corporation is at all times serving as an independent contractor under the terms of this Agreement. Client shall neither have nor exercise any control or direction over the methods by which The Promotion or others employed by Corporation perform their work and duties.

C. This Contract constitutes the entire agreement between the parties and cancels and supersedes any and all prior oral or written understandings between the parties and may be modified or changed only by writing.

D. This Agreement and all its terms, conditions and stipulations shall be binding upon and insure to the benefit of, the parties hereto and their respective heirs, executors, administrators, personal representatives, successors and assigns and shall be governed by the laws of the State of

_____.

E. Any dispute, controversy or claim arising out of or under this Agreement shall be submitted by the parties to conclusive and binding arbitration in ___(city and state)___, in accordance with the rules of Commercial Arbitration of the American Arbitration Association then existing and judgment on the arbitration award may be entered to costs and reasonable attorneys' fees from the other party.

THE DATE OF THE PERFORMANCE WILL BE RESERVED FOR CLIENT AND THIS AGREEMENT SHALL BE BINDING UPON THE PARTIES ONLY IF THE PROMOTION RECEIVES A DULY EXECUTED COPY OF THIS AGREEMENT EXECUTED BY CLIENT AND CLIENT'S DEPOSIT, AS PROVIDED IN PARAGRAPH 2, BEFORE _____.

IN WITNESS WHEREOF, the undersigned have executed this Agreement on the day and year first above written.

THE PROMOTION

_____ (University) _____
Client   President of Corporation

SPONSORSHIP CONTRACT

THIS AGREEMENT is made this _____ day of __(month and year)__ by and between __(Sponsor)__, INCORPORATED, "SP," a __(state)__ corporation with its principal offices in __(address)__, and UNIVERSITY ("U"), a non-profit institution with its principal offices in __(address)__.

WHEREAS, U wishes SP to be the principal sponsor of the U intercollegiate athletic program (the "Program"); and

WHEREAS, SP wishes to be the principal sponsor of the Program;

NOW, THEREFORE, in consideration of the mutual covenants herein set forth, the parties agree as follows:

1. THE PROGRAM. SP shall be the principal sponsor and the exclusive beverage sponsor of the Program and the events and activities which are the subject matter hereof.

2. ADVERTISING AND PROMOTION.

(a) SP shall have the right to engage in any advertising or promotional activities which it may reasonably determine with respect to its sponsorship of the Program.

(b) U hereby grants to SP the following sponsorship rights with respect to the Program:

(i) *19xx–xx Men's Basketball*

(1) SP identification (furnished by SP) to be displayed on all ticket brochures and pocket schedules;

(2) Two 3' by 22' SP banners (furnished by SP) to be displayed in prominent locations at all home games;

(3) Subject to the approval of Facility management, a large no-slip SP decal to be displayed on the floor of __(facility)__ at all home games;

(4) Ten (10) choice season tickets and five (5) preferred parking passes;

(5) 4-color advertisement (copy furnished by SP) on the back cover of all press guides, yearbooks and programs; and

(6) Mutually agreeable sponsorship rights to two (2) promotions conducted by U at its expense.

(ii) *19xx Men's Soccer*

(1) SP identification (furnished by SP) to be displayed on all ticket brochures, ticket booklets and pocket schedules;

(2) Ten (10) season ticket booklets;

(3) SP identification (furnished by SP) to be displayed on five

hundred (500) t-shirts (furnished by U) to be given away at __(coach's)__ soccer camp;

   (4) 4-color advertisement (copy furnished by SP) on back cover of all press guides and programs; and

   (5) Four (4) 4' by 24' SP signs to be displayed at all home games.

  (iii) *19xx Spring Golf Tournament*

   (1) Two (2) foursomes in the Tournament;

   (2) Official sponsor status for Product;

   (3) One (1) SP banner and giant inflatable balloon (furnished by SP) to be displayed in prominent locations at the tournament site; and

   (4) 4-color advertisement (copy furnished by SP) in the program.

 3. SPONSORSHIP FEE. SP shall pay to U the total sum of Forty Thousand Dollars ($40,000) on or before December 31, 19xx.

 4. TERM. The term of this Agreement shall start on December 1, 19xx, and unless sooner terminated in accordance with the provisions hereof, shall end on November 30, 19xx.

 5. TERMINATION.

 (a) Either party shall have the right at any time to terminate this Agreement, effective upon the other party's receipt of termination notice and without prejudice to any other legal rights to which such terminating party may be entitled, if:

  (i) the other party commits a material default of any of the provisions of this Agreement, which default is not cured within fifteen (15) days following written notice of such default to the defaulting party; or

  (ii) any of the representations or warranties made by the other party in this Agreement shall prove to be untrue or inaccurate in any material respect.

 (b) If SP terminates this Agreement pursuant to the provisions hereof, U shall refund to SP, within ten (10) days after its receipt of termination notice, a pro rata portion of the sponsorship fee paid by SP hereunder.

 (c) Termination of this Agreement for any reason provided herein shall not relieve either party from its obligation to perform up to the effective date of such termination or to perform such obligations as may survive termination.

 6. RIGHT OF FIRST REFUSAL. SP shall have the right to purchase the several rights granted under this Agreement for a 1-year period from and after the expiration hereof and U shall propose to SP in writing the terms and conditions therefor on or before August 1, 1986. SP shall have until the later of September 1, 1986 or thirty (30) days after receiving U's proposal within which to accept the same. If SP does not accept such proposal within such time, U shall be free to contract with any third party with respect to any or all of such rights, but not on more favorable

terms than those offered to SP without again giving SP a thirty (30) day right of first refusal concerning the same.

7.   WARRANTY.

(a) U represents, warrants and covenants to SP as follows:

(i) It has the full right and legal authority to enter into and fully perform this Agreement in accordance with its terms.

(ii) This Agreement, when executed and delivered by U, will be its legal, valid and binding obligation enforceable against U in accordance with its terms.

(iii) The execution and delivery of this Agreement has been duly authorized by U, and such execution and delivery and the performance by U of its obligations hereunder do not and will not violate or cause a breach of any other agreements or obligations to which it is a party or by which it is bound.

(iv) U is not a retailer of alcoholic beverages and has no ownership interest in any alcoholic beverage retail license.

(v) No monies paid by SP for the advertising purchased under this Agreement are intended to be or will be passed on by U to any alcoholic beverage retail licensee for or in any manner as an inducement to any such retailer to purchase any alcoholic beverage produced, sold or offered for sale by SP.

(vi) There is no agreement or understanding between SP and U that, as consideration for SP's purchase of advertising under this Agreement, U will require any alcoholic beverage retail licensee to purchase any alcoholic beverage produced, sold or offered for sale by SP.

(vii) The advertising purchased under this Agreement is being purchased by SP at a rate no higher than that at which such advertising is available to other advertisers.

(viii) In addition to being true as of the date first written above, each of the foregoing representations, warranties, and covenants shall be true at all times during the term hereof. Each of such representations, warranties and covenants shall be deemed to be material and to have been relied upon by SP notwithstanding any investigation made by SP.

(b) SP represents, warrants and covenants to U as follows:

(i) It has the full right and legal authority to enter into and fully perform this Agreement in accordance with its terms.

(ii) This Agreement when executed and delivered by SP, will be its legal, valid and binding obligation enforceable against SP in accordance with its terms.

(iii) The execution and delivery of this Agreement has been duly authorized by SP, and such execution and delivery and the performance by SP of its obligations hereunder, do not and will not violate or cause a breach of any other agreements or obligations to which it is a party or by which it is bound.

(iv) This Agreement is entered into solely for the purchase of advertising as described herein and for no other purposes.

(v) SP's purchase of advertising under this Agreement is in no way conditioned on any agreement or understanding that U will require any alcoholic beverage retail licensee to purchase any alcoholic beverage produced, sold or offered for sale by SP.

(vi) By the purchase of advertising under this Agreement, SP does not agree, expect, or intend to induce the purchase of any alcoholic beverage produced, sold or offered for sale by SP by or through U or any alcoholic beverage retail licensee.

(vii) SP has no agreement with any alcoholic beverage retail licensee related to or respecting this Agreement.

8. TRADEMARKS. The SP trademarks, label designs, product identification and artwork as referred to herein (collectively "SP Trademarks") shall remain the property of SP. Any and all rights in the above under trademark or copyright law or other property rights shall inure to the benefit of and be the exclusive property of SP. SP grants to U the right to use the above during the term of this Agreement in accordance with the provisions hereof; provided, however, that said right is nonexclusive, nonassignable and nontransferable. All proposed uses of SP Trademarks shall be subject to SP's review and prior written approval.

9. EXPENSES. Except as otherwise specifically provided in this Agreement, each party shall be responsible for any expenses incurred by such party in connection herewith.

10. INSURANCE. U shall provide SP, on or before November 1, 1985, with a certificate from its qualified and licensed insurer certifying that U has a comprehensive liability insurance policy in force with at least One Million Dollars ($1,000,000) single limit liability at all times during the term hereof. The certificate shall also certify that SP is an additional insured under the insurance policy, which poicy shall include a contractual liability endorsement to cover U's obligations under Paragraph 11 of this Agreement. The evidence of coverage shall specifically state that coverage as it pertains to AB shall be primary regardless of any other coverage which may be available to SP. The policy shall be written so that SP will be notified of the cancellation or any restrictive amendment of the policy at least fifteen (15) days prior to the effective date of such cancellation or amendment. U shall not violate, or permit to be violated, any conditions of said insurance policy, and U shall at all times satisfy the requirements of the insurance company writing said policy. Failure to provide such certificate in the manner and time required or to maintain the insurance coverage specified herein shall be deemed a material breach of this Agreement. It shall be a condition precedent to the enforcement of SP's obligations hereunder that U shall have furnished to SP the insurance certificate as aforesaid.

11. INDEMNITY.

(a) U will indemnify, protect, defend and hold harmless SP, its parent, subsidiary and affiliated corporations, and their respective directors, officers, employees and agents, from and against any and all claims, liabilities, losses, damages, injuries, demands, actions, causes of action, suits, proceedings, judgments and expenses, including, without limitation, attorneys' fees, court costs and other legal expenses, arising from or connected with (i) any alleged or actual breach by U of any provision hereof or the inaccuracy of any warranty or representation made by U herein, and (ii) any act or omission to act by U, its employees and agents in the performance of this Agreement or otherwise in furtherance of the purposes of this Agreement.

(b) SP will indemnify, protect, defend and hold harmless U, its parent, subsidiary and affiliated corporations, and their respective directors, officers, employees and agents, from and against any and all claims, liabilities, losses, damages, injuries, demands, actions, causes of action, suits, proceedings, judgment and expenses, including, without limitation, attorneys' fees, court costs and other legal expenses, for libel, slander, invasion of privacy, improper trade practices, illegal competition, or infringement of copyright or trademark, resulting from SP's use and/or display of SP Trademarks as contemplated hereby.

(c) Each party shall give the other party prompt notice of any claim or suit coming within the purview of these indemnities. Upon the written request of an indemnitee, the indemnitor will assume the defense of any claim, demand or action against such indemnitee and will upon the request of the indemnitee, allow the indemnitee to participate in the defense thereof, such participation to be at the expense of the indemnitee. Settlement by the indemnitee without the indemnitor's prior written consent shall release the indemnitor from the indemnity as to the claim, demand or action so settled. Termination of this Agreement shall not affect the continuing obligations of each of the parties as indemnitors hereunder.

12. INDEPENDENT CONTRACTOR. The parties shall be and act as independent contractors, and under no circumstances shall this Agreement be construed as one of agency, partnership, joint venture or employment between the parties. Each party acknowledges and agrees that it neither has nor will give the appearance or impression of having any legal authority to bind or commit the other party in any way.

13. COMPLIANCE WITH THE LAW. Should the SP Legal Department, in its reasonable opinion, determine that this Agreement or any provision hereof violates any federal, state or local law or regulation with respect to the advertising or sale of alcoholic beverages, then the parties shall promptly modify this Agreement to the extent necessary to bring about compliance with such law and/or regulation; provided, however, that if such modification would cause this Agreement to fail in its essential purpose or purposes, it shall be deemed cancelled by mutual

agreement of the parties. In the event of such cancellation, payment shall be made only to the extent of a party's performance to and including the date of cancellation, and any payments which shall have been made and which are applicable to future time periods shall be refunded pro rata to the date of cancellation, and neither party shall have any further obligations or liability with respect to this Agreement.

14.   NOTICES.   All notices required or permitted hereunder shall be in writing and shall be deemed duly given upon receipt if either personally delivered or sent by certified mail, return receipt requested, addressed to the parties as follows:

If to SP:	If to U:
Sponsor	University
(address)	(address)
Attn: Vice President—Brand Management	Attn: Athletic Director

or to such other address as either party may provide to the other in accordance herewith.

15.   SUCCESSORS AND ASSIGNS.   Neither party shall assign its rights and/or obligations under this Agreement without the prior written approval of the other party. This Agreement and all of the terms and provisions hereof will be binding upon, and will inure to the benefit of, the parties hereto, and their respective successors and approved assigns.

16.   MISCELLANEOUS.   Each of the individuals executing this Agreement certifies that he or she is duly authorized to do so. This Agreement constitutes the entire understanding between the parties with respect to the subject matter hereof and supersedes all prior or contemporaneous agreements in regard thereto. This Agreement cannot be altered or modified except by an agreement in writing signed by authorized representatives of both parties and specifically referring to this Agreement. The paragraph headings set forth herein are for convenience only and do not constitute a substantive part of the Agreement. This Agreement is entered into in the state of _____ and will be governed by and construed under the laws of such state, without regard to its principles of conflicts of laws.

IN WITNESS WHEREOF, the parties hereto have caused this Agreement to be executed as of the date first above written.

SPONSOR, INCORPORATED

By _____
Executive Vice President

UNIVERSITY

By _____

Title _____

Essentials of Amateur Sports Law

GAME CONTRACT

THIS AGREEMENT made and entered into this _____ day of _____, by and between the athletic authorities of (the first) University and the athletic authorities of (the second) University, stipulates:

FIRST: That the <u>basketball (men's)</u> teams representing the above named institutions shall <u>meet and play at (site)</u> on <u>(day and month)</u>, 19____, and at (site) on (day and month), 19____.

SECOND: That in consideration of playing this game,
(1) That the Host Team shall provide the Visiting Team one rights-free radio outlet for the broadcast of the game by its designated radio station and/or network:
(2) that television rights to the game remain the property of the Conference and the University;
(3) That the Host Team shall provide the Visiting Team with forty (40) complimentary tickets;
(4) That a minimum of 200 tickets shall be made available for sale to the Visiting Team, but that unsold tickets be returned to the Home Team no later than 72 hours prior to game time.

THIRD: That officials for the game shall be provided by the Conference.

FOURTH: That the game shall be played under the eligibility rules of the respective institutions.

WITNESSED BY: HOST UNIVERSITY

_____   _____
Business Manager of Athletics   Associate Director of Athletics

WITNESSED BY: VISITING UNIVERSITY

_____   _____
Business Manager of Athletics   Visiting Institution

                                       _____
                                       Director of Athletics

Appendix C

SAMPLE FINANCIAL AID AGREEMENTS

METRO FINANCIAL AID AGREEMENT

From:_____(University)_____ Date _____

To:_____(Name of Applicant)_____ ☐ Initial   ☐ Renewal

_____(Street Address)_____ Date of Entrance in:
University _____

_____(City and State)_____ Sport _____
College Period _____

1. This Financial Aid Agreement is subject to your fulfillment of the admission requirements of this institution, and its academic requirements for athletic competition and financial aid.

2. This Financial Aid Agreement covers the following as checked:
    ____(a) Full Grant: includes tuition and fees, room and board, and use of necessary books in your selected course of study.
    ____(b) The following items as checked:
        ____(1) Tuition and fees in your selected course of study
        ____(2) Board
        ____(3) Room
        ____(4) Use of necessary books in your selected course of study
        ____(5) Other explanation of Award: _____

3. You will be eligible for consideration to renew this Financial Aid Agreement according to this University's renewal policies at the end of its term if you are academically qualified for intercollegiate competition.

4. If you wish to accept this Financial Aid Agreement it will be necessary for you to return two signed copies of this form NO LATER THAN _____

Signed _____ Signed _____
Director of Athetics   Scholarship Officer

ACCEPTANCE

I accept the Financial Aid Agreement which appears above on this form. In doing so, I certify that I have not accepted another Financial Aid

685

Agreement from a member of the Metropolitan Collegiate Athletic Conference. I am also aware that:

(a) I will forfeit my athletic eligibility if I receive any financial assistance from any source other than as provided for in this award, or my family and governmental agencies, or in the form of an award having nothing whatsoever to do with my athletic abilities or interests.

(b) I am aware that any employment earnings by me during term time and any other financial assistance, except from my family, but including academic scholarships must be reported by me. Any such earnings or assistance, in combination with the aid provided through this Financial Aid Agreement, may not exceed basic educational costs at this University.

(c) The aid provided in this Financial Aid Agreement will be cancelled if I sign a professional sports contract or receive compensation from a professional sports organization.

(d) This Financial Aid Agreement may not be signed prior to March 1, 19XX.

Signed _____
　　　　　　　　Student　　　　　　　　Date and Social Security Number

Signed _____
　　　　　　　Parent or Legal Guardian　　　　　　　　Date

If you wish to accept this Financial Aid Agreement you are to sign all copies.

FINANCIAL AID AGREEMENT

Name _____ Sport _____

This agreement is an acknowledgment of the receipt of a conditional educational grant from the department of athletics. The conditions of this agreement are that I maintain eligibility as outlined by the Constitution and Bylaws of the NCAA.

I understand that this grant can be cancelled for the following reasons.

A. If I render myself ineligible for competition.

B. If I file a fraudulent application for admission or letter of intent.

C. If I am involved in serious misconduct which warrants disciplinary action by the institution.

Cancellation shall mean the termination of the grant during the period of its award.

I understand that the award of the educational grant is for a period of one year initially and for a maximum of one-year thereafter. The minimum period of award (after the initial year) may be from term to term.

I understand that the option of renewing the scholarship following each period of award shall be at the discretion of the institution. The reasons for nonrenewal may include:

- A. Voluntary withdrawal from participation in the sport for which the grant was awarded.
- B. The evaluation of my athletic ability and potential to contribute to the success of the team.
- C. My inability to participate because of an injury (the athletic department may indicate that its general policy is to extend the grant for athletes who are injured, but they are not legally bound to that extension).

I understand that I am expected to participate in athletics as a condition of this grant, but that such participation is not required. This stipulation affirms the scholarship as an educational grant and subsequently does not affect my status as an amateur athlete, assures that the grant is not taxable by the Internal Revenue Service, and voids any employee relationship which might be construed between myself and the institution.

I understand that my financial aid for this term (Fall ____ Winter ____ Spring ____) 19 ____ is accepted in the following amounts:

Tuition: $_____   Board and Room: $ _____

Books (on loan): $ _____   Non-Athletically
Related Work: $ _____

In addition to accepting the conditional education grant, I agree to report campus and off-campus employment to the Director of Athletics.

_____   _____
Date   Athlete

_____   _____
Coach Administering Agreement   Director, Financial Aid

Source: Herb Appenzeller, *Sport and Law: Contemporary Issues* (Charlottesville, Va.: The Michie Company, 1985).

STATEMENT OF FINANCIAL AID

1. I understand that under Conference Rule 7 I will be ineligible for intercollegiate athletes if I accept financial aid other than (a) from my family; (b) from the university under a Tender; (c) in the form of a grant-in-aid or scholarship having nothing whatsoever to do with my athletic

interests; (d) work other than provided in a Tender at which I actually earn the going rate of pay; or (e) bona fide loans.

2. I also understand that if I am receiving financial aid under a Tender I must report the receipt of non-athletic grants or scholarships and term-time earnings from employment because they reduce my eligibility for aid under a Tender.

3. The following is a record of all of the forms of financial aid I received last year, and have or will receive this year:

TENDER LAST YEAR ☐   TENDER THIS YEAR ☐

OTHER GRANTS OR SCHOLARSHIPS, INCLUDING GOVERNMENT GRANTS

	Name of Award	Sponsor of Award	Basis of Award	Amount
This Year				
Last Year				

LOANS

	Source and Address	Repayment Terms	Amount
This Year			
Last Year			

OTHER (Working Spouse, ROTC, Insurance, Etc.)

This Year (Explain) _____ Amount _____
Last Year (Explain) _____ Amount _____

LAST SUMMER EMPLOYMENT

Name and City and State of Employer	Type of Work	Weeks Worked	Rate of Pay	Total Earnings

4. I understand that if for any reason the sum of unearned financial aid, grant in aid, and earnings from term-time employment exceeds the maximum amount outlined in Rule 7, scholastic credits and graduation certificates may be withheld until restitution of the excess has been made.

5. I certify, upon penalty of ineligibility for intercollegiate athletics and loss of athletic financial aid, that the above statements are complete and accurate, and that I am familiar with and in conformity with Conference Rule 7 governing financial aid to athletes.

Signed _____

6. To the best of my knowledge the foregoing is a complete and accurate statement.

Signed _____
Coach

Source: Metropolitan Collegiate Athletic Conference.

SAMPLE WAIVERS AND RELEASES OF LIABILITY

WARNING, AGREEMENT TO OBEY INSTRUCTIONS, RELEASE, ASSUMPTION OF RISK, AND AGREEMENT TO HOLD·HARMLESS

(Both the applicant student and a parent or guardian must read carefully and sign.)

I am aware that tackle football is a violent contact sport and that playing or practicing to play tackle football will be a dangerous activity involving MANY RISKS OF INJURY. I understand that the dangers and risks of playing or practicing to play tackle football include, but are not limited to, death, serious neck and spinal injuries which may result in complete or partial paralysis, brain damage, serious injury to virtually all internal organs, serious injury to virtually all bones, joint, ligaments, muscles, tendons, and other aspects of the muscular skeletal system and serious injury or impairment to other aspects of my body, general health and wellbeing. I understand that the dangers and risks of playing or practicing to play tackle football may result not only in serious injury, but in a serious impairment of my future abilities to earn a living, to engage in other business, social and recreational activities, and generally to enjoy life.

Because of the dangers of tackle football, I recognize the importance of following coaches' instructions regarding playing techniques, training and other team rules, etc., and to agree to obey instructions.

In consideration of the Seattle School District permitting me to try out for the _____ High School football team and to engage in all activities related to the team, including but not limited to trying out, practicing, or playing tackle football, I hereby assume all the risks associated with tackle football and agree to hold the Seattle School District, its employees, agents, representatives, coaches, and volunteers harmless from any and all liability, actions, causes of action, debts, claims, or demands of any kind and nature whatsoever which may arise by or in connection with my participation in any activities related to the _____

689

High School football team. The terms hereof serve as a release and assumption of risk for my heirs, estate, executor, administrator, assignees, and for all members of my family.

DATE _____, 19XX   _____
                                             Signature of student

I, _____, am the parent/legal guardian of _____ (student). I have read the above warning and release and understand its terms. I understand that tackle football is a VIOLENT CONTACT SPORT involving many RISKS OF INJURY, including but not limited to those risks outlined above.

In consideration of the Seattle School District permitting my child/ ward to try out for the _____ High School tackle football team and to engage in all activities related to the team, including, but not limited to, trying out, practicing, or playing tackle football, I hereby agree to hold the Seattle School District, its employees, agents, representatives, coaches, and volunteers harmless from any and all liability, actions, causes of action, debts, claims, or demands of every kind and nature whatsoever which may arise by or in connection with participation of my child/ward in any activities related to the _____ High School football team. The terms hereof shall serve as a release for my heirs, estate, executor, administrator, assignees, and for all members of my family.

DATE: _____, 19XX   _____
                                             Parent or Legal Guardian

OFF-SEASON PARTICIPATION CONSENT FORM

The __(team name)__ ("Team") hereby grants permission for __(Player)__ ("Player") to participate in a game or exhibition of basketball in __(location)__ from (or on) __(date)__ to __(date)__. It is acknowledged that the Player's participation is not part of an NBA or team event. Although the Team's consent for the Player to participate, as required under paragraphs 6 and 17 of the NBA Uniform Player Contract or any amendments or modifications thereof, is being given to the Player, such consent is granted solely on the condition that:

THE PLAYER WAIVES ANY AND ALL LIABILITIES AND OBLIGA-
TIONS WHICH ARE REQUIRED OF THE TEAM UNDER PARAGRAPH
6 OF THE CONTRACT OR ANY AMENDMENT OR MODIFICATION
THEREOF, AND THE PLAYER FURTHER WAIVES ANY PROTEC-
TIONS OR GUARANTEES ENTITLING THE PLAYER TO THE PAY-

MENT OF SALARY, BONUS AND/OR DEFERRED COMPENSATION UNDER PARAGRAPH 2 OR 20 OF THE CONTRACT OR ANY AMEND-MENT OR MODIFICATION THEREOF, SHOULD INJURIES TO THE PLAYER RESULT FROM PARTICIPATION IN SAID EVENT.

The Player understands and acknowledges this waiver. Should any injury occur to keep the Player from playing basketball next season, the Team will not be responsible for paying any medical expenses or for paying the Player's contract that season or any other season for which the Player cannot play basketball.

_____	_____
Player	Date

_____	_____
Team Representative	Date

Valid upon Team's receipt of Player's signature.

PARENT/GUARDIAN PERMISSION
AND RELEASE FORM

CHILD'S NAME _____

ADDRESS _____

TOWN _____ ZIP _____

PHONE NO. _____ GRADE _____

DATE OF BIRTH _____ AGE _____

DATE OF LAST PHYSICAL _____ DR. _____

PHYSICAL RESTRICTIONS: Yes ☐   No ☐
   (If yes, please explain below.)

_____ DIV. _____

Franchise area   Team Name

I, as parent/guardian of the above named child, do hereby give my approval to his/her participation in the game of _____ under the direction of the Central Massachusetts Youth Athletic Association, Inc. (CMYAA). I assume all risks and hazards incidental to such partici-pation including transportation to and from the activities, and I do hereby waive, release, absolve, indemnify and agree to hold harmless the CMYAA and each town participating in CMYAA programs and the organizers, supervisors, coaches, participants and persons transporting my child to or from activities for any claim arising out of any injury to my child, except to the extent and in the amount covered by the accident or liability insurance provided through the CMYAA.

I assume all responsibility and certify that my child is in good physical health and is capable of participation in the above mentioned sport.

I agree to return upon request any uniforms and/or equipment which may be issued in as good condition as when received except for normal wear and tear.

I will also furnish upon request a certified birth certificate and/or doctor's health certificate as may be required by the CMYAA or the town in which my child is a participant.

Parent/Guardian _____ Date _____
                               Signature

(Describe physical restrictions, if any, or any other information which you may feel would be appropriate.)

Source: Central Massachusetts Youth Athletic Association, P.O. Box 321, Southboro, Massachusetts 01772.

HEALTH INFORMATION RECORD

Fighting Illini Summer Camps Medical Statement & Release
(Please Print)

We are enrolling our son/daughter ___(name)___ in the FIGHTING ILLINI ___(name of sport)___ Camp to be held in Champaign on ___(date)___ .

I state to you that my son/daughter is in excellent physical condition and that in no way should his/her activities be limited, or participation hindered because of any physical ailment. I assume full responsibility for my son's/daughter's physical condition and you should proceed with him/her in all activities with full confidence in my statement. If my son's/daughter's physical condition should change between the time of this statement and the time your camp begins, I will notify you. During the time that my son/daughter is at your camp, if any emergency arises involving the physical well being of my son/daughter, I give you full permission and authority to take such steps as are reasonably necessary, in your own good judgement, to protect and assist my son/daughter. I ask that you proceed in the way you would if your own son/daughter were involved, and I release you from all responsibility for such actions. I agree that I will pay any hospital expenses, doctor bills, or any other expenses that may be incurred as a result of treatment given my son/daughter for camp related injuries in *excess of that provided by the "Camper's Insurance."** I understand that the *"Camper's Insurance" does not cover any expenses incurred as a result of illness.* I make these statements and commitments as consideration for your allowing my son/

daughter to be enrolled in your camp and to take part in all of its activities.

_____

*Camper's Insurance
$1,000.00 maximum Accidental Injury
$ 150.00 maximum Dental Injury

_____
(Signature of Parent/Guardian)

_____
(Date Signed)

THIS STATEMENT MUST BE PROPERLY SIGNED AND RETURNED *BEFORE* THE FIRST DAY OF CAMP

Home Address (street) _____ (city) _____ (state) _____ (zip) _____

Telephone Number (___) - _____ Date of Birth _____

Parent/Guardian (name) _____ (business phone) _____

Occupation (street) _____ (city) _____ (state) _____ (zip) _____

Name of Family Physician _____ Telephone Number (___) - _____

Medical History:

	Yes	Year		Yes	Year		Yes	Year
Heart Condition			Epilepsy			Allergies		
Asthma			Diabetes			Other		

1. Injuries and/or operations during the past year? (Include Dates) _____
2. Has your physical activity been restricted during the past year?
   _____ (Reasons & Duration)
3. Is your son/daughter taking any medication?
   If yes, why? _____ Name of medication _____
4. Has your son/daughter ever taken any sulfa drugs? _____
5. Adverse reactions to any drugs? _____
6. Date of last tetanus immunization? _____

Appendix E

SAMPLE STANDARD PLAYER CONTRACT

NATIONAL BASKETBALL ASSOCIATION UNIFORM PLAYER CONTRACT

(ROOKIE OR VETERAN—TWO OR MORE SEASONS)

THIS AGREEMENT made this _____ day of _____, 19_____ by and between _____ (hereinafter called the "Club"), a member of the National Basketball Association (hereinafter called the "Association") and _____

whose address is shown below (hereinafter called the "Player").

WITNESSETH:

In consideration of the mutual promises hereinafter contained, the parties hereto promise and agree as follows:

1. The Club hereby employs the Player as a skilled basketball player for a term of _____ year(s) from the 1st day of September 19_____. The Player's employment during each year covered by this contract shall include attendance at each training camp, playing the games scheduled for the Club's team during each schedule season of the Association, playing all exhibition games scheduled by the Club during and prior to each schedule season, playing (if invited to participate) in each of the Association's All-Star Games and attending every event (including, but not limited to, the All-Star Game luncheon and/or banquet) conducted in association with such All-Star Games, and playing the playoff games subsequent to each schedule season. Players other than rookies will not be required to attend training camp earlier than twenty-eight days prior to the first game of each of the Club's schedule seasons. Rookies may be required to attend training camp at an earlier date. Exhibition games shall not be played on the three days prior to the opening of the Club's regular season schedule, nor on the day prior to a regularly scheduled

Source: National Basketball Association

game, nor on the day prior to and the day following the All-Star Game. Exhibition games prior to each schedule season shall not exceed eight (including intra-squad games for which admission is charged) and exhibition games during each regularly scheduled season shall not exceed three.

2. The Club agrees to pay the Player for rendering services described herein the sum of $——————— per year, (less all amounts required to be withheld from salary by Federal, State and local authorities and exclusive of any amount which the Player shall be entitled to receive from the Player Playoff Pool) in twelve equal semi-monthly payments beginning with the first of said payments on November 1st of each season above described and continuing with such payments on the first and fifteenth of each month until said sum is paid in full; provided, however, if the Club does not qualify for the playoffs, the payments for the year involved which would otherwise be due subsequent to the conclusion of the schedule season shall become due and payable immediately after the conclusion of the schedule season.

3. The Club agrees to pay all proper and necessary expenses of the Player, including the reasonable board and lodging expenses of the Player while playing for the Club "on the road" and during training camp if the Player is not then living at home. The Player, while "on the road" (and at training camp only if the Club does not pay for meals directly), shall be paid a meal expense allowance as set forth in the Agreement currently in effect between the National Basketball Association and National Basketball Players Association. No deductions from such meal expense allowance shall be made for meals served on an airplane. While the Player is at training camp (and if the Club does not pay for meals directly), the meal expense allowance shall be paid in weekly installments commencing with the first week of training camp. For the purposes of this paragraph, the Player shall be considered to be "on the road" from the time the Club leaves its home city until the time the Club arrives back at its home city. In addition, the Club agrees to pay $50.00 per week to the Player for the four weeks prior to the first game of each of the Club's schedule seasons that the Player is either in attendance at training camp or engaged in playing the exhibition schedule.

4. The Player agrees to observe and comply with all requirements of the Club respecting conduct of its team and its players, at all times whether on or off the playing floor. The Club may, from time to time during the continuance of this contract, establish reasonable rules for the government of its players "at home" and "on the road," and such rules shall be part of this contract as fully as if herein written and shall be binding upon the Player. For any violation of such rules or for any conduct impairing the faithful and thorough discharge of the duties incumbent upon the Player, the Club may impose reasonable fines upon the Player and deduct the amount thereof from any money due or to

become due to the Player during the season in which such violation and/
or conduct occurred. The Club may also suspend the Player for violation
of any rules so established, and, upon such suspension, the compensation
payable to the Player under this contract may be reduced in the manner
provided in the Agreement currently in effect between the National
Basketball Association and National Basketball Players Association. When
the Player is fined or suspended, he shall be given notice in writing,
stating the amount of the fine or the duration of the suspension and the
reason therefor.

5. The Player agrees (a) to report at the time and place fixed by the
Club in good physical condition; (b) to keep himself throughout each
season in good physical condition; (c) to give his best services, as well as
his loyalty to the Club, and to play basketball only for the Club and its
assignees; (d) to be neatly and fully attired in public and always to conduct
himself on and off the court according to the highest standards of honesty,
morality, fair play and sportsmanship; and (e) not to do anything which is
detrimental to the best interests of the Club or of the Association.

6. (a) If the Player, in the judgment of the Club's physician, is not in
good physical condition at the date of his first schedule game for the
Club, or if, at the beginning of or during any season, he fails to remain in
good physical condition (unless such condition results directly from an
injury sustained by the Player as a direct result of participating in any
basketball practice or game played for the Club during such season), so
as to render the Player, in the judgment of the Club's physician, unfit to
play skilled basketball, the Club shall have the right to suspend such
Player until such time as, in the judgment of the Club's physician, the
Player is in sufficiently good physical condition to play skilled basketball.
In the event of such suspension, the annual sum payable to the Player for
each season during such suspension shall be reduced in the same proportion as the length of the period during which, in the judgment of the
Club's physician, the Player is unfit to play skilled basketball, bears to
the length of such season.

(b) If the Player is injured as a direct result of participating in any
basketball practice or game played for the Club, the Club will pay the
Player's reasonable hospitalization and medical expenses (including doctor's bills), provided that the hospital and doctor are selected by the
Club, and provided further that the Club shall be obligated to pay only
those expenses incurred as a result of continuous medical treatment
caused solely by and relating directly to the injury sustained by the
Player. If, in the judgment of the Club's physician, the Player's injuries
resulted directly from playing for the Club and render him unfit to play
skilled basketball, then, so long as such unfitness continues, but in no
event after the Player has received his full salary for the season in which
the injury was sustained, the Club shall pay to the Player the compensation prescribed in paragraph 2 of this contract for such season. The Club's

obligations hereunder shall be reduced by any workmen's compensation benefits (which, to the extent permitted by law, the Player hereby assigns to the Club) and any insurance provided for by the Club whether paid or payable to the Player, and the Player hereby releases the Club from any and every other obligation or liability arising out of any such injuries.

(c) The Player hereby releases and waives every claim he may have against the Association and every member of the Association, and against every director, officer, stockholder, trustee, partner, and employee of the Association and/or any member of the Association (excluding persons employed as players by any such member), arising out of or in connection with any fighting or other form of violent and/or unsportsmanlike conduct occurring (on or adjacent to the playing floor or any facility used for practices or games) during the course of any practice and/or any exhibition, championship season, and/or play-off game.

7. The Player agrees to give to the Club's coach, or to the Club's physician, immediate notice of any injury suffered by him, including the time, place, cause and nature of such injury.

8. Should the Player suffer an injury as provided in the preceding section, he will submit himself to a medical examination and treatment by a physician designated by the Club. Such examination when made at the request of the Club shall be at its expense, unless made necessary by some act or conduct of the Player contrary to the terms of this contract.

9. The Player represents and agrees that he has extraordinary and unique skill and ability as a basketball player, that the services to be rendered by him hereunder cannot be replaced or the loss thereof adequately compensated for in money damages, and that any breach by the Player of this contract will cause irreparable injury to the Club and to its assignees. Therefore, it is agreed that in the event it is alleged by the Club that the Player is playing, attempting or threatening to play, or negotiating for the purpose of playing, during the term of this contract, for any other person, firm, corporation or organization, the Club and its assignees (in addition to any other remedies that may be available to them judicially or by way of arbitration) shall have the right to obtain from any court or arbitrator having jurisdiction, such equitable relief as may be appropriate, including a decree enjoining the Player from any further such breach of this contract, and enjoining the Player from playing basketball for any other person, firm, corporation or organization during the term of this contract. In any suit, action or arbitration proceeding brought to obtain such relief, the Player does hereby waive his right, if any, to trial by jury, and does hereby waive his right, if any, to interpose any counterclaim or set-off for any cause whatever.

10. The Club shall have the right to sell, exchange, assign or transfer this contract to any other professional basketball club and the Player agrees to accept such sale, exchange, assignment or transfer and to faithfully perform and carry out this contract with the same force and

effect as if it had been entered into by the Player with the assignee club instead of with this Club. The Player further agrees that, should the Club contemplate the sale, exchange, assignment or transfer of this contract to another professional basketball club or clubs, the Club's physician may furnish to the physicians and officials of such other club or clubs all relevant medical information relating to the Player.

11. In the event that the Player's contract is sold, exchanged, assigned or transferred to any other professional basketball club, all reasonable expenses incurred by the Player in moving himself and his family from the home city of the Club to the home city of the club to which such sale, exchange, assignment or transfer is made, as a result thereof, shall be paid by the assignee club. Such assignee club hereby agrees that its acceptance of the assignment of this contract constitutes agreement on its part to make such payment.

12. In the event that the Player's contract is assigned to another club the Player shall forthwith be notified orally or by a notice in writing, delivered to the Player personally or delivered or mailed to his last known address, and the Player shall report to the assignee club within forty-eight hours after said notice has been received or within such longer time for reporting as may be specified in said notice. If the Player does not report to the club to which his contract has been assigned within the aforesaid time, the Player may be suspended by such club and he shall lose the sums which would otherwise be payable to him as long as the suspension lasts.

13. The Club will not pay and the Player will not accept any bonus or anything of value for winning any particular Association game or series of games or for attaining a certain position by the Club's team in the standing of the league operated by the Association as of a certain date, other than the final standing of the team.

14. This contract shall be valid and binding upon the Club and the Player immediately upon its execution. The Club agrees to file a copy of this contract with the Commissioner of the Association prior to the first game of the schedule season or within forty-eight (48) hours of its execution, whichever is later; provided, however, the Club agrees that if the contract is executed prior to the start of the schedule season and if the Player so requests, it will file a copy of this contract with the Commissioner of the Association within thirty (30) days of its execution, but not later than the date hereinabove specified. If pursuant to the Constitution and By-Laws of the Association, the Commissioner disapproves this contract within ten (10) days after the filing thereof in his office, this contract shall thereupon terminate and be of no further force or effect and the Club and the Player shall thereupon be relieved of their respective rights and liabilities thereunder.

15. The Player and the Club acknowledge that they have read and are familiar with Section 35 of the Constitution of the Association, a copy of

which, as in effect on the date of this Agreement, is attached hereto. Such section provides that the Commissioner and the Board of Governors of the Association are empowered to impose fines upon the Player and/or upon the Club for causes and in the manner provided in such section. The Player and the Club, each for himself and itself, promises promptly to pay to the said Association each and every fine imposed upon him or it in accordance with the provisions of said section and not permit any such fine to be paid on his or its behalf by anyone other than the person or club fined. The Player authorizes the Club to deduct from his salary payments any fines imposed on or assessed against him.

16. Notwithstanding any provisions of the Constitution or of the By-Laws of the Association, it is agreed that if the Commissioner of the Association, shall, in his sole judgment, find that the Player has bet, or has offered or attempted to bet, money or anything of value on the outcome of any game participated in by any club which is a member of the Association, the Commissioner shall have the power in his sole discretion to suspend the Player indefinitely or to expel him as a player for any member of the Association and the Commissioner's finding and decision shall be final, binding, conclusive and unappealable. The Player hereby releases the Commissioner and waives every claim he may have against the Commissioner and/or the Association, and against every member of the Association, and against every director, officer, stockholder, trustee and partner of every member of the Association, for damages and for all claims and demands whatsoever arising out of or in connection with the decision of the Commissioner.

17. The Player and the Club acknowledge and agree that the Player's participation in other sports may impair or destroy his ability and skill as a basketball player. The Player and the Club recognize and agree that the Player's participation in basketball out of season may result in injury to him. Accordingly, the Player agrees that he will not engage in sports endangering his health or safety (including, but not limited to, professional boxing or wrestling, motorcycling, moped-riding, auto racing, skydiving, and hang-gliding); and that, except with the written consent of the Club, he will not engage in any game or exhibition of basketball, football, baseball, hockey, lacrosse, or other athletic sport, under penalty of such fine and suspension as may be imposed by the Club and/or the Commissioner of the Association. Nothing contained herein shall be intended to require the Player to obtain the written consent of the Club in order to enable the Player to participate in, as an amateur, the sport of golf, tennis, handball, swimming, hiking, softball or volleyball.

18. The Player agrees to allow the Club or the Association to take pictures of the Player, alone or together with others, for still photographs, motion pictures or television, at such times as the Club or the Association may designate, and no matter by whom taken may be used in any manner desired by either of them for publicity or promotional purposes. The

rights in any such pictures taken by the Club or by the Association shall belong to the Club or to the Association, as their interests may appear. The Player agrees that, during each playing season, he will not make public appearances, participate in radio or television programs or permit his picture to be taken or write or sponsor newspaper or magazine articles or sponsor commercial products without the written consent of the Club, which shall not be withheld except in the reasonable interests of the Club or professional basketball. Upon request, the Player shall consent to and make himself available for interviews by representatives of the media conducted at reasonable times. In addition to the foregoing, the Player agrees to participate, upon request, in all other reasonable promotional activities of the Club and the Association.

19. The Player agrees that he will not, during the term of this contract, directly or indirectly entice, induce, persuade or attempt to entice, induce or persuade any player or coach who is under contract to any member of the Association to enter into negotiations for or relating to his services as a basketball player or coach, nor shall he negotiate for or contract for such services, except with the prior written consent of such member of the Association. Breach of this paragraph, in addition to the remedies available to the Club, shall be punishable by fine to be imposed by the Commissioner of the Association and to be payable to the Association out of any compensation due or to become due to the Player hereunder or out of any other monies payable to him as a basketball player. The Player agrees that the amount of such fine may be withheld by the Club and paid over to the Association.

20. (a) In the event of an alleged default by the Club in the payments to the Player provided for by this contract, or in the event of an alleged failure by the Club to perform any other material obligation agreed to be performed by the Club hereunder, the Player shall notify both the Club and the Association in writing of the facts constituting such alleged default or alleged failure. If neither the Club nor the Association shall cause such alleged default or alleged failure to be remedied within five (5) days after receipt of such written notice, the National Basketball Players Association shall, on behalf of the Player, have the right to request that the dispute concerning such alleged default or alleged failure be referred immediately to the Impartial Arbitrator in accordance with Article XXI, Section 2(h), of the Agreement currently in effect between the National Basketball Association and National Basketball Players Association. If, as a result of such arbitration, an award issues in favor of the Player, and if neither the Club nor the Association complies with such award within ten (10) days after the service thereof, the Player shall have the right, by a further written notice to the Club and the Association, to terminate this contract.

(b) The Club may terminate this contract upon written notice to the Player (but only after complying with the waiver procedure provided for in subparagraph (f) of this paragraph (20)) if the Player shall do any of the following:

    (1) at any time, fail, refuse or neglect to conform his personal conduct to standards of good citizenship, good moral character and good sportsmanship, to keep himself in first class physical condition or to obey the Club's training rules; or

    (2) at any time, fail, in the sole opinion of the Club's management, to exhibit sufficient skill or competitive ability to qualify to continue as a member of the Club's team (provided, however, that if this contract is terminated by the Club, in accordance with the provisions of this subparagraph, during the period from the fifty-sixth day after the first game of any schedule season of the Association through the end of such schedule season, the Player shall be entitled to receive his full salary for said season); or

    (3) at any time, fail, refuse or neglect to render his services hereunder or in any other manner materially breach this contract.

    (c) If this contract is terminated by the Club by reason of the Player's failure to render his services hereunder due to disability caused by an injury to the Player resulting directly from his playing for the Club and rendering him unfit to play skilled basketball, and notice of such injury is given by the Player as provided herein, the Player shall be entitled to receive his full salary for the season in which the injury was sustained, less all workmen's compensation benefits (which, to the extent permitted by law, the Player hereby assigns to the Club) and any insurance provided for by the Club paid or payable to the Player by reason of said injury.

    (d) If this contract is terminated by the Club during the period designated by the Club for attendance at training camp, payment by the Club of the Player's board, lodging and expense allowance during such period to the date of termination and of the reasonable travelling expenses of the Player to his home city and the expert training and coaching provided by the Club to the Player during the training season shall be full payment to the Player.

    (e) If this contract is terminated by the Club during any playing season, except in the case provided for in subparagraph (c) of this paragraph 20, the Player shall be entitled to receive as full payment hereunder a sum of money which, when added to the salary which he has already received during such season, will represent the same proportionate amount of the annual sum set forth in paragraph 2 hereof as the number of days of such season then past bears to the total number of days of such schedule season, plus the reasonable travelling expenses of the Player to his home.

    (f) If the Club proposes to terminate this contract in accordance with subparagraph (b) of this paragraph 20, the applicable waiver procedure shall be as follows:

(1) The Club shall request the Association Commissioner to request waivers from all other clubs. Such waiver request must state that it is for the purpose of terminating this contract and it may not be withdrawn.

(2) Upon receipt of the waiver request, any other club may claim assignment of this contract at such waiver price as may be fixed by the Association, the priority of claims to be determined in accordance with the Association's Constitution or By-Laws.

(3) If this contract is so claimed, the Club agrees that it shall, upon the assignment of this contact to the claiming club, notify the Player of such assignment as provided in paragraph 12 hereof, and the Player agrees he shall report to the assignee club as provided in said paragraph 12.

(4) If the contract is not claimed, the Club shall promptly deliver written notice of termination to the Player at the expiration of the waiver period.

(5) To the extent not inconsistent with the foregoing provisions of this subparagraph (f) the waiver procedures set forth in the Constitution and By-Laws of the Association, a copy of which, as in effect on the date of this agreement, is attached hereto, shall govern.

(g) Upon any termination of this contract by the Player, all obligations of the Club to pay compensation shall cease on the date of termination, except the obligation of the Club to pay the Player's compensation to said date.

21. In the event of any dispute arising between the Player and the Club relating to any matter arising under this contract, or concerning the performance or interpretation thereof (except for a dispute arising under paragraph 9 hereof), such dispute shall be resolved in accordance with the Grievance and Arbitration Procedure set forth in the Agreement currently in effect between the National Basketball Association and the National Basketball Players Association.

22. Nothing contained in this contract or in any provision of the Constitution or By-Laws of the Association shall be construed to constitute the Player a member of the Association or to confer upon him any of the rights or privileges of a member thereof.

23. This contract contains the entire agreement between the parties and there are no oral or written inducements, promises or agreements except as contained herein.

EXAMINE THIS CONTRACT CAREFULLY BEFORE SIGNING IT

IN WITNESS WHEREOF the Player has hereunto signed his name and the Club has caused this contract to be executed by its duly authorized officer.

Witnesses:

_____

_____   By _____

                                                Title:

_____   _____

                                             Player

             Player's Address _____

MISCONDUCT OF OFFICIALS AND OTHERS

35. (a) The provisions of this Section shall govern all members, and officers, managers, coaches, players and other employees of a member and all officials and other employees of the Association, all hereinafter referred to as "persons." Each member shall provide and require in every contract with any of its officers, managers, coaches, players or other employees that they shall be bound and governed by the provisions of this Section. Each member, at the direction of the Board of Governors or the Commissioner, as the case may be, shall take such action as the Board or the Commissioner may direct in order to effectuate the purposes of this Section.

(b) The Commissioner shall direct the dismissal and perpetual disqualification from any further association with the Association or any of its members, of any person found by the Commissioner after a hearing to have been guilty of offering, agreeing, conspiring, aiding or attempting to cause any game of basketball to result otherwise than on its merits.

(c) Any person who gives, makes, issues, authorizes or endorses any statement having, or designed to have, an effect prejudicial or detrimental to the best interests of basketball or of the Association or of a member or its team, shall be liable to a fine not exceeding $1,000, to be imposed by the Board of Governors. The member whose officer, manager, coach, player or other employee has been so fined shall pay the amount of the fine should such person fail to do so within ten (10) days of its imposition.

(d) If in the opinion of the Commissioner any other act or conduct of a person at or during a pre-season, championship, playoff or exhibition game has been prejudicial to or against the best interests of the Association or the game of basketball, the Commissioner shall impose upon such person a fine not exceeding $1,000 in the case of a member, officer, manager or coach of a member, or $10,000 in the case of a player or other employee, or may order for a time the suspension of any such person from any connection or duties with pre-season, championship, playoff or exhibition games, or he may order both such fine and suspension.

(e) The Commissioner shall have the power to suspend for a definite or indefinite period, or to impose a fine not exceeding $1,000, or inflict both such suspension and fine upon any person who, in his opinion, shall have been guilty of conduct prejudicial or detrimental to the Association.

(f) The Commissioner shall have the power to levy a fine of $1,000 upon any Governor or Alternate Governor who, in the opinion of the Commissioner, has been guilty of making statements to the press damaging to the Association.

(g) Any person who, directly or indirectly, entices, induces, persuades or attempts to entice, induce, or persuade any player, coach, trainer, general manager or any other person who is under contract to any other member of the Association to enter into negotiations for or relating to his services or negotiates or contracts for such services shall, on being charged with such tampering, be given an opportunity to answer such charges after due notice and the Commissioner shall have the power to decide whether or not the charges have been sustained; in the event his decision is that the charges have been sustained, then the Commissioner shall have the power to suspend such person for a definite or indefinite period, or to impose a fine not exceeding $5,000, or inflict both such suspension and fine upon any such person.

(h) Any person who, directly or indirectly, wagers money or anything of value on the outcome of any game played by a team in the league operated by the Association shall, on being charged with such wagering, be given an opportunity to answer such charges after due notice, and the decision of the Commissioner shall be final, binding and conclusive and unappealable. The penalty for such offense shall be within the absolute and sole discretion of the Commissioner and may include a fine, suspension, expulsion and/or perpetual disqualification from further association with the Association or any of its members.

(i) Except for a penalty imposed under subparagraph (h) of this paragraph 35, the decisions and acts of the Commissioner pursuant to paragraph 35 shall be appealable to the Board of Governors who shall determine such appeals in accordance with such rules and regulations as may be adopted by the Board in its absolute and sole discretion.

EXCERPT FROM BY-LAWS OF THE ASSOCIATION

3.07 *(Waiver Right.)* Except for sales and trading between Members in accordance with these By-Laws, no Member shall sell, option or otherwise transfer the contract with, right to the services of, or right to negotiate with, a Player without complying with the waiver procedure prescribed by these By-Laws.

3.08 *(Waiver Price.)* The waiver price shall be $1,000 per Player.

3.09 *(Waiver Procedure.)* A Member desiring to secure waivers on a Player shall notify the Commissioner, and the Commissioner, on behalf of such Member, shall immediately notify all other Members of the waiver request. Such Player shall be assumed to have been waived unless a Member shall timely notify the Commissioner by telegram and telephone of a claim to the rights of such Player. Once a Member has notified the Commissioner to attempt to secure waivers on a Player, such notice may not be withdrawn. A Player remains the financial responsibility of the Member placing him on waivers until the waiver period set by the Commissioner has expired.

3.10 *(Waiver Period.)* If the Commissioner distributes notice of request for waiver at any time during the Season or within four weeks before the beginning of the Season, any Members wishing to claim rights to the Player shall do so by giving notice by telephone and telegram of such claim to the Commissioner within 48 hours after the time of the Commissioner's notice. If the Commissioner distributes notice of request for waiver at any other time, any Member wishing to claim rights to the Player shall do so by sending notice of such Claim to the Commissioner within ten days after the date of the Commissioner's notice. A team may not withdraw a claim to the rights to a Player on waivers.

3.11 *(Waiver Preferences.)* In the event that more than one Member shall have claimed rights to a Player placed on waivers, the claiming Member with the lowest team standing at the time the waiver was requested shall be entitled to acquire the rights to such Player. If the request for waiver shall occur between Seasons or prior to midnight November 30th, the standings at the close of the previous Season shall govern.

If the won and lost percentages of two claiming Teams are the same, then the tie shall be determined, if possible, on the basis of the Championship Games between the two teams, during the Season or during the preceding Season, as the case may be. If still tied, a toss of the coin shall determine priority. For the purpose of determining standings, both conferences of the Association shall be deemed merged and a consolidated standing shall control.

3.12 *(Players Acquired Through Waivers.)* A Member who has acquired the rights and title to the contract of a Player through the waiver procedure may waive such rights at any time, but may not sell or trade such rights for a period of 30 days after the acquisition thereof, provided, however, that if the rights to such Player were acquired between schedule Seasons, the 30 day period described herein shall begin on the first day of the next succeeding schedule Season.

3.13 *(Additional Waiver Rules.)* The Commissioner or the Board of Governors shall from time to time adopt such additional rules (supplementary to these By-Laws) with respect to the operation of the waiver procedures as he or it shall determine. Such rules shall not be inconsistent with these By-Laws and shall apply to but shall not be limited to the mechanics of notice, inadvertent omission of notification to a Member and rules of construction as to time.

GLOSSARY OF LEGAL AND SPORTS TERMS

Acceptance   the offeree's notification to the offeror that he agrees to be bound by the terms and conditions of the offer.

Accommodation   adjustment or settlement.

Accrue   increase, add to, become due.

Addendum   addition and/or change.

Adjudicate   have a court make a decision or decide a dispute.

Administrative law   law which affects private parties, promulgated by governmental agencies other than courts or legislative bodies. These administrative agencies derive their power from legislative enactments and are subject to judicial review.

Advance   to give or grant funds.

Aff'd (affirmed)   to affirm a judgment, decree, or order is to declare that it is valid and right and must stand as rendered by the lower court.

Affidavit   a written statement or declaration of facts sworn to by the maker, taken before a person officially permitted by law to administer oaths.

Agent   one who is authorized by the principal to make contracts with third parties on behalf of the principal.

Amateur athletic union   an amateur athletic association.

American Bar Association   national association of lawyers in the United States.

American Basketball Association   defunct corporation which operated a professional basketball league in the United States from 1966–1970, and which eventually merged with the National Basketball Association.

American Football League   defunct corporation which operated a professional football league in the United States from 1960–1966 and which eventually merged with the National Football League.

Amicus curiae   friend of the court; a third party who presents a brief to a court on behalf of one or the other of the parties in a case.

Annotations   (1) statutory: brief summaries of the law and facts of cases interpreting statutes passed by Congress or state legislatures which are included in codes; or (2) textual: expository essays of varying length on significant legal topics chosen from selected cases published with the essays.

Appeal   a request from the losing party in a case that the decision be reviewed by a higher court. Acceptance of the request and issuance by a writ of appeal is mandatory for the higher court.

Appeal denied   a refusal by the higher (or appellate) level court to review a lower court decision for error.

Appeal filed   a request for a higher (or appellate) level court to review a lower court decision for error.

Appellant   the party who appeals a decision from a lower to a higher court.

Appellate court   court of appellate jurisdiction.

Appellee   the party against whom an appeal is taken.

Arbitration   the hearing and settlement of a dispute between opposing parties by a third party. This decision is often binding by prior agreement of the parties.

Arraignment   the appearance of a defendant to a criminal charge before a judge for the purpose of pleading guilty or not guilty to the indictment.

Assault   an unlawful, intentional show of force or an attempt to do physical harm to another person. Assault can constitute the basis of a civil or criminal action. *See also* **Battery.**

Association of Intercollegiate Athletics for Women   defunct amateur athletic association which governed women's intercollegiate athletics before the National Collegiate Athletic Association assumed those duties in the mid-1980s.

Assumption of the risk   knowledge by one of the parties to an agreement of the risks to be encountered, and that party's consent to take the chance of injury therefrom.

Attorney general opinions   opinions issued by the government's chief counsel at the request of some governmental body that interpret the law for the requesting agency in the same manner as a private attorney would for his client. The opinions are not binding on the courts but are usually accorded some degree of persuasive authority.

Authority   refers to the precedential value to be accorded an opinion of a judicial or administrative body. A court's opinion is binding authority on other courts directly below it in the judicial hierarchy. Opinions of lower courts or of courts outside the hierarchy are governed by the degree to which it adheres to the doctrine of stare decisis. Authority may also be either primary or secondary. Statute law, administrative regulations issued pursuant to enabling legislation, and case law are primary authority and if applicable will usually determine the outcome of a case. Other statements of or about law are considered secondary authority, and thus not binding.

Battery   an unlawful use of force against another person resulting in physical contact (a tort); it is commonly used in the phrase "assault and battery," assault being the threat of force, and battery the actual use of force. *See also* **Assault.**

Bill   refers to a legislative proposal introduced in the legislature. The term distinguishes unfinished legislation from directly enacted law.

Bona fide   real, true, and actual.

Book value   The value at which a security is carried on the bank's balance sheet. Book value is often acquisition cost, plus or minus accretion or amortization, which can differ from market value significantly.

Branch banking   The right of banks headquartered in some states to take deposits, cash checks, and make loans at more than one location (branch) in the state. Where branch banking is not allowed, "unit banking" prevails.

Breach of contract   the failure to perform any of the terms of an agreement.

Brief   in American law practice, a written statement prepared by the counsel arguing a case in court. It contains a summary of the facts of the case, the pertinent laws, and an argument of how the law applies to the facts supporting counsel's position.

Business unit   A part of a bank managed and accounted for as a self-contained, independent business, serving customers outside the bank and/or other business units in the bank. These units are encouraged to innovate and contribute to corporate profits, while remaining consistent with corporate policies and objectives.

Case book   a textbook used to instruct law students in a particular area of substantive law. The text consists of a collection of court opinions, usually from appellate courts, and notes by the author(s).

Case law   the law of reported appellate judicial opinions as distinguished from statutes or administrative law.

Cause of action   a claim in law and in fact sufficient to bring the case to court; the grounds of an action. (Example: breach of contract.)

Certiorari   a writ issued by a superior to an inferior court requiring the latter to produce the records of a particular case tried therein. It is most commonly used to refer to the Supreme Court of the United States, which uses the writ of certiorari as a discretionary device to choose the cases it wishes to hear. The term's origin is Latin, meaning "to be informed of."

Cert. (certiorari) denied   a decision by an appellate court to refuse to review a lower court decision.

Cert. (certiorari) granted   a decision by an appellate court to grant a hearing to review a lower court decision.

Citation   the reference to authority necessary to substantiate the validity of one's argument or position. Citation to authority and supporting references is both important and extensive in any form of legal writing. Citation form is also given emphasis in legal writing, and early familiarity with *A Uniform System of Citation*, published by the Harvard Law Review Association, will stand the law student in good stead.

Cited case   a case which is referred to in a court decision.

Civil law   (1) Roman law embodied in the Code of Justinian, which presently prevails in most countries of Western Europe other than Great Britain and which is the foundation of Louisiana Law; (2) the law concerning noncriminal matters in a common law jurisdiction; (3) one form of legal action for enforcement or protection of private rights and prevention or redress of private wrongs.

Claim   (1) the assertion of a right, as to money or property; (2) the accumulation of facts which give rise to a right enforceable in court.

Class action   a lawsuit brought by a representative party on behalf of a group, all of whose members have the same or a similar grievance against the defendant.

Code   by popular usage a compilation or a revised statute. Technically, the laws in force are rewritten and arranged in classified order, with the addition of material having the force of law taken from judicial decrees. The repealed and temporary acts are eliminated and the revision is re-enacted.

Collective bargaining   the process by which the terms and conditions of employment are agreed upon through negotiations between the bargaining representative of the employees (union) and the employer (management).

College football association   an amateur athletic association composed of NCAA Division IA members who compete in football.

Common law   the origin of the Anglo-American legal systems. English common law was largely customary law and unwritten, until discovered, applied, and reported by the courts of law. In theory, the common law courts did not create law but rather discovered it in the customs and habits of the English people. The strength of the judicial system in pre-parliamentary days is one reason for the continued emphasis in common law systems on case law. In a narrow sense, common law is the phrase still used to distinguish case law from statutory law.

Compensatory damages   a money award equivalent to the actual injury or loss sustained by plaintiff.

Complaint   the plaintiff's initial pleading and according to the Federal Rules of Civil Procedure, no longer full of the technicalities demanded by the common law. A complaint need only contain a short and plain statement of the claim upon which relief is sought, an indication of the type of relief requested, and an indication that the court has jurisdiction to hear the case.

Compromise   an agreement reached by each party giving up part of its claim(s), right(s), or property.

Congressional documents   important sources for legislative histories, which are often necessary for proper interpretation of statute law. Congressional documents are most accessible through specialized indexes and include hearings before congressional committees, reports by or to House or Senate committees, and special studies conducted under congressional authority.

Consideration   something to be done or abstained from, by one party to a contract in order to induce another party to enter into a contract.

Constitution   contains the fundamental law of any organization possessing one. Most national constitutions are written; the English and Israeli constitutions are unwritten.

Continental Basketball Association   a corporation which operates professional basketball leagues in the United States.

Contract   an agreement between two or more parties, a preliminary step in making of which is an offer by one and acceptance by the other, in which minds of parties meet and concur in understanding of terms. The elements of an enforceable contract are competent parties, a proper subject matter, consideration, and mutuality of agreement and obligation.

Contributory negligence   the negligence of a plaintiff which contributes to or enhances the complaining party's injuries. Contributory negligence is a bar to recovery at common law in some jurisdictions.

Corporation   an artificial person or legal entity created under state corporation statutes.

Counterclaim   a claim made by the defendant against the plaintiff in a civil lawsuit; it constitutes a separate cause of action.

Counteroffer   the offeree's response to an offer, in which the offeree proposes different or additional terms than were contained in the original offer. A counteroffer is construed as a rejection of the original offer, and a new offer by the original offeree.

Covenant   an agreement or promise of two or more parties.

Criminal law   one form (division) of legal action by which the state (federal or state) treats crimes and their punishments, usually by imprisonment, fine, or both.

Damages   monetary compensation awarded by a court for an injury caused by the act of another. Damages may be *actual* or *compensatory* (equal to the amount of loss shown), *exemplary* or *punitive* (in excess of the actual loss and which are given to punish the person for the malicious conduct which caused the injury), or *nominal* (less than the actual loss— often a trivial amount) which are given because the injury is slight or because the exact amount of injury has not been determined satisfactorily.

Data base   the accumulation of textual or other material available to the user of an on-line computerized information service.

Defamation   anything published (libel) or publicly spoken (slander) which injures a person's character, fame, or reputation by false and malicious statements.

Defendant   the party against whom legal action is taken; particularly, a person accused or convicted of a criminal offense.

Deposition   the testimony of one witness taken out of court before a court reporter and under oath.

Discharge   to release, usually from an obligation.

Discovery   a method by which opposing parties may obtain information from each other, to prepare for trial and to narrow the issues to be presented at trial.

Diversity jurisdiction   that aspect of the jurisdiction of the federal courts which applies to suits between residents of different states.

Docket number   a number, sequentially assigned by the clerk at the outset to a lawsuit brought to a court for adjudication.

Due care   the legal duty one owes to another according to the circumstances of a particular case.

Due process of law   a term found in the Fifth and Fourteenth Amendments of the U.S. Constitution and also in many states constitutions. Its exact meaning varies from one situation to another and from one era to the next, but basically it is concerned with the guarantee of every person's enjoyment of his rights (e.g., the right to a fair hearing in any legal dispute).

Endorse   to sign.

Equal protection   the constitutional guarantee that no person shall be unreasonably discriminated against legally.

Equal Rights Amendment   a proposed amendment to the U.S. Constitution to guarantee equal rights to women which did not get ratified in the early 1980s but which certain states have adopted.

Equitable   just; fair; reasonable.

Equity   legal rules, remedies, customs, practices, and principles devised by courts of law to supplement those of the common law.

Et al.   and another; and others.

Evidence   any form of proof presented at trial through the use of witness records, documents, and concrete objects, and used to assist the trier of fact in making his determination of the case.

Ex parte   a hearing or examination in the presence of only one of the parties to a case.

Ex rel.   on behalf of, in the name of; a legal proceeding instituted by a state on behalf of an individual who has a private interest in the matter.

Federal question   a case which contains a major issue involving the U.S. Constitution or a provision of an act of Congress or a U.S. treaty. The jurisdiction of the federal courts is governed, in part, by the existence of a federal question.

Felony   a serious criminal offense, as distinct from a misdemeanor. Typically, those crimes for which the punishment may exceed one year in jail.

Forbearance   refraining from doing something which one has a legal right to do.

Health, Education and Welfare Department   a former cabinet department in the federal government that oversaw TITLE IX compliance.

Governmental activity   one which can be performed only by the state.

Hearings   extensively employed by both legislative and administrative agencies and can be adjudicative or merely investigatory. Adjudicative hearings can be appealed in a court of law. Congressional committees often hold hearings prior to the enactment of legislation; these hearings are then important sources of legislative history.

Hearsay evidence   evidence not based on the personal knowledge of the witness but from the mere repetition of what one has heard another say.

Holding   the declaration of the conclusion of law reached by the court as to the legal effect of the facts of the case.

Immunity   a condition which protects against liability (tort) or prosecution (criminal law).

Incur   to take on or accept.

Independent contractor   one who contracts to perform work according to his own methods and without being subject to the control of the employer except for the result of the contractor's work.

Indictment   a formal accusation of a crime made by a grand jury at the request of a prosecuting attorney.

Induce   to urge on or to lead into.

Injunction   a judge's order that a person do or, more commonly, refrain from doing a certain act. An injunction may be preliminary or temporary pending trial of the issue presented, or it may be final if the issue has already been decided in court.

In personam   against a person. A legal proceeding instituted to obtain decrees or judgments against a person.

In re   in the matter of, concerning; usual method of entitling a judicial proceeding in which there are not adversary parties.

Instruction to the jury   a statement by the judge to a jury of the applicable law.

Instrument   usually a document, such as a contract.

International Olympic Committee   world sanctioning body for the Olympic Games; it is located in Switzerland.

Interrogatories   return questions directed to a party or witness, who must serve return answers to the questions under oath.

Jurisdiction   the power of a court to hear and determine a given class of cases; the power to act or a particular action.

Jurisprudence   (1) the science or philosophy of law; (2) a collective term for case law as opposed to legislation.

Laches   wrongful or unwarranted delay.

Legislative history   provides the meanings and interpretations (intent) of a statute as embodied in legislative documents. Also, citations and dates to legislative enactments, amendments and repeals of statutes are sometimes imprecisely identified as legislative histories. More accurate designations of these citations of legislative changes, as included in codes, are historical notes or amendatory histories.

Lexis   the pioneering computerized full text legal research system of Mead Data Central. The data base organizes documents into "libraries" and "files." Documents may be court decisions, statutory, or administrative provisions.

Liability   the condition of being responsible either for damages resulting from an injurious act or for discharging an obligation or debt.

Libel   written defamation of a person's character.

Major Indoor Soccer League   corporation which operates professional indoor soccer in the United States.

Majority opinion   an appellate court decision, in which the holding of the court is not unanimous.

Major League Baseball   corporation which operates professional baseball in the United States and Canada; it is located in New York City.

Malfeasance   the doing of an act that is wrong and unlawful.

Malpractice   professional misconduct or unreasonable lack of skill. This term is usually applied to such conduct by doctors and lawyers.

Misdemeanor   a minor criminal offense, as distinct from a felony.

Misfeasance   performance of a legal act in an illegal manner.

Mitigation of damages   a requirement in contract law that a plaintiff alleviate the damages of the one who has breached a contract.

MLB Players Association   represents professional union players in Major League Baseball.

Modified   changed; a decision altered by the introduction of new elements or the cancellation of existing elements.

Moot question   a case which, because of changed circumstance or conditions after the litigation was begun, no longer contains a justiciable question.

Motion   a formal request made to a judge pertaining to any issue arising during the pendency of a lawsuit.

National Association for Intercollegiate Athletics   an amateur intercollegiate athletic association for small-sized four-year colleges; it is located in Kansas City, Missouri.

National Basketball Association   corporation which operates professional basketball in the United States; it is located in New York City.

National Collegiate Athletic Association   the major intercollegiate athletic association for men and women in the United States; it is located in Mission, Kansas.

National Football League   corporation which operates professional football in the United States; it is located in New York City.

National Governing Bodies   governing bodies for individual sports sanctioned by the U.S. Olympic Committee.

National High School Athletic Association   amateur athletic association for interscholastic athletics in the United States.

National Hockey League   corporation which operates professional hockey in the United States and Canada; it is located in New York City.

National Junior College Athletic Association   amateur intercollegiate athletic association for two-year colleges in the United States; it is located in Colorado Springs, Colorado.

National Reporter System   the network of reporters published by West Publishing Company; these reporters attempt to publish and digest all cases of precedential value from all state and federal courts.

NBA Players Association   a union which represents professional players in the National Basketball Association.

Negative covenant   an understanding in a deed or contract whereby a party obliges him or herself to refrain from doing or performing some act.

Negligence   the failure to exercise due care.

Negotiation   the deliberation, settling, or arranging of the terms and conditions of a possible transaction.

NFL Players Association   union which represents professional union players in the National Football Association.

NHL Players Association union which represents professional union players in the National Hockey League.

North American Soccer League defunct corporation which operated professional outdoor soccer in the United States from 1968 to 1985.

Obligation debt or duty.

Offer an act on the part of one person giving another the legal power of creating the obligation called a contract.

Offeree one to whom a contract is made.

Offeror one who makes a contract offer.

Opinion an expression of the reasons why a certain decision (the judgment) was reached in a case. A *majority* opinion is usually written by one judge and represents the principles of law which a majority of the judge's colleagues on the court deem operative in a given decision; it has more precedential value than any of the following. A *separate opinion* may be written by one or more judges in which he or they concur in or dissent from the majority opinion. A *concurring opinion* agrees with the result reached by the majority, but disagrees with the precise reasoning leading to that result. A *dissenting opinion* disagrees with the result reached by the majority and thus disagrees with the reasoning and/or the principles of law used by the majority in deciding the case. A *plurality opinion* (called a "judgment" by the Supreme Court) is agreed to by less than a majority as to the reasoning of the decision, but is agreed to by a majority as to the result. A *per curiam opinion* is an opinion "by the court" which expresses its decision in the case but whose author is not identified. A *memorandum opinion* is a holding of the whole court in which the opinion is very concise.

Option clause in sports law, the club's right to renew a contract for a one-year period under the same terms and conditions as the previous year of the contract, including another option year, except that the option year of the contract will not contain an option clause. The only term which may differ in the option year is the salary, which varies from league to league, according to provisions set forth in the contract and/or collective bargaining agreement.

Option contract a contract which binds the offeror to hold his offer open for a specified period of time in which the offeree must give consideration for the option.

Ordinance the equivalent of a municipal statute, passed by the city council and governing matters not already covered by federal or state law.

Parallel citation a citation reference to the same case printed in two or more different reports.

Per annum per year.

Per curiam by the court. An opinion of the Court which is authored by the justices collectively.

Per diem per day.

Per se by itself; inherently; in isolation.

Petitioner the party who brings an action; the party who seeks a writ of *certiorari*.

Plaintiff the party who brings an action; the complainant.

Precedent a case which furnishes an example or authority for deciding subsequent cases in which identical or similar facts are present.

Prima facie at first sight; on the face of it; presumability; a fact presumed to be true unless disproved by some evidence to the contrary.

Proprietary activity one which is done by the state but could be undertaken by the private sector.

Proximate cause the act which is the natural and reasonably forseeable cause of the harm or agent which occurs and injures the plaintiff.

Punitive damages compensation in excess of actual or consequential damages. They are awarded in order to punish the wrongdoer, and will be awarded only in cases involving willful or malicious misconduct.

Ratification the adopting or confirming of an act which was previously executed without authority or an act which was voidable.

Regional reporter a unit of the National Reporter System which reports state court decisions within a defined geographical area.

Regulations orders issued by various governmental departments to carry out the intent of the law. Agencies issue regulations to guide the activity of their employees and to ensure uniform application of the law. Regulations are not the work of the legislature and do not have the effect of law in theory. In practice, however, because of the intricacies of judicial review of administrative action, regulations can have an important effect in determining the outcome of cases involving regulatory activity. U.S. government regulations appear first in the *Federal Register*, published five days a week, and are subsequently arranged by subject in the *Code of Federal Regulations*.

Relinquish to give up, surrender, or turn over.

Remand to send back for further proceedings, as when a higher court sends a case back to a lower court.

Reports (1) *court reports* are published judicial cases arranged according to some grouping, such as jurisdiction, court, period of time, subject matter or case significance; (2) *administrative reports* or *decisions* are published decisions of an administrative agency; (3) *annual statements of progress, activities or policy* are reports issued by an administrative agency, or an association.

Rescission cancelling, annulling, voiding.

Reserve clause in sports law, the club's right to renew a contract for a one-year period under the same terms and conditions as the previous year of the contract; the only term that may differ in the option year is the salary, which varies from league to league according to provisions set forth in the contract and/or collective bargaining agreement.

Res ipsa loquitur rebuttal presumption that defendant was negligent, which arises upon proof that instrumentality causing injury was not defendant's exclusive control, and that the extent was one which ordinarily does not happen in absence of negligence.

Res judicata an adjudicated matter; a legal issue that has been decided by a court.

Respondent the party against whom legal action is taken; the party against whom a writ of certiorari is sought.

Rev'd a decision by an appellate court which voids a lower court decision based on some error made in the lower court. Often times the case is also remanded (sent back) to the lower court with instructions.

Right that which a person is entitled to keep and enjoy, and to be protected by law in its enjoyment. A right constitutes a claim when it is not in one's possession. The word "right" also signifies an interest when used in regard to property. "Right" in this sense entitles a person to hold or convey his property at pleasure.

Shepardizing a term that is the trademark property of Shepard's Citations, Inc. and is descriptive of the general use of its publications.

Slander oral defamation of a person's character.

Specific performance an equitable remedy, whereby the court orders one of the parties to a contract to perform his duties under the contract. Usually granted when money damages would be an inadequate remedy.

Standard of care the level of caution that one should exercise.

Standing the qualifications needed to bring legal action. These qualifications relate to the existence of a controversy in which the *plaintiff* himself has suffered or is about to suffer an injury to or infringement upon a legally protected *right* which a court is competent to redress.

Stare decisis to stand on what has been decided; to adhere to the decision of previous cases. It is a rule, sometimes departed from, that a point settled in a previous case becomes a precedent which should be followed in subsequent cases decided by the same court.

Statutes acts of a legislature. Depending upon its context in usage, a statute may mean a single act of legislature or a body of acts which are collected and arranged according to a scheme or for a session of a legislature or parliament.

Statutes of limitations laws setting time periods during which disputes may be taken to court.

Strict liability   liability regardless of fault. Under tort law, strict liability is imposed on any person who introduces into commerce any good that is unreasonably dangerous when in a defective condition.

Subpoena   a court order compelling a witness to appear and testify in a certain proceeding.

Summary proceeding   a judicial action, usually a judgment or decision, which is taken without benefit of a formal hearing. Summary decisions of the Supreme Court are those made without the Court having heard an oral argument.

Supreme Court   (1) the court of last resort in the federal judicial system. (It also has original jurisdiction in some cases.) (2) in most states, the highest appellate court or court of last resort (but not in New York or Massachusetts).

TACTRUST   trust account established to protect amateur athlete's amateur status in which monies received by athletes are deposited and expenses drawn from and which is governed by the Track Athletic Congress.

Terminate   to end or bring to an end.

Tort   a civil wrong which does not involve a contractual relationship. The elements of a tort are a duty owed, a breach of that duty, and the resultant harm to the one to whom the duty was owed.

Track Athletic Congress   amateur athletic organization that governs amateur (nonintercollegiate or interscholastic) track competition in the United States.

Trademark   a name, a device, or symbol which has become sufficiently associated with a good or has been registered with a governmental agency; once established, the manufacturer has a right to bring legal action against those who infringe upon the protection given the trademark.

Trial court   court of original jurisdiction.

Unfair labor practice   activities by management or the union under the National Labor Relations Act which the National Labor Relations Board determines to be in violation of the act.

United States Basketball League   corporation which operates professional basketball in the United States during the spring and summer months.

United States Football League   corporate organization that operates professional football in the United States.

United States Olympic Committee   amateur athletic association that governs Olympic competition and eligibility in the United States. It is located in Colorado Springs, Colorado.

U.S.C.   United States Code. A compilation of Congressional statutes and their amendments organized into 50 subject titles.

U.S.C.A. United States Code Annotated. A commercially published edition of the *United States Code*.

Vacated annulled, set aside, cancelled, or rescinded; the cancelling or rescinding of an entry of record or of a judgment.

Venue the particular geographical area where a court with jurisdiction may try a case.

Void having no legal effect and not binding on anyone.

Voidable that which may be legally annulled at the option of one of the parties.

Waiver the voluntary relinquishment of a known right.

Westlaw a computerized data base and legal research system available through West Publishing Company. The data base contains statutory material and cases from components of the National Reporter System.

Women's Basketball Association defunct corporation which operated a professional women's basketball league in the United States from 1978 to 1982.

World Football League defunct corporation which operated a professional football league in the United States in the 1970s.

Writ a written order, of which there are many types, issued by a court and directed to an official or party, commanding the performance of some act.

Writ of certiorari an appellate court proceeding reviewing an action of an inferior court.

INDEX